COLLECTED WORKS OF A.M. KLEIN

BEYOND SAMBATION:
SELECTED ESSAYS AND EDITORIALS 1928–1955

A.M. KLEIN
Beyond Sambation: Selected Essays and Editorials 1928–1955

EDITED BY
M.W. STEINBERG AND USHER CAPLAN

UNIVERSITY OF TORONTO PRESS
Toronto Buffalo London

© University of Toronto Press 1982
Toronto Buffalo London
Printed in Canada

ISBN 0-8020-5566-4

_____

Canadian Cataloguing in Publication Data

Klein, A.M. (Abraham Moses), 1909–1972.
Beyond sambation
ISBN 0-8020-5566-4
I. Steinberg, M.W. (Moses Wolfe), 1918–
II. Caplan, Usher, 1947–   III. Title.
PS8521.L45A16 1982   c814'.52   c82-094050-X
PR9199.3.K63A16 1982

_____

Frontispiece
Klein speaking about his journey to Israel, Europe, and North Africa, at a
Canadian Jewish Congress convention 24 October 1949. *Courtesy Jewish
Public Library of Montreal*

This book has been published with the help of grants from the Canadian
Federation for the Humanities, using funds provided by the Social Sciences
and Humanities Research Council of Canada, and from the Publications
Fund of the University of Toronto Press.

Contents

x   Contents

'When the years were ripened, and the years fulfilled, then was there fashioned Aught from Naught. Out of the furnace there issued smoke, out of the smoke a people descended. The desert swirled, the capitals hissed: Sambation raged, but Sambation was crossed ...'
    The Second Scroll

'Here were lions ... Here anthropophagi most ravenous ... Here desert where we ate mirage, and were sustained ... Sambation here ...'
    'In Praise of the Diaspora'

Introduction

Although A.M. Klein's fame as a writer rests very largely on his poetry, his prose writings, which extend over a period of more than a quarter of a century, also represent no mean achievement. For the most part, these writings are in the form of editorials, articles, and book reviews prompted by contemporary events during the time that Klein served as editor of *The Judaean, The Canadian Zionist*, and *The Canadian Jewish Chronicle*. Even though during most of this period he was a practising lawyer and held various other positions, such as consultant for Seagram's Ltd and lecturer in English at McGill University, he took his responsibilities as journalist very seriously. During his editorship of *The Canadian Jewish Chronicle*, for example, he contributed weekly a page or two of editorials and a section of commentary on current events, often very incisive and witty; he frequently added articles on such subjects as humour, folklore, poetry, and the Bible; and in addition he wrote long book reviews and contributed poems, occasional short stories, and translations from Hebrew and Yiddish literature. Many of his editorials were written in response to ephemeral local events, often out of a sense of duty to the community and its agencies, and at times written in haste to meet printers' deadlines, but they seldom descended to the level of mere hack work. These prose pieces, written regularly week by week, constitute, in effect, an intellectual and to some extent literary autobiography of A.M. Klein.

In an editorial reviewing the achievement of *The Canadian Jewish Chronicle*, Klein singled out two functions of such a press as deserving special mention. 'The first was the fact that it served, and serves, as a means of bringing to our English-speaking population a knowledge of the traditions of the past and an awareness of Jewish problems in the present. The second was as a means of communicating with our non-Jewish fellow citizens who first learned of the reaction of our community to current events only from its columns.'[1] In this statement Klein indicated two of the central responsibilities he had accepted on assuming the role of editor. He saw himself as an educator whose task it was to teach his own people, especially the young North American-born segment, about their rich cultural past and to heighten their consciousness as Jews and their pride in their Jewishness, and at the same time to make them more aware of their current dangers and responsibilities. He wrote many articles and editorials on great contemporary Jewish writers and statesmen such as Herzl, Achad Ha'am, and Tchernichovsky, and he drew constantly on his knowledge of the Bible, the Talmud, and the works of rabbinic sages and Jewish philosophers and poets of the past. Jewish holidays, as they occurred in the cycle of the year, were carefully noted and commented upon. Whether Purim or Passover, Yom Kippur or Chanukah, the meaning of each was developed, given its full historic significance and contemporary relevance. The annual public campaigns for Zionist causes, for welfare and other philanthropic institutions, for Hebrew schools, Jewish libraries, and rabbinic colleges were supported vigorously, the editor prompted by his own commitments and sense of duty. Klein's editorials on these subjects often read like sermons, exhortatory and admonitory, at times fervent, at times witty, nearly always learned.

The cause to which he devoted himself as a journalist most constantly and energetically was Zionism. He believed that at a time when Judaism was becoming increasingly pluralistic, cultural Zionism would provide 'a new principle of coalition,' a more effective means of preserving Jewish unity. He shared Achad Ha'am's dream of Zion as a renewed cultural and religious centre from which the Jewish contribution to civilization would be made in more specifically Jewish terms, reflecting what he believed to be the characteristic, individual genius of the people. In one of his earliest articles, written at the age of nineteen, Klein stated: 'It is to arouse the just recognition of the Jew to his own abilities, and to prompt him to use it for the creation of his own culture, that this Zionism exerts all its efforts. A culture not of one language (for in the Diaspora that is an impossibility), but of one thought, a literature not of one style, but of one spirit, a product singularly Jewish and yet remarkably cosmopolitan – that was the dream of Achad Ha'am, that is the goal of cultural Zionism.'[2] This culture had to be rooted in the soil, in a Jewish homeland, but it had to be more than a product or an expression of an agricultural undertaking, or of a political-economic arrangement; it had to be concerned with 'the redemption of a spirit.' This ideal, this vision of an Israel restored to its homeland, as a spiritual centre, persisted even though the rising menace of Nazism and the threat of physical annihilation of European Jewry made him emphasize the need for a Jewish state more urgently in terms of rescue and freedom from persecution.

Throughout the late 1930s and 1940s, Klein, though an admirer in most respects of the British people, its institutions and its spirit, criticized the British government for its vacillating policies and its tactics in the Middle East and for its failure to implement the Balfour Declaration. In the force of his denunciations, as in the unqualified rejection of the Peel Commission plan in 1937 to partition Palestine, Klein went beyond the public utterances of most Jewish communal leaders, and displayed the integrity and boldness of a crusading journalist. The fulfilment of the Zionist dream, the achievement of Jewish statehood in 1948, was the happy culmination for Klein of years of dedicated labour on its behalf, an event made all the more solemn and exhilarating, momentous, almost Messianic in meaning, by the Holocaust in Europe that preceded it. Klein's response to that event found lyric expression in his 'Notebook of a Journey,' a diary-like account of his journey in 1949 to the new state and to some of the older communities in Europe and in North Africa from which immigrants flocked, an account that formed the basis of his novel, *The Second Scroll* (1951). Klein's support of the new state continued undiminished to the end of his career as a journalist.

At the same time, however, that Klein praised every achievement of the fledgling state and urged other nations and Diaspora Jewry to aid it, he was not uncritical of a small chauvinistic element in it that tended to disparage the non-Israeli Jew and the culture of Diaspora Jewry, contemporary and historical. He felt the need to reaffirm the positive values of Judaism developed during twenty centuries of exile. His own learning provided him with such an appreciative awareness of the Jewish heritage and its contributions to religious and philosophical thought, to science and the arts, that he dismissed the superficial negation of the Diaspora experience as unrealistic and unjust. In an article entitled 'The Dangers of Success' he angrily attacked this negation as divisive, calling it wicked and pernicious, because it undermined the Jewish unity that he hoped the attainment of Zion – a spiritual, cultural centre – would reinforce. It set up an 'aristocracy of residence' and an 'abominable class distinction' between Jews who returned to the homeland and those who remained in the countries where they lived. 'The *primum mobile*,' Klein insisted, 'is neither land nor language; it is people. It is the folk – and all of it everywhere – which is of the essence. Domicile, status, speech, etc., these are but adjectival; the substance is *Amcho* – thy people.'[3]

Klein's criticism is sound and in the prevailing circumstances, timely, but the force of the attack against a relatively insignificant group in this article and in a subsequent one only two months later, 'Of Jewish Culture,'[4] might suggest that it was in part also an attempted subconscious justification for his own unwillingness or unreadiness to live in Israel. The whole bent of his life, the essence of it as expressed in his writings, indicated that he should, but timidity and a deep affection for Canada weighed against such a step. In a later essay, 'In Praise of the Diaspora,'[5] he again movingly recounted the manifold achievements of Diaspora Jewry, the creation of a culture and a spirit that would live on through a renascent Jewry, but the central theme of his earlier essays on this subject – the expectation of a fruitful interplay of Israeli culture and Jewish Diaspora culture – is missing. The tone of this essay, one of Klein's finest pieces of prose, is nostalgic; the praise, a graveside eulogy. The Diaspora, he asserts, the conditions that prompted great Jewish creativity in scattered lands, is dead. Clearly there was a serious ambivalence in his feelings about his own position, and perhaps a sad foreshadowing of his own not too distant withdrawal from life.

Almost as significant to Klein the journalist as his espousal of the Zionist cause was the task of alerting his people to the gathering dark forces from within the local scene and from abroad that threatened their security and even their existence. This constant concern was addressed not only to his Jewish readers, but to the non-Jewish public as well. He felt it incumbent on himself as journalist to take up the challenge shrilled vituperatively by antisemites from public platforms and in the press. Passionately and logically he made the case for his people to those whom reason and sincere feeling could reach, countering the lies and innuendoes of the antisemites, and condemning antisemitic action, whether vandal acts by a misguided mob or the calculated policy of civic politicians. He denounced restrictive covenants and other discriminatory practices in Canada, and he replied to the slanderous antisemitic attacks by the Coughlinites and the isolationist policies of the America Firsters in the United States which favoured Nazi Germany. His dislike for Soviet Russia on ideological and humanistic grounds, deepened by his resentment at its anti-Zionist stance, was related to what he recognized as its deeply ingrained anti-Jewish bias, which existed despite the state's lofty proclamation to the contrary. Jewish cultural genocide was no more palatable to Klein than physical oppression, and he foresaw and warned against the connection between the two.

His greatest concern, however, was over the increasing manifestation of antisemitism, discriminatory and violent, in eastern and central Europe, by the governments and people of Poland, Rumania, and Hungary, and above all of Nazi Germany. In his journalism, as in his poetry, he reviled the cruel policies and barbarous acts. He appealed to the moral conscience of western nations and was deeply outraged at the relative indifference shown by the so-called liberal democratic nations of the western world to the plight of the victims in Europe and the refugees drifting on land and sea. The moral apathy of the world at large distressed him and may well have contributed to the deep depression from which he subsequently suffered.

The moral concern so clearly shown in Klein's articles and editorials on antisemitism and the refugee problem was not limited to matters Jewish. Scattered throughout his journalism are vigorous condemnations of harsh and arbitrary treatment of other minority groups. For example, he denounced the policy of 'apartheid' in South Africa, the unjust policies of the Canadian government towards its Japanese citizens on the west coast, and of the Quebec government towards the Jehovah's Witnesses sect. Klein was equally ready to criticize his fellow Jews when their actions in his view deserved censure. Thus, though he shared the ultimate objective of the militant Irgun and Sternist groups for an independent Jewish state, he unequivocally condemned their acts of terror in the Middle East as conscienceless betrayals of morality. This concern over political and social abuses, voiced frequently in his prose, found parallel expression, stated or implied, in poems published in the 1930s such as 'The Soirée of Velvel Kleinburger,' 'The Diary of Abraham Segal, Poet,' or 'Barricade Smith,' and again in several poems from the forties. It underlay his political stance, that of a liberal socialist. Though for most of his life he was not active in political parties or political processes, he did let his name go forward as the CCF candidate for Montreal Cartier in 1944, a riding with a heavy Jewish vote, but he subsequently withdrew it. In 1949 he was again prevailed upon to stand for the CCF in the federal election and this time he fought an unsuccessful campaign. Although his defeat was not unexpected, the task of electing a CCF candidate in Quebec at that time being virtually impossible, he had reason to be deeply disappointed in view of his record of service to the community.

Klein's journalism largely reflects his views on public affairs and his involvement in them, particularly in matters pertaining to Jews, but it also manifests another important aspect: his interest in literature. Although the journals that he edited and to which he contributed most of his prose non-fictional writings were directed chiefly to a Jewish public and perforce dealt with topics that interested them as Jews, Klein used the opportunity afforded him as editor to publish many reviews and articles on literary topics. Frequently these writings, too, dealt with Jewish themes, such as the Bible as literature, or Jewish folklore, or with books by or about Jews, but Klein wrote also about literature in general.

His journalism reflects specifically his interest in the Canadian literary scene. Paralleling his increased involvement in the 1930s in Jewish affairs was his valued association with Leo Kennedy, A.J.M. Smith, and Frank Scott, the group known as the 'Montreal Poets,' whose achievement, according to Klein, marked the emergence of a modern, sophisticated literary culture in Canada. In the 1940s Klein's association with P.K. Page and Patrick Anderson, the central figures in the *Preview* group of writers, and with Irving Layton, John Sutherland, and Louis Dudek, the *First Statement* group, attested to his continuing close connection with literary circles in Montreal. The strong moral sense in his response to public affairs is also revealed in his judgment of writers and writing. Thus he condemns Ezra Pound, T.S. Eliot, and Robinson Jeffers as poets on moral grounds, even though he finds much that is praiseworthy in the art of the last two. Similarly, his admiration for certain qualities of Karl Shapiro's poetry is overshadowed by his angry criticism of what he considered to be Shapiro's negative, even hostile attitude towards the Jewish tradition. On the other hand, his high praise for poets such as E.J. Pratt and Chaim Nachman Bialik was earned not merely by their technical craftsmanship and their artistic skill, but also by the fact that they wrote within a national tradition and expressed clear and unequivocally strong moral values. His literary comments and criticism, however, written over a period of two decades, are only marginally represented in this book, as they constitute a sufficiently substantial and coherent body of material to warrant publication in a separate volume.

The material chosen for this book comprises less than one-tenth of Klein's journalism. Specifically excluded, as a category, as just mentioned, are his articles and reviews that deal primarily with literary topics. In making our selection for this book, we were governed by two major considerations. First, we wished to represent as best we could the full range of Klein's ideas and interests, historical and contemporary, the opinions that he brought to bear upon current events, and the values, religious and secular, by which he judged these events. The task of the journalist, according to Klein, was to be not merely the eyes and ears of the world, reporting its activities, but also a sensitive conscience, for which beliefs and values provided necessary standards. Furthermore, the journalist had to be prepared to commit himself to act with the power at his command on behalf of those causes to which his conscience compelled him. In a review of Pierre van Paassen's *The Forgotten Ally*, Klein scornfully provided a simple diagnosis of what he termed the classic ailment of reportage: 'a pseudo-impartiality, a cynical hard-boiledness, a spectatorial and olympian aloofness from the realities which are presumably the journalists' metier. At such a one you can level no greater insult than to say that "he takes sides." It is his proud and pathological boast that he never takes sides, that he can describe the workings of iniquity with the same dispassionate unconcern with which he retails the philanthropies of virtue, and that he is, essentially and by definition, *au dessus de la bataille.*'[6] Klein was well aware that the journalist, in taking sides or espousing a cause, might become a propagandist, or seem to become one, but this possibility the journalist had to risk. Facts for him were merely indicia; he had to search for conclusions and in his search he had to be guided by conscience and personal judgment. Klein sums up his views on the responsibility of the journalist by referring to van Paassen's quotation from a letter of Alfred Loisy to Pope Benedict: 'No one has a right to be neutral in moral questions. Whoever pretends to be indifferent is in reality siding with him who is wrong.'

A second consideration that shaped our selection was the desire to choose from the abundance of material, much of which reiterated views on the same themes, those articles that had special literary merit, or gave evidence of particular qualities, admirable or otherwise, that characterized the style of the author. Because of this second consideration, we included, at times, articles which might not be regarded as in themselves substantial, or which repeated ideas or topics already represented.

Much of Klein's journalism is, as might be expected, ephemeral in nature, though many articles transcend the occasion that prompted them. All, however, are part of the history of the times, recording and commenting on the grim and exhilarating decades that saw economic depression and growing international tension; the cancerous growth of Nazism with its accompanying horrors – the plight of the unfortunate refugees, uprooted and drifting, and the monstrous fate of the still less fortunate, the millions who perished in the Holocaust; the events of World War II and their happy termination; and the struggle for a Jewish homeland which saw the emergence of the Jewish state. Whatever new events and public figures the passing years brought to the fore, most of these subjects constantly recurred, and the point of view – the events seen largely in terms of their impact on the Jewish condition – remained more or less the same through the decades.

Stylistically, Klein's editorials, articles, and reviews differ markedly, but together they reveal the qualities that characterize Klein's writing, many of which are to be found in his poetry as well. He loved words, the sound and the sense of them, mouth-filling, polysyllabic words, teasing words that playfully become puns or homonyms, words that create pictures and extend the imagination. His notebooks reveal that his search for novel, strange diction, technical or obsolete or rare, was constant, and his essays and articles show the result of this search. He seasoned his writing with foreign words, Latin and French, Hebrew and Yiddish, and with historical allusions, often quite esoteric and remote, with the result that his writing is frequently overspiced. His play with language is one form of his pervasive wit. His satire is another form, usually sharp, a quick plunging flash, but at times heavy and obvious, a verbal mallet. His tone and mood were varied. He could build up a case logically, writing in a cool, dispassionate manner, but much more often he indulged in rhetoric, the mannered, argumentative stance of the debater, a pose that he loved, or the swelling, denunciatory tones of the angry attacker or desperate defender, the spokesman committed to a cause dearer than life itself. In his strident passages Klein's comment on the Soviet journalist Ilya Ehrenburg applies to himself, for he, too, 'is the Jew who writes with passion, with the memory of atrocity perpetrated against his kith and kin, with invective and malediction last heard of only in the *tochacho* pages of Deuteronomy.'[7]

Klein's prose is frequently flawed structurally and grammatically, a consequence undoubtedly of the haste in which he wrote many of these pieces. Klein's sons relate that frequently he was composing at the very last moment, even as he was hurrying to the typesetter. Often he would dictate to his wife, seated at her typewriter, an entire editorial or article, with virtually no pause in the dictation and no time for revision. One stylistic consequence of composing in this way is that such writing bears the impress of the spoken word. In these works Klein's prose rhythms are speech rhythms and the language is simpler, more colloquial than that of his more polished or more carefully wrought essays.

Klein's journalism suffers somewhat from more serious flaws than those of careless grammar. He is at times too self-consciously 'clever,' and rhetorical to the point of artificiality. His unusual diction and abundant learned allusions, which clearly reflect his mastery of language and his knowledge of Jewish and non-Jewish culture, also suggest at times an unawareness of the limitations of his readers, or of the fact that they might be distracted or bored by his frequent use of foreign expressions, or English words that are archaic or pedantically rare. Perhaps it would be more correct to speak of his unconcern – for he must have been aware – an unconcern that reflects a degree of indifference to the level of his readership and an occasional readiness to subordinate his journalistic responsibility to his literary impulses. While on the one hand it is to his credit that he never wrote down to his public and that he tried to be himself in his writing, saying what he had to say in the manner that best suited and pleased himself, these characteristics of his style suggest a measure of intellectual ostentation, and his indifference, insofar as it existed, perhaps indicates an aspect of cultural snobbishness, or at least conscious distancing, that seems to have been an element in Klein's complex make-up. His sense of verbal play and his obvious delight in the exercise of an agile, sophisticated mind, qualities which endear him and his writing to us, could at times become a compulsion to be witty at all costs, so that his humour strikes one at such times as forced or misplaced. But such lapses, seen in perspective, are really minor matters and do not significantly detract from the overall achievement of Klein the journalist.

In an editorial celebrating the centenary of the *London Jewish Chronicle*[8] Klein mentioned two other purposes of an ethnic press, not unrelated to the purposes discussed earlier. The pages of such a journal, by chronicling the daily or weekly events of a community, serve as an authentic history of the community, but the journalist, he adds significantly, must not only record this history but also, in a sense, make it. Klein's writings constitute a truthful though not dispassionate account of the times. They did more. His journalism, which for him was not separable from his participation in the work of the Zionist Organization of Canada and of the Canadian Jewish Congress, or from his literary activities, undoubtedly helped to make the history of his community.

It is difficult to assess the impact of a writer on his generation, but we can safely affirm that Klein's influence was pervasive and widespread. As editor of the leading Anglo-Jewish journal in Canada for very many years, at what was probably the most critical period in post-biblical Jewish history and indeed in world history, he reached a large reading public and on the whole successfully expressed their feelings and helped to shape their responses. His wide reading, sensitivity, and intelligence made him a perceptive observer and an able analyst of current political developments, while his command of effective language, his passion, rhetoric, and wit made him an eloquent spokesman, on most occasions, for his people. These qualities put to the service of his people, particularly in their struggle against anti-semitism and on behalf of Zionism, enabled Klein in his journalism to carry out admirably the responsibilities, as he saw them, of chronicler and champion.

In a tribute to Israel Rabinovitch, editor of *The Canadian Jewish Eagle (Der Kanader Adler)*, the Yiddish counterpart of *The Canadian Jewish Chronicle*, a journalist for whom Klein had the highest professional respect and personal admiration, Klein wrote: 'Many of the essays and columns which he has written are, of course, of an ephemeral nature; such, alas, is the unhappy lot of all journalists – they must wait for history to bring perspective to their necessarily one-dimensional work; but many, a very great number of Rabinovitch's essays, are of lasting worth and merit. A selection from his columns of the last number of decades, would constitute to our mind, not only a kaleidoscopic view of the developing Jewish community, but also a date by date revelation of an interesting and genial personality. Even divorced from theme and subject-matter, they could stand on their own feet, as literary creations of enduring value.'[9] Almost ten years later he urged the publication of a selection of Rabinovitch's journalism on the grounds that such a volume would serve a double purpose: 'it would put between covers,' said Klein, 'and make accessible to all, the best that Rabinovitch has written, and would thus rescue the ephemeral column back into literature; and would afford to the general reader an incident-by-incident survey of the creation of Canadian Jewish history.'[10] The applicability of this praise to Klein's own journalism is obvious, and its force for the English-speaking reader at least is even more apparent. The history to which he refers, it is clear to us, is part of the large mosaic of Canadian history with its pattern of interweaving patterns.

Klein's journalism, moreover, is more than a survey of Canadian history, Jewish and general: it constitutes a chronicle and a commentary by a sensitive, well-informed Canadian on events of world-wide import. For the student of literature, these writings have in addition a particular significance, for they are in themselves a body of prose writing of genuine literary merit, and because they relate frequently in substance and language to his poems and fiction, they provide a very useful background, a context for the study of his creative writing. Furthermore, in a more general sense, by revealing aspects of Klein's personality, ideas, values, and commitments, they contribute to our understanding and appreciation of A.M. Klein the poet-journalist.

MWS

NOTES

1 *The Canadian Jewish Chronicle* (subsequently referred to as CJC) 12 May 1944
2 'Notes on Cultural Zionism,' *The Judaean*, November 1928
3 CJC, 18 March 1949
4 CJC, 13 May 1949
5 CJC, 9 January–27 February 1953
6 CJC, 28 January 1944
7 CJC, 22 September 1944
8 CJC, 21 March 1941
9 CJC, 27 April 1945
10 CJC, 31 December 1954

Editorial Principles

The opening eight pieces in this selection are taken from *The Judaean*, the monthly magazine of Canadian Young Judaea which Klein edited from 1928 to 1932. All the remaining essays and editorials appeared originally in the weekly *Canadian Jewish Chronicle*. Klein contributed to the *Chronicle* occasionally during the early and mid-thirties, and then served as its editor and principal columnist from 1938 to 1955.

The arrangement of the material in this volume is chronological, with two exceptions. 'Notebook of a Journey,' which was serialized from August to December 1949, is brought together as one unit beginning in August 1949. 'In Praise of the Diaspora,' a long essay published in serial form in 1953, is presented at the end of the volume, because it complements and recapitulates some of the central themes in this selection. Unlike most of Klein's journalism, it is a polished and highly formal piece of writing.

Many of Klein's essays and editorials in *The Canadian Jewish Chronicle* appeared under his full name or over his initials. His unsigned editorials, both in *The Judaean* and the *Chronicle*, are easily attributable to him simply on the basis of style and diction. No distinction has been made between Klein's signed and unsigned editorials.

In the interests of readability, the editors have opted for a completely clear text. Notes and emendations are provided at the back. The running heads on the pages of end notes help locate the references, and emendations are located by page and line references. Some of the more important Hebrew and Yiddish terms are listed not only in the notes but also in an alphabetical glossary. In the case of proper nouns and personal names, the index is often helpful in tracking down the first occurrence in the text and the location of the note. An explanation of how the notes have been prepared appears on page 487.

One difficult problem in editing Klein's writings from *The Judaean* and *The Canadian Jewish Chronicle* stems from the fact that the original texts are riddled with typographical errors, grammatical slips, and inconsistencies of style – the combined results of hasty writing and inaccurate typing and typesetting. In dealing with these various sorts of flaws, the guiding principle has been to interfere with the text as little as possible and not attempt to improve it.

Obvious typographical errors, misspellings, and confusing mispunctuations as a rule have been emended silently. All other changes made by the editors are noted in a list of emendations beginning on page 479. Some of these listed emendations may appear rather obvious, but it was thought better to err on the side of inclusiveness.

In the list of emendations, the expression preceding the bracket sign is the word or phrase established for use in this edition. The second expression, following the bracket sign, is the word or phrase as it originally appeared in the newspaper version. In a number of cases, an expression was listed not because any emendation was made but simply in order to suggest a possible alternative. Such alternative readings are introduced by the phrase *sic, maybe*. In several other instances, an emendation has been made and in addition an alternative has been listed in brackets, introduced by *maybe*. Emendations based on Klein's own revisions and corrections of his tearsheets (now in the Public Archives of Canada) are followed by a *K* in brackets. The use of an oblique (/) in the emendation list indicates the end of a newspaper column line.

At no point have the editors inserted the expression *sic* into the text itself. Where it appears, it is Klein's own expression.

There are several places in the original newspaper text where a line seems to be missing, either a line of Klein's manuscript or a line of newspaper type. If any attempt has been made to repair such a gap, the change is noted in the emendation list. Otherwise, there is a pair of brackets around three dots wherever such a break is suspected to have occurred.

Many emendations made by the editors have been based on a reconstruction of Klein's handwriting, which was often misread by the typesetter. For example, a loop in his *w* can make it appear as *ev*, or two narrow *e*'s can become a *u*. In several instances, emendations have been based on the assumption that Klein dictated a particular piece to a typist – usually his wife – and that the word was not misread but rather misheard.

Various types of grammatical errors occur in Klein's newspaper writings. Perhaps the most frequent is lack of agreement between subject and predicate, either in person or in tense. Where no reasonable case could be made for retaining the original, a correction was made in the simplest and most conservative manner possible, often silently if the error seemed attributable to a mere typographical accident, such as the dropping of an *s* at the end of a word. Errors in diction and syntax have been more difficult to deal with. A number of expressions, so convoluted that meaning was obscured, were emended with as little alteration as possible. In many other cases, however, Klein's usage has been retained, awkward though it is, provided that the general sense of the passage is sufficiently clear. A number of errors occur in Klein's use of foreign expressions, but as a rule no attempt has been made to correct such solecisms.

Some of Klein's solecisms in English also have been retained, mainly as examples of his stylistic quirks. Two recurring examples are his frequent spelling (and no doubt pronunciation) of *beneficent* as *beneficient*, and his quotation of the Shakespearian expression 'counterfeit presentment' (from *Hamlet*) as 'counter presentiment.' Klein rarely invented neologisms or new spellings, but he sometimes gave an archaic or foreign twist to words, as in his preference for the more Hebraic-sounding *Jerusalmite* over the usual *Jerusalemite*.

Errors in Klein's quotations from books and periodicals have not been corrected unless the meaning is seriously impaired. Where corrections have been made to quoted passages, they are based wherever possible on an examination of the source.

Klein's use of italics was somewhat inconsistent, and his habits changed over the years. Some italicization of foreign terms has been introduced. For borderline cases, roman type has been preferred, especially in the cases of proper nouns and foreign terms that have come into use in English. Some inconsistencies still remain, but an effort has been made to standardize usage at least within a given piece. Sometimes it has been necessary to determine whether Klein was using quotation marks instead of italics to indicate a foreign term. If it seemed that he was, then italics have been substituted. However, if there is some likelihood that the quotation marks were deliberately intended as such, then they have been retained along with the added italics.

Generally speaking, Klein's punctuation has not been tampered with, except in cases where clarity is seriously impaired. His punctuation sometimes reveals the use of outmoded forms, but more often it seems that he simply disregarded rules and punctuated according to the sound of the sentence as it might be spoken. His overabundant commas are often merely rhetorical pauses, and in retaining them the editors are also highlighting the distinctly oral qualities of Klein's prose.

There are several different ways of transliterating Hebrew and Yiddish words into English, and in Hebrew there are different ways of pronouncing certain letters depending on dialect. As a rule, Klein's inconsistent spelling of Hebrew and Yiddish terms has been retained. The notes give some of the potentially confusing variants in parentheses.

Single quotation marks and small capitals for abbreviations and acronyms have been used in this edition, in conformity with University of Toronto Press style.

Acknowledgments

The editors are grateful to their fellow members of the A.M. Klein Research and Publication Committee – Dr Gretl Fischer, Professor Tom Marshall, Professor Seymour Mayne, and Dr R.J. Taylor, as well as Klein's sons, Colman and Sandor Klein – for their valuable help and advice at every stage in the preparation of this book. Important assistance of various kinds was also received from Rabbi William Altshul, Sandra Campbell, Sonia Caplan, Mark Finkelstein, Dr Carole Gerson, Ruth Huberman, Sharon Katz, Professor Zailig Pollock, Esther Steinberg, and Susan Taylor.

The Public Archives of Canada was most helpful in making available its A.M. Klein Collection and in providing special use of its facilities. Other institutions whose research collections were used during preparation of the manuscript included the Jewish Public Library of Montreal, the University of British Columbia Library (Vancouver), the University of Western Washington Library (Bellingham), Jews' College Library (London, England), and the Hebrew University Library (Jerusalem).

The introduction to this book, slightly modified, appeared in *Canadian Literature* 82 (Autumn 1979) 21–30.

Biographical Chronology

1909
born to Kalman and Yetta Klein, orthodox Jews, in Ratno, a small town in the Ukraine, and brought to Montreal, Canada, with his family probably the following year (officially claimed to have been born in Montreal, 14 February 1909).

1915–22
attended Mt Royal School. Received Jewish education from private tutors and at Talmud Torah.

1922–6
attended Baron Byng High School.

1926–30
attended McGill University, majoring in classics and political science and economics. Active in Debating Society with close friend David Lewis. Founded literary magazine, *The McGilliad*, with Lewis in 1930. Associated with 'Montreal Group' of poets and writers, including A.J.M. Smith, F.R. Scott, Leo Kennedy, and Leon Edel. Began publishing poems in *The Menorah Journal*, *The Canadian Forum*, *Poetry* (Chicago), and elsewhere.

1928–32
served as educational director of Canadian Young Judaea, a Zionist youth organization, and edited its monthly magazine, *The Judaean*, in which many of his early poems and stories appeared.

1930–3
studied law at the Université de Montréal.

1934
established law firm in partnership with Max Garmaise, and struggled to earn a living during the Depression. Served as national president of Canadian Young Judaea.

1935
married Bessie Kozlov, his high school sweetheart.

1936
active in publicity and educational work, and on speaking tours, for the Zionist Organization of Canada, and editor of its monthly, *The Canadian Zionist*.

1937
moved to Rouyn, a small mining town in northern Quebec, to join Garmaise in law practice there.

1938
returned to Montreal, and re-established law practice in association with Samuel Chait. Assumed editorship of *The Canadian Jewish Chronicle*, to which he contributed numerous editorials, essays, book reviews, poems, and stories.

1939
began his long association with Samuel Bronfman, noted distiller and philanthropist and president of the Canadian Jewish Congress, working as a speechwriter and public relations consultant.

1940
first volume of poems, *Hath Not a Jew ...* , published by Behrman's in New York.

1942–7
associated with the *Preview* group of poets – F.R. Scott, Patrick Anderson, P.K. Page, and others – and with the *First Statement* group, in particular Irving Layton.

1944
The Hitleriad published by New Directions in New York. *Poems* published by the Jewish Publication Society in Philadelphia. Nominated as CCF candidate in federal riding of Montreal-Cartier, but withdrew before the election of 1945.

1945–8
visiting lecturer in poetry at McGill University.

1946–7
wrote his first novel, an unpublished spy thriller, 'Comes the Revolution' (later retitled 'That Walks Like a Man'), based on the Igor Gouzenko affair.

1948
The Rocking Chair and Other Poems published by Ryerson in Toronto.

1949
published the first of several articles on James Joyce's *Ulysses*. Ran unsuccessfully as CCF candidate in the federal election of June 1949. Awarded the Governor-General's Medal for *The Rocking Chair*. Journeyed to Israel, Europe, and North Africa in July and August, sponsored by the Canadian Jewish Congress, and published his 'Notebook of a Journey' in *The Canadian Jewish Chronicle*.

1949–52
travelled widely in Canada and the United States, addressing Jewish audiences, principally concerning the State of Israel.

1951
The Second Scroll published by Knopf in New York.

1952–4
increasing signs of mental illness. Hospitalized for several weeks in the summer of 1954 after a thwarted suicide attempt.

1955
resigned from editorship of *The Canadian Jewish Chronicle.* Ceased writing and began to withdraw from public life.

1956
resigned from law practice and became increasingly reclusive. Awarded the Lorne Pierce Medal by the Royal Society of Canada.

1971
death of Bessie Klein, 26 February.

1972
died in his sleep, 20 August.

BEYOND SAMBATION:
SELECTED ESSAYS AND EDITORIALS 1928–1955

The persistence of the Jews as a nation throughout centuries of persecution and in countries remote one from the other is a riddle baffling to the ethnologist. To him it holds something of the miraculous and the incomprehensible; he declares it an important exception to an important rule. Edom and Ishmael, Ammon and Moab, the Canaanite and his six neighbours, all of these, contemporaries of the early Israelites as they were, have now passed into mythology, have vanished from off the face of the earth, have become bywords of ephemerality. We alone have preserved a distinct and continuous national character. What then has been the reason of our unbroken existence? What was the force that for a twenty century long exile has protected us from the external onslaught of intolerance and the internal inclination to assimilate? What is the power that has given us the secret of perpetual motion, and what is the blessing that has made us, to use Shelley's phrase, pilgrims of eternity?

Simply has the enigma been solved – up to the middle of the nineteenth century it was religion that was the main factor in maintaining our national consciousness. All Jews felt that even if they were not granted civic rights in the respective countries wherein they dwelt they still were compatriots of a higher state – theirs was the kingdom of heaven. The very derivation of the word religion is an indication of its coalescing utility – most etymologists derive it from the Latin word meaning, 'to bind.' Religion, therefore, is not only that which binds man to God but also that which binds man to man. Accordingly it is impossible to over-estimate the value of the synagogue (Greek for meeting-place) in creating that spirit which prevented national disruption and ultimate annihilation. It was not merely a place of worship – it was also a fortress. One is thus driven to the historical conclusion that it was the belief in one God that kept us as one people.

There came a time, however, when creed was assailed by the incredulous. Then it was that some asserted that the Yiddish language would prove the salvation of cosmopolitan Jewry. Yiddish was to be the Esperanto of the Jews of the whole world – we were to be united in speech. The mother tongue, they believed, would make us all brothers. Uniformity of language, they argued, would produce a national entity; a language was to hold a people; a nation was to live on words.

This, too, proved illusion and fantasy. Statistics show that Yiddish as a spoken language is on the decline. Language alone, the Yiddishist must declare with a defeated bitterness, cannot suffice to preserve a national being – one cannot, if I may be permitted the expression, hold a nation by its tongue.

It is these circumstances and these factors which have in the past served their purpose of preserving a unity among Jews. But now that religion is solely a matter between man and his God, Jewry being divided into orthodox, reform and agnostic elements, and now that Yiddish has no serious significance for the purpose in hand, a new principle of coalition, a new raison d'être must be sought. We must discover a new basis of existence. That is cultural Zionism.

The chief sponsor of the idea of cultural Zionism was Achad Ha'am (Asher Ginsberg). He realized that there is in the Jew a talent all his own, a characteristic ability, an individual genius. This must be encouraged and fostered. This must be cultivated. It is obvious that for such a circle of activity we must find a centre, a cultural centre – out of Zion must come learning, and the word of God from Jerusalem. The Jew must cease to be a '*luftmensch*' – he must anchor his culture in the soil. Achad Ha'am deplored that Zionism of his time which concerned itself mainly, almost solely, with political and economical interests. The revival of Jewish nationalism must not only be agricultural, it must also be cultural. The redemption of Palestine was not merely a real estate scheme; it was rather the redemption of a spirit, the succour of an ideal. If Zionism was to degenerate into a series of philanthropic manifestations, a succession of charitable donations, if it was to be a pocket-cleansing rather than a soul-cleansing movement, it was foredoomed to failure. Not by bread alone do we live – there must also be that which Schopenhauer called 'the will to live,' – the national consciousness.

It must not be understood that one is here arguing for a financeless movement. Even the most fantastic idealist must concede that without money we are without power to convince, not ourselves, but our enemies. In a world where possession is nine points of the law our claims, our ancestral claims, must be gilded. It is inevitable. What the cultural Zionist does object to, however, is the undue emphasis that is placed on this item in disregard to all others. He objects to the attributing of an exaggerated importance to its political aspect. He condemns an unjust accentuation of its economic phase. He would rather harmonize these, he would rather build political Zionism on a foundation of cultural Zionism.

As has been before suggested, this cultural Zionism must be definitely associated with some locality having not only economic but also emotional appeal. It is for this reason that Palestine is suggested as our cultural centre. What Athens was to Greece, Rome to the Empire, Paris to the world of Louis XIV, London to literary England, that Jerusalem, figuratively speaking, is to be to the Diaspora. Too long have the Jews donated their genius to the creating of foreign cultures. Ingratitude has, in such cases, always been the reward. As soon as fame smiles upon a Jewish musician, newspapers conveniently herald him as a German genius; as soon as critics speak favourably of a Jewish artist, they miraculously discover in him traits and characteristics of Russian talent. Of the Jew it may be said what Dr. Johnson said of Oliver Goldsmith – '*nullum quod tetigit non ornavit'* – nothing that he touched he did not adorn; and yet this statement, just as in the case of an able Jew, was made only after his death. Thus the Jew has for these many years contributed to strange cultures, exerted his efforts for alien literatures, given his best for that which was not his own. The situation is well expressed in the Song of Songs – 'they made me the keeper of the vineyards, but mine own vineyard have I not kept.'

It is to arouse the just recognition of the Jew to his own abilities, and to prompt him to use it for the creation of his own culture, that this Zionism exerts all its efforts. A culture not of one language (for in the Diaspora that is an impossibility), but of one thought, a literature not of one style, but of one spirit, a product singularly Jewish and yet remarkably cosmopolitan – that was the dream of Achad Ha'am, that is the goal of cultural Zionism.

In this respect it is futile to attempt to educate our elders – if they, imbued with a spirit which has had its beginning in no American environment and which is so strongly implanted in them that it defies assimilation, if they are content to concentrate on the economical and financial side of Palestine, they have a perfect right to do so, and they carry our hopes and our blessings. It is to the youth, brought up in an environment foreign to his nature, continually in danger of losing his national consciousness, always in peril of being boiled into an unrecognizable glue in this relentless Melting Pot, that we must turn with the ideal of cultural Zionism. If they wish to borrow from the surrounding cultures, by all means let them do so, yet let them at the same time preserve the Jewish hallmark.

It is in Young Judaea that we must emphasize this point of view above all others. Let us remind ourselves (if it is possible to forget such a thing) that we are Jews; Zionists we will be as a natural consequence. Let our Judaeans know not only that they are Jews by genealogy, but also by psychology. Let their Jewishness be written in their hearts; let the *Mogen Dovid* be pinned in their minds, not only on their cravats; let them wear phylacteries on their souls.

The Hebrew University   March 1929

It is a belief cherished by those who know these things that what is more important to a University than even the novelty of its discoveries is the antiquity of its traditions; and by traditions they mean not only the set of principles and the series of precedents governing and inspiring its generations of students, but also those familiar little details of that University's architecture and environment which endear it to the subsequent students. Thus the turrets and the cloisters of Oxford or of Cambridge, of Heidelberg or of the Sorbonne, made venerable by age and lovely by association, create in themselves, without the aid of erudite professors and purblind scientists, a heavy and almost sacred atmosphere of age-old learning. The student points at the dusty portraits in its halls and feels an elevated affinity to these his now-famous predecessors; he discovers through the information of the antiquarian that it was in this precise spot that Newton first saw the apple fall, or in that precise room that some scientist, now renowned, achieved his glory; he scrutinizes the half-blurred inscriptions upon the ancient desks and reads the idle marking of Shelley or of Tennyson, and senses towards them the relations that one senses towards classmates. These century-old Universities, therefore, succeed in evoking in their devotees a spirit which transcends all time and which succeeds in resurrecting all its former students to make its ennobled forerunners familiar companions, and its present scholars further links in the golden chain of its history.

Pertinently may it be asked – can this be said of the Hebrew University? Can we attribute to this University, with its two or three buildings, its brand new benches, its polished furniture, and its modern laboratories the attractions and the dignity of an antique tradition? Have we as yet, on the University campus, spots that we can point to as ground hallowed by definite associations or sanctums made immemorial by some now vanished presence? And can we discover, in a University which is about to celebrate merely its fourth birthday, a directed principle and a definite motive worthy of being termed a tradition?

Paradoxical as it may seem, the Hebrew University even in its birth already bore the burden of such a tradition. If the House of Learning on Mount Scopus were merely a school for the city of Jerusalem or even for the land of Palestine, the last assertion would be exaggerated; true it is, however, because this Institution is not merely for Eretz Israel but for the whole world. It is a University in the true sense of the word – it is universal, and as such the laying of its first foundation-stone already saw the imposition of a duty and of an ideal to be attained, in fine, of the perpetuation of a tradition for ages sanctioned and sanctified by the People of the Book.

It is no idle fancy to imagine the lecture halls of the Hebrew University haunted by the spirits of those who have in the past made Jewish learning a byword among the nations. Here we may see the ghost of the patriarchal Jacob listening attentively to Einstein on relativity; here the Kennesseth Hagadola jostling their way *en masse* to attend Professor Klausner on the Sopheric Age, the while they cast knowing glances one to the other; here the spirit of Ecclesiasticus wanders from Greek to Hebrew lecture and is happy in the realization of the union of that which once had been diametrically opposite – the union of the glory that was Greece and the sanctity that was Jerusalem; there the shade of Josephus hovers over the shoulder of a young pioneer construing his *Contra Apion*; there the ghosts of Rabba and Abbaya, having sallied from their tables of disputation to enter this modern atmosphere to allow the new dust of learning to settle upon their already dusty selves, are descried fiercely gesticulating; yonder the phantom academicians of Pumbeditha discussing violently are, in their proverbial manner, drawing elephants through the eyes of needles; further on the turbaned wraith of Maimonides mystically passes from the Institute of Jewish Studies, his first love, to the microbiological laboratories, his second passion; even the thin soul of an already quiet Cabbalist flutters about some heated test-tube, seeking to discover the difference between this alchemy and his of long ago; and there the lean apparition of a *Yeshiva bocher*, who in his mundane days studied the Law and ate uncertain meals on his allotted '*teg*,' mingles with the pioneer students of to-day who, like him, three days a week toil in their studies, and two labour with the pick and spade. Thus all time sheds its spirit over the tradition of the Hebrew University, and thus the culture of every country from the fiery creeds of Persia to the frigid marble-beauty of Greece throws its glamour by contact and association over a tradition now regaining new vigour.

It is because the Hebrew University has this universal character that Canadian Young Judaeans feel the almost personal interest in its progress. A University which, though distant in space, is near, is intimately near, in relationship, will need no propagandists to evoke in the hearts of every Judaean an enthusiasm for its success. Not only is our affinity to the Hebrew University one of general culture but also one of special activity, insofar as Young Judaea has always concentrated its efforts on the educational side of the Zionist movement. We feel sure that Judaeans, realizing the especial significance of our campaign for a Canadian Young Judaea scholarship fund for the Hebrew University, will enter upon this task with a vigour and an energy worthy of that special significance.

Our Language   November 1929

One of the three things which according to Haggadic tradition achieved for our people the release from Egyptian bondage, was the fact that they did not change their language. Even in the fleshpots of Mizraim they spoke in a sanctified tongue; the syllables of the Hebrew language were ever on their lips, a continual reminder that they were strangers in a foreign land. Their vocabulary pointed to a future of freedom; their diction in itself was prediction ...

Even after the Destruction of the Temple, the Hebrew language continued to be spoken and taught. Though our country was taken from us, our language could not be stifled. If, through the necessities of commerce, we adopted and developed other languages, always was it understood among the self-conscious Jews that the arrangement was merely a temporary one; always did we wait for the opportunity when we would be able to lift up our voices, and utter accents all our own. That opportunity has come.

Though there be some who maintain, whether through the love of an adopted tongue, or through hatred of their own, that Hebrew is a dead language, their contentions are only superficially true. The Hebrew language, though discarded as a speech between men and men, ever continued as a speech between men and God. All liturgy is phrased in its words; all messianic aspiration received shape in its syntax. Tradition, moreover, has it, that Hebrew was the Holy Tongue, – God's language, – so that in the case of the Jews we have a true enough example of 'vox populi – vox Dei' – the voice of the people is the voice of God. To such an extent, in fact, did this opinion hold that during the period of the Hebrew Renaissance there were some fanatics who were against using Hebrew as a daily speech because, so they alleged, daily speech profaned its holiness. That attitude, of course, is gone; a new one takes its place. For if ever it is again asserted that Hebrew is a dead language, one may retort that if so it is buried in the hearts of our people, and demands immediate disinterment.

The process of reviving our language in the countries of the Diaspora must begin, if it has not yet begun, immediately. Our exile has buried the language alive in a coffin of materialism; it is for us to withdraw the nails from its lid. A language of our own is an invincible antitoxin against assimilation. If the Middle Ages have done to us spiritually what they did to our ancestors physically – plucked their tongues out – it is for us now to remedy our speechlessness. Without the Hebrew language, we are, as a nation, dumb.

Certainly we must not adopt as our mother tongue the languages of our environment. As for Yiddish, by one to whom that language is dear, a decision can not be made without a pang of anguish – he recognizes the importance of its literature, he acknowledges the appeal that it has to him, both because of itself and of its associations, he basks in its typically national idiom, but he must in the final analysis put it on the same level as Ladino and the other languages acquired in the exile years. It is with Hebrew that our past is bound; it is with Hebrew that our future must bind itself.

If Englishmen are proud, and justly so, in 'speaking the tongue that Shakespeare spake,' what pride should be ours, who could, if we would, speak the tongue that Isaiah spake, repeat the rhythms that Koheleth shaped, sing the songs that the sweet singer of Israel sang? Speech is the gift whereby man is elevated above the beasts, and language the gift whereby nations are elevated above their former selves. For that purpose, to us, the people of the Book, is allotted the language of the Book.

The movement for the revival of our language should justly begin in our Judaean clubs. Already have there been formed in some of our centres groups where the tongues of the exile are at least temporarily forgotten, and where at least the words spoken are Palestinian. That this plan should be followed wherever possible goes without saying; if it is impossible to form regular Hebrew-speaking clubs, Hebrew study groups should be formed, Hebrew courses should be given; but whether in the one way or the other, let Hebrew, by all means, be spoken.

This is, in a way, attempting like the magicians of old, to conjure up a spirit by means of an incantation of sacred Hebrew words; this is, we admit, attempting to build a nationalism upon a dictionary. It is, therefore, of necessity artificial. But that is inevitable – just as the acquiring of the languages of the Ghetto was in the first stages artificial, so our redemption from them, in the first stages, must be artificial. Once that is passed, however, the path is smooth for a national, and yet a universal language.

A universal language – the word is pregnant with possibilities! If the Hebrew language is adopted, as it should be, by all Jews all over the world, we have the achievement of the universal language, towards which all linguists and statesmen have been striving. A Hebrew Esperanto, a medium of world-wide communication. But perhaps the ambition is as yet too lofty and too distant. Still may it be cherished as an ideal to be attained.

It is customary among our people that when Jew meets Jew his first words are 'Sholem Aleichem' – a Hebraic salutation. Let it be your purpose, Judaeans, to so develop yourselves, and to so acquaint yourselves with your language that when you meet, your Hebraic salutation may be followed by Hebraic contents. Then in truth will one be able to reply to you 'Aleichem Sholem' – Peace is with you, – a peace and a truce to the struggles against your environment.

The Modern Maccabee   December 1929

We are a people of peace. From our earliest youth, the ideal of friendship and of brotherhood has been implanted in us. Our laws enjoin it; our prophets urge it; our poets proclaim it. Those of our enemies who have titled us aggressive have never even in their moments of deepest hatred, termed us bellicose. Trite would it be indeed here to repeat the threadbare dictum that the power of Esau is manual, and the power of Jacob vocal; so common is this knowledge that it is lisped even by the sucklings of the kindergarten. We rattle no sabres; we throw no gauntlets. If we have chosen any of our symbolism from a military vocabulary, it has been the symbolism of defence rather than of offense – in the whole language we have glorified not the javelin of Saul, but rather the Shield of David.

To-day, too, when diplomats discuss disarmament and world peace, it is from our prophets that they glean the strange companionship of the wolf and the sheep, the serpent and the child, the ploughshare and the sword – we are related to truce, not to truculence.

And yet this is not through want of courage. There are times when it takes more bravery to be a pacifist than it does to be a warrior. And warriors we have had not a few. Samson, whose strength vanquished the hordes of Philistines in many a single-handed exploit, and whose defeat came only because his strength hung on a hair; David, who stood up, mere midget, against the giant Goliath, and shot into his brain the pebble of victory; Saul, who entrusted his life to his armour-bearer rather than to his foe; Daniel, who faced lions because of his faith in the Lord; Bar Cochba, who plucked feathers from the Roman eagle; Rabbi Akiba, leading twenty-four thousand disciples in defence of the Word – all of these, and more, are names which show that heroes and Israel are not antonyms. And not only heroes – our women, too, have, when the crisis demanded it, sacrificed themselves and displayed masculine fortitude, strengthening feminine devotion. Deborah, the bee who stung first and then hummed so melodiously; Esther, who with remarkable courage saved Israel from Ahasuerus the fool and Haman the knave; Judith, who left Holofernes with his height ending at his neck; Hannah, who herself a heroine, exemplary mother in Israel, brought up seven sons who defied Antiochus the Madman. The very holiday which we celebrate this month is in commemoration of the indomitable Hasmoneans, the Maccabees, Mattathias and his five sons who flaunted the behests of the pagan Greekling and saved their country from invasion and their temple from pollution.

The tradition of heroism extends from the conquest of the Kings of Canaan up to the expulsion of the Jews from Palestine, despite the revolutions of Bar Cochba, by the Roman legions. With the diaspora, however, courage was not squeezed out of the Hebrew heart – it merely transformed itself from active heroism which it had been hitherto, into a passive one, a heroism of endurance.

Throughout the Middle Ages, wandering over every unwelcoming corner of the world, we have been a people of mute bravery. It has been the heroism of endurance, of long suffering, of martyrdom. No statistician, armed with every mathematical device, will ever compute how many of our kin, rather than forsake their creed and their truth, have gasped out the *Shma* in noisome dungeons, shouted it from the points of spears, murmured it from the embers of autos-da-fé, and no epic written in stone eroded by tears, can do justice to this heroism, not of the triumphant erectness but of the bent back, this heroism, not of the victor, but of the vanquished. The courage of submission which scoffed at the faggots of the priest and scorned the knouts of the Cossack is once more with the emancipation of our people and with their return to Palestine being transformed from passive endurance to active resistance, from martyrdom to Defence – *Haganah*.

With the return to the Homeland, the spirit of invincible defence has returned. We Jews are no longer allowing ourselves to be made living sacrifices upon the altar of some Moloch of intolerance. Our blood, if it must be shed, must be shed dearly. Joseph Trumpeldor and his comrades, in nineteen hundred and twenty, at Tel-Chai, manifested before the whole world that bravery and courage and fortitude had not vanished from the heart of the Jew, and in the recent massacre, too, the Yishuv, the new settlements, continued the tradition of the Maccabees, and if some fell, they fell not in retreat.

In Palestine there grows a little red flower called דם המכבי – the blood of the Maccabee, and legend says that wherever the Hasmoneans spilled their heart's gift upon the Holy Land, there these scarlet blossoms grew. We come to Palestine not to sow these blooms of blood, but rather to sow wheat, to build terraces, to plant orchards. We come with a message of peace; we say to our cousins, quoting the words of him whom they call Suleiman, 'How good and how sweet is the dwelling of brothers together.'

But if there be those who reject our offers of friendship and spurn our messages of good-will, answering the outstretched palm with the brandished scimitar, then do we declare that the spirit of the Maccabees is not dead in us, and that if we must defend ourselves, the Shield of David is at hand.

Messiah in Our Days   January 1930

The charlatans and fakirs who for centuries imposed themselves on a nation of such despairing pessimists that at any moment, so extreme was their feeling, they could be driven to an exalted but ephemeral optimism, form an essential part in the evolution of the national Idea. It is upon the phoenix-ashes of the Messiah-belief that Zionism is born; and it is thus that our national endeavours have in them, without any of its sensationalism and dupery, all the sublimeness of a messianic enterprise. Herzl is merely a saner and a sincerer Shabbathai-Zebi.

Yet it is not for us to scoff at that sorrow and that faith which put its trust in self-appointed Redeemers. So dark was the night that it is no wonder that the meanest firefly was heralded like the dawning sun. The Messiahs were the straws to which the drowning men clung. Every Ghetto, every *Judenstrasse*, was eager and ready to prepare goodly welcome for anyone who brought tidings from the hills of Judaea; our ancestors placed such colossal faith in men, because they cherished an even greater faith in God. Did not the writings of the prophets foretell an end to Israel's woe? Did not Isaiah of Babylon cry 'Console ye, console ye, my people,' and were not these Redeemers the *Menahems*, the Consolers in the Exile? Did not tradition foster the belief, and were there not Cabbalists who tore out the very secrets of the sacred script, prophesying by their curious *gematria* the exact day, even the exact hour, of the messianic appearance? In an era when their mediaeval neighbours believed in satans and demons, were they not justified in believing in Messiahs and Redeemers? The omens of the times encouraged such credence; their own hearts palpitated in rhythm to the echoing trotting of the white Horse of Messiah.

Alas, that they were doomed to discomfiture and disillusionment, and that in all in whom they trusted they were deceived! The wonder is not that Messiahs found followers, but rather that after the first terrible disappointments they should still succumb to others, – indeed, many there were who, after the first deception, abandoned their Judaism and became either Christians or Moslems, – the wonder is that after the first discords of failure they should still find the *Shofar* of the Ephraitic Messiah melodious, and that after the departure of one pseudo-Messiah, they should still prepare themselves for another. The explanation lies in their environment – it lies in the fact that living in times of futility, protracting miserable existences through an age, the Hebrew persecutions of which have been tabulated merely in bare outline by Zunz in a book of tens of pages, the slightest ray of hope, the most meagre modicum of consolation, was cherished with fanatic fervour.

Not so to-day. Although we can admire the beauty and the sincerity of the belief in the miraculous intervention of Divinity Itself in our affairs, still rationalism forbids us to stand with arms akimbo, stolidly awaiting the Courier of the Lord. God helps those who help themselves. Our aspirations towards the Homeland must be achieved by our own personal efforts, and not by a blind expectation of another's aid. The Roast Leviathan which is to be in Messiah's days, in our days shall be savoured in Palestine! Every *Chaluz*, every farm-lad in the Emek Jezreel driving the cattle to pasture, is himself in charge of messianic horses! The trumpet of the Redeemer is placed to the lips of each of us! Every Jew is to-day his own Messiah!

But My Own Garden I Kept Not   May 1931

There are a number of Jewish writers for whom it is a continual source of pride and gratification to point out that such and such a great one was of their own race. They delve deeply into genealogies to seek some root in the family tree of the renowned which sprung from Palestine; they analyze the blood of the great, and gloat when they discover that a drop of it is Jewish; they take the most heathenish of names and juggle and twist it until they are ready to proclaim a scion of David discovered. Nothing pleases them more than to choose some man of eminence and announce him, despite his own vociferous protestations, a Semite. They stalk through the Pantheons of the world, and stop before every statue, crying: 'Jew.'

Thus, though Charles Chaplin may wave his cane and shake his derby in emphatic denial, they will insist that he is Hebraic. They will dig up archives and announce to a listening world that Columbus was a Jew. And if Leif Erickson had discovered America they probably would have Judaized him, too.

From gentiles who are obviously not Jews, they pass in admiration to Jews who would like to be recognized as gentiles. Though Disraeli was confirmed in the Church of England at the age of thirteen, and though he considered his own race as a race whose only destiny was to adorn a novel, these hero-worshippers continually hail him as Jew, and cherish his primrose as if it were the very Rose of Sharon itself. Heine, too, who advertised himself as a Hellene and who wept that Judaism was not a religion but a misfortune, is gathered by the same idolators into the very bosom of Abraham. And Sir Isaac Isaacs, now Governor-General of Australia, who denies that he is a son of a tailor, and a Jewish tailor at that, is heralded nonetheless as a true son of Israel.

We are not averse to honouring our own great men, provided they are proud of the affiliation with their race. But when they deny us, it is a matter of self-respect for us no longer to insist upon the relationship. If they exclude themselves from the congregation of Israel, so much the worse for them; we have enough talents and geniuses in our midst to spare ourselves the ungrateful labour of exhorting renegades to return to the fold.

And yet this whole situation is but a sign of the times. Just as there are those who seek to conceal their Jewish origins, so there are those who would be pleased to have them known, but who are doomed to be considered as anything but Jews. A Jewish fiddler remains a Jewish fiddler, but a Jewish virtuoso loses his adjective as soon as he gains his fame. Thus in literature, too, the Jew has neglected his own heritage and tilled fields not his own. Georg Brandes is recognized as a Dane; Marcel Proust and Catulle Mendès are Frenchmen, and Heijermans is a Dutchman. But all of them were Jews when they began. In art Mark Antokolski is a Russian, William Rothenstein an Englishman, and Camille Pissarro a Frenchman; or so at least the art-histories declare them to be. But they, too, were Jews when they began. Mendelssohn-Bartholdy, Meyer-beer, Offenbach, Frederic Cowen, Mischa Elman, Ephraim Zimbalist and Fritz Kreisler and Jascha Heifetz, all of these have been claimed by different members of the League of Nations. But all of these, too, were Jews when they began.

These two phenomena – the Jew seeking his brother where he is not, and the Jew forced to deny himself even where he is, are due to a single fact, – the

Jews have been a people, but not a nation. They have contributed of their best efforts to foreign cultures because their own culture has been put away in storage for centuries. Some of them have been forced to abandon the arts which are particularly national and take up the sciences which are generally international. Out of a dozen Jewish winners of the Nobel prize at least ten have won it for science, and the one who was awarded the prize for literature in 1928, Henri Bergson, really received an award for philosophy rather than for belles lettres.

The dice are loaded. As long as the Jew remains in exile he will reap very little profit out of his own labour. He is bound to remain a servant in the house of those who will proclaim themselves his masters. And it is time for him to become master in his own.

Theodor Herzl   June 1931

On July fifth the whole Jewish world will commemorate the anniversary of Herzl's death. In no more than three decades, within the period of a single generation, Theodor Herzl has already become a legend and a symbol. He has won for himself so exalted a place in the Jewish heart that if canonization were a Hebrew practice the Jewish calendar would have already been graced with a Saint Theodor. Yet though Herzl is universally admired and his memory everywhere respected, few if any have been able to fathom his enigmatic personality, and he has remained a 19th century sphinx.

In one of the early entries into his diary Theodor Herzl wrote: 'The worst that they could say of me is that I am a poet.' It seems to us that this self-accusing epithet may be turned into the supremest of compliments, for only when we recognize the poetic principle behind the labours of the Hebrew Hercules, is the riddle that was Herzl in some small way solved. In Theodor Herzl we behold the last of the Jewish romanticists and therefore by a strange paradox the first of the Hebrew realists. Here is a poet and a man of action in one, a dreamer and a doer, a man who took the rock that the builders rejected and made of it a cornerstone.

HERZL THE POET

Let it be understood at the outset that Theodor Herzl never wrote a line of poetry in his life, except a few verses that he scribbled for the delectation of his children. How then are we justified in calling him a creative poet? That depends entirely upon our definition; and though we shall not attempt accurately to define the nature and functions of a poet – that would be like seeking to cage the nightingale or dissect the rose – still there are certain characteristics that we may, with impunity, permit ourselves. The word poet comes from the Greek – *poieio* – to make. The poet, therefore, is he who makes. He creates. With magic incantations he conjures up, like the witch of Endor, the spirits of the past; with the spell of his language he brings into life that which but a moment ago was not and yet now is. Words he takes, words undistinguished in themselves, and by a mystic combination fashions of them a glorious thing. The poet is like a cocoon; in him the caterpillar of the past finds rest, and from him the butterfly of the future emerges.

And yet in the character of Herzl the fiery imagination of the poet is tempered with the cold practicality of the statesman. Before him there had been false Messiahs, blowing their raucous trumpets; poets who wept and were dissolved in tears; mediaeval rabbis whose only conception of a Jewish parliament was that the House of the Lord was the Hebrew House of Commons; statesmen, too, but statesmen in the employ of foreign empires – the Don Josephs, the Ibn Nagdelas and the Beaconsfields who were made keepers of the vineyards, but their own vineyards they kept not. Not until Herzl appeared upon the scene did the Jewish world witness its first diplomat and statesman.

The kings and emperors received him as the exception to the general run of Jews whom they imagined to be hunch-backed wretches with unkempt beards and ludicrous ear-locks and contaminated caftans. Here – *mirabile dictu* – was a Jew who looked like a gentleman. Herzl himself was continually conscious of the impression he made. Before the First Zionist Congress he had a long argument with Nordau, insisting that the latter should wear a frock-coat – for the impression. It is in the same spirit that Herzl records with meticulous detail how he had his right hand ungloved in his audience with the Kaiser, how he casually refused to kiss the Pope's outstretched hand, and how the king of Bulgaria in accidentally stepping upon his toe, had asked his pardon. A king asking pardon of a Jew!

HERZL AND ANTI-SEMITISM

To be received by the powers of Europe was not enough to make a hero out of Herzl. A purpose and a goal was necessary, an idée fixe. Every poet can create out of great sorrow and out of great joy. What Aristotle called catharsis, the element that purges with pity and with terror, must enter into the person of the poet and, as it were, recreate him anew. This solvent of experience the Germans called *Erlebnis*. Without it the voice of the poet is an echo; with it it becomes a trumpet and a prophecy. This *Erlebnis* in Herzl's life was the Dreyfus case. It is true that Herzl had known anti-semitism before; he had once passed through a German town and had had the words 'Hep Hep' shouted after him; and the

Albia club to which he had belonged in his student days had excluded Jews, whereupon Herzl himself had resigned; but these were but slight manifestations of the colossal animosity which Sokolow has called the 'eternal hatred of the eternal people,' slight as compared with the blatant anti-semitism evident in the Dreyfus case.

Herzl was a changed man. The poet had suffered the caldron of experience, and what he had suspected before, now he knew. At this juncture a comparison between Moses the prophet and Herzl the poet is tempting. Moses too was brought up in the court of Pharaoh, and saw the misery of his brethren from the comfortable altitude of a palace window. Moses, too, was something of a poet, for without this presumption the incident of the burning bush remains incomprehensible. Moses, too, went forth into the fields and realized that he was in Egyptian bondage, and discovered that the God of the Hebrews was called 'I am what I am' and not as the assimilated would have it: 'I am what I try to be.' But in one respect Herzl's task was more difficult than that of Moses: Moses made water come forth from a rock with the help of a rod; Herzl achieved the same miracle, only he had no magic wand.

THE JUDENSTAAT

After the Dreyfus case Herzl set to working on the creation of his epic. Other poets in creating their masterpieces have invoked the moon, enjoined the nightingales and uprooted the rose. They have conjured up all things that are in themselves beautiful. Herzl dreamt of a land of almond blossoms and orange vineyards, a land of the proverbial milk and honey, but began to realize his dream in a prosaic, economic treatise: the *Judenstaat*. The *Judenstaat* is an epic of industry where, instead of the song of the turtle dove in the land, one hears the whir of dynamos, instead of the falling waters of the Jordan one listens to the noise of irrigation canals, and instead of gardens one beholds orchards. It was then that Herzl wrote in his diary: If the romance does not become a fact at least the fact can become a romance. But he realized that as yet he had no firm foundation for his work. Therefore he wrote: Great things do not need to have a firm foundation. An apple must be put on a table so that it should not fall. The earth swims in space. For Herzl began the struggle alone and unaided. The philanthropists were not with him. They thought in terms of orphanages, not states. And Herzl detested philanthropy. To him it was the alm which the lazy rich give to the workless poor. Charity is indeed the method whereby those who have nothing else to recommend them attempt to bribe the gate-keeper of heaven for entrance. It is the baksheesh of the celestial gates. In the final analysis it is the bone that one throws to the underdog. It was no wonder then that Herzl wrote: What have we got to do with charity organizations, the community boards and all the Jewish Pickwick clubs? The dear gentleman who wrote to the *Times* simply does not understand our movement, he does not know what the rebirth of a nation is. On another occasion Herzl declared the difference between himself and Baron de Hirsch: They beg from him but do not love him; I am loved by the beggars. That is why I am the stronger.

But his very position as a statesman was a contradiction: a statesman without a state; a leader without a following; a voice crying in the wilderness for a wilderness. He founded a state with words; he established it with a slogan; he solved the Jewish problem with a formula. When he went to the chancellories of Europe, when he interviewed the Sultan, shadow of God upon earth, when he negotiated with great powers, he had opposition before him and indifference behind him. He had no sabre to rattle like the Kaiser. He had no money to offer, for at this early period the Rothschilds and the De Hirsches were still interested in philanthropy not state-building. Yet with words alone he was able to achieve what the millions of the Rothschilds achieved not and with words to conquer what an army terrible with banners could not conquer. Theodor Herzl was the Jewish will to live, working under a pen-name.

INTERNATIONALIST AND NATIONALIST

Another paradox presents itself in the life of Theodor Herzl: before he could be a nationalist he had to be a virtual internationalist.

The man who was destined to become the supreme patriot of his generation began as a typical cosmopolite of the 19th century. Before Herzl had penned a single line of his *Judenstaat* he had already been in Roumania where pogroms are a national sport; he had lived in Austria where Jew-baiting was a hobby of the upper classes and a modus vivendi of the lower; he had passed through Spain where a man with Herzl's imagination could still sense the smoke of the autos-da-fé in the pestilential air; he had dwelt in Italy where but a generation earlier the vicars of Christ on earth had amused themselves by choosing the fattest Jew in the Ghetto to run an annual race with the city prostitutes; and he had been to Paris, scene of the Dreyfus affair. 'My removal from Vienna to Paris was historically necessary so that I might learn the meaning of migration.'

Famous *Zaddikim* used to take upon themselves the *ol galuth*, the yoke of exile; one can see in the wandering of this modern Jew something like an unconscious acceptance of this yoke – before his life would be over his foot would have trod upon three continents. The anaemic personality of the cosmopolite who dislikes every country with equal impartiality was to be changed into the vigorous one of the nationalist who loves all peoples, but his own the most.

For hitherto Herzl had been a literary dabbler, a typically cultured gentleman of Paris and Vienna, the dilettante citizen of the world. He frittered away his energies in the concocting of epigrams, he wasted his time in preparing dialogues for contemporary plays. Suddenly he realized that the monologue of woe which was his people was of far greater consequence than the scintillating dialogues of his ephemeral plays; suddenly he realized that he did not have to write dramas – a drama was before him; suddenly he was aware that a volcano should not spend itself in festival fireworks, and that a Jew should not write feuilletons when tragedy stalks before him.

Inspired with a desire to help his people and armed with the ammunition of European culture Herzl the poet appeared on the Jewish scene. There is a painting of Theodor Herzl by Solomon J. Solomon, one of his contemporaries, in which the bust of the man is portrayed against a dark background. From the general blackness of the picture but two things emerge – Herzl's dark flaming eyes and the immaculate whiteness of his starched shirt-front. It was because Herzl came to the Kaiser in a starched shirt-front that he was so acceptable to him and because he appeared before his people with those flaming eyes and that Messianic beard that he was so acceptable to them. In those early years Herzl's beard did more for the advancement of Zionism than a hundred manifestos.

HERZL AND THE RABBIS

Did he represent the Rabbis? Only a few. The vast majority, especially the reform rabbis, who had made their *siddurim* read like Protestant hymn books, who had deleted all references to the Homeland in their prayers, and who thought that to be a patriot in Germany one had to be a renegade in Israel, these, bitterly opposed him. Herzl carried on a strenuous fight against these 'protest rabbis' as he called them, whose sole function was to lament and protest when pogroms were perpetrated; the official mourners and diplomatic undertakers in Israel. In a memorable epigram Herzl squelched them; you 'protest rabbis' live *on* the Jews; I *for* the Jews.

Were the masses behind him? At first not. Miserable masses in Eastern Europe were so deeply affected by the Jewish problem, that they knew no Jewish problem. A man in delirium does not know the nature of his own disease. The only solution that has been offered was the rather unconsoling one of Pobyodonostieff, the Russian minister who suggested that a third of the Jews of Russia should be baptized, a third forced to emigrate and a third pogromized.

And so at first Herzl was alone. Even more justly than Louis xiv, could he say: *L'état c'est moi*, the Jewish state, I am the Jewish state; for he was at that time its leader and its first and only citizen. It is true that the Chovevei Zion had been before him and that Moses Hess and Rabbi Hirsch Kalischer, communistic and orthodox rabbis, had come to the same national conclusions; but with them the goal was a colony, not a state.

It was not till later that the masses came over to Herzl, the masses in London as well as those in Vilna. At first they knew not Herzl, for to them he was a stranger, but in the course of time they began to understand the man. In dealing with the Jewish people Herzl's humour and charm was of inestimable value. He who tries to lead the Jews and has no sense of humour is bound to die of heart-failure several times a day; and even the sparkling Herzl died at forty. At times Herzl was so disappointed in the apathetic attitude of his generation that he suggested as an epitaph for himself: He thought too highly of the Jews.

HERZL'S DIFFICULTIES

In a memorable passage in his diary Herzl describes his difficulties as being so many eggs which he had to handle with care: 1, egg of the *Neue Freie Presse,* a statesman without a state could accept no pay; 2, egg of the orthodox Jews; 3, egg of the Austrian patriotism; 4, egg of Turkey and the Sultan; 5, egg of the Russian Government; 6, egg of the Christian Sects with regard to Holy Places; 7, egg of Edmond Rothschild; 8, egg of Chovevei Zion in Russia; 9, egg of the colonists; 10, egg of envy and jealousy.

Tragic is the fate of the poet who not only has to be a statesman, but also a juggler of eggs.

THE FIRST CONGRESS

Herzl then called the first Zionist Congress. If he had done nothing else he would have already gained for himself a place in Jewish history. The first Zionist Congress was a gathering of the exile, a convention of the Diaspora. Israel Zangwill describes it thus: 'A strange fantasmagoria of faces. A small, sallow Pole, with high cheek-bones; a blond Hungarian, with a flaxen moustache; a brown hatchet-faced Roumanian; a fresh-coloured Frenchman, with eyeglasses; a dark, marrano-descended Dutchman; a chubby German; a fiery Russian, tugging at his own hair with excitement, perhaps in prescience of the prison awaiting his return; a dusky Egyptian, with the close-cropped curly black hair, and all but the nose of a negro; a yellow-bearded Swede; a courtly Viennese lawyer; a German student, with proud duel-slashes across his cheek; a Viennese student, first fighter in the University, with a coloured band across his shirt-front; a dandy redolent of the best Petersburg circles; and one solitary caftan-Jew, with ear-locks and skull-cap, wafting into the nineteenth century the Kabbalistic mysticism of the Carpathian mountains.'

The Congress was inspired by Herzl, and Herzl inspired the Congress. It was then that he inscribed in his diary this new motto: My life is now no romance, but the romance is now my life. He dedicated all his energies to a single purpose, he gave all his time to one ideal, he saw before him once more the burnished domes of Jerusalem.

He felt himself the trustee of an exalted mission and yet not for a single moment did the poet believe himself, as he might well have done, a Messiah.

Herzl is like Napoleon, completely unmodern in the sense of the timeliness of his personality. It is for this reason that one can easily imagine Herzl as a Messiah. But with a difference. A messiah came on a white ass, blowing a ram's horn; Herzl came in a Viennese calèche and spoke with the still small voice of the Hebraic conscience. Messiahs came promising 410 future worlds, Herzl promised only 8,800 square miles. He was a poet who used hyperboles, but his hyperboles were restrained within the limits of creative reason.

HERZL'S DEATH

He was the Susskind von Trimberg of the 19th century. He was a troubadour and a minnesinger recounting the epics of his people, and out of history making history. In the courts of Europe, before emperor and pope, before sultan and king, he wove the tapestry that was his people's future. Behind this wandering poet seeking a lodging for his folk there moved the shadows of the other characters in the poem. Newlinski, the Polish emigré, Vambery, who was a priest in ten cults and then ended by becoming an atheist, and Hechler, who thought that Herzl was a forerunner of the Messianic era, all of these characters create a picture somewhat fantastic. Before the very eyes of our fathers there transpired this romance which reads like an excerpt out of the Arabian Nights. Behold in him a dramatist finding an actual denouement for the plot in which his people were so ravelled; a literary man creating, like the holy spirit, the world out of the *logos*, the state out of a word.

He died in 1904. The poet laid down his pen; the statesman gave up his work. He had striven so long to recapture the original metre of his nation's song that at length his own heart lost its rhythm and he died singularly enough of arrhythmia. But he left a legacy greater than the millions of the Rothschilds; he had left a heritage that was Palestine. His monument is more lasting than bronze, and it is not situated in the cemetery of Vienna. In the conscience of his people is it engraved; and in the tombstone standing in the heart of Israel is written this message, a message that is at one and the same time an inheritance and a last will and testament, a legacy of words – *Wenn ihr wolt, ist es kein marchen* – if you will it this is no fable.

Zionism – Our National Will-to-Live   May 1932

When words have too many meanings, they have none. They then become ambiguous, equivocating, dangerous. They beget misunderstandings which beget conflicts. They mean one thing to Berach, another to Zerach, and still another to Terach. A babel ensues. Men find themselves in the position of the two knights, who meeting on the highway beneath an ensign, engaged in an argument as to whether the shield was red or blue, an argument which was settled only in trial by combat. As a matter of fact, the sign-post was red on one side and blue on the other. The quarrel, therefore, arose only out of the interpretation of the word 'ensign': each knight meant by ensign only half an ensign, to wit, the side which he himself beheld. It may be said without fear of exaggeration that the origins of most wars are to be found in a dictionary rather than an encyclopedia. The exact enunciation of the significance of Godhead has splintered religion into many factions; the precise meaning of 'balance of power' has set nation at the throat of nation. They could not elicit the same meaning out of the same phrase. One blessed the evening star and the other hailed the dawn. Says a Jewish proverb: The tongue has no bones.

Definitions therefore are imperative. Before one can discuss Nationalism, or Zionism, one must first make clear the meaning of the word nation.

NATIONALITY

There are a number of factors which go to make up the idea of nationality. Similarity of physical features, of mental outlook, race, language, country, religion are some of them. A number of these are mere coincidences to the idea of nationality; others are absolute essentials. What are these essentials?

Is a nation characterized by the fact that its members are all of one religion? Most certainly not. The Germans and the English are both distinct nations, yet both are Christian people. If all those who believe in the same religion constituted a single nation, then the last war was really a Civil rather than an International one, because Christian fought against Christian. Furthermore, members of a single nation may confess to different creeds: South-Germany is Catholic, while North-Germany is Protestant.

Is a nation to be identified merely by its language? Again the answer is in the negative. The Swiss people declare French, Italian, and German to be among the national languages. Dutch and English are both spoken by the citizens of South Africa, French and English by those of Canada. The truth is that a nation makes a language, but a language alone does not make a nation. Is there such a group as an Esperanto nation?

Must a nation have a land of its own? All the nations that we see about us have. Those who have lost their land have either disappeared from off the face of the earth, or have degenerated into a gypsy folk, a nomadic tribe. The Jews, due to their strong national character, and life-sustaining traditions, did not exactly become a band of sixteen million gypsies, but they did become what are called *luftmenschen*, that is to say, people up in the air and fixed with no roots in the soil.

We mentioned our strong 'national character'; and this perhaps will lead us to the fashioning of an exact definition. We must first of all admit, however, that although religion and language are not essential elements of nationality, they are important assets to it; and that although a nation may exist even for twenty centuries without land, it cannot live in landlessness for ever. The fact that we have existed in exile for such a long period of time is no argument that we will continue to do so. I know a man who had a weak heart and lived until he was fifty. But without it he might have lived longer; and more fully.

In the final analysis of what is meant by national character it will be found that the best description of a nation is this: *A group of people, acknowledging a common past and tradition, and having a will-to-live as such a group.* For us that past and that tradition is the heritage of our prophets, the legacy of the Talmud, and the epic memory of our heroes and our sages. That thread which was so cruelly snapped at the beginning of this era must be continued, we say, and must be woven into the glorious tapestry of our future.

But this can be achieved only through a national will-to-live. This term is a philosophical phrase but a natural feeling. Everybody acknowledges it. Without it we would succumb to despair and ultimately to suicide. And if a nation wishes to preserve itself from the ignominy of suicide, it too must cherish this will-to-live. One of the elementary ways in which an individual expresses his desire to continue to live is in finding shelter for himself. That same spirit of self-preservation, too, urges a nation to seek shelter and sanctuary in its ancestral land.

For Jews in the Diaspora are threatened on all sides by foreign influences, and inharmonious elements. The language that we speak is not our language. The studies that we undertake are not our studies. The customs that we adopt are not our customs. As a nation we are becoming paralysed, and are unable even to make a national gesture. The words of the Song of Songs can be very aptly applied to Jews in the exile: They have made me a keeper of the vineyards, but my own vineyard have I not kept. Our great men, for example, dedicate their efforts to strange cultures. Literature written by Jews is usually accredited to the language in which it happens to find expression, and is seldom considered as an interpretation of the Hebraic genius. Our artists rarely work upon Jewish lines, and our musicians sell their birthright for a song.

PREVIOUS SOLUTIONS

Most assuredly this is a dismal picture of our life in the *Golus*. Our wandering staff is being used as a rod wherewith to beat us. To solve this problem many attempts have been made, and most of them have resulted in failure. Thus, there were a group of people who thought that in view of the fact that we were (or so they thought) doomed to be pilgrims over the face of the earth forever, the best thing to do under the circumstances, would be to make peace with their environment, to lose themselves among the nations of the world. They are the assimilationists, who foolishly maintained that the only way to save yourself from being murdered nationally, was nationally to commit suicide. Their plan, of course, suffers from great and chronic ailments. First of all, to deny your nationality is hardly a self-respecting thing to do. When one considers the great gifts which our Rabbis and philosophers have bestowed upon humanity, then to deny one's relationship with the nation to which they belong appears to be not only a sign of self-imposed disgrace, but also of actual ignorance. And in the second place, experience has shown that even when these assimilators deny their origin, the people with whom they wanted to mix, rejected them just the same.

On the other hand, there have been some who thought that by creating a strong national feeling in the exile, without the support of a homeland, they might be able to solve that most intricate of puzzles, the Jewish Problem. Before the emancipation of the Jews from ghetto life, this was easily achieved. The uniformity of religion was a uniting force in Jewish life. As a matter of fact the word 'religion' by derivation means 'to bind together'; it bound man to God and Jew to Jew. It is true that during the Middle Ages we did not have a parliament or any kind of representative institution, but for us the House of the Lord was our House of Commons. The synagogue was very frequently our fortress, not only in a metaphorical, but also in a physical sense.

During the nineteenth and twentieth centuries, however, Jews began to mix more and more with the inhabitants of the countries in which they happened to live. Moreover, our religion, too, began to suffer schisms, breaks, divisions into factions and groups. All the efforts of our spiritual leaders, sincere and zealous though they were, have resulted in the creation of what at best seems to be an artificial Judaism. It is a Judaism which is not creating any new values, and which is forced from time to time to make compromises with its environment.

Between the utter absurdity of assimilation on the one hand, and the inadequacy of a Judaism unsupported by a national life and national homeland we are somewhat in the same position as the man who tried to avoid the numerous bankruptcies and failures which are the indices of our current events, with this original idea: He rented a double parlour, and in one room he established a bakery, and in the other an undertaking business. If people lived, he argued, they must have bread, and if they died, they must have burial. Coming or going, he had them both ways. But the result was that he went bankrupt just the same. Why? Because in these days *nisht me hot gelebt en nisht me iz geshtorben*. People neither lived, nor died; they just continued to exist.

So, too, we Jews, between the devil of assimilation and the deep sea of a profound though unplumbed Judaism, continued to exist by half-measures. We are neither here nor there, because we are everywhere.

Zionism, however, maintains that to regain our national self-respect, to make possible the continuance of our culture, and to offer us the opportunity to work out our own destiny, we must have a land which is our own. We frequently hear about the conflict between Hellenism, a form of assimilation, and Judaism, and we read in the story of the Maccabees how our ancestors overcame this menace to their national integrity. It may be stated here that Hellenistic philosophy is very attractive; its message of recklessness and carefree life found eager votaries among the weak-willed. Hellenism, moreover, has cast its charm over many nations of Europe. We do not know how our ancestors would have been able to cope with this cultural spell if they had been in exile. It is precisely because they were fighting against Antiochus for their religion and their customs upon their very own soil, and for their very own soil, that they were able to muster to their ranks such zealous and such self-sacrificing soldiers.

OUR WORK IN PALESTINE

Already we see that those who have actually settled in Palestine are happier than they could possibly be in any corner of the Diaspora. They are creating a new life, a new culture, a new environment. They are what no Jew has been before the appearance of Zionism: the masters of their souls and the captains of their fate. When we remember by what self-sacrifice this bounty is attained, when we recall what difficulties they have to face, we cannot help but apply to these men of blood and iron the noble lines of Rupert Brooke.

> Blow, bugles, blow, they brought us for our dearth,
> Holiness lacked so long, and love and pain;
> Honour has come back, as a King, to earth,
> And paid his subjects with a royal wage;
> And Nobleness walks in our ways again;
> And we have come into our heritage.

INFLUENCE ON DIASPORA

But how can Zionism help those who are forced by circumstances to remain in the countries of the exile while their brethren go to Palestine? In this respect the importance of Eretz-Israel lies in the spiritual influence it will have and already has on the Diaspora, as a cultural centre, as a vortex of Jewish life. It radiates to every corner of the dispersion its glowing warmth, and brings to every forlorn *minyan* a knowledge that they are not merely a crew without an anchor. They then become not exiles with the mark of Cain upon their brows, but self-willed and proud expatriates, who could, if they wished, return at any moment to the land which is ready to welcome them. The position of the Jews in exile is like the position of the flower known as the heliotrope, which gets its name from two Greek words meaning 'to turn to the sun.' No matter where this flower grows, whether vertically on a straight field, or horizontally from a crevice on a cliff, it always turns its petals to the sun. Without the sun it would cease to grow; growing, it lifts its face to its life-giver. Need we say that exiled Jews, too, will live in the knowledge of a revived Palestine, and will turn to Eretz-Israel, not only as a religious obeisance but also as one who turns to the source of his life-blood.

HISTORICAL NOTE

The ideal of Zionism, of course, did not crop up overnight. Jerusalem, like Rome, is not built in a day. Zionism is as old as the exile itself. There is an old Jewish legend which expresses this in poetical language, saying that on the very day the Temple was destroyed, the Messiah was born. In the course of centuries this ideal has undergone many developments: first, Messianism, when Jews thought that a personal Messiah would arise and would, with the help of God, lead them back to the Holy Land; then came the Pre-Herzlites, composed mainly of the Chovevei Zion who without getting political guarantees for a Jewish state in Palestine, none the less undertook the establishment of colonies and settlements; then Theodor Herzl, the Father of political Zionism, who with unswerving loyalty to his ideal, and with an inspirational fervour carried on negotiations with prince and potentate on behalf of the Jewish state; later the Zionist organization, and today the extended Jewish Agency, which embraces in its ranks both Zionists and non-Zionists. Thus Zionism is a national movement with a world influence. The fact that, if all the news pertaining to Zionism and Palestine were to be left out from the Jewish Press, the press would remain with practically nothing but advertisements and blank space is an indication of the influence that Palestine has upon the Diaspora, and the interest the Diaspora evinces in Palestine.

SOME DISTINCTIONS

Nationalism, however, must be distinguished from Imperialism. Whereas the Nationalist contents himself with the will-to-live, the Imperialist expresses a will-to-power. He is not satisfied with merely ruling himself, he seeks also to extend his beneficient government (so he thinks) over others. We as a nation have never entertained hopes of imperialistic expansion, we do not wish to rule others, nor do we wish others to rule us. Our motto in Palestine is – not to dominate, nor to be dominated. Zionism is a declaration of Israel's equality among the nations. We will strive to excel and surpass, it is true, but only through intelligence, character, and idealism. When Disraeli was asked how he expected to win his election, and on what ground he stood, he answered, 'I stand on my head.'

Because these are the principles on which our Nationalism is based it follows that our movement is also an international one. Internationalism certainly does not mean the mixing of nations into a single undistinguishable mass; as a matter of fact, internationalism presupposes separate nations to begin with. As such we Zionists are ever-ready to take up our burdens and our privileges amongst international groups.

But Zionism to us is not only a political plan, an economic solution, or a cultural way of life. It is also a faith. We are positively convinced, and we firmly do believe that we can no longer continue without a country to call our own. A French nationalist was once asked what he would do if the Atlantic flooded France. He shrugged his shoulders, in a gesture of despair. A Zionist was asked what he would do if the Mediterranean would suddenly inundate Palestine. He said: 'I would learn to live under water.'

Such must be our credo, and such our undaunted determination.

The Twin Racketeers of Journalism   8 July 1932

Several years ago, out of a clear blue sky, there fell upon the Jewish community of this province, a series of evil-smelling and malevolent thunderbolts. With that sufferance which is the badge of all our tribe, we at first dismissed these puerile explosions as one dismisses the firecrackers of irresponsible street-gamins. For we knew their origin. We knew that two professional mud-slingers, two double-jointed acrobats leaping from one political party into the other, had appeared upon the journalistic scene and were auctioning off their bankrupt souls to the highest bidder. The sulphurous fumes of slander which filled the atmosphere and which reeked to very heaven, had an unmistakeable odour. We knew who emitted it. And the mire and dirt which was slung at the Jewish name had an obvious explanation: mud-masseurs were trying to make a living. Such, at first, was our greeting to the unscrupulous *gemini* in the political zodiac.

If we did feel chagrin and bitterness at these attacks, our misery at least had company. There was hardly a public man in this province, in either party, who at one time or other did not see himself besmirched by the katzenjammer kids of French-Canadian journalism. For their slanders, no accusation was too low, and no personality too exalted. Not only did they level their aim against living French-Canadians – Taschereau, David, Bourassa, to name but a few – but they spared not the dead, and wrothful against the patriotic spirit of L.J. Papineau, for that he was instrumental in obtaining Jewish emancipation in Quebec, recently exhumed and dissected him in their columns. Their position was a clear one. Calumny was their business, and the only condition was cash, no questions asked. Their overhead expense was covered by their underground income. And the turnover was excellent. They throve.

They throve to such an extent, indeed, that soon one single sheet sufficed not their all-embracing needs. They established, therefore, an unholy trinity of journals, the calibre of which can be easily surmised from their names. Of the *Goglu*, – Bobolink – the Prime Minister declared, in a famous speech before the legislature of the province, that it fed on dung. The humped anatomy of the *Camel* is too well known to require further elaboration; and the *Mirror*, which published their distorted reflections, was of that type, commonly seen in circuses, which elongates the object into ridiculous gauntness, or broadens it to elephantine obesity. With these as mouthpieces, our worthy wights sallied forth, inundating the Jewish community beneath slander, and occasionally sending a libellous expectoration in the direction of their political foes.

These knights, *sans coeur et sans approche*, then looked about them for matter lurid and sensational. Accordingly, out of the museum they dragged the entire panoply of mediaevalism, and out of the archives all the Judaeophobic lampoons of the Dark Ages. Reviving the bigotry of seven centuries of barbarism, they accused the Jew of every crime in the criminal code; and when these gave out, invented new ones. The Jew, they wrote in their mad frenzy, infects the merchandise in which he deals. The Jew sprouts horns. The Jew poisons his environment. The Jew plots the overthrow of the world, and so on *ad nauseam*. The only mediaeval accusation which they omitted, and this probably through an ignorance of Latin, was that of the *fetor Judaicus*. Their propaganda, in fine, read like mediaeval manuscript.

To give it the touch of modernity, however, the editors brought their defamations up to date by reiterations of the notorious *Protocols of the Elders of Zion*. They filled their papers with slander as headline, garbled quotation as footnote, and forgery as space-filler. The contents of their pages, moreover, when analyzed, proved that what its publishers could not invent or copy, was supplied to them by a syndicate of anti-Semitic propaganda, trafficking in synthetic venom and co-operative hate. Its headquarters seemed to be Germany: when Hitler sneezed, they caught cold. Thus, the pest of Jew-hatred, like the bubonic plague, was being brought from continent to continent, through the medium of rats.

As this inciting propaganda progressed, we did repeatedly warn the community that it might have a deplorable result, and we urged upon our representatives the necessity for action, immediate and drastic. Apart from the Bercovitch Bill, which died in child-birth, no action was taken. The race-cry continued unchecked.

Our patience and endurance, however, broke its bounds when we read the most recent copy of *Le Miroir*. Plastered across its front page, in letters as black as its intent, there cried the statement that all Jews are murderers. The ritual-blood accusation, in all its horror and gruesomeness was being revived here, in a British country, and now, in the twentieth century. We could not believe our eyes. Was it for this climax that the three great C's of history, civilization, culture, and Christianity had conspired? But there they were – the article incarnadined with blood-accusations (Jews killed Lindbergh's baby), and a gory cartoon, depicting a creature with horns and beard, presumably a Jew, slitting the throat of a Christian child! This issue, moreover, was dramatically timed so that it should coincide with our centennial celebration of Jewish emancipation. What a grand finale!

If ever there was a necessity for action, it is now. This evil growth which was not nipped in the bud, must be lopped off before it becomes a veritable apple of Sodom. This is a duty which amounts to a categorical imperative. These attacks are preludes to we know not what. The situation is serious; it merits drastic action. Barbarism cannot be dismissed with an epigram, nor murderous demagogy with a jest. Now is not the time to adopt the Wilsonian attitude and say that we are too proud to fight – the battle is in our hands, and the law courts are open.

It is a curious anomaly of our law, however, that whereas to belabour an individual constitutes libel, to slander an entire community is merely fun. In vain our geometrical theorem that the whole is made up of its component parts; in vain our logical proof that the calumny of a race does a thousand times more harm than the insult of a single person. *Dura lex, sed lex.*

Nonetheless, the fact remains that the aforementioned sheets are liable to prosecution even within the narrow limits of our statutes. They have slandered and libelled Jewish businessmen; they have heaped calumny upon our prominent communal leaders; they have cast opprobrium upon our representatives; they have urged boycott; they counselled measures in restraint of trade. Their misdemeanours, moreover, have smacked of the lowest kind of blackmail ever perpetrated. Did a Jewish business man advertise in their pages, he was boosted and proclaimed a leader in Canadian progress; did he withdraw his ad, he was forthwith converted from a captain of industry into a deserter and renegade.

The case is a clear one. If ever libel was committed, it was committed in the columns of these journals. The injured parties, men whose business enterprises have been irreparably hurt, must take immediate action, if not in their own interests, then in the interest of the Jewish community in which they play a prominent part. Those who are wedded to the Jewish cause cannot declare that they are powerless; impotency, apparent and manifest, is a ground for annulment of marriage.

Not only must action be taken on the part of individuals, but the public opinion in this province and in the Dominion, too, must be roused to condemn these reprehensible attacks upon an innocent minority. Jewish youth in this city cannot stand with arms akimbo, and watch the progress of this chauvinistic charlatanism; a definite stand must be taken. The Canadian Jewish Committee, now firmly established, with a constitution modelled upon that of the Board of Jewish Deputies, must emulate also the line of action of that Board. French and English journalists, mindful of the high tradition of their calling, ought also to take measures to crush the yellow scribblings which can but tend to bring their profession into disrepute. The statesmen, too, the statesmen, and not the politicians, of our country, if they are concerned with the moral standards of Canadian life, must bring all their power and influence to bear down upon the two malaria-spreading mosquitoes of Quebec journalism.

We know full well that the journals of which we have written at great and bitter length represent but a negligible minority in this Province. The general attitude of the country towards its Jewish citizens is much more adequately expressed in the Centennial Issue of the *Canadian Jewish Eagle*, appearing to-day. But the fact remains that even microbes are dangerous. The stone which one fool throws into a well, ten wise men cannot withdraw.

An irreparable wrong has been done to the reputation of the Jews of this province. An indelible blot has been cast upon the name of Quebec. Measures must be taken; and redress must be done.

The German Elections   5 August 1932

Despite the depreciating references with which the Left press has greeted the Nazi victory on July 31st, the fact remains that the Hitlerites have appreciably increased their strength in the German Reichstag. Previously represented with only 143 seats, they now have won for themselves 230; and the franchises which they received from a nation victimized by the Versailles treaty and burdened with debts which visit the sins of the fathers upon the third and fourth generations, have been quadrupled since 1928. If Hitler is not yet comfortably seated in the saddle, he has begun at least to mount the governmental charger.

It is wrong, we believe, to explain the spread of the Nazi epidemic as due entirely to the proliferation of the antisemitic germs. The Communist conquest of Berlin, for example, a city in which the Reds bested all their electoral competitors, most certainly cannot be attributed to the spread of Jew-hatred in the Capitol. Besides, antisemitism is not the main plank of the Nazi scaffold; in their operatic farce it is merely an impolite aside, and in their academic training only an extra-curricular activity. The overwhelming success of German Fascism was caused, it seems, by the despair of an oppressed people, which, like a captured beast, now groans under twenty yokes, branded and muzzled. In their darkness and agony, it is no wonder that they put their trust in false prophets. Hitler is an orator, and Hitler promises salvation.

It is idle to conjecture now as to what will be the fate of the German republic. Seers and visionaries rise on all sides; some prophesy a return of the Kaiser, when the hewer of wood at Doorn will come to the rescue of the drawers of water in Germania; others declare that the Centrists under Bruening will make an alliance with the Hitlerites against the Communists and Socialists; others again, prognosticate the outlawing of the Communist party, thus giving the Nazis an unquestionable majority; and still others, foresee a continuation of the von Papen dictatorship. But all of these forecasts are matters of doubt. Only one augury is a matter of certainty: the fate of the Jews in Germany is not a happy one.

For although we declared that antisemitism was to the Hitlerites an extra-curricular activity, it is a well known failing of human nature that man spends more energy on his hobbies than on his vocations. The Jew now stands condemned in Germany as the eternal alien; the deluded mobs who voted for the Brown Shirts now know where to find a scapegoat on which to vent their wrath and explode their indignation. It is a scapegoat with a beard; it is a Jewish scapegoat. Hitler may be powerless to legislate for the good and welfare of his Arians, but his henchmen undoubtedly can now act more freely for the confusion and discomfort of Hebrews.

The Nazis, indeed, assure the world that they will put Germany on her feet again; but, to parody the worst line in the bad poetry of Cicero, it would be 'an unhappy fate of the German state its birth to date from the Semite hate.'

The whole situation, especially as it concerns the Jews, seems to be an irony of facts, a national atavism, a prank of Him whom Heine called the Greater Aristophanes. For the German Jews, the first in our history to accept in theory and in practice the doctrine of assimilation, are now being rudely rejected even by those to whom they made amorous racial and cultural advances. The Germans of the Mosaic persuasion evidently persuaded no one but themselves. To-day they are disillusioned, disillusioned but not completely. Dr. Kaufman, of Hamburg, still thinks that it is the East-European Jews who have 'invaded' the German cities who are responsible for the Fascist reaction.

We do not wish to gloat over the misery of German Jewry, nor do we desire to use its bleeding wounds as the proof of a nationalist thesis. The truth, however, is that many German Jews are beginning to go back to the gods of their fathers; and are reconciling themselves to the idea that Jews they were born, and when they die, especially in Germania, it will be as Jews. Many of them are becoming even Zionists, and are attempting to enter Palestine, despite the numerous immigration restrictions. Sokolow's prophecy is already being fulfilled; so much so, indeed, that entrance into Erez Israel on the part of the erstwhile Germans of the Mosaic persuasion is being essayed even through indirect channels. The Hebrew legend has it that in the darkest hour of Israel's need the Messiah will appear, and that when he appears the bodies of the dead will roll underneath the earth until they rise in the Holy Land. The darkest hour, it seems, is at hand; and the spiritual corpses are already crawling towards the East.

Balfour! Thou Shouldst Be Living at This Hour   9 July 1937

It has happened! The blow which hovered over the head of Jewry, has at long last fallen. Seven months of adjournments, postponements, and procrastinations, have finally ceased. The judgment of the Royal Commission, although at time of writing, not yet officially issued, has been widely publicized. This procedure is not surprising; it is an old diplomatic custom whereby the *sotto voce* secrets of the embassies are the black-type headlines of the international press. The summary of the wisdom of the Royal Commissioners – if such wisdom can indeed be summarized without loss of some invaluable pearls of sapience – indicates that the honourable gentlemen who last December went to sit on the Palestinian egg have, after a half-year's brooding, finally hatched a duckling. It will be dubbed *partition,* and it is no mean achievement; for mathematicians and geographers will readily concur that the partition of Palestine constitutes a masterpiece in the division of the infinitesimal.

This, then, was the Report which would be an echo of the very voice of Justice! This was the climax for which with bated breath we waited all these many months. For all the good that it will achieve, we are inclined to believe, that it would have been better to have postponed such sage counsel indefinitely. This Solomonic wisdom – we use the adjective advisedly, Solomon, in a *cause célèbre* also suggested partition, – is not to our taste. But that is not important. It is to the taste of Royal Commissioners with whom partition has developed into a habit. First it was the cutting off of Transjordania in 1922, and now it is the splitting of Palestine itself. Tomorrow, perhaps, there will be the partition of the partitioned part of the partitioned part; and some time in nineteen hundred and sixty, we suppose, the ninetieth stone of the Wailing Wall will be divided by a Royal Commission of six months' pensiveness.

We have often wondered as to the exact functions of Royal Commissions in British legislative history. Now we know. By the same token that a trader's commission is a ten per cent cut, a Royal Commission is a sixty per cent cut.

Even prior to the issuance of the Report of the Royal Commission, a couple of preliminary betrayals were perpetrated. It appears, first of all, that the Cabinet has so expressed itself upon the contents of the Report that there will be no vital debate upon the subject either in the House of Commons or the House of Lords. Members of the House will not be able, in view of the espousal by the Cabinet of the dicta of the Commissioners, to express a free opinion without precipitating a vote of confidence in the Government. The party whip will, no doubt, co-operate with the commission lash to avoid such a contingency.

If the action of the Cabinet constitutes pre-judgment of a case without hearing of counsel, the action of the Commission constitutes something tantamount to false pretense. For it was clearly understood that the terms of reference of the Commission excluded any discussion of the Mandate. Such was the explicit assurance of the Colonial Secretary. In the light of these assurances, the Jewish Agency, in testifying before the Commission, confined itself to evidence which naturally assumed as its major premise, the fulfilment of the Mandate. Partition means the murder of the Mandate. Upon the vital *considerants* of its judgment, the Royal Commission not only dispensed with counsel; it also avoided the handicap of testimony.

With this basis for its conclusions, the Royal Commission then enters into an analysis of the case. The ambitions of Jews and Arabs are incompatible, say the Commissioners, because the Arabs want an empire and the Jews a home. Accordingly, it seems, justice demands that the home should be cut in twain so that the Arab empire should increase in size. It is inconceivable, is the exclamation of horror, that 400,000 Jews should hold subject a population of one million Arabs. It is forgotten, of course, that this number of Arabs are not natives, but immigrants who have come into the country as a result of that impartial policy which limited the entry of Jews to economic absorptive capacity and the entry of Arabs to their facilities of walking across the border. The Commission, composed entirely of gentlemen, criticizes the weakness of the British Administration in controlling the riots; indeed, reprimands the policeman for inefficient handling of the criminal – and then punishes the victim by making him pay in land, fine and costs, and suffer imprisonment in the cell which is to be called the new Jewish State.

For Palestine is to become a state, – nay, three of them. There will be a Jewish state extending on the west, along the coast, from Ras en Nakura in the north to Beer Tuvia in the south – the modern translation of *from Dan to Beersheba*; on the north along the Syrian frontier; along the east down to the Jordan unto a spot north of Beisan, then indenting in a semi-circle, so as not to touch, forsooth, Jenin and Tulkarm. The British will rule over Jerusalem – half of it, or all of it, it is presently a subject of negotiation – Bethlehem, Nazareth, a corridor from Jerusalem to Jaffa, and will also go mandating over the railways therein contained. The Negev, too, will be mandated territory. The rest of the country goes to the Arabs, to widen the territories of Emir Abdullah. Thus, Palestine, like Gaul, is classically divided into three parts.

It thus appears that the Balfour Declaration, once a headline across the pages of Jewish history, has been reduced to less than a footnote. For in 1917, the promise – how ironic that word now sounds! – envisaged an area on both sides of the Jordan, of 45,000 square miles. By the verdict of 1922, that area was drawn and quartered; and 10,000 square miles were left in Erez Israel. Now, still another amputation takes place; and the final area of the Jewish state will be about 7% of the original promise. Such may well be the settlement of a bankrupt; but certainly not that of the British Empire.

An examination of the maps – there are, it seems, two appendices to the report: (a) maps, (b) battleships – will disclose some startling anomalies. It becomes obvious, first of all, that the Jewish territory consists mainly of land already bought. Nonetheless, Daganiah, Gesher, and Naharaim, by one of those quirks which characterize arbitrary map-slicing, will become Arab territory. Jericho, despite benefit of trumpets, swells the realm of the Emir. Hebron and the resting place of the Patriarchs goes to sanctify Pan-Arabia. Shechem, now called Nablus, becomes, over the protests of Simeon and Levi, Arabic territory. The Dead Sea, with its great chemical riches and the Rutenberg electric plant, will be interred in the Arab State.

And now the lion and the lamb can lie down together. Except that there doesn't seem to be much room for the lamb, unless he really be an inconspicuous muttonhead. Moreover, there does not seem to be much devoted belief that this report, advertised by the Commissioners as a panacea, as soothing and pacifying balm in Gilead, will truly accomplish that end. Surely the warships now rushing to the Palestine coast are not travelling there for the playful purpose of shooting off a salvo of jubilee?

Indeed, the Royal Commissioners, with regal munificence, recommend a grant of ten million dollars and an additional unspecified contribution for the transfer of Arab population from within the Jewish State into Transjordan. That, it appears, is a price for harmony. It marvels us, however, that if the perspicacity of the Commissioners feels that a grant of ten million will satisfy the Arab demand in the Jewish State as *they* have constituted it, why could not a proportionate sum have satisfied those demands in the Jewish State as presently constituted?

The issuance of the Report is timed with a sense of the macabre. Particularly at a time when in Poland, in Germany, and in other countries where legislation and statistics have rendered our people a surplus population, thousands of Jews are clamoring for entry into their Homeland, particularly at such a time, is it cruel and callous to constrict that Homeland to the dimensions of a strait-jacket. For the Royal Commissioners have, in fact, not recommended a Jewish State; it is a Jewish suburb that they are setting up, a ghetto on the Mediterranean. For while the Churchill White Paper lopped Palestine into the size, as the Yiddish saying goes, of a yawn, the Peel Report has diminished it to the size of a sneeze. Once upon a time, as the fairy tale reads, Palestine was designed as a foothold for the Jewish people; the modern commentary has been written; it will be a foothold – for toe-dancers.

In the interval, until the Jewish State is finally set up – it has already been upset – the acquisition by Jews of land in future Arab territories and by Arabs of land in future Jewish territory will be prohibited. Observe the impartiality of the Commissioners' phrases; both will be prohibited. That Arabs don't buy land from Jews is irrelevant. The Jewish State, moreover, will still, during the transitional period, a period which is usually more elastic than rubber, be governed as to immigration by the Simpsonian principle of economic absorptive capacity.

There are some Jews, to whom sufferance is the badge of all their tribe, who adopt a pose of practicality, shrug their shoulders, and say: We accept. Such an attitude is impossible. It can not be sincere. It is, it must be accompanied by the *arrière pensée*. We accept, these seem to say, temporarily; in our heart of hearts we can not ever abandon hope of redeeming what is being taken from us. We accept because we are helpless to do otherwise. We accept because we hope by peaceful penetration, and by the accidents of circumstance, to penetrate into territory forbidden to us. We will make treaties with Abdullah, we will, from the vantage point of our pedestal (that's all it will be) play a role in international politics. Our economics will achieve what our politics failed to achieve.

We submit that this attitude is not only defeatist but also illusory. It is, to our observation, the policy of a provident man not to forego his possessions readily, simply because he can mentally console himself that perhaps, maybe, somehow, he will get it back. Nor does one have to be a maximalist to insist upon that minimum of 10,000 square miles. For acceptance implies not only dispossession, but also thanks to the bailiff. Moreover, when Transjordan was sliced away, we accepted; the world now beholds our reward. The Arabs never accepted, they contend, the implications of the Balfour Declaration; behold *their* reward!

The Peel Commission Report is a complete reversal of British policy. It is a breach of English promises, a denial of the commitments that Albion (adjectives are unnecessary) has made to the Jewish people. The neat compliments and pious hopes which the Commissioners have included in the Report, in no way alter its nature. Balfour has been betrayed. And not only Balfour.

The Twentieth Zionist Congress will have to deal with this situation with dignity and firmness. After forty years of political Zionism, this is the result; after forty years of wandering in Palestine, we land in the wilderness.

The Report can not be accepted! One cannot afford to delude oneself with mental reservations and bosom-solatium that its effects will be temporary. The old spectre of the *Nachtasyl* – of half a slice better than none – must not be resurrected. The Congress must live up to its traditions in Jewish life. Remember Uganda!

Vandal and Victim   18 November 1938

The entire world still stands aghast at the monstrous happenings in Germany which have in the past week disgraced the name of civilization. Because an irresponsible Jewish youth, aged seventeen, maddened by the reports of what was happening to his near kin in Germany, went forth and assassinated the secretary of the German Embassy in France, such vengeance was wreaked upon the entire Jewish population in Germany as has no parallel, either in the annals of barbarism or in the dossiers of gangsters. Spontaneously – the word is Goering's – assault upon Jews and arson on synagogues were perpetrated throughout the length and breadth of the German Reich. So miraculous was the spontaneity, that the pogroms began in every city at the same hour, ceased simultaneously, and began again at a given moment, the whole with robot-like precision. The business was as spontaneous as a schedule; the organized massacres of Czarism were blunderingly amateurish compared to this orgy of Nazi sadism. Germany appeared in its true colour – the Jack the Ripper among nations.

Lest the cup of bitterness of German Jewry be not full, the geniuses of Aryan malevolence set about to pass a series of draconian edicts. All Jews were expelled from every institution of learning; the ghetto is being re-established; and a collective fine of over four hundred million dollars – a devil-send to the depleted German finances – was imposed upon the entire Jewish population. German Jewry has been condemned to pauperization, madness, and suicide.

Civilized countries have already reacted to this saturnalia of bestiality by horrified indictments which have branded the Nazi regime as a government of outlaws with whom it is contamination to treat. It remains to be seen whether the foreign policy of the democracies will keep in step with its public opinion. Already President Roosevelt has recalled his ambassador from Germany, an unusual procedure which must be regarded by the Germans as a direct condemnation of the Olympic savagery they recently permitted themselves. Will this action be followed up by other activities designed to manifest to the Nazi bandits that they cannot forever go on 'beating the rap'? What are the thoughts to-day of those who have been extending their hand of friendship to this government dyed in blood? Is a rapprochement with murderers the objective of European appeasement? Do not amiable negotiations with them constitute the negotiators accessories after the fact?

The Allied Powers may now well pause to reflect as to what would have been their fate had Germany won the war. If the treatment visited upon helpless Jews, a nation of hostages in the hands of political racketeers, is any kind of criterion as to their manner with the conquered, then the treaty of Versailles was a monument of generosity compared to the *vae victis* terms which Germany would have imposed upon its victims. To co-operate in the extension of the influence in Europe of this citadel of barbarism, therefore, is to betray the interests of humanity; to accord them new colonial territory is callously to throw some additional sacrifices into their cauldron of hatred.

In the meantime, it must be made clear to the German Reich that there is a limit to patience, a boundary to forgiveness, a point at which civilized countries can no longer maintain their polite aloofness, and keep faith with their conscience. And that point has been reached!

For let no one imagine that in the cesspool of iniquity beyond the Rhine, these things happen only to mere Jews. To-day it is the Jews who have been reduced to serfdom, decreed into helotry, made lower than the worm. But to-morrow? Consider the fate of Cardinal Innitzer, whose home lies in ruins, the work of Nazi hoodlums. Consider the fate of Cardinal Faulhaber, in daily terror of his life. To-morrow? To-morrow it will be Catholics, the Protestants, all Christians whose doctrine of love is anathema to the savages who have sprung up upon the seats of the mighty in Germany. There is a lunatic abroad in Europe; and the world had better give heed.

The world had better give heed to the glaring fact that, under the Nazi regime, the principles of international law have been abolished. A conquering nation does not treat its prisoners of war with that ruthlessness with which the German Reich has treated its Jewish citizens. Decency is exiled from that land; honour has been expelled from it; civilization has been placed in a ghetto. If ever there was a case of violent insanity which merited segregation, it is the case of the German leaders, mad with Hitlerics; if ever there was a source of pestilence which deserved quarantine, it is that of the German pirate ship of state.

For the immediate moment, however, the urgent problem is to take measures towards the salvaging of the ruins of German Jewry. Those countries which have hitherto maintained a closed-door policy cannot now afford to turn a deaf ear to those who are agonizingly calling from the depths of their despair for aid and succour. Until now, refugees were merely a category of people in the records of the League of Nations; to-day a refugee is the symbol of the eternal scapegoat, a living appeal to the heart of decency, a human invocation to its conscience. One cannot, one must not, slam the door in the face of a man escaping from a burning house in the cold and darkness of night!

Insofar as Jews happily situated in a free country on this side of the

Atlantic are concerned, it is our duty, in this our hour of sorrow, to manifest to the world at large, by organized meetings of Jew and Gentile and by responsible utterances, that our brethren in Germany are not utterly forsaken, and that not in silence and submissiveness do we accept the cruel fate that barbarians have visited upon them. Let Canadian Jewry remember those who in this day and age, died *al kdushas hashem*; let them remember the synagogues burned, and the scrolls polluted, the victims in concentration camps, and the victims not yet in concentration camps, walking the earth, as in a nightmare; let them remember the tears and the agony of our flesh and blood in the land of the Hamaniac, and let our voice issue in sorrow, in anguish and in protest, so that the conscience of civilization which has been dead may live again, and so that in this cosmic Sodom the righteous may be heard again!

Le Devoir Sees Its Duty   2 December 1938

On Friday, November 24, the *Le Devoir* announced to its breathless readers, that on the next day would appear a magnum opus on the Jews in Germany. The readers were insomniac with impatience. Then the next day came; *Le Devoir* dutifully arrived. And Pelletier oped his lips to speak.

He began by shedding a couple of paragraphs of crocodile tears on behalf of the German Jews, and by damning the Nazis as naughty, naughty. They really shouldn't have done such things. It simply wasn't nice. He then enumerated – just to show that he knew what was happening – the abominations which the German Fascists had perpetrated, made the proper gestures of disapproval, and uttered a sigh – perhaps it was only a belch – for stricken Jewry. Then he proceeded to reveal what was really on his mind.

What did *The Star* mean, he asked, by extending an invitation to Jewish refugees? Did not Mr. Chamberlain say that they could go to – Tanganyika? Then why should *The Montreal Daily Star* speak of vast virgin territories suitable for Jewish colonization?

Indeed, M. Pelletier ventured an opinion as to why *The Star* was, to use his own perspicacious phrase, so concerned over Jews. It was – M. Pelletier, managing editor of *Le Devoir*, evidently judged all by his own standards – because *The Star* already had many Jewish advertisers, and sought more.

We overlook for the moment a base insinuation, no doubt born of envy, which attributes to a distinguished contemporary newspaper such low motives upon an issue of such importance as to constitute in the reactions to it, the true test of humanity. For *The Montreal Daily Star*, it must be remembered, did not content itself with merely analyzing the situation of German Jewry to say *Too bad, it's really not sporting; The Montreal Star* adopted the attitude which lay in the premises, an attitude which required, by all the standards of decency, that something should be done, and not merely that something should be prettily said.

That, however, is not M. Pelletier's idea. His solution to the problem would be that a transcript of his paragraphs of consolation be sent to the Jews in Germany so that it furnish reading material wherewith to while away the lazy hours in a concentration camp.

The Star had ventured to suggest that Jews might colonize certain areas of Canada. Effectively, this was like waving a red flag in front of the sensitive Pelletier. It immediately brought out the scholar and statistician in him, and he set about proving, like two and two makes five, that Hebrews never can be colonists. Who ever heard of such a thing? Suddenly, however, the thought rushed through Pelletier's mind that perhaps Jews are successful colonists in Palestine. Out came the impulse of generosity, the dictum of chivalry, the utterance of Nature's nobleman: *The Jew can cultivate Palestine? Why, let him go there!*

Once Pelletier works himself up to this inspired mood, the rest follows easily. He calculates the number of Jewish lawyers in Montreal, finds them many, and like a new creative god, sees that it is not good. The number of Jewish doctors also taxes his mathematics.

Finally, – indeed, not soon enough – he concludes in language that is a veritable incitement to attack. We translate, verbatim: 'If one wishes to open the doors of this country to this new strange element, let one say so clearly! Let one not use towards true Canadians false and absurd representations, subterfuges easily unmasked! Let one also realize the danger inherent in this policy. Canadians will all too soon become disillusioned before the influx of newcomers to our cities where certain groups, already at the end of their patience – unemployed vainly seeking work, young men without jobs annoyed at seeing the newly-arrived take their places – may be tempted to give themselves over to anti-semitic excesses, regrettable it is true, but nonetheless explicable in the premises. Let them not be provoked!'

If this Pecksniffian mode of writing is not in itself an incitement to provocation, then incitement has no meaning. M. Pelletier knows well enough that the type of journalism of which he is herein guilty is twin brother to the pasquinades in the Nazi press which preluded the arrival of Hitler.

It is very difficult to argue with M. Pelletier. Of what use will it be to inform him that the arrival of new blood into his sparsely populated country will not deprive people of jobs, but will increase the possibilities of employment among the general population? What purpose can it serve to draw to his attention that new cities will be built, new colonies established, new industries introduced? It is not to these that he really objects. We strongly suspect that what he objects to is the 'new foreign element,' to wit, Jews. The words are the words of Pelletier, but the psychology is the psychology of that same racism which he says that he decries.

The attitude of Pelletier is particularly disappointing as coming from the editor of a newspaper renowned for its piety. In what part of the Holy Evangelists did Pelletier learn the phrase 'foreign unassimilable elements'? Surely the founder of his religion – a religion which is being as vigorously attacked in Germany as the Jewish, and about which attacks Pelletier has been singularly silent – surely that founder considered all men brothers, and did not speak luridly of 'strangers.'

Assuredly there can be no polemic between individuals who do not agree on fundamental definitions. Pelletier's definition of decency, if any, baffles us. We must content ourselves therefore with drawing to his attention the parable of the good Samaritan. Let him remember what is written in the New Testament about that man, who when he beheld a fellow-man, beset by thieves and murderers, bleeding and sore afflicted, turned his head and crossed to the other side of the street. For that is precisely what Pelletier has done.

The Mahatma and the Jewish Question

16 December 1938

Mahatma Gandhi, hearing that by dictatorial ukase, the Jews of Germany have been added to that caste, has just realized that there are untouchables elsewhere than in India. An authority on that subject, he proceeds to give advice to the parties concerned. But his advice, we regret to say, is a peculiar admixture of Hindoo mysticism and Anglophobe realpolitik.

In the first place, he produces from the capacious folds of his loin-cloth, that great weapon of his invention – passive resistance; and he counsels German Jewry to swing this instrument against the Nazis, and not to leave the frontiers of Allemania. We admit forthwith that there would be something noble, heroic, and self-sacrificial about such an attitude; but there would also be a great deal of the foolhardy and stupid therein. What would passive resistance of Jews in Germany mean? It would mean that the victims of Nazi oppression would continue to be robbed, murdered, thrown into concentration camps, and all for the noble and altogether futile purpose of making Hitler blush. We feel that such an approach is entirely out of the question; only a fanatical mystic could propound martyrdom as a revenge upon the oppressor.

The entire fallacy of Gandhi's suggestion lies, of course, in the fact that this erstwhile Indian lawyer has forgotten how to draw distinctions. The passive resistance of a majority against a minority – the people of India against its

British officials – is, of course, very frequently a formidable weapon; but the passive resistance of a minority against a majority – the Jews of Germany against the German Government – is purely suicide, with trimmings. So much for Gandhi's mysticism.

The mahatma then proceeds to doff the veils of the metaphysical to don the cap of realpolitik. The Jews, he says, ought not to go to Palestine because there are Arabs there. They should, of course, stay in Germany and supply an elevating example of saintly self-sacrifice. It is wrong to impose the Jews upon the Arabs. Gandhi, of course, assumes that this is an imposition. Being a mystic, he is not concerned with the fact that it is the Jews alone who maintain the Palestinian treasury, nor with the fact that many Arabs themselves, not having heard of the Hindoo philosopher's opinions, do not consider the arrival of Jews as unwelcome.

In brief, the sum total of Gandhi's advice to Jewry in its hour of need is to turn its other cheek to the oppressor, and to keep its feet off the Holy Land. Rochefoucauld was wise, indeed, when he noticed how easy it is to bear with equanimity the troubles of another.

The Feast of Lights   23 December 1938

The celebration of the feast of Chanukah this year is not that occasion for festivity which it might be. For we have ourselves become a sort of Chanukah symbol, – a nation of pancakes scraped on the grate of antisemitism, and fried upper and nether, a people of *dreidlach*, spinned this way and that, and falling towards the four sides of the wind.

Nonetheless, in the very midst of our trial and tribulation – while our brethren in Germany see themselves compelled to give to the tyrant an enforced Chanukah *gelt*, and while the swine enters onto the altar of our synagogues, with no Mattathias to stop him – we do still recall, from the pages of the glorious epic of the Hasmoneans, that not always have we suffered defeat. Victory, too, has been ours; and as Tennyson once said, 'Sorrow's crown of sorrows is – remembering the happier things ...'

To-day we find ourselves in an age of inverted miracles. Whilst with the Maccabees that cruse of oil which was thought sufficient for one day did, in fact, last eight, to-day our science and our education, the perfection of twenty centuries of intellectual light, is not sufficient to dispel the darkness which has spread, as it were, overnight. Perhaps, however, this is because the oil of the Hasmoneans was sanctified oil, and the light of contemporary science, preparing its poison-gas, and lighting its bombs, is profaneness itself.

Howbeit, it is from the might of our past that we draw strength for our future. We are not of those Jews who, as a class, consist of 'outlivers' – we have outlived the Pharaohs, we have outlived Haman, we have outlived etcetera – we believe that our national destiny lies in living, not merely in outliving; nonetheless, we must draw a great deal of consolation from the fact that others have wickedly risen up against us, have sought utterly to destroy us, and to-day their memory is no more than an obscure historical allusion.

Who was Antiochus Epiphanes? If he is remembered at all, he is remembered as one who talked himself into believing the Aryan theory of his day. We, who issue from an old and tried people, do tell people that those sons of Belial who presently lord it over an intimidated world and who think that they are already writing the history of the future, will be mentioned in that history, if at all, in a footnote on the twentieth century Chanukah, yet to be celebrated.

Mr. H.G. Wells: Crystal-Gazer   23 December 1938

Mr. H.G. Wells has again sallied forth into the realm of imaginative literature. Having with the precision of an eye-witness described in his previous masterpieces the mores of Mars and the men in the moon, the Admirable Crichton of the twentieth century undertakes to tell what is wrong with the Jew, and the Jew that he describes is as mythical a character as the milkman of the Milky Way.

In the current issue of *Liberty* – a magazine which is a sort of literary Grand Hotel in whose printed lobby one encounters Leon Trotsky rubbing shoulders with Vicki Baum, and Douglas 'Wrong-Way' Corrigan backing himself into Princess Kropotkin – Mr. Wells, having doffed the toga of the historian and the undergarments of the romancer, speedily enwreathes himself in the seven veils of prophecy, and in Sibylline tones, tells *Liberty*'s millions of readers what is the future of the Jews.

And what, pray, is the sum total of the wisdom of the oracle? That Jews have no future, unless – they cease being Jews. They must, wherever possible – even Wells must have read in his *Outline of History* that it is not everywhere possible, – assimilate. The solution to the Jewish problem, if we may paraphrase him, is dissolution.

The Jews, he says, display a 'certain national egotism.' If a desire to survive is a manifestation of 'national egotism,' Mr. Wells himself, we venture to say, is a prize example of selfishness. But let Mr. Wells utter his own nonsense. 'They (the nationalist Jews) have intruded into an Arab country in a mood of intense racial exhibitionism. Instead of learning the language of their adopted country, they have vamped up Hebrew. They have treated the inhabitants of Palestine practically as a nonexistent people ... The Jews think that they are peculiar and chosen. The Germans have produced a very good parallel to Zionism in the Nordic theory.'

Here, then, issuing from the pen of one who pretends to be a scholar, though the pretense of being a gentleman is abandoned, is a powerful heap of fallacious twaddle. The Bible, as Ben-Gurion once pointed out, is the Magna Carta of the Jews to Palestine, a charter which has been redundantly confirmed by fifty-two nations – one for every week in the year – but still historian and international student Wells dubs their arrival in their Homeland as 'intrusion.' If they return to Palestine as 'intruders,' where, may we ask, do they not intrude? Or is it to be assumed that the great humanitarian holds that their very existence upon this planet is an invasion?

What 'racial exhibitionism in Palestine' means, we must admit, escapes us. Are we to gather that once having 'intruded' into their home, the Jews should have hid themselves in the caves of its mountains, in the bulrushes of its rivers? Does Mr. Wells, in his country, conceal his light under a bushel? He doesn't; in fact, he sends that light across an ocean, and it sheds more shadow than illumination.

For according to his lights, Palestine is an 'adopted' country, where Jews sin, among other things, in a shameless vamping up of Hebrew. Delightful phrase, that! Worthy of a man of letters and a lover of the rights of small people! Can you imagine the gall of this unsocial race – they insist on speaking their modernized Hebrew! O for a vamped up Wells! A Wells who would not so far forget truth as to accuse Jews of treating the Arabs as non-existent people. The indictment, of course, is not horrific; is it still better than to be convicted of exploiting other peoples. But still, is it an accusation which betrays either ignorance or falsehood. It is trite to repeat that the whole Jewish economy in Palestine has brought untold benefits to the Arab population. However, Wells would still have us believe that for the past two years, the Jews of Palestine have been oblivious to their surroundings, and have been defending themselves against the invisible bombs of phantom bandits of a non-existent people!

And where did Mr. Wells pick up the notion that we regarded ourselves as the Chosen People? We are chosen only in the sense that every scribbler can choose to foretell our future, and analyze our phrenology. Jews have never maintained that they were the salt of the earth, the cream of society, the supermen. They are amply content if they are accorded the equal rights of human beings.

We have little to say of Mr. Wells' comparison between Zionism and the Nordic theory, save that it is a colossal piece of blind Zion-hating effrontery. What concentration camps have the Zionists established in the name of their Zionism? What races have they reduced to sub-human levels by reason of being, to use Wells' phrase, history-ridden? The parallel is unscientific, shameless, and venomous.

By way of solution to world problems, Wells suggests the panacea, Education. In this we agree. Only education can remove Antisemitism; and Mr. Wells may well begin with self-instruction. If he wishes to write on the sources of Jew-hatred, let him take the advice of Sir Philip Sidney on the art of poesy:

Look in thy heart and write!

Conquest à la Carte   30 December 1938

The latest incidents in German realpolitik manifest very clearly that the sense of aesthetic refinement which the Bavarians lack in their culinary sauerkraut-and-frankfurter art, they do possess in their diplomatic pot-pourri. For the history of the past five years has shown that the German Reich has proceeded towards the gobbling up of Europe with the deliberate savoir-faire of a political gourmet. The repast of Hitler began naturally enough, with some juicy hors-d'oeuvres snatched from off the plate of Versailles, the whole preceded by an introductory cocktail sipped in the re-occupied Rhine. This was later followed by the agglutination of a submissive wienerschnitzel, and temporarily completed by a munching of the upper crust of Czechoslovakia. That this light diet, we may add, is most agreeable to its participants is amply evidenced by the comfortable proportions of Goering.

Hunger, however, grows apace. The maître d'hôtel of the Reich, considering how the clientele is smacking its lips at the toothsomeness of the territorial tid-bits, now announces the pièce-de-résistance of the glutton's menu – the Ukraine.

As early as the days of the first composition of *Mein Kampf*, Hitler has dreamed of the wassail cup which he would at some future date quaff down within the borders of the fat lands of the Ukraine. Now, belching with the semi-satisfied noises of the half-fed, he ponders the Ukraine as a tasty morsel, and has invited for its preparation the help of those cooks best suited for the preparation thereof.

He finds them in Paris, in Paris where the union of chefs and the society of waiters is composed almost entirely of abdicated monarchs and pretending princes; for bad Russians, like good Americans, when they die, even if only politically, go to Paris.

Accordingly, Count Vladimir has become an aide of Hitler for the purpose of giving artificial respiration to a moribund Ukrainian nationalism, later to be used as a Nazi vanguard. The plan, of course, is full of uncertainties and pitfalls.

A renascent Ukraine will certainly not please Poland, so-called ally of Germany, between whom there is a ten year treaty of undying love. King Carol, too, sits jittery on his throne, fearing that German propaganda is going through that ancient pastime of speaking of the wheat of the Ukraine and meaning the oil of Rumania.

We need hardly mention the reactions of the Russian bear. We doubt very much whether the Nazis will have that picnic wresting territory from the u.s.s.r. that they have had in obtaining free lunches from Central European powers. It may be true that Soviet Russia is considerably weakened by the liquidation of some of its generals – in Russia, evidently, generals do not die in bed – but it must be remembered that when the captains go, the soldiers remain, and that in fighting Russia, the Reich will meet not only with the resistance of a proud proletariat, but also with the repulses of a resurgent Russian nationalism, which evokes, even from such reactionary quarters as those of the White Russians, led by Denikin, expressions of inverted patriotism.

In fine, the totalitarian regime in Germany will have to wait a while until it has thoroughly masticated and digested the victims of 1938, before attempting to swallow down its proposed quarry. Hitler will have to ponder the possibility of choking on black bread and being scalded by the borsht of the Ukraine. In the meantime, the world may consider the desires of the Nazi regime as but another instance of that Shakesperian truism about those whose appetite grows with what they feed upon. And it is a truism which the democratic countries ought well to bear in mind; for we believe that even the acquisition of Russian territory, if ever that day should come to pass, will not sate the continuously famished digestive tracts which have fed too eagerly upon that appetizer, the Will to Power. Indeed, we are inclined to believe that having cleaned up the table of Europe, the Nazis, tooth-picks in teeth, will look around for a tasty dessert and like that character in the fairy tale, will sing forth 'Fee, Fi, Fo, Fum – I smell the blood of an Englishman.'

War: The Evolution of
a Menagerie   10 February 1939

Mad warriors have frequently maintained with that perverseness which is the characteristic of the intelligence called military that methods of warfare have been the most important factors in the development of civilization. One has but to read the classic Oman's History of organized killing to come to the conclusion that the instruments of battle, and their application, have considerably altered – not civilization, forsooth, – but the chronicles of man.

The great terror which now agitates the human mind is not so much the terror of war, as of that terribly horrific, new instrument of destruction – the bombing plane. For us there appears to be a general evolution in the methods which men have devised in killing each other, methods which they have borrowed from the animal kingdom.

The caveman, undeveloped and uncivilized (?), fought with fists and feet, the method of the most undeveloped animal. To escape this, the victims hid behind stone walls; man, therefore, went again to the animal kingdom, and for the purposes of siege-work, devised the battering-ram, imitation of the goat. The knights of the Middle Ages, with their coats of mail, and lances, fought precisely like elephants, or rhinoceroses, with tusks and pachyderm. The swifter methods of the bow-and-arrow are a servile imitation of the porcupine's protective measures. The octopus, which squirts its bag of ink, before it uses its tentacles, is the obvious inspirer of the military smoke-screen and camouflage. None but the skunk suggested warfare by gas. The submarine – is not that the sword-fish of battle? And the tank owes its existence mainly to the admirable example of the tortoise, which suggested a method of defence even to the great Caesar. But the greatest of these, the most destructive, the most annihilating, is the warplane – the hawk of destruction.

It is the talons of this new bird of prey which hover over entire cities filling them with terror and alarm. This, then, is the apex of military civilization, the supreme peak of humanity's evolution.

What a commentary upon mankind, which instead of evolving from the ape, devolves to the beast, instead of clothing itself, as is its religious destiny, in the pinions of angels, attires itself with the shells of tortoises and fits itself with the claws of eagles.

Pope Pius XI   17 February 1939

Although we are not of the faith, our sorrow at the passing of His Holiness, after a valiant battle with the Angel of Death, is no less than that of our good Catholic friends. For Pope Pius XI was one of the finest spirits that ever reigned over the Holy See, a reign which coincided with a most difficult period for the world in general, and religion in particular. Scholar, statesman, scientist, His Holiness while adhering meticulously to the traditions of the Fathers of the Church, nonetheless kept intimately in touch with the many inventions of its sons. By speech, by audience, by encyclical, the Pope who has gone to the holiest See of all, exerted in his lifetime a most salutary influence over the three hundred million Catholics who acknowledged his spiritual suzerainty.

We, as Jews, owe a particular debt of gratitude to the late Master of the Vatican for the truly noble attitude which he adopted with reference to that persecution of Jewry which in many countries is the first symbol of a relapse to paganism. Even to the very last days of his life, this octogenarian Pope inveighed with all the spiritual fervour at his command against that idolatry which, spurning the doctrines of a religion based upon humanity, turned to Wodin and Thor to find benediction for their savage instincts. He saw the new ethnological theories as a reversion to the heathenry of the wilderness which worshipped blood. When he beheld about him that deformation of his religious symbol, the swastika: cross with claws, he was sad and sore afflicted, and like the founder whose vicar on earth he was, he wept.

One time librarian of the Vatican, the Pope was naturally familiar with the culture of the Christian centuries. He looked about him and beheld, like some of his predecessors, the barbarian marching on the gates of Rome. It was then that he warned his flock that the race theories were a menace not only to Jews, but to the whole Catholic hierarchy. Of the Jews he said in one of those historic utterances which have the dignity and force of a Beatitude: 'We are all spiritual Semites.'

Truly he earned that finest epithet of the occupants of the Vatican: servant of the servants of God.

Little Red Riding Houde   24 February 1939

Camillien Houde rides again. He rides from meeting to meeting, and stops at each long enough to reveal to all who will listen, his new discovery of an ethnological America, – the true form and content of the French-Canadian soul. Wearied with the heavy realities of municipal finance, Camillien has decided to take a fling at folklore; his plump diminutive form stanced upon a Y.M.C.A. platform, the mayor, a born raconteur, recently delivered himself of his latest masterpiece in nursery fiction; he spoke of the nature and essence of French-Canadian blood. And his fairy tale was Grimm.

For like the little girl in the childhood book, Camillien addresses himself to a creature of his creation, and says, 'My! grandmother, what a blood pressure you have!' and, ventriloquially, the mayor replies in behalf of this beldame, 'The better to Fascist you, my dear!' There, says the first magistrate, there is the legal proof that the French-Canadians are fascist by blood, if not in name!

It is highly regrettable that M. Houde should, at this late hour, have fallen for the so-called 'blood-science.' Surely, we had thought, any person living in a democracy, and certainly the mayor of a metropolis, should know that these racist theories, these red generalities, are nothing more than a twentieth century version – but not a harmless version – of the fairy tales of Prevost and Grimm. Readers will recall how the ogre in one of these anecdotes of infancy, rushes into his castle and shouts, 'Fee-fi-fo-fum, I smell the blood of an

Englishman.' That, perhaps, is quite proper in the world of imagination, – but how the mayor of a city upon this continent can afford to indulge, despite his sensitive and capacious nostrils, in sniffing at blood theories, is certainly beyond comprehension.

Moreover, – and this is of the utmost importance – Houde's statement about the French-Canadian being congenital fascist is simply not true; it is a downright slander of all those democratic forces, those liberal minds which the French-Canadian peoples, in a great history of struggle for constitutional principles has produced. The late Sir Wilfrid Laurier a Fascist by blood? The heroes of '37 fascist by blood? Merely to put the question is to hear the echo of its absurdity. And are we to understand, too, that *le petit gars de Ste. Marie*, is also a fascist by blood? Houde does his own self a great injustice.

Be that as it may, we cannot help but feel that in this statement, the Houdini of Montreal politics – dubbing himself that 'old fool Camillien,' has caught himself in a straightjacket from which he will find it extremely difficult to extricate himself. It is true that the Conqueror of Concordia, seeking to bolster up his watered blood theory, spoke also of the French-Canadians as being Latinized Normans. Confusion worse confounded! Is it to be assumed, *mon vieux*, that in the Latin veins there run specific corpuscles which are pregnant with quotations from *Mein Kampf*? Or that in the blood vessels of all Latins there flows haemoglobin which will pulsate only to a totalitarian tempo? If this is so, then Mazzini, Garibaldi, Matteotti, and camillions of other Latins, must have been, to say the least, anaemic.

We pass over in uncomfortable silence the remarks which Houde made anent French-Canadian loyalty, an example of horrifying bad taste and verbal gaucherie. We prefer rather, to believe the numerous denials which have issued from every representative section of the French-Canadian population.

So what motivated the Mayor to make these palpably erroneous statements? It is difficult to guess; the ways of the Mayor are mysterious to man. They are all the more mysterious when they issue from a man who was once a bank teller who should know that one ought not to issue notes of opinion which will come back with the remark – Not Sufficient Funds of information. For Houde's statement already has proved to be a rubber cheque; it has come back with a snap. Perhaps, however, the Mayor, like another fat boy in Dickens, only wanted 'to make our flesh creep'?

Of Him Whom We Envy   10 March 1939

We doubt whether there will be any who will find it in their hearts, after a reading of the following lines, to either compliment or condemn us – depending upon the point of view – as being too religiously fanatic. We know at least that our Rabbi would not hold us up as an example of purity, and a paragon of fervour. We doubt whether we are fitted to enter into the company of the saintly. For us our religion has been a purely personal affair, modelled upon the dictum of Heine: *Dieu me pardonnera, c'est son métier* – The Lord will forgive me; He makes a living out of forgiveness.

The fact is that the sophistical and much-too-rational education to which we have been subjected has altogether unfitted us for the sweet simplicities of the unquestioning faith. At the universities which we have attended, the training has been such that although we have been formally introduced to the élan vital, the First Cause, the One Increasing Purpose, and the rest of that philosophic family, the Creator Himself has remained charmingly incognito. Indeed, were it not for those glimpses of deity which were vouchsafed to the clear unmotivated eyes of our youth, we would still be under the impression that the Lord was merely a pronoun.

It is because rationalism has so removed us from the spiritual that we to-day look with a consuming envy upon those blessed souls who in these times of trial and tribulation, can find comfort and confidence in the bosom of their belief. How happy, indeed, is that orthodox Jew, who considers the world, its savages rampaging upon the stage, the righteous suffering, and the wicked prospering, and who loses not his optimism, who abandons not his faith, knowing that the ways of God are mysterious to man, and that it does not behoove the simple soul to seek to analyze the inscrutable methods of Providence. To him, Hitler is not so much knave as fool; fool, who for the empty glory of a day of noise, abandons all rights and forfeits all privileges in the World to Come. He regards that monster, therefore, not so much with hate as with pity; for is it not written: 'The wicked, they are like the chaff which the wind driveth away. He that sitteth in heaven laugheth, the Lord hath them in derision'?

For such a one, therefore, the *Weltschmerz* is a simple ailment. He does not fear annihilation; he belongs to a nation of 'outlivers.' It has outlived the Pharaohs, it has outlived Antiochus; it has seen Haman vanish into thin air; it has watched the Inquisition disappear in smoke; it has beheld the Tsars vanish in a cellar; and no doubt it will be present at the obsequies of all those who to-day bark and bite at the heel of Jewry. These are truly the chosen who can boast that sufferance is the badge of their tribe.

Not so, in these days, to use the phrase of Paine, that try men's souls, is the logician, the rationalist. He, alas, can find but little consolation in a syllogism, but small solace in a theorem. His strength lying in his mind, he is helpless before a world which has lost its head. He rushes to the Temple of Reason, and finds it empty, with a sign on the door, reading: Closed for Repairs.

But until those repairs ensue, where is he? Recently we had occasion to listen to Mr. Baruch Zuckerman, who proclaimed himself a Marxist, but who nonetheless, was driven, after an analysis of the Jewish situation, to seek refuge in an optimistic mysticism. It is true that he has transferred his mysticism from the Heavenly Host, to the Holy Land; but mysticism it remains.

Indeed, the agony of our people is so great, that mysticism seems to appear as the only alternative to that manifestation of despair, pessimism. Many will recall that after the Russian Revolution of 1905, the participants were so disillusioned that they gave themselves over to a hedonistic philosophy of 'let us drink, eat, and be merry for to-morrow we die.' When analyzed to its fundamentals, this is a terrible and fruitless *Weltanschauung*, which must end in more melancholy than merriment. Neither the man of intelligence, nor the man of faith can accept it.

The above-mentioned mysticism, of course, does not mean a grovelling in Cabala and a juggling of the Zohar. We imagine – although we are no authority on the subject, – that it rather means a return to those traditions which have sustained our ancestors in the days of their ordeals, a return to the radiant horns of the altar, to the primeval sanctities, the cleansing beliefs.

But we note that we are delivering a sermon, and have already exceeded our commentator's jurisdiction. What we really set out to say was that we envied the man of faith – and so to envy is in itself an act of faith.

Stalin: The Man of Flexible Steel   17 March 1939

For weeks prior to the Soviet Congress which is presently taking place in Moscow, the Communist press heralded and prognosticated messages that would prove of great interest and importance to the proletariat of the world. No doubt democrats in all the free countries of the globe waited in anticipation for the gospel about to be uttered from the Kremlin. Now, they must have said, we will hear, not the shilly-shallying temporizing of realpolitik, the smug clichés of diplomacy, but the true word and accent of democracy. The fearless Russians are about to speak; surely they will tell the totalitarian states where and what is their place.

Alas, that Stalin, that man of steel, is as flexible as the other politicians of Europe. No word of defiance to Hitler and Mussolini came from the Georgian's lips; instead – who would have thought it? – intimations and indications that the Marxist and Fascist were considering an entente. Hitler, said Stalin, is not aiming at Russia. His barbs and plans are directed at others; upon Russia he has no designs. Indeed, one almost got the impression that Adolf was really, in spite of his declarations and policies, terribly infatuated with the Soviet States. The paragraphs of his *Mein Kampf*? – They were merely window-dressing. His intrigues with the Ukrainian Monarchists? Those were purely a pantomime, designed to lull the capitalistic countries into a false sense of security. Hitler's persecution of Communists, Socialists, democrats, non-Nazis? That is a trifle, it concerns internal administration; it has nothing to do with foreign policy.

So spake Stalin. That there is a spiritual affinity between the dictator of the extreme right and the dictator of the extreme left does not occasion very much surprise. After all, a brown tyrant, as all who have dealt with colours know, is merely a red tyrant with some green in him. But that the eagle and the bear should lie down together, that Stalin should be considering, even a platonic affair, with one whom the world has seen as his biggest enemy, indicates definitely that the Russian dictator is no more in favour of democracy than is the madman of Munich.

We pity the Stalinite. Every time he gets accustomed to a new change of policy, the policy is changed yet again. The impresario of Moscow keeps his Russian ballet dancing on their ideological toes. Already had they almost persuaded the world that Russia was the true saviour of democracy, in the forefront of the fight against Fascism, when the maestro himself goes and kisses Adolf in public. What are they to do? Once they were taught the doctrine of permanent revolution. Stalin liquidated that. Then they were taught the principles of the United Front, and in their naiveté, imagined that what Stalin meant was a united front with the democratic parties. Nothing of the sort! The new policy is a united front, with Fascism!

At any rate, we are glad that Stalin has made clear what has for a long time been suspected. Stalin is first a Russian, and foremost a dictator. Democrats of the world have nothing to hope for, and nothing to gain from this emotional twin of Hitler. He has put Marx in the straitjacket of realpolitik; he is ready to betray all liberty-loving persons for the sake of his unholy Russia, and his sacred self.

Let us, therefore, not hear any more of those shibboleths emanating from Communists about the Soviets being the true bulwark of democracy, no more of those exploded clichés with which the versatile propaganda machine of the Kremlin has confused and befuddled men of good will. Let Stalin and Hitler dance their joint waltz and mazurka, seeing that they are now headed in the same direction, a direction which is as far from democracy as possible. But let no wise dialectician – even Hegel, with his thesis, antithesis, and synthesis, would not have been able to reconcile that which the Man of Steel has reconciled – give us any more of that feeble cant and outworn piffle about Russia and the fight for freedom.

The White Paper   26 May 1939

The British House of Commons has, at this writing, reluctantly and half-heartedly approved the notorious White Paper as an expression of future policy in Palestine. The injustices expressly detailed and indirectly implied in that cynical document shall henceforward be the law of Government in the Holy Land; Mr. Chamberlain, without expense of plane-fare, has achieved another Munich. The shadow of the umbrella falls across Erez Israel.

That this new declaration has brought bitterness and disappointment in its wake is easily understandable. Jews have been shocked by this volte-face of a many-faced policy, emanating from that quarter in Downing Street which they had hitherto regarded as a political Holy of Holies. The White Paper now marks zero across all those sacred promises and sacrosanct commitments which issued without compulsion and which were acted upon as if they were as solid as the Rock of Gibraltar used to be. It is a complete nullification of an era of British foreign policy in the Near East, a sad commentary upon the life and works of the late Lord Balfour, a wanton toying with the value and weight of an English word of honour, a colossal betrayal, not only of Jewish labour and sacrifice in Erez Israel, but of the finest impulses and the noblest motives of England in whose 'green and pleasant land, Jerusalem was to have been builded again.'

One does not have to examine the White Paper under a microscope to see how the true seal and signature of Britain has been forged on it. One examines a diamond, – not a piece of glass – for flaws. The entire document is one huge flaw. It seeks to reduce Jewry in Erez Israel to the permanent position of a minority; it attempts to crystallize – a better word is petrify – the Jewish population at one-third of that of the entire country. A ghetto is planned where a homeland was contemplated. The Foreign Office, liquidating the Near East, offers to its most co-operative creditor a settlement of thirty-three per cent; for the balance, *stop payment* is marked across the cheque. As for the Arabs, hitherto seeking to enforce what at best was a litigious claim by threat, intimidation, murder, and arson, they are favoured with a fraudulent preference. Lest this policy fail of achievement by the sheer force of economic law, the White Paper further enjoins restriction of land-sales and limitation of immigration, two sacrilegious blows aimed at the *shel rosh* and *shel yad* of Jewish development in Palestine. That Jewish refugees from Central Europe and pauperized Jewry in Poland have received this latest billet-doux as tantamount to a death-warrant serves well to emphasize the full and bitter implications of Malcolm MacDonald's venture into the art of juggling. One recalls the storm of protest when Malcolm's father issued his famous MacDonald letter; the White

Paper is infinitely worse; 'my father did chastise you with whips, but I will chastise you with scorpions.' *Hinc illae lachrymae*: hence these prayers and fasts, these petitions and protests, this Jewish arsenal of tears and letters and memoranda.

We cannot help, too, but comment upon the manner in which military authorities in Palestine sought to stifle 'with an iron hand' the demonstrations of Jewish dissatisfaction. If three fingers of that iron hand had been directed against the Arab terrorists, the entire situation might well have been avoided. The best comment upon this strange phenomenon came from members of the Black Watch in Palestine: 'We thought,' they said, 'that we were sent here to put down Arab riots; instead we find ourselves shooting at Jews.'

And so *finis coronat opus*; twenty-two years after that famous letter to Lord Rothschild in which His Majesty's Government contributed an Isaiah-like verse to the Bible, one finds the British Cabinet by terror unmanned, Palestine about to be unmandated, and precious British-Palestinian documents expurgated and unbalfoured!

Nonetheless, although we can understand the weeping and gnashing of teeth, we feel, first, that this White Paper is not the doing of the English people, and second, that it is not even the whole-hearted work of Chamberlain's cabinet. Indeed, Chamberlain's entourage are more to be pitied than condemned; its policy is dictated solely by expediency, the wisdom of which may perhaps be questioned, but not its motivation. There has, to our mind, been no change of heart in England; there has been a change in the world situation, impelling the British Government to seek friends by giving gifts. Purely and simply, the White Paper is a White Flag hung out before the Arab world.

It is precisely because the White Paper is so grounded in expediency and based upon temporary convenience, that its issuance is not the tragedy which it otherwise might be. Our claims to Erez Israel are based upon principle; principles are eternal. Expediency, however, changes from occasion to occasion. Our destiny is not determined by stationery of no matter what imprint or color. A white cloud, born of the vapors of international hatred, has passed across our sky; clouds are not permanent.

Surely it is stupid and false to talk of anti-Semitism on the part of the British Government. By whatever motive the Paper was issued, it certainly was not issued on account of Jew-hatred. Let who will number the friends of Jewry among the nations of the world; there is no doubt as to whose name is among the leaders of the list. For sensation-seeking journalists, therefore, to speak of boycott and war against Britain is dangerous, irresponsible, prima-facie demagoguery. The battle against the White Paper is to be fought, not with boycott and anglophobia, but with all those instruments and modalities which the Government opposition, for example, employs against unjust legislation of Governments in power.

For Jewry, though the hour is a sad one, all is far from being lost. The striving and effort for a Jewish National Homeland went on before the Balfour Declaration; it can and will go on without it. We have not travelled the circuitous route around the world and back to Erez Israel so that now we might be stopped by a heap of paper in our path. The explosions of Arab bombs have not frightened us away from our Homeland; surely the crackling of foolscap will not terrorize us. Zionism understands peace, not appeasement, and we who have withstood fire and sword, can not and will not collapse before ink and umbrella.

The White Paper, moreover, speaks of self-government for the Arabs in the distant future. The term is ten years, but that term is hedged with so many conditions and provisos that it is no cause for immediate alarm. It must be remembered that autonomy was promised to India about twenty years ago; and has not yet been fulfilled. As for loopholes and lacunae, the White Paper is full of them. If the Balfour Declaration could have been bent, the White Paper, after remaining folded for ten years, will no doubt be broken.

Our rights to Erez Israel are based upon the incontrovertible dictates of justice. Weizmann the statesman did truly don the mantle of the prophet when, in discussing the White Paper, he predicted that it 'must crash beneath the weight of its own unrighteousness.' Unrighteousness, indeed! Ironical and full of significance is the fact that on the anniversary of the granting of Torah – epitome of justice – the British House of Commons sanctioned the White Paper. It was as if amidst the thunder and lightning of Sinai, someone tried to light up the scene and add to the awe-inspiring roar by – striking a safety match!

Rejoice, Ye Bulls of Bashan   26 May 1939

Let no one despair of the race of man. It is most surprising in what quarters one is liable to discover virtue, and in what breasts humanity throbs. Hearken to this tale. An offer by bull fight promoters to give a benefit performance in the Madrid Arena with the best bulls and fighters in the country has been rejected by Generalissimo Francisco Franco. Why? You would never guess, dear readers. Why? Because in the new Spain – actually more second-hand than new – in the new Spain, blood sacrifices even in the form of horses and bulls must not be intermixed with patriotic celebrations!

Now, I ask you, isn't that sweet and lovely of Little Lord Fauntleroy Franco? Isn't there something humane even in the worst of the breed? Who would have thought that this Franco who caused the destruction of millions of his fellow-countrymen, who brought his native land to ruin, whose firing-squads have not yet, at this late hour, become silent, that this great heroissimo would suddenly grow soft on us, and break down at the prospect of shedding a bull's blood? It is, as Sherlock Holmes might, in like case, have opined, remarkable, most remarkable!

We can see him now before us in his new guise – yesterday's slaughterer and to-day's St. Francisco of Assisi! 'Suffer little bulls to come unto me,' he says in his benign falsetto, as two horns make a halo above his head. 'You may shed the blood of Pedro and Diego, Miguel and Juan, but woe betide him who touches the least hide of Ferdinand the Bull! Our Italian guests may playfully throw bombs at Spanish babes, but anyone who annoys a little calf, let him beware!' At this point the sensitive and sentimental Franco, stepping out of character, goes into appropriate song-and-dance. He sings:

> I do not adore
> A toreador,
> Nor do I pick
> A picador!

Dignified again, he continues: 'Patriotism – and the bull! What a fitting combination. It is a union which none will destroy. The Madrid Arena must be protected from the thrust of Bolshevism. For I, Francisco Franco, and Ferdinand the Bull, have this in common – we both go mad when we see red. It is my duty, therefore, to protect my bovine brother; as long as the new Spain remains polished off under me, I will permit no sport with animals. Besides, the killing of bulls is really a pretty tame pastime, but any one who wishes a first-class thrill for his blood-system, visit one of my recently organized concentration camps – there he will see the real McCoy. The Madrid Arena pales into namby-pamby in comparison; the bull-fight is a pink-tea by contrast, a sissified entertainment. No, my good friends.

> Let us go horn by horn
> With our brothers sworn,
> And hand in hand
> With Ferdinand!'

And having delivered himself of these pious sentiments, Franco, as is his custom, knelt and prayed: 'Our Fuehrer which is in Berlin, thy kingdom, come; we will be done out of earth, as we have been out of heaven; give us this day our daily dead; and forgive us our debts; and lead us by imitation forever into evil; for thine is the kingdom, sour and gory, Amen.'

'Luftmenschen' and 'Wassermenschen'   9 June 1939

That anti-Semitism which for centuries relegated Jews, by dint of economic laws, to the position of a 'Luftmensch,' a being neither rooted in the soil where he dwelt nor consigned to the heavens which he desired to enter, has now come upon a new development. The economic race-juggling is complete; the political one is well on the way. Refugee Jewry, battered from pillar to post, can find no place of sanctuary. Booted out of one country, it cannot find refuge in another; doomed it is to linger, like a personification of the evil conscience of the world, outside the pale. Going down, like its ancestors, to the sea in ships, it is rejected from one port after another. Refugee Jewry is being transformed into that awful unspeakable nightmare – 'Wassermenschen.'

This, indeed, is what happened several months ago when Jews, shipped out of Germany, could find no country, no port, no harbour, which would receive them. Like the spirit of God, in an ungodly world, Jewry brooded upon the face of the waters of the Danube. If the Jews of Zbonshyn, driven from Hitlerland and not permitted into Poland, found themselves in a 'No Man's Land,' those Jews who upon many waters constitute a pitiable and unconsigned human cargo, bereft of bill of lading, find themselves in an even more horrible 'No Man's Sea.' 'The waters,' if we may translate Holy Writ literally, 'have risen up to the soul.'

Even when these hapless bottoms, freighted with Jewish tragedy and bewilderment, finally reach, by many circuitous routes and after much travail, the ports of Palestine – the Homeland! – they meet not the hospitality and sanctuary which is their due, but the dour customs official and the unsympathetic immigration officer, and impersonal police. But yesterday, two ships, bearing about 1,400 souls brimful of jubilee at the prospect of finally finding a foot-rest upon their own small strand in 'God's sweet world,' were stopped and passengers and crew arrested. Here was the Paradise which these scorned and rejected had hoped to enter; alas, it was not to be! Over the gates of this Eden, there stands an official, 'with a flaming sword which turneth all the day.'

At the other end of the world, there floats a similar ship of human misery. The Ancient Mariner who hailed the wedding-guest with the startling revelation: 'There was a ship,' quoth he, could have put no greater poignancy into his story than the mere telling of the unadorned facts of what happened to those poor unfortunates who, leaving Germany for Cuba with landing permits in their possession, came to Havana to find those permits rescinded. A wave of attempted suicide broke out on board ship. The ship is about to return.

Sodom and Gomorrah were Sunday schools compared to the planet Earth in the twentieth century! The earth itself must cry out against this inhumanity, the waters of the seven seas must boil with wrath! Driven from their home to the highways, and from the highways to the high seas, these black ships cross the waves, going from port to port, even as the thought of these must cross the minds of human beings, like a bad dream, a cauchemar that couldn't occur in the light of day, but could find being only in the darkness of the night, the darkness of that night which now envelops a world which once was civilized.

We are not fond of sermons; but wickedness such as stalks rampant across the face of the globe, ought at least to be reprimanded. If the pecadilloes by comparison, of the generations preceding Noah, were punished by a divine justice with a flood, where is that all-seeing Eye and powerful Hand to punish this abominable sin by water with the just retribution of flood? For this is, indeed, the last string of humanity torn, the last bulwark broken, and after – *après nous, le déluge!*

A Modest Proposal   14 July 1939

Many readers no doubt will recall that the great satirist Dean Swift, in seeking to heap ridicule upon his contemporaries, suggested by way of 'modest proposal' a *reductio ad absurdum* of the customs of his fellow-men then current. Having neither the wit nor the Irish of the Dean, it does seem to us, nonetheless, that there is a crying need for such a 'modest proposal' anent the destiny of the Jewish homeland and the fate of Jewish refugees.

It appears that great numbers of the wanderers have willy-nilly taken to the high seas. The *St. Louis* floats upon the Atlantic for two months, freighted with unhappy human cargo. Another ship leaves some Greek port, and arrives in Palestine only to see its passengers interned in a concentration camp. But a little while ago there came to the shores of Erez Israel a ship which Jews in Danzig had bought and manned, and directed to the Holy Land; when they arrived at the Port of Haifa they were towed out of the harbour and left floating along the sea-coast.

Here then is the opportunity for some grim humorist to win himself a place in immortality beside Dean Swift. Let him suggest a homeland for Jews upon the face of the waters!

If there was room for a 'Jewish Territorial Movement,' perhaps a Hebrew Oceanic Society can be organized!

Perhaps, too, the British Government, realizing the error of its ways, will revise the Balfour Declaration, and issue a new one, a liquid one: 'His Majesty's Government views with favour the "floating" of a "National Jewish Homewater," anywhere upon the surface of those waves which Britannia rules, and will use its best endeavours to facilitate the achievement of this proposal, it being clearly understood that nothing will be done to injure the rights of non-Jews in the said waters.'

Upon the issuance of such a proclamation, shiploads of Jews would issue. They would always stay at anchor, a floating state joined, ship to ship, cruiser to cruiser, liner to liner, a floating state.

A couple of years thereafter, as this naval country would begin to prosper, the British Government would send forth a Royal Commission to investigate. The Commission would bring in a report that the Jewish Homewater was not properly docked, and that the Jewish ships were destroying the national independence of the neighboring fish. Tons of pamphlets would then be circulated about the problem of 'the landless fish.' The chairman of the aforementioned Commission would insist, with all the logic he could muster, that the phrase 'nothing will be done to injure the rights of non-Jews,' obviously referred to the local marine life, which apparently did not subscribe to the Mosaic creed.

Ship-building would continue, and the Homewater would expand. Another Commission would be then sent to examine the area of 'Yom Yisroel' and would look with disapproval upon the 'immigration waves.' Recommendations would be made that there should be a Partition of the waves, the learned Commissioner, indeed, would support his viewpoint by citing from the biography of Moses who performed a similar procedure on the Red Sea.

But the Homewater would still flourish. 'Yom Yisroel Chai!' would be the slogan of a national Jewry. Whereupon the Colonial Office, completely fed up with the manner in which these *chalutzim* would be making a success even out of water, would begin to study the above-mentioned Declaration again. Finally, it would issue a White Paper, made out of rubber – the better to float with, my child. The gist of this White Paper would be that when the Government promised a Homewater on the surface of those waves which Britannia rules, it really meant a different thing entirely. Instead of 'on the surface,' read, 'at the bottom'; otherwise they stick by all their commitments.

Comrade Hitler and Fuehrer Stalin:
Heil Tovarisch   25 August 1939

We are fully aware of the possibility that as we pen these lines, European developments, which move at such an infernal pace, may completely contradict every single line, jot and tittle. In the light of what is transpiring, the safest formula for wisdom is silence; for those who once believed that two parallel lines would never meet except in infinity, must now either recognize the arrival of that infinity, or revise their Euclidean geometry.

For the two lines have met. Nazi Germany, whose favourite sport since 1933 has been the baiting of Russian Communists and the incarceration of native ones, and Soviet Russia, whose entire propaganda, internal and external, has been geared on the premise that National-Socialism is the bitterest enemy of the Soviets, have now signed a trade treaty and a non-aggression pact. Those who for years have declared that Nazism and Stalinism are the two sides of the same drum, to-day see their analysis confirmed: the Russian Bear and the German Eagle do lie down together. The red dictator has found his soul-mate, the brown one; the totalitarian colour-scheme is complete.

There is no doubt that the world has been temporarily stunned by this new turn of events. The creation of a 'Berlin-Moscow Axis' was a possibility which was used to bait the Marxian; but no one ever really believed that such a contingency could arrive, no one, except Stalin. The new alignment, rigid or elastic as its terms may reveal it, coming as it does at a time when protracted pourparlers have been going on towards the solidifying of the Peace Front, is probably one of the greatest treacheries perpetrated in the history of diplomacy at its most treacherous. In comparison, the agreement at Munich a year ago was a gesture of supreme honour. Chamberlain should sell his umbrella to Stalin.

For surely, the last thing that one expected from the preachers of the 'Front Populaire' and the creators of a 'democratic constitution' was that they should establish a dictatorial front with him whose plan of campaign in *Mein Kampf* sees Russia as the first enemy of the Reich. Nor can the diplomatic nuptials be explained as a *mariage de convénience*, for it obviously postulates a new dismemberment of Poland which would deprive Russia of a much-needed buffer state.

There are some who seek to explain or apologize for Fuehrer Stalin by declaring that the mésalliance was motivated by chagrin at Chamberlain for being left out of the Munich negotiations. It is quite clear that if Stalin contributes nothing else to the Communist movement, he certainly does, by his numerous volte-faces and perpetual acrobatics, induce the mental agility of apologia. But do these apologists, otherwise such realists, believe that international alliances are based upon personal peeves? And are they really convinced that whereas Stalin may dislike Chamberlain, he is positively in love with Hitler? The height of servile stupidity is reached indeed, in the declaration of the Communist Party of England that the new arrangement is 'a victory over the war-plans of the Fascist and pro-Fascist policy of Premier Chamberlain.' For Hitler it is presumably a defeat!

The effect of this hammer-and-scythe and swastika policy has already created repercussions everywhere. Britain and France have reiterated their pledges to Poland, which stands today in greater danger than it ever did before.

Tokio, too, is discovering that it is not precisely Aryan, and that the anti-Comintern Pact was, as they say in Japan, a diseased silkworm. The Pope, speaking for all Catholics, sees an alignment of the atheist and the pagan. It is only Italy which has remained somewhat silent, wondering what booty it will gain out of the new set-up.

There are however a number of factors in the situation which somewhat alleviate the seriousness with which one is inclined to regard it. In the first place, the terms of the arrangement are not clear, and there are rumours to the effect that it will have as many loopholes and escape clauses as is worthy of the temperaments of the two negotiating Houdinis. In the second place, the whole procedure may be nothing more than a trial balloon, a significant gesture. It appears that the negotiations between Britain and Russia had been held up because the British delegation would not make sufficient concessions. No doubt one of the reasons motivating the British attitude was the feeling that as between Chamberlain and Hitler, Stalin had a Hobson's choice. The new pact which, according to communications from Moscow, is already concluded, may be merely an indication that Russia does have a choice, an indication thus given for the purpose of eliciting better terms from Britain and France.

And finally, a treaty between Hitler and Stalin must be considered rather as a gesture than an agreement. We do not believe that either of them has any illusions about the other's sincerity, and each will await the first favourable opportunity to denounce it. Each is entering into the pact, full of mental reservations, and ulterior motives; both are seeking to dupe the other; and both feel that the treaty which they have announced with such éclat, is probably better honoured in the breach than in the observance.

Be that as it may, the international situation is to-day confusion worse confounded. It is difficult to recognize the friend; it is hard to distinguish the enemy. And for the Jew, the situation is full of tragic significance when it is recalled that in Russia and Poland there are more than five millions of our brethen.

The Issue Is Clear!   8 September 1939

The issue is clear! The war which the madman of Europe has forced upon the world permits of no misinterpretation. It is befogged by no imperialist analysis; it is beclouded by no complicated *realpolitik*. It is purely and simply the conflict between Mazda and Ahriman, between day and night, between light and darkness! Futile will be the attempt to analyze the pros and cons; and empty the desire to weigh and measure arguments and counter-arguments. No slogans can help us, no shibboleth of propaganda can aid us. A child can understand the cause of this, the second, and we hope final, World War!

Born it was in the corrupted soul of one man, nurtured by his ambition, fed by accidents, advanced by intrigue, and launched forward with perfidy! His objective is apparent – the domination of the earth, and the establishment of that his unspeakable tyranny of which he has already shown the abominable example. His means are identified – the metal vulture that flies through the air, the iron animal that crawls on earth, the motorized fish that swims beneath the surface of the waters. His victims are not kept secret – the fine, the noble, the free, men, women, and children. His motivation is clear – the aggrandizement of an insane and bestial personality, flung up from the dregs by post-war pressure, and presently harbouring Napoleonic ambition. His philosophy, if that melange of lunacy peppered with hatred can indeed be called a philosophy, is certain – the destruction of liberty, the cancellation of equality, and the enslavement of the world to an already enslaved Germany!

Equally certain must be his defeat and obliteration!

Surely every effort for peace that could have been made, has been made. Surely no man could have shown a more Job-like patience, a more commendable long-suffering than did Prime Minister Chamberlain. Well did the British Cabinet understand that conflict with the uncontrolled and arrogant Attila would lead to a holocaust of stupendous proportions; it sought therefore, by unwilling compromise and unwelcome concession, to create about the infected area a *cordon sanitaire*, hoping in its humanity to confine the disease to the Nazis who inoculated themselves therewith. But Hitler, like a madman confined to a padded cell, has upset Europe with his horrifying escapes. Yesterday he wreaked havoc upon Czechoslovakia, the day before he destroyed freedom-loving Austria, today he is foaming at the mouth at Poland. And to-morrow?

The world has realized that there must be no to-morrow for Hitler! Either he is destroyed, and with him all who have bent to his will and served his purpose, and the world can continue along the even tenor of its way, in peace towards progress; or he is permitted to continue his course unrestrained, until the world is rendered safe for dictatorships, and mankind relapses back to the age of Neanderthal.

Indubitably it is the conflict between civilization and barbarism!

If this, reader no longer gentle, is the reaction of the world at large, what is the reaction of Jewry at this momentous hour? The reaction of Jewry permits of no ambiguity. For six years the Nazis have carried on a relentless war against our people, a war directed against the defenceless, inspired by no reason save the instincts of savagery, and conducted without let-up, without restraint, without quarter. Its objective has been shouted from the roof-tops, and has been echoed across the world – the utter destruction, the complete annihilation of Jewry. Upon every occasion and at every opportunity it has vented its bestial *schrecklichkeit* against the blameless and innocent of our people. And when it has not had the opportunity granted by geography, it has sought to create it by conquest!

The terms of the battle have been clearly enunciated. There is no room upon the face of the earth for both Hitlerism and Jews! Should the gangster of Germany emerge victorious – may the Lord forfend! – then that victory spells the end of our people, its culture, its religion, its individual lives.

Now, even now, the bombing planes of Germany are launching their attacks upon three and a half million of our brothers and sisters, kith and kin. Poland is a victim that Hitler is particularly enjoying – it satisfies his craving for bloodshed, and it has the additional zest of Jewish corpses.

They cry to us across a continent and an ocean, to us who by an accident find ourselves here in a land of freedom, who might as easily have missed the boat and remained there! They cry to us from the darkness of the concentration camps at Dachau, from the ghettos of Prague, from the encampments of refugees! They cry to us for succour and aid from the monster who is goose-stepping upon their lives! Shall their cry remain unanswered?

The Jews of Germany went down with a whimper; the Jews of Czechoslovakia expired with a groan. Jews of the lands of freedom must meet the enemy with a battle-cry!

Our loyalty to our country demands it! Our loyalty to ourselves insists upon it. The fight that the British Empire is today waging is a fight for freedom, for tolerance, for liberalism. It is our fight! We shall not survive a British defeat! We desire not the enslavement that such survival would mean!

Past wars have seen our people, brave and loyal, fighting in opposing camps. No such divided allegiance disturbs us now. In the ranks of the enemy there are no Jews, save hostages, prisoners, and cadavers.

The issue is clear! Clear is the answer of Canadian Jewry. Every effort will be bent, every ounce of energy will be spent, every sacrifice will be made, to see to it that we – all of us – people, and country, and Empire – emerge victorious. The challenge has been made, and the answer will be given. We are fighting a fight for survival, and our courage will be as high as our stake is great!

The Fuehrer's Fury   22 September 1939

The oration which Adolf Hitler delivered from Danzig, and which was permitted to be heard in all the democratic countries, – there is not here, like in Germany, a death penalty for listening to foreign propaganda – throws considerable light upon the mentality of the Fuehrer. In the first case, the manner of its delivery indicates that honours and power have brought no sanity to the madman who rules the Reich; beginning, with a prima donna's histrionics, in a low voice, the Fuehrer in his peroration rose to such a crescendo of dementia that one could almost see the froth and foam issuing out of the radio. Adolf has a habit of mesmerizing himself with rhetoric; statements which in the calm of his Berchtesgaden eyrie he knows to be damnable lies, he utters with so many vibrations in his voice that he sounds as if he almost convinces himself. Did not the world know that his previous protestations of saint-like innocence and Job-like patience were enunciated with the same one hundred and forty-eight vibrations, his present tremolos might sound quasi-convincing.

The general tenor of the talk was that of an incoherent pot-pourri of variegated billingsgate. There was nothing statesmanlike about it at all. It was a high-school boy, boasting about a still undigested victory, and seeking to make points out of an opponent's *obiter dicta*, whilst ignoring main issues.

Surprise has been expressed in certain quarters at the fact that the Canadian Broadcasting Commission saw fit to permit the relaying of this Nazi propaganda issuing out of the *sanctum sanctorum*. We think that this permission redounds to the credit and intelligence of the departments concerned, not because – forsooth – it is an example of freedom of speech – we are under no obligation to accord the enemy such liberty – but because it indicates that the authorities are working under the assumption that Hitler is Britain's best propagandist. And indeed it is so. One who heard the raving of the lunatic must understand, better than by a thousand editorials, why we are at war, and what our objective is. Certainly the Fuehrer can win no converts in our ranks by referring to Eden and Churchill as war-mongers, or dubbing the leaders of the Empire 'British criminals.' Certainly the working class can see things in their proper perspective when it listens to the love-lyrics which the Fuehrer indites to Stalin, and which Stalin so graciously accepts. Certainly the man on the street will know how to estimate Hitler's protestations about 'mutual confidence' when he hears his raucous cries at the same time as he has before him the figures of Polish casualties. Indeed, one way of propaganda is to call the opponent a madman and a liar; the better way is to allow the opponent to demonstrate the accuracy of the accusations.

Does Hitler really want peace? It is quite likely; and it is indeed gratifying to hear from his lips the indirect admission that he is not prepared to conduct anything more than a blitzkrieg, and that he would prefer to call the whole thing off. Such gestures are always considered a sign of internal weakness, even though the author seeks to cover them up with the pantomime of defiance and the bravado of threat.

The Allies, however, will understand the Nazi peace – the peace that passeth all understanding and frontiers. They are treating them with the respect which they merit, the respect due to the promises of a blackmailer, betrayer, liar and lunatic. They are preparing the answer to the oration, an answer which will thunder forth from the Maginot line, which will descend from the skies, and not via pamphlets, and which will be brought home to the German sieg-heilers by British ships.

For the only treatment for the violently insane is the straitjacket.

'He Sent a Letter to His Lover'   20 October 1939

Readers, no doubt, will recall this pleasant line from a pleasant little nursery rhyme. This stanzaic doggerel is being to-day repeated in international relations. The latest report has it that A. Hitler has recently sent, by special courier, a love-letter to one J. Stalin. What the contents of it are, we do not know; but we can well imagine. We present herewith a draft thereof:

My dear Joie,

Since our last communication to you, time has dragged heavily in my hands. I have tried, with the technique which both of us discussed last time, to get the democracies to fall for my peace-plan, but it seems that after these many years, the stupid democrats are getting wise to my game. So it looks as if the war will have to continue.

You know very well that I can't continue it myself, and that your help will be deeply appreciated. I can see, for both of us, a glorious future, resulting from this co-operation. It is true that for a while it looked as if we didn't agree; but really, it was ony a lovers' quarrel. In the final analysis my National-Socialism and your Marxism are really one and the same thing. Let us not, therefore, quibble over technicalities.

I would like you, immediately upon receipt of this letter, to send me those things you promised me, you know, the wheat, the oil, and the other stuff required to give our love-bond a lasting foundation.

By the way, Joie, have you ever really thought of the Jewish problem? If you could only see eye to eye with me on this subject, we could conquer the world. Besides, if you are going to have any difficulties in your household about your association with me, you could always use the Jews as a good safety-valve.

I do hope to hear from you soon; in the meantime, do me a favour and stop grabbing up Balkan and Baltic territory; it looks terrible, not only for you, but also for me. People are wondering whether you are sincere in your intentions toward me.

Yours as ever,

Adolf

No Concealed Assets   20 October 1939

It is gratifying in newspapers lugubrious with war news and melancholy with peace offensives to read an item which at least serves to increase the gayety of nations. Of course in these times it could hardly be a completely light-hearted piece but it is the next thing to it – sorrow with undertones of laughter. We refer, ladies and gentlemen, to the report announcing that Miss Sally Rand, the famous bubble dancer, has gone bankrupt.

The record of her case, we feel, should create jurisprudence. Held, that a person who began her business with assets consisting only of the fact that she had not a stitch of clothes on her said person, can nonetheless be reduced to a state of bankruptcy. Held, that a practitioner of the jactitating bubble dance may properly and legally avail herself of the Winding-Up Act. Held, that the stock-in-trade of a fan-dancer, saving the fan, is not divisible among the most of creditors.

The facts of her case, narrated in the current press, present, indeed, some interesting problems. Her assets were valued at $8,067 – what did these assets consist of? Surely not merely a fan, a bubble, a peacock feather? Has, in fact, Sally Rand made full and complete disclosure?

It would be interesting to know, too, whether the California law accepts the doctrine that the trustee in bankruptcy becomes vested with the assets of the bankrupt; and, if so, how the trustee purposes to dispose of the said assets at public sale; and, if so disposed, how the dividend will be declared and distributed.

Will, in fine, the much advanced jurisprudence of our time be baffled by this new problem in bankruptcy, and seek, in desperation, a solution in the old Roman law of the Twelve Tables whereby the debtor was personally divisible among the creditors?

Polish Jewry   3 November 1939

The imagination of the most macabre author could hardly conceive fictions more horrible than the facts which are daily issuing out of Poland, describing the fate of its unfortunate Jewry. For a while, during the progress of the war, many naive souls consoled themselves with the fond hope that perhaps the German army was made of finer stuff than the storm-troop rabble which perpetrated the notorious November tenth of 1938. It was hoped that the great military traditions of Germany would prevail over the contemporary bestiality introduced into German life; facts reveal that that hope was doomed to disappointment. Indeed, if ever there were any elements in German life, civil or military, in whom some vestiges of humanity remained, they have long since been either 'concentrated' or liquidated. The case of von Fritsch is one in point. It appears that he was one of the few who did not see eye to eye – or monocle to eye – with the Nazi commissars; under most unusual circumstances he was killed, and given the dubious solatium of a military funeral.

Accordingly, the hordes that rushed into Poland, as onto a picnic ground, were pure unadulterated votaries of *schrecklichkeit*. That the military campaign itself was accompanied by outrageous barbarities is already public knowledge; the facts that arrive now speak of the leisurely sadism of the occupation.

For this diabolic vengeance, the Jews of Poland have been singled out as specially juicy victims. Over a million and a half Jews in German Poland are undergoing slow but sure starvation. While rations are being distributed to the rest of the conquered population, entire towns and cities of Jews are being left without any sustenance whatsoever. Whatever possessions were left to them after the army of Huns passed through, have already been confiscated. Those who are not perishing of starvation, are succumbing to disease, and those who perchance escape both these fates, usually find themselves among the summarily shot. Executions take place without trial or accusation; it is an orgy of murder, in all its forms. Even women are not safe from the Nazi sadism. Jewish women are taken away from their children and compelled to work at hard labour for periods of forty-eight hours, without cessation. Death releases them more frequently than do their tormentors.

One could continue to pile up instance after instance of German atrocity – not Macedonian – in Poland. At the sight of this rod with which Moses is beaten, a stone would shed, not water, but blood. Jewish Poland sees the schedule of Germany's November the tenth become the order of the day, and of every day.

We who receive these communications become more and more convinced with every report that our duty is clear and unambiguous – to bend every effort toward the crushing of Hitlerism, to adopt every means to destroy this new reign of Genghis Khan, to wipe off from the face of the earth this twentieth century regime of Sodom and Gomorrah. Surely that smug imperialist statement of Molotov – 'One can disagree with Nazism, one need not fight it' – is of the essence of heartless hypocrisy. Surely a callous and mephistophelian recipe to offer Polish Jewry – 'you may disagree with Nazism' – when Nazism is systematically putting that Jewry in the horizontal position where it can disagree with no one.

There can be no room to-day for pacifism. Pacifism is a doctrine which may be used as a gesture of nobility to appeal to some vestige of nobility left in the enemy. The enemy to-day is utterly and completely ignoble. Pacifism therefore is merely a lazy man's form of suicide. To-day the situation demands an unrelenting prosecution of the war, with all the resources, physical and material, at our command, a prosecution of the war in which the Empire in all its component parts, with all its varied peoples, stands as a valiant knight in defense of the just and the true, a prosecution of the war which shall not close until victory is attained, and the dark shadow which hovered over the earth for six years removed from the horizon forever.

M. Jean-Charles Harvey and Pan-Americanism   19 January 1940

M. Jean-Charles Harvey, editor of *Le Jour*, which by its weekly appearances proves that its name means, not The Day, but The Light, has delivered himself of a speech before the Toronto Empire Club which constitutes perhaps one of the sagest comments upon the essence of true Canadianism that has been heard for many a day. Repudiating all those slick formulas, those provincial clichés, the hackneyed parochialisms which are the usual stock-in-trade of dispensers of nationalism, M. Harvey not only defined the true nature of this phenomenon, but recommended a number of points which would serve to weld together a nationhood far from sectional and racial prejudices.

With a liberalism which was as well-thought-out as it was rare, M. Harvey said: 'Unless we can look forward to a time when racial passion shall have disappeared in Canada, then the future we have to work for is not worth bothering about. Unless we can remember the ideal the founders of North American white civilization had before their eyes when they formed the constitution of this Dominion and of the United States, we must condemn our children and our children's children to life in an atmosphere constantly darkening, as men develop deadlier and deadlier means of fighting one another in the name of race or ideology.'

How refreshing, indeed, are these words when contrasted to the Anglophobia and Francophobia current in certain quarters! How civilized are these utterances when placed side by side the benighted fulminations of an Adrien Arcand or a Bouchard!

Nor are these expressions the result of a mere doctrinaire and utopian emotionalism. M. Harvey not only examines carefully the actualities of the day; he wisely foresees the necessities of the future. In analyzing the present ethnic constitution of the Dominion, M. Harvey emphasized the fact that no one race made up a majority of the population of Canada. Of 11,000,000 people in Canada only 5,000,000 were of Anglo-Saxon descent, 3,500,000 were of French origin, and 2,500,000 were made up of various other races. Said he: 'We have got to make up our minds that we can have no national spirit only on a basis of compromise. You will never persuade or force 3,500,000 French-speaking Canadians to give up their language, their religion, their schools or their customs. You will never persuade or force 5,000,000 English-speaking Canadians to give up their language, their democratic tradition, or their system of non-denominational education ... What Canada must do – and this cannot be done by law – is to develop a new, purely Canadian mentality, adjustable to all these various national personalities, without destroying their distinctive characteristics.'

M. Harvey looked also to the future. Post-war conditions, he told his audience, will bring problems of assimilation of immigrants who must be brought to Canada to serve industries bound to come to this country; and if these are to become part and parcel of the Canadian body politic, a start must be made now to create such a healthy body.

It was, therefore, in the light of these premises, that M. Harvey made his recommendations. Among these recommendations we especially signalize the following: to launch a campaign of education to teach Canadians to think nationally; to propagandize against all movements tending to set up groups against each other; to bring about unification of educational methods and certain textbooks; and to uphold democratic principles and the power of the Central Government.

All in all, it was a most enlightened address. It was a blue-print for Canadian unity, the manifesto of Canadian solidarity. Now more than ever before, now when our country is tested in the crucible of war, M. Harvey's suggestions came as golden counsel. The movement of Pan-Canadianism, launched by M. Harvey some time ago, and inspired as it is by the high and noble purpose above indicated, deserves the unanimous support of all citizens of the Dominion. It is, indeed, a formula for civilized patriotism.

Jewish Writers in Poland   23 February 1940

The facile phrasemakers are wont to speak of that hackneyed contrast – literature and life, as if the two concepts, instead of being complementary, were mutually exclusive. To-day, with reference to the sorry lot of all those who in Poland earned their meagre livelihood by the pen, they are amply justified. Literature and life are mutually exclusive.

The fate of Polish Jewry in general is a bitter and a tragic one; but the fate of those who built up Jewish culture in Poland until it fed the world, and all for a paltry pittance, is even bitterer and more tragic. There are no more Jewish printing presses in that country; no one there can now live by the sanctifying and ennobling word. But, whereas a tradesman, fleeing from one country to another, may orientate himself in his old trade, or a similar one, the Jewish journalist or writer is completely déclassé. Indeed, refuge is more difficult for them than for others; on account of their prominence in days past, they are singled out for special visitations of the invaders' wrath.

In the light of this situation, we are not surprised that there is a feeling among many that some special effort ought to be made on behalf of these particular victims of Nazi persecution. We note, from newspaper reports, that a number of these declassed journalists, still left in Warsaw, have betaken themselves to the profession of glaziers. They walk up and down the streets of that city, and put panes into the windows shattered by the bombs of Hitler's messerschmidts; and they eke out for themselves their crust of bread. How symbolic this situation is! Creative writers work and plan to open up new windows through which the world may look; and along come the barbarian eagles and convert the whole into magic casements opening on the foam 'of perilous seas forlorn.' And then yesterday's genius walks up and down the streets, with glass and putty, to make clear again the outlook upon life.

Upon re-reading these paragraphs, we realize again how truly tragic is the Jewish situation in Europe, for how tragic is tragedy when one measures its degrees, and compares its intensities!

Crocodile Tears   15 March 1940

The jackals have started their chorus again. Since August of last year when Tsar Joseph the First allied himself with Adolf, the Soviet press, when it has not been silent on the Jewish question, has been enigmatically ambiguous. Indeed, upon frequent occasions before that ominous date, the henchmen of Stalin have maintained a guilty taciturnity about this problem. When refugees were scattering all over the face of Europe, seeking a place of refuge from the wrath of the madman, the so-called bourgeois states gave them whatever asylum they could: it is true that they were not absolutely saint-like in their attitude, but at least they made a gesture. It was left to the great saviour of small people, the protector of minorities, the monopolist of the working class to slam the door in the face of the refugees.

When the infamous pact between the world's pioneer Jew-baiter and Stalin was consummated, then the cat was out of the bag. Then one knew that Russia was as imperialist as any other European state, and that in its expansionist realpolitik, it would throw overboard any and all of the ideals which it carried as ornamental baggage. Hence the silence in the Soviet press on the Jewish question.

Now, however, with the recent land ordinance issued in Palestine, the Communists have regained their tongues. The old song and dance is worked again; again one hears the taunts about Zionists serving for and being victimized by British imperialism. The Soviet lackeys, indeed, assume an attitude of heart-rending sympathy; 'too bad,' they say, 'that the British should have so betrayed you. We are really sorry.'

We, frankly speaking, are not impressed by these crocodile tears. We remember too keenly and too bitterly the attitude of the Soviet theoreticians when the riots of 1929 took place. Then it was that the *Freiheit*, with a despicable heartlessness and treachery which it has since, for reasons of convenience repented, announced to the world at large that the uprising of the Arab bandits was a revolutionary movement. Then it was that they would have had us believe that the *Yeshiva-bochur* of Hebron was a reactionary capitalist, that the *Chalutz* of Galilee was a tool of imperialism, and that the *shamas* of Petach-Tikvah was working hand in hand with international finance. Accordingly, they justified the arson, the murder, the slaughter. It was not a pogrom, they said; it was a loftily-inspired revolution!

To-day, they dissolve in tears because a land ordinance has been passed. Their sensitive hearts cannot stand it; the woe of Israel is their woe!

We repudiate this foxy sympathy. We scorn these uncouth subterfuges designed for soul-catching. That the land-ordinance is unjust we still maintain; but surely it is no reason for us to repudiate or to dissociate ourselves from the British Empire which to-day is carrying on a fight for the fundamentals of democracy and decency. Surely no Jew can think of extending the hand of friendship to one whose hand is already bloodied with Hitler's handshake!

Jews realize that ordinances are by their very nature temporary and ephemeral. They certainly do not constitute eternal law. But the threat of Hitler, and of all those who co-operate with him, *is* a threat against the eternal verities. Should Hitler emerge victorious, then the land ordinance assumes indeed a ridiculous insignificance, a fillip compared to a bomb-explosion.

Certainly, though Jewry is to-day hard beset, it has not yet lost its sense of proportion. A prohibition to purchase land is one thing; but a prohibition to live is yet another. Unhappy fate of Israel that it should be confronted with a choice, but once the choice is presented there is no doubt which shall be chosen.

The Brenner Rendez-Vous   22 March 1940

Speculation is rife as to what actually transpired on Monday upon the high Brenner Pass when the two worthies of European politics, the pseudo-Demon and the quasi-Pythias of Fascism, had their rendez-vous of love. They had not seen each other since 1938, alas; but since that time much water has flowed under many bridges. That great friendship about which both of them prated at every opportunity, had somewhat cooled; the wintry blasts about the Brenner altitudes constituted a fit atmosphere for the reunion.

What did they speak about in that two-hour interview? Nobody knows, except the two conversationalists and their respective shadows, Count Ciano and von Ribbentrop. Did they fondly reminisce about the Rome-Berlin Axis, which nothing, of yore, could break, and which since has been considerably dented and bent by a Russian hammer and sickle? Did they shiver in the railway-train, so that Benito could make a significant reference to the non-arrival of German coal, intercepted by the British blockade? Did Adolf catch on to the point intended by the master of ceremonies of this get-together, when he arranged that it should take place on Italian soil? Did Mussolini, realizing what happened to all others who went to interview the Fuehrer on home ground, insist that this time the Mohammed of Fascism should come to the mountain? And was there any special lesson to learn from the fact that the meeting took place at the Brenner Pass, a boundary which Hitler, after the taking of Czechoslovakia, proclaimed as sacred, sacrosanct?

Reporters, with that shrewdness which is the badge of all their tribe, venture two guesses. They say, these smart fellows, that Hitler and Mussolini, discussed one of two things – peace or war. The war-guessers opine that, like Alexander and Napoleon, the Fuehrer and the Duce had a long talk, dividing Europe between them. We do not doubt that this subject, under any circumstances, is a most entrancing theme of conversation; but we doubt whether that was really the gist of that tête-à-tête. Eye-witnesses who saw the conclusion of the interview report that Mussolini emerged smiling, and Adolf somewhat pale. This is a most peculiar shade of countenance for Hitler; usually it is he who emerges grinning, as witness the famous post-Munich photographs. The only conclusion one can arrive at is that for once the Fuehrer did not have entirely his own way; and Benito is not as malleable as one supposed. Mussolini is beginning to enjoy the position of fence-sitter.

Those who suggest that it was a peace-plan that was being discussed have a number of combative factors to support their case. In the first place, peace-plans are now quite the vogue in Europe; four out of five have it. In the second place, Mr. Sumner Welles' presence in Europe is a high incentive. In the third place, nothing would please Hitler more than to have a peace declared now which could give him time to solidify his position, organize his conquests, and after a spell, go back to unfinished business. Mussolini, too, could use peace discussions for the purpose of some private Italian blackmail; a concession here, a concession there, it all adds up and it costs nothing.

The difficulty, however, appears to be, that the peace terms which can issue from these two Katzenjammer twins, will not be acceptable to the Allies.

Already the Paris press has declared, in no uncertain terms, that it will not hear of any peace which leaves Czechoslovakia enslaved, Poland conquered, and Europe still threatened.

So, perhaps, the interview in the Brenner Pass was merely a social call. Perhaps, it was merely an attempt by husband Hitler to explain to his spouse Mussolini, that his flirtations with the Marxian concubine were really not serious, and that, after all, he still loved Benito. Why then was he reported as 'pale'? Perhaps, the Duce with callous heartlessness interrupted his protestations of love, with the crass interjection: 'What is there in it for me?'

The Shadows Move   10 May 1940

It would be laughable, were it not so tragic, this latest pre-occupation of the Polish Government in Exile. Faced with great national issues, a country under the heel of a foreign dictator, and their countrymen conquered and oppressed, the geniuses of Polonia seem to have no other fit subject for the exercise of their gigantic intelligences, than the paramount question: 'What will they do with the "surplus Jews" in Poland after the war? How will they be evacuated?'

We can think of no parallel to this example of combined gall and stupidity. At a time when the Nazi legions are treating all Poles as if they were surplus humans, the Warsaw Anders junta thinks only of the surplus Jews; at a time when the Nazi gauleiters are arranging for wholesale evacuation of Polish families, the Polish leaders who have been crying injustice plan how they can best emulate this example.

Indeed, what is this term 'surplus'? By what criterion, by what standard is one human being declared to be essential, and the next, surplus? Did not even General Haller, man of an unsavoury past, go touring up and down this continent declaring that in the new Poland, Jews and Poles would be given equal rights of citizenship? And while he was making the easy promises, couched in a facile verbiage, the Polish leaders who evacuated themselves from Poland are planning ways and means of evacuating the Jews who remained in the land!

That the Pans should think in this fashion, is, of course, not surprising. Long centuries of training have gone to make up this mentality. But that they should have the gall to extend to Jewish leaders an invitation to discuss ways and means of kicking Jews out of Poland, is certainly a sure indication of their superb arrogance and supreme stupidity. No Jewish leader, worthy the name, could possibly enter into such pourparlers. For such discussions are all based upon the despicable premise that the Jewish population of Poland are interlopers, interlopers who have lived in Poland for at least nine centuries!

However, the shadows continue to move. The Becks and the Smigly-

Ridzes are gone, but those who are left, carry on. They carry on a tradition which they should long ago have abandoned, which, since the war, they surely should have abandoned. But, like the Bourbons, they never learn. *Plus ça change, plus ça reste la même chose.*

Sermons in Bombs   7 June 1940

The bombings which recently took place in southern France, particularly in Marseilles, are being interpreted, not as a military but as a diplomatic move. It is, of course, difficult to understand what there is of the diplomatic in the tone of an exploding bomb; but this, it appears, is a special occasion. As Mussolini sits upon his fence, plucking a daisy – he loves me, he loves me not – the Fuehrer wishes to hasten his decision. Accordingly, he sends his bombers to the Mediterranean with 'a message for my love' – 'See,' he seems to say, 'jump in, the water's fine! And if you need any further help, why, my Messerschmidts will be along.'

It is, O gentle reader, a new language, Hitler's Esperanto, the Nazi code. Let the enfeebled democracies speak of the language of flowers; let the mollycoddled Allies read meanings into the rose and the forget-me-not. The hardy sons of Germany have a more powerful tongue. They communicate with each other by means of devastating bomb, destructive tank, eloquent flame-torch. Ah, sweet mystery of the Heinkel, at last I've found thee!

And so Benito is a much puzzled man these days. Like a fat Cassius, he sleeps not o'nights. He dreams of Rubicons; cast dice go cluttering through his brain, as on a barbotte table. 'Heinie-meinie-meeny-mo, to the battle shall I go?'

Certainly the Duce understands the meaning of bombs over Marseilles. It means that the German Air Force can reach southern France. Would that it meant only that, thinks the Duce. But it means also that French planes can leg it over Leghorn, can turn on Turin, can roam over Rome. After all, 'See Naples, and die' is advice which Italians give to other people. They do not relish being put in that spot themselves.

The Bluebirds   26 July 1940

There was something greatly pathetic and symbolic in the arrival in America of the latest refugee from Europe, Mr. Maurice Maeterlinck. The famous dramatist was accompanied by his wife and two bluebirds. The bluebirds, suspect of carrying infectious diseases, were not admitted, they were released from their cage to continue, like birds during an earlier deluge, their wanderings over the face of the waters.

The old dramatist, age 77, was himself a pitiable figure. The man who had so great a joie de vivre, the man of imagination and poetry, could not understand what had happened. For a person accustomed to bluebirds, the vultures who had recently swept over Belgium were strange birds, indeed. All the old man could think of was that his possessions in Belgium had been taken, his native land laid waste, and all those values which for almost fourscore years he had so highly prized, had been laid low. He must indeed, have felt like a relict from a forgotten world, a denizen of an older civilization who had somehow neglected to die. Pathos, with a vengeance.

And the bluebirds! Those feathered beings, symbol of happiness, theme of Maeterlinck's greatest play, they, too, had been refugees. Where the eagles of Hitler had arrived, there was no room for these brightly-coloured birds. Even the land where the pursuit of happiness is part of the constitution, the bluebirds were prohibited. It appears, ornithologically speaking, that the world is governed by vultures, using gulls, for the suppression of – doves.

One can eke out consolation only from the fact that not even the sparrow falls without the concern of Providence.

Shadow and Substance   2 August 1940

Dr. Chaim Zhitlovsky enjoys an extraordinary reputation in Jewish letters. At the risk of being dubbed a Philistine, and in spite of Zhitlovsky's ponderous volumes, we venture to say that that reputation is grossly overestimated. For the learned doctor, despite his sesquipedalian vocabulary, has ever dealt only in platitudes and half-truth. His erudition has been but of the shallowest kind, its shallowness disguised in a mongrel Yiddish which is a composite of German and Latin, designed to impress only those who have not had the benefit of that European culture which Zhitlovsky presumably conveys to the Hebrews.

Indeed, there is no creative contribution which the doctor has made to the realm of thought. Instead, he has taken and badly digested the truisms and the semi-truisms of European thought and has placed them before a people hitherto fed only on religious literature. The result was that the ex-*yeshiva-bochurim* who constitute Zhitlovsky's chief readers, imagined that they were getting the secular gospel right from the horse's mouth. The fact was that these pseudo-philosophic essays have no more real cultural value than the popularizations which are printed from time to time at a publisher's orders. This, of course, is not to detract from him the merit of having at least opened for Jewry those magic casements of general western civilization, but this achievement is not to be confused with that of having assimilated or embellished the view thus revealed.

It is our impression, indeed, that the intellectuals of Zhitlovsky's day – that is, of a bygone day – were so grateful for the fine slogans of nineteenth century thought, that they accepted them at their face value, as if the words themselves had something magical and potent within them. Tolerance, for example, is treated not as a concept subject to analysis, but as an incantation for the life of the philosophic medicine-man. How much keener were the thought processes of the late Max Nordau who declared that every European constitution felt it necessary to include a clause about liberty, fraternity, etcetera, albeit no one intended to use said clause, 'much as a respectable bourgeois family places a grand piano in the drawing-room although there is no one in the house to play it.' Nordau looked for the substance beyond the shadow; he did not merely read a constitution and say Hallelujah.

These remarks are motivated by a recent article written by the learned doctor Zhitlovsky in which he reproaches Jewry with not having sufficient tolerance. The reader will naturally interject – tolerance for whom? Well, Dr. Zhitlovsky would like to be tolerant of Hitler. We must, he says, understand his viewpoint.

We feel that this reproach is unworthy to issue from the lips of this man. It is indeed, Jewry that understands Hitler, and not the doctor, despite his cultural background, who does so. For a Jew to speak of being tolerant of Hitler, may perhaps result in raising that Jew's estimation of his own prophetic messianic self, but it certainly is unseemly in one who seeks above all things to be rational. 'Love good, and spurn evil,' said the holy writers; one cannot be platonically fond of both. He who is tolerant of Hitler, is intolerant to Hitler's victims.

But Dr. Zhitlovsky is apparently not living in the 1940's. He's still thinking the thoughts of those pre-war days when merely to be a pacifist was to be considered an intellectual giant. Behold then the distinction between the philosopher and the pseudo-philosopher. Zhitlovsky still mumbles the clichés of tolerance for Nazis; he does not stop to consider the substance behind the shadow; Bertrand Russell, a much profounder person, who underwent personal sacrifices for his ideal, no longer speaks of tolerance toward the murderers of Berlin.

All in all, Zhitlovsky's thesis is a disgraceful phenomenon. We know how we in British countries react to it; we wonder how our brothers in Poland, the refugees in France, the victims in Holland, would react to the glorious and noble gospel of the saintly and pious doctor. They, too, would feel, no doubt, that the professor was pouring metaphysical salt on physical wounds.

Vladimir Jabotinsky   9 August 1940

Haboker, in commenting upon the great loss which Jewry has just suffered in the passing of Vladimir Jabotinsky, says: 'An eagle has fallen from the skies.' This is no mere oriental hyperbole, motivated by the injunction to speak only good of the dead. Keen-eyed, upward-soaring, the late Jabotinsky was a veritable eagle in Israel. It is true that he frequently swooped down upon those whom he considered of the lesser breed; it is true that frequently he kept himself aloof in the great eyrie of his idealism; but certainly he always flew high, certainly he ever saw far.

He was a man of no mean talents. His literary activities, from the days when he was associated with *Razviet* until the very hour of his last writing, were a world's marvel. He touched nothing but what he also adorned it. A lord of language, he was equally at home in Russian, English, French, Yiddish and Hebrew, the which tongue he acquired only at an advanced age, and forthwith stepped from its primary letters to the creation of its literature. He translated the poetry of Chaim Nachman Bialik into Russian, and with consummate irony, he rendered Dante's *Inferno* into Hebrew, a tongue already replete with melancholy classics.

Powerful as were his writings, his speech was even more so. His oratorical genius is of the great tradition; it is an integral part of the Zionist Renascence. No one who heard him forgot thereafter either the vigour of his [...] echoes of his perorations still ring in the hearts of Jewry.

But he was not merely a man of words; on the contrary, he was essentially a man of action. The creation of the Jewish Legion during the last war was mainly the result of his activities; at the very time of his death, he was busily engaged in the mustering again of a Jewish 'co-belligerent' army, which was to take its place in the vanguard of the legions of civilization.

His dynamic activism, moreover, was not, as is frequently the case, frittered away in half a dozen contradictory efforts; for him, nationalism was the 'one increasing purpose.' He was the Jewish maximalist par excellence, and in an age characterized by appeasement and compromise and minimalism, it was frequently refreshing, yes, and inspiring, to witness his valiant battles, sometimes Quixotic, against great odds.

Because of his uncompromising nature, he naturally aroused the opposition of the powers that be. It is ironical, almost literary, to reflect that the great fighter for a Greater Palestine should, like Moses, have been prohibited, for the last decade, domicile in the Promised Land. Technically a man without a country, he travelled on a Nansen passport, and when asked his nationality, described himself as 'The Wandering Jew.' His peripatetic activities were almost as geographically-embracing as Herzl's; both these leaders, in the true tradition of our people, suffered personally the *ol galuth*, the yoke of exile, so that the redemption might the sooner come.

Perhaps the most significant contribution of Vladimir Jabotinsky to the life of his contemporaries was the magic of his personality, a personality which appealed to the inward nostalgia of all Jewry. Jabotinsky was the active subconscious of all Israel, the personification of its longings; in fine, he was in an iron age that which lesser Jews could be only in a golden one. In great measure this explains the powerful hold which he had over the imagination of Jewish youth, particularly in Poland. He it was who took Bialik's thesis in verse, adumbrated in 'The City of Slaughter' in which Bialik reviled that pseudo-pacifism which was really inertia, and rendered it into prose. That there were great practical difficulties in the realization of this approach was immediately noted by his doctrinaire and prosaic opponents; no one, however, can gainsay the fundamental kernel of truth therein inherent.

His opponents attempted to make much of the fact that he was the man of 'the grand gesture,' that he did many things for effect, that he thought grandiloquently, and entirely out of proportion to possibilities. While there may have been considerable truth in this evaluation, it nonetheless remained incontrovertible truth that the 'grand gesture' approach influenced the imagination and was worth to the Zionist movement a million pamphlets.

Even his bitterest opponents admit that he was, par excellence, the sincere and devoted nationalist, given over to the cause of Zion as an idée fixe, and uttering out loud hopes which the rest of Israel cherished in its bosom. His reach exceeded his grasp; 'aye, but a man's reach *should* exceed his grasp, or what's a heaven for ...?'

Jabotinsky is dead. He leaves behind him a great heritage, the heritage of a colourful life, richly lived. His was the poetry of action of the Hebrew Renascence; already he belongs to our mythology. Our people will always remember him, as a young man, – the eternal youth of the eternal people – who flashed across our sky, like a meteor, a brilliant anachronism, but a gratefully accepted one, who permitted us, at one and the same time, to live in the golden age of Israel's leaders while treading through the contemporary slough of despond. The odds were against him; the realities were opposed to him, but

> Is it not fine to fling against loaded dice
> Yet to win once or twice?
> To bear a rusty sword without an edge
> Yet wound the thief in the hedge? ...
> To be cast into a prison damp and vile,
> And break bars, with a blunt file?
> To defy the tyrant world, and at a pinch
> To wrest from it an inch?

To engage the stars in combat, and therefrom
Pluck a hair's breadth of room?
Is it not fine, worthy of Titans or gods
To challenge such heavy odds?

Indeed it is; and all honour to the man whose life was such a gallant battle with heavy odds. Nor has he lost.

Of Wine and Water   6 September 1940

The latest decree emanating from the lawmakers of Vichy concerns prohibition. Still bewildered at the cause of French defeat – look in thy heart, and write? – the junta of Vichy now announces that the French republic collapsed because the republicans drank too much wine. Alcohol, therefore, has been the doom of 'la belle France.' Not Pétain undermined the state, but Pernod, the manufacturer, of absinthe. If only the French people had not drunk wine, their resistance might have been greater. Such at least, is the thesis which the solons of unoccupied France wish to advance, as they prohibit the consumption of alcohol in the land.

We doubt very much whether it was to this factor that the temporary conquest of France is attributable. We cannot subscribe to the theory that it was the pressed grape which demoralized the poilu, that it was absinthe which made the heart grow fond. The Vichy Government, however, is happy to be able to accept any excuse, any alibi, so long as suspicion does not fall upon her. Let liquor take the blame; let Laval et al. be exculpated.

It is this law itself which indicates how alien, how unrepresentative the Vichy Government really is. Could one ever conceive a truly typical French regime prohibiting the imbibing the juices of the warm south, the beaker of Provençal wine? It is only a group of usurpers, a set of Nazi agents who can suggest that France in defeat be deprived of even the consolation of drink.

No, France is really wine, fervour, sentiment; it is only Pétain who is water, Vichy water.

Einstein and God   20 September 1940

The distinguished Dr. Einstein, it appears, has graduated himself from relativity to theory. Deprived of his laboratory by the Nazi regime, the minute scientist is attempting to smuggle himself into the Lord's test-tube and retort presence. Such, at least, is the impression which is gained by the learned doctor's most recent address delivered in a paper presented at the Conference of Science, Philosophy and Religion at the Jewish Theological Seminary of America. Here it was that, like a new Moses on an American Sinai, he urged the ministers of the Lord 'to give up the doctrine of a personal God.'

Although ourselves intended by fond parents for spiritual leadership in Israel, we have for some inscrutable reason, sedulously avoided matters theologic. We have not sought, except in an extra-curriculum way, to divine the divine. Our relationship with Divinity has been a purely personal one, based on a variation of Heine's dictum: *Dieu me pardonnera; c'est son métier.* Profounder subjects we have left to the specialists in the field.

The author of the theory of relativity rushes in where angels fear to tread. We are, be it noted, not commenting upon Einstein's disquisitions about the essence of deity; what we are commenting on, however, is the strange place he went to, to urge the abandonment of a personal God – right in the throne of the synagogue! After all there is such a thing as tact, as a sense of the fitness of things. After all, there is a theory of relativity!

Einstein's theory, moreover, is particularly inopportune at the present moment. It is indeed, excessively cruel to urge civilized mankind to forsake its last pillar of consolation, and to seek refuge in Einstein's God, a God who is merely a concept, composed of mathematical formulas and natural laws. Even Voltaire was kinder – he said, in his blasphemous manner, that if there were no God, it would be necessary to invent him.

However, we doubt whether the Conference of Science, Philosophy and Religion will adopt Einstein's credo. They will feel that a magnifying glass, a table of logarithms, and a test-tube are not, Einstein notwithstanding, the Urim and Thummim of the twentieth century.

Sermons and Stones   27 September 1940

We had occasion some time ago to comment upon an editorial which appeared in the Toronto *Globe and Mail* in which its author, using the smooth style in which blessing reads like malediction, set himself up as a mentor to Jewry, and lectured Israel – of course, in the most refined language – upon its duty in time of war. The gratuitous sermon of the Toronto journal was evoked by an announcement from 'The New Zionist Organization' that a plan was afoot to organize a Jewish army. While the Montreal *Daily Star* used this announcement as an occasion to pay tribute to the contribution which Jews had made to the last war, and to this, the Toronto newspaper wrote a complete essay, the substance of which was to say that it was high time, and American Jews included.

It is true that the writer of that editorial does not seem to be, even upon superficial reading, very well informed. He declared, for example, that there were *thirty million* Jews in the United States from which the Jewish Army might be drawn! Of all the errors of that editorial, this was the only one which was subsequently corrected; the *Globe* did not want people to think that it saw ten Jews where only one stood. Accordingly, the statistics were altered; but the prejudice remained. And *The Globe and Mail* devoted itself to subsequent editions.

But the evil which men do lives after them. This last week *Le Canada*, charmed by the subject, decided also to write a homily on the Jewish army. And what was simpler than to reprint the paragraph'd wisdom of *The Globe and Mail*, stud it with some philosophy of its own, and then serve it up, in bold and in italics! *Le Canada*, moreover, despite the benefit of the correction which appeared in *The Globe and Mail*, reprints the unadulterated original. *Le Canada*, indeed, misses nothing important; it too, makes as its own, this priceless paragraph of the Toronto bombast: 'The accusation which Jews ought to answer is this: That having been the most vigorous in demanding that the British Government put an end to the aggressions of Hitler, they are to-day the principal beneficiaries of the prosperity which certain industries enjoy as a result of the war. When one sees the mortal foe of Jewry fought at the price of so much Anglo-Saxon blood, the prestige of the Jewish people upon this continent will not be heightened unless the armies of Judaea take their place upon the field of battle.'

What a fine-flowing sentence, full of the oil of rhetoric, with not a little vinegar of prejudice! The reference to prosperity and its beneficiaries, for example, which is untrue, irrelevant, and utterly despicable. And as for the amount of blood shed, apparently the blood of Polish Jewry, fighting violently in the legions of Poland, and Czech Jewry, and French Jewry, is water, and not blood!

It is high time, indeed, high time that those self-appointed censors, those arrogating Catos were told to learn the facts before they rush to spread insinuation and innuendo over the breakfast table. It is high time that they learned of the part which Jews are already playing in the armed forces of the country, soldiers who are slandered by lucubrations of the above-described kind. It is high time, too, that they were reminded that immediately at the outset of war, a Jewish delegation visited Ottawa for the purpose of organizing a Jewish Unit, the which project was deemed inadvisable by the Government. As for the Jewish army of the New Zionist Organization, it was announced as a *plan*, and apparently has not yet received the approval of the British

Government. (The New Zionist Organization may learn from the editorials the benefits of hasty publicity.) The only plan which the British Government did approve was for the organization of a Jewish unit in Palestine, for which the Jewish Agency had clamoured for about a year, and indeed, three days after the opening of its roll, the full number of required volunteers was reached!

Jews are doing and will continue to do their full duty to the country in which they are equal citizens, and this without instruction from anyone. No one need teach them the meaning of Hitlerism, and the necessity to combat it. Nor do Jews consider themselves above criticism; they are entitled, however, that any criticism should be based on facts, and not on rumour, inaccuracy, prejudice, and worse. It is against this very psychology that the Empire is engaged in mortal combat.

The Isles of Greece   1 November 1940

From the shores of the Mediterranean there sprang the two great sources of our culture and civilization, the Hebraic and the Hellenic strains. While the one contributed our concepts of morality, ethics, right being, the other brought to light the concepts of art and beauty. Together, in an almost impeccable amalgam, they gave western civilization both its form and its substance.

Against this culture, the axe-bearers of the Axis are implacably set. They began their onslaught, naturally enough, against what they termed the Semitic in European life, i.e., against the Ten Commandments, against the teachings of the prophets, major and minor, against the doctrines of Christ, who in his sympathy for the meek and the heavily-laden is far too Judaic for the hard hearts of the blond beasts of barbarism. Towards this task they dedicated all the ingenuity of their propaganda and all the force of their concentration camps. Fortunately they have not yet succeeded; but ere they complete that nefarious objective, they have already set themselves against that other source of European culture – Greece.

Symbolically enough, the onslaught begins with a bombing of Athens! How fitting! There where Phidias showed the beauty of the human form divine, there the sons of Mussolini drop their bombs to see that form open up, to use their own delectable phrase, 'like a rose.' There where Plato and Aristotle fathomed the workings of the human mind, the Fascists now display the workings of the mind not so human.

At this writing, the Greeks are putting up a valiant resistance. All that Mussolini has struck so far has been the ruins of Greece; the people of Greece are by no means decrepit. And to their aid has come, as in the days of Byron, a navy full of Byrons of our day, who conjure up again the glory that was Greece, and whose reflections to-day are those of the noble land of a century ago.

> The mountains look on Marathon
> And Marathon looks on the sea,
> And musing there an hour alone
> I dreamed that Greece might still be free.

If the world needed but another instance revelatory of the true character of the foe, this is it. The fight in the Balkans well may be but another recrudescence of that ancient ever-unfulfilled German policy – the *Drang Nach Osten*, the Berlin-Bagdad mirage; but it is also more than that – it is an attempt to clear away from the path of marching barbarism this unpleasant recollection of one of the temples of that culture which the Axis so profoundly despises.

It is said that the current adventures of Adolf and Benito are designed also to embarrass Roosevelt in his forthcoming election. If this was an incidental consideration of the plan, there can be no doubt but that the plan has 'gone aglae.' The American people, nurtured upon Greek thought in extent only second to English thought, will know how to react to this most recent attempt at aggression of a peaceful nation.

It is reported that the British fleet is now ubiquitous among the Aegean Isles. This is gratifying. At long last the arm of the Navy will be able to reach out, and meet the Italian forces which hitherto have made the practice of turning tail a military strategy. Already it is conceded that the campaign of General Graziani in Northern Africa has proved a fiasco; cut off from his sources of supply, and meeting the inclemencies of the desert, not to speak of the R.A.F. and the periodic fire of the Navy, Graziani has discovered that this time he is not campaigning against Haile Selassie. It is to be hoped that now another coup de grâce will follow in the Isles of Greece.

Certainly our cause had a number of setbacks. The extension of the conflict to the Balkans, however, unfortunate as it may be to the countries involved, increases the opportunities of meeting the foe in that combat we so heartily desire. And in no place better than in Greece can one evoke the words which Byron once wrote of that country's struggle:

> For freedom's battle, once begun
> Bequeath'd by bleeding sire to son,
> Though baffled oft, is ever won.

A Finger of God 15 November 1940

The Bible, written in anthropomorphic terminology – *l'shabair eth ha-ozen*, as Maimonides explains it – has a remarkable expression for events of an inner symbolism. They are called 'fingers of God.' Such a one was lifted last week for all to see. And timely it was, indeed. Whether it will serve to point the lesson intended, or not, is quite another question; but as the novelists say, you have been warned.

For the earthquakes in Rumania, extending as they did not only throughout that country but far beyond its borders, should have written a message not only upon Europe's seismograph, but also upon its conscience. In these quakes, indeed, there is inherent a symbolism as powerful as that which startled the banqueting guests of biblic times when all of a sudden, at the height of revelry, they read the writing on the wall, *Mene, mene, tekel, upharsin.* To nations and peoples strutting upon the face of the earth in the arrogant panoply of war, and particularly to dictators, flaunting the moral laws and considering themselves, Nero-like, as gods, the rumblings of the earth – *Deus sive Natura* – should be heavily fraught with the ominous forecast of doom. How puny, indeed, do the most perfectly co-ordinated blitzkriegers appear in comparison to this mere sneeze of Nature, this petty hiccup of the earth!

It is, however, highly dubious whether those for whom the lesson is particularly intended will take it to heart. We cannot conceive of the puffed-up Belial of Nazi Germany possibly concerning himself with the theological implications of what Ribbentrop will explain to him as a purely scientific phenomenon. Even the Rumanians, first victims of the upheaval, do not appear to have noted the moral indications of this calamity. Latest reports from that country announce that 120 million lei have been allowed – not for relief to the stricken, but for division among 'blood-Rumanians' wherever these creatures may be. These millions represent some of the booty of confiscation from Jewish estates.

To some an earthquake is not sufficient catharsis. Like the Bourbons, they must also have a deluge.

The Balcony Warrior 15 November 1940

There was a time when the gullible were easily impressed by one Benito Mussolini. All the Duce had to do was jut out his jaw, and the discontented and the undiscriminating immediately began to rave about 'the strong man.'

Indeed, it was a popular sport within the democracies themselves to hold up the picture of Benito as an example of the man 'who gets things done.' All those who at one time or other flirted with Fascism, dressed in the seven veils of business efficiency, idealized the Duce, and spoke wistfully about the appearance of that prototype in their own countries.

The war has considerably diminished the glory which surrounded that renegade upstart. Time showed that the Duce was neither a strong man, nor yet a silent one. As for the railway schedules which presumably ran on time in Italy since the advent of Benito, that, too, appears to have been an optical illusion; for was there not a train schedule planned for northern Greece, by the Duce himself, the which schedule has considerably backfired.

Even as a warrior – and Benito ever maintained that if a man was not a warrior, he was nothing – Benito has proved a flop. It is true that he conquered Haile Selassie; but no self-respecting European would consider that a great achievement. Now his forces are bogged in Northern Africa, and as for Northern Greece, the Duce is so infuriated, so chagrined at the defeats which his crack warriors have been suffering that he seeks refuge in his usual sanctuaries – the piazza or the balcony.

Whenever the Italian fuehrer has an important pronouncement to make – and to him all are important, and every pronouncement is in itself an achievement – he picks himself a cosy little balcony facing onto a square. It is a tradition, no doubt, borrowed either from the ancient tribunes of Rome, or the balcony-climbing of Romeo of literature, – no matter; what a beer cellar is to Adolf, that a balcony is to Benito. Accordingly, as the news of the war developments lay heavy upon Musso he sought himself out a hall – apparently no balcony was at hand – and he delivered a speech to the 'provincial hierarchy of Fascism.'

And what a speech! Caesar, whom the Duce seeks to emulate, never uttered the like. Apart from the fact that oratory issuing from one who has been singularly barren of accomplishment is disgusting in itself, Mussolini's protestations that he is telling the truth are unparalleled in the history of falsehood. Before he has had occasion to make any real statement, Benito, as if engaged in mind-reading, shouts: No, it's the truth! Even the Fuehrer, notorious liar, does not preface his remarks by announcing that he is not lying.

Equally comic-opera – indeed, the whole Mussolinian performance ought to have been accompanied with music – was the announcement that 'the Greeks hate us.' Really! The speech was not broadcast outside of Italy, and so we cannot tell whether the Duce's voice broke at this juncture; but surely the accusation came from the depths of the Fascist heart. We wonder what General Metaxas is supposed to reply in answer to this indictment – that the Greeks love the Italians? Or is the reply given at Korizza entirely adequate, at least for the moment?

The speech, of course, had the usual peroration. Let ordinary militarists rattle their sabres; when the Duce rattles, he rattles eight million at a time! Writhing with discomfiture at the Hellenic setbacks, Benito again threatens the world with his eight million bayonets. One has yet, of course, to see these bayonets in action. Thus far, all one has observed, to use the language of President Roosevelt, is a little bit of Fascist dagger-work in the back of France. That, no doubt, is the reason the Duce boasts about breaking the *back* of the Negus, breaking the *back* of Greece. He is an expert on *backs*. During the last war did he not himself receive shrapnel in his own posterior?

The trouble, of course, is that the Greeks are not showing their backs. That display, therefore, has been made only by the crack divisions of Mussolini!

A Strange Apologist   10 January 1941

We have no quarrel with those who insist that the eclipse of France is merely temporary. Indeed, no one who has the slightest vestige of faith in the vigor of militant democracy, can believe otherwise. This great people, which first gave to the world the example of democracy, which enriched civilization with the priceless gift of its culture, and which even in military matters ceded to no one – until it was taken by surprise – has merely had its history interrupted, certainly not ended. The reports which issue from unoccupied France, moreover, tend to further confirm this estimate of the élan vital of the French people. Defeated, they are not crushed; surprised, they are not overwhelmed. Accordingly, we have no polemics to exchange with anyone who expresses – even as mere wishful thinking – a belief in the future of France, a premonition of the rise of the phoenix.

But this type of statement, however, is entirely different from the apologetics which engages itself in whitewashing the architecture of Vichy. Even the blindest, even the most uninformed, have learned to make a distinction between those who temporarily sit in the seats of office, and the vast people of France. Because one is unhappy about what the Lavals and the Beaudoins sought to accomplish, one ought to be mercifully silent. One certainly ought not to assume that the de facto sub-rulers of France can do no wrong.

And this is precisely what M. André Maurois assumes in a recent article in *Life*. Mr. Maurois' career has hitherto been characterized by a sort of unofficial ambassadorship between the English and French speaking peoples. He it was who popularized the lives and ideologies of a number of distinguished English writers. He was the interpreter of the '*entente cordiale*.' He was this, not only metaphorically, but actually; he served, before the debacle, as liaison officer between the English and the French forces.

Now, dwelling in America, Maurois has undertaken – certainly a much more difficult task – to explain the men of Vichy to the United States, which apparently refuses to understand. To estimate Maurois' homiletics, it is important to remember one fact – Maurois is a Jew. In France itself to-day, Maurois would not be permitted to publish the article, to write for *Life*, even were it ten times as exculpatory, as laudatory – precisely because he is a Jew. And this prohibition against Jewish journalism – albeit couched in the most stylized French, and signed by a Gallicized name – prevails not only in occupied but also in unoccupied France.

However, Maurois, with a tolerance which is angelic, prefers to ignore this fact. He ignores other facts too. He writes, for example, as if the entire government of France consists only of Pétain, and Pétain was the hero of Verdun. One would never suspect, from the article, that that government included also the Lavals and the Flandins, and the Cagoulards of yesteryear. Pétain is the name with which he conjures. Maurois ignores also the farcical trials which the henchmen are planning for Reynaud, Daladier, Mandel, Blum. One can hardly refrain from remarking that if Maurois had remained in France, he doubtless would have found himself amongst the minor accused, but amongst the accused.

Having escaped the fate of an accused, Maurois voluntarily assumes the office of advocate for the advocates of the prosecution. How much better, and more honorable, it would have been for Maurois to have remained silent until the soul of France itself would speak! Or if silence to him was intolerable, how much more harmonious would have been his voice if lifted in utterance with the forces of de Gaulle! Why, even that old man, Bergson, refused, not only to sing the praises of the new regime, but even to indulge in pure philosophy under its protection! Maurois voluntarily applies for the position of 'court-Jew.'

No one denies that the Pétain regime has its difficulties and its dilemmas. But to say this, and to say that everything that the Pétain regime has done is good, are two different things. Moreover, if the government at Vichy must have apologists, let others than Maurois accept the dubious honor. For one must inevitably be offended by the spectacle of one who under Vichy is considered a third-class citizen, singing the praises of his scornful masters.

A Splendid Precedent   17 January 1941

The last week-end beheld in Toronto an event unprecedented in the history of Canadian Jewry. It is difficult for us, being part of the said event, freely to comment thereon; the natural modesty of the undersigned handicaps accurate description. The precedent, however, is of such a nature, that it behooves us, in the larger communal interest, to fling humility to the winds, and to sing, in unembarrassed numbers, the eisteddfod of the Central Division of the Canadian Jewish Congress.

This, then, is what occurred. Let it be writ in large letters that all who run may read, and all who read may in their footsteps halt. The Canadian Jewish Congress, Central Division, preoccupied though it continually is with problems of greater practical moment, decided that it was high time to acknowledge the days and works of its literary men. It noted with approval that the last year saw the publication of three volumes of creative endeavor – a book on Jewish music by I. Rabinovitch, a volume of Yiddish poetry by I.I. Segal, and a volume of English poetry by the writer of these lines. Under the inspiration and guidance of its president, Mr. A.B. Bennett, the Central Division of the Congress was instrumental in encompassing a triple miracle.

In the first place: it invited from Montreal the aforementioned triumvirate so that they might participate in an assembly dedicated solely to matters cultural and literary. This, it was felt, would be a gracious genuflection in the direction of the purveyors of the 'word.' It is to be noted that the three wise men of the East so to be honored were – *mirabile dictu* – still alive! Immortal they were only in the sense that mortality had not yet caught up with them. It is further to be noted that the evening for which they were invited was to be untrammelled with pragmatic purposes – no campaigns, no propaganda – merely belles lettres pure and undefiled! The thing was hitherto unheard of in remembered history.

The first miracle brought in its wake a second. The three literary musketeers, contrary to established custom and routine, waited not to be coaxed, cajoled, persuaded, into accepting the invitation. Indeed, the alacrity with which all three availed themselves of the opportunity verged upon rank betrayal of the so-called literary etiquette.

And then the three journeyed together to Toronto – two bards, and one editor who is also a musicologist. The two bards fought no duels; such amity existed between them that the impartial spectator might indeed have doubted as to whether these were really literary gentlemen. More than that: they did not even conspire against the editor. The harmony which welled from the musicologist pervaded the atmosphere.

The three arrived – to discover – O manna from heaven! – O dew from Hermon! – O precious ointment that runneth down upon the beard! – that the *Hebrew Journal*, under the editorship of S.M. Shapiro, was dedicated practically in its entirety to the three by this time much inflated guests. It is true that the journal of that issue had some references to the war, but these were obiter dicta; it was quintessentially a literary issue. Sam Abramson, cicerone, immediately bought out a considerable portion of the issue, and handed it to the logos-bearers. Here the three literary men reverted to type; each searched for articles upon himself, and they read, and their cups ran over.

Shall one speak of the gatherings, the assemblies, the sittings of brothers together that followed the next day? Are they not writ in the chronicles of the three who ate? Surely it was as the crier in the Book of Esther would say: So is it done to them in whom the King – *Amcho* – delighted!

(Reader, forgive; the writer keeps on forgetting that he was one of the three!)

And then the final pièce de résistance – the eisteddfod itself at the Bellevue Theatre. Certainly it was filled to capacity; if as Walt Whitman said – To have great poets, one must have great audiences – then the inspired word ought not to be lacking in Israel. There they were: Segal, with that piety with which he approaches the written word, reading an essay on the essence of literary creations – a Yiddish *sefer yetzirah* – and concluding it, as becomes a disciple of the Master of the Good Name, with two poems, one about the Baal Shem Tov, and the other about a magnanimous thief; Rabinovitch, with his genial humor, expounding the origins of Jewish music, and instructing not only with informal exposition, but also with melodious examples; and Klein – the politico will out – rhapsodizing about that latter-day Elizabethan, Winston Churchill, and mouthing curses at Hitler in bloodcurdling rhyme. Over it all presides Rabbi Sachs, a just and equitable *arbiter dicendi*, and beside him beams Archie Bennett a benedictine beam. Nor is Sam Kronick absent, himself in Toronto representing the government-in-exile of the Litvacks.

But hold, enough of this pure reportage. Let the editorial clarion sound out loud. It will say that the Central Division of the Congress has established an excellent precedent – although yours truly is bound to remark, the purpose of gagging Satan, that perhaps one third of it was misplaced – that he who conceived the gesture was a scholar and a gentleman, and that those who executed it were men of no mean parts. Certainly A.B. Bennett, whom we at this opportunity embrace as fellow-columnist, is unique among presidents. May his tribe increase!

A Nazi Boast   31 January 1941

At last the Nazi press has pleaded guilty – not without arrogance – to the accusation par excellence which the democracies level against it. Many years ago, when Edgar Ansel Mowrer first analyzed the nature of the Nazi regime, he published a book called *Germany Puts Back the Clock*. That was sometime in 1933. Since then it has been clearly demonstrated that it is not merely a clock which the Fascists have put back; they have torn up the whole calendar of contemporary progress.

Accordingly, it is no mere propaganda to say that the ambition of contemporary Germany is to lead the world back to the Middle Ages. Time was when such an accusation constituted a most humiliating slur to any people which considered itself civilized. It was equivalent to dubbing them barbarians. Not so to-day in Nazi-land. The *Voelkischer Beobachter*, the official cesspool of Hitlerian ideology, accepts the accusation as a compliment! Certainly it would greet the return of the Middle Ages! They were, were they not, a period of great cultural achievement?

It is true that the Middle Ages are characterized by a certain cultural progress, the most distinguishing feature of which was its religious art. Certainly it is not this aspect which appeals to the soul of the gauleiter! What is there in common between Hitler's barracks, pointing guns, and the great cathedrals of the fourteenth century, pointing fingers up to God? Are not these achievements of that age anathema to Hitler? As for the religious hierarchy which dominated that period, it is not to that regime that Adolf would revert. The whole world knows what Streicher et al. say of Roman Catholic priests, and in what manner they are treated under the Third German Reich.

What things mediaeval do they so admire? Its chivalry? It is to laugh. What chivalry is there in a regime co-ordinated by the Gestapo? Is it chivalrous for many to attack one? Is it chivalrous for a whole nation to concentrate its fury upon its minorities?

We venture to suggest that what has so enamored the Nazi leaders with the mediaeval way of life is the tyranny on the one hand, and the submissiveness on the other, which eminently characterized it. A regime which considers all its subjects as so many chattels in the service of the state is but a transposition of mediaeval feudalism with its serfs attached to the glebe. Such a system eminently suits our Adolf. Hitler as lord of pre-eminent domain, his vassal Quislings serving him in the duchies, and the huge population of Europe reduced to villeinage – is this not the blueprint of the New Order, made upon illuminated manuscript?

There are of course some minor details of mediaevalism which have their special charms. The suppression of freedom – a sine qua non; the elimination of free investigation – a veritable insurance policy; and the tortures, the inquisitions – delectable sport. One need not mention the mediaeval treatment of Jews – if the Middle Ages hadn't thought of that treatment, the Nazis certainly would have invented it.

How deformed must be that government which boasts of its own iniquity!

Even the Tsarist regime felt deeply offended when it was called mediaeval. But not so Hitler's. Wickedness, indeed, knows no deeper depth than that it should not recognize its own wickedness.

Perhaps, however, there is a saving feature in the Nazi boast. The chief metaphysician of the Reich, Alfred Rosenberg, it will be recalled, has been preaching for many years a reversion to paganism. The system that he would introduce into Germany would be that which prevailed in its forests during the first and second centuries of the Christian era. The painted hairy barbarians of the days of Vercingetorix are his ideal, Thor and Wodin his gods. It is not surprising therefore that in comparison with such political concepts the Middle Ages should appear to the editor of the *Voelkischer Beobachter* as an age of progress and civilization.

Immortal Speech   14 February 1941

Of the spirit which activates the Prime Minister of Britain, all know from the example of his sturdy leadership in the most troubled time of England's island story. Of his plans, his policies, his programs, are they not written in Hansard, reported in the press, and told in all places where speech is not stifled nor fettered the human mind? Like the true pedant which we are, we propose to write of the speech, the language, which gives form to his imperishable thought.

No leader of Britain, within the memory of living man, has been such a master of the inspiring utterance, finding the singular word for the common thought, and endowing even a statistical report, or a narrative of troop deployment, with all the heroism of British tradition, and all the idealism of human aspiration. Here is language that is as if taken out of Holy Writ, the homely parable, the apt quotation, the ironical aside – all the verbal characteristics bespeaking the man endowed with a purpose and brimming with confidence.

Indeed, a single speech of his is compact with history, replete with allusion, allusion not obscure, like that of the professor, but allusion known to all men, a thing familiar. His military reports sound as if they were pages out of Caesar, the same compactness, the same activity, the same marching towards a purpose, full of grandeur, yet business-like. Has Nemesis ever been more implacably, more classically described? 'In order to win the war, Hitler must destroy Great Britain. He may carry havoc into the Balkan states; he may tear great provinces out of Russia; he may march to the Caspian; he may march to the gates of India. All this will avail him nothing. He may spread his curse more widely, throughout Europe and Asia, but it will not avert his doom ... The British Empire, nay in a certain sense, the whole English-speaking world – will be on his track, bringing with them the sword of justice.'

He has, indeed, the capacity to endow even a weather-report with a touch of the heroic. It is a common observation that the days are now growing longer. But this is how Churchill says it: 'We have broken the back of the winter ... The daylight grows, the Royal Air Force grows, and is already actually master of the daylight air.'

Speak of the classic touch! His whole speech echoes with fragments of the classics. When, perchance, he needs must refer to Hitler, always he gives him the same epithet – 'that wicked man' – a complete characterization, Homeric, as who should say, 'pale-eyed Athene,' or 'rosy-fingered dawn.'

Nor is it merely the pithy epigrammatic sentence which he has mastered. The rolling period, heaping Ossa upon Pelion, marching, like an army with banners, to a triumphant destination, is also his. Listen to this menacing rhetorical rumble, the sound of thunder before the storm: 'It is right (*fas est*) that the Italian people should be made to feel the sorry plight into which they have been dragged by Dictator Mussolini; and if the cannonade of Genoa, rolling along the coast, reverberating in the mountains, has reached the ear of our French comrades in their grief and misery, it may cheer them with the feeling that friends, active friends, are near, and that Britannia rules the waves.'

He is, too, a stylist, deeply steeped in tradition. He creates, but he is also the heir of creators before him. Does he have to issue an order to General Wavell to attack, it is from his Bible – how Cromwellian! – that he takes the order, verbatim. 'Knock and it shall be opened to you.' General Wavell knocked, and it most certainly was opened. Does he wish to describe the tinsel nature of might unsupported by right, it is from Byron that he picks his phrase: 'Those pagod things of sabre-sway, with fronts of brass and feet of clay.'

His great·contemporary, President Roosevelt is also steeped in the same tradition. He writes to Churchill with the words of Longfellow:

> Sail on, O ship of state!
> Sail on, O union strong and great!
> Humanity with all its fears,
> With all the hopes of future years,
> Is hanging breathless on thy fate!

Singularly enough, Churchill replies with prose, not poetry, prose of his own making. Well might he have aroused the transatlantic greeting with those British lines of 'Invictus' concerning mastery of one's fate and captaincy of one's soul. Churchill's prose, however, is equally vigorous: 'We shall out-wit, out-manoeuvre, out-fight and out-last the worst that the enemy's malice and ingenuity can contrive.'

It is an immortal cause speaking immortal speech.

Dove Conquers All   28 February 1941

Somewhere in his 'Don Juan,' Byron has occasion to describe a character as 'the mildest-mannered man that ever slit a throat.' We recalled this masterly description as we read of the latest cooings of Japanese diplomacy. Major Kumo Akiyama, it appears, has decided ornithological opinions about contemporary politics in the Pacific. Addressing a press conference recently, he declared that the British and Americans 'were snakes placing snakes' eggs in a dove's nest.'

For those who may be obtuse in catching the implications of this oriental imagery, it may be explained that the dove's nest is the Pacific – which the dove would like to feather entirely for herself – and that the dove – believe it or not – is none other than the contender, the Empire of Japan. The eggs, we presume, are the Australians recently sent to Singapore, and not bad eggs at that.

We suppose that this type of zoological imagery goes over big in the orient. The classics of the east are full of such Aesopian parallels. But the essence of an analogy, we were always taught, is that it must be apt. Otherwise, no matter how ornamental, it is mere efflorescence. And nothing, to our mind, can be less apt than picturing the sabre-rattling, axis-shaking samurai as so many cooing doves, bent upon missions of peace. For it is not olives – unless of Mussolini's vintage – upon which the Japanese have fed, but sour grapes which has set their teeth on edge. It is to be wondered what General Chiang Kai-shek must think of this latest outburst of anti-vernal poesy; now he knows that the cities of China lie in ruins, because his country was not sufficiently prepared with anti-dove guns.

As for us, we must say that we put but little credence in the columbine protestations of the Japanese. Not they are the turtle-doves heard in the land, heralding, as the Canticum has it, the advent of the spring. If, however, dove-ism is the new Japanese foreign policy, so be it; if not, there may be heard again, to use Tennyson's picturesque phrase

The moan of doves in immemorial elms.

Samuel Bronfman   7 March 1941

Sincere, laborious for the common weal,
Able, of heart capacious, broad of mind,
Militant for his country, of great zeal
Unto the human of earth's humankind,
Excellent in most wise philanthropy,
Leader well-chosen for his people's need,

Bringing where union was not, unity,
Resolving acts to implement the creed –
Out with it, Sonneteer, reveal his fame,
Name him, that all may know this kingly man,
Fervent of purpose, lofty in his aim!
Merit reveals him! His achievements scan
And thus acknowledge him by deed and name,
Name that does honor both to chief and clan!

It is in the words of the above sonnet, forming part of the illuminated address presented to Samuel Bronfman on the occasion of his fiftieth birthday, that a poet – a dear friend of ours – reviving the acrostic form which so flourished in the Golden Age of Spain, paid tribute on his own behalf and on behalf of his contemporaries – to the official spokesman of Canadian Jewry. It was not a mere poetizing sonnet, performing the routine courtesies of a festive occasion; it, indeed, reveals, in its cryptic phraseology, packed into the fourteen links in which this literary form chains its practitioner, illuminating facets of the career and character of the man of the day.

'Sincere' – perhaps no word in the language goes so trippingly off the tongue, and is so often devoid of any real significance. In the case of Samuel Bronfman sincerity amounts almost to a passion. He calls it sincerity of purpose and in that phrase he combines all the meanings which Matthew Arnold implied in his formula – 'seeing life clearly and seeing it whole' – coupled with that additional purposefulness which is so strong a trait of the subject of this editorial. It is interesting, moreover, to note, in the pedantic fashion which is a weakness of this writer, that the word 'sincere' is derived from two Latin words – *sine cera* – meaning 'without wax.' It was customary among the ancient Romans to send their friends gifts which usually took the form of busts or other pieces of sculpture. To good friends one sent busts of pure Carian marble; to second-best friends one sent busts where an ear or a nose had been chipped off, but where the missing members were stuck on to the original marble in the form of wax. A fake article, therefore, was an article with wax. Sam Bronfman is sincere in the sense that there is no sham about him, no pose – without wax – an authentic person.

Certainly the term laborious – full of labor – may be aptly applied to him; no one has more good works to his credit. Whether it be his years of leadership of the Federation of Jewish Philanthropies, or his labors on behalf of the Jewish Hospital, or his guidance of the Canadian Jewish Congress, or his direction of the United Jewish War Relief and Refugee Agencies, or his participation in the national patriotic endeavors of his country – energy, industry, talent, are exercised to the full.

All who have come into contact with him personally, or judged of his efforts from afar, can testify to his ability. Of his general personality, that and his sincerity are the two undebateable features par excellence. As for the capaciousness of his heart, is it not recorded and measured in the treasuries of all the fraternities of good work?

Men of wealth, although of humble origin, very frequently acquire certain prejudices which from time immemorial have been associated with the possession of worldly goods. It redounds to the honor of Sam Bronfman that he has acquired capital, without picking up plutocracy. In Canadian Jewish life, indeed, he has placed an unremitting insistence upon the democratic function. Not that he seeks ostentatiously to bridge a gap between classes – he doesn't even think in terms of classes. He thinks in terms of Canadian and Jew.

Such a psychological approach, it will be readily agreed, is most adapted to bring about that which Sam Bronfman, as president of the Canadian Jewish Congress, has set out to do. Unity is an idée fixe. As he so aptly said in his address of thanks the other night, 'Unity, not uniformity; we are big enough to share many ideas and aspirations; we are too small to be broken and parcelled into groups and factions.' This, indeed, is a view which is total, as distinct from totalitarian.

'Militant for his country' – the remarks made by Sam Bronfman about the relation and position of the Jew in the British Empire will probably go down as one of the finest utterances on the subject. Certainly in this time of crisis and struggle, his words are the echo of that which is in the hearts of all his compatriots. 'If, as it has been said, the true barometer of a people's civilization is its treatment of Jews, then the British Commonwealth of Nations is the most civilized in the history of mankind. Here it was that our people provided a Prime Minister to the Mother Country, viceroys to the Dominions beyond the seas, and most important of all, a mass of good law-abiding citizens ... The Empire upon which the sun never sets never withheld from us its beneficial sunshine. In times of peace we manifested our gratitude by the service, the contribution, the loyalty of daily good citizenship. Now in times of war, shall we not say, we its citizens, say in words of the good book: *Whither thou goest, I shall go, and where thou lodgest, I will lodge. Thy people shall be my people; where thou diest, I will die; the Lord do so to me if aught but death part thee and me.*

We recommend in fact, to all Jews, the close reading of that address which is published in full in another part of the journal. It is a complete credo, indicative of a well-thought-out way of life.

Mr. Bronfman's remarks on the duties of citizenship, on philanthropy, his tribute to the early pioneers of the country, his concept of the Canadian mosaic – 'bringing where union was not, unity' – his description of the nature of the contemporary world struggle, his traditional remembrance of Zion, and his inspiration within the heritage of his people – 'Let us consider the generations which have gone and the traditions which they have left us; let us consider the generations yet to come and the tradition they will expect from us' – manifest a personality which is at once of his people and for his people.

This journal is, indeed, happy to join with Canadian Jewry in the felicitations which it has extended to Samuel Bronfman on the occasion of his fiftieth birthday. His deeds in fact 'do honor to his clan.' It is our sincere wish that long years may still be given to him to continue these labors in which he has already so signally distinguished himself, and further these aspirations and ideals which, in his position of leadership, he holds as trust from the thousands who loyally place confidence in him.

And in the Spring
a Young Man's Fancy ...
21 March 1941

As we write these lines, our city is tied with ropes of wind and knotted with gordians of snow. Nonetheless, the calendar informs us that since the ides of March has passed in routine fashion, unlucky only for the latter-day pseudo-Caesar who watches Africa fade into darkness before him, the twenty-first day of the month will arrive, and astronomers will squeak: Spring.

It used to be a word to conjure with. Poets used to wait for that day, much in the same fashion as cloak-makers wait for the early fall; it is their 'season.' Young men impatiently attended its arrival because these self-same poets had informed them of an unbreakable bond between spring and love. All in all, it used to be a blithe season of lambkins frolicking, and buds bursting, and even of stodgy bears stirring in the dawn of their hibernation.

Alas, it is not so to-day. The vernal season has only iron implications. One thinks of young men and their fancy turned to the stratagems of war; of campaigns and plans; of mud, and its influence upon battle terrain; of sunshine, and its convenience for air-raids; of moonlight, and murder from the sky. At such a time, indeed, bitterness becomes poignant; and fancy turns not to thoughts of love, but to thoughts of hate, hate for the barbarians who seek to turn day into night, virtue into vice, who distort the very purpose of man, who profane his language, pollute his thoughts, and corrupt the very beauty of God's marvellous seasons.

The Journalist in Chains   4 April 1941

In another of a series of articles by Mr. Demaree Bess, appearing in the *Saturday Evening Post*, that author, having despatched Norway, writes about 'Poland in Chains.' We had occasion to remark concerning his last lucubration that it was a perfect example of how words can be used to conceal and not to reveal thought. It is, of course, always understood that writing from Germany, every comma of the peripatetic journalist is being censored; it was, indeed, precisely because Mr. Bess sought to give the impression in his last article that he was free to go where he pleased and say what he pleased that even the editors of the *S.E.P.* found it necessary to write an editorial tantamount to an apology for publishing the impartial correspondence.

The new apocalypse, 'Poland in Chains,' is introduced by a note which declares that what Mr. Bess fails to say therein may be as significant as what he says, 'and may be read between the lines.' This is the first time in journalistic history that we have met with an editorial board which takes credit not only for its printed words but also for the blank spaces between them. Nonetheless, it is at best worthy of note that this time the editors do not trumpet forth their Bess-seller as the real McCoy and the inside dope.

We recommend to all lawyers with a bad case the examination of the method employed by the *Saturday Evening Post* correspondent. It is not that he prevaricates; it is not that he conceals; it is the tone in which he speaks of these things about which he writes. Be it said at the outset that there are no facts in this article which can not be found elsewhere; if Mr. Bess thinks that his information was given to him as a special favor to his genius, he is grossly deceived. Practically every newspaper on this continent has published amongst its items – and always as a piece of macabre mediaevalism – a description of the Warsaw ghetto.

It remained, however, for Mr. Bess to describe that relapse into barbarism, that undertaking in efficient *schrecklichkeit*, to read as if it were ' a social experiment,' a New Order institution. Certainly the Warsaw ghetto, 'modelled on the Indian reservation,' is neither social nor an experiment. It has been tried before; and any attempt to so describe it is nothing more than a gratuitous (?) service rendered to the goose-stepping Nazis.

It is true that Bess puts all his explanations of 'The Forbidden City' into the mouth of an individual most inappropriately called Herr Schoen. It is he who explains – so scientifically and so falsely – that Jews are immune to typhus; it is he who speaks of mass uprooting of families as causing 'some confusion and hysteria,' and it is he who announces that the rabbis were helpful in persuading their people to accept the plan 'without quibbling.' (A man who objects to being flung from one end of the country to the other – quibbles.)

But the manner of writing, and above all the omissions, are all Bess's own. The whole thing reads as if what Bess was writing was not a report of one of the greatest tragedies of our day, but a description of ways and means adopted for routine slum clearance. The man has even so light a heart that he cannot refrain from introducing humor to brighten up his literary style; with the air of one cracking jokes at a funeral, he tells of Warsaw residents referring to the Jewish quarter as Hollywood 'because every inhabitant is a star' – Star of Judah – get it? So funny!

Here is a typical Demaree paragraph: 'In all of Germany's plans for a New Order in Europe, there is nothing else that can be compared precisely with the political and social organization of the General Government of Poland. That organization grew out of an emergency, and it is being improvised constantly to meet changing conditions.'

What does this mean, in man's language, and not in the tongue of weasels? It means that out of the whole baggage of totalitarian barbarism, the re-establishment of mediaeval ghettos is beyond parallel in contemporary civilization. These ghettos moreover, are made more and more mediaeval as political exigency requires; as for example, the threatening of American Jewry with dire punishment to be inflicted upon the Polish Jewish hostages.

We must admit that we are at a loss to understand why any American citizen, brought up presumably under a tradition of democracy, could perpetrate this type of reportage. Perhaps Mr. Bess will have a different manner of telling his story when he returns to a free country; certainly in his published article one hears such clinking as can come only from a journalist in chains.

And It Was at Midnight   11 April 1941

One of the most ingenious and loveliest of the poems included in the Passover service is that which has as its continual refrain: *And it was at midnight*. Its author, with a versatility reminiscent of the Alexandrian school, and a faith typical of the mediaeval one, enumerates in verse culled from Holy Writ the various occasions when a divine Providence wrought at mid of night on behalf of an oppressed Israel. This flower of poetry which finds its proper place in literature's greatest anthology of liberty – the Haggadah – still serves to-day to cast its fragrance upon a most unredolent world, to give to Jewry, hard-beset, a scent of the bouquet of hope.

For in many parts of the world hitherto considered illuminated, our people find themselves at 'mid of night.' We are, indeed, encompassed by what Milton vividly called the 'darkness palpable.' Black are the skies; wherever stars do appear, they look like nails on the floor of the firmament. For what indeed, could be darker than the ghetto of Poland, where curfew tolls at nine o'clock, but where night descends the whole day long? What is more symbolic of the fate of European Jewry, than these refugee camps where the hunted dwell in houses that have no windows? From the great depths of the night our brethren are heard to pose the anguished question: When will the morning-stars again sing in the heavens?

The answer we find implicit in the distinguished pages of history which stand alone in having been sanctified into theology – the record of our redemption from that land of bondage which a dictator sought to render *Judenrein* by establishing a *numerus clausus* on Jewish births. There shall we find many parallels to the contemporary madness which has infected the world. Our ancestors had built Pithom and Ramses, even as our fellow-Jews have erected edifices of art and science – to be rewarded, in the end, by being requested, indeed compelled, to drown their pride and themselves in the waters of the Nile – or the Rhine, or the Vistula, or the Danube. The Egyptians, too, utilized as the excuse for the anti-semitic policy the fear 'lest they multiply and dominate us.' Concentration camps were established then, as now, and Jews filled them.

Says the compiler of the Haggadah: *In every generation, the Jew must behold himself as if redeemed from Mizraim ... for not only were our ancestors emancipated, but also ourselves.* History repeats itself, and the saga of the exodus from Egypt is the forecast of the saga of the exodus from the dark contemporary Mizraim. The Haggadah is the exemplar, the prototype; the place-names are changed, but the formula of preservation remains the same.

The same, too, must remain the formula of redemption. It is the formula of self-sacrifice. It is that injunction which bids one abandon the flesh-pots of Egypt, and go wandering – for how long no one knows, through a wilderness, beneath the glaring sun, in search of a promised land. Is not this, indeed, the order of the day? One must rouse oneself from the sloth of peace, re-dedicate oneself again to the hardship of the great struggle whose final reward is the destruction of Pharaoh and all his chariots, and the attainment of the freer life of justice and equality.

For if Passover is to be characterized by a single concept, it is that of liberty. It comes in the season of *Aviv*, the spring time when the whole world is released from the cold hand of winter, from the bondage of the unfertile season. It commemorates, too, the classic revolt of our people against their taskmasters, the throwing-off of the chains of slavery, and the re-shaping of the national destiny. It is a festival which is at once a trumpet and a prophecy; and this year, indeed, thousands of Jews scattered all over Europe will greet the Passover with a keen realization of its symbolism and hope, and thousands in the free countries of the globe with a rededication to that task, initiated by Moses of old, often interrupted, but always continued – the task of winning for our people its proper place upon God's world.

The Son of Belial   9 May 1941

Milton somewhere has a phrase descriptive of the arrogantly wicked – he calls them 'the sons of Belial, flown with insolence and wine.' Certainly the ranting rhetoric of the Fuehrer, delivered at the Kroll Opera House on Sunday, qualified him for that description. It may perhaps be a source of comfort to the illegitimate Schicklgruber to learn that he is somebody's son, even if only Belial's. Be that as it may; every word of the dictator was full of the triumphant arrogance, the orgulous gloating of the typical wicked who prosper.

And yet, despite the obvious rubbing-of-palms which characterized Adolf's speech, one sensed certain *arrière-pensées* of misgivings. In the first place, the Fuehrer did not, as he has so often before, promise the German people a speedy victory. Indeed, in boasting with barbarian pride about the efficiency of German armament, he made a point of promising even better munitions next year. This must have been disappointing information to an audience which so frequently had hoped for rest during 1941. What the morale of the audience is like, is further indicated by another aspect of the Fuehrer's speech. Hitler does not trust the German people; why else should he find it necessary so shamelessly to lie about the extent of German casualties in the Greek war? Apparently no one knows better than he that the Nazis can't take it. Again, Hitler feels quite disturbed about what Churchill only last week called 'the west where the sun shines bright.' Accordingly, Adolf indulged in a bit of rhetorical whistling in the dark. Said he: 'Germany is superior in power to any conceivable coalition and will have only one answer to democratic agitators who threaten to throttle the Nazi state.'

The most revealing aspect of the Fuehrer's speech, however, was his private little feud with Winston Churchill, a feud to which he gave vent time and time again in the course of his speech. From all of these petty jibes of a petty man, one thing was eminently clear. Hitler had met his superior, and was peeved at the prospect. Once he had dealt with Schuschnigg; and Schuschnigg was now an incognito somewhere in Austria; again he had poured all the phials of his wrath against Beneš, and Beneš was now a refugee in Great Britain. He had dealt with a dozen minor princelings and leaders in Europe, and brought them under his thumb. Even the great Mussolini, whom he so admired in the days when he was in the wilderness himself, even he was now a satellite and a hanger-on of the Fuehrer. Only one man had stood up valiantly against him, and rallied behind him all the force of the democracies. Only one man – Churchill – had called the bandit by his proper name, and supported his epithet by force of arms. Worse, only one man was there against whom he delivered blows, and who rose from these blows mightier than before.

The Fuehrer cannot understand it. Says he of Churchill: 'No other man could have survived the defeats which he has suffered.' Quite true; the Fuehrer well knows that he himself could not survive a single set-back, even an isolated defeat. The Fuehrer knows that for the first reverse he encounters he will himself have to pay with his head. He cannot understand, therefore, the good fortune of Churchill, and *hinc illae lachrymae.*

It is simple to comprehend the reason for this difference in psychology. Churchill holds his position by force of moral power; he stands arrayed in the right; he can suffer a reverse on the battlefield, and still remain impregnable in the strength of righteousness. Churchill can lose only with the last loss. Hitler loses with the first. Behind him is no moral armament, only the Krupp Works; no ideal to be fought for; only the goose-stepping legions. At their first misstep, they fall. Hitler's tirade against Churchill was an avowed and public confession of envy.

It is characteristic of the smallness of this dwarf who has temporarily stolen the giant's clothes, that he should make these personal references to the leader of his opponents. A big man does not act that way. It is only the small man, who cannot see world issues, but only personalities, who does not understand world forces, but only personal competition, who can permit himself – indeed who cannot resist this international billingsgate.

We can well imagine Mr. Churchill's reaction. Certainly he will not enter into any personal polemic with Attila. He will no doubt bide his time – amused at the antics of the man who presumes to emulate Napoleon – and in his next address he will refer to him, as he always has, not by name, not by designation, but by that mustardy epithet which at once recalls the cause of our fight, and envelops in well-known anonymity the monster it describes – 'that wicked man.' The son of Belial deserves no more.

The Russian Pooh-Bah   16 May 1941

We do not know whether it is as a result of the Russian-Japanese pact or from some other inscrutable cause, but the customs of the land of the chrysanthemum, as described by Gilbert and Sullivan, are already being manifested in the domain of the bear. Of particular interest is the latest imitation of Japanese mores – the institution of the Pooh-Bah.

It will be recalled by those familiar with *The Mikado* that one of its most fascinating roles is that of the Pooh-Bah, the high executioner, advocate, judge, and general factotum. His vocation is changed according to the exigency of the moment. Like Cleopatra, he has an infinite versatility.

This character is now being emulated by Comrade Stalin. On certain occasions the occupant of the Kremlin is content to be known as merely the Secretary of the Communist Party. On certain other opportunities, particularly birthdays, he is 'the father of peoples.' Frequently he appears on the world stage as a dictator but faintly distinguishable from Adolf Hitler. He has, indeed, emulated – as in the case of his old friends the liquidated Bolsheviks – the office of high executioner. And now, his latest role is that of Premier of Russia.

Let not the reader be deceived into believing that this constitutes a promotion of Stalin by Stalin. It is nothing more than a wardrobe change. *Plus ça change, plus ça reste la même chose.* The dictator remains dictator, as always. Only now he wants a new uniform.

To be more precise, it appears that Hitler wants a new uniform for him. Rumor hath it that Joseph Stalin has been anxious for an interview with the Fuehrer, but the Fuehrer apparently is reluctant to meet anyone who has no official character, anyone who merely unofficially oppresses his people. 'Why,' says Stalin, 'an official character – that is very easy to arrange; character would be an entirely different matter.' And so he makes himself Premier, and Molotov stutters out his resignation.

To show how easy it is for him to adjust himself to a role written by Adolf, Stalin has just gone through his first rehearsal. It was a simple one, though his heart may have bled, and his spirit gone humiliated, as he performed the motions. This little act consisted of informing the Ambassadors of Norway, Yugoslavia and Belgium, that they were no longer accredited to the Kremlin since their countries had lost their sovereignty.

That this was 'business' – as the play-actors say – dictated by the Fuehrer is obvious from the fact that Norway and Belgium, it seems to us, have been without sovereignty – whatever that means in diplomatic jargon – since last year. Nonetheless Comrade Stalin acts as if he had just noticed it. Apparently being merely Secretary of the Communist Party, the matter had not come to his attention, but now, having looked through the files – as Premier – he is astounded to discover this sensational fact. Having discovered it, his duty – how meticulously Stalin sticks to duty – is to cease recognition of these two countries.

A Premier – a Russian Premier – must have a conveniently short memory. How else can one explain the gross ingratitude, the typical Marxian immorality of this latest Kremlin gesture? How else can one explain the fact that Stalin seems to have forgotten that Belgium was the first country in the world to recognize Soviet Russia – this at a time when all other nations looked at her but professed not to see her, just as to-day they all see her, but can't look at her?

The case of Yugoslavia is even stranger still. Here are no remote Flemings and Wallons, removed by a continent from the good Slavs of Russia. Here are brother Slavs, and what brother Slavs! So fraternal were they, indeed, that Stalin even encouraged them to resist Adolf, even went so far as to promise them help, and as a matter of fact gave sanctuary to Yugoslavian flyers. Now, suddenly smitten with political amnesia, he no longer recognizes them, brothers or no brothers.

But a role is a role. The show must go on. And trouper Stalin is not one to let the stage manager down. Accordingly Pooh-Bah assumes the new character of Premier. It is all part of the play, and the denouement, we feel sure, will be a surprise, not only to the audience, but even to the actors, too. After all, when a principal actor keeps on changing his role with such confusing frequency, it is not surprising if some of the other participants do sometimes miss their cue. As for us, it behooves carefully to watch this Stalin and his peace and cues.

Mr. George Bernard Shaw
and His World   20 June 1941

There is nothing more pitiable than the spectacle of a man, once famous, long outliving the years of his glory. The full vigor of his youth is gone, the fire of his genius is burned out, and all that remains is a memory and a faded laurel wreath. Indeed, the longevity, which otherwise might be considered a blessing, turns into a curse, and the last years of life into a slander upon that life itself.

These sombre reflections occur to us when we contemplate the life and work of George Bernard Shaw. Once 'twas a name to conjure with; all of wit and all of wisdom was therein incarnate. But lately the man has degenerated into a clown, concerned, as the world falls in ruins, with his vegetarianism, praising, as the dawn firing squads play their gruesome aubades, the deeds and doing of the greatest death musician of them all – Joseph Stalin.

Such a eulogy indeed appears under the Shavian signature in last week's issue of *Liberty*; it is entitled 'The u.s.s.r. and the World,' and the man 'greater than Shakespeare' gives himself over to a paean of the Caucasian bandit which pales not even before the worst oriental laudations of *Pravda*.

The mutilation of Finland is pardoned; the Moscow-Berlin pact is condoned; the purges are overlooked; the regimentation is forgotten; and the maker of these things is hailed as genius, saint, statesman. The Soviet regime is held up as another paradise, Joe is not a dictator, says Shaw – he is only secretary of the party, and can be forced out any time. What naiveté, what childishness of second childhood! This 'removable secretary,' however, appears to be very efficient himself in 'removing' the members of his secret executive; and when Stalin removes, it is to be noted, the candidate is never again subject to re-election.

Poland? Shaw has an explanation for that, too. When the Soviets stepped across their frontier to cut in two the prostrate body of Poland, Stalin – marvel, all ye who are uninitiated – did it to save at least half of Poland from the clutches of Hitler. Shaw does not discuss the aesthetics of Stalin shaking hands with those clutches. He confines himself only to a Shavian version of Molotov's famous apologies about rushing into Poland to save the 'brother Slavs.' In Finland there were no blood-brother Slavs; but no matter; in Yugoslavia there were plenty of brother-Slavs, but no rushing.

As for Stalin – hearken to Shaw's description. 'He is not a dictator, nor a president, nor a pope, but simply the Secretary of the Russian Thinking Cabinet which can sack him at a day's notice.' The fact is, however, that all that thinking cabinet is now liquidated. Stalin has purged thousand upon thousand of his 'thinkers,' until today there is not a thinker nor a thought left in Russia.

These are statements which are being written by a pseudo-intellectual leader at a time when his country is being daily bombed in a war which has been brought about principally by reason of Stalin's neutrality. The world will know how to estimate Mr. George Bernard Shaw – not as simply an enfant terrible, but as a reckless individual, inconsiderate of the highest and noblest of principles so long as he can write something original.

Shaw intended to write a tribute to Stalin. The thing will inevitably boomerang. It turns out really to be a tribute to the Empire which he professes to scorn. In no other country, indeed, would he be permitted to write in the tone and in the words which he has adopted. Imagine, for example, a Russian writer, temporarily out of a concentration camp, sending *Liberty* an essay of such fulsome prose, concerning, let us say, Mr. Winston Churchill. We venture to suggest he wouldn't keep his head, let alone his beard, for an half hour after publication.

Those whom the gods love, die young. Mr. Shaw, who has himself stated that every man over forty is a scoundrel, has really merited the enmity of the deities. And that enmity is being turned into action; for those whom the gods would destroy, they first render mad.

The End of the Honeymoon   27 June 1941

The Fuehrer of the Nazi Reich, his patience with Soviet Russia now at an end, has declared war upon that country, and as these lines are being written, bombs are dropping on both sides of their common frontier. To many, this new turn in the tide of events has something macabre and strange about it; to us, reluctant as we are to ejaculate: 'I told you so,' the entire event has been postulated by previous circumstances. The break between the two cronies had to come; it was merely a question of time. It was also a question as to who would make the final attack; it has turned out that Hitler, blown up and inflated with a premature sense of victory, has been the first to 'lose his patience.'

Certainly we shall shed no tears over Stalin's dilemma. He made his bed, and for two years he slept therein a restless and disturbed sleep. Our sympathy goes to the Russian masses, who, now called upon to defend their hearth and home, are not as prepared as they might have been had their leader been more perspicacious than he has turned out to be. Stalin and Molotov, now fighting a defensive fight against their great friend of yesterday are reaping only what they have sown. Yesterday's declaration of war is the direct result of the pact of 1939 – the private little Munich of Russia. Whether Stalin's policy to date was motivated by a desire to see Britain and Germany exhaust themselves, or whether his neutrality was based upon territorial ambitions of his own, his period of appeasement and fence-sitting is at an end. It does not redound to his credit that this change in policy is compelled upon him, and is not a voluntary act.

Speak of the blindness of the Chamberlain era! Stalin had far more signs and portents wherewith to prognosticate the event which has now come to pass. It is here, and he is not as prepared as he should, in duty to his country and his ideals, have been. The anti-British propaganda which he has carried on for years, the doctrine of the inspired press that this is not an ideological war, the liquidation of his generals and administrators, the use of his extra-territorial Comintern to weaken the democratic opposition to Hitler, all of these things must leave him to-day with impaired morale and decreased military efficiency.

But he is resisting Hitler. That is all we know, and all we need to know. The declaration of Winston Churchill that Britain would lend all aid to Russia is an understandable – and indeed the only possible policy. We, at least, foresaw this contingency, and our attitude towards it was determined in advance. Communism is not our ally; Russia is our co-belligerent. Whoever is willing or forced to fight Hitler, fights our fight. We ask for no references, we inquire into no antecedents. We look only for military strength, and strategic advantage. There is in Russia a potential of fifteen million soldiers; their guns and bayonets face Hitler; it is an attitude which we commend. There is in the geographical position of the Soviets an obvious strategical benefit; we shall not overlook it merely because it is the scene of a regime distasteful to our concepts. With Communism as an ideology – particularly as practised by Stalin, we will have no truck nor traffic; of it, as of Nazism, we say with Heine – *der alle beide stinken*. With Russia, as a resister of the Nazi juggernaut, we are bound, by the interests of civilization to march shoulder to shoulder.

Certainly, if British soldiers will fight on Russian soil, it will not be to preserve Stalin in power; it will be to wipe Hitler from the face of the earth. In this great battle, every soldier is an asset, even a mercenary; every co-belligerent a source of strength, even if not a spiritual partner. We consider Stalin in no loftier category than that of a stool-pigeon; in our effort to maintain peace and order, and destroy the world's arch-enemy, it is good police method to use also him.

That this hostility between Russia and Germany gives us new military strength – its actual worth will appear in the course of time – is a source of gratification. It is equally a source of gratification to learn that Hitler – patience aside – found himself compelled to attack Russia. If he weren't compelled by dire necessity, he could have bided his time and made the attack at a later date, for make it he must. That it is made now shows that the war is having its effect upon his military economy. It indicates that he is feeling the pangs of hunger and is looking for food in the Ukraine, and feeling the pangs of mechanical thirst and looking for oil in Southern Russia. It indicates, too, that he is in a hurry; that he realizes that his powers of endurance are limited, and that he must win shortly, or never. It demonstrates, moreover, that the attempt at the invasion of Britain is postponed; no German can think without a shudder, of fighting on two fronts at the same time. It is obvious, too, that win or lose, he will be engaged in Russia for some time; that time will assuredly not be wasted, either by Britain or the United States. It is equally obvious, that the eastern part of Germany will now receive a real taste of war, and that bombing of the Reich will now be a complete territorial job.

It is suggested in some quarters that one of the minor objectives of the attack upon Russia is to divide in opinion the democracy of the United States which is most loath to consider Stalin's regime as a partner. Certainly common sense will see to it that that objective does not prevail. Military allies are not chosen for the same reasons as one chooses a wife. Love and honor and obedience are not absolute sine qua non. Only one factor is essential – common battle against the common foe. When Russian arms strike at the Nazi foe, they must receive our blessing. It is only after Hitler is defeated, that we will be able to afford the luxury of that pleasant military order: 'As you were.'

The Party Line   27 June 1941

There is one group of political thinkers (?) whom we do not envy at all these days. We refer to the cis-Atlantic Communists. Consider the agonizing acrobatics to which they have been subjected during the last six years: first, the period when all who differed with them, even Socialists, were dubbed Social-Fascists; then, that blithe interregnum of the Popular Front, when the

Communist party all but embraced religious orthodoxy; later, the flirtation with Hitler, and finally the consummation of the Berlin-Moscow pact. Certainly these periodic volte-faces evoked a great deal of mental agility on the part of the perennially faithful. The Moscow voice sounded, and come hell and high water, the New York larynx echoed. There was not a prestidigitation of the Kremlin which the local myrmidons did not attempt to rationalize; there was not an ukase issuing out of Holy Mother Russia, but the native Marxists considered it, 'and saw that it was good.'

For the last two years, they gloated that the policy of Stalin was one which would exhaust 'the imperialist powers,' the whole to the greater glory of the Soviets. Hitler was bad, but he was no worse than Churchill; in fact, while the wickedness of the Fuehrer was a mere mental reaction, the capitalism of Churchill was shouted from the columns of *Pravda* and *Izvestia*. For every turn and quirk and detour of Soviet foreign policy, the Marxist apologists had an explanation and a theory. It was, in fine, the inscrutable cunning of Stalin which would confound and plague 'both your houses.'

Came the dawn. Germany attacked Russia. Were the American Communists crestfallen and abashed? Did they beat their chests and cry *Peccavimus*? No, they are right again, and still right. Such at least is the impression which one gains from the manifesto just issued by William Z. Foster, chairman of the Communist Party.

Says he, without blush or hiccough: 'Since its inception the Soviet Union has consistently and courageously fought for peace among the nations, for preventing war and checking aggression.' If this is so, what happens to the theory that Stalin's objective was that the imperialist powers exhaust themselves in mutual battle? Or was that theory reserved for the edification of fellow-travellers, and the new one designed for democrats? Foster says not a word of the economic aid given to Germany, not a word of the propaganda barrage loosed against the democracies, not a syllable about Communist strikes organized in war industries. 'In the fight for the working class' – Foster's phrase – the c.p. perforce united itself with such liberals as Colonel Lindbergh, Burton Wheeler, and Henry Ford. Now, however, they are the incorruptible champions against the Fascist gangsters!

He who seeks water in the desert is as wise as he who seeks consistency in the c.p. The party line is by no means Euclidean; it travels like lightning, sulphurous, and zigzag.

These comments, of course, are not to be construed as advocating that Russia be allowed now to stew in her own juices. We reserve our opinion about the men in the flying trapeze who dictate Communist policy. The fact, however, still remains that to-day's objective of Russia is also our objective. Our consistency certainly can and ought to be made to co-operate with Russian inconsistency.

Arma Virumque Cano   8 August 1941

We do not know whether the Duce has appointed any one to act as the official chronicler of Italian war effort. It is a job we would not wish our worst enemy. For the military historian, it must be noted, can exercise his talents only in the narration of victories, or even of defeats, if they be glorious. Alas, that the annals of Italian military history are singularly deficient in such exploits.

How, indeed, is one to sing in inspired numbers, the ignominious defeat of Caporetto, the classic example of the last war which has so frequently repeated itself in this? What touched lyre can one lift to sing of the arms and the men who beat all speed records at the Guadalajara? Is it not better that silence shroud those Italian ignominies beheld by the Libyan sand, or that empty reputation melted with the Albanian snows? Surely the Duce whose favourite boast in peace-time was of the eight million bayonets which he commands is a better rhetorician than a military leader.

But the worst was yet to be, – last week a British battalion captured 200 Italians and loaded some of them into a captured Italian truck. On the way to the British lines, it broke down and the British were forced to abandon the prisoners. Not long after they reached their own lines they were astonished to see a truck streaking for their camp, and even more astonished to find that the Italian prisoners had repaired the vehicle and made their way in alone!

Sometimes, one feels, indeed, that it is an asset to the Allies that Mussolini is a partner to the Axis. Certainly, Italy, shaped as a boot, is the Achilles heel of the unholy partnership of Fascism.

Why should this be so? We are not of those who like to make national generalizations tending to prove that the Italians are poltroons and incompetents. Such a statement, considering past history, would be simply silly. The reason appears to be merely that the Italian people have not their heart in this war at all. It is Mussolini's adventure, not theirs. Perhaps the boner which the young student pulled in translating the first line of Virgil, explains the situation. Said he: *Arma virumque cano* – Arms and the man, and a dog ...

Letter to Benito Mussolini   15 August 1941

Duce:
I address you by your self-imposed magniloquent title and by no other, not forsooth, because I wish to hail you as leader, but because by your actions, by your attitude, by your entire outlook on life, you have reduced yourself from

being a man to being merely an occupation. And to-day I particularly wanted to address the father in you, hoping that something paternal might still be lingering in that ambition-distorted heart and power-corrupted brain of yours.

For certainly you have long since ceased to be a father. I do not refer to your fifty-eight heavy years which you so sedulously keep a state secret. I do not refer even to the reluctance with which after siring your first child, you became the husband of its mother. I emphasize merely the fact that to you your children have become state-appendages – your daughter the attaché of your foreign minister, and your sons the mere symbols of the wicked ideals which you have set up for all the bambinos of Italia.

You will remember – were you not proud of them? – the exploits of your son Vittorio? He not only imitated your bloodthirsty practices; he even copied your ugly melodramatic literary style. How proud you were of his description of his murder of helpless Ethiopians – so proud, indeed, that you publicized his immortal words in all the columns of your subservient press. You grinned and jutted out your jaw as you read that Vittorio flung bombs from his plane, and then saw Ethiopian flesh bursting in all directions like a flowering rose. The image was pretty, was it not? 'Worthy of d'Annunzio at his most decadent.' Indeed it was on a par with your own declarations that war is the permanent condition of mankind.

Such was the doctrine that you implanted unto your sons. Death – the next man's death – was beautiful; and the agonies of the flesh – the flesh of the other man – was a sight superbly aesthetic! Who else but the spawn of your loins and your brain would ever conceive of God's image on earth being torn by diabolic explosive as a rose-tree in blossom.

To-day, the reward of your doctrine lies before you. Your son Bruno has fallen from the skies and been killed. He, too, was taught to 'live dangerously,' in the service of 'your destiny.' Of course, he is only one of thousands who has paid and will continue to pay the price of your megalomania. But the others have touched you not at all. Your own flesh and blood might.

And so, Benito, as you sat in vigil over the corpse of your son, did you, then, also think of a shower of petals from heaven? Did you poeticize, then, also, of the human manna flung into the mouth of your Moloch? Was the odour in your nostrils the sweet savour of roses, or did you at last catch the stench of carrion?

And Vittorio, gardener of Ethiopia – how did he meet the news of his brother's calamity? Did he suffer what Joyce calls the 'agenbite of inwit'? Or has his conscience been so completely dulled, under your tutorship, that there is no room for remorse in it?

It is reported that you spoke to Bruno's plane-companions, who survived him, and that you said that Bruno was well and had nothing further to fear. Is this the pass to which you have come, what with your destiny and your loud talk – that only he is well who is dead, and only he has nothing to fear who is no longer among the living? Are we to take this as a revelation of your own mental terrors? Are you, too, being haunted by the ever-pursuing dagger of the mind?

Fathers console disconsolate fathers. But we have no consolation to offer you. You have sowed the whirlwind; as yet, you have reaped only the wind. If Bruno, your son, is no longer with you, the author of his death is known. Surely he was the victim of his father.

Italy has many sons. Some day, and not far hence, they will realize the full implications of the theories which you have propounded. No, they have no objection to 'living dangerously' – there is nothing reprehensible in that alone; on the contrary, there is something noble and alive about such a 'modus vivendi.' But living dangerously – for what? Surely they will one day say that if the fathers have eaten sour grapes, let *their* teeth be set on edge!

Sic Semper Tyrannis   5 September 1941

There is no doubt but that in the concepts of western civilization as we know it there is no room for the principle of 'tempering government by assassination.' In the first place, it is a practice which is repugnant to the high ethical instincts of civilized men; in the second place, it seldom achieves that for which it is perpetrated. Moreover, it sets up against one form of arbitrary tyranny – that of the despot – another form, that of the assassin. Certainly it runs counter to the general principle enunciated by the Talmudists – *dina d'malcutha dina* – the de facto law is the law.

Nonetheless, it is not in the light of these high concepts that we are to judge the deed of the young man who attempted the life of Pierre Laval, arch-quisling of France. Indeed, a good case could be made out to establish that acts such as Colette's – the would-be assassin – are inspired by a loftier ethics than that known to the sermonizing text-books.

Let us examine the true nature of the case. This cannot be understood unless one understands the nature of the foe against whom the bullet was aimed. The totalitarian regime which, imposed by Berlin and executed by Vichy, menaces the very future of the entire French people is not a milk-and-honey affair. It is not trammelled by obsolete notions of chivalry. It is not handicapped by a crippling sense of 'cricket.' It is, to say the least, direct. It devastates countries without the formality of a declaration of war. It plights its honor (*sic*) with the fixed intention of betraying it. It advances bellicosely – with tourists; its only gallant charger is the Trojan horse.

In a word, it breaks every rule of the most rule-less of human enterprises – warfare. It does so because it is motivated by totalitarian objectives; hence totalitarian means – nothing excepted – are used. Such an abominable foe cannot be met with protocol. Against such an enemy one does not exercise the controlled refinements of international ethics. To do so would be to doom one's self to defeat at the outset. Certainly the man who encounters a wild beast in a forest has things to think about other than the Queensberry rules.

If this procedure is justifiable against a foe such as we have described, how much more so is it permitted against a traitor from within, who allies himself – unnatural crime – with the jungle-beast. Certainly no one man is more responsible for the condition in which France finds herself today than the bartender Laval who for years served his people the absinthe of appeasement. He it was who went through the pantomime of fighting the Nazis when all the time he was consumed by a passion for Fascism. There has, moreover, been no ideology which he has not betrayed. Socialist, Bourgeois, Radical – he has been – and for a time led – almost every shade of French political thought, only to abandon it when his career required a change of trains. Presently he is travelling, first-class, on the express to Berlin. Even now, we believe his voyage to be more of a business trip than a pilgrimage.

It was against this man that young Colette fired the lead message – *sic semper tyrannis*. Note well: Colette is no Communist despite the attempt of the Vichy propagandists to paint him as such. Colette, son of ever-independent Brittany is a French patriot who could no longer suffer the betrayal of not only France's interests, but her honor. He belongs to the undaunted spirit of unconquered France. He is of the tradition of the French Revolution. For him *La Marseillaise* had never been proscribed.

Apart from the fact that the attempted assassination is indicative of the fact that not all of France has been lullabied into torpor by Grandfather Pétain, it has wider significance as a warning both to the Nazi overlords and their Fascistophile henchmen, that even a conquered people is not utterly helpless against the oppressor. Surely no one attempts assassination who is wallowing in the trough of luxury and benison; it is only despair which removes the pistol from its holster, the dagger from its hiding place. True, these attempts will lead, have already led to reprisals; but reprisals, on the Hun basis, must inevitably lead to further assassination. The gauleiters of conquered Europe may feel arrogant behind their Gestapo and their armaments; but ' a hand may still be put forth to touch them in their bone and their flesh.'

The New Year   19 September 1941

New Year editorials run to a monotonous standard. Invariably one recognizes the formula which created them – a swift fleeting glance upon the past, an olympian survey of the present, and a jubilant greeting of the future – and the literary ceremonial is fulfilled.

But while this is true – platitudinously true of the level and extended days of peace and ennui, it is only superficially true of the days through which we are presently passing. There is no hour which sounds upon the clock which is not full of forebodings and omens. There is no incident which is not pregnant with the ripe implications of history. Nobody can complain of boredom. These are verily the days 'that try man's soul.'

And in the trying of souls, none has been more grievously tried than ours. The attacks directed against our people by the Pharaohs and Hamans of bygone days are but as skirmishes compared to the bitter onslaught which Hitler is directing against us, and against all of civilized mankind. For the madman of Berlin is no half-measure maniac – his phobia is, indeed totalitarian. While Haman could set as his objective the uprooting and destruction of Jewry, he was after all merely employing a literary flourish, a grandiloquent hyperbole. The contemporary Haman, however, means it in dead earnest; and has reduced his hatreds to a science and an art.

One has but to consider the works of the man, to gather the full force of his intentions, as they apply to our people. Of the Jews in Germany, he has made a tribe of slaves and hostages; the Jews of Poland he has reduced to animals in a cage called a ghetto. From Czechoslovakia he has not stayed his hand. French Jewry, too, is beginning to feel the full terror. Presently he is on his cannibalistic tour of Russia. Of all the policies enunciated in his original demagogic platform, he has deviated, wandered, transgressed – it is only in his implacable hatred of our people that he has remained ignominiously consistent.

Turn the pages of our varied history. Certainly we have been often and in many places in grave national danger. *B'chol dor v'dor*, in every generation, says the Haggadah, there is one of these Hamaniacs who rises up, seeking to destroy us. But at no time has the hatred been so purely psychopathic – that is, impossible of compromise – and so armed and panoplied with the most modern instruments of warfare.

The High Holy Days are the season set aside, not only for a personal spiritual accounting, not only for the individual searching of the soul, but also for national introspections and national trial balances. As we stand upon the threshold of a New Year and survey our present and our past, with what emotions and with what aspirations do we face the future?

The liturgy of the High Holy Days has supplied the answer. With truly poetic inspiration – an inspiration whose chief characteristic is that its significance does not vanish with the mere passage of time – the contributors to the *Machzor* have divided the prayers into three distinct categories – *Malcioth, Zichronoth, Shofroth*.

The *Malcioth* prayers concern themselves with the laudation of the royal omnipotence of the King of Kings. What sounder message can be received by Jewry and, indeed, by all oppressed peoples than the message of the greatness and power of Him before whom the mightiest of tyrants, the most powerful of despots, are but as vassals and slaves? Let the petty satraps lord it for their dog's day. Let them strut about upon their shaky stages imagining themselves as almost divine. Firm is the knowledge, strong is the conviction, that there is none to rule over men save God alone!

This is a trust and faith which is mightier than armour-plate, and stronger than all the mechanical toys of the war-lord.

Malcioth has yet another significance in its original tongue. It means kingdoms, dominions, powers. Jewry derives great strength and solace from the fact that *we are not alone*. Great powers and dominions are also suffering their days of trial and tribulation, – and their cause is our cause.

The section on *Zichronoth* concerns itself particularly with remembrances. It is a catalogue of all those historic incidents where at a dark moment, divine intercession brought the ray of light. While it is true that a sorrow's crown of sorrow is remembering happy things, there is also a type of memory of the affairs of long ago which strengthens and fortifies the spirit. Certainly our epic recollection of the troubled days of our past invariably ending in triumph and salvation should stand us in good stead in this era of difficulty. We are a people with a long tradition and a great past; the formula of the present we have already encountered before; and we know – and in this is our strength – how that formula was resolved.

It is an indication of that kind of future that the liturgical anthology of *Shofroth* enters our catalogues. It is the poetry of the trumpet-blast, the prophecy of the ram's horn. In our ritual the ram's horn has been a symbol most pertinent to our time: it is with the ram's horn that the jubilee of liberty is blown. So it was with reference to Hebrew slaves emancipated at the end of their indentureship, and so it is, in other times, and in other fashions.

Upon the cover of this issue appears a drawing in which the *shofar* plays an important part. It evokes the fall of the city of Jericho which was taken, not by might, not by power, but by the trumpet-blowing perambulation of the children of Israel about the city. A trumpet-blast – mere air, a thing intangible, effusion most non-material, and yet strong against a walled city! What is that but an ennobling and inspiring symbol of the force of spiritual values, the indomitable strength of conviction and faith?

Certainly it is not with mere faith alone that we will resolve the problem of the day. For while the *Machzor* liturgy emphasizes the importance of prayer and fasting, and remembrance and *Shofroth*, the principle emphasis is still upon the deed and the act. At the same time that deed and that act is without potency unless also energized by religious fervor and unbreakable faith!

We face the New Year, therefore, with the firm hope that kingliness will yet come back to earth, and that the events of our lives will yet create *Zichronoth* worthy to be remembered, and that the *shofar* of jubilee will yet sound, in our time and day.

He Is Not Alone!   26 September 1941

The 'Lone Eagle' is far from being the solitary creature the newspapers and hero-worshippers have made him out to be. The fact is that he flies with the rest of the vultures. His recent speech, in which for the first time, the idol of yesteryear shamelessly raised the race-cry to advance his isolationist propaganda, now demonstrates that he is of the same feather as those birds in Berlin. Comparatively lonely he is only in America where his denunciation of the Roosevelt regime and the Jews has aroused condemnation from all truly American citizens.

Indeed, the worthy flier is not even an eagle. His ornithological antics more closely resemble those of the parrot. The words which for weeks he has been aching to utter, and which he did finally blast out, are no different, either in tone or in content, from the usual ravings of Streicher and Goebbels.

For the past week now, the American public has found it difficult to recover from the stunned consternation effected by the Colonel's stupid Judaeophobia. The papers have been full of statements condemning the idol of the twenties as a disturbing force in American life. Certainly in a country nurtured on the traditions of Patrick Henry, Thomas Jefferson, Abraham Lincoln (no Arian has yet discovered that that Abraham was a Semite), the blather of Charles Lindbergh is a most cacophonous intrusion. It brings for the first time into American political life the despicable voice of the Jew-baiter. The clean-cut young hero – the Spirit of St. Louis – now has the dubious honor of being the mid-wife of political anti-Semitism in the United States.

Fortunately, the midwifing of Charles has produced only an abortion. It is just as well that the child was not born viable; it was conceived in sin, and spawned in corruption.

The incident, apart from revealing the fact that an anti-Semitic movement in the United States is doomed from the outset, also indicates exactly where the America First Committee stands. Ample opportunity was given to these so-called defenders of American democracy to repudiate the shameful statement of the august Lindbergh. No such repudiation has been forthcoming. Indeed, one recalls that it was really Mr. Gerald P. Nye who first raised the race-issue, only he did it with greater skill and more finesse. It was left to the clumsy flier to come into the parlor and burst out the conversation of the coulisses.

The America First Committee, therefore, is clearly an instrument of Nazi technique. Until yesterday it sought to achieve its appeasement objectives within the limit of the democratic four-corners. It soon saw itself destined to defeat. The howling at all things British, and the singing of Sweet Adeline to all things German, did not find favor in the eyes of the American public. The cry of 'Jew, Jew' was undertaken as a measure of desperation. It, too, has failed.

What will be the next demagoguery of the American-Firsters? Will they now outburst again, in more lurid terminology, the fomenting of race-hatred? Or will they now see what they can do with the Free-mason cry? After all, Roosevelt has just been 'unmasked' as a Free-mason. Perhaps they will merely resort to the old chestnut of Communism.

In the meantime, everybody now knows where Lindbergh stands. 'The wave of the future' has washed all the veneer from him. He is revealed as the American who today has the greatest potentialities – for being a quisling. All his talk about Americanism is now proved as so much window-dressing. He is the typical Nazi, made in U.S.A. It used to be one of Hitler's most convincing of lies that Fascism was not an exportable article; we can now see why; it does not have to be exported, when it grows native.

We reflect again upon that novel of Sinclair Lewis which several years ago was such a best-seller because it postulated in such an interesting fashion what everybody nonetheless felt to be an impossibility: *It Can't Happen Here*. The point of the story was that it could happen here. Charles Lindbergh wanted to put it to the test. He did; he travailed like a mountain, and produced a mouse, or a rat. For the time being, public opinion has caused that creature to scamper back into the dark hole whence it came. It is to be hoped that public opinion will keep it there.

Hess Won't Eat   10 October 1941

Latest reports from the place of incarceration of Rudolf Hess indicate that that worthy is presently on a hunger strike. It was the last method to which, we imagined, he would resort, inasmuch as hunger strikes are peculiarly proletarian weapons, and certainly to be scorned by the aristocratic supermen of the Reich. Besides, it is unlikely that Hess's gaolers will be much concerned about his voluntary limitation of diet, inasmuch as supermen, by definition, can get along without food.

Nonetheless Hess – during the ten days of penitence, and no doubt also on Yom Kippur, is fasting. His grievance is that he is being treated as a prisoner, and not as 'a special envoy.' It is difficult to see how Hess can justify his position of 'enemy extraordinary.' Where are his credentials? To whom was he accredited? By whom was he sent? His own Fuehrer declared, immediately after his disappearance, that Hess had gone crazy, and had been for some time. Accredited, therefore, he is only to Bedlam; and that is not where he is being kept.

And so Hess is keeping a stiff upper lip and a closed lower jaw. We are not much disturbed. It will only prove that Hess has become so acclimatized to British environment that he is himself willingly extending the British blockade to himself. Could naturalization go farther?

Hess won't eat. The colossal gall of those Nazi overlords is a thing to wonder at. Uninvited, he flies to England. He is received and obtains the fullest hospitality of English officials. And the churl, rejects the welcome which is given to him, although he came as a gate-crasher!

The reason for this hunger-strike perhaps lies deeper. It is, in the final analysis, the result of his peeve. Hess realizes how bitter was his mistake, how seriously he underestimated the English. He thought that all he had to do was show his benign presence in England, do his song-and-dance about the two Nordic races, and the Russian menace, and Churchill would fall over his neck, embrace, and peace – and another bloodless victory. But Churchill didn't bite; so Hess can't eat.

'That Jewish War'   31 October 1941

The isolationists and the fifth columnists still persist in their malevolent characterization of the great conflict upon which the outcome of civilization depends. Once upon a time, it was the delight of the great strategists to term the battle a 'phoney war'; all for the purpose of undermining the morale of the belligerent countries. Time, of course, has shown that there is nothing phoney about it. The refugees of Europe, the widows and the orphans, the concentration-camp residents, the crippled and the maimed, all of these by way of example, fail to appreciate the adjective 'phoney.' There is nothing phoney about death.

And so a new tack was taken. It is a Jewish war. That, in fact, would appear to be an even more demoralizing accusation than the previous one. The implications of this charge, for it is said as if it were an indictment – are that no one really has an interest in the defeat of Hitler except the Jews.

That this characterization is a malicious falsehood emanating from Berlin, and worthy only of Berlin, has been amply proved time and time again. The fact does remain that for seven years while the Jews of Germany were being outrageously persecuted, no one lifted a finger in their defense. Equally incontrovertible is the fact that the actual *casus belli* was Poland – remember the slogan of the French appeasers: Die for Danzig? – yet no one has as yet said that this is a Polish war. No one has termed it a Czech war, or a Belgian war, or a French war, and so on ad nauseam. The true characterization of the cataclysm is that it is a war of all free peoples, fighting on behalf of their freedom.

There is one sense in which it is a Jewish war, and in this sense it is symbolic that the two great objects of Hitlerian wrath are the British Empire and the Jewish people. As a people we are to-day joined with the Empire not only by common physical danger, but by a shared spiritual heritage. Even as we are the people of the Book in Hebrew, so are the British the people of the same Book in English. This spiritual affinity – Oliver Cromwell's soldiers marching to battle, singing the psalms of King David, are typical – resulted throughout the centuries in a Jewish Prime Minister in Britain, a Jewish viceroy, and in general, patriotic participation on the part of Jewish citizens in all the achievements of the Empire.

The war, accordingly, is not a battle for *lebensraum*, for colonies, even for the truly phoney theories of racism. It is a war by the peoples of the Book, for the maintenance of the principles of that Book. These principles are simple: they are the Ten Commandments.

Every one of these commandments has been broken by Adolf Hitler. Instead of the doctrine of monotheism he imposed upon his people a crass paganism, a despicable heathenry, which consists in the worshipping of one man, and that man a beast. The prohibition against taking the name of the Lord in vain, has been violated at least twice annually by the Fuehrer himself in his numerous 'solemn declarations.' 'Thou shalt not steal' – the whole German policy is based on theft and robbery. 'Thou shalt not murder' – it is the Reich which has made murder a strategy of conquest. The policy of one-hundred-for-one, introduced into occupied France, is the most blatant example of the doctrine of *schrecklichkeit* promulgated by the international bandits. 'Thou shall not covet' – the megalomaniac ambitions of Adolf towards world-domination are nothing more nor less than one continued unremitting breach of this prohibition.

These breaches of the moral law and civilized order are the very premises of the Nazi ideology. It is for the maintenance of the very elementary and very essential principles of the Decalogue that the free world is fighting to-day. Once these principles were purely Jewish ones; they have entered the fabric of civilized thought throughout the world. Said the Pope: We are all spiritual Semites.

This, of course, does not establish the present war as a Jewish war in the sense that Hitler's agents would like to establish it. It merely shows that instead of being a war between nations, it is a war between principles. And even as once these sacred principles were issued from Sinai, to the accompaniment of thunder and lightning, so to-day they are being reiterated, amidst *blitzkrieg* and *donnerwetter*.

Weizmann's Plea and Protest   14 November 1941

The present world situation, it will be readily agreed, is full of riddles; but of all the enigmas which defy logical analysis, none is more tantalizingly sphinx-like than the attitude of the British Government in refusing to permit the organization of a Jewish army to fight the common foe of mankind. One would have imagined that such an offer would have been gladly accepted, accepted both because it would mean an increase in military strength and also because it would add another banner – and an ancient and honorable one – to those already raised in defiance against the modern Attila. Certainly such was the response when, a quarter of a century ago, the Jewish Legion was organized under Colonel Patterson, and was gladly received into the great company which then gave civilization another lease on life.

Something has happened to alter that situation. Since the outbreak of the war, Dr. Chaim Weizmann, president of the World Zionist Organization, a man whose services to Britain in the last great conflict are still remembered, whose services have not ceased to this day, and who, better than any one else can speak on behalf of the Jewish people, has been trying to get the permission of the government to accomplish this end. To no avail. The frigidity with which his plan was received by the Chamberlain Government has changed, with the passage of time, only to the lukewarmness of the Churchill Government. An offer which in other circumstances would have been hailed – and justly so – as the proper attitude of an honorable people, is to-day frowned upon in silence, gestured away, either refused outright, or procrastinated into frustration.

Why? Is it not but right and proper that that people which has been the particular object, the special target, for the attacks of the barbaric paganism of Hitler, should take up arms, and under their own flag, at least change murder into battle, persecution into conflict? Is not this – the manly right to bear arms – a right, mind you, not only a duty – the least which the civilized world owes to Jewry? Must the Jewish people, specifically attacked because it is Jewish, be doomed to play, in this glorious struggle, forever a passive role? Are the ghettos, the concentration camps, and the execution walls, the only terrain upon which Jewish sacrifice is to be made, and is the field of honor to be prohibited area for them? Is it, indeed, indelibly written in the chronicles that our people must be martyrs; soldiering is too good for us?

We are, of course, aware, that thousands of young Jews are now playing their worthy role in the armies of the democracies. In the battalions of Britain, of Canada, of Poland, of Czechoslovakia, they march valiantly beside their comrades of other faiths. Nor would we have this situation altered. This is essentially not a war of nations; it is a war between two conflicting ways of life –

one that strives ever upwards, and the other which seeks to push mankind nearer and nearer to the jungle. Nor is this a war of religious creeds; it is a war between all the creeds which admit the fatherhood of God, on the one hand, and that creedlessness which subscribes only to the bestiality of men. All men, therefore, be they but men, may well enough belong, to use the military vernacular, to the same outfit. In those countries where conscription is the law, there certainly is no room for a Jewish army; in these lands, however, where the army is recruited on a voluntary basis, the suggestion offers great possibilities; in non-belligerent countries, such as the United States, it is, to put it mildly, a consummation greatly to be desired; and in Palestine – there, one would have imagined, it would have been a foregone conclusion.

Attend, therefore, to what Dr. Weizmann says: 'I have nothing to report – with reference to a Jewish Army – except disappointment and frustration. We had to fight a political battle before Palestinian Jews were permitted to bear arms! And the battle is not over even now ... At first the British would accept recruits in Palestine only for non-combatant duty. Later, it was decided to enlist Palestinians for combatant service but only on the condition of numerical parity between the Jews and Arabs.'

It certainly is ironical that the first decision of the powers that be, as to the role which Jews should play in the fighting forces, is not much different from that of the Nazis who also relegate their Jews to 'noncombatant service,' albeit for different reasons. The concession which was later made is, indeed, the work of a master-mind. He surely was a genius who first conceived of measuring Jewish duty by Arab enlistment! One still remembers the ridiculous theories once advanced by Palestine administrators to keep out Jewish immigration, particularly the theorizing about the 'economic absorptive capacity' of the country. To-day a new theory has been invented – that of 'patriotic absorptive capacity'!

Alas, it is a poor standard! As Dr. Weizmann said, no doubt thinking of Iran and Iraq, 'As the keenness of the Palestinian Arab is not equal to the occasion, this rule restricted Jewish numbers to a mere fraction of what the total would otherwise have been.'

Since that time, however, the parity rule has been relaxed, with the result that Palestinian Jews have supplied 10,000 men to the British forces and are still supplying them. But that is by no means enough. Said the spokesman of Jewry: 'There is, however, one supremely important aspect on which so far, we have been refused any satisfaction. Like all nations, the Jews desire to serve under their own national name and flag, doing honor to their national badge, the Shield of David, which the Nazis tried to convert into a mark of shame. But the name of "Jew" seems to be shunned as much by those who accept our services as it is flaunted by our enemies. We Jews are being penalized for loyalty and devotion. There is obviously the feeling that we require no encouragement and we are refused the rights of every nation to its name and flag ... And even now I say, addressing myself especially to the Palestinian Jews: Enlist in ever-growing numbers. Work and fight, even if nameless. You are working and fighting for a great cause.'

The whole story sounds quaint and incomprehensible. The legions of Judaea wish to rise again; only a condition is imposed – they must do so anonymously. All the free flags of the world march forward against the Nazis, like Nemesis itself – on that flag, and that badge which has been most insulted and degraded by the enemy, is not permitted to wave in the air. Reasons are not given; they can only be surmised.

It is to be hoped that the Government headed by Mr. Churchill will still give the matter further consideration, consideration in the light of those principles which run through all his speeches and which informed the eight points of the famous Atlantic Charter. Jewry knows that it is fighting for its life, and so, perhaps, it may matter little under what flag it fights; but it is also fighting for its national honor, and that can be preserved only under the Shield of David. During the last war, as Jews enlisted in all the allied armies, there was also, in addition a Jewish fighting force. The British Government encouraged that fighting force, and indeed, supplied its officers. Is a Jewish army less desirable now because the enemy's menace is greater? Let us hope that this era which has produced its Hamans and its Tituses will yet produce its Hasmoneans and Bar-Cochbas. We have had enough of the halo of martyrdom; prithee, a sprig of laurel ...

Max Nordau: A Tribune to His People
5 December 1941

Review of *Max Nordau to His People* (New York: Scopus Publishing Company 1941)

No one who studies national traits and character can overlook the fact that the majority of the early protagonists of political Zionism were what may be called for want of a better term, literary men. Diplomats without a state, they manifested their statemanship mainly in the republic of letters. Herzl, the greatest of them all, the supreme leader, began his career remote from the Jewish tragedy – in the feuilleton columns of the *Neue Freie Presse*. His first impulse towards Jewish nationalism, indeed, was a purely inspirational one; it was only after being confronted by the brutal reality of the hard facts of the Jewish problem that he showed, not only the great vision of the dreamer, but also the cold practical perspective of the realist. Zangwill, too, was another of the same school; an early disciple of Herzl, his very Zionism was a literary corollary; a sort of practical epilogue to his Dreamers of the Ghetto. When subsequently he became a mere territorialist, it was no doubt because the King of Schnorrers was in the ascendant. And, as a last example, Nordau's return to his people was also the result of a latter-day realization of the eternal values inherent in his people's traditions.

Nor is this close association between moral standards and political activity a new phenomenon in Jewish life. It is, indeed, of the heritage of the prophets. They, too, were the statesmen, the king's counsellors of their day; and they, too, determined their *realpolitik* on the basis of the great verities, and couched their advice in the immortal language of inspired literature. In this respect we are – we say it without chauvinism – unique among the peoples of the world. Very few states, in sooth, determined their foreign relations upon the basis of moral truth. With them, quite a different standard prevails. Certainly the primer which Machiavelli compiled for the use of princes, a primer which even to this day serves as text-book for despots, is as removed from an ethical catechism as day is from night. Certainly Bismarck was never suspected of confusing the doctrines of righteousness with the practice of politics. The fact is that the motivating principle of all international relations has been, and is, temporary opportunism as opposed to eternal salvation. That diplomat who to-day suggested that his country, in moulding its foreign policy, should be guided by 'truth, honor and chivalry' would be dismissed from his functions, if not immediately consigned to the care of an alienist.

Perhaps the insistence of Jewish statesmen upon moral values is not the result of a natural piety, but rather of the constantly unhappy position in which our people find themselves. It is quite possible that our devotion to ethical values has been motivated, as it always is in the case of the underdog, by self-interest. Be that as it may, the utterances of Max Nordau, delivered at the opening of ten Zionist Congresses, and here for the first time collected in English version, in a single book, constitute one of the finest amalgams of national *realpolitik* and international morality.

Like Herzl, Nordau did not graduate into Jewish nationalism from the ghetto. Neither of them was a ghetto-Jew. Indeed, Dr. Nordau, long before he fell under the influence of Theodor Herzl and the concept of a Jewish state, was that true cosmopolite of whom Tennyson speaks in such flattering terms. Perfectly at home in all the literatures of Europe, he was, for at least two decades, the giant arbiter of the literary values of continental culture. His magnum opus – *Degeneration* – ruined at least a dozen reputations, and made his own. Tennyson, Baudelaire, Rossetti, Nietzsche – all fell victim to his scriptic analysis, an analysis which was most intolerant of the *fin de siècle* literary quiddities which masqueraded as profound thought. The theory of art for art's sake – always unacceptable to the Jewish mind – revolted him and brought forth from his pen the accusatory epithets of degeneration. In this approach, Nordau, the European, was typically Hebraic. From time immemorial our culture has placed the greater value upon content, not form. It was Yehuda Halevi, who, at once poet and philosopher, summarized the national reaction. Said he: 'Greek art is like a flower, which blossoms, and then fades. Hebrew art is also like a flower, but a flower which turns into fruit.'

It was not, however, until Nordau espoused the cause of Zionism that he was able to say: 'My life now has an aim and content.' The very first Zionist Congress, which took place in 1897 (the same year saw the publication of Chamberlain's precursor to *Mein Kampf* – *The Foundations of the Nineteenth Century*), he was the strong right arm of Herzl. For Jewry he was its mighty organ-voice. One of his principal functions appears to have been to summarize for the assembled delegates of the honored Congress the contemporary condition of Jewry.

Hinc illae lachrymae. It is these summaries which constitute the skeleton framework – the word is used in more than one sense – of the ten addresses of this book. If they contained but factual reports concerning the sorry state of Jews and Judaism in the years between 1897 and 1911, they would make sad reading, indeed. The fact is that almost invariably Nordau begins his address by apologizing for the Job-like tenor of his speech, as if he were personally responsible for the discrimination and failure and pogroms which made the central theme of his orations. It is however, when Nordau doffs the character of Jeremiah and dons that of Isaiah that he rises to his true stature. Then the thinker, the philosopher, the statesman, becomes apparent in every epigram; the mere mourner has vanished from the scene, and in his place, upon the Congress platform stands a proud Jew, heir of the prophets.

The tragedy which Nordau describes is, of course, pale in comparison with that which encompasses Jewry to-day. But the philosophy, *weltanschauung* is as contemporary as to-day's headlines. Some of his epigrams have in them the glow of a great and revealing brilliance. 'The Jew strives after superiority, because equality is denied him' ... 'They protested that they were *auch Juden*; I say they are merely *bauch Juden*' ... 'The Zionists are no party; they are the Jewish body itself' ... 'Our friends assert that we render services and are useful. The indifferent say: "What services do the Jews render? What use are they to us?" No one however, seems to notice how monstrous this standpoint is. Of what other nation in the world has anyone presumed to ask: "What use is it?" A people is an ultimate end' ... 'It was once humorously asked what would have become of Liszt and Paganini if they, with their specific genius, had come into the world before the invention of the piano and the violin. Herzl supplies the answer ... He was a born statesman, without a state' ... 'Zionism is a beneficent movement, not a benevolent movement.'

The speeches are studded with these brilliants. Others, equally illuminating, are not, on account of their length, as susceptible of quotation. His description of the *luftmensch*, his analysis of the difference between volcanic and glacial evolution as it affects a people, his characterization of the Jewish beggar-student – these will forever remain *loci classici* in our thinking literature.

It is regrettable that the editor, Mr. B. Netanyahu, who writes a very interesting introduction to the speeches, has confined himself merely to Nordau's Congress speeches. His essays, and his addresses delivered upon other occasions should yield ore as rich as that which is here included. Certainly the reader, in putting down this book, will ask, like Oliver Twist, for more.

It may be noted by way of addendum that this book on Nordau constitutes but one of a series planned by the Scopus Publishing House. The object of this series is to introduce to English readers a general survey of Zionist thought and Hebrew literature. It is a consummation greatly to be desired.

Notes on a 'Court Jew'   12 December 1941

Those who are familiar with Jewish history will no doubt recall that upon an unhappy time there appeared in its Polish annals a certain Jacob Frank, a pseudo-messiah, who in dark and dismal days held out to his contemporaries the light of hope – the deceptive firefly of his personality. Like the careers of all such panacea-bringers, his, too, ended at the baptismal font.

'Aye, but that happened,' as Marlowe would have said, 'in a different age, and in another land.' True, but if Jewry for a moment thought that it was forever rid of the Frankist psychology, and all that it implies, it was bitterly disillusioned when it read last week the leading article in *The Saturday Evening Post*. In the author of that lucubration one beheld a new Frank who had arisen, not a patriarchal one whose name was Jacob, but a patristic one whose name was fittingly enough Jerome. And this new Frank also had a gospel which he wished to preach, if only by indirection, to his fellow-Jews.

The gospel, of course, was not a new one; it had the familiar assimilationist ring. Hundreds of such articles have been written by the kind of Jews of whom it is typical: by the Hellenists of the days of Antiochus who announced in bad Greek that they were not Jews; by the Jewish upper crust on the Tiber who boasted that they were citizens of no mean city; by the assimilationist Russifiers who sought to exchange their *tzitzith* for a Czarist knout; and finally by the Germans of the Mosaic Persuasion who until 1933 shouted their Aryan patriotism. Indeed, we would not be surprised if in the Nazi library for the study of the Jewish problem, there is catalogued under the heading of 'slavishness,' a word-for-word German version, written by a German Jew, of the article which now sees English publication from the hand of Jerome Frank.

For our readers whose national long-suffering has not been taxed by a perusal of the sabbatical thesis, it will be fair to state that Mr. Frank no doubt intended his essay as a piece of masterly apologetics. Apparently he wished to clear the Jews of the charge, made by Wheeler and Lindbergh, that they were interventionist, and so found himself, as a result of his enthusiasm, vigorously asseverating that American Jews were not Jews at all, but only Americans. Already history has played its practical joke upon Mr. Frank's apology for what he calls his ex-isolationism; the Japs have already made his polemic a matter of interest, if any, purely academic.

No matter; it is not Mr. Frank's debate with Wheeler which is interesting; it is his analysis, which is revealing of the slavish, sycophantic, obsequious depths to which an assimilationist will sink in seeking to prove to his querulous neighbor that he is true blue and to the manor born. To this end, it is necessary, first of all to prove that Mr. Frank has nothing in common with European Jews, with the *Ost-Juden*. Says he, and apparently with pride: 'I was often asked by Gentiles how I, a Jew, could advocate American isolationism. My answer was that I was an American, and that however much I might be anguished at the plight of oppressed peoples in other countries, Jew or gentile, I did not believe that America should sacrifice its welfare to rescue them.'

Please note, gentle reader, if gentle you can still remain, the charming impartiality with which Mr. Frank is oblivious to the suffering of both Jew and gentile. It is a tribute to the judicial qualities of this legal light – Mr. Frank is a distinguished jurist – that he can so maintain *mens aequa in arduis* – an equable temperament under adversity, the adversity of others! President Roosevelt could well quote Abraham Lincoln to the effect that the world cannot be half-slave and half-free; but not Mr. Frank. After all, the president is, in the final analysis, a Dutchman, and Jerome Frank – an American!

It might be well, before we further pursue the wisdom of our Saint Jerome, to inquire as to who he is. He is – his protestations to the contrary notwithstanding, a Jew. What kind of a Jew remains to be seen; but certainly *goyim*, if not Jews, will always consider him – not quite a *goy*. The American *Who's Who* informs us that his father's name is Herman and his mother's name Clara; his wife's, before she became a Frank, was Kiper. Mr. Frank has had a brilliant legal career, specializing in traction settlement, and practising in Chicago from 1912–1929. Apparently he was an isolationist in 1917, too, when his slogan was not 'Save America First' – the title of a book he published in 1938, but 'Save Chicago First.' He is a Phi Beta Kappa. The *Who's Who* note boasts no Jewish letters. In the Roosevelt administration he is deemed to be a brain-truster, which tempts us to define that species as being one whose brains are taken on trust. It would seem that it is this proximity to the throne which contributes to his *hof-Jude* psychology. Mr. Frank is also the author of a book *Law and the Modern Mind*, a book which, together with those of Thurman Arnold, seeks to speak of law in the terminology of folk-lore and basic myths. It is ironical that Mr. Frank's book is introduced by Judge Julian W. Mack, a noted Zionist. This enables Mr. Frank to say that some of his best friends are Zionists.

This is the man; his theory – that the Jew in America is also a basic myth. He proceeds to analyze. Taking the juiciest morsel first, Mr. Frank discusses the Jewish Communists. He concludes that they form an insignificant fraction of American Jewry, and that anyway, they aren't Jews. The reader will wonder why Mr. Frank included them at all; certainly he should have been guided by his own maxim: *De minimis non curat lex*. Mr. Frank, however, needed a *red* herring; and the Communists fulfilled that function admirably – even if they were only a minnow.

Having disposed of the Communists, Mr. Frank then continues his discussion of what he calls the other hyphenates. Of all the varied punctuation in English grammar, Mr. Frank hates the hyphen most; he prefers to that obnoxious line, anything, even a question-mark. The Zionists, he says, are mostly not hyphenates. Mr. Lloyd George, Mr. Winston Churchill, President Roosevelt, the American Senate, will all be greatly relieved at this concession; if Mr. Frank had not been so generous, they might have been embarrassed on account of their part in the conspiracy of the missing hyphen. Mr. Frank even concedes a gracious nod in the direction of the late Mr. Justice Brandeis, of whom he would say, no doubt, that his Zionism and Americanism were lovely and pleasant in their lives, and in their death they were not hyphenated.

'But,' says Mr. Jerome Frank, 'there is a small group of fanatic Jewish nationalists who have identified themselves completely with Zionism. Zionists of that type are not American Jews, but Jewish sojourners in America. They regard themselves in effect as refugees longing to return to what they consider their native country.' Here, at last, Mr. Frank really does invoke a basic myth. Among the four million Jews in America, of how many Jewish sojourners does he know? Certainly he will find nowhere in the doctrine or propaganda of American Zionism this policy of emigration. That some American Jews may wish to settle in Palestine is conceivable; if there are a hundred such in the whole United States, we would be surprised. A view of American Jewry does not stop at such a negligible, infinitesimal phenomenon – not unless the writer wishes to direct slanderous insinuations against the 99.9% of Zionists whom he faintly praises!

That Frank's statement is subject to misunderstanding is apparent from what happened in the offices of *The Saturday Evening Post* itself. 'The Red, White and Blue Herring' – Jerome Frank's fish story – according to newspaper rules, required illustration in the form of photographs. Accordingly, over the caption 'The author charges a few fanatic Zionists are not American Jews, but Jewish sojourners in America,' the editor of the *S.E.P.* publishes a cut of a Zionist rally. Upon the platform one can see Felix Warburg and Governor Herbert Lehman! They are sitting firmly in their seats; and not at all like sojourners.

Mr. Frank discusses also another category of Jew – the rich Jewish Fascists, who love Hitler and Mussolini, and would embrace them, except that those two worthies have slipped up on the Jewish question. Of those we are not in a position to speak; we have never met any. Mr. Frank's associations, no doubt, have given him better opportunities. We do fear, however, that Mr. Frank is perhaps distorting a Jewish opponent of the New Deal, into a Semitic gauleiter.

And finally, Mr. Frank reaches his *pièce de résistance*, the true Jewish majority. He describes it as follows:

'The majority of American Jews have adopted a "hush policy." They have been, undertandably, sensitive to criticism and have feared that any discussion of "the Jewish question" would activate anti-Jewish feeling. As a consequence, they have mistakenly allowed the more intense Jewish nationalists among the Zionists and certain "professional Jews" to do most of the talking in public about American Jewish attitudes. That "hush policy" assumes that Jewish silence will prevent the American public from thinking about the Jews. It recalls Mark Twain's story of the little boy who was told to stand in a corner and not to think of a white elephant.'

We recognize the 'hush-hush' Jews at once. They are not at all a majority; in fact, they constitute definitely a minority, albeit not a negligible but on the contrary a powerful minority. Their silence is by no means due to the fact that they are tongue-tied; these Jewish leaders are unlike Moses, in addition to other dissimilarities, in that when they wish it, they are most articulate. They may not then shout from the roof-tops; that is impolite and very oriental, but they are masters of the insidious whisper. 'Hush-hush' they are only about their Jewishness; about their non-Jewishness they are practically rah-rah! Witness Mr. Frank's article, in which he displays his separation from Jewry before three million readers!

To break the silence of these hushed Jews, Mr. Frank invents a spokesman, a *deus ex machina*, one Arthur Klein, speaking his *lingua franca*. He it is who presents the assimilationist viewpoint, a viewpoint which, in its desire to emphasize the American, minimizes and nullifies the Jewish. All the Kleins, thank God, are not alike.

From then on, the article is written by a composite of Arthur Klein and Jerome Frank. According to them, it is only the immigrants who cling to the baggage of Judaism; the third and fourth generation have had unadulterated Americanism visited upon them. It is true that even a third generation

American Jew is barred from fraternities, or from hotels or clubs. But Jerome Frank is a sport. He accepts 'such social disabilities with a sense of humor.' Kick him out of the golf-club because he is a Jew; he doesn't mind; he is really an American. It wasn't he who was kicked out; it was only his grandfather.

Of orthodox Judaism, Frank speaks with scorn. The ritual is merely Godified custom. The whole affair is an anachronism. In fact the more Jewish a group is, the greater hostility it arouses. 'Intense Antisemitism and intense Jewishness are twins.' How fundamentally false this statement is to anyone who has given the matter the slightest thought! In the first place, there is no relationship at all between Antisemitism and Jewish qualities or characteristics; if Jews were to be as angels for virtue, as saints for piety, and as Franks for patriotism, Antisemitism would be not one whit the less. On the contrary, such paragon qualities would exaggerate Jew-hatred. But be that as it may; the fact is that Antisemites have only incidentally resented Jewish Jews; it is the would-be marranos that they have really hated. The whole German propaganda considers the orthodox Jew as merely a funny Jew; it is the assimilationist that it considers really detestable. We need not say that we hold no brief for this hatred even of the assimilationist; but if Mr. Frank wishes to be a realist, let him look at the platitudinous fact, and not the epigrammatic fiction.

The rest of the article is devoted to proving that Judaism in America is dying, dying as a religion, as a heritage, etc., and that one ought not to shed tears over the prospective demise. Will not that spiritual and national death result also in the death of the hyphen? Let a people perish, so long as that ominous hyphen perishes with it! For out of its ashes, there will rise the phoenix of pure unadulterated unshackled Americanism. First cultural assimilation, then assimilation by marriage – and all the time, no doubt, prohibition of immigration, and the Jewish problem will be solved!

The whole tenor of this thesis – solution by dissolution – reads like a learned paraphrase of Will Cuppy's recent book: *How to Become Extinct*. We cite a passage therefrom, so that you may get Frank's objective in Cuppy's language: 'Becoming extinct has its compensations. It is a good deal like beating the game. I would go so far as to say that becoming extinct is the perfect answer to everything and I defy anybody to think of a better. Other solutions are mere palliatives, just a bunch of loose ends, leaving the central problem untouched.'

Mr. Cuppy, of course, is a humorist; and Mr. Frank only unintentionally so. Actually, the Frank article is a tragic document, manifesting the intellectual and spiritual bankruptcy of a certain pseudo-Jewish viewpoint. For it certainly is not a Jewish viewpoint, and it is even less an American viewpoint. No responsible American leader (gentile) has ever declared that a man's Judaism was a handicap to his Americanism. On the contrary, a man's loyalty to his race and religion is an additional guarantee of his loyalty to his country. Let Mr. Frank re-read his article and he will soon realize that he who has so much to say about 'professional Jews' is himself very like a 'professional American.' True Americanism does not protest so much. True Americanism does not involve denying one's ancestors, or thwarting one's posterity. True Americanism asks of its citizens only that they 'be themselves.'

Mr. Frank leads off his three herrings with a picture of Stephen Wise before a microphone. Two weeks ago we heard Dr. Wise speak before another microphone in Baltimore. If Mr. Frank did not hear him, he would do well to take his words to heart. He said: 'As for those pitiable Jews who deny their Jewishness, who seek to cancel their relation to the Jewish people and the Jewish faith, I am almost tempted to warn countries against such Jews. Jews who are disloyal to Jews, who, for the sake, whether of security or comfort or peace or power or prestige, try to cut themselves off from the Jewish bond, may prove equally disloyal to their national lands, new and old ... If they represent little loss to the Jewish body, I am sure that they bring no gain to those faiths and peoples to which they relate themselves through ruthless disavowal of their past and present.'

The Sun Comes Up
Like Thunder ...   12 December 1941

The dastardly attack launched by the Empire of the Rising Sun against a country with which it was at peace – with which, in fact, it was at the very moment of the hostile preparations and onslaught, negotiating for a pacific settlement – will go down in history as the classic example of perfidious double-dealing. The records of civilized mankind, even its records of conflict and bitterness, contain no incident comparable in treachery to the cunning Japanese scheme which preceded their brutal attack. The negotiations for peace, the bland smile, the sending of the two special envoys, the flowers from the flowery kingdom – all this while the submarines were taking up their stations, and the battleships streaming out on their deadly missions, and the plane-motors in action, constitute a course of conduct the odour of which stinks to high heaven, even the heaven of the Emperor, its illustrious son.

That the attack was not an impulsive act, brought about by a sudden decision, is evident from the area over which it was made, the manner in which it was timed, and the method by which it was conducted. The result of long premeditated treachery, the scheme was designed to be a super-blitz, a military typhoon such as sometime rages over the China Seas. Hawaii, the Philippines, Hong Kong, Malaya are simultaneously attacked; and without any warning, without any ultimatum thousands of persons killed. Certainly the warlords of Japan had laid their plans carefully; the third gangster of the Axis was muscling in with a vengeance.

One need not dwell at any great length upon the moral quality of the Japanese acts. It is high time that we of the democracies realized once and for all that we are faced by enemies in whom we shall see neither chivalry, nor gallantry, nor fair play, nor even ordinary common garden variety of decency. These are bandits who do not get embarrassed at the cry of *shame!* To meet them with Queensberry rules is criminal madness and suicidal folly.

The war is now a World War in earnest. No part of the globe is removed therefrom. It is indeed, symbolic that those very South Sea Islands, once considered the ideal refuge for those seeking escape from reality, are to-day the actual scene of combat. Even those countries which as yet have not declared war, are not certain that war has not been declared against them, the news whereof, with the charm of contemporary international etiquette, is being kindly kept back from them.

We shall not attempt to essay a calculation of the new military set-up created by the events of this week. We shall not rush in where even the President of the United States has not yet trod. There are, however, a number of factors that can be immediately estimated. In the first place, with the entry of Japan, all the big cards have been played, the little Jap being, no doubt, the knave of bomb. In the second place, it is now established definitely that any and all surprise methods, including those learned outside of Sunday School, are trumps. In the third place, the United States enters the war as one nation, a mighty land shaking off the easy-going manners of a week ago and rising in power and in anger for the defense of its very existence. At its side there stands practically the entire continent. And in the fourth place, the two great democracies fighting the powers of darkness are no longer in relationship of creditor and debtor – they are partners – allies.

Certainly we are beholding to-day the battle of Armageddon itself, the conflict of Gog and Magog. Never before was so much at stake, and never before did such a conflict rage simultaneously over so all-inclusive a terrain. To be more extensive than it already is, the war would have to turn into a battle of planets; a battle of hemispheres it is already. The first blow of the Japanese attack has caught the continent somewhat unprepared; it will not be long, however, before it will regain its equilibrium, realize its lesson, and dedicate itself totally, unremittingly, to the maintenance of the right, and the elimination of the triple plague which has beset the world.

Rabbi Steinberg's
Four Principles

2 January 1942

The *Contemporary Jewish Record* is an excellent periodical, published under the auspices of the American Jewish Committee. Since its inception several years ago, its writers have contributed to American Jewish thought a series of treatises upon a number of subjects which have almost invariably been thorough, studied, and profound. The only faults which we have found with the *Record* is that some of its authors have apparently written under the assumption that to be serious is to be dull, and to be factual is to be pedantic. To the reading of the *Record* one must bring not only a broad mind, but also a tolerant seat; to express it as the *Record's* pundits might, its deductions are all *a posteriori* ... O for a bit of verve, a suggestion of wit! The reader looks for these in vain. Despite its anti-Germanism of content, we know of no journal which is in style as professionally Germanic, as heavily Teutonic, as the *Jewish Record*. Published ostensibly as a magazine, it is doomed, we fear, at worst not to be read, and at best merely to be referred to. For on the very day of its publication, its format, its style, its approach condemn it not only to being mere '*record*'; it positively appears, even with the ink still fresh upon it, as dignified but unreadable archive. It is regrettable that the *Menorah Journal*, the only other periodical which is as ambitious in scope as the *Record*, has itself become – since it doesn't go out often enough – so anaemic; time was when it could have given the *Record* a most salutary blood transfusion.

The fact is that not everybody thirsts after knowledge like the writer of these lines, who has more than once sat down to read some of the *Record* articles by sheer force of will-power, seeking the nuggets of fact which some erudite professor has concealed in the considerable ore of circumlocution and ponderosity. Others there are who rush, like Cadmus, to read, and end up like Homer, nodding – nor is it the nod of assent. Accordingly, we suspect, much of the excellent material of the *Contemporary Jewish Record* is bound to be read, alas, only by an elect and determined minority.

And it is the great majority which should have the benefit of Rabbi Milton Steinberg's article in the December issue of the *Contemporary Jewish Record*. Under the heading 'First Principles for American Jews,' Rabbi Steinberg enunciates four cardinal premises for an approach to what is called the Jewish problem. We must admit that, under other circumstances, we would be prejudiced against such mathematical enunciations of Jewish principle. Certainly, we might feel, that what with Ten Commandments, and Thirteen Credos, and Ten Wilsonian Dicta, and Eight Atlantic Points, that there ought to be a moratorium on the ideologies which not only count but are counted. But Rabbi Steinberg, while not exhausting the number of sociological principles, has nonetheless indicated four cardinal ones. They are not new; but they are worth repetition.

Principle 1. – The rights and opportunities which Jews enjoy in America are theirs as of right, and not through the sufferance or toleration of anyone.

A decade ago, anyone who enunciated the above dictum would have been looked upon as a great sayer of the superfluous. For the principle was part of the constitutions of every civilized country of the world. It is true that in many instances it was a principle more honored in the breach than in the observance; but the breach was never brazen; it was accomplished by excuses, by apologia. To-day, the principle itself has been brought into question by the concerted propaganda of the Axis powers. All the printing presses and radios of the Reich are dedicated to its denial. The tragedy of the Jewish situation is that we should to-day find ourselves in the position where so elementary, so fundamental a declaration has to be reiterated. In fact, the tragedy is even greater than at first suspected; for the principle must be re-emphasized – to Jews! One of the most insidious effects of Hitler propaganda, indeed, has been the fact that in it lay a constant danger that the Jew himself might lose his *tzelem-elohim*. Too many of our co-religionists, we feel, have been if not converted, at least made dupes of the Goebbels doctrines. We have been almost persuaded into speaking in whispers, into submerging our personalities, and into being content with the mere crumbs of civil rights. It is from those that there springs the what-will-the-*goyim*-say psychology. A politician who treated us as if we were human beings we have considered, out of the gratitude of our defeat, as a forward-looking history-making progressive and liberal. Well is it, therefore, that matters are brought into proper perspective, and our civil rights placed, as they are, on a par with that of any other citizen.

Principle 2. – *Antisemitism is not created by the behavior of Jews.*

This does not mean, as Rabbi Steinberg hastens to point out, that all public relations work is a labor of supererogation. It does serve, however, to destroy that illusion which some Jews entertain, that if all Jews acted like angels, if adults were saints and the children little Lord Fauntleroys, Antisemitism would vanish, like a fog lifting in the sunshine. The truth is that Antisemitism, like love, has 'reasons Reason does not have'; that where it is grounded in religious and economic soil, its uprooting requires not a Jewish but a Christian act, and that when it is not so grounded, but exists as a pestilential miasma in the air, its effluvium emanates from the concoctions of demagogues seeking a philtre to win the adoration of the susceptible masses. German propaganda, indeed, has declared more than once that if the Jew-as-ogre did not exist, he would have to be invented; and invented he was, without restrictions to patent rights. Antisemitism is, as Rabbi Steinberg says, 'the projection not of Jewish behavior but of broad social forces.'

Principle 3. – *Antisemitism cannot be controlled by the Jews.*

Antisemitism, having such an origin – an origin not within the Semite, but extraneous from him – the remedy to this disease of the twentieth century does not lie with the Jew. Certainly the Jew, like any other citizen, may make a contribution towards the alleviation of those social ills which bring about the unsocial hatreds. But Antisemitism, taken by and large, cannot be controlled by Jews; for Antisemitism, as we have said elsewhere, is but the delirium of a social disease.

Principle 4. – The Jews need to-day, as never before in modern times, a vital and significant Judaism.

Antisemitism affects different Jews differently. When an assimilated German Jew begins to feel the full impact of the racist madness, he presents, indeed, a pitiable aspect. Suffering all the punishment of the damned, he suffers yet the additional agony of knowing that he is innocent of the accusation for which he was condemned. He is a Jewish martyr without ever having been a Jew. Going unwilling to the sacrifice, he is immolated for something about which he has not the slightest concern, in which he has not the slightest interest. The denizens of Dante's Inferno know paradise compared to the hopeless hell which is his.

The source of his weakness lies, of course, in that he has no internal resources wherewith to meet the foe. He can never be opponent; he can only be victim. Not so the Jew – as for example the orthodox Jew – who knows that if he is suffering, he is suffering *al kiddush ha-shem*. His martyrdom is not mere biological discomfort; it is theological ascension. His calvary, unlike that of the assimilated, has meaning, although it is not the meaning of the oppressor.

The appeal – by implication – which Rabbi Steinberg issues to American Jews – to thy tents, O Israel! – is not the first of its kind, nor have these appeals been confined to the rabbinate. Time and time again have we heard during the past dark years, Jewish public speakers, some of them professional sceptics and vaunting agnostics, paint a picture of the contemporary Jewish scene, and then, groping for a comfort-ye-comfort-ye-my-people peroration, finding none save an exhortation to return to the traditions of our religion, and embrace the faith, be it sociological or theological. For the declaration that man does not live by bread alone is not simply a dietary truism; it is a profound spiritual truth. Bread may be rationed; Faith cannot be – it is all or nothing.

American Jewry ought to be grateful to Rabbi Steinberg for having re-iterated and expounded the principles which we have so sketchily paraphrased. They are foundation corners for an American-Jewish civic *Shulchan Aruch*.

Report from Warsaw

23 January 1942

The news which has issued out of the former Polish capital has for many days been of a most tragic nature. The number of deaths taking place in the Warsaw ghetto daily, the unsanitary conditions imposed by the German overlords, and the general sadism which has characterized the Nazi administration, have been matters which have justly caused grave concern for the future of Polish Jewry.

It is heartening therefore to obtain from that dark quarter whatever ray of light may emerge. One such ray is the fact that though all the Jews of Warsaw may be under the heel of the Nazi tyrants, their spirit is far from being broken. Indeed, there has developed, in the midst of all the misery and tragedy engendered by the madmen of the Reich, a recrudescence of spiritual strength unparalleled even in the history of Warsaw – for centuries a strong fortress of the Jewish spirit. According to a report issued by the Agudath Israel, religious activities in the Warsaw ghetto are, despite Nazi-imposed restrictions, on the increase. The orthodox seminaries now have long waiting lists, and the synagogues are better attended than ever before.

It has always been so. In times of darkest despair, our people has invariably found strength and spiritual sustenance in the great reservoir of its tradition. Here one was able to oppose against the temporary misfortune, the consolation of the eternal verity; here one was able to learn from the pages of the past those lessons which were so vital to a survival in the present; and here one was able to view the evil of the day in the light of one to whom a thousand years were but as yesterday, as a watch in the night when it is past. Above all, here, at the horns of the altar, in the bosom of tradition, misfortune and un-happiness took on meaning. It was not, as in the case of assimilated German Jewry, pointless and meaningless. Hitler may confine the Jewry of Warsaw to the durance vile of its ghetto; the spirit of Jewry, strengthened by the flame of its tradition, escapes his grasp; it rises to heights undreamed of even on the altitudes of Berchtesgaden.

The Long Voyage Home –
The S.S. Struma   27 February 1942

If any single incident were required symbolically to illustrate the dire plight, the utter hopelessness of European Jewry to-day, that which occurred five miles out of the Bosphorus in the Black Sea has amply supplied it. For while it is true that in time of war, and particularly during a war of the present dimensions, there is a danger that one may become callous to tragedy, and unmoved by loss of life, the fate of the seven hundred who perished with the Struma has not failed to stir to their inmost being all those to whom the news has been brought; for here is tragedy without the usual redeeming feature of necessity, here is loss of life which was futile, purposeless, empty of meaning.

Out of the horror of Nazi-occupied Rumania, where the bandits of Antonescu and the storm-troopers of Hitler joined in making holiday by means of barbaric pogroms and unspeakable massacres, out of the ghettoes of Czernovitz where the populace, flown with blood and conquest, was indulging in an orgy of *shechita* in which Jews were killed like cattle, there fled seven hundred refugees. Somewhere, after much cajoling and imploring, they boarded ship. The builders of that craft – the *S.S. Struma* – had intended it for one hundred and twenty passengers. Into it, there crowded 769 Jews, apart from the crew. The captain gleefully rubbed his hands; he had never dreamed of such a profitable – it cannot be called a passenger list – such a profitable cargo. And the refugees remembering whence they fled, and whither they were going, were happy too. For were they not on their way to Palestine?

We do not know whether the log-book of that voyage had been preserved. If faithfully kept, its contents would reveal such suffering and hardship unheard of even in the agonized annals of mediaeval seafaring. Many of the passengers fell sick; two of them went insane. A storm damaged the ship's motors, and put its radio apparatus out of order. Throughout the voyage the passengers were continually manning the pumps.

Finally, at long last, the *S.S. Struma* reached Istanbul. Soon, soon, they would enter Palestine, the haven of their refuge, the home of their ancestors.

The Palestine administration refused them entrance.

The Turkish Government would not grant them sanctuary.

Even the appeal of the Jewish Agency that they be *interned* in Palestine was rejected!

The story moves like a nightmare. The refugees were to be returned – to Rumania! And they were to make the voyage home (?) on the same motor-less water-leaked unseaworthy *S.S. Struma*!

It was when the ship and its miserable cargo was being *towed* out of harbor, that it apparently struck a mine, and exploded. All lives were lost.

Does this narrative require editorial comment? Does not its pity and its terror rise up from every incident, crying to God that He look down to see what man does to man, not his enemy? Do the Turkish authorities who ordered the return of the broken vessel, who turned away the weeping and helpless suppliants from their door, sleep well at night? And if their rest is somewhat disturbed, how goes it with the smug schedule-quoting colonial officials who refused to the Jews even the sanctuary of a desert concentration-camp?

A Great Talmudist – Rabbi Pinchas Hirschprung Interviewed
13 March 1942

There is no doubt that the ravages of the contemporary Hamaniacs have left their mark, for generations to come, not only upon the physical appearance of the European continent, but also upon its cultural character. That the face of Europe has been changed, no one can deny; one only has to be referred to the scarred physiognomy of Rotterdam, or to the pock-marked countenance of Warsaw, to see that of the Hun it may be well said that he found a Europe of stone, and left a Europe of rubble. But the change has gone into the very essence of life; the virus has entered the soul itself.

If this is true of European life in general, it is even more pointedly, more poignantly true of Jewish life on that continent. One after the other, the great centres of Jewish learning have fallen before the barbarian foe. The *Yeshivas* of that continent have been converted into wandering groups of scholars; the scholars and rabbis, into harried and driven refugees. Poland is no longer that strong fortress of the Lord it used to be; that country which saw the birth and labor of so many profound exegetes, so many distinguished rabbis, so many intellectual giants who moulded the life and law of all the communities of Europe, 'now doth sit solitary, and weepeth sore into the night.' Her scholars have not that settled abode – those tents of Jacob – so necessary for learning, and the golden chain of the Hebrew tradition groans beneath the strain of circumstance.

As a result of the efforts of various American and Canadian agencies – the United Jewish Refugee and War Relief Agencies with which are associated the Federation of Polish Jews and the Joint Distribution Committee – a number of the rabbis and scholars have found sanctuary in our country. Insofar as the Jewish tradition is concerned, it is a movement which knows no parallel – for cultural significance – save in the movement of Renascence learning into Europe after the Dark Ages. Certainly it will be admitted that American Judaism, whether regarded from one aspect or another, has suffered a kind of pernicious anaemia; the advent to our shores of the great scholars – the spiritual heirs of the Tosafoth – should serve as a most refreshing blood transfusion. Nor is it a question of re-duplicating here in America, the Jewish life of Poland; history does not stand still; changes must ensue; but changes do not take place in a vacuum. They take place round and about a set of cultural values; and it is these values which the new Canadians bring to our Jewish life.

Among the recent scholar-refugees who have settled in our midst is Rabbi Pinchas Hirschprung, with whom we had the pleasure of a two hours' conversation in the presence of my good Talmud guide, Mr. Suchachevsky. We have seldom, if ever, met with such a vast erudition in Judaica as is represented by this rabbi, twenty-seven years of age. We are told, indeed, that already in Galicia and in Poland, his abilities and knowledge had won the admiration of the greatest scholars of the day. We had occasion to see that this reputation was in no way exaggerated.

The Talmud, it is known, is published to-day exactly in the same format and with the same pagination as appeared in the edition of 1572. In the centre of the page is printed the text of the Talmud proper; to right and to left, the commentaries of Rashi and the Tosafoth. As a result of the disquisitions of centuries, there are in addition, other commentaries, explaining the first, exegesis upon exegesis. There are eighteen volumes, and each volume has an average of about two hundred pages, each page bearing one number, side *a*, and side *b*. The text, it must be remembered, is unpunctuated, and the language, a composite of Hebrew and Aramaic, full of technical phraseology, makes the reading thereof even more difficult. Moreover, as a result of mnemonics and cryptic speech, a page of Talmud text actually represents much more intellectual matter than would appear in any other kind of text of the same size. The content, moreover, is of a most varied nature – law and legend, proverb and anecdote, argument and statement, all mingle and flow one into the other, cohering together only by an unbroken chain of logic. Well has the Talmud been called a Hansard of Jewish spiritual life.

It is this which has constituted the impedimenta of the wandering scholars, only Rabbi Hirschprung, it is to be noted, did not have to declare his Talmud to the customs officer. For such is his phenomenal memory – so photographic in perception, so sponge-like – to use a Talmudic simile – in its retention – that he carried it all in his head!

Seventeen years ago, upon the passing of the late Rabbi Simcha Garber, of blessed memory, we wrote of him, our mentor, and of his erudition, the following lines:

> When will there be another such brain?
> Never; unless he rise again,
> Unless Reb Simcha rise once more
> To juggle syllogistic lore.
>
> One placed a pin upon a page
> Of Talmud print whereat the sage
> Declared what holy word was writ
> Two hundred pages under it!

Rabbi Hirschprung's is 'another such brain,' and like the late Rabbi Garber, of the same modesty. We had, indeed, heard from others of the young Rabbi's memory; but, coming from Missouri, we wished to be shown. After directing the conversation into the proper channels which would make our request not seem rude, we brought the Rabbi to the stage where he was reciting, word for word, entire pages chosen at random from various volumes of the Talmud. Whether it was from *Kidushin*, or *Baba Bathra* or *Chulin*, the Rabbi was able, at the mere prompting of a page number, to present a verbal photostat of the entire text, and to give the content of the Tosafoth commentaries thereto appertaining! To complete the virtuosity of these mental jousts, Rabbi Hirschprung was able, by merely regarding three words at the bottom of a page – the rest of it concealed – to cite the source, volume and page!

Nor is it merely with a phenomenal memory that the young rabbi is endowed. If that were so, we would be inclined to be amazed, but cynical at its manifestation. Together with this stupendous memory, he enjoys also great mental agility. There was hardly a gesture, or an *obiter dictum*, during our conversation for which he was not able to conjure up a pertinent quotation, either from Holy Writ, or world literature.

For unlike the usual product of the *Yeshivas*, Rabbi Hirschprung has drunk deeply from the Pierian springs. Proficient in the Polish language, with a knowledge of German and as much Latin as Shakespeare had, the culture of Europe has not been foreign to him. During our talk, which touched upon many subjects, the Rabbi had occasion to refer to the writings and doings of such varied worthies as Diogenes, Plato, Spinoza, Heine, Shakespeare, Lessing, and Kant. Of the writings of Freud he has made a special study, and, indeed, has written several articles on the professor's dream-theories for the Polish press. Nor is he unfamiliar either with the products of *Haskala*, or of the German *Yiddische Wissenschaft*. Rabbi Hirschprung, moreover, has found time to co-operate with the Jewish Scientific Institute, in whose premises in Vilna he enjoyed a special office.

The adventure of his flight from German-occupied Poland would make very interesting reading, had the Rabbi a mind to write autobiography. The despicable tactics of the Nazi herrenvolk, their sadistic invention (the Jewish elite of a captured town were always chosen to sweep the streets and clean the privies), his sojourn in a concentration camp, where the taskmasters always shaved the orthodox Jews half the beard, half a mustache and one eyebrow – would make a Tosafoth to modern *Kultur* such as has not been written. But in this country, Rabbi Hirschprung is devoting himself to a continuation of those studies he had so brilliantly conducted until the savages interrupted them. Already he has been appointed as Rabbi for the Adath Yeshurun Synagogue, which honors both him and itself in its choice. Rabbi Hirschprung is a definite asset to our cultural life, and the Montreal Jewish community is fortunate in his presence here.

The Fifth Column on Parade! 27 March 1942

The shameful precedent – was it a precedent? – which was established some time ago when rowdy gangs of juvenile hoodlums, emerging from a pseudo-political meeting, went rioting through the streets of Montreal, was repeated again on Tuesday night. As in the first case, the ruffians followed the same formula which characterized their first exploit. A meeting under the auspices of 'The League for the Defence of Canada' was convened to discuss the forthcoming plebiscite. Demagogues harangued the audience; they spoke soft words and noble phrases; they knew, with all the instincts of the sophist, that sometimes one can inflame one's listeners better with understatement than with vituperation. They knew also, being of the League for the Defence of Canada, that there are Defence of Canada Regulations which might touch their own precious skins. Accordingly, on the first occasion Mr. Henri Bourassa, called back from his pious philosophic retirement, uttered the words of patriotism, and gestured the innuendoes of disunion; and on Tuesday, Mr. J.F. Pouliot, of Temiscouata, known both for the originality of his metaphors, and the strangeness of his opinions, addressed his meeting in perfect parliamentary style.

But the outcome of the session was far from parliamentary. The voice which was lifted for anti-conscriptionism by Mr. Pouliot was apparently not enough; a blow had to be struck for this cause. And the organizers of the affair had decided that the blow must fall, for reasons inscrutable, upon the Jews of that city whose motto is: *In harmony there is safety.*

What took place at this juncture is already well-known. Inflamed with rhetoric and basking in the approval of their elders, the young men pursued a wild odyssey, from the place of meeting at Jean Talon, down Park Avenue, as far as Mount Royal, west on Mount Royal to St. Lawrence, and down St. Lawrence to Pine – the main streets of the Jewish district. Nor did they content themselves with an isolated march; groups converged on this district with strategical talent, which might better have been used elsewhere, from various directions. Placards bearing anti-conscriptionist slogans were prominent. From time to time, the marchers burst into song, singing *A Bas la Conscription* to the tune – believe it or not! – of *God Save the King.*

After the musical and rhetorical *hors d'oeuvres* there came the *pièce de résistance.* Shouting *A Bas les Juifs,* the heroes set to smashing windows, stopping street-cars, assaulting pedestrians.

From the circumstances of this incident (*sic*) a number of deductions can be made. In the first place, this demonstration was by no means a spontaneous manifestation. It was planned; it was arranged. How else explain the prepared placards? How else explain the choice of terrain for the 'forced march' of fifteen blocks? Who are the fifth-column generals who stay at home incognito while their deluded dupes indulge in this despicable goose-stepping? Who are the geniuses who conceived these slogans, for conceived beforehand they certainly were?

We must say frankly that the conviction is growing in many quarters that these meetings are convened, not to produce a platform for speakers, but to serve as a rendezvous for rioters, a central point for the gathering of those elements which are bent on creating in our midst that dissension which is so necessary to their treacherous purposes. Conscription is made, by dint of the peculiar workings of the demagogic mind, an occasion to preach antisemitism; and antisemitism itself is conceived as a tool for wider political objectives. The technique is not a new one; he who wishes to study it need only refer to the early career of Hitlerism.

Without preparation, the riot never would have begun. Without official slackness, it never could have continued. These ruffians had no permit to hold 'a parade.' They constituted, without doubt or question, an unlawful assembly. Their slogans and their cries threatened assault. Why were they permitted to continue along their unruly way, stopping street-cars, damaging property, insulting and assaulting people, for fifteen blocks, without interference by the police? There were in the meeting hall, we are told, five policemen! And this after the edifying example of the Bourassa meeting. During the march, these dwindled to two, in a police-car! It was not a law-enforcement body, it was an escort. Only after the riot began to take on what seemed serious dimensions, did a squad of policemen arrive, and they arrested – youngsters, nine!

We cannot refrain from expressing the opinion that there is too prevalent amongst some an attitude of mild-mannered tolerance to this so-called ebullience of youth. Certainly if the penalty for rioting is to be $3.50 a session, the fool and the knave may well be encouraged by this low price-ceiling to purchase so exciting a commodity. It may well be that the young men involved in the actual disturbances considered it no more than 'good clean fun'; but let no one be mistaken into underestimating the implications of these meetings, marches, and assaults. A hand, as yet unseen, directs them; it is the same hand, which when less cowardly, lifted itself in Fascist salute to Adrien Arcand, and to the things for which he stood.

For this is Fascism, simple and unadulterated – native-born, home-made Fascism. Like its European model, it tries its hand first against the Jews; successful there, it proceeds elsewhere. We disagree vigorously with the *Montreal Daily Star* which declares that 'those young men should not be taken seriously.' We imagine that the *Munich Daily Star* – if we may be forgiven the comparision – also in 1932 wrote such editorials about the misled storm troopers of Adolf Hitler. Certainly in the vocabulary of the demagogues it is but a step from *A Bas les Juifs* to *A Bas les Anglais*, and *A Bas Anyone Else* who may fit into the pattern of required tactics.

We believe that it is high time that constituted authority should act to see to it that a repetition of these incidents is made impossible. The safety of our citizens, the reputation of our province, the future of our war-effort, is at stake! If the municipal authorities are unable, for one reason or another, to cope with the situation, then certainly the provincial forces of law and order have a duty before them. As for the Federal Government, the Royal Canadian Mounted Police might well evidence some curiosity as to the organizers and authors of these demonstrations. For they are aimed not at St. Lawrence Boulevard, although it is the windows of that street which were smashed; they are aimed at other buildings, other thoroughfares, the roads which lead to Ottawa. It will profit Canada little to have a defeated Fascism abroad, only to discover its ugly snake-head lifted at home!

The *S.E.P.* Mounts Again   1 April 1942

The *Saturday Evening Post*, either because of its sabbatical name or for purposes of circulation, has set itself, during the last winter season, the task of solving the Jewish problem. We need hardly report that despite the glowing limelight which the *S.E.P.* focussed upon this question, the matter still remains penumbrated beneath the triple shadow thrown by its three illuminators – Messrs. Jerome and Waldo Frank, and finally Mr. Milton Mayer. Of Mr. Frank's contribution to the subject, we have already written at great and painful length. Our readers will remember that the learned judge disposed of the case by declaring the Jews a legal fiction; and presto – there being no Jews, but only Americans, there could be no Jewish problem.

Subsequently, the *S.E.P.* followed up the somewhat philistinish disquisition of Jerome Frank, by a high-class intellectual contribution of Waldo Frank. Mr. Waldo Frank is known in American literature as a great authority on Spain – and his article, as was almost to be expected, reads like a confession of a marrano. We mean this in no derogatory sense, for Mr. Waldo Frank enjoys our greatest respect. But having dealt for so long in commodities metaphysical and eternal, he apparently approaches the realistic Jewish question handicapped by his usual philosophic impediments. His thesis, in a word, is that the Jew must remain Jew *malgré lui*; that he is born with a heritage, and that that heritage he carries within him, willy-nilly, nolens-volens, waldo-naldo. What that heritage is, he does not say; all that one gathers is that it is some *Je-ne-sais-quoi*, some *tertium quid*, which distinguishes a Jew, even unbeknownst to himself, from his fellows. There is nothing much that can be said of this theory of Hebraic atavism except that it sounds mysterious and exotic, as becomes a philosophic analysis, but that it fails to convince all those who come from Missouri and its remotest environs. But while the hypothesis that the Jews are forward because they are throwbacks may be palpably fallacious, it is comparatively innocuous. At worst, it is but a negative definition of Judaism; a Jew, according to Waldo, is one who carries in his *subconscious* the memory of his ancestry; nothing more; nothing affirmative; as inevitable and irresistable as a birthmark cinque-spotted mole.

The last of the trinity to say his say on the Jewish question was one Milton Mayer, of Chicago, who previously appeared as the author of an article: 'I'll Sit This One Out.' The *S.E.P.* in a footnote to the *Mayer-bal-haness* article assures us it is the last; a great sigh of relief resounds through Jewry. For from such diagnoses, as this magazine has had its experts make, comes the worst disease. They have done more to darken, to confuse, to obfuscate the issue than any other single piece of American hocus-pocus within our generation. And the shuddering I-will-make-your-flesh-creep essay of Mr. Milton Mayer is a fitting finale to the *danse macabre*, in three movements, sponsored by the literary heirs of Benjamin Franklin.

In the first place, Mr. Mayer, just to show that he is a restrained and understanding fellow, titles his lucubration: 'The Case *Against* the Jew.' Lest you be deceived by the mute ingloriousness of this *Milton*, we inform the reader forthwith that the Chicago Mayer, like the Talmudic one who also used to find seven-score reasons for his sophistries, is a Jew. When a Jew, therefore, tells the readers of the *S.E.P.* that he is going to reveal, at last, the case against the Jew, one may well be justified in expecting the real low-down.

And low-down it is; right from the ass's mouth!

Mind you, we admit forthwith that Mr. Mayer writes well; he has a knack of wrapping his half-truth in the cellophane of epigram. You get a general view of blurred transparency; you hear a pleasing crackle; but you really don't *see* what's behind the cellophane. When this fails to convince you, he tells an anecdote, preferably about a Jew. Something happens to this apocryphal anecdotal Jew, and you are supposed to deduce therefrom that it is happening to *all* Jews. Logicians used to call this the fallacy of deducing from the particular to the general; but reporters – Mr. Mayer is a reporter – call it writing for the *Saturday Evening Post*.

Mr. Mayer's article is properly divided into two parts. In the first part he attacks the assimilationist Jew; in the second part, he hands out his recipe for a kosher future for Jewry. With his remarks about the assimilators, their cowardice, their knavery, we are in accord – one hundred per cent. This Milton has done a good job on them; in ten paragraphs he has written their paradise-lost. So far, so good; so far, he has served as an excellent antidote to the saccharine smugness of Jerome Frank. But our author is not content with merely being a critic; he must also be *Mayer ha-golah* – light to the exile.

And so having proved that certain Jews are no-good and worrisome things – to wit, the assimilators, the exploiters – he issues his *ukase* against *all* of Jewry. Does it wish to solve the Jewish problem? When it first sat down to the piano, did men laugh? Enclose ten cents – the new price of the *S.E.P.* – and a self-addressed envelope, and the solution will be sent to you! In six easy lessons! By such learned scholars as Isaiah, Amos and Milton Mayer!

For after convicting 'three Jewish industrialists' and 'forty-three Jewish editors' of assimilatory tendencies, secret admiration of Fascism (antisemitism deleted) and of tolerance of exploitation, Mayer feels himself justified to tell all the American Jews what is wrong with them, and how to right it!

The answer, my friends, is righteousness! Let the Jews be righteous and antisemitism will disappear! Let them cease being exploiters! And love will well forth from a thousand fountains! Let them read and obey the Bible, and Christians will practice towards them the Golden Rule! Let the Jew save his own soul, and he will be saved!

We must admit that when we first read the outburst of latter-day evangelism, our first thought was that the *S.E.P.* was purposely publishing this insulting balderdash to find out, by the written reactions, how many people were still reading the journal. 'Cease being exploiters!' That, as they say in Chicago, is a hot one! Tell it to the Jewish masses, Mr. Mayer, tell it to the members of the Amalgamated Clothing Workers of America, tell it to the East Side, shout it from the roofs of Jewish tenements! Pick up the relief rolls of New York, Detroit, Chicago, and points west, and send to its Jewish names, your exhortations against exploitation! They will just love your plea that they turn righteous! And they will most certainly appreciate your own righteousness, a righteousness which leads you to perpetrate the cheapest trick known to the demagogue – giving friendly advice, which by implication suggests that the advice is needed!

Mr. Mayer, you are an authority on Jew-hatred, since you are both a Jew and a hater of yourself. Do you imagine that if all Jewry was to take your advice, and become, all sixteen million of them, better than the angels, as saintly as St. Francis of Assisi, a whole nation of Isaiahs, do you imagine that antisemitism would decrease? Would not the contrary be true? Would not the whole world rise up in justifiable animosity against those paragons of virtue, even as the reader who knows you not is filled with a loathing towards your righteousness?

Besides, how come you issue these moral adages, these copy-book maxims, to Jews only? Virtue is not national; morals belong not to one group. It is true that you invariably modify your superfluous sermonizing by adding that it is intended also for the gentile; but the fact remains that your epistle is addressed to the Jews. Why then do you seek to give the impression that it is Jewish exploitation, Jewish assimilation, Jewish unrighteousness, that constitute the 'case' against the Jew?

Have you realized, Mr. Mayer, the full implications of your 'burden of Jewry'? Has it occurred to you that the thesis you have sought to maintain is different only in degree, and not in kind, from those which see the light of day in the *Voelkischer Beobachter*? Has it occurred to you that your advice that Jews be righteous can take its place beside the usual inscription over the gates of German concentration camps: *Work makes free*? That also, is, in the abstract, good advice; but in its context is, like yours in its context, a cruel irony, a sadistic joke.

We are not at a loss to know why the *Saturday Evening Post* publishes these pseudo-friendly articles. It is looking for some adrenalin for its circulation; the more sensational, the better! Certainly it is not looking for enlightenment – one can name a dozen men, who know the problem and are not free-lancers taking a stab at it, who are authentic Jews and not Jeromes, Miltons and Waldos, who could have really contributed something to the subject. But not that was what the *S.E.P.* was after.

As for Mr. Mayer himself, he is we fear, a case. Was he prompted by desire to be a one-day wonder – a Jew who spat in his own face, and piously uttered the *bracha* for rain? Or is he himself a victim of 'The Jewish Case,' indulging in 'the self-flagellation of the righteous,' the masochism of the sick? We do not know. We only know – and we are grateful – that the *S.E.P.* is not admitting any more of these invalids to its journalistic ward. Milton Mayer – the righteous Abou-ben-Adam, may his tribe decrease! – will now be able to sit them out.

The Plebiscite   24 April 1942

On April the twenty-seventh, the people of Canada will go to the polls to declare their democratic will concerning a problem which is of vital importance to the future of our war-effort. They will be asked, at this historic moment, whether they are for or against the release of the Government from the pledges which it had made prior to its entry into office.

It will be remembered that during the last election, both contending parties, conjuring up before them the picture of disunity which had resulted from the conscription issue during the last war, committed themselves to a recruiting policy which excluded overseas service. Behind this attitude, there were profound psychological and historical inhibitions. When it is further recalled that at the time the Government bound itself with these pledges, the war had not yet assumed the terrifying dimensions which it shows to-day, it will be clearly seen that a change of policy may, at any moment, become an urgent and imperative necessity.

The fact is that the Government presently enjoys full powers to make whatever decision it sees fit. The Government, however, believes that it must keep faith with the people, and that although the pledges are merely (*sic*) morally binding, they require, in a democratic country, the voluntary release of the electorate. In such manner, it is thought, the errors of 1917 will be avoided, and a decision will be arrived at which will not disrupt the unity of the country. Hence the plebiscite.

In the manifesto which has been issued by the Canadian Jewish Congress, the attitude of Canadian Jewry on this question is clearly indicated. As

Canadians standing on guard for the integrity of our country, and as Jews fighting the totalitarian menace, Canadian Jewry will most certainly vote *Yes*; a war against a ruthless foe cannot be fought with restrictive measures, and, as it were, with one hand tied behind one's back. Against totalitarian aggression, the only answer is total resistance!

Certainly Jewry cannot, not in any way, feel disposed towards a mollified and trammelled warfare against the foe. This is not said by way of concession to those despicable fifth-columnists, who go about prating about 'a Jewish war.' The sorry fact is that for six years Hitler carried on unrestricted, unhampered, and unmolested warfare against our people, without the slightest interference from any of the Governments of the world. Against the machine of terror which he set in motion, our brothers overseas were absolutely helpless; they were not opponents – they were victims. As the greed and power-lust of the Nazi maniac spurred him on to further experiments in aggression – after all, his experiment against Jewry was carried out with impunity – his plan of world-conquest became all too painfully clear. War was declared; to-day Jews, citizens of the democracies which are pledged to the destruction of Hitlerism, find themselves no longer helpless and unarmed. The use of these arms, by all who fight in the legions of freedom, ought not to be restricted!

The nay-sayers have, indeed, made great to-do about the defence of Canada, as if they, and they only, were concerned about that matter. The fact is that to wait to defend Canada in Canada is to extend an open invitation to the enemy to make of our land a battlefield, and to deprive ourselves – voluntarily – of one of the greatest of strategical assets – the carrying of the war to the foe. It is, moreover, a sorry spectacle to behold much platform-pantomime about civilization, decency, justice, etc., and at the same time, announce that our concern over these magniloquent concepts does not extend beyond the three-mile limit. It would certainly afford the enemy great comfort and consolation to know that while he may roam throughout the world in predatory search of booty, his Canadian opponent is tied, as with rope, to a given circumference.

We shall not dwell at any length upon the dictates of honor, since they are so obvious. Canada fights not alone; there are the United States, the United Nations, and the sister-Dominions of the Empire. None of these are shackled and fettered by such commitments as bind us. But we all fight for the same cause. Can we turn to the United States and say: 'If need be, you will come to our aid, since you are not bound by restrictions; as for ourselves, we cannot reciprocate, since we are restricted.'

Honor, safety, justice – all cry out for a Yes answer from the people of Canada. We are convinced that Canadian Jewry will live up to the urgencies of the hour, will take yet another step towards the forging of victory, and will vote to our Government a full and unrestricted mandate in the prosecution of the war. To judge by the temper of the people as it manifests itself before the day of election, there seems to be no doubt but that the affirmative will carry the plebiscite by a majority. In a plebiscite of this kind, however, it is not enough to have merely a mathematical majority; intended as an instrument of unity, the plebiscite should carry by an overwhelming majority. It devolves therefore, upon every citizen, not to rely merely upon the prognostication of the Gallup poll, but to add his ballot to the affirmative avalanche which must ensue on the 27th; and in that decision Canadian Jewry must play the part which both its Canadianism and its Judaism demand!

A Symphony of Three Cities: Vichy – Delhi – Tokio   24 April 1942

THE THIRD MOVEMENT

We are told by those who know that the great musical masterpieces of the symphony are built about the technical variations of one or two or three major themes. While it may be stretching a point, we do believe that contemporary history may well be compared to such a symphony; not that there is anything in the news of the day which is particularly melodious, or elevating, or sweetly musical. As a piece of history-making music, current events may rather be compared to one of those ultra-modern masterpieces, characterized by strident chords and much din and clangour. Indeed, the valley of the shadow through which we are passing may make a fit subject for a new Grand Canyon Suite. It is only in its deeper undertones, only its profounder implications of 'Fate knocking at the gate' that one sees a parallel to Beethoven's Ninth.

We trust, moreover, that this symphony is now at least at its third movement, the one preceding the finale. In it, we believe, one can already distinguish the dominant themes; and each is represented by a city, a snatch of raucous discord heard from Vichy, an unrealistic note issuing out of Delhi, and a succession of panic tremolos heard from Tokio. What is the relation of each piece of music to the other remains to be seen; it is in the hands of the Great Composer.

ON Y DANSE

At Vichy, the French collaborationist puppets seem to be dancing once again, and with greater vigor, to the tune called by Berlin. With the arrival of Pierre Laval, the dance assumes a new Teutonic frenzy. The old puppet-master Pétain, although still retaining a palsied hand over the strings, no longer directs the show. The real boss is now the man who has dedicated his life to the betrayal of his Fatherland, the man who already has won the first round of applause in the shape of a bullet. How his music will end nobody knows – whether in the shape of a sea-chanty to accompany the deliverance of the French fleet to the German masters, or whether to the accompaniment of those shrill arpeggios which usually illustrate tight rope walking, remains to be guessed. One thing is certain – the music of an impending crash is inherent in the playing of Laval.

The withdrawal of the American ambassador from Vichy was, of course, a foreseeable event. Admiral Leahy could not carry on any responsible negotiations with a group of second fiddlers, who acted according to the wave of a baton swung in Berlin. With this break in Franco-American diplomatic relations occurs the first ceasure in a harmony which has existed ever since the French Revolution.

But the spirit of the French Revolution is no longer understood in Vichy. Marshal Pétain now speaks of a new authoritarian order, the architect of which is Hitler, with Laval as supervising engineer. The stirring melody of the *Marseillaise* no longer finds utterance upon the lips of Pétain who, like all old men approaching second childhood, suffers a change of voice.

CARROTS AND VITAMINS

Carrots, we are informed, by the authorities on the subject, contain the vital vitamin which is so necessary to good eye-sight. Perhaps it was for this reason that Sir Stafford Cripps, the carrot-eating lawyer, was sent to India – great vision was required in the solution of that problem. But that vision, it appears, should have been directed towards India many decades ago. The strained relationship of centuries, it seems, has blurred, for the Indians at any rate – the British have shown a clear aftersight – the precise contours of the contemporary picture. We are inclined to believe that the leaders of India, mesmerized by the shibboleth which they have uttered [...] prayers, have missed, in the negotiations with Sir Stafford a great opportunity for that sub-continent's future. In the meantime the status quo is maintained. The symphony, instead of being altered to the minor key of Asia, remains in the major key which prevailed to date. Sir Stafford, it is to be noted, has not abandoned hope of better relations with India. His final remarks pointed to the great possibilities of post-war negotiations. The music dies, but the melody lingers on.

MODERN BUTTERFLY

No other creature can better symbolize the mood of Tokio to-day after the mysterious bombings which took place during the week-end. To judge by the radio broadcasts issued by the Axis pal in Berlin, the emotions of the Japs are a charming combination of terror and bewilderment. In the last five months, they had thought themselves snug and safe in their tight little isle; now, all of a sudden, out of a clear blue sky, and in broad daylight, came planes to bomb Tokio and the surrounding suburbs. Where do they come from? Air-craft carriers. Then why does not the Japanese navy deal with these carriers? Could it be possible that the Americans have planes which could come all the way from Los Angeles, or even Corregidor? Madame Butterfly wraps herself in her kimono, and shudders.

As for the United Nations, the news of the Tokio bombings has sent a thrill throughout the free world, Now, at last, the yellow Aryans may have a foretaste of that which lies in store for them. The atrocities of Nanking, the treachery of Pearl Harbor, the savagery of Hong Kong must and will be avenged; and the bombs which fell over Kobe announce the march of that vengeance.

Of course the Japs, adopting the 'Stop, thief' technique have already whimpered into their radios about the children who were casualties of the bombing raids. It would appear that the unknown airmen purposely avoided the military targets of Nippon. We therefore, offer to the Air Command a free and gratuitous suggestion; let the next raid be directed against neither a military or civil target; but let the bombs rain into the craters of the neighboring volcanoes! God and nature will do the rest!

THE FINALE

We shall not undertake the old art of prophecy. No one may foretell the theme of the final movement of the great historical composition which is being shaped before our very eyes. We cannot help but feel, however, that the fact that Germany requires and insists upon further close barber-shop harmony – 'I shave you, and you clip yourself' – the fact that Tokio has uttered its first cries of pain, and the fact that India's co-operation still remains pledged to the war-effort, private differences notwithstanding, that all of these facts can be summed up to augur something of good for the future.

As for the final coda, it is Wagner, that great hero of the Nazis, who has himself written it. Hitler, who rushes off to his eyrie in the Bavarian mountains to listen to the mighty chords of Wagner, never mentions this composition. He prefers the *Nibelungenlied, Parsifal,* and all the other musical apotheoses of lust and power. But this particular composition of Wagner's he eschews like the plague. Its melody, however, haunts him from day to day. It is the melody of 'Rule Britannia.'

Non-violent and Non-Co-Operative Resistance

8 May 1942

There was a time when the formula of resistance, invented by Mahatma Gandhi out of the whole cloth of his mystical consciousness, and applied against the British Government in India, had in it a modicum of naive charm, and even of simple practicality. As applied against the mild-mannered English officials, this method of warfare by nuisance, was sometimes effective. This was so, not because Gandhi's passive resistance can seriously be considered a means of opposition, but because the British bureaucracy, consisting of gentlemen to the manner born, allowed their *noblesse oblige* to bow before the Mahatma's fastings, and before the symbolic weaving of his followers.

Certainly we could have expected that faced with the menace of Japan and Germany, even so doctrinaire a spirit as Gandhi would soon realize that his prayers and his pacifism ought now to be discarded, and replaced by a more vigorous form of resistance. Alas, the groove in which the fanatic mind moves, inevitably becomes a vice which holds. The National Congress of India, dominated by the Zend-Avesta personality of Gandhi, has declared its intention to persist in the milk-and-water formula of resistance against Japan. Said the Congress: If the hordes of Japan descend upon India, they will be resisted by methods of non-violence and non-co-operation!

How nice! What a relief to the war-lords of Tokio! How comforting to be told in advance that should the samurai of Nippon enter India, they will meet no Indian bullets, no resisting sword! It is true that it will be somewhat uncomfortable for the Japanese to feel the embarrassment of non-co-operative resistance, but that is, after all, a misfortune that can be borne even by the most sensitive of souls. And the Japanese soldier is not a sensitive soul.

We can readily imagine the roar of Wagnerian laughter which must echo through the corridors of Berchtesgaden as this piece of priceless military strategy is being discussed. The people of India are going to *shame* the Axis into going away! The people of India will not speak to the vile attackers! Teutonic endurance will surely snap beneath the strain!

And yet Hitler, no doubt, can not help but express the wish that all his opponents follow the example of India. How simple everything would be! What a saving in steel and oil! All one would have to do would be to walk through a country, meet – at worst – its icy stare – and then settle down for good. Once one is settled down, the silence of a people – we quote the Gestapo – can easily be broken.

The fact is that this non-violent non-co-operative resistance is but another name for passive co-operative non-hostility. One requires merely to equate the negatives to arrive at this conclusion – a conclusion which merely underlines the fact that the Congress formula is but one step removed from the fifth-column technique. Surely the goose-stepping *herrenvolk* will not sit down to weep at the prospect of India wilfully submitting to enslavement. They know full well that if the English haven't got the methods to break the backbone of a 'non-violent resistance,' they have. They surely, will not be as sensitive about the Mahatma's starvation diet as the British viceroy is. In fact, they might even apply that diet to the millions of his followers, leaving them, by the way of consolation, the benefit of Gandhian philosophy.

The Appeal of the *Yeshivoth*   22 May 1942

The appeal on behalf of the two *Yeshivoth*, recently established in Montreal, which is to be launched in all synagogues during the Shevuoth festival should evoke a wholehearted and sincere response from all those who are concerned about the future of Judaism in this country. No event, it has been wisely said, is wholly evil; the disturbances which have been visited upon Europe by the abominable tyrant are no exception to the rule, for they have resulted – albeit we would have wished that the result had been consummated in some other fashion – they have resulted in the establishment in our midst of two important academies of learning, academies dedicated to the continuance of those traditions by which our people has survived the centuries. It is the pride of Montreal that during the last war there was published by the editor of the *Canadian Jewish Eagle*, the last edition of the Talmud; it is a source of similar pride that during the present troublesome times there have been established in our city two schools of learning which are dedicated to translating that *Shas* into living action.

Ever since the days of Rabbi Yochanan ben Zakkai, Torah has taken the place of Temple as the fortress of our people. It was the *Yeshivoth* of Sura and Pumbeditha which gave to our tradition a vitality which continued for centuries after the dispersion; it was the academies of eastern Europe which preserved that vitality until yesterday. History, it appears, has ordained it that this new continent should see the further development of the old doctrine.

There are some, we know, who speak of the *Yeshivoth* as if they were obscurantist institutions. The fact remains that without a solid basis in the teachings which have so glorified our past, contemporary Judaism is a make-believe sham, a hollow mockery, a voice and nothing more. Judaism does not exist in a vacuum; it grows; it has sources; no one can expect to see the tree splendid with foliage, and at the same time cut out the roots!

It is to be noted that the two academies, founded in Montreal, have objectives which go beyond the four walls of their places of learning. It is not solely to be a pilpulistic hair-splitting Talmudic rationalism to which they are dedicated, but also to the dissemination of good doctrine, high morals and pious deeds. Already the Academies Tomchai Tmimim and Mercaz Hatorah have exerted their respective influences upon our youth; as yet small in scope, there is no doubt that the future holds still a wider sphere of influence. The Jewish community of Montreal, in supporting the *Yeshivoth*, supports its own Jewish future, the allegiance of its youth, and the integrity of its traditions.

Your Picture in the Paper

Gutenberg has been sufficiently cursed for having invented the printing press. Let him stay, therefore, unmolested by us in his printers' heaven, listening to the loved hosannah of the linotype, and inhaling the ambrosial odors of printer's ink. But upon him who invented the process of reproducing photographs in newspapers, and upon all those who have corrupted his good intentions, if any – may their destiny be an after-life when all is a blur, and existence itself a faded negative!

The bitterness of our soul wells up at the thought of the monstrosities which are daily perpetrated by means of this diabolical invention. Weekly we receive upon our desk, a varied assortment of Canadian Jewish publications, printed in Yiddish and in English. Of their contents and their literary style, we shall say nothing. But who is so great a master of self-control, who has that yogi temperament, that he can remain silent at the distasteful display of some of the cuts and photographs therein contained?

Certainly it is not that the faces are unhandsome. The daughters of Israel whose beauty is displayed on glossy paper, in black and white and even sepia, are frequently of an outstanding comeliness. The heads of prominent Jews who peer from the newspaper columns are often, indeed, impressive with a charm obviously induced by counsel of the photographer. Not this is our grievance, not this our complaint. It is the corpses and the children who have moved us to these lines!

This article certainly should have been written a long time ago. The fact is that we have for many weeks cherished a secret hope that Mr. A.B. Bennett, that distinguished commentator upon Canadian Jewish mores, would some day dip his pen into the appropriate acid, and indite a satirico-metaphysical treatise on the most objectionable phase of Canadian-Jewish journalism. Mr. Bennett, however, seems for the nonce to be concerned with matters of trifling import, such as Canadian-Jewish unity and Zionist realpolitik. What is a profile to him who anatomizes not only the face, but the entire Jewish body politic?

Accordingly we have decided that where the Jewish Cato is silent, we shall lift our voice. Let Troy fall, let Ilium go down in flames, but at long last we will say our say about the pictures in the paper. Too long have we endured it, this disgrace to Jewish journalism, these profiles and full-faces which bring the blush of shame to the countenance of even the most callous of spectators.

Take for example certain Jewish newspapers of the west. We receive them with gratitude, they are so full of communal news, and so informative of the fine Jewish life which characterizes our western communities. Then, as we are engrossed in a column of Mark Zelchen, or an article by Salem Miller, or a learned and humorous disquisition by L. Rosenberg, and with our eyes still on the paper, but our hand looking for the sugar for the coffee, we suddenly alight upon a reproduced photograph of an elderly gentleman staring fixedly from between two ads. Who, we ask ourselves, is this venerable worthy? We read the sub-title, and discover that he has been dead these three years, that he is distinguished in having thoughtful children, and that to-day is his *yahrzeit!* We push the coffee aside.

Now, we ask, what macabre morbidity is it that prompts editors to accept these unearthed cadavers, to display them, with a *Chevra Kadisha* expertness, upon the weekly galleys? We mean no disrespect to the dead; some of our best friends are corpses of long standing – if that is the word. But why should it not be enough merely to mention the fact of the anniversary, together with the appropriate verses, and call it a day of filial piety? Why the touching addition of a photograph – dressed in the latest style of 1909 – of a man or woman who has departed this life and all its vanities full many a year agone? They have gone to their Eternal Rest; must that rest be disturbed? Is it really necessary that this additional *chibut hakever* be so mercilessly inflicted? Or is it an apology for *Kaddish?*

As for the reader, innocently led into this charnel-house, are not his feelings to be considered at all? Not every one, it must be remembered, dotes on having a *memento mori* at his breakfast table. There is, indeed, something eerie and uncanny about looking across your cup of coffee to see the spirits from beyond calmly returning your gaze. The editor who inflicts such spectral company upon his reader expects a degree of fortitude not usually met with in that gentle tribe. The Fourth Estate sinks to a low one, indeed, when it permits its hallowed ground to be converted into cemetery plot.

Let no one imagine that we are callous to the fine human sentiments which prompt the heirs and assigns of the deceased to ask for these funebrial insertions. Filial respect is a virtue at all times. But, as a wiser one once said, there is a time and a place for everything; and the press, we submit, is not the proper place for these pious *yahrzeit* pictures. An editor should resist the persuasions which bring about this abominable breach of decency and good taste. Otherwise the Rabbinical Council may find itself compelled to interdict the Yiddish press to *Cohanim* under the prohibition against trespassing upon burial-ground.

And there is yet another class of reproduced picture that arouses in us the mingled feelings of pity and despair. We refer to those festival issues of the Anglo-Jewish press which go in for a veritable orgy of de luxe photography, flattering only to the subjects thereof. The ante-nuptial art which displays brides hiding behind lilies, and bridesmaids – they must be homelier than the bride – flanking the scene, the while a little flower-girl brings up the rear, may be tolerated. The picture of Mrs. X pouring tea for her sister-in-law – with whom she has not been on speaking terms for years – also may be forgiven. These things, we are given to understand, are of the matters which constitute 'Social News.'

It is, however, the periodic display of the photographs of one-year-old infants, usually swimming upon some fur rug, their posteriors seen in profile, which reaches the climax of journalistic dotage. Again we must interject a disclaimer; we are definitely not against infants; we believe in them with a firm and practising faith. We love the darling tots. We even dote on photographing them. But stop short at publishing the photographs. What, in heaven's name, we ask, is newsworthy about Mrs. Cohen's two-year-old, entered into the Rosh Hashanah classic? Is Mrs. Levi really interested in seeing the excerpts from Mrs. Cohen's family album? Does it add to universal enlightenment? Is it literature? Is it, is it art?

Of course it gratifies Mrs. Cohen to see her bambino displayed in the public prints! And if it is a good photograph, it gratifies also the photographer who may forthwith expect an invasion of his studio by all the mothers of the neighborhood gang, equally desirous of immortality. But should – and here is the crux of the ethical question involved – the august representative of the Fourth Estate cater to those purely private, albeit laudable since maternal, cravings of his readers?

We understand, of course, the impulse which frequently drives an editor to accept these lovely pictures. Sometimes they are paid for, and there is really no reason why Borden's Elsie should be photographed and not Mrs. Gordon's Elsie. Again, the plea of a mother is difficult to resist; hell knows no fury like a woman spurned. Frequently, too, there is a dearth of news; and space-filler is required. Why not fill it up with faces that can launch a thousand ships? And finally, everybody's doing it ... Our point is that they shouldn't.

P.S. – Any and all descriptions of journals or photographs hereinabove included are not intended to resemble anything or anybody within hearing.

Should such similarity or resemblance, however, actually occur, it is to be taken as purely coincidental.

    P.P.S. – Any and all opinions anent the above momentous subjects are purely personal, and do not in any way involve this journal which no doubt has its own ideas on the subject, which may or may not agree with those of the writer.

Remember Lidice!   19 June 1942

It may be a difficult name to remember. The pronunciation of Czech consonants does not, after all, flow trippingly from our tongue. We may be remembering a sound which means nothing to Czech ears. But to the world at large the very letters of that word, its mere unuttered orthography speaks with a message it shall never forget!

Remember Lidice! There are so many places to remember in these unforgettable years. There is Dunkirk, for the callous might of the Nazi war machine; there is Rotterdam, for the ruthless savagery of its Luftwaffe; there is Pearl Harbor, for the treachery of its yellow partner. But Lidice symbolizes the essence of the entire German psychology, its paganism, its disregard of life, its wantonness, its Assyrian *schrecklichkeit*!

Not since man emerged from palaeolithic barbarism, has any nation made itself the author of a deed so nefarious as that which transpired at Lidice, about twenty miles from Prague. Everybody is already sadly familiar with the abominable details. The hangman Heydrich met a well-deserved end at the hands of unknown Czech patriots. One could hardly have expected him to die yawning in his bed. The savagery and bloodlust with which he oppressed the Czech people cried out for an avenger. His ordered executions, his firing squads, his concentration camps, were already beyond human endurance. Only men of putty could submit indefinitely to the regime of blood and iron for which he stood. Accordingly, there occurred once more what has always occurred in human history when the love of freedom, crushed for a moment, rises again, and with the same retribution lifted aloft, cries the age-old cry of Nemesis – *sic semper tyrannis!*

With poetic justice, as if designed in heaven, Heydrich lingered on for about a fortnight. This was as it should be. After all the favorite slogan of the Gestapo which Heydrich headed was that quick death was too good for its victims. 'Let them ask for death as for sweet release' – that was the standing instruction to his co-ordinating butchers. To him, too, death came as final dismissal from his detestable office. In the meantime, his expiring agonies were accompanied by daily slaughters of innocent women and children, arrested because they did not like their Nazi overlords. (This is not an understatement: the German despatches definitely declared that the executed found their fate because they did not approve of Heydrich.)

With the passing of Heydrich, Nazidom decided that something must be done 'which would make the skin creep.' Insofar as the deceased himself was concerned, he was given a splendid funeral – no doubt *pour encourager les autres.* But something was necessary to shudder the Czechs with the horribleness of the deed. Nazi officialdom, so reckless of the lives of its own millions flung upon distant battlefields, now began to feel the pin-prick in its own skin. The assassination of Heydrich was an attempt not only against that particular butcher – it was the forecast of the doom which awaited all the other tyrants, grand and petty.

Hitherto, the German policy had confined itself to the execution of single hostages, a method of reprisal which is as unjust as it is savage and bearing not even the tinsel of judicial process of law. For the killing of hostages is admittedly the killing of innocent persons – murder unashamed and vauntful, perpetrated only for the sake of showing the murderers' murderousness. Now the German brain trust decided to promote itself from the retail hostage business to the wholesale field. Lidice was chosen as the scene of an experiment that civilized mankind had thought had vanished from its annals with the disappearance of the cavemen, with the passing of the oriental satrap.

Under the pretext that this town, hitherto unheard of, and henceforth to be a clarion-call for all free men, had broken some regulation imposed by the conquerors, all the male inhabitants of Lidice were executed, its females banished, its children taken to 'institutions' and the village itself razed to the ground. Horrible! horrible! horrible! The full unspeakable atrocity of the New Order shows itself, clear, crimson as blood. Beyond this, bestiality could not go. The beasts that walk like men act according to their natures.

Wiped off the map, Lidice now lives in the heart of mankind, a heart at once full of pity for its sad fate, and full of hatred crying that that fate be avenged. Lidice now becomes the opposite symbol of Sodom; Sodom has murdered Lidice, Sodom shall sleep no more!

Remember Lidice! When the day of victory comes, let not that same lassitude, that same milk-and-water inertia which took hold of the peacemakers in 1918, take hold of them then. Much criticism has been levelled against the Treaty of Versailles; the real fault with that treaty, we believe, was the fact that it resulted from divided minds, a mongrel document, a hybrid peace. At the green tables of peace, one can adopt either of two policies; one can, in a spirit of amnesiac forgiveness declare that bygones shall be bygones, and that the culprit is liberated, so only he go and sin no more; or one can adopt the rigorous attitude demanded by the circumstances, and announce implacably *Vae victis.* The error of the Treaty of Versailles was that it was neither of these things, but a poor amalgam where pity for Germany was ousted by considerations of conquest, and where the demands of security were thwarted by misdirected compassion. Remember Lidice! The treaty that is to be written after this war must be one which will re-establish Lidice, as much as it can be re-established, and eliminate forever the authors of its destruction. Let us not ever again be befuddled by doctrinaire shibboleths applied in favor of an enemy who will only use our 'effete pity' as an invitation to leap at our throats again.

There is yet another thing which we must remember when we remember Lidice; and that is, that incidents of this kind do not occur in a vacuum. Somebody causes them; they are not the result of spontaneous combustion. In the past, the rigors of the victor have always been imposed upon the shoulders of the masses; reparations, diminution of territory, blockade – these have been the punishments visited upon the indiscriminate followers of aggressive leadership, but not upon the leaders themselves. The leaders either retired, like Hohenzollern, to an estate in a foreign country where they live to a ripe old age, or at worst, got themselves an island, like Napoleon, with all modern conveniences, including medical attention. That error must not be perpetrated again. Such impunity of leadership will serve only as an encouragement to other would-be tyrants who feel, that at worst, they risk only the next fellow's neck. The Heydrichs, the Goebbels, the Goerings, the Himmlers, and Hitler must be brought to account – personally. The fiction that the destroyers of civilized life in Europe are merely fulfilling the injunctions of a *de jure* and *de facto* government merely puts a premium upon such savagery. Let it be determined now that when the day of victory comes, abdication will not solve the problem of Hitler and his gang. Any other approach to the issue in question is a stupidity and a sham.

It is a sham because to permit the slaughter of millions while the instigators of the slaughter go scot-free, is a sham. And it is stupidity, because should Hitler emerge victorious, there is no doubt as to how he would act towards our leaders. One knows of his expressed intentions with regard to Beneš; one knows of his accomplished fact with regard to Schuschnigg.

Lidice is off the map of Europe. But three hundred widows remember it, and at least as many orphans. Remember it, too, will the conscience of the world, which will not rest until the blot which Germany has flung upon mankind's name will be effaced, and avenged.

The Mystery of the Mislaid
Conscience   17 July 1942

There has never been a crisis in human history but it brought forth in its wake of misery and suffering some great utterance, some inspired declaration which either articulated a new truth or reiterated an old one in danger of being forgotten. Always at the moment when the world seemed to lapse into the corruption of Sodom and Gomorrah, some voice was lifted which informed the world that the human conscience was still alive, that moral values still counted for something, and that injustice, if it had to be perpetrated, would be perpetrated not in shameful silence, but over and against noble protest. Thus, in the last century, when a whole continent seemed unconcerned about the terrible fate of the Armenians, they found a doughty, if solitary, champion in the person of William Ewart Gladstone. Thus, again, when one innocent man was about to be left to his fate on Devil's Island, the thundering voice of Emile Zola was heard, fulminating his *J'accuse*. And thus, finally – we give an instance within the memory of living man, when a whole wandering nation, after two thousand years of homelessness, sought a resting place from its weariness, it was the late Lord Balfour who spoke out for the best impulses of mankind.

It is to be noted, in all of these instances, that the righteous deed, although almost invariably the act of a single individual, mighty in his moral integrity, needed but initial example to inspire the approval and support of the many. The world recognizes the right when it is shown; but the world somehow always requires some great personality to make the first revelation, some titanic moral force to set in motion the moral momentum which would carry all before it. Had Zola remained silent, Dreyfus might have indeed spent his days in ignominious torture. Had Gladstone kept his peace, the Armenians might have been no more; and had some inspired spirits within the British Cabinet sealed their lips against utterance of the age-old iniquity against Israel, and its righting, the little which this people has might not have been. One there was in history who averted his face at the spectacle of wrong-doing; the name of Pontius Pilate is still remembered as that of the man who washed his hands but sullied his soul.

From that cesspool of wickedness which is the German Reich, abysmal iniquity has flowed over the globe. The doings of Sodom are as the driven snow compared to its red horrors; the evils of Gomorrah are as innocence itself. Against some of its atrocities the world has reacted in a manner befitting a world which calls itself civilized. Against others, it has remained silent, an uncomfortable silence which is eloquent of nothing so much as of a sense of its own guilt.

Let us cite instances. When the hatchetmen of Hitler razed to the ground the city of Lidice, and murdered all able-bodied men found therein, there was felt throughout the democratic world a feeling of revulsion at the deed, and shame at the thought that the perpetrators of it were bipeds, and in all points like human beings. Save in humanity. When reports of the dire straits in which the Norwegian people find themselves under the Quisling heels reach civilized people, headlines are made in the journals, and the blood of men grows hotter, and the brimstone of vengeance is in the air. When White Papers touching on German atrocities against Poles are made public, one senses everywhere a determination that those things shall not be again, and that those who made it possible even once shall be punished in such manner that repetition of the offense shall forever be impossible.

And these feelings of protest and sympathy are, of course, as they should be. It would be a sorry world, indeed, if the narrative of these bestial iniquities left its hearers unmoved and untouched. The fact is that the course of German barbarism so runs counter to the most elementary notions of human conduct that they stir even the most callous of souls. One need not be a sensitive plant to react against these perpetrations, nor a mighty organ-voice of humanity to speak out against them. To be human is sufficient.

And yet there is daily before our eyes a record of atrocity, a plan of barbarism, authored by the German butchers, which might well harrow up the human soul. It is the record of systematic destruction which the Nazis are levelling against the Jewish people. Lidice is cruelly sensational and un-ashamed; but its effects are no more devastating than the less sensational but equally murderous methods adopted by the Nazi gauleiters against the ghettos of Poland, or the conquered cities of Russia. Moreover, in the one instance, a city is destroyed for the purpose of terrorizing the survivors into submission; in the anti-Jewish policy, however, it is not mere terrorism which is the objective; it is total destruction, the methodical and complete annihilation of a people. To achieve this one uses not only the brutality which shudders the beholder; one also creates conditions where famine and disease may enter as silent partners into the axis scheme.

To-day the cables bring reports of the pogrom which lasted for two days in the city of Lemberg. Yesterday Slovakia – Nazi-dominated – boasted across the airwaves that it would soon be *Judenrein*. A week ago came the belated news of the continued and daily massacre of Jews in the Baltic countries. A month ago, the world heard of the holocaust in Kiev where forty thousand Jews were destroyed. A year ago, one read the report of the *schechitos* in Rumania.

We recount these atrocities, as if they were the items in a Cook's Tour Catalogue, the peregrinations of murder. It is in this same matter-of-fact fashion that the general press reports these matters. They are relegated to a footnote, a small item in the back page, these which should furnish the headlines of the day. It is as if the press of the world were economizing in space, and were printing synoptic obituaries.

Where, we ask, is the thunderbolt of invective which these events should call forth? Where are the keepers of the world's conscience, its intellectual leaders, guardians of the progress of the ages, and where the as-yet-unuttered *J'accuse* of our generation? Who is the Zola who has spoken out against these atrocities? The Armenians had their Gladstone – what impartial voice speaking for it has Jewry?

It is true that it may be answered that the Jewish tragedy is part of a world tragedy and that concerning the latter and all its moral implications much has already been said by the wise and the noble of our generation. That is irrefutable. The 'four freedoms' of President Roosevelt, and the Atlantic Charter of Winston Churchill do speak in general terms of the foundations of the world to come. It is significant, however, that in addition to the general teleologies, voices are raised on behalf of the Czechs, the Poles, the Norwegians, the Yugoslavs, the Greeks. All have friends at court; for all some great personality, other than their accredited leaders, says the winged word, some powerful influence is somewhere exerted. For Israel, however, no one – save the victims – has yet spoken.

At the beginning of the war, it was sometimes stated that the leaders of the democracies did not desire to make any special point of the Jewish plight, lest 'they open the mouth of Satan' and lend a foundation to the slander that this was a 'Jewish war.' The march of events has shown even to the most obtuse how ridiculous that fabrication is. Too many nations are vitally involved – involved as to their present and their future – for any one seriously to countenance that notion that the Armageddon was either created or is being continued for Jews. The fact is that for seven years before the actual outbreak of hostilities, when Jews were the helpless victims of the Nazi savagery, no one intervened – the plight of German Jewry was, in the eyes of the world, purely a domestic incident. This 'Jewish war' bogey is no longer an excuse for silence. If silence continues, it can only be interpreted as the uneasy conscience of the democracies themselves. Certainly it is high time that the leaders of the United Nations show an aware-ness of the abominations that are being perpetrated against a part of mankind, high time that the German government is told, and not merely by implications, that the democracies are not indifferent to the fate of the thousands of Jewish hostages in Nazi hands. Liberty is indivisible; democracy is not a rationed article. Jews, although not represented as such among the United Nations, are also of the family of mankind. One still awaits some indication that this elementary fact has somewhere been noted among the councils of the mighty.

Shall Never the Twain Meet?   14 August 1942

The Indian leader, Nehru, addressing an open letter to Americans in which he sought to win u.s. sympathy for the Gandhi sabotage of the military efforts of the United Nations – ventured to express the opinion that although the western countries were justly credited with great material progress, it was to the East – to India, to China, that the world ought to turn to learn the true art of living. We must admit that this contrast between occidental materialism and oriental spiritualism is not an original idea with Nehru; the point has been made before.

It is a point, moreover, which to our mind receives too ready an acquiescence not merely in eastern circles to which it is flattering, but even in occidental groups, critical of the lack of perfection in our way of life. It is, indeed, too facile an antithesis, this between the continents where science has plucked from nature all its pragmatic secrets, and yet no happiness is; and those continents where life has not changed since Buddha last visited the earth, and yet – so we are told – the shining faces of contentment are everywhere to be seen.

It would be well, indeed, that before this counter presentiment is estimated, we looked, as Shakespeare bids us, on this picture and on this. What is meant by this 'crass materialism of the West'? No doubt that pejorative is intended to describe the state of affairs which exists in western countries, and in which despite the introduction of many utilitarian comforts, there is a singular absenting from felicity. The indictment would appear to run somewhat as follows: You men of the west have certainly changed the face of the earth, and no doubt for the better, but have you introduced a new happiness into your souls? Admitted that your houses are fitted with better plumbing conveniences, does this scientific cleanliness bring you any nearer to godliness? Admitted that your many inventions – your telephones, your radios, have achieved the miracle of conquering space, have you not failed dismally in your attempted conquest of time, not to speak of eternity? Is it not a fact that your latest and most sensational invention – the machine that flies like a bird – until the day before yesterday, your proudest boast, has brought misery into the world more than any other conglomeration of sticks and stones known to history? And is it not, moreover, true that in the wake of the petty advantages, the puny successes which your scientific efforts have won, there has followed a host of maladies and discomforts hitherto unknown to much-afflicted man? The speed with which your wheels move you has brought also both a new dizziness and a distortion of perspective; the labor-saving devices which you have thought up, have perhaps eliminated a number of industrial gestures, but certainly increased the sum total of regimentation. And as for sanity, no place in the world sees so many cases of social maladjustment as there where science was to have ushered in the millenium.

The devil's advocate of westernism would do well if he stopped there, at the point where his indictment reaches its climax. But usually he seeks also to paint his client in the most glowing of colors. Changing his character from prosecutor of the west, to apologist for the east, he seeks to conjure up a picture of oriental bliss. Look, he says, pointing to the millions of Asia, look how everyone lives at peace with his environment. The Chinese passes his life in philosophic content, unmoved by the hurly-burly of the ambitious, and cynical of those who expect from their mundane existence more than the minima of sufficiency. The Indian spurns the world and all its troubles; he has his regard fixed on higher things. It is his immortal soul, and not his standard of living, which is his chief pre-occupation. Not feasting, but fasting, is his pleasure; not wealth, but poverty, his ambition. Between him and Nature, the great and fertile goddess, he lets no multitude of wheels, no jungle of pistons, no labyrinth of valves, intervene. He sees nature clearly, and he sees it whole. The world is not too much with him; he does not lay waste his powers; he has not given his heart away, a sordid boon.

It is, indeed, a very happy and idyllic picture. And would that it were true! It is a picture, moreover, which has been painted *ad nauseam*. But recently Professor Lin Yu Tang wrote a best seller in which he portrayed the Chinese people as admirable stoics, suffering with a bland smile. Throughout his book, indeed, there seemed to run a continual refrain: All is vanity. Nothing, *sub specie aeternitatis*, was really worth getting excited about, except, perhaps, a piece of roast pig, or the moon reflected in the Yangtse River. One could not help but wonder, after reading this analysis, what all the Chinese fighting was about!

We are not a protagonist of the beauty and charm of Western industrialism. We do agree that it would be much better for our civilization if its spiritual resources were treated at least with the same respect accorded to its outward material appurtenances. We would not even be vigorous in denying the contention, so frequently advanced, that the sorry pass to which we have come has been in large part due to the sloth, gluttony, and other cardinal sins engendered by our mode of living. (Actually we are of the opinion, that if we had had more of that materialism – more planes, more tanks – the sorry pass too would have been avoided.)

But all this is not to agree with Nehru, and his invitation to learn about life from the East. The unhappiness current in our midst has ensued not because of our material progress but in spite of it. The plane is an excellent instrument for inter-communication between peoples. Alas, it can also be used to drop bombs. But there is hardly anything invented by man which cannot be used to man's discomfiture. The bread-knife is a lovely thing, apportioning, as it does, the requisite parts of the staff of life. But wrathful husbands have been known to use this instrument to slit their spouses' throat. To blame the knife is to evoke the mediaeval theory of deodand – whereby the instrument itself which causes death was punished by being taken out of circulation.

No one can make this writer believe that an ox-cart is a better means of transportation than a Chevrolet, and that he who rides in one is ergo nearer to the secret arcana of Nature. No one can convince this writer that because an individual dispenses with the 'modern conveniences' that go with western real estate he is therefore in a better position to grasp the eternal verities. And we see nothing spiritual about eastern concepts of hygiene. It is quite true that the bather in the Ganges may feel and appear perfectly happy, in contrast perhaps happier than the Sunday-picnicker on Coney Island, but this certainly is not due to the fact that the one gets home by subway and the other gets home by pilgrimage.

And as for the art of living! We really have not much to learn from Nehru's India. A non-materialistic people, it seems to us, should have been able centuries ago to discover, out of its spiritual meditations, the crying injustice which it perpetrates against the millions of untouchables. Even the very, very spiritual Gandhi has never led a passive resistance movement on their behalf. We leave, for want of corroboration, unmentioned the many charming descriptions of the Indian 'art of living' to be found in Mother India. We stop only to wonder how much happiness is to be found among this lowest of castes, untainted though it is, by western materialism.

As for the Chinese art of living, we hesitate to make odious comparisons touching our gallant ally. The fact, however, remains that whatever art there does appear in Chinest living, has come into it only under Chiang Kai-shek; and that even under him we read that the law whereby rich Chinese could make a contribution in money instead of serving personally in the army, was abolished only six weeks ago. Moreover, we cannot resist the thought that the Chinese art of living, such as it is, would have enjoyed considerable additional advantages if it had additional materialism, such as hangars, planes, and ammunition.

The fact is that the reverse of Nehru's theorem is true, and that the sum total of the world's happiness is increased, rather than decreased, by the progress of the professors and the chemists. It is, of course, true, that progressive advances make their beneficiaries more critical and fastidious, thus resulting in imperative discontent, and additional progress. But one must not confuse the cud-chewing contentment of the cow with felicity.

It is not the machine which is the guilty party. Burns' truism still holds good – the source of misery 'is man's inhumanity to man.' And that inhumanity, it appears, knows no distinction of occidental or oriental. If it is to be alleviated, it will be alleviated by eliminating the causes which induce it, and mainly the competition over the world's comforts. In this respect, 'materialism' with its objective of increasing those comforts, is a factor for greater happiness.

Certainly, the real truth of the situation lies not in a contrast between that spiritualism of the East and materialism of the West, but in an amalgam of the two world-outlooks. When the twain will meet, it will assuredly redound to the advantage of both the party of the first part and the party of the second part.

The Jewish Unitarian   28 August 1942

No doubt the unitarian, as hereinafter defined, exists also among what the old scribes called 'the nations of the world.' We are impelled to write, however, about the Jewish unitarian because when the general characteristics appear in the Hebrew they are, by some unknown pathological law, exaggerated into classic characteristic. And when so exaggerated, gentle reader, this unitarian is indeed a weariness to the flesh and a bore.

Let us define the term. By Jewish unitarian we do not in any manner or wise refer to theological credos. In the final analysis, all Jews are unitarians, since by virtue of the *Shma* they all believe in the one God, omnipotent and everlasting. Concerning these pious monotheists we have nothing but good to say; in a world of many idols, they hold to the great pure intangible truth.

The unitarian who to-day rouses our wrath is that worthy, who surveying the whole duty of man, whether from the religious or ideological aspect, invariably comes to the conclusion that he has the answer and that it is a very simple one, indeed. His is the one-track mind par excellence. For every problem, for every situation, he has some single panacea, some isolated nostrum, some inclusive cure-all. That his solution does not answer all the aspects of the problem, does not seem to concern him; he loves the geometry of unity, oneness has a certain mystical charm, it is inconceivable to him that life, and its problems, are varied and ramified, and that therefore its answer is never expressed, like a reply to a proposal, in a monosyllable.

Examples will illustrate our complaint. Jews there are who believe that all of Judaism – its six hundred and thirteen injunctions and additional minor fardels – are answered by this isolated practice of philanthropy. To them Judaism is no longer a religion, a creed, or even a culture; it is an eleemosynary institution. Heine once declared that Judaism was a misfortune; they opine that Judaism can exist only on misfortune. Abolish the poor, and the recipients of their charity, and you abolish their Judaism, with a decree more draconic and effective than any Antiochus could devise. Time was when the good Jew, seeking to establish his worthiness in the eyes of God and of man, recorded to himself, in a silent *cheshbon hanefesh*, the manner in which he had observed or failed to observe, the sundry traditions of his race and his creed. The *cheshbon hanefesh* of those who wrap up their Judaism in a single activity is expressed only by budgetary calculations as to donations made.

Mind you, blessed are the hands that give. From of yore charity was for Jews a cardinal virtue, if we may use that adjective. We, certainly, would never wish to put a stumbling block in the path of those who come to the aid of the orphan and widow. What we do say, however, is that philanthropy is not the be-all and end-all of our creed. To deem it so, is to deem it lop-sided. Moreover, if this were so, the poor, who cannot enjoy this *mitzva* would be left most cruelly out of the pale of Judaism, existing solely for the purpose of affording the rich an entry into heaven.

There is yet another type of Jewish unitarian, equally myopic, only this latter places all his emotional emphasis, not upon a single *mitzva*, but upon a single ideology. The favorite slogan of this philosopher announces, as if it were a paraphrase of the Talmudic dictum: 'The Tishbite will answer all questions and difficulties' – that socialism will solve all problems. That to this writer there is a great deal of incontrovertible truth in the announcement does not alter his opinion that as a general statement it is fallacious and misleading. We believe that it has been observed by others wiser than ourselves, that even after all the economic grievances are satisfied, there still remains a vast field of human relations, untouched by the laudable cure. Particularly when applied to the Jewish problem, does this one-sidedness appear, not only as an error, but also as a positive danger. It is, for example, the credo of the aforementioned gentry that the striving of Jews for a homeland is a work at once stupid and supererogatory. Will not the economic millenium solve all problems, those of Jews included? That, until that happy occasion comes to pass, Jews are left homeless and landless, appears to be overlooked. There is a doctrinaire solution, and if it is late in coming, let the people which boasts itself to be eternal, learn to wait. It has plenty of time. This attitude to our mind is as logical as that of the man who refused to concern himself with the trials and troubles of an evicted family because the social revolution would reinstate them anyway. All they had to do was park on the sidewalk and wait for history to march by.

The social unitarian has his counterpart again in the Zionist one. Ignorant of the true aims and objectives of this most important movement in Jewish history since the dispersion, the fellow weakens his case by exaggerating it. Instead of approaching Zionism as a vital, and most vital contribution to the Jewish problem, he dubs the solution one and indivisible. That even after the establishment of a Jewish commonwealth in Erez Israel there will be millions of Jews still living in the *galuth*, still facing their own local problems, is a viewpoint he cannot grasp. Overcome by an inexplicable mysticism, he seems to be of the opinion that as soon as a Jew has crossed the frontier into Erez Israel he is thereby elevated, in historic value, above his lowlier brethren still denizen of the ghetto. Accordingly, to all things he brings a purely doctrinaire viewpoint; all things he views with spectacles made in Tel Aviv. Thus, if a convention, let us say, of economists meets in Patagonia, he reserves his judgment upon it until he discovers whether it did or did not pass a Zionist resolution. That the Patagonian economists had no more reason to pass such a resolution than to pass one approving Einstein's theory of relativity, is no concern of his. He has one standard: Did they or did they not utter the *Shmoneh Esra* prayers touching the return to Zion?

We have not, by any means exhausted the list of unitarians, the blessed spirits who walk about as if they had cornered the market of truth, as if their *idée fixe* was the Archimedean lever with which they would move the world. All of them, however, have this in common: they do more harm to their own viewpoint than good. The noble soul who identifies Judaism with philanthropy only, casts a shadow both on his faith and on his charity. The bellicose zealot who flings realism to the winds, and holds that his ideology, and that only, is the answer to the riddle of the sphinx is himself a poor and misguided exponent thereof. And the Zionist who cavalierly pretends to ignore the exile-doomed, brings his own viewpoint into disrepute.

In the final analysis, the three unitarians described above are really not complete persons. Each is some single attribute of a person, one the spirit of confined goodness, the other that of social striving, and the third that of national aspiration. Perhaps if all three individuals were compressed into one they would make a complete man.

Manifold and complex are the problems which man faces. No single rule can answer them, no hard-and-fast regulation can control them. For us, the best philosophy is the eclectic one, that way of life which meets the difficulties with solutions fitted for the occasion, and not that philosophy which measures cloth by weight, or wheat by measurements. We subscribe, indeed, wholeheartedly to the exposition of Judaism so well developed by Professor Mordecai M. Kaplan. To him Judaism is not merely a series of dietary laws, or a calendar of festival occasions, or a financial statement of a welfare agency. It is these, of course, and more; it is a complete way of life, concerning not only the exalted mood but also the pedestrian routine, providing spiritual sustenance not only for the fortunate lying at ease in Zion, but also for those in travail in *galuth*. The aspiration towards a better social order is an integral part thereof, even as is the return of the homeless to their home. Of philanthropy it conceives a higher purpose than that of providing soup-kitchens and hospitals. In its theology, philanthropy takes on its original philological meaning – love of man – not the olympian love of the mighty man throwing sustenance to the mean, but the love of man which exists as between equals, and which manifests itself in the thousand kindnesses to which human relationship gives scope. That philanthropy, too, is a kind of unitarianism – it considers all of Judaism a unit, and does not emphasize a part at the expense of the whole. It is a complete view, not a narrow perspective. It is a world of ideas, and not of the *idée fixe*. It is unity in universalism, and not in exclusion.

Advertising Declares War   4 September 1942

The art of advertising, we have been told, consists in making everybody buy what nobody wants. The malice prepense behind this dictum appears to assume that it is the function of advertising not so much to direct the reader to the destination where his wants may be best satisfied, as much as to create in him a want for something he might not desire without the copy-writer's verbiage.

Although there is much truth in this statement, it is much less than a half-truth. The fact is that there is no barometer which so clearly reflects the mentality of the public as the advertising slogans which are aimed at it from day to day. You may tear up, or delete, all the reports and news items to be found in our daily or weekly journals; if you but leave the ads intact, the historian of the future will therefrom alone be able to conjure up an accurate picture of the customs and mores of our day.

For the copy-writer has a more impelling motive to gauge that public's interests and predilections than the mere editorialist or reporter. The reporter is merely doing a job; he tells a story, and he is done. The editor inditing his piece of wisdom, is aiming no doubt, at his meed of immortality. If he gets it, well; if not, he'll try again. But the copy-writer is driven by the most impelling necessity of our American life – he must sell! Immortality and human interest are all very well, in their place; but no sales force earns its salary with these commodities.

As a natural consequence, it is this worthy – the magician whose incantations are ads – who is the true medicine-man of our age. He it is who ever keeps his finger on the public pulse; he it is who holds it with his glittering eye. He lets nothing by which can help him in this project; all is grist that comes to his mill.

Is there some important sporting event which has captured the public imagination? You can count on it; it will soon crop up, with pictures, in some ad. Is there a movie idol who is the talk of the country? You may give odds that ere long that idol will be persuaded, with one persuasion or more, to endorse a commodity seeking the public favor. Is there a statesman who has uttered some colloquialism which has entered the popular parlance? It is ore for the copy-writer; in a week he will dish it up as the punchline of an ad, advancing the interests of some very pedestrian article.

Now all of this is very well in its time and in its place. Everything is fair in love, war, and advertising. The end – the noble end – to wit, increased sales – sanctifies the means. Accordingly, if the commodity requires that its literary puff contain some 'snob' appeal, snob appeal it will have – the ad will announce to all and sundry that this particular article is being used by those who count. The implication, of course, is clear – if you want to count, buy. If you don't, you don't count. Others again, work on the reader's fear. Four out of five have it, the ingenious copy-writer announces. If you want to make sure that you're not one of the eighty per cent, use such-and-such. The hardiest reader, the most resistant purchaser, we are informed, succumbs before these tattle-tale menaces, these pink-brush phobias.

There is no fear, no vanity, which the copy-writer will hesitate to use. All of human psychology is his instrument; and he plays upon it, as it were a fiddle. We do not complain; frankly we find ads as entertaining as essays. We do not intend to buy; we do not buy; but we read. It is a glorious game of barren window-shopping that we play with our newspaper. And the windows are well-dressed. It is no wonder that some of our most distinguished starving poets have at last found their daily bread in the large advertising agencies.

But there was one angle of mass-appeal that we hoped would be immune to the copy-writer's ravages. Alas, we were doomed to disappointment. These fiddlers fiddle even while Rome burns. It is to the shame of the advertising art – or artifice – that it has in recent months launched upon the world a veritable plethora of ads, all hailing their products, lauding their merchandise – not because they wish to sell them forsooth, perish the base thought! but because they wish – believe it or not! – to advance the war effort. Now, if ever the supreme in cant, the apex of hypocrisy, was achieved, it is in this wise achieved.

We take an issue of a contemporary magazine at random. Into its ads have gone the best talent, both in the literary and graphic arts. What do we find? We find that all of the advertisers, for one reason or another, have wrapped themselves in the flag. One would imagine that until war broke out they were completely indifferent to selling their merchandise. It is only the fight for freedom – if you would believe them – that spurns them on in their attempts to persuade you to buy.

Here, for example, is a shoe-manufacturer. He looks for a war-angle in which to perch his shoes. At last, he has it! In essential industry, he announces in capital letters, shoes are essential! Apparently before Pearl Harbor, everybody went barefoot. Another advertising genius, aware of the fact that the public is war-conscious, heads his ad with the ominous words, in bold black letters: Secret Service. You would imagine that here you were going to be made privy to some hair-raising revelations. You read. The secret service is a confidential matrimonial agency!

The food advertisers, too, are not totally unconscious of the existence of a state of hostilities. Checking with the rations given in the Army, those purveyors of edibles have included in their self-laudations the announcement that the army marches on their food. What did they expect, that the military authorities would boycott civilian vitamins?

Did you know that tobacco increases the war-effort? So it is, indeed; tobacco, says the ingenious copy-writer, steadies nerves. In war and in industry steady nerves are an asset. Ergo, tobacco is our secret weapon! The same type of logic is exemplified also in the boasts of the paper-trade ... 'It takes more than a whistle to start production,' announces a paper-manufacturer; and he illustrates his thought by showing a picture of assorted papers, made into plots, reports, plans, etc. Nothing fazes the copy-writer; he'll make a case even for red-tape.

We wondered, when we first noticed this advertising phenomenon, how the advertising men would meet the challenge of soap. Soap, as is well known, contains in quantity elements used in war-production. It was reasonable to expect therefore, that with the war-effort in mind, the consumption of soap should be decreased. Not such, however, is the opinion of the paid agents of soap. On the contrary. Frequent rinsing in soap preserves clothes, and conserves material. The use of more soap is an act of economy. One inspired bard of advertising even found a romantic angle to his blurbs. Women are being employed more and more in war-industry. They still, however, wish to remain feminine. After the grime and the oil of ammunition labor, do working wives still wish to keep their hands enchanting? Use so-and-so's Soap!

The Hon. Mr. Ilsley has addressed the nation on several occasions urging the virtue of thrift. A naive listener would have taken him to mean that a good citizen is to spend less. Not, however, according to the commentary of the advertising megaphone of a certain department store. According to him, he who would practise economy should buy more and more at his client's emporium. It is cheaper. Therefore, a purchase at that particular establishment is a blow struck for freedom!

The number of examples could be multiplied *ad infinitum* and *ad nauseam*. One has but to turn the pages of any periodical, note the soldiers, sailors, and airmen, featured in the most outlandish places and attitudes, to realize how the copy-writer has taken over the function of the High Command. It is, to put it mildly, shocking. We recall the time when Captain Britton made the V for victory symbol famous. There ensued a veritable scramble, on the part of the grocers, the bakers, and candle-stick makers, to usurp this symbol for their mercenary purposes. The abuse threatened to assume such proportions that the law intervened, and forbade the use of this symbol for trade objectives. That law, we suggest, should be widened to include also other aspects of the fight for the four freedoms. We are not battling to provide merchants with catchy slogans. Their own consciences, their own sense of proportion should have bid them stop on approaching this sacred territory. It hasn't. Legislation, therefore, should teach the copy-writer that the historic struggle is not just another sporting event, and its participants not movie-stars. Some things there are that are sacred.

The Canadian Jewish Daily Eagle – Thirty-Five Years of Creative Journalism
11 September 1942

Thirty-five years ago – on August 30, 1907, to be precise and historical – there was founded in the city of Montreal, the first Yiddish newspaper in the Dominion, our distinguished contemporary, *The Jewish Daily Eagle*. Of its original founders, all, with the exception of one, saw their journalistic ardor quenched by the vicissitudes of newspaper pioneering. One lasted a fortnight as a tycoon of the Fourth Estate; after that his five hundred dollars gave out. Another discovered that he was not by temperament suited to the struggle involved in bringing a journal to birth. Still another discovered, in those early trying weeks, that despite the governmental tax upon all imported journals, the couch of the local infant industry was not, therefore, a bed of roses. Only that hardy communal worker, that born fighter of the two secret weapons – humor and stick-to-itiveness – Mr. H. Wolofsky, survived those parturitional ordeals, controlling and directing the *Eagle* from the day when it first tried its pinions through all the thirty-five years of its flight. To him, and to this all-inclusive institution, our sincerest felicitations!

It is impossible, indeed, to over-estimate the role which this paper has played, during its third of a century of existence, in moulding and reflecting the character of the Jewish community in Canada. It will be recalled that the first decade of this century was characterized by an extraordinary flow of Jewish immigration, impelled by the outrageous pogroms which were making the Czarist regime a stench in the nostrils of mankind, and facilitated by the liberal policies initiated by the late Sir Wilfrid Laurier. Seeking freedom and a livelihood, the immigrants of that day came in such numbers that they soon found themselves to be a community. They did indeed find that freedom they sought; they gained, not without struggle, the livelihood they required. Still there was felt the lack of a communal life, a congregational solidarity, an organ which should express their concepts of citizenship, their religious and racial individuality. The frequent meetings and gossip-sessions which took place in Chenneville Park – Peanut Park as it was so descriptively called – were a poor substitute. Even the opportunities afforded by the sabbath and festival meetings in the double-parlor synagogues were perhaps, a satisfaction to the Lord, but not to His servants. The Sunday morning assemblies at union-headquarters, too, were as yet a thing of the future, and would be facilitated only after this first want was fulfilled – a Jewish newspaper.

Of the trials and tribulations of that creative effort, it is not for us to speak here. Are they not written in the chronicles of its publisher, and in the memoirs of its compositors? (*The Eagle* always employed literary compositors, who, alas, too frequently sought to edit their editors!) Suffice it to say that at long last – scheduled for the 7th, it appeared on the 30th – *The Eagle* mounted from its nest at 508 St. Lawrence Boulevard. By way of symbol of victory, there was placed in the window of the printing plant, the linotype machine which had done it – the first Jewish linotype in Canada.

Already in the first issue – written in the quaint Germanized Yiddish of that day – there was set forth a program and a policy which has been steadfastly observed throughout the years. Jewish citizenship, philanthropy, Jewish education, and the communal scene in all its ramifications – these were the declared concerns of the editors of the *Eagle*. It is no exaggeration to say that several generations of Jewish readers have been brought up and nurtured by the ideology of this paper. No other single institution has left its mark upon Jewish communal life as indelibly as this journal which directed its thought and expressed its hope for three and a half decades.

It is, indeed, a splendid galaxy – the cultural mentors for whom the *Eagle* was both a platform and a pulpit. To identify the individuals associated with its editorial and literary columns, is to conjure up a host of names the recollection of whom still echoes in the hearts of its readers: Mr. H. Hirsch, Wortsman, Michael Aronson, Dr. A.A. Roback, the late Reuben Brainin, Moishe Leib Halperin, Konrad Bercovici, etc. Presently with the journal, are such distinguished journalists as Mr. I. Rabinovitch, master of the genial columnist style, and noted musical and dramatic critic; B.G. Sack, distinguished historian of Canadian Jewry, associated with the journal from its very first day; I. Medres, feuilletonist and labour authority; M. Ginsberg, communal commentator; L. Cheifetz, news editor; the distinguished poet, I.I. Segal; N. Gottlieb, essayist and novelist; Dr. Stilman, medical columnist; and Melech Ravitch, internationally known author. Over all, guiding and planning, here winning a point with a pertinent anecdote, there adorning a tale with some apt Talmudic quotation – the publisher, to whom a good editorial is even as gratifying as a fine profit-and-loss statement.

It is, however, not the authors it encouraged, or the new literary styles it may have introduced, that have won for this journal the place it occupies in Canadian Jewish history. It is rather because of its participation in every worthwhile local and Dominion-wide Jewish movement that the *Eagle* assumes its importance, not merely as a journal but also as an active communal force in itself. Certainly the future historian who will seek to describe the development of Jewish life in Montreal during the last thirty-five years will find no better source-material than the old bound copies of our contemporary. But he will find also more than that. In addition to reportage, he will find that the *Canadian Jewish Eagle* has itself been one of the prime movers in Jewish communal endeavor. Well may it take for its own the words of Ulysses: Cities and men and deeds have I beheld; and I have been a part of them!

In the development of philanthropic organizations, it was the *Jewish Daily Eagle* which played an important and constructive role. The dissatisfaction with the status quo which existed prior to the organization of the Federation of Jewish Philanthropies finds expression, time and again, in its columns. Indeed, without the *Eagle*, the organizations of that day would have existed in a vacuum. True to its original program, it also initiated and advanced every aspect of Jewish national life. Already in the very first issue, we discover an editorial on the Jewish National Fund. It is an interest and a loyalty which it has preserved throughout the years. There is no issue of Zionist policy which has agitated the public mind which has not been debated in its pages. When the Zionist ideal had no official organ, the *Eagle* served that purpose.

Nor has this journal concerned itself only with the national issues. The interests of the masses, its most faithful and constant readers, have ever been its interests. It is true that when the *Eagle* was first founded there was one spirited soul, here remaining anonymous, who hoped, in one fashion or another, to make it a Socialist paper. He did not succeed; because the *Eagle* had no intention of dedicating itself to a single party ideology. Its policy was the inclusive one: *Nihil Judaicum me alienum puto.* But workers' interests lost nothing because of this non-affiliation. As is well-known, great numbers of the early immigrants fluctuated to the needle-trades. Indeed, it was Jews, both as employer and employee, who established this industry. During the early years, however, during the era of the sweat-shop, labor conditions in these factories were deplorable beyond description. Here, therefore, the *Eagle*, had an important function to fulfil. The hard-won rights of Montreal Jewish labor would have been impossible without the co-operation of the *Eagle*. As one thumbs through old editions, one is struck by the fact, time and again, that in every important strike which marked the progress of the labor movement, the *Eagle* acted as mouthpiece of the workers. It made itself bitter enemies in the persons of the recalcitrant manufacturers; but it was a people's voice, saw the right, and fought the battle – until it was won.

In the religious community, too, the *Eagle* fulfilled its role. The organization of the Vaad Ho'ir, and the introduction of organized *Kashruth*, with its by-product of educational stipends, is a direct result of the initiative of the *Eagle* and its publisher. That there was opposition on the part of vested interests against these reforms, can readily be verified by reference to the history of those days; the *Eagle*, however, pursued its way, until its purpose was achieved.

The Jewish community is justly proud of the positions which it has won for itself on the political field. But these positions were not won with a magic fiat, or a set of prayers. A Jewish public opinion had to be organized, the political issues had to be explained, the sense of citizenship further developed; and here the *Eagle*, from election to election, stood ever on guard. One still recalls the valiant battle it fought in the Jewish School question, a battle in which it well may have emerged a victor, were it not for the constitutional interpretations of the Privy Council. In retrospect to-day, however, that battle assumes importance for the splendid expression of Jewish educational and national principles which found its expression in the pages of this journal.

Nor have the *Eagle's* flights been confined merely to the local and Canadian. In the field of world-wide Jewish culture, the *Eagle* has to its credit the publication of the first American edition of the Talmud – a feat which put its press in the same classic category as that of Rom and Soncino. When it is recalled that the pagination of the Talmud follows set rules, and cannot be deviated from without bringing chaos and confusion into the entire realm of Talmudic commentary, one may get an inkling of the nature of this achievement.

Mainly a first-generation community, Montreal Jewry had flesh-and-blood ties with many parts of Eastern and Central Europe. The *landsmanshaften*, the old-town brotherhoods which flourished everywhere, and which have persisted to this day, always knew the *Eagle* to be their house-organ. When the post-war pogroms stirred the whole world with their atrocity, it was the *Eagle* which clamoured for a movement on behalf of the refugees and the orphaned. The *Eagle* has never, as certain Parisian papers, adopted as its slogan the omniscient *Je suis tout* – but it can, without exaggeration arrogate to itself: *Je suis partout!*

Thirty-five years of this endeavor have passed. The *Eagle* and its publisher still guard the old truth, the ancient principles. They have been thirty-five – almost twice *chai* – anniversaries of fruitful and constructive endeavor, redounding to the benefit of the community, which gave it birth, served, and was served by it. They have demonstrated the power of the written word as an influence for good; and they have illustrated the truth that no community is complete unless it have an organ where its joys and sorrows can come to utterance. It is no mean record. It is Canadian history; it is Jewish history; and long may it continue!

An American Tragedy   25 September 1942

A peculiar nemesis seems to pursue certain of the practitioners of the literary art. Launching upon the world their figments of imagination, they walk arrogantly in their creativeness, until a retributive irony turns them themselves into the prototypes of their writing. Thus, Mr. P.G. Wodehouse, who brought to life that supreme example of a gentleman's gentleman is to-day himself a butler, a valet, a Mr. Jeeves to his German captors. And thus Mr. Theodore Dreiser, who several years ago wrote a powerful novel about 'An American Tragedy,' decided that he himself should perform a tragic role.

Toronto was the scene of his disgrace. Invited to address a meeting at the Eaton Auditorium, Mr. Dreiser could not contain himself. He must perforce give out his overbrimming wisdom in an interview to the press, in which he regaled his auditors with some of the delicious tidbits which he intended later to elaborate in banquet measure. The tidbits were enough. They revealed such anti-British poison, such typical fifth-column ideology, that all Canada was shocked at their colossal gall, their abysmal bad taste. Enjoying the invitation of hospitality and the presumable immunity of a stranger, Mr. Theodore Dreiser clearly intended to avail himself of his opportunity to preach treason and disaffection.

He came to Toronto as a friend, of course. If he declared himself an enemy, he would never have been invited. Under the guise of friendship therefore, it was that Dreiser came to sow his insidious poison 'on behalf of Allied Victory.' Arriving upon British soil, the great literary genius found it meet and fitting to begin with a well-directed insult at his hosts. He spoke of 'unbelievable gall and brass of the English who have done nothing in this war except borrow money, planes and men from the United States.' Note, it is Dreiser who speaks of unbelievable gall! We do not intend to enumerate the sacrifices which Britain has made for the common cause; to do that would be to descend to this marrano-nazi's level. It is sufficient to point out at this junction that the task which Herr Dreiser took is precisely the one prescribed by Doctor Goebbels for just such an occasion; and the words themselves a direct quotation of Berlin rhetoric.

Lest there be any doubt as to where Mr. Dreiser stands, Theodore dissipated it himself. 'I admire Colonel Lindbergh and follow right along with his ideals.' Confusion becomes worse confounded. One might have imagined at first that Dreiser's peeve at the British was caused by a pro-Soviet impatience with the delay in opening a second front. This declaration of allegiance to Lindbergh shows that all is grist to his treason-manufacturing mill; and that if need be, he will pose either as a friend of the Russian people, or as a friend of the enemy of the Russians, or as both.

Returning to the pro-Soviet angle, Mr. Dreiser undertook to make a declaration also for Mr. Churchill. 'He has no intention of opening a second front. He's afraid the Communists will rule the world, so he does nothing except send thousands of Canadians to be slaughtered at Dieppe. He didn't send any English as far as I know.'

It is fortunate for Mr. Dreiser, né Dresser, that he escaped from his hotel room in time. The above-cited remarks are not the innocent ravings of a misled man. They are the malicious German-inspired technique of the fifth-columnist, highly placed, – the playing off of one against the other, the breeding of dissension, the German wedge-strategy applied to psychological warfare.

Several years ago Mr. Dreiser indicated in no uncertain terms what he thought about the Jewish people. Readers then thought that this outburst of anti-semitism was one of those *enfant terrible* aberrations which one is inclined to tolerate in geniuses. Subsequent events put no such easy interpretation upon Mr. Dreiser's ideology. His is not the anti-semitism of Voltaire, but of Goebbels. It follows the pattern of Berlin. It is one with his utterances in

Toronto. It is of a piece with his discipleship of Lindbergh. Should we fail, we now know who would be our gauleiters, and who our intellectual leaders.

For the remarks of Mr. Dreiser can be interpreted only one way. They were anti-British obviously; but they were also anti-American. And despite their phraseology, despite Dreiser's protestations, they were not pro-Soviet. That was merely a front, a peg to hang his cloak on. They were however, definitely pro-German.

The Jew behind the Times   20 November 1942

Mr. Arthur Hays Sulzberger is, in one more than one sense, the Jew behind the *Times*. He is, in the first instance, the publisher of that powerful organ which releases only the news that's fit to print; and he is, in the second instance, a Hebraic Canute seeking with a gesture and a speech to halt the march of Jewish national resurgence. Despite careful perusal of his own journal he has not, apparently, yet realized that the aspirations of the Jewish people for a homeland of their own are so deep-rooted in his co-religionists' psychology, and so essential because of the sorry plight in which millions of his brethren find themselves, that no speech of his can alter a reaction which is brought about by forces greater even than those of a forceful newspaper publisher.

For many years the *New York Times* has been sedulously anti-Zionist. The achievements of the Yishuv have been deemed as of those subjects not fit to print. The owner of this journal, indeed, has always prided himself as being an American, pure and simple, first and foremost; and his Judaism, save in a quasi-ritual fashion, did not even take second place. It is true that the Antisemitic press, in maligning the *Times*, frequently reversed its name to read *Semit*; but this was always an indictment which was as malicious as it was unjust. Throughout this period of *obiter dictum* anti-Zionism, of understatement anti-nationalism, the publisher of the *Times* maintained a discreet silence, preferring rather to permit his editorial servants to do, behind the anonymity of their articles and the pseudo-impartiality of their manner, the work which he felt it not necessary to do for himself.

During the years of the war, it must be admitted, the *New York Times* has done an excellent job for the improvement of British-American relations. To no other u.s. newspaper is Britain as indebted as it is to the *Times*. Here was its most perfect, most articulate friend at court. The *New York Times*, indeed, had become even more pro-British than the London one.

Returning from a trip to England where no doubt due tribute was paid to him for his efforts on behalf of the cause, Mr. Sulzberger, it appears, has begun to feel that he has the rights of a minister without portfolio in the British Cabinet, and has undertaken to give gratuitous advice as to the manner in which Britain should conduct itself in relation to his co-religionists.

To deliver himself of his nation-making and nation-breaking opinions Mr. Sulzberger could choose no better forum than the pulpit of Rabbi Morris Lazaron, from of yore an eloquent enemy of Zion. The report of Mr. Sulzberger's speech shows that his address was very carefully prepared, so that its anti-Zionism should obtain the flavor of a delectable cosmopolitanism, and so that Sulzberger should appear to be an idealist not content with the narrow confines of Eretz Israel, but seeking rather the scope of the entire world.

Said Mr. Sulzberger: 'What Jews want far more than a home of their own is the right to call any place home.' Who can deny this? But the remark is completely irrelevant, and moreover carries implications that are as false as they are wicked. Do the Zionists advocate, in their zeal for a Homeland, that all Jews in the Diaspora abandon their natural civil rights as citizens? Does the Englishman to whom his home is his castle, and his homeland the finest piece of earth, for that reason entertain the notion that if one of his kin adopts American citizenship, he is to be treated as a second-class citizen? The incontrovertible truth is that Englishmen abroad enjoy the rights which they do only because they have a home which they can call their own.

Said Mr. Sulzberger: 'In finding a new home, justice must be done those who already dwell where the newcomer would live.' Jewry finds in Eretz Israel not a new home, but an old one. To insist on justice being done to those who already dwell there is to imply that such justice is not presently being done. Mr. Sulzberger can discover from reading any and all other journals save his own that such is not the case. Since the advent of Jewish settlement in Palestine, the lot of the local inhabitants has been indescribably improved. An appeal for justice on the part of Mr. Sulzberger is tantamount to putting the *Times* into the service of the most reactionary elements of Palestine, the pro-Nazi henchmen of the Mufti.

Continues Mr. Sulzberger: 'I would not have you think that I am unaware of the need for refuge for many peoples, including the Jews, after this war is over.' (Mr. Sulzberger is very observant.) 'I know too that many Jews will seek the Holy Land. But let us keep it a Holy Land. Let us make sure that we do not transfer it merely into another nation, jealous of its own national rights.'

Mr. Sulzberger perorates with his own plan for a Jewish homeland. He is not content with leaving the position of Jews in such a Homeland to chance, or to natural development. He wants to make sure. He wants to make sure that they will remain in a minority. Says Sulzberger: 'It would seem to me that this could be done if, when the time comes, there is created a great state out of several countries in that section of the world. I would make it sufficiently large so that the Arabs would welcome its might and never have cause to fear that the Jews who move there would upset the numerical balance of power.'

It is difficult to find words to describe this plan of a *numerus clausus* for Palestine, devised by a Jew comfortably located in New York. One also finds the term 'numerical balance of power' a concept somewhat outmoded in the contemporary world, and certainly strange in the mouth of one whose paper is continually preaching the idealism of the Atlantic Charter.

'And into the enlarged state I would welcome all who wish to come' (but Jews, apparently, only in a certain proportion) 'and the Arabs would join in such a welcome secure in the knowledge that they would not be outnumbered. Such a plan would provide the refuge we all seek to establish. I would, however, deny Jewish statehood; but in a world already plagued by too many nations, is that not right?'

It most certainly is not. It's not the little nations which have been plaguing the world, but the big ones. The little ones are content if they are but left alone. We wonder, too, why the *Times* is so eloquent on behalf of the Czechs, the Yugoslavs, the Norwegians, the Greeks, little nations all, and not on behalf of his own little nation. We wonder, too, what Greeks would think of a fellow-Greek, or Norwegians about a fellow-Norwegian, who wrote about their national aspirations as Mr. Sulzberger writes about the national aspirations of his people?

It is, indeed, so easy for Mr. Sulzberger to be altruistic about his people's aspirations. It costs him nothing. He is so nicely ensconced in his position, that Palestine seems to him to be but the fad of a bunch of ghetto-Jews. But Mr. Sulzberger − the ghetto-Jews are many, and the Sulzbergers are few. In the concentration camps of occupied Europe, in the ghettos of Lublin and of Warsaw, it is the hope of Zion, and not the word of Sulzberger, which brings strength and endurance in the hour of suffering. To them a passport to Eretz Israel is conceived of, not in terms of narrow nationalism, not in terms of anti-Arab feeling, but as simple unadulterated national and personal salvation. After all, into America and its Johnson acts, they cannot come, despite the preachings of the *Times*. The Americans, we suppose, have a right to adopt the Sinn Fein policy − the land of the free for ourselves alone. But to Palestine, we come as of right, and not by tolerance or quota. These are facts which cannot be altered, by the arguments even of one who describes himself, as Sulzberger does, as an American, albeit of the Jewish faith.

The New Order: Murder
and Ransom
27 November 1942

The defeats to which German arms have been of late subjected, both in Russia and in Africa, have not served to bring to the Reich that feeling of contrition which comes from the sense of imminent doom. Perhaps it is too early to expect that these sentiments will have any currency among the hardened criminals and arrogant slaves who constitute the *herrenvolk*. Instead there is everywhere apparent, desperation and fear. But it is a desperation as yet unaccompanied by remorse.

On the contrary; the bandits of the Reich, in fear lest the measure of their wickedness may not be completed before the way of reckoning arrives, rush with barbaric haste to perpetrate the atrocities as yet unfulfilled. The case of the Jews in the occupied lands is one in point. Hitherto, as the Prussian generals laid low one country after another, the butchers of the Reich proceeded towards the extermination of the thousands of Jews who fell into their grasp, in a leisurely and unhurried fashion. They had all the time in the world to 'liquidate' the Jewish problem, and the more time it took, the more fun it would be. It would be a sheer waste of opportunity to kill off all the Jews at one fell swoop; sadism preferred the lingering tortures, the protracted agonies. Besides, the control over large populations of Jewry, preserved for yet a while from murder, had its uses. It showed the world that the Nazis were not entirely savage; and it furnished a steady supply of hostages.

With the recent turn in events, however, feelings of misgiving have arisen in the bosoms of the supermen. Only a month ago Hitler spoke of not doing what the Kaiser did; but he thought of the Kaiser's end sufficiently to refer to it, albeit by way of contrast. Accordingly, Herr Himmler has come to the conclusion that he and his abattoir-members can no longer afford the luxury of merely toying with murder on off-days. Life is short, and art is long. Let us pluck Moses while we may. To-morrow may be a moral day.

The order has therefore been issued that to German *schrecklichkeit* there will now be added German mathematical precision. Half the Jews of occupied Poland are to be killed within the year. Already the policy of murder has begun on a systematic basis. From time to time, the executioners of the Reich appear in the Polish ghettos, snatch men from their homes, take them to the marketplaces and make them the victims of wholesale slaughter. Others are packed into cattle-cars, sent to unknown destinations, where, those who are still alive after the foodless, airless travel, are taken out and shot. Callous, mathematical extermination of Jewry is the avowed and practical policy of the Reich. With the change in the fortunes of war the tempo has increased. One hesitates to imagine what the tempo will be in the weeks before the inevitable debacle.

Yet another sign of desperation, of the same quality, but in a different sense, is the Reich-sponsored policy of extortion and ransom which has lately assumed great proportions. Hard-pressed for foreign exchange, Hitler is willing to sell even his human victims for the precious commodity. Of late there has been a considerable traffic in the occupied countries where potential refugees obtain sums of money from relatives abroad to pay their captors for permission to leave the country. At first it was thought that this was the usual process of bribing underlings to render favors which were illegal; it has since been discovered that this traffic in human souls is being conducted with the approval and under the inspiration of Nazi authorities. Cash is needed; to a state which has millions of prisoners, it is nothing to spare some wealthy ones so that funds may be obtained to perpetuate the captivity of those remaining.

There have been wars before. They have not been beautiful things. They have been cruel; they have brought in their wake much suffering, great human agony. But in these wars, murder of civilians and of prisoners, and traffic in civilian prisoners have been – at least since the abolition of slavery – the aberrations of war, and not its normal conduct. It was left to the Aryan *herrenvolk* graduating from the Black Forest to introduce into contemporary warfare the methods and the morals of primitive man, and to worsen them with scientific improvement and twentieth century organization.

Drapeau Holds an Inquest   11 December 1942

We were surprised, as we turned on our radio last Sunday evening, to hear the voice of Jean Drapeau, 'the candidate of the conscripts,' holding forth in a post-mortem dissertation upon the results of the election in Outremont. At first our surprise was confined to a single motivation; we found it strange that a defeated candidate, who barely saved his deposit, should carry his humiliation beyond the frontiers of his constituency, and subject himself to a process of verbal self-flagellation by analyzing the statistics of his defeat. We felt, however, that if an aspirant to political office, repudiated by his electors, did entertain such a passion for publicizing the circumstances of his downfall, it was his right, and he could, particularly since the League for the Defence of Canada paid for the time, make his confidences to the air-waves to his heart's content.

But as Mr. Drapeau – how fortunate for this hero whose very name is a flag! – continued the inquest upon his own deceased electoral body, it became quite apparent that the gentleman was not so interested in revealing political statistics as in continuing the racial propaganda which disgraced his campaign. We listened with amazement, wondering all the time at the standards which the censors had applied in permitting this obvious piece of demagogy. Mr. Drapeau began his address by informing his listeners that he and his henchmen were being martyred for their opinions; why, one campaign organizer of his had just received his first letter (for military service) and he had received his second. He did not make clear why he or his associates should enjoy any particular exemption or immunity; but left his listeners with the impression that he was being called up, as a piece of personal revenge. After this charming premise, he launched into the *pièce de résistance* of his thesis; to wit, that all of his votes were French-Canadian, and all of Major-General LaFleche's were the result of 'an Anglo-Jewish bloc.' From then on he made the usual racist deduction; he even went so far as to insert into his talk a veiled threat that the time would come when the French-Canadians would remember the manner in which 'the Anglo-Jewish bloc' interpreted the Atlantic Charter. What particular relationship there was between the Atlantic Charter and the constituency of Outremont was not made clear; one was left only to assume that if all the electors of Outremont had voted for Drapeau and his parochial isolationism, that would have been a vindication of the Atlantic Charter!

We do not wish to enter into any competitive analysis. But we do wish to express our astonishment at the fact that the speech was granted the liberty of the air-waves. We recall that only a week ago, an attempt was made to obtain permission to broadcast the Conservative leadership address to be delivered at the forthcoming convention in Winnipeg; and that this permission was refused for that it came under the category of controversial matter. We do not approve or disapprove that particular decision. But if that decision was well-founded, then certainly the address of Mr. Drapeau, too, should have been either prohibited, or more carefully censored. For his remarks are not to be judged as coming under the usual rule of freedom of electoral campaigning; the campaign was over, and the decision was rendered. Moreover, the content of the speech made quite clear the purpose which Mr. Drapeau had in mind: to keep the home fires of racial dissension burning, to set up creed against creed, and people against people. To have permitted such a talk on the air-waves was to have been guilty, to put the mildest construction upon it, of an inexplicable laxity.

The Slaughter of the Children   11 December 1942

It is almost an act of foolishness to comment upon German barbarism. Certainly one does not find the fact that the jackal feeds on carrion, or that the vulture swoops down on the dead, a fit subject of editorial expatiation. That the Nazis are beasts, and that their entire policy towards Jews and other victims is bestial, is already one of the truisms of European life. To remedy the situation, one does not lecture the beasts; one merely takes one's hunting rifle.

Yet, are there degrees in bestiality, and stages in savagery. A new depth of depravity reached by the Prussian hangmen is indicated in the recent incident at the Medem Sanatorium in Poland, one of the finest humanitarian institutions in that country. According to a report issuing from Warsaw, the Nazi butchers entered the institution and ordered all the children and their teachers into the ghetto. This was, of course, a decision which was tantamount to a death-sentence, particularly for the invalid children. Upon the refusal to obey this order, the German apaches murdered all the inmates of the Sanatorium, teachers and children alike!

One is filled with a feeling of overwhelming rage at this barbarian orgy. Yet it is futile to argue with those monsters, futile even to threaten and to warn. It must have dawned upon the Nazi murderers long ago that the only thing which will save them from the hand of vengeance will be either their triumph or their suicide. For us, there remains only to engrave these incidents upon the tablets of our memory, to put before us ever and without interruption the sacred duty of avenging these and other innocents, and to labor incessantly to wipe out this abomination from off the face of the earth.

The Politics of Gesticulation   15 January 1943

How often, indeed, is a concept more lucidly interpreted by a gesture rather than by a word! You have only to put this assertion to the test to discover how frequently individuals prefer the almost intuitive facility of a gesture to the labor and care required for definition. Ask your neighbor to define the word 'accordion' – a common enough instrument of dubious music. Your neighbor will not halt to pick and choose the exact phraseology which will convey to you the form, shape, and function of an accordion: he will simply move his hands back and forth, now slowly, now quickly, as if holding something between them, and probably for further elucidation, humming a tune in tempo with his pumping arms. Note: he has told you what an accordion is – and has avoided language.

A similar reaction will result if the word 'spiral' is used. We will give, happily and in wild amazement, our Oxford Dictionary to any one who, unwarned and uninstructed answers that spiral, in the words of the said dictionary means 'winding continually about and constantly receding from a centre, whether remaining in the same plane like a watch-spring, or rising in a cone.' We make the offer with impunity. The invariable answer on the part of the questioned will be not a reply in words, but a hand or a finger gesticulating a spiral out of and into the thin air.

And why this excursus on gestures? *Mai ka mashma lun* – as the Talmudist would say, and which translated roughly means: So what? We wish simply to apply this method of mental behavior so characteristic of the many, to the world of ideologies. Ask the same neighbor – if you have not yet exceeded the hospitality of interrogation – to define Nazism. In all likelihood he will fling his right arm upward at an angle of forty-five degrees with his shoulder, and will then – and only then – use language unutterable in the Reich; and here only unprintable. In Nazi Germany, the upflung arm is the total explanation of totalitarianism. It is so simple; it eliminates lengthy disquisition and complicated soul-probing. One merely flings one's arm skyward, and one is a philosopher!

It is ironical that it should be the antisemitic parties which have given themselves over to gesticulation as a form of political thought; it was always the favorite technique of the antisemite to deride Jewry by cartooning it as a nation of gesture-throwers. Now the whole philosophy of Adolf Hitler, if such it can be termed, is summarized in the single gesture and expostulation: Heil Hitler! Mussolini, too, has reduced a nation of born gesticulators to but one single bodily movement – the Fascist arm outstretched and perfunctory wrist-flap.

We animadvert to these facts at a time when the subject is further emphasized by the new calisthenics of the Mexican Fascists. They, it appears, have developed a new salute, a novel gesture: It consists of a movement of the right arm upward until level with chest, and then the forearm instead of being extended is deflected backward so that the fingertips point backward over the left shoulder. It makes a fine geometric design, and is no doubt very effective in building the biceps, if not the brains.

It is to be noted that the democratic philosophy has not yet been simplified into a definite manual exercise. For it is a philosophy, not of a static and authoritarian nature, but of a dynamic and ever-evolving progressivism. It will not be confined within a single movement, for it is at once the warmth of the handshake, the embrace of brotherhood, the palm of benediction, and even the jerked-back thumb of the comradeship of the road.

Willkie on Idolatry   22 January 1943

We are most happy to move a sincere vote of thanks to Mr. Wendell Willkie for thoughts recently uttered, and laudable for both lucidity and timeliness. We have long felt that the statement should have been made, and no one could have made it with greater verve and less objectionableness than Wendell Willkie whose motive in this instance could not be suspect.

The courageous and incontrovertible dictum of Willkie is worth quoting verbatim. Deploring what he called ' a trend toward what is called leadership – but what is really nothing more than the idolization of individual men,' Mr. Willkie said: 'In Russia there is Joseph Stalin, in China Generalissimo Chiang

Kai-shek, in Britain Winston Churchill, in the United States Franklin D. Roosevelt. The stature of these men in every case is out of the ordinary and they deserve the high positions they have won. And yet dare we say that any of them is indispensable? The moment we say that, our world may change.'

Precisely. There is no gainsaying the steel constitution of a Stalin, the ineluctable conscience of a Roosevelt, or the dauntless courage of a Churchill; but these qualities of the men are to be considered not personal monopolies which they enjoy over and above their countrymen, but rather symbolic assets which they hold in trust for all their people. The courage of Churchill would have been mere wind and rhetoric without corroboration in action by his unsung and unnamed countrymen. The ideology of Roosevelt would be but as a voice crying in the wilderness were it not known that that voice is the echo of the heartbeat of all Americans. And even the clanging will of Stalin is but a description of the clanging resolution of Stalingrad, and not a *ding an sich*.

Of course leadership is important. But in a democracy a leader is one who gives articulation, not to his own whim, but to the people's will. In a dictatorship, it is of course the other way around. One must therefore be on continual guard lest one day we find that the leader is translated into *Der Fuehrer*, or the *Duce*, or some other version of the rugged individual man of destiny. There are no men of destiny, there are only ideas of destiny.

The Dark Decade   5 February 1943

The week-end which passed marked one of the gloomiest milestones in world history – a decade since Adolf Hitler's accession to power. To mankind at large it has been a period in which the world witnessed one of the most powerful attempts to push civilization back 'into the dark backward and abysm of time'; a period during which there rose to influence and to might a philosophy which was a complete denial of all that men had ever worshipped or cherished; a period in which a talented but demented people repudiated international morality, scorned both public and private right, oppressed religion, abolished freedom, and sanctified blood and the shedding of blood. As one looks back upon the years which preceded the great madness and on those which were informed by it, one realizes how often and with how little effort, the Nazi pest might have been curbed. Here and there a date rises, and noting it, one cannot but reflect: Here the deathblow might have been given to the Nazi bandits. Unfortunately, the attitude of *laissez-faire* was adopted, with the result that the man who was laughed at in 1933 as a clown, appeared in 1939 as almost an emperor.

If to mankind in general, this decade is a sorry decade, what tragic word, what heartbreaking phrase shall describe what it has been to Jewry? Never in our history – and our history has been marked by the atrocity of more than one tyrant, the cruelty of more than one pogrom – has so implacable and unrelenting an enemy risen against us. Here was no mere discrimination motivated by difference of religion – the Nazis were opposed to all religion save the paganism which worshipped the idol at Berchtesgaden – here was no measurable antisemitism fostered only by social and economic prejudice; here rather was a definite and unmistakable racial enmity elevated to the status of a philosophy, a bloodlust aggrandized into a destiny, murder made into a political policy. For six years before the world even seemed to realize that the Nazis were toothed and clawed, already the body of Israel was being torn and mutilated by the savage beasts. First German Jewry and then in rapid succession the Jewries of Austria, Czechoslovakia, Poland, France, and occupied Russia fell prey to the marauding denizens of the Black Forest. Nor was this policy aimed at the extermination of an entire people the result of a momentary frenzy, a passing rage, brought on by wine, or misery, or war; it was rather a coldly-calculated scheme, worked out with precision and shamelessness, reckoned to its minutest details and as totalitarian in its technique as it was in its objective. Other tyrants have sought to conquer, to penalize, to enslave; the madman of Berlin is content only with complete extermination of men, women and children. How brazen is the brow of this ruthless murderer is evidenced by the cynical notations which appear on returned letters addressed to Jews in Poland: *Died during the liquidation of the Jewish problem*. And the liquid is blood.

That the chief bandit of Europe is reaching the end of his rope is evident from many a sign of the times. One would have imagined that the tenth anniversary of his accession to power, would have been a grand occasion for Hitler to deliver one of his rhetorical outbursts, which are more orgy than speech. The great day, however, passed; and the Fuehrer was singularly silent. He couldn't find his voice; there was, apparently, a lump in his throat. The victories in Russia which he had held out to his people as *faits accomplis* had yet to happen; on the contrary, German arms had just suffered their greatest defeats at Stalingrad and Leningrad. In Africa, too, his Rommel was on the run; in Italy his ally had reached the very nadir of his morale; and at home, a nation accustomed to speedy and easy victories was beginning to realize that this was a war in which there were combatants, and not merely aggressor and victim.

That the Nazis have realized that they have lost the initiative, and that their eventual defeat is merely a question of time and of mode, was apparent from the addresses which were delivered, delivered at the same hour as British bombs. Pitiably, Herr Goering directed his entire verbal attack against Bolshevism, with not a word to say against Britain or the United States or even the Jews. His was apparently a hope to lead the United Nations to believe that he had no quarrel with them, or at least to make Stalin believe that the United Nations were open for a proposition. Of course, the Casablanca declaration took the powder out of that explosive. Dr. Goebbels, too, made a speech which was defeatist to the n'th degree; comparisons between 1918 and 1943, made by a German orator, hardly contribute to the creation of a mood of triumph.

The United Nations, of course, have yet to achieve the inevitable victory. But the end of the road is nearer. It is in this spirit, indeed, that people are beginning to think more and more of the nature and character of the peace that is to follow the defeat of the Axis. That the task of reconstruction, both physical and moral, will be one which challenges the abilities and the goodwill of the people of the world, goes without saying. That the task of Jewish reconstruction will be one of gigantic proportions cannot be gainsaid.

Certainly it will take much effort and sacrifice and humanity to undo, wherever that is possible, the evil which the Nazis have been doing for ten years. Much of that evil can be undone only by the miracle of resurrection. But even those who survive the pogroms, cold and hot, of the Nazi regime, will present a problem of appalling proportions. Uprooted, debilitated, broken physically and spiritually, European Jewry will constitute a population of invalids. How to bring back life, and security, and dignity, to those broken shreds of humanity is a matter to which all Jews, placed in happier position, must give thought.

That Jews are already giving thought to the morrow is evident from the proceedings which took place at a conference of the Canadian Jewish Congress and the United Jewish Refugee & War Relief Agencies which took place this week-end in Montreal, and which was addressed by Dr. Leon Kubowitski, leader of Belgian Jewry. The picture he painted of the plight of European Jewry was such as to harrow up the soul. Yet he dealt not with emotionalism, but with statistical fact. It was at this conference, too, that Mr. Samuel Bronfman, President of the Canadian Jewish Congress, reporting on the achievements of Canadian Jewry towards the war effort, directed his listeners' attention to the post-war problems, not only of individual Jews, but of Jewry itself. Advocating a wholesale solution, and not merely the palliatives motivated by temporary pity and passing compassion, Mr. Bronfman postulated, as a premise to Jewish reconstruction, not merely the rebuilding of Jewish lives, but the reconstruction, on a permanent basis, of Jewish national dignity.

There is no doubt but that the misery of Jewry during the past decade will be an empty sacrifice, a vain oblation, if out of all this tragedy there does not emerge a world-formula which will assure to the Jewish people the minimal national rights which inalienably belong to all nations and peoples on the globe. The guaranteeing of minority rights, whatever form it may take, will achieve a great deal towards eliminating hitherto rampant injustice; but this will, at best, be but a negative achievement. Positive solutions can come only from positive attitudes. The aspiration towards a Homeland is such an aspiration. Then, and then only, can we expect the dark decade to be followed by the centuries of light.

Will the World Accept the Challenge?   5 March 1943

Once again there came to articulate expression, at Madison Square Garden, the great challenge which history has flung at our civilization. Will the world stand by – even a world at war – while an entire people, helpless and unarmed, is systematically and ruthlessly exterminated? Will those nations who form part of the compact of anti-Nazi warfare, look on as the enemy dooms to wholesale destruction an ancient and innocent race, and content themselves with saying: *Our hands have not shed this blood?* Will they postpone the rescue of those who can now be saved until such time as all can be saved? Or will they extend, even under arduous circumstances, the hand of help and hospitality to those who may still find their way out of the Hitler gehenna?

Thus far, we regret to say, this challenge has been answered, if at all, in an almost inaudible whisper. In many places there has arisen a clamor from exponents of the best standards of contemporary civilization that some pressure be brought to bear, either by exchange, or negotiation, to induce the Pharaoh 'to let the people go.' From many hell-holes of Europe they have, by some miracle, achieved the miraculous boon of exit; but they are thwarted by the tragic absence of a place of ingress, an asylum, a city of refuge.

Time was when the word of the Lord came out of Zion; this week the conscience of humanity spoke from Madison Square Garden. In a demonstration which reflected the most liberal sentiments of the most liberal representatives of the United Nations, a strong appeal – whether it was irresistible remains to be seen – was made to the world to do something about this shameful phenomenon which disgraced our century. Sir Norman Angell, who spoke with that spirit of humanity which has characterized his whole career urged the United Nations 'to give evidence of their sincerity by making it plain that those who can be rescued now will find sanctuary among us; that we will not erect barriers of red tape; that we will not pass the buck to the other.' His language of the negatives to be avoided in the future constitutes an accurate description of the conditions which prevail in the present. Mr. Wendell Willkie sent a message in which he declared that 'not to take every possible measure consistent with our war effort to give sanctuary wherever possible to the Jews ... is unthinkable.' Alas, that much iniquity is perpetrated without thinking. Sir William Beveridge contributed the following: 'The issue raised by the latest persecutions of the

Jews is a test of the capacity of the United Nations as a grand alliance to make up their minds on the problem for whose solution the alliance exists, and in hopes of whose solution it fights. It is a test of the humanity of all of us, of our power to act together, and to act quickly.' It is with ominous misgiving that one reflects that Sir William's first Beveridge plan has already been postponed until after the war.

Gratifying, and concrete, was the news communicated to the mass gathering by Viscount Halifax that the British Government had completed negotiations with the Bulgarian Government for 4,000 Jewish children and 4,000 Jewish adults to leave that country and go to Palestine. The British Government, in fact, has undertaken to receive in Palestine, if the necessary arrangements can be made, up to 29,000 Jewish children with a proportion of adults, by March 31, 1944.

But this, of course, is but a drop in the ocean of misery. Millions remain, and await salvation. Out of the demonstration there was adopted an eleven-point program of action to achieve its purpose. The resolution will be presented to President Roosevelt, and other leaders of the United Nations. It remains to be seen whether the imperatives of humanity will over-ride the temporary excuses of inconvenience. Certainly there is no doubt but that when the future comes to judge of the present *sub specie aeternitatis*, its judgment will in large measure be determined by the manner in which the mighty of this generation came to the aid of its weak and its persecuted.

Erlich and Alter   5 March 1943

The news which has just been released that Henrik Erlich and Victor Alter, world-renowned Socialist leaders of the Polish working-class, had been executed last December by – of all people! – the Soviet authorities evokes mingled feelings of sadness and embarrassment; sadness, that so terrible a fate by so incongruous an execution should have been visited upon these men – and embarrassment that it was the government of a valiant people which perpetrated this deed. It will be remembered that Alter and Erlich had been arrested by the Communist authorities immediately after they took over their part of Poland. Subsequently, after intercession on their behalf, by leading Socialists of the world, they were released.

It now appears that they were re-arrested, presumably under the accusation of having carried on anti-Soviet activity, an accusation which is made more specific by an official statement to the effect that 'they sought to encourage defection in the Soviet Army, and advocated a peace with Hitler.' It is an indictment which is the very zenith of incredibility. One is surprised at the lack of imagination in the Russian propaganda department which believes that such stories will be believed, without even the formality of a public trial.

Our colleague of the *Jewish Daily Eagle*, Mr. I.R., commenting upon this tragedy in a manner which reveals his disappointment in every line, sets up the hypothesis that no doubt Erlich and Alter were guilty of associating with 'oppositional forces' in Russia, and that, under the Soviet Code, is treason. The fact is, however, that we have long been led to believe that all oppositional forces in Russia had been liquidated, that this was achieved in the well-remembered Moscow trials, and that because of this very liquidation the Soviet regime has been singularly free of Quislings. If this is so, with what oppositional forces did the two Socialists conspire?

Mr. I.R. – apparently not convinced by his own assumption – then goes on to take a last-ditch stand by saying that in war-time many things are done with which one could never reconcile oneself in peace-time. '*C'est la guerre,*' is the phrase which he uses to summarize the apologia. But the fact is that *ce n'est pas la guerre*. In war one shoots one's military enemies, not one's political opponents. The men who dedicated their entire careers to the advancement of the interests of the working-class were not friends of Hitler; the men who spent time in Czarist and Polish prisons because of their socialist opinions were not traitors to the social cause; and Erlich who, as lawyer, defended gratuitously many an accused Communist, was not an enemy of the Soviet Union.

The whole incident is regrettable. It can be attributed to nothing less than the exercising of an executive animosity arising out of difference of opinion, despite agreement as to fundamentals. The authors of the deed, moreover, have done a grave disservice to the reputation of the Soviet Union, which through the Red Army and the Russian people, has won itself friends and supporters throughout the world. Very often, indeed, a petty bureaucracy can undo in a moment the good which a great people has achieved in a year.

The City of Chelm   5 March 1943

Childhood is not childhood unless it possess its imaginary town of fools. They were shrewd men, indeed, the mythologists of every people who invented for the sake of their babes and sucklings these legendary habitations of stupidity, the exploits of which served, *a contrario*, to teach the infants wisdom and the way wherein they should go. The little children of Greece had their Boeotia, renowned for the simplicity of its denizens; Englishmen had the city of Gotham; and Jewry has its town of Chelm. All of these municipalities grew famous in the imagination of youth by the tales of the laughable doings of those who dwelt in them; and they remained forever after as an undying memory of a topsy-turvy kingdom, whose citizens perpetrated all kinds of foolishness but were never hurt beyond being laughed at.

For childhood, these places of invented travel served a double purpose. In the first place, they provided for the mischievous effervescence of that age, an innocent outlet. Pranks played in the imagination upon personages imaginary can do harm to no one; they provide the mind with a titillation, free of charge; the animal spirits explode, with a bang, but without damage. And in the second place, the unhappy fate of the legendary victims instructs by example how humiliation is to be avoided, and proportion and perspective maintained.

To us, the capital of childhood was the great metropolis of Chelm. Here lived, as a result of the creative transportation of the folk-fancy, a group of Jews whose sole purpose seemed to be to do everything up-side-down, and thus afford the rest of Jewry both gaiety and edification. Warsaw might have its scholars, Vilna might boast its pundits, Odessa its intellectuals, but in all the cities and hamlets of Russia, there was no place which had more to offer by the way of instruction in the perils and pitfalls of ordinary day-to-day life. If ever a stupidity were possible, rest assured it happened in the town of Chelm; all you had to do was to read the archives of that renowned habitation to be forewarned and forearmed.

They were archives – these non-existent records of fantastic half-wittedness – which lightened up our youth with joy and laughter that not all the comedians of all the stages have ever been able to rival. Was one glum and unhappy about a thought awkwardly conceived, a phrase badly expressed, an attitude unthinkingly adopted – go to Chelm, thou sluggard, and see thy foolishness out-foolished. Always we could hear, wherever two Jews gathered for the honored sport of anecdotage, the laughter – rare, indeed, in the ghetto – which paid tribute to some recently discussed masterpiece of Chelm. It was in gratitude to these memories – and without the sponsorship of the aldermen of that fine city – that we wrote the following lines, for the greater glory of the immortal town –

On a little brown pony, a little boy rides
Over cobblestone roads through strange countrysides;
He rides to and fro, and he rides up and down,
Asks milkmaids and blacksmiths how far 'tis to town,
    To topsy-turvy town.

His grandfather told him that would he be wise
He must see the fool's town with his very own eyes;
See Jews catch the moon in a bucket for cheese,
And find the next night that moon stuck in the trees –
    That moon stuck in the trees.

See the simpleton settling high matters of state;
The rabbi a-scratching his dubious pate,
Watch the baker knead rolls out of dough made of lime,
Since it never turned sour, and kept a long time,
    Because it kept a long time.

And hear the philosopher in the town-hall
Drone nothing is nothing, and that is all,
And also the poet who bawled out a song
Which proved that the heat stretched the summer day long,
    Did stretch the summer day long.

So into the hamlet the little boy rides –
Oh, even his pony is holding its sides!
The little boy smiles to the Jews of the realm,
Nods right and nods left to the burghers of Chelm,
    The simple burghers of Chelm.

In such wise did we think of that strange city, such were our memories of this city *aim b'Yisroel*. Its roofs shone in the imagination with a crazy splendor, its streets were murmurous with the hubbub of nonsense, its mayor stood before us, a genial clown. It was a place of fun, and merriment, and laughter without malice.

We no longer think of Chelm in that happy-go-lucky fashion. For there is an actual city in occupied Russia known as Chelm. The Jewish Encyclopedia describes it as a lumbering centre. For some reason or other – a thing inscrutable within the imaginative workings of the race – this Chelm was taken as the prototype of madly-rollicking towns. But it is, to-day, no longer rollicking, and only mad. It is no longer a place of fun and merriment; not laughter, but malice is heard through its streets.

For the Germans, according to latest reports, have chosen, perhaps with diabolic aptness, this city of Chelm as one of their principal extermination-centres. Thither are sent all those thousands who are deported to destinations unknown into Eastern Poland; and here there functions the dread *Extermina-tionskolonnen*. The city of joy and laughter is reduced to an abattoir and a charnel-house. How is she fallen, who was full of joy and frolicking! How is she become a place for the murder of old men and the stifling of infants, she who once brought back youth to the aged, and gave to the child its wisdom!

Now Chelm is the seat of carnage, and the habitation of slaughter. It is the Nazis who are to-day the grim pranksters of Chelm. Their trick – it is a simple one, typical of the savage childhood of the race – is to administer gas, in wholesale quantities to its chosen victims, the aged and the young of Jewry.

(The able-bodied are subjected to a more difficult form of extermination, labor in the concentration camps, under conditions of starvation and exposure.) The 'king of Chelm' is the Nazi gauleiter, Fey – more bloodthirsty than Rosenberg, crueler than Streicher – the master of the experiment in murder. He calls himself the 'Father of Chelm,' and like a barbarian god, he lives upon 'his children.'

We do not know by what accident or 'inspiration' the Nazi sadists chose Chelm as the locale of their unending crimes. It has in it a grimness which is shuddering, a gruesomeness which sets the hair on end. To pick the sunlit ever-smiling Chelm as the scene for the suffocation of old men, women and children, horrible beyond the expression of words, brings out in the sombrest of colors the heinous crime which Hitler and his myrmidons are perpetrating. If murder can be enhanced, this enhances it. This is murder in the very temple of innocence!

Yet is there a certain appropriateness in the choice of Chelm as slaughter-house and asphyxiation centre. Chelm is topsy-turvy town. What, indeed, could be more topsy-turvy, more contradictory of the eternal verities by which civilized men live, than the Sodom wickedness and Gomorrah iniquity of the Nazi regime? Here kindness is a crime, and pity a misdemeanor. Here the cultured city is misplaced, and only the jungle reigns supreme. Here the accents of humanity are foreign; native only the savage gutturals of the Black Forest. What is righteous throughout the world, is in German Chelm unrighteous and wrong; what is recognized as law and justice in other parts, in Nazi Chelm is scorned and despised. The world stands on its head. Chelm is, for once, literally upside-down, for man, divine man, is lowered into the cold earth, while the beast stalks above, king and master of the devastated city.

The world must set it right. Lidice was a challenge; Chelm is both a challenge and a symbol. We are all Hamlets now:

The time is out of joint. O cursed spite
That ever we were born to set it right!

The Bermuda Conference 23 April 1943

The Bermuda Conference, called under Anglo-American auspices, to discuss ways and means of solving the acute and tragic problem of the refugee, has already sat for a number of days. Under ordinary circumstances one would have been justified in seeing a symbolic forecast of liberation in the fact that the sessions of this loftily inspired meeting take place on the days of Passover, season of emancipation. But the provisos which have thus far hedged this conference, and the cautious and nullifying reports which have thus far issued of its deliberations, give even to the most sanguine no grounds for optimism. With every news release one is confirmed in the impression that what the world is witnessing is not a serious and aggressive effort at solving this weighty problem, but a mere humanitarian pantomime.

One has but to consider the pronouncement which precedes the conference to realize that doubt as to its sincerity is not an out-of-hand piece of incredulous cynicism. Lest anyone should imagine that the United States would be a fit sanctuary for refugees, Secretary of State Cordell Hull invoked, even before the conferors sat down, the sacrosanct American immigration quota. Lest anyone should be under any illusions as to the refugee absorptive capacity of England and its Dominions, a statement was issued showing how many aliens were already so quartered; and this statement included the figures of war-prisoners! Lest a whisper should be breathed about Palestine as an asylum for the hunted and persecuted, officials have taken the opportunity of declaring that the quota of 29,000 for Eretz Israel is fixed and unelastic! With so many preliminary negatives, the scope for positive action, to put it mildly, is considerably restricted. Remains only a discussion of the *nachtasyl* which may be furnished by neutral European countries, such as Sweden, Switzerland, Spain. We have seen nowhere that these countries are reported at the conference.

It is of course argued by the sponsors of the conference that it is 'purely exploratory,' and that its recommendations are in no way binding. Aye, there's the rub! What, in this year of grace 1943 is there to explore? Whether there are any unhappy sufferers who require asylum? Certainly governments which indicate in their figures as pertinent to the Bermuda conference how many refugees they have received since 1933 are fully aware of the extent of this greatest of challenges to the world's conscience. Then it must be as to territories which may serve as refugee asylums that the exploration is to take place. But from the advance remarks of the delegates to the conference, one gathers that that voyage of discovery has taken place long before the conference began, and that certainly no New America will be discovered in old Bermuda. It is true that a number of shipping reports have been cabled to the scene of the meeting; one really cannot escape the thought that the shipping of the reports was an act of supererogation; two cables could just as easily have revealed the possibility.

Nor are our misgivings laid all out by the fact that representation of the press has been seriously curtailed; indeed, what the press has hitherto published has all the indicia of prepared 'hand-outs'! Even more serious is the fact that no delegations are being permitted to Bermuda lest their tragic importunities upset the too-too-impersonal character of the deliberations. Whatever will be decided, it appears, will spring from the original sources of wisdom and the private impulses of humanity of the members of the conference. One can only think that Wilson must be turning in his grave at this example of 'open-and-shut covenants secretly arrived at.'

Most disturbing, too, is the fact that there appears to be, to judge from the Bermuda newspapers, a pitiable touchiness, a morbid hyper-sensitivity lest the conference be misinterpreted as an attempt to save Jews. Almost every newspaper reference touching the gathering goes out of its way to insist that this is no pro-Jewish venture. The whole attitude of the publicity-agents of Bermuda shows that they themselves have become victims, in a new and peculiar fashion, of the racist mentality. Is it really necessary, we ask, to apologize if there is a possibility that the conference might come to the aid of Jews?

It is not to be denied that, representing the American Government, there is Mr. Sol Bloom. We do not think, however, that anybody is going to be embarrassed by Mr. Bloom's Jewishness. A worthy gentleman, Chairman of the House Committee on Foreign Affairs, Bloom has endorsed many a cause – save that of his co-religionists. His attitude to the Jewish problem is simple in the extreme; there are people suffering, he says. And among the people are Jews. No more, and no less. Would that some of the problems of this Bloom had impregnated the gauleiters of Europe!

It would seem, therefore, that the Bermuda talks are merely an instrument to prove to the world, at no expense and without any commitments, how humanitarian we are as compared to others. Others actually perpetrate atrocities; and we only ignore them. It is a construction of the conference which we, for the present at any rate, refuse to adopt. Despite all the gloomy omens, despite all the encompassing negatives, we refuse to believe that two great Governments having enunciated as their war objectives idealisms unparalleled, would do other than meet on this subject in a spirit of high seriousness, and with a knowledge that the manner in which they seek to solve present problems will be taken as a criterion of the manner in which they will implement their post-war promises.

The Warsaw Ghetto   21 May 1943

As the much-vaunted forces of the 'invincible' Rommel were surrendering in their tens of thousands in North Africa, the German military machine was not entirely helpless and forlorn. There were still fronts where its blitzkrieg methods availed for something; there were still battlefields where additional glory and honors for the Reich could be won. One of these immortal battlefields was the ghetto of Warsaw, where, after ten days of warfare, in which the fire and metal of the German army was directed against the blood and flesh of unarmed civilians, a great victory was registered in Hitler's name; the ghetto was liquidated.

To those who, despite the savagery of the foe and the ruthlessness of the methods against the unresisting, have felt a secret admiration for the so-called bellicose qualities of the Nazi soldier, the contrast between the stand of von Arnim and those of the ghetto can well serve to refocus matters in their proper perspective. In Africa, still supplied with much material of war, still extant as a military body numbering thousands, the German soldier, despite instructions to fight on to the last man, ignominiously capitulated as soon as it beheld, for once, the superiority of the enemy. No Stalingrad resistance can be marked up to the credit of the German army in Africa. The myth about the common soldier's self-sacrifice on behalf of his Fuehrer was buried forever in the sands of Cape Bon. Vigorous, implacable, the Nazis are only against those whose resistance collapses.

How different was the attitude of the untrained thousands of the ghetto! These, certainly, never had the military training afforded by the great slaughter-academies of Germany. No stock of even primitive ammunition, beyond that which was supplied by sympathetic Poles, was available for them. With their bare hands and unarmored bodies, – unprotected by planes, unshielded by tanks, – they stood up against executioners armed to the teeth. And the campaign against the ghetto of Warsaw took as long as the campaign against France – ten days of Hitler's precious schedule were expended upon this glorious venture.

Of course, the issue was never in doubt. No one knew that better than the Warsaw Jews. That flesh cannot stand up against explosives is an axiom in both the physical and military fields. But knowing this, the valiant of Warsaw preferred rather to fight inch by inch through the tortuous ways of the ghetto to being led out, like cattle, onto the unknown and macabre highways where the Nazi extermination squads do their heinous work. They died, but they exacted a price.

As for the Nazis, they will no doubt enter into their military annals the tale of the victory over the Warsaw ghetto. Something, after all, must atone for the ignominy of Tunisia; the victory over the spectres of Warsaw can well serve that purpose.

Quebec City Gets Another Park   18 June 1943

We do not know whether the Municipal Council of the good City of Quebec has yet seen fit to pass a resolution of gratitude to its Jewish community for being instrumental, if only indirectly, in contributing towards the scenic embellishment of that fair metropolis; but certainly such a resolution has long been overdue. No other group of citizens, to our mind, has recently done more towards the increasing of parks and playgrounds than the Jewish community in its futile quest for a site for its synagogue. Our readers will no doubt remember that for the last several years, Quebec Jewry has been desirous of building itself a place of worship in that pious city. Every time a site was purchased, however, the city fathers of Quebec found, in their inscrutable wisdom, that a building permit could not be granted. Accordingly, the Ark of the Covenant, as in biblic days, was compelled to see its hopes for a resting place moved from city lot to city lot.

Recently, it appeared – vain mirage! – that at last a building permit would be issued allowing construction to begin in the latest site chosen. Alas, *dis aliter visum*! The municipal lordlings have otherwise decided. Although there is a park in the vicinity of the new synagogue-site, the aldermen desire to expropriate also the synagogue-land to be used as a park. The fact is that the synagogue question has already been converted into a political playground; remains only to transform the lot itself into a public recreation area. Indeed, it appeared plainly from the debate which was held in the Municipal Council that should the Quebec Jews find other land for their long-projected synagogue, that too will be expropriated for parks and playgrounds! Truly, no other Quebec group is doing more for civic improvement than this Jewry and its ever-frustrated place of worship!

To what mediaeval depths certain of the councillors of Quebec City have fallen can be seen from the shameless suggestion made by an alderman, one Drolet. In a British country, and in the twentieth century, this individual had the effrontery to suggest that the city council adopt a resolution that no synagogues be built within the city limits of Quebec. No doubt Drolet had ready in hand the text of the resolution; he need only have copied it from the statutes of Nuremberg. It is to be noted, however, that the other members of the council were somewhat better instructed in the spirit of British law, and knew that such a resolution was palpably and blatantly illegal. Accordingly, they preferred to achieve their purposes behind the poetic protection of park foliage.

We do not know what the upshot of this impasse will be, whether the Lord will in time soften the hearts of the municipal councillors, or whether they will persist in their bigoted obstinacy. We do know that in the meantime, the incident serves to give the city an unenviable reputation among the cities of America. For certainly as one reads of these goings-on, and one reflects, one has a right to query, with Keats: Do I dream or wake? Has the fate of Rip Van Winkle overtaken Quebec, and are its councillors the long-dormant relics of the Middle Ages? Are the councillors of Quebec City aware of the fact that a war is being fought for the four freedoms? Or does Quebec fight for only three of them?

Lessing 'Lackland' Rosenwald   9 July 1943

As we read in a recent issue of *Life* the infuriating and sycophantic contribution made by Lessing Rosenwald to the discussion which that magazine has been publishing about the aims and objectives of Zionism, we could not help but reflect how prejudice so frequently distorts the meaning and implication of the simplest of words. Take the word 'landlessness' as a pertinent example. To most people, the word implies a condition which is far removed from felicity. Our readers no doubt will recall the John Lackland of English history, the tragic figure of a disinherited prince. Everything else about him is forgotten; one remembers only that he was unique in that he was dispossessed of his land. The distinguished French poet, Ivan Goll, also accepts the word in its natural connotations. Publishing a series of poems describing the sorry plight of contemporary Frenchmen, he titles it *'Jean Sans Terre.'*

But Lessing Rosenwald, who can afford such luxuries, has a dictionary made entirely for himself. In that dictionary 'landlessness' is a synonym for the blessed state in which Jewry finds itself in desperation. Apparently losing himself in the Reform doctrine that Jewry has a 'mission' – to propagate its lofty ideals among the peoples of the world – Lessing finds that Jewish wandering constitutes a decided advantage to such intellectual peddling. That the same thing might be achieved – if such achievement is indeed a consummation so devoutly to be wished – by the mail-order technique of his own family, with distributing centre in Palestine, has not yet occurred to Mr. Rosenwald. He contents himself for the moment with the dubious distinction that both he and Ibn Saud of Arabia, are both against Zionism, and both for the same pious religious reasons, taken, of course, by each out of his respective Koran.

For Lessing Rosenwald, too, believes that Jews are doomed to eternal wandering, – and a good thing it is, too. Being the votaries of a world religion, Jews are not entitled to the possession of any specific country. That Christianity is a world religion, that Mohammedanism is a world religion, and both numbering a much greater discipleship than Judaism, apparently does not lead Rosenwald to the conclusion that also Christians and Mohammedans should, forsooth, be deprived of their respective homelands. That privilege he reserves only for his co-religionists; that, no doubt, is his interpretation of the singularity of 'The Chosen People.'

Still mouthing pieties, the American Lessing goes on to fortify his argument with the thesis that it is undesirable that Jews should be in possession of a country which has holy places sacred to all three religions. The gentleman has not read, or has forgotten, the terms of the British Mandate over Palestine which categorically guarantee the untouchableness of all the sanctums of the Holy Land. It is to be asked, moreover, whether Rosenwald really believes that if Palestine is not granted to the Jews, that it will therefore remain a no-man's land. Surely some people, whether Christian or Mohammedan, will enjoy sovereignty over that domain. Does Rosenwald believe that Ibn Saud can be entrusted with the guaranteeing of Christian and Jewish holy places, but that Jews can not?

There are other arguments with which Mr. Rosenwald entertains the readers of Life. He feels, for example, that the acknowledgement of the fact that Jews as a people are entitled to a Homeland, would make precarious the position of Jews living outside of Palestine. It is the typical appeal to fear which characterized the attitude of the pre-war German-Jewish anti-Zionists; and with what results everybody knows. That the position of the Irish-American in New York is not rendered 'precarious' by the existence of Eire is, of course, admitted. The same logic, however, Mr. Rosenwald refuses to apply to his own people. Indeed, it has not yet occurred to Lessing that the Palestine Homeland would lift the Jews of this diaspora out of the position of being an inferior nomadic tribe to the full dignity of nationhood.

How great is Rosenwald's phobia lest he be thought a Jew, and not merely an 'American of Mosaic persuasion,' is evidenced by his gratuitously-offered theory that Zionism is a 'racist' doctrine. By that the 'protector of the Jewish religion' would imply that the aspiration of the hunted and harried refugees of war-torn Europe to establish a Homeland which they could call their own and where they could rebuild their broken lives and continue their national traditions is but another version of – Hitlerism. There can be no words too strongly condemnatory of this piece of malicious impertinence. To inform the millions of gentile readers of Life that in the midst of Jewry there exists to-day a movement to Hitlerism is to render a grave disservice to his 'co-religionists' and to be disloyal both to truth and to his people.

It would have been much better if Rosenwald had confined his literary efforts to the Sears-Roebuck catalogue. At least there his words would have had some value, if only at bargain prices. But to rush in where angels fear to tread, to treat a subject where his prejudices are rivalled only by his ignorance, was a piece of effrontery which is unparallelled since Jerome Frank's trailing of the red herring. If Mr. Rosenwald wished to dissociate himself from the hope of millions of Jews, that is his privilege. National landlessness apparently means little to one who is compensated by private property. 'What's Hecuba to him, or he to Hecuba?' – what does he have in common with the Jews of the ghetto of Warsaw, or the Jews of the Yishuv in Palestine? No one asked him for his sympathy or help. But neither did anyone ask him to use the accident of his Jewish birth as an excuse to pose as an authority on Jewish destiny.

The Feast of Tabernacles 13 October 1943

The celebration of the Feast of Succoth, with its picturesque ritual and ancient memories, comes again to grace the Jewish calendar, a living parable for the very days of our years. A composite religious and national festival – the occasion for the ingathering of the harvest and the seasonal ceremonial evocative of Israel's wanderings – its symbolism is but half-pertinent to our contemporary history. For no one who gives thought to what is everywhere transpiring about us can see, we know, any sign or vestige of anything even faintly resembling a cornucopia harvest for Jewry, – unless it be the grim poison of the Angel of the Scythe.

Insofar as the Feast of Tabernacles commemorates a dwelling in booths, however, its symbolism does give an accurate and poignant picture of the low estate to which Israel has fallen. In no place of the world, not in Europe, and not even in Palestine under the White Paper, does our people own a certain and secure habitation. Everywhere it dwells in booths, which an evil wind or wicked marauder may with ease and impunity destroy. Not the case of ancient Israel do we memorialize in these booths, but our own bitter contemporary plight.

Hope lies only in the belief that history repeats not only its unpleasant chapters, but also its happier ones. The dwelling of our ancestors in their shaky booths, it will be remembered, was but a phenomenon of transition. It passed; and after its passing, there followed the long sojourn in their own Homeland, 'every man under his vine, every man under his fig-tree.' To the thousands across the Atlantic who languish, when free, in booths, and otherwise in cells, the only ray of light in their great darkness, is this hope that they may, in God's good time, exchange booth and cell, for home and homeland. Then, indeed, will the feast of Succoth, not only constitute a happy memorial of old unhappiness – *olim meminisse juvabit* – but also the symbol of the true rejoicing of harvest time.

The Mosley Affair 26 November 1943

The release of Oswald Mosley, Britain's arch-fascist, from the internment for the duration to which he was condemned at the beginning of the war, has raised a storm of protest throughout the length and breadth of England which promises to spread to other parts of the Empire. These protests, to say the least, are understandable. Why special clemency should be exercised in the case of a man who for years was the pledged enemy of democracy, the loudest British admirer of Hitler, and the most dangerous potential fifth-columnist on the island, passeth the understanding of all minds save the acrobatic ones of the sponsors of his liberation.

In explaining, – we should say in apologizing for his act, – the Home Secretary Mr. Herbert Morrison, invoked humanitarian reasons as justification. It would appear that the dear little boy – one of our own native supermen – was not feeling very well; his continued confinement, it was further suggested, would make him feel worse. One would imagine that Mosley was the only person who was ever indisposed as a result of imprisonment; there have been thousands, and humanitarianism has invariably dictated that they be treated in prison hospitals. Why then this exception in the case of the man who aspired to be Britain's Laval, Britain's quisling? We are not at all surprised that the straightforward plain-talking man can not follow the ratiocinations of the Home Secretary.

The general public, moreover, is uneasy about the implications of this unfortunate precedent. If this is the loving kindness with which an internal enemy is treated after four years of colossal sacrifice on the part of the people, what guarantee has it got that when the day of retribution for the Hitler criminals arrives, there will not be another resurgence of pseudo-humanitarianism? The fact is that to apply the word humanitarian to such an act is to slander humanity, for to be kind to evil, is to betray the good. No one will deny that in time of war, at a time when we are waging a life-and-death struggle – humanitarianism must be rationed. Moreover, it is subject to certain priorities. If one has to be 'humanitarian,' such feelings, we feel, could with greater justice have been lavished upon the victims of the *Struma* and the *Patria*, who came to watery graves, because hard-hearted officials would not let them land in their own Homeland. Certainly, if there are to be candidates for release from internment now, Mahatma Gandhi is more deserving than Oswald Mosley. We are not to be misconstrued, moreover, as advocating wholesale releases from internment; but certainly if a beginning is being made, that beginning emphatically should not be Oswald Mosley.

The Perfect Man   24 December 1943

It is refreshing to read, in a world full of frailties and decrepitudes, of a valiant professor, located, of all places, in Chicago, undertaking to describe the aspect of the brave new world in general, and in particular, so that all may hear and be heartened, the shape and form of 'the perfect man' of the future. The search for this flawless specimen of mankind is not a phenomenon new to either professors or philosophers; from time immemorial the human mind has dwelt wishfully upon an era when the flesh would be rid of its corruptions and life itself would take on an ineffable perfection. Despairing of ever achieving such a consummation here in the valley of the shadow, the earliest philosophers, theologians all, discovered or invented the Life Beyond; there, indeed, all would cease from troubling, and time itself, would move from one felicity to the next. To some, this paradise of perfection, this domain of the *ne plus ultra*, was a place of continuously ravishing religious music; to others, an inexhaustible festive board upon which the roast leviathan lay heaped in platters, pregnant with the tastes of all food, including that of the all-inclusive manna; and to others again, it was celestial seraglio, where man must needs be perfect indeed.

Unfortunately none of these habitats of 'the perfect man' were subject to either geographical scrutiny or scientific description. Located all beyond 'the bourne from which no traveller returns,' inquisition into their mores was primarily a matter of metaphysics aided by intuition bolstered by vanity. Of exact information there was none.

Hard upon the heels of the clerics came the scientists. They had beheld the futile homunculi allegedly created by chanting cabbalist formulae, and felt that the golem could only with difficulty be dubbed a paragon. Of the dubious perfectionism beyond the grave, they knew nothing, and, like scientists, expressed no opinion. But out of their test-tubes and retorts, out of the mechanistic paraphernalia of the laboratory, they volunteered, in the fullness of time, to develop that final flower of perfection which all so zealously desired.

Thus far, none has achieved this self-set task. But a number of years ago, Mr. Aldous Huxley, in a novel which gave new currency to the phrase 'brave new world,' undertook to describe the lot of a humanity, science-begotten and science-bred. It was not an appetizing picture. Artificial insemination, communal incubation, and Pavlovian education, constituted an unholy trinity which provided the leaders of the state – themselves superior votaries of old-fashioned manners – with a mass of conditioned robots ready to do their will. Significantly enough, time, in this wonderful new world, was indicated as such-and-such a 'year of our Ford.'

Now, hotly heaven-bent, comes Dr. James Shelly Thomas, technologist and economist, former president of the Clarkson (N.Y.) College of Technology and the Chrysler Institute of Engineering, former University of Chicago economist, and presently also among the prophets. Addressing a meeting of the Chicago section of the American Chemical Society, Dr. Thomas gave his audience the benefit of his prognostications touching the man of the next century. 'He dipt into the future, as far as human eye could see, and saw the vision of the world and all the wonder that would be.'

First of all, he saw that the average man of the next century would be at least six feet three inches in height. Apparently, he had to be that tall to be seen at a distance of one hundred years ... What is significant is that the learned professor thus establishes height as the first criterion of perfection. It is to be wondered whether this is not a typically American fallacy, brother to the logic which invariably associates better with bigger. It sounds almost as if one took the German pejorative *untermensch*, too literally. By such a standard, the Nordics, a tall group, must be forthwith acknowledged as a superior race, and the Greeks and Latins, who, we believe, have also rendered some service to civilization, of the lesser breeds. By such a standard, indeed, the giraffe looms very high upon the evolutionary tree. In the light of this description of perfection, we cannot resist curiosity as to the measurements of the professor himself. If he is tall, his theory is sheer personal vanity; if he is short, one has listened to the effusion of an inferiority complex.

Dr. Thomas goes on to indicate that the man of the future, moreover, will never grow grey, nor fat, and will live to one hundred and twenty-five years. The perfect life will thus be deprived of the distinction of grey hairs, the pleasantness of the plump, and the sweet tragedy of those who depart this world young and untainted. All of this is to be brought about, saith the sage, by the tremendous strides about to be taken in the medical, chemical, and dietary sciences. They have not yet been taken; at present, as the world conflict goes on, science, poor handmaiden, is engaged in cutting down the size of men, inducing premature greyness, and decreasing the span of life. Only on the restriction of fat has its task really begun.

Nor is the professor sparing of details as to the general picture of the shape of things to come. Soon after the war is over, he predicts, there will be millions of new houses that will cost $1600 and contain dozens of new developments. These may eventually include unbreakable glass plumbing (a feature not without its disadvantages), filters that transform noises from outside into music inside, refrigerators that have everything including murals (the apple will be both eaten and painted), and a living room that can be redecorated merely by pressing a button.

We shall not say that these quiddities are entirely without charm. But surely it is not with improvements such as these that the perfect life is ushered in! It is not the size of the human being, nor his furniture, which determines the question of happiness or unhappiness in the world. No doubt much misery is caused by some of the defects which, Dr. Thomas assures us, the next century will correct; John Keats was acutely sensitive about being only five feet tall, a 'human pentametre' he called himself; and many are the tears which have been shed over illness, early death, and inadequate household goods. But the great cosmic tragedies do not flow from these causes; they flow from the faulty relationship *between* men, from the faulty and greedy distribution of the world's goods; it is not that the size of man is puny, but that his heart is narrow.

Such an ailment is not cured by chemistry, and is not answered by a cornucopia of plastics. At the risk of appearing pietistic we recall him who enjoined the circumcision of hearts. But of an improvement in human relations within the next century, the professor says nothing. And it is precisely here that the great task of perfectionism is so imperatively urgent. For the better world to come is a problem neither of mechanics nor of chemistry, but of psychology.

In vain will all these improvements in the body beautiful be achieved; in vain these lean girths and lanky builds, this vitamin-stirred circulation and this scientifically-perfect complexion. The man of the future with all his perfection, will show but a face which will be 'faultily faultless, icily regular, splendidly null.' Not from his fatness his failure, not from his face his misfortune. For the statistics of centuries show that the greatest burden of unhappiness has come from one principal source: that the arm of every man is lifted up against his brother.

Oscar Wilde tells a parable of the porcupine. Unable any longer to suffer the stings and quills of his fellow-porcupines, the hero of the fable retired to the loneliness of the mountain-top. Here, however, he found his solitude unbearable. He descended back into the woods. Again the society of his brothers was intolerable. Again to the mountain-top. So was he ever torn between the anguish of solitude and the agony of society.

The happiness of mankind will be advanced, not with the formulae of Dr. Thomas. The happiness of mankind will be advanced only when the above antithesis – between man the lonely one in a wide world and man the unsuccessful social animal, is finally resolved.

In Memoriam: Rabbi Levi Yitschok of Berditchev   7 January 1944

As the tanks come rolling to the rescue of the city which you have made famous in our memory, I think of you, O wonderful Rabbi, again and again. Almost have I expected to hear your name mentioned in the war-communiqués, to hear it sounded from the radio, to see it headlined in the newspapers: *Rabbi Levi Yitschok of Berditchev wins his debate with God.*

But never a word was repeated of your doings. Berditchev is mentioned, but not the one by whose ineffable merit Berditchev lived. Secrecy surrounds you, as if you, arrayed in your *tallis* and *tfillin*, were one of those guerrilla heroes who fight from forest and cave; silence encompasses you, as it does always the fame of the Unknown Soldier. Where have you been, O crony of the Lord, familiar of heaven?

For I have remembered you, as you have stood always in our legend, full of a pious audacity, addressing the Lord as if He were your intimate. I have recalled again that glorious occasion when you issued your fiat against the Heavenly Throne itself, when before the entire gathered congregation of Berditchev, convened to its devotions on the sacred day of Rosh Hashanah, you spoke to the *Rebono shel Olam*: 'Lord of the World, if today Thou writest the name of Thy people Israel into the Book of Life – good; for the saving of life annuls the prohibition against writing either on the Sabbath or on Holy Days. But if such is not Thy intention – behold, I, Rabbi Levi Yitschok, Rabbi in Berditchev, do forbid unto Thee this the contravention of Thine own law.'

Where, O spirit of Levi Yitschok, was that saintly boldness of yours the day that so much evil befell your brethren, shepherdless and alone? Have you not seen, have you not heard of the many inventions the sons of Belial have invented to destroy us? You who heard the infants' babbling of the *aleph-bais*, and forthwith hastened to your God, saying: 'Behold Thy sacred children, how they con Thy holy letters even before they utter complete words,' have you not heard the agony of *Shma Yisroel* rising all about you, bursting the walls of prison, overwhelming the salvo of the firing-squad, sounding above the thunder of the cattle-cars? And what message have you reported to The-Holy-One-Blessed-Be-His-Name?

Even your own congregation, Rabbi of Berditchev, is no more. With fire and sword destroyed, its buildings razed, its sons murdered, its memorials put to shame, both God and Israel have been exiled from that place. 'O, how is she become, she that was Jerusalem in Volhynia, how doth she sit solitary that was full of people, she weepeth sore in the night.' You, who heard holiness even in the chaffering of the little merchantmen at the fairs of Berditchev, have you not heard, from your tomb, the sanctification of the Name that fills the air?

Or is it that the barbarian has laid his bloodied hands also upon your resting-place?

Then, the cry, the agony, the importunity of your plea, should have been mightier still! For surely if there was one who could have brought our sorrow and our affliction before the Heavenly Throne, you were he, you were that man! Who else, among the saints, who else among the holy ones of Israel, ever spoke to the Almighty and called Him: Thou. 'I will sing thee a Thou-song,' you said, 'East-Thou! West-Thou! North-Thou! South-Thou! Everywhere and always, Thou! Thou and Thou only, O Lord, God of the World!'

Where were your theeings and thouings in the hour of our need, O Rabbi Levi Yitschok? Was not this the time for you to break in upon the *Pamalyah shel maalah*, with clamour and accusation, to silence the hosannas in the court of heaven, to hush the angels, and to remind the Lord Himself of your name and of His? *Derbarimidiger* – the Compassionate One!

A time there was, O Rabbi, when you were wont ever to sing the praises of the Children of Israel. Jewels they were, you said, in the Crown of the Lord. O, consider them, how they have been broken and flawed! The chosen ones – who have been chosen for suffering! Those who brought tidings of God – for whom no tiding now is heard! And still you are silent!

We have heard it from our fathers, O son of Rabbi Meir, and we have told it to our children, how upon a day as you stood in the synagogue of Berditchev, your caftan girdled with ram's horns, you made preparation to blow the *shofar*. You blew once, but no sound issued; you blew again, but only raucous noises as if a thousand demons resided in that horn. You tried again – again to no avail. Then it was that in discomfiture, you put aside your *shofroth*, and said: 'If my blowing of the *shofar* is not acceptable to the Lord, then let the *shabbos-goy* blow it! Let us see, O Lord, how the heathen will blast Thy fame!'

We have seen it, Rabbi Levi Yitschok. And we have seen also how the *shofar* of Israel, soundless, lies broken in the dust!

And yet from you – no word; no sign anywhere that you, emissary of your people, have spoken the required word. It is still time, still time for you to repeat, one century later, the prayer you uttered at *Ne'ilah* in the synagogue of Berditchev when another tyrant's soldiers over-ran the Pale: 'Napoleon,' you said, turning to the Ark of the Covenant, 'Emperor of France, proclaims that the entire world is his; but I, Levi Yitschok of Berditchev, declare, *Yisgadal v'Yiskadash Shmai Rabah!* Great and Holy is the Name of the Lord!'

Can it be, O Rabbi, that you have forgotten those to whom you were protector and guide here below? Can it be that now enjoying your heavenly reward, the affairs of the valley of the shadow are no longer your concern? Is it possible that now, since you dwell in a day which is wholly Sabbath, the mundane week-days are beyond your ken?

So be it. Still, you in your Sabbath may again intone for us the litany that you once composed for Israel's week-days. For certainly for us, the Sabbath has departed, if even only for a while, and we stand facing the long and heavy labour of days without glory or holiness. Illuminate our darkened week with your prayer. Intercede for us, as you were wont to intercede, in these your holy words:

'O God of Abraham, Isaac, and Jacob, spare thy dear people Israel from all evil, and even as the Holy Sabbath departs from us, vouchsafe unto us a week of faith, and wisdom, brotherly love, and communion with the Creator, Blessed Be He; strengthen us in our belief in the Thirteen Credos, and in the Redemption of Israel, and in the Resurrection of the Dead, and in the vision of Moses our Teacher of blessed memory! *Rebono shel Olam*, Thou who givest strength to the weary, grant strength and endurance to Thy children so that they may praise Thee and serve Thee. Grant also that this week come towards us with health and benediction and loving kindness, to us and to all of Israel. Amen.'

O Rabbi Levi Yitschok, the hour of *Ne'ilah* is not yet arrived, and the

Gates of Compassion still stand ajar. Already the breath of pity is wafted from that door, as the armies of rescue march towards your own city. Regain your voice, and speak again in those accents which always before won the verdict from the Heavenly Court!

Deep in the Heart of Texas 21 January 1944

Things most strange, most passing strange, according to song and story, do happen in the state of Texas. Not the least of these astounding occurrences, to our mind, took place a fortnight ago when after the subject had been mooted for the necessary forty days and forty nights, the Houston Beth Israel Congregation finally agreed upon what, with a gallant disregard of the meaning of words, it was pleased to call 'The Basic *Principles* of Reformed *Judaism.*' The reportage touching this latter-day apocalypse does not, unfortunately, reveal what scruples of conscience, what *agenbite of inwit*, prompted this brand-new testament. That we are left to surmise for ourselves, as we listen to the voice speaking from the sage-brush, even as in the days of Moses:

'We are Jews by virtue of our acceptance of Judaism. We consider ourselves *no longer* a nation, but we are a religious community. We expect neither a return to Palestine nor a restoration of any of the laws concerning the Jewish State ... Our nation is the United States of America. Our nationality is American. Our flag is the "Stars and Stripes." Our race is Caucasian ... We accept as binding only the moral laws of Mosaic legislation and Prophetic teaching. We reject the rabbinical and Mosaic laws which regulate diet, priestly purity, dress, and similar laws which originated in ages and under influences of ideas and conditions which to-day are entirely unsuited, unnecessary and foreign to progressive Judaism in modern America.

'The Hebrew language has become unintelligible to the vast majority of our co-religionists; therefore, it must make way to intelligible language in prayer. The basis of unity among the Jews throughout the world is Religion. Hence, it is our duty to help our co-religionists whenever and wherever the need may arise, even as we must help all mankind that may be in need, in accordance with the principles of our faith.'

Such is the new Torah – thunder and lightning, please! – descended from Houston, for its purity first vouchsafed to the Congregation of Beth Israel (who smuggled this Hebrew *Beth* into the house Caucasian?) and offered to the rest of Jewry through the ministry of the orthodox cantor's son, Rabbi H.J. Shactel. (Methinks this Shactel doth not smell of Mayflower!) The new laws, moreover, are not to remain merely theoretical, a rabbi playing solitaire with a deck of credos; upon those who fail to observe the word of God as revealed through the unconsumed sage-brush, sanctions are imposed, not excommunication which is mediaeval, but disenfranchisement which is modern and in the spirit of progressive Judaism. Wherefore, he who will not subscribe to the new gospel will be deprived of his congregational vote; he of the Congregation who is offered a tasty pork-chop, whose fat, as in the Psalms, runneth over, handed to him by his *shochet*-sired rabbi, and in his Asiatic stiff-neckedness refuses to eat thereof, he will be an outcast in Israel, deemed forever unbasic, unprincipled, unreformed, and unJewish!

This is not a mad fantasy which we are describing, a Swedenborgian nightmare; the thing did come to pass even as described. In fact these principles and their penalties, not being of divine inspiration – concession to the age of enlightenment, – were put to a vote. Only one hundred and sixty-eight of the parishioners of Beth Israel voted for the status quo; six hundred and twelve, however, greeted the new negatives of Shactel with overwhelming approval. By a strange cauchemar of democracy, befitting the pathological nature of the event, the six hundred and thirteen of *Taryag*, Torah, were swamped by the six hundred and twelve of Houston, Tex.!

Now, the writer of these lines does not hold himself out to be a saint in Israel. 'So many good years him, how many transgressions he has transgressed.' But certainly he is not so soul-less a reprobate as to erect his sinning into a theology, or magniloquize his guilty conscience and alien's complex into a gospel and creed. Surely if the worthies of Houston, the purity and piety of whose Judaism is revealed by their vote, consider the burden of being a Jew too heavy for their feeble shoulders, the solution to their problem is simple. Let them, then, have the courage of their evictions. But let them not bear upon their backs an inflated balloon, full of nothingness, and groan, so all may hear: The weight of Judaism is upon us!

For certainly, after Shactel, son of cantor, no doubt scion of some bearded *shochet* who gave the family its name, has been at work with his own little progresso-moderno-reformist blade, there is not much left of the winged thing called Judaism. To a nation it does not belong, not any longer; at what precise date Jews ceased to be a nation to become a committee of 612, the Rabbi does not indicate. We assume, knowing the thought-processes of this type, that it is his opinion that Roman conquest ended Jewish nationality. It would now be logical for the Houstonites to invite the Czechs, the Danes, the Poles, the Dutch, and the French – all temporarily conquered – to join with them in their 'basic principles' and make of their ideological orgy a real international national-suicide pact.

Nor are the Jews a race – that propaganda which Hitler and his henchmen have been carrying on with such misguided fervour is not truly anti-semitism; they don't know it, but they are really anti-Caucasianists!

There must follow, after such devastating negatives, something affirmative and positive. If only by the process of elimination, Judaism must be – something! Judaism is – you guessed it, – a religion, but not the religion you thought it was ... For at this point in the analysis – the thing moves like a nightmare – the Texas theologians are beheld methodically eliminating the entire body of Jewish rite, custom, and ceremonial, burning Maimonides in effigy, flinging through the windows of their temple *mitzva* after horrible *mitzva*, until of Judaism, as of the vanishing Cheshire cat, there remains only an empty Freudian grin, a grotesque surrealist 'moral law,' a dangling unrooted kindliness towards 'our co-religionists.' However, as the authors of basic principles write of 'their duty to help their co-religionists whenever and wherever the need may arise,' they suffer a lucid interval, they realize that they are also Americans, even humans; whereupon the principle is extended 'to all mankind that may be in need.' Certainly we do not quarrel with this principle; it is so elementary that a Talmud Torah kindergarten pupil could expound it better; but where, we ask, is that particular called Judaism? And is it necessary to build a synagogue to enshrine this platitude, or to support a rabbi to rehearse it?

One may also pardon our curiosity as to whether 'the help which it is the duty of the Congregation Beth Israel to give to our co-religionists whenever and wherever the need may arise' also extends to the thousands seeking sanctuary and homeland in Palestine? Or are they – a lesser breed, to be excluded because, non-swine-eaters, they are, by definition, not co-religionists? But to mankind, since not to porkdom, they surely belong? The anti-Zionism it seems does not tally with the humanitarianism.

This Judaism of Shactel's is difficult to understand on yet another ground. For if it has been reduced to a single imperative – help those in need – that, and no others, what religion remains to the poor who cannot afford the sole solitary *mitzva*? Indeed, are they who have been deprived of the things of this world also to lose, ipso facto, the blessings of the next? Are only the moguls among the prophets, and for the widow and the orphan is there no portion in Israel? If that is the import of the Texas revelation, then we must say it clearly and unambiguously: these principles are the most unprincipled ever put to paper, this Judaism is truly deformed, [...] Calf!

Were these 'basic principles' but the empty theorizings of a rabbi seeking to employ his leisure they would still constitute a strange psychological phenomenon; it is, however, the attempt to put them into practice which evokes the revulsion inevitable. For surely there is nothing more macabre than this spectacle of a congregation in Israel searching out its members to make sure that they contravene the very laws of that religion in whose name it professes to speak. This is not Judaism, but its cruel travesty, a pathological distortion, the delirium of the schizophrenic.

We can, indeed, imagine a typical initiation rite of the Congregation Beth Israel. A candidate comes forward; and a committee is forthwith appointed to investigate whether he is not a secret marrano, a Jew of the tradition seeking to smuggle himself into the company of the lone stars of Texas. Has he ever been guilty of fasting on the Day of Atonement? Is there hidden somewhere in his dark past a criminal observance of the Sabbath? Has he in an unguarded moment spoken well of Zion? Are his children barbarically circumcised? Does Dunn and Bradstreet's rate him, or is he a heathen? Should the investigation completely exonerate the candidate of these suspicions, he will be put to the supreme test. Before the whole gathered congregation, he will be given a ham sandwich. 'But I don't like ham sandwiches!' he may say. 'You must eat it just the same: – the categorical imperative of the basic principles!'

Then, and then only, may he be admitted to his religious estate, heir of Sinai, legatee of Houston, endowed with ballot. But should he fail these tests, then he shall forever remain in outer darkness, permitted, perhaps, to watch the bliss of his happier brethren, but himself, not of the sodality, a stranger, and non-voter!

Surely those whom the gods would destroy, they first make insane! Surely these inventions of this reformed Judaism do not belong in the histories of religion but in the treatises of Havelock Ellis. For the motivation of the basic principles is clear; these people don't want to be Jews, and are still inhibited from becoming Christian or agnostic. Accordingly they invent a religion which is a revolving door; standing in it, one makes exit and entrance simultaneous. It is not Ezekiel's circumcision of the heart; it is Shactel's castration of the soul. Ironically enough, it was left to Jews to sterilize their creed, to emasculate it of everything potent and positive, to convert it into a set of abstract nihilities, demoralizing negatives. If these disquisitions had constituted merely the evangels of some new sect, the shakers of Texas, holy-rolling away from the creed of their fathers, we would have dismissed the whole thing as but another manifestation of the natural phobias of troubled times. But the parishioners of Beth Israel, who are so concerned about *giving* help to the needy, apparently do not have troubled times; and moreover, it is in the name of Judaism they speak. That is their crime, and that their cowardly treachery; that is the dagger which they seek to drive deep into the heart of Jewry.

Pierre van Paassen:
The Remembering Friend   28 January 1944

Review of Pierre van Paassen, *The Forgotten Ally* (New York: Dial Press 1943)

The temptation to divide the continuum of history into stages clearly defined and easily identifiable, has been, it would appear from the writings of both scientists and poets, ever irresistible. Thus, the bard, surveying the vast backward and abysm of time, has, in many notable instances, bethought him of metals, base and noble, and has accordingly designated the ages of history as being either golden or of iron; and thus, too, the scientist, borrowing his imagery, not from the mineral but the animal kingdom, has distinguished one period of time from the other by attributing to each the name of some predominating and characteristic beast. It is, of course, true, that in the final analysis, both seer and sage, have found that their categories were not completely air-tight, that the golden often merged into the iron, creating an alloyed age, and that the chronological bestiary oft-times became confused and mingled, breeding eras which were unquestionably hybrid; but, by and large, their reliance upon a single adjective, a single phenomenon, to characterize an age, has indisputably had its uses.

Reflecting upon these thought-processes of both the literary and statistical historian, it has occurred to us that frequently history, to symbolize its nature and activity, evokes not the image of a metal or of an animal, but that of a human, and personalizes its cultural atmosphere – in a vocation. No one will deny but that the principal intellectual trait of the first half of the nineteenth century was its Byronism; it was the poet Byron then, even as in the Victorian era it was the poet Tennyson, who best summarized, both in their works and days, the trends and aspirations of the times. During the flighty fevered years of the twenties, when prosperity answered completely the material needs of the American people, creating, by contrast, an obvious spiritual vacuum, it was the movie actor Valentino and the evangelists Aimee Semple McPherson and 'Billy' Sunday – to each people its typical prophets – who symbolized the uncouth longings of that era.

With the passing of the halcyon days, and with the advent of the doubt-divided decade, – the years of ideological conflict, the period of the unreduced contradictions – another group of characters mount upon the stage, a new vocation becomes the symbol and the expression of the times, a vocation whose votaries, like some ancient Greek chorus, are always caught either in the act of recording things past or announcing things to come. The reader, no doubt, will recognize in this description the ubiquitous journalists, the peripatetic correspondents, dubbed foreign, but everywhere at home. It may be fairly stated, we believe, that at no time in history has a single calling more signally answered the intellectual demand of its time. For in the ever-constricting world of our day, the psychological quality which most people have shared in common has been curiosity – a thirst for knowledge, knowledge not so much of the arcana of nature, or of the subtleties of the human psyche, but knowledge of the way things move in this complicated world, of human relationship, of people and their governance.

Hence, the legion of journalists, professional interviewers, occupational cable-senders, the eyes and ears, as the cinema sub-title would have it, of the world. For the most part, this tribe has catered to one single public appetite – curiosity. It has travelled, interviewed, reported, all with one purpose in view – to satisfy the normal man's desire to know what's going on. It is a tribe which has produced some very distinguished practitioners, men who have not gone entirely unrewarded by their contemporaries, whose books are best-sellers, and whose views are second in importance only to the opinions of those statesmen whose dicta they relay.

At the same time, the typical occupation has produced its typical occupational disease. No medical term has yet been applied to this classic ailment of reportage, but its diagnosis is simple – a pseudo-impartiality, a cynical hard-boiledness, a spectatorial and olympian aloofness from the realities which are presumably the journalists' *métier*. At such a one you can level no greater insult than to say that 'he takes sides.' It is his proud and pathological boast that he never takes sides, that he can describe the workings of iniquity with the same dispassionate unconcern with which he retails the philanthropies of virtue, and that he is, essentially and by definition, *au dessus de la bataille*. His self-designating vaunt is that he is 'only eyes and ears.' If he were more, he fears, he would be accused of being a propagandist. To propagate even righteousness, it would appear, constitutes an unseemly partiality.

We have written this rather lengthy prolegomenon to a couple of reviewing paragraphs only to make the point that Pierre van Paassen, although one of the world's best international correspondents, is not of this calibre. It is a point which we have found it necessary to make simply because so many of the reviewers of his latest book: *The Forgotten Ally*, seemed to sneer, if only between the lines, at his passionate espousal of a cause, and appeared to consider the inclusion of ethical values within the scope of his reportage as an unprofessional and detracting intrusion. The fact is that it is precisely this quality which endows the writings of van Paassen with more than an ephemeral importance; it is by virtue of the fact that he is not merely big eyes and open ears, but also sensitive conscience, that he stands head and shoulders above his fellows. He is as far removed from the pseudo-impartiality of the statistical reporter as a man is from an adding-machine, a human from a canine 'seeing eye.'

As natural consequence, he never contents himself merely with the narrative of fact. Facts are indicia, and van Paassen legitimately searches for conclusions. In the case of the theme which he has chosen in this book, the conclusions are not far to seek. For the first time after five years of war, a voice is lifted on behalf of Jewry – the forgotten ally, the mislaid associate. Daily the press reports the many inventions which the savage Hamaniacs seek to visit upon a helpless people, no doubt for a while they provided to the reader a new and shuddering frisson; and after a while, they ceased to provide even that. To

Pierre van Paassen, precisely because he is more than eyes, ears, nose, and throat, this colossal tragedy contains the true Aristotelian qualities – pity and terror. But van Paassen, unlike the majority of his non-Jewish contemporaries is not content merely to sympathize with, or shudder for, our unhappy people. He knows, as everybody knows, how thousands of them may be saved and rehabilitated; and he knows, as so many find it difficult to realize, that the obstacle in the path of this salvation is the new appeasement-inspired foreign policy of Britain with reference to Palestine.

The indictment which van Paassen levels against both the Palestine administration and those doctrinaire imperialists at Whitehall whom the Lukes and the Keith-Roachs look to for inspiration and support, is one of the most devastating that has ever been launched against those equivocal and equivo-cating tactics which have for twenty-five years, not facilitated, but impeded the establishment of a Jewish Homeland. At times the intensity of van Paassen's *J'accuse* reaches the scathing proportions of prophetic utterance at its most vitriolic. Indeed, there have been some who have complained that due to an improper emphasis the British regime emerges only slightly less wicked than the Nazi regime. To think so is to misinterpret the entire tenor of van Paassen's thesis; it is precisely because he so intensely admires so much of the British tradition and standard of government – van Paassen is a naturalized Canadian, born in the Netherlands – that his wrath is the greater at this the betrayal of those standards and traditions. As for Hitler being the principal enemy, – of course, this is so; but we have reached a stage where it no longer requires temperament to hate Adolf, nor vision to berate fascism. But it does require enlightenment, and righteous indignation, to reveal and unmask to the innocent masses of the democracies these 'secret covenants secretly arrived at' which are this very day sealing and signing away the fate of Jewry and of Palestine.

Jewry ought to be grateful to van Paassen for yet another reason. No Jew could possibly have written van Paassen's book. He would have been held back from speaking frankly and with passion, as van Paassen does, either because of present discretion or old gratitude; in the final analysis, we would have read a petition and not an indictment. Yet an indictment was imperatively necessary at the present moment, before too much damage is done by that unremitting and energetic cabal of Baghdad effendi and Kenya bureaucrat. We are grateful that before these impending iniquities, Pierre van Paassen did not remain silent, but spoke out, as was befitting to one who believed in both God and man. Time was when the late William Butler Yeats complained, in a memorable poem, that 'the good lacked all conviction,' and only the wicked proceeded with a 'passionate intensity.' *The Forgotten Ally* constitutes, at last, a gratifying example of 'passionate intensity' dedicated to good, and not to evil, to Truth's partisanship, and not to Truth's ambiguous neutrality. Indeed, the mood, the temper, of van

Paassen's book is best revealed in the lines he quotes from a letter of Alfred Loisy to Pope Benedict: 'No one has a right to be neutral in moral questions. Whoever pretends to be indifferent is in reality siding with him who is wrong ...' Van Paassen has chosen his side; it used to be called the side of the angels; it is the side of the weak, and the wronged.

The Last Jew of Danzig   3 March 1944

A laconic note in the Polish Socialist newspaper *Rabotnik* reports that but recently the dread Gestapo finally liquidated the last Jew of Danzig. It will be remembered – it certainly has not been forgotten – that early in the spring of 1940, the goose-stepping sons of Belial, blown up with insolence and blood, celebrated their then current victories with a veritable massacre of the Jews of Danzig, an orgy which was at once a thanksgiving to their pagan blood-swilling gods and a first instalment upon their plan to make Europe *Judenrein*. In this massacre, conducted with German savagery and German thoroughness, no one was spared, no one except the lone anonymous sculptor Mr. X. It is this Mr. X whose name now marks the last spot on the Gestapo's dossier of murder.

The tragedy which has enveloped European Jewry during the last four years, it has been seen by all, has assumed a hundred gruesome shapes, a thousand macabre forms. The most diabolic inventions of the most satanic playwrights have never, it is clear, equalled the infernal techniques of torture, the hellish designs of degradation which the Hitlerite demons have prepared and visited upon their Jewish victims. Here, indeed, has been one field of endeavour in which throughout the years of the war they have never had recourse to ersatz; of indignity and terror which they have provided for Israel, they have furnished only the most thorough and the most effective. Not even Dante could complain about the authenticity of their fiend-fashioned inferno.

The students of sadism – and there *are* such; ponderous tomes, most unflattering to the reputation of mankind, have been written about the many inventions, from thumbscrew to air-bubble injector, which have been devised to advance (?) man's inhumanity to man – the students, we say, will be hard put to it to indicate which of the techniques of Himmler's butchers best represent the Aryan temperament at its most ingenious and most hardy. There are so many to choose from, for such as are interested in that kind of choice, so many methods of murder worthy of the coveted Iron Cross. Yet to us the fate of this anonymous sculptor Mr. X seems to represent the last word in the refinement of torture, the ultimate syllable in the agonies of degradation.

The Jew X was apparently spared – permanently, he thought, – because his captors wished to commission him to do some artistic work for them. The Nazis, it is well known, are great art-lovers; there is not a museum in Europe which they have not robbed. When they discovered, therefore, a Jewish talent in Danzig, they decided to be merciful, and suffer yet a little while the existence of the accursed *Jude*. It is not revealed what kind of work was demanded of the sculptor X, – it is not difficult, however, to imagine that in all likelihood the call was for busts, heroic statues of the conquerors of Danzig, the butchers of his brethren immortal in marble. *For there they that carried us away captive required of us a song; and they that wasted us required of us mirth, saying, sing us one of the songs of Zion ... How shall we sing the Lord's song in a strange land?*

It is for the psychologist to expatiate upon the emotions which agitated the artist X, both when the proposal was made to him, and during the months of his labour. How did his aesthetic spirit react to so ignominious a task? How did the conflict go, the inevitable conflict between his natural artistic integrity and the irresistible and therefore abominable will-to-live? How, indeed, did he manage to conceal his true feelings as he stood, chisel in hand, before his arrogant equestrian sitters? Was he not tempted, ever, to use his short instruments upon that material, only slightly softer than stone, that sat before him? When, at what point, did he first begin to suspect, from the gesture, from the attitude of his 'clients,' that as soon as his work was done, he, too, would be? Did he, at that point, begin, to prolong his work, lingering over his hammer-blows, delaying his cuts, accidently breaking his marble and beginning over again, sculpturing against time? Did he fail in his tasks, and was therefore punished by death, or did he complete his labours, to be in the same way rewarded?

There are no answers, as yet, to these questions. The anonymity of Mr. X, the very absence of details as to the circumstances preceding his death, agonize the imagination. Here, indeed, was an example of Bialik's commiseration for those 'who sink their blood into the foreign stone.' For the sense of worthlessness which he must have felt at the realization of how he was buying his life, together with the ever-present sense of fear that in the final accounting the bargain would not be, as it was not, kept – these beggar description. They are emotions – this pity and this terror – which properly belong to a tale of Edgar Allan Poe.

Now, it is reported that the Jew X is dead. His commission completed, he was hanged from a tree.

At last the news item reveals itself in its true colours! It is not the Jew X who plays the role of artist therein; it is the German executioner who is the real sculptor, sculpturing in the anonymous limbs of the last Jew of Danzig, stiff with rigor mortis, the figure and emblem of the New Order! Against the windless horizon, it hangs rigid, statuesque, its head somewhat on a side, as if listening to final instruction, – the supreme effort, the highest reach of German art! This is their Apollo Belvedere, not, perhaps, the symbol of the body beautiful, but certainly the pendent token of suffering humanity; – the contribution of the Gestapo chisel-men to the pantheon of art!

No one knows the name of the Jew X, member of the race unmentionable, the race unremembered. What, indeed, is one Jewish corpse among three million already lying in the European charnel-house, that his name should be noted? Even the X of his designation seems too individual, too particular. Yet in his very anonymity he is universal, the universal symbol of both the ordeal suffered by a helpless people, and of the abattoir tenets and hangman doctrines of the Prussian supersavages. It is a symbol the memory of which must not be obliterated. That swinging sculpture moving over the air of Danzig must hang also from the rafters of the human mind, until the day when the iniquity it betokens shall be avenged! The very winds which touch it bring its tidings throughout the length and breadth of the continent! The birds of prey, waiting for its descent, caw aloud the wickedness which has been done!

When shall that wickedness be effaced, atoned for, revenged? Only on the day when that hanging statue, the corpse of the Jew X, whom no Pygmalion can bring to resurrection, shall have for company the bodies of his persecutors – the bodies of Hitler, Goebbels, Himmler, and all their blood-stained henchmen, hanging from trees, stiff with rigor mortis, the pendent statues of Nemesis, the final and completed sculpture of the anonymous artist X, last Jew of Danzig! Then, and not earlier!

Of the Purim to Be   10 March 1944

It was none other than Adolf Hitler who, to a Jewry celebrating the discomfiture of Haman and the triumph of Israel, furnished the perfect thought for the occasion. With a knowledge of Jewish lore which is not surprising in one who for years has specialized in discovering and slandering all things Semitic, and with a natural intuition which for once seemed to have a solid background, *der Fuehrer* expressed the conviction that world Jewry stood by eagerly awaiting the opportunity to commemorate his downfall with a new Purim. We believe that for once, Hitler diagnosed our sentiments correctly. He spoke not merely as a politician; he spoke like a prophet, a seer proclaiming the inevitable.

Certainly the Hamanism which the Nazi overlord represents is such as to cause that of the original son of Hamdatha to pale into comparative insignificance. Where the one was a tyro, the other is a professional; where the one relied only upon his hatred, the other relies also upon his typical German organization and skill; where the one sought massacre on an occasion, the other seeks massacre as a system and with a purpose. The descendant of Agag is for anti-semitism, as a dwarf compared to the illegitimate scion of the Schickl-grubers.

Wherefore, if joy followed the hanging of Haman upon a pillar fifty cubits high, what joy and jubilee shall ensue when Adolf meets a similar fate? Surely the Purim of the Book of Esther will be as a minor festival compared to the grand unforgettable date of the new Purim to be!

We can already foresee the ritual of its celebration. Naturally a *megillah* will have to be composed, recounting the narrative of *der Fuehrer's* rise and fall. We leave it to the inspired scribes of the future to determine the form and content of this new *megillah*, the final negating appendix to *Mein Kampf*. In the synagogues, therefore, the story will be repeated, and every time the name of Adolf will appear therein, the *gragers*, as of old, will sound again – only this time they will be *gragers* simulating the noise of Stukas, dive-bombing against the memory of their creator, the Stuka with which he thought to conquer the world, and now become a child's bauble. When the names of Adolf's henchmen – since, impotent, he had no sons – will be uttered by the reader of the scroll, it will be in one breath that they will be uttered, even as is now done unto the names of the ten sons of Haman. No doubt, too, to cap it all, the Jewish housewife will invent some *Hitlertaschen*, tasty in content, symbolic in form.

Unfortunately, there is a rigorous routine to be followed in the fashioning of a new Purim. There can not be – as is evidenced by tradition and law – a feast of Purim unless it is preceded by a fast of Esther. It is through that period that we are now passing, a period of fasting and self-sacrifice, of abnegation and mortification of the flesh. The great ordeal of war to which all of us have been subjected is that preliminary fast. We have no doubt but that despite the anguish of its endurance, despite the agony of its ritual, the faith in all of us remains firm, a faith that the morrow will be followed by the triumphant victorious celebration of a new, and, it is hoped, the final Purim. This new Purim, moreover, is one which all of the peoples of the earth, and not only Israel, will zealously and piously observe. Even as Adolf suspected, and as all of us hope, may it come soon and in our day!

The Feast of Passover   7 April 1944

Again the annual feast of Passover comes, not as a commemoration of events belonging to the remote and romantic past, but as the symbol of the very incidents of the current all-too-realistic day. Indeed, as one reads both the first twenty chapters of Exodus and the embellishing narrative of the Haggadah, one is struck again and again by the fact that the story told is far more contemporaneous than historical. It is as if the headlines of today and tomorrow had been foretold in the chapters and verses of Holy Writ. We would not be surprised, in fact, if one of these days newspaper editors, seeking to save that rationed paper, suddenly decided to communicate their news only by the means of biblic references.

The truth is that the authentically fundamental writings of mankind have always had this quality: their verities are eternal. Until wickedness and the hatred of man for his brother utterly vanish from the earth, those opening chapters of the Book of Exodus must remain the dubiously classic formula for anti-semitism. It is true that during the centuries, this Judaeophobia received here and there some new quirks and improvements (?); Haman made his contribution to the science of Jew-hatred, and subsequently lesser worthies, too. But fundamentally the technique for the oppression of a minority was definitely blueprinted by the wizards of Pharaoh.

Even the arch-antisemite of history, Adolf Hitler, has not altered the technique; he has only cast it into the mould of a scientific and organized world. He, too, began by raising the patently false cry that the Jews must be destroyed 'lest they rise up against us'; and then revealed both the hypocrisy and savagery of his attitude by refusing to let the people go. Obviously, from the point of view of efficiency, the Gestapo agent is an improvement upon the taskmaster, and the patented gas-vans and air-bubble-injectors a scientific advance over death by drowning in the Nile. Obviously, even the sages and counsellors of the Pharaoh could never hope to achieve so thorough and methodical a system of mass-murder and scheduled slaughter as in the throaty boast of the Black Forest pagans. But in objective and motive, both historic periods and both megalo-maniac tyrants are one and indivisible – aggrandizement marching forward upon the golgotha of its victims' skulls.

Certainly all of Europe today – and not only its Jews – languish in a veritable Egypt. The only Goshens remaining are these concentration camps crowded with our co-religionists; and these, too, are fast disappearing, liquidated, vanishing into their mass-graves, the last air-raid shelter of the oppressed. Those who survive are used, as in the historic parable, for the erection of the contemporary Pithom and Rameses, the gigantic fortifications of the continental prison. And carrying out the historic parallel to its last agonizing detail, even the straw is not provided for the bricks. The pool of slave-labour of Germany, fashioning under duress its own shackles, does not even receive the minimal fodder accorded to beasts of burden.

Bondage it is, as Egyptian and as Pharaonic as ever bondage was. Fortunately, the similarity does not end with the prospering of the wicked. Until a year ago, it is true, it did look as if the modern version of the story of Exodus was to have a speedier and unhappier denouement; but recent history has repeated the ancient. Already the plagues are being visited upon the hard-hearted one, and all his domain. It is true, that unlike prototype, most of these plagues are of his own creation; and do fall upon him out of poetic justice. The darkness that envelops his land was by himself called forth; the hail of bombs that devastates his cities are but the imitation of his own diabolic invention.

The exodus itself is not far off. Already there is being proposed the final destruction of the hosts of Pharaoh and all his chariots. On the eastern front he is in continual retreat; when the western front is finally opened, there will be no place for retreat, – only defeat. Then, indeed, will all those who have suffered beneath his oppression be freed again, all those little countries, brought into the orbit of his enslavement freed again, and all those populations, agonized beneath the lash of their gauleiters, be men and free again. True it is that before that day dawns much blood will yet be shed, many miracles will yet have to be performed; Pharaoh will relent and harden his heart again, relent and seek some new negotiated subterfuge for the attainment of his purposes; but clear it already is that his inevitable end is already writ large in current event.

Nor will the epilogue to the Passover tale of to-day be any different from that of yore. Again, with the emancipation there will come, out of the thunder and lightning, the re-emancipation of those principles by which civilization has endured and marched forward. The ten commandments which Hitler and his myrmidons have sought to abrogate will come into their own again; the fundamental tenets of decent human behavior first given to our ancestors at Sinai, and later incorporated into all the moral systems of the world, will be once more vindicated.

Some time ago Hitler ventured the opinion that when he would be defeated, all Israel would celebrate his downfall with another Purim. Although we never really did think much of Adolf as an inventor of Jewish ritual, or as a proclaimer of Jewish holiday, we did, at the time, consider his suggestion – and prophecy – the first statement which the Fuehrer had made with which we could agree. We feel moreover, that we can't have too much of a good thing; and that Purim is not enough. A latter-day Passover would also add both to the joy of the Jewish calendar and to the general gaiety of nations. May it come soon, *b'mhairo b'yomainu.*

The Three-Fold Exile   5 May 1944

That the Jews of Poland, even in the halycon days of peace, did not in that country lie at ease in a bed of roses, is a historic fact which requires no elaborate proof. The newspaper headlines of the Thirties supply sufficient illustration. Nonetheless, in the common misery which befell all the citizens of the Polish Republic, Jewry was ready to forget – at least for the duration, it hoped, forever – the unhappy things of yesterday, the economic discrimination, the ghetto-benches, the uniforms of the Endeks, the bloodless pogrom and the occasional bloody one, too, – forget, indeed, the entire system and schedule of persecution which made Poland to one tenth of its population a place of indubitable exile. The Polish Government went into exile; into exile, too, marched the remnants of its army. The people within Poland fought on. For a while it did appear as if out of the ordeal of a shared calamity, there would emerge a Poland purged of its racial prejudice, a Poland which out of the heroism of the Warsaw Ghetto, out of the sacrifice of the Polish underground, would rise again, cohesive, united, brotherly with the brotherhood of common suffering.

There was good ground to believe that this hope would someday be realized. Poland was, after all, the only occupied country in which arose no Quisling who would prostitute himself to the conqueror's will. No Laval, no Delacroix, no Seyss-Inquart, appeared in Poland to besmirch its record. There was, however, a Quisling, which did not bear the image of a human, who did appear – that was the Quisling of Polish antisemitism.

The whole democratic world has been shocked by the Polish court-martial in England which recently 'convicted' thirty Jewish 'deserters.' The crime of the Jewish soldiers serving loyally in the Polish Army consisted of their refusal to continue to bear arms under officers and among troops who shared and uttered the anti-semitic notions of the very enemy whom they were supposed to fight. The incidents which have disgraced the Polish Army would seem incredible were they not so thoroughly substantiated by the testimony of eye-witnesses. On one occasion, it is reported, Polish soldiers cheered and jubilated over the story of the Warsaw Ghetto – not, mind you, over the humiliation of the German forces which required six weeks to subdue unarmed and starved civilians, but cheered the massacre of the Warsaw Jews! On another occasion, officers of the Polish Republic announced to their soldiers that Poland could hope for nothing from Churchill because 'he had been sold to the Jews.' On a third occasion, the same gallant comrades-in-arms announced that when the day of liberation came they would have as many bullets for the killing of Polish Jews as for the killing of the German invader!

Such sentiments, surely, are not to be considered as expressing merely the natural exuberance of soldiers fighting the battle for democracy. They reveal, indeed, an intellectual cancer which not all the radium of their own Madame Curie could ever eradicate!

Is it surprising, therefore, that Jewish soldiers refused to continue to serve any longer in the ranks of these marrano Nazis, these delayed Hitlerites? Certainly the Polish Jew, wearing the uniform and the wounds of the Republic, stood here in threefold exile; an exile in Poland, an exile again with the Polish Army in England, and a third time an exile in the very ranks of his fellow-soldiers!

He would, indeed, have been a slave, a helot, a mere mercenary, if he did *not* insist upon his soldier's right to equal and fair treatment. As for 'desertion,' let the facts make clear the nature of this desertion. The thirty accused did not seek discharge from the Army so that they could return to the calm and quiet of civilian life; they sought a transfer into the British Army! They wanted to continue the good fight; but under auspices more in harmony with the avowed objectives of the United Nations. How great must have been the degradation of these thirty, how bitter their suffering, how shattered their hopes if they wished to change the comradeship (?) and the customs of their own forces and their own language for service in an army whose soldiers they did not know and whose language they would have to learn! Only weeks, months, of spiritual agony and disillusion could bring soldiers to such a decision, and only the Quisling – antisemitism – could bring about such a shattering ordeal.

The court-martial, therefore, which found these men guilty – guilty of wanting to fight better with the British! – was neither a court, nor was it martial. For the objectives by which it seemed to be motivated were neither those of justice nor of army morale. Certainly it is not just that men should be sentenced to two and three years imprisonment because they seek in their own ranks the symptoms of those ideals for which they are sent out to shed their blood; and certainly it is not in the interest of the morale of the Polish Army, or of any other army, that racial discrimination should flourish, and flaunt its ugly face among comrades presumably fighting for the four freedoms and the brotherhood of man.

A court-martial certainly should have been held; but the accused should have been the antisemitic officers, those quasi-Gestapo men who dared to introduce into the barracks and the mess-halls of the armies of liberty those traitorous opinions and those quisling attitudes which could have been born only out of secret intellectual traffic with the enemy!

Apparently, no such courts-martial were held; or if they were, their effect was not very salutary. Certainly the Polish Government which does not miss an opportunity of publicizing its acts of tolerance and its gestures of magnanimity did not see fit to give these courts-martial (if any) their due publicity. No doubt the fate of the thirty Jewish soldiers would have been kept equally secret, if it had not been that the trials took place in England, and England is a country of healthy public opinion.

The entire incident, with its revelations and its mealy-mouthed apologies, points moreover, to a situation more serious than appears on the surface. The Jew-baiting that went on in the Polish Army, after all, were the acts of minor officers and privates; but the decision of the court-martial is that of majors and generals. Indeed, one has a right to assume that the corporal would not permit himself the luxury of the antisemitic sport if he did not think that his superior officer was of one opinion with him. It is this suspicion which ought to cause the greatest concern to those who consider themselves the architects of Poland's future.

Poland needs the goodwill of the democracies. Her entire future depends upon the regard of her allies. That good will can not be won by reports that officers in the Polish Army are awaiting 'Der Tag' when they can indulge in an orgy of pogroms, nor by reports that Jewish soldiers find life so intolerable under the love and affection of their Polish buddies that they must seek admission into another army to achieve the objectives of this war. To convict men for rebelling against the antisemitism which infects the Polish Army is to make oneself party to that antisemitism, is to range oneself on the side of the enemies of democracy. The judges who sat on the now notorious court-martial did a grievous wrong to the thirty accused; an equally grievous wrong they did to the good name and the future of Poland.

The Eleventh Commandment   19 May 1944

Review of Walter Clay Lowdermilk, *Palestine: Land of Promise* (New York: Harper and Brothers 1944)

It was the late Chaim Nachman Bialik, poet laureate of the Hebrew Renaissance, who once made so bold as to declare that to him, despite his literary loyalties, a book on Palestinian fertilizer was a much more welcome phenomenon, at this period of the Homeland's development, than the finest masterpiece of belles lettres. This dictum – which reveals that even poets are sometimes visited with a sense of reality – came to our mind as we read the highly factual and extremely fascinating book of Mr. Lowdermilk. It is a book which for its treatment of the agricultural and industrial potentialities of the much-promised and much-maligned land would most certainly have made glad the heart of our Bialik.

Even to the writer of these lines – fit only to hold a translator's bushel over Bialik's light – it was a relief, after years of feeding upon the Zionist literature of rhapsody – the lyrical travelogues, the dithyrambic prophecies, the ecstatic analyses – to come upon a book which at last goes back to first things, and considers – inevitable task! – the very fundamentals of Palestine's future, its soil and its moistures. Of the other two elements of the famous four, of fire from the Palestinian sun and of the air which according to Talmudic statement 'maketh its inhaler wise,' we are content to let the seers and the sweetsingers have their say; of its earth and its water, it is but right that an expert should speak; and Mr. Lowdermilk is such a one.

Sent in 1939 by the United States Department of Agriculture to make a survey of the use of the land in Palestine for the purpose of deriving therefrom whatever lessons might be pertinent to the problems of American land conservation, Mr. Lowdermilk made a detailed study of almost all of the economic and industrial aspects of the country. One of the principal points of the book, dramatically enough, is that its author concludes by applying lessons learned from American experience to the specific problems of Palestine; the most important of these suggestions is a great reclamation project, tentatively called the Jordan Valley Authority, along the lines of the Tennessee Valley Authority.

Mr. Lowdermilk, as we have already said, gets down to fundamentals. He is prosaic enough – and realistic enough – to declare that all civilization is based on food; that the source thereof is the soil; and that in a constricting globe the only frontiers still open lie beneath our feet. It is inspiring to watch him delve into the biography of the Palestinian soil; it is even more inspiring to see him lift his handful of the good red earth and hold it aloft – a symbol of the pregnant future. So impressed is the author with this vital relationship between man and his habitat, that he takes the liberty of devising an Eleventh Commandment, so pertinent to the past, present and future of Palestine, that we give it here in full:

'Thou shalt inherit the holy earth as a faithful steward, conserving its resources and productivity from generation to generation. Thou shalt safeguard thy fields from soil erosion, thy living waters from drying up, thy forests from desolation, and protect thy hills from overgrazing by the herds, that thy descendants may have abundance forever. If any shall fail in this stewardship of the land, thy fruitful fields shall become sterile stony ground or wasting gullies, and thy descendants shall decrease and live in poverty or perish from off the face of the earth.'

Lowdermilk's book is really an extended commentary, a piece of elaborate Rashi on this text. He shows how the inhabitants of Palestine for century after century failed to observe this unwritten commandment; how only with the advent of the *chalutz* was this *mitzva* finally performed; and how, in the future, the additional injunction can receive full implementation through projects of great scope and vision. His tribute to the achievement of the Yishuv – a tribute given without benefit of conjuring adjectives but solely through scientific matter-of-fact statement – coming as it does from an impartial source, constitutes most gratifying reading. The victory over the anopheles mosquito, more terrible than the mufti; the resurrection of the Dead Sea; redemption of swampland; the conquest, as in Tel Aviv, of the sands; the development of citrus agriculture where every orange and lemon tree, so dearly beloved, have each their recorded case-history; these are epic chapters more glorious than armies with banners. For here, 'in an area of a province which has the soil and conditions of a continent,' to use Sir Herbert Samuel's phrase, a people come from all corners of the world has frustrated the neglect of centuries!

Mr. Lowdermilk, moreover, is a soil conservationist, and not an archaeologist. He is interested in the evidences of the earth, not merely for what they reveal of the past, but also, and principally, for what they indicate for the future. The present low condition of the land, he is convinced, is the result of centuries of wilful neglect and criminal unconcern on the part of its rulers. Palestine, he deduces from facts which come to his attention, both in ancient texts and in extant ruins, once held a population of at least four million people. Palestine, he deduces from that which has already been achieved by its Jewish inhabitants and from what may be achieved by following modern methods of reclamation, can again feed and support at least so great a population. These prognostications, moreover, are not based upon wishful thinking; the author indicates, with everything except actual blueprint, how the country may again become a land, if we permit ourselves the phrase, flowing with Lowdermilk and honey.

His principal suggestion is one which involves the application of emergency techniques so admirably used in the United States. With a grand system of irrigation, involving the diversion of the Jordan waters, with their damming at critical points, and release at the proper time, the whole aided by a proper system of soil conservation, involving the terracing of hillsides, the leaching of saline earth, the draining of swamps, much of the vital plenitude of nature's resources which to-day goes to waste may be used for the increased fertility of the land, and the added felicity of its added inhabitants. Joined to this, the utilization of the Dead Sea depression, the deepest natural trench upon the face of the earth, the Grand Canyon of the East, for the purpose of creating power-producing waterfalls between the Mediterranean and the Dead Sea – and another source of inestimable riches, with the resurrection of the Negeb as a consequence, is wrested from topography. The plan inflames the imagination; as with a mighty hand, it pushes aside horizons.

Mr. Lowdermilk has much to say about the industrial achievements and possibilities of Palestine. Everywhere he is factual; and everywhere thorough. Nothing is overlooked, neither silt nor salt; the expert gets his data before he enunciates his desiderata. Even the social aspects of the Yishuv – its co-operative colonies, its semi-industrial villages, its sense of the dignity and worthiness of labour, all play a part in his description and in his promises for the future. Lowdermilk's book is beyond doubt one of the most down-to-earth and reach-the-sky analyses of the Palestine problem which we have seen since time beyond remembrance. No Jew should be without it; its author is for Palestine the guide par excellence; for he is at once practical and a man of vision. If you have not up to now, go now and seek out his company, he will tell you many things, why springs trickle from limestone, and why the clouds over the Dead Sea are blueish-white.

Incendiary Antisemitism   26 May 1944

It is with a deep sense of sadness and with a shocking realization of the truth as it is glaringly revealed in the flames playing about the newly-erected Quebec synagogue that we must here record that that dubious honour – the burning of synagogues – which hitherto characterized only Nazi cities is now shared by the capital of our province. There is, moreover, hardly an enlightened Canadian, of no matter what religious persuasion, who does not at this moment join with us in our wrath and bitterness at the thought that in a democratic country, engaged in a life-and-death struggle for the fundamental principles of religious freedom, such things should occur!

It has been said that the hands which set fire to the Quebec synagogue were the hands of criminals. Of course. Heroes and saints they were not. But the act of these ruffians was beyond doubt the result of preliminary causes; it most certainly was not a case of spontaneous combustion. Clearly the arsonists perpetrated only the last explosive act of a series of preliminary incendiary preparations.

What were these preparations? The preparations consisted not so much of the act of pouring gasoline upon the synagogue walls as of the continued and unrelenting dissemination, by careerist demagogues and bigoted misleaders, of the highly inflammable oils of antisemitism. When the City Fathers of Quebec took one unconstitutional step after the other to prevent the construction of a place of worship for a group of its citizens, they did, in fact, prepare the intellectual (?) background to acts such as finally occurred. When certain influences, week in, week out, invoked all the shibboleths of mediaevalism and went rampaging in a veritable orgy of Jew-baiting, they did, in fact, without benefit of torch or phosphorus, prepare the milieu for a deed such as was finally perpetrated. The hand which did the actual dirty work of arson may have been that of some uncouth and criminal hoodlum; but certainly other hands, dipping their pens in Judaeophobic poison remote from the scene of crime, must bear the real responsibility.

That there has been created, by those fomenters of race-hatred, so ugly a mood in Quebec City is further evidenced by the fact that a rabbi coming from out of town to the consecration ceremonies could not obtain a taxi to take him to the synagogue premises. Anywhere else, the chauffeurs told him, they would drive him, but not thither. Such an attitude demonstrates clearly that the Jew-baiting demagogues have done their work well, and that their virus has been inoculated far and wide. It is also to be noted that at the actual consecration ceremonies which, despite flood of petition and fire of arson, did take place, no minister of any church came to express his sympathy at the desecration which had been done.

That an attempt – and a serious one – should be made to discover the actual criminals and to uncover those who sent them to do their illuminating work goes without saying. But that is not the crux of the matter. Once and for all, a stop must be put to the fomenting of racial hatred which is rampant in our province, and which is being practised with shameful impunity. As the law exists at present, every little careerist, and every big one, too, finds it an adventure most profitable to conduct campaigns of racial hatred and religious intolerance. As long as this antisemitic circus is open to all and as long as so-called respectable elements enter its precincts to go through their Jew-baiting antics as preliminary to the selling of their particular political or doctrinal wares, so long will there be found elements from the underworld who will seek to emulate their betters (?) in the manner in which their crude literalism must dictate.

Authority must speak out. The Jews of Quebec City in erecting their synagogue were exercising a right which is accorded to all citizens of free countries. Their first project to build themselves a House in which they could worship God was met by libel both defamatory and blasphemous. Now the consecration of their synagogue is heralded with arson. What next? There lies a heavy burden upon authority, both legislative and moral, to speak out against the iniquity which has been done in our midst.

Cherbourg

16 June 1944

We have no doubt but that General Montgomery, now leading the attack upon the beaches of Normandy, has frequently had occasion during the last seven days, to recall many of those passages of Holy Writ, so appealing to his temperament, so pertinent to his destiny. For 'Monty' is, almost as much as he is a general, a Bible-man. With equal skill does he wield both the avenging sword and the consoling text. Son of an Archbishop, he bears with him, even into the smoke and fury of battle, the lore which he gathered at his father's table. So was it when he pursued across the length of Northern Africa his famous adversary Rommel, dubbed 'the desert fox'; then did his despatches read like veritable gleanings from the Book; and so must it be now, as probing into the lairs and secrets of the Atlantic Wall, he seeks out 'the foxes, the little foxes, that spoil the vines.'

It is the sixth chapter of Joshua which today must be uppermost in the mind of the spiritual descendant of Cromwell's Roundheads, who did also go forth into battle to the singing of Psalms. They are the trumpets of Jericho which must be echoing, across the centuries, in his ears. Having landed upon the shores of France, having completed the agenda of D-Day ('*Der Tag*' of the Germans, in reverse), and now paying back to Normandy a visit which was once made at Hastings, it is the port of Cherbourg that the might and power of the United Nations is encompassing. They are not trumpets which clamor about that besieged city, but the more compelling persuasion of artillery; it is not merely with continual prayer that the fall of Cherbourg is sought, although the prayers which rise from millions of homes, beseeching divine intercession for sons and brothers does today fill the courts of Heaven with a perpetual plea; the hosts of liberation stand upon the European shores.

As we write these lines, the battle still rages in all its fury. The first great thrill of enthusiasm which swept the free world – yes, and the enslaved world, too – at the news that the invasion had begun, has settled down to the more earnest and grimmer business of daily warfare. Towns have already been taken; bridgeheads have been established; Cherbourg is about to fall. As in some movie-house, where a whimsical operator, himself a thwarted dramatist, turns the machine backwards, the entire scene of Dunkirk is being shown again, – only this time the actors move in an opposite direction. Yet Cherbourg is not the Jericho which must fall; the Jericho which must receive its just doom is that great city of dreadful night which exists behind the Atlantic Wall, the Nazi domain builded on the misery of oppressed peoples, the grim metropolis of golgotha fashioned by all the gauleiters of Europe. That city, in the course of time must be razed to the ground; and 'cursed will be that man before the Lord, that riseth up and buildeth this city Jericho: he shall lay the foundations thereof in his first-born, and in his youngest shall he set up the gates of it!'

In the meantime, the battle continues apace. The armed men are passing, to compass the city. The sound of the modern ram's horns – what mighty horns from what battering rams! – fills the land. The first day has passed, and the second, and the third; but much still remains to be done. A high seriousness, a solemnity, confident but not of lightheartedness, takes hold of us; for the order of Joshua is the order of the day: 'Ye shall not shout, nor make any noise with your voice, neither shall any word proceed out of your mouth, until the day I bid you shout; then shall ye shout.'

Of Lowly Things

Of the sweetsinger in Israel it is written that he did once cause his lips to speak evil of the spider, God's creature. Out of the disgust of his soul, he, the psalmist who had so richly praised the world and all that is therein, did abhor this ugly creeping thing, of the six legs all ambulant, as if filth would embrace the compass, and of the little bloated belly weaving the gray filaments of corruption, – belly and legs, a retching for the eye.

The writing, however, goes on to say that later when King David was pursued by his enemies, and sought refuge in a cave, he did, for three days, sit watching a spider weave its web over the mouth of his hiding-place. Then, when his pursuers came seeking him, and fell upon this cave wherein the King, with held-in breath, in darkness sat, they beheld the labour of the spider upon the cave's mouth, and they said: He has not been here, for, look, the spiderweb hangs over the entrance and it is whole. Wherefore they went upon their way.

Then was King David glad, he breathed again, recanting his slander of the spider, praising the spider, singing a psalm for the spider that in the hour of his need had made him a buckler and shield.

The rabbis tell this story because it is a lesson in humility; and therefore they preach that everything which appears on the face of the earth, and in the bowels thereof, or anywhere visible to the eye, is not to be despised, not the spider, nor the speck that lives upon the spider, nor anything that has a being; for that being is from the earth's foundations, ordained by God's decree. Its purpose may not be known, its origin not known, its reason inscrutable; but there it is, by fiat extant, and not to be contemned.

For is it to be thought that the creatures that crawl upon the earth, the pale pullulation that swarms beneath a lifted stone, the uglinesses little and monstrosities large that inhabit the deep, were fashioned merely to arouse in the human beholder derision and disgust? Was it for this – for the entertainment and catharsis of the nobler generations – that Godhead laboured six days of Creation?

Surely there are things which to our own eyes have neither meaning nor purport, yet to the eyes of our children's children may shine with glory newly discovered, significance freshly snatched, even as today there are many things which we hold precious and cherished which to our ancestors were but clods and rubbish! The world is truly born anew; the inventory of yesterday's earthly riches is not today's, but increased; for that which in ignorance was spurned is now for knowledge held dear, and that which was flung in a heap as of no worth is presently, out of deeper vision, prized above rubies.

Consider the lumps of coal, black, hard, and of no beauty, fit for the furnace, a source of cheap warmth. Nor is this, its humble use, to be disdained. Yet there came a day when because of wisdom in man, a new element was therein discovered, banishing mysterious diseases, mighty and merciful; and look! out of this stone, this soot, a new Creation. The power of the compressed centuries is loosed; the secret, which was never a secret save for ignorance, is revealed; and the sun, fettered in the clefts of the dark rock, unshackled, – again beneficient, salutary, radiant!

Even those dwelling in the darkness of superstition have surmised this truth – that out of things lowly and graceless, things worthy, and healing to man, might issue. Recall the incantations of witches, dancing bony dances about their brews, flinging into the sacrilegious cauldron their thesaurus of disgust, eye of newt and toe of frog, fillet of a fenny snake, wolf tooth and lizardleg, owletwing and goatgall, all things at once frightful and sickening, the very broth of nausea. True, this is mere heathenry, and darkness; yet is it the invention of a man. It is man's invention and guess, even as were those balms prescribed by the salving doctors of long ago, composed of urine and earwax and other defecation, laid to the body of the sick to bring it health.

It is no wonder; see, see those million candles lighting the earth, wafting a sweet incense, flowers with their roots in dung and ordure!

It is a text which everyday is written in the Book of Life. Until yesterday many afflictions and diseases came upon man to destroy him. Against their ravages there was no cure, no salvation, only the bandage of the winding-sheet. Such was that foul trituration which comes from the accidents of venery, such that rotting of the limbs infected announcing itself with prophesying stench, and such many other ailments, shaming the doctors. Now is discovered penicillin. It is the remedy that stays corruption and takes away the hunger from the eating wound. Whence is it? What marvellous new gem is it that with its potency palsies the crawling fingers of Death? What noble element, what richness of wealth itself, is this elixir?

It is mould.

The green mould that gathers upon bread, the feculent fur of cheese, the mushrooms of rot – this, is our *physic nonpareil*! The pus of food! This is what stays disease, and brings wholeness to gangrened limb, brings resurrection. This is resurrection's scum!

Is there not here a homily from which all may learn King David's lesson? Out of the lowly cometh exaltation, and out of the rejected healing. Who would have imagined that this despised mould, so nauseating in appearance, so ugly in origin, would be lifted to such useful heights? Yet those who sought these uses, found them, and what yesterday was spurned by the foot is today taken into the very stream of the blood, as a talisman, a cure, a saver of life.

For this whole world is like a great nursery room which the Lord, upon his sixth day, had left for the entertainment of his children. He filled it, moreover, with every manner of toy, with varied gadgets, playthings of a simple and of a difficult kind. Into this nursery He made to enter His children so that they might discover the workings of the infinity of things with which it is filled. When, out of the curiosity of their minds, they succeed in unravelling the plentiful puzzles, the Lord is glad, like a Father in the growth and intelligence of his children. When, however, they sit gaping at the things intended for their delight, making no effort to discover the operation of their nursing furniture, then is He sad, like a Father whose children are behind their years.

There must have been joy in heaven, therefore, at the disclosure that at last a son of man had found the plan and purpose of that thing which so many generations had spurned. Another one of the mysteries of the earth had been solved; the children of men were growing, God bless their bones!

Might one not add another moral to the tale? There are men, too, who may be likened to mould, rejected by their fellows, universally despised, considered as of no use. Surely there must be in them, even as in their parallel, some of the magic penicillin, if only one knew how to extract it, if only one had the intelligence to see it. Indeed, revelations such as those of penicillin now occur with such frequency that one is compelled to the belief that there is nothing – neither among things animate nor those inanimate which may be considered lowly, but that all things and all people stand equal in the great and universal design.

Where's Adolf?   17 November 1944

No doubt our readers are familiar with that famous Canadian advertising cartoon which, announcing the charms of a certain beverage, daily startled the engrossed public with the challenging query: Where's Joe? Invariably the self-satisfied answer was forthwith provided by the advertiser: Gone for a beer.

The same sort of act has been taking place, it would appear, in the world press, curious about the whereabouts of Adolf Hitler; it sets up hypotheses, it reports rumours, it piques curiosity, all on the question of what has happened to Adolf. These questionings, moreover, are not entirely unjustified: upon certain unpleasant occasions throughout the year, Adolf Hitler, it was known, was wont to address his German *volkstum*. Having created a calendar of holidays commemorating the sordid incidents of his own ignoble life, Adolf, at these gatherings used to be the principal celebrant. Now, for a period of almost six months, the Fuehrer has not opened his lips. Ever since he was so miraculously saved (*sic*) from the attempt made on his life, a deathlike silence appears to have settled upon him. Hence the interrogation: Where's Adolf?

By almost unanimous consent, the reporters and the newspaper commentators have chosen as their guess the same answer as that of the abovementioned brewer: Gone for a bier. The Fuehrer is dead, the Fuehrer is dying, the Fuehrer is about to die. The desirable prospect is conjugated in all its tenses. Some there are who maintain that he has gone mad; but how they can tell nobody says. Others surmise that he is now a prisoner of the Gestapo, which is planning to blow up Berchtesgaden (with Hitler in it) and thus make out of their leader an immortal legend. Still others conjecture that he has already gone to his reward, but that Himmler is keeping the news secret until his own *coup d'état* shall have been prepared.

It must be stated that in all of these conjectures and surmises one notes a tone of joy, the accent of triumph. To our mind it is a mistaken jubilee. The natural and premature death of Adolf Hitler would be a grave miscarriage of poetic justice. The proprieties of retribution demand that he should survive at least until the day of reckoning. His personal presence is required for the last scene.

It is for this reason that we are somewhat heartened by the subsequent news that it is not insanity or death which is preventing Adolf from making an appearance, but rather a tumor in his throat, brought on no doubt by his special type of oratory, and now a handicap against further rhetoric. Such a possibility, indeed, is more in line with what nemesis requires. Certainly there is a satisfying irony in the fact that the first personal affliction to come upon the author of this holocaust should come in the form of a punishment against that organ which was his principal instrument for capturing power. This, indeed, is poetic justice with a vengeance. It is the penalty of Balaam all over again. His heart bursts with hatred against 'international Jewry' and against 'eastern Bolshevism'; he would fain deliver, as of yore, one of his Nuremberg masterpieces against the twin menace; but the heart may burst, for the throat refuses to articulate. Wickedness eager to perform its deed, but the body too weak to accomplish the will – it is a condition dantesque in its horrific justice.

So Hitler could not arise to curse. Wherefore it was fitting that on November the seventh, Himmler should speak. When Balaam falls silent, it is the ass that brays.

The Smoke of a Pistol   24 November 1944

While one can understand the great personal feeling, the strong pressure of a shocked public opinion, and the natural reaction to an abominable deed, all of which impelled Prime Minister Churchill to make his recent statement upon the assassination of Lord Moyne, one cannot but help a feeling of regret that Mr. Churchill's remarks were not, to say the least, couched with the usual felicity of his expression. Indeed, one cannot but entertain a suspicion that Mr. Churchill's penchant for antithetic and dramatic rhetoric led him to give an impression that was totally unwarranted by the facts, and to adopt a stand whose implications run counter to the most elementary dicta of British justice.

Said Mr. Churchill: 'If our dreams for Zionism are to end in the smoke of the assassin's pistol and our labors for its future to produce only a new set of gangsters worthy of Nazi Germany, many like myself will have to reconsider the position we have maintained so consistently and so long in the past.'

This type of language, it must most respectfully be stated, is entirely gratuitous. It is, indeed, the perfect example of a diplomatic *non sequitur*. Between 'the position which we have maintained so consistently and so long in the past' – presumably a support of Zionism – and the irresponsible act of the two terrorists, there is – to use the jargon of the law – absolutely no *lien de droit*. With the proposition that murderers should be punished, everyone is in complete agreement; but the proposition that the fate of Zionism should depend upon a total good behaviour of every single Jew everywhere – a proposition which Mr. Churchill seems to accept – is to elevate the taking of hostages to an international principle. When Crippen, the notorious English wife-murderer was hanged, no one advanced the theory that all Englishmen because of this deed, should forever be deprived of the bliss of matrimony. Crippen was a case; and as a case was judged. The same certainly should apply to the two deluded youngsters who did perpetrate this unspeakable crime.

It is gratifying to note, amidst the entire picture where nothing else that is gratifying appears, that the British press has been far more moderate and more logical in its appraisal of the situation than the Prime Minister. Many Englishmen have not failed to note that acts of terror do not usually spring up out of a vacuum or out of a paradise, that reprehensible as they are, they do frequently reveal a situation for which those sinned against are in no small measure to blame. The real names of the two assassins at Cairo were – *Struma* and *Patria*! It is this 'position maintained so consistently and so long in the past' which, if anything, should be reconsidered.

One cannot but recollect, too, that during the many years of Arab rioting and murder, organized by the leaders of Arab life, no British statesmen ever found it necessary to declare that because of these deeds – and they were inspired, and not irresponsible, systematic and not isolated – Britain was to reconsider its position with regard to the Arabs. That Mr. Churchill should now deem it opportune to threaten a whole people because of a crime of two of its members, is the most unkindest cut of all. That he should, for the purpose of tying a knot in his lash, imply also that Zionism 'is producing a set of gangsters worthy of Nazi Germany' is oratory as superfluous as it is misleading; not

Zionism, but that same policy of political expediency and appeasement which produced the original Nazi prototype has produced these unexpected imitations.

The stand of Mr. Churchill, moreover, is all the more incomprehensible when it is realized that the Palestine settlement has spoken out in no uncertain terms against the terrorists of the Stern group. The fact is that the accredited leaders of Zionism, the members of the Jewish Agency, are themselves possible targets for the pistols of this intransigent band. Public opinion in Eretz Israel has been most condemnatory against these political hoodlums; the fact, however, is that the maintenance of peace and order in Palestine is not in Jewish but in the mandatary's hands. When the Jewish Agency asked for arms to combat the 'Sternites,' these arms were refused.

Moreover, when Mr. Churchill spoke – in the manner of an enraged prosecutor putting an entire people in the prisoner's dock – he already had in his hands a letter from Dr. Weizmann, whom he described as 'a very old friend.' He quoted Dr. Weizmann as saying that the executive of the Jewish Agency had called upon the Jewish community 'to cast out the members of this destructive band, to deprive them of all refuge and shelter, to resist their threats and to render all necessary assistance to the authorities in the prevention of terrorist acts and in the eradication of the terrorist organization.' It is difficult to imagine what more could have been stated or done. What was Mr. Churchill's comment? 'We must wait for these words to be translated into deeds.' We have seen the occasion when Mr. Churchill has put greater trust in brand-new friends.

For four years, as it suffered the grimmest ordeal of its history, Jewry has been consoled by the hope that soon, soon Mr. Churchill would issue a statement about the future of Palestine. We do hope that the remarks quoted above do not constitute that long-awaited statement, nor the basis of such a statement. Certainly it would be a grave injustice if the deed of the two assassins were made the excuse for a further juggling with the sanctuary and future of Israel. Let crime be rooted out with its perpetrators; but let not an entire people, let not an age-old hope, an honorable international commitment be sacrificed for the indignation, no matter how righteous, which should be directed only against the authors of the crime.

The Zionist hope is not to go up in smoke, of a pistol shot or of any other combustible. That is the way it was born, out of the smoke of a desecrated Homeland, out of the flames of Jewish sacrifice throughout the ages. We have had enough of it. Nor do we see anything apt in making the pistol-shot a symbol of our aspirations. Our symbol is, and always has been, the thunder of Sinai, which, among other things thundered forth *Thou shalt not kill,* a thunder whose echoes *we* spread throughout the world. We resent the unnecessary reverberation of that echo.

Weizmann at Seventy 8 December 1944

The numerous tributes which during the past fortnight have been paid to Dr. Chaim Weizmann, president of the World Zionist Organization, felicitations which came to him from all free countries and from the representatives of almost every political point of view, should be not only a source of satisfaction to himself, but also a source of pride to all Jews everywhere. Certainly his leadership, despite criticism levelled at it by the intransigent and the impatient, has been such as to win him the support of the vast majority of the Jewish masses. There is, indeed, no doubt but that the position of preeminence which Dr. Weizmann has kept for so many years has been primarily due to the fact that he, more than any other Jewish leader, was always able to divine the feelings of his people on any given subject, to articulate their aspirations, to symbolize their common sense – to become, in a word, the living incarnation of Jewish folk-feeling.

At no time was this quality of his better exemplified than in his memorable disagreement with the late Judge Brandeis. Mustered against Weizmann's point of view, there stood the architects and controllers of American Jewish life; almost alone, save for the help of the late Shmaryahu Levin, he was able to win over to his democratic and national view the American Jewish masses. But to use the term 'win over' is an inexactitude – all Weizmann did, really, was to give leadership and expression to a conviction which was there all the time.

This phenomenon is all the more remarkable when it is noted that about Dr. Weizmann there is nothing of the demagogue. His speeches are never flamboyant; not the wide gesture, but the *sotto voce* aside is the characteristic typical of his oratory. Nor can it be called oratory; it is always something more in the nature of a *shmoos*, a 'come-let-us-reason-together' discussion in which to situations intensely emotional in their significances Dr. Weizmann brings the cold logic of a Talmud exposition. When it is further considered that Weizmann's particular *forte* is scientific investigation, the paradox of the super-sophisticate leading a movement which is so much centred about the Jewish heart is again accentuated. The truth is that Dr. Weizmann is an outstanding composite of both the cerebral and the emotional; a composite which occurs in the case of national leaders of no other people.

It is for this reason – this paradoxical combination of the rational and the emotional – that Dr. Weizmann has so unfailingly mirrored and expounded Jewish hopes and aspirations, for Jews themselves are in psychology just such a composite. We find nothing startling in the joinder of *hithlahavuth* and *pilpul*, ecstasy and syllogism; in our history, the combination is classic.

It is true that Dr. Weizmann has been often compelled, by virtue of the hard dictate of necessity, to effect compromises; in no other man, perhaps, would these compromises have been tolerated; but here again, his pliability was not original but a reflection of the national desire and need. Dr. Weizmann, in a word, is more than an individual personality; he is prototype of the Jewish personality.

For the last number of decades, moreover, he has been and still is, the living embodiment of Jewish aspiration toward a Homeland in Eretz Israel. We can think of no other personality who has typified better the national hopes of Jewry than Dr. Weizmann, the direct continuator of the tradition of Herzl. Certainly it would not be wrong to declare that, even as the latter half of the nineteenth century was pre-Herzlite, and the first part of the twentieth Herzlian, that the era from 1917 onward is the Weizmann period. It has been a period which though beginning with the great promise of the Balfour Declaration, suffered numerous setbacks; it must not be forgotten, however, that it has been also a period of definite achievement, achievement unparalleled since the dispersion; and this achievement has been in very large measure due to the inspiration and leadership of Dr. Weizmann.

Surveying the columns of the world press, full as they are with justified adulation of Dr. Weizmann's personality, sincerity, and intelligence, we could not help but reflect upon the occasion when Dr. Weizmann first stepped onto the stage of international diplomacy. Lloyd George, who is of the opinion that Dr. Weizmann was the cleverest of the representatives of smaller nations at the Versailles Peace Conference, rivalled, if at all, by the late M. Venizelos of Greece, tells the story in his memoirs. Having made by scientific inventiveness, a vital contribution to the war effort during the last crusade against the Germans, the British Government wished to reward him. Dr. Weizmann, it would appear, wanted no personal reward or honors; he wanted something done for his people. One could, of course, be doing an injustice to the British Government, to the Jewish people, and to Dr. Weizmann himself, if one were to reduce the Jewish claim to Eretz Israel to merely such a simple *quid pro quo* transaction; but the story is revealing, nonetheless.

Would it not, we reflected, be an equally laudable move if now, after the attempt had been made by several Palestine administrations to nullify the Balfour Declaration, after the faithful co-operation of Dr. Weizmann for a period of over twenty-five years, after the indescribable suffering of our people during the last decades, that Dr. Weizmann's seventieth birthday be honored with the gesture *par excellence* – the abolition of the White Paper and the establishment of a Jewish Commonwealth in Palestine?

Surely such an announcement would be the only fitting greeting to the venerable leader of three score years and ten. We sincerely hope that such a contingency will be realized early, and in Dr. Weizmann's time. Canadian

Jewry, by whom Dr. Weizmann is deeply cherished, earnestly hopes that this will come to pass, and to its congratulations to its inspired mentor adds also the devout wish that the present president of the World Zionist Organization may enjoy long life as the first leader of the Jewish Commonwealth.

The Tactics of Race-Hatred   29 December 1944

From time to time, various publications, published in the other eight provinces of this Dominion, and in the United States, have 'gone to town' on the province of Quebec. With a self-righteousness which was apparently blind to things transpiring under their very noses, and with a crusading fervour which was not always pure and undefiled, they have set themselves up as critics and castigators of what they termed the peculiar mores of the province of Quebec. By way of adding a coronative feather to their Galahad-plumes, they have, – with justice, – railed against the anti-semitism which prevails in our region, and spoken – with an unpardonable hypocrisy, – as if that anti-semitism were a Quebec monopoly.

Now, let us make ourselves clear: that there are certain forces in this province which seek to exploit race-hatreds and religious bigotries for the benefit of their own political or commercial purpose, has been all too blatantly demonstrated and on far too many occasions in our provincial annals. That these forces ought to be unmasked, and shown to be what they really are – arsonists against the public peace, traffickers in intellectual narcotics – goes without saying. Both the protection of minorities and the welfare of the province demand it. Insofar as progressive newspapers, here and outside the province, contributed towards this objective, their efforts are to be welcomed and applauded.

But it is quite another thing when editorial writers go out of their way to give the impression that the entire province of Quebec is a domain of intolerance, and every one of its citizens – and the adjective 'French-speaking' is invariably added to make their intention and their purpose clear – a carrier of the antisemitic virus. This is simply not the truth; and one has a right to question the motive of such wholesale prosecution. In many such instances, one of two things, we believe, will be revealed: either the pious defence of a discriminated minority is being used as an instrument of denigration against the French-Canadian minority; or the crusader, adopting the tactic of *Stop, thief*, is pointing to Quebec anti-semitism only to draw attention off his own. In some cases, both objectives are sought.

Thus we have encountered periodicals whose editors were by no means distinguished by their love and affection for Jews, who suddenly berated the province of Quebec – the whole province of Quebec – presumably for publicly manifesting prejudices which they entertained only privately. Examination of other columns of the same periodicals revealed that antipathy to Quebec was motivated by an entirely unrelated set of excuses. And thus, too, we have noted – to name a less offending name – *Time* magazine devote entire sections of its space to a discussion of Quebec's race-hatred only to follow it up later by an extensive use of the 'Clear-it-with-Sidney' slogan – anti-semitism's transparent mask, used during the last presidential election.

We believe that it is high time that things should be called by their right names. Anti-semitism is a danger to the public welfare not because it stems from Quebec or from Ontario; it is reprehensible wherever it lifts its ugly head; and the geography of its manifestations, unfortunately, is not restricted. The attack should be levelled against the fomenters of anti-semitism themselves, and not against their residential addresses. To use the defense of one minority, solely as a means of attack against another, is still to participate in the dissemination of race hatreds. The struggle for democratic principles is not a struggle between areas; it is a struggle between the forces of light, everywhere, against the forces of darkness, everywhere.

In Memory of Martyr and Hero   16 March 1945

It is not our intention here to enter into a theological discussion of the salutary effects wrought upon the spirit by the discipline of periodic fasting, or of the inward rewards offered by penitence, or of the beneficent moral consequences of contrition. The day of fasting which was Wednesday proclaimed and observed throughout the Jewish world was not, essentially, a day of penitence and contrition; it is not Jewry which in this instance has reason for repentance, but Jewry's oppressors; the fast-day was primarily a day of mourning and remembrance.

Certainly it was meet and proper, while many arduous duties still lie ahead, and many difficult determinations remain to be settled, for Jews, individually and as a group, to take record of the havoc which has been wrought in our midst. It is not an easy inventory to make, this inventory of our slaughtered saints who fell. No other people on the face of the earth has, during the past decade, suffered losses such as ours; one quarter of our world population – at conservative and optimistic estimate – has been destroyed. No other nation has endured such an amputation.

These solemn thoughts, moreover, are given an additional bitterness when it is realized that the great majority of these casualties did not have even the opportunity for self-defense. Helpless and without aid, they are truly the martyred of our generation.

What are the reflections which pass through the minds of brothers as they sit upon their mourning benches, in *shiva* for a brother passed away? Invariably, the thought must come to them: Now we must be more firmly knit together than ever before. Such, too, must be the reaction of surviving Jewry, touching the great calamity which has befallen our people.

Yesterday, a fast-day; today, and tomorrow, and the day after – days of healing, of binding of wounds, of reconstruction. One shudders to think at what the day of complete victory in Europe will reveal concerning the plight of our brothers. It will be a challenge such as has never before been presented to Jewry. The broken will have to be made whole again, the scattered gathered to a home that they can call their own. Another link in the continuing chain of our history will have to be forged. Surely it is at this moment of solemn prayer and sombre fast that it behooves all of us to dedicate ourselves to the tasks that lie ahead, to a Jewish future that shall never again be marred by fast-days such as this.

Israel Rabinovitch (On the Occasion of His Fiftieth Birthday) 27 April 1945

There is, in our unceremonial time, nothing sacrosanct about birthdays. The clock ticks off its number of hours, the days pass, the calendar pages are torn and flung away, and there it is: another anniversary. But even in this latter day, birthdays still possess the charm that they do provide the formal occasion for the utterance of tribute which somehow, in more pedestrian days, remains unsaid. It would be, we venture to platitudinize, a happier world if these things were said all the days of the year; failing that, however, it is at least a consummation that they are uttered once in a lustrum, once in a decade, once in a jubilee. We rejoice, therefore, that such opportunity is now given us, upon this page whereon during the past several months we have published the translation of Rabinovitch's masterly work on Jewish music, to undertake appreciative commentary touching the man, his work, and his continuing influence upon the community in which he plays so leading a part.

This influence he exercises primarily with his pen. Although among the tools of art the violin, his first love, is perhaps his more cherished instrument, although it was through one of those fortunate accidents by which happy marriages are made that he entered into the field of Jewish journalism, it is his pen, flourished across the front page columns of *The Canadian Jewish Eagle*, that is at once his weapon of polemic, his baton of organization, his wand of magic. This is the sword with which, we might say after Shakespeare, 'he opes his oyster'; only we cannot imagine Rabinovitch at home with a sword, and much less with an oyster. Certainly the daily opinions of no other man have counted for so much in our community as the 'Good Morning,' and 'Day In, Day Out' comments of 'I.R.' (There was a time when, in our ignorance of the identity of the author, and in our awe before his reasoned and compelling logic, we imagined that these initials, in their Yiddish translation, stood for *Yoshaiv Rosh*, and in their English, for *Imperator Rex*.)

Now, it is no easy task to write a column fresh for every dawn. That Rabinovitch has succeeded in having these his daily essays read with such eagerness and interest is a tribute to the qualities which inform both his manner of thought and his style of writing. Here, when he wishes logic to prevail, he can be, even upon the most excitable of themes, cool and dispassionate; here, with humour, he carries a point miles further than heavy-breathing seriousness can; his invective, usually couched in understatement – key to the man's personality – is devastating. But above all, – quality so rare and so priceless – he possesses an unfailing sense of proportion, an inevitable good taste.

It is for this reason that his writing, despite the pressure of daily production, remains so purely and authentically Yiddish; its tone, its spirit, is of the folk; now a text from Holy Writ, now a proverb, now an anecdote, all essences much relished by the people, the true hallmark of the classic style, all come to point the moral or adorn the tale. It is a style pure, native, and without those blemishes which the intrusion of alien elements invariably effects. When, in his writing, an Anglicism or an Americanism intrudes itself, it is not allowed to stand, stiff-necked and at home in the sentence, but is immediately confined within quotation-marks – so that it may know its place. This, we regret to say, is not the habit of the so-called cosmopolites of the New York Jewish press, who disregarding the purity of the tongue, permit all manner of alienisms to clutter their paragraphs, until the writing is not Yiddish but polyglot.

The same good taste, moreover, guides Rabinovitch not only in the manner of his speech, but also in the content thereof. Never will he write, even upon the most sensational of subjects, merely for sensation's sake; never does he succumb to that easiest of journalistic temptations – the urge to write *pour épater le bourgeois*. Always will he bear in mind the full implications and corollaries of his remarks; and govern himself accordingly. If, in the larger public interest whose guardian he is, something ought not to be said, Rabinovitch, though fully aware of how effectively and how beautifully it could be said, will simply not say it. It is left, perhaps, to be read between the lines; and writing of such interlinear literature, it must be admitted, is of the highest and most exacting.

And there is, of course, in addition to the matter and style of his essays, their mood. Here we may well borrow, for the characterization of the variety of his writings, the nomenclature of the modes of Jewish music, modes upon which in previous issues of this journal, Rabinovitch has expatiated. First, there is the *Adonai Moloch* mode – now and again, in the midst of discussion of the most bitter manifestations of Jewish tragedy, there surges, above the description of iniquity, over and above the implications of despair, an overwhelming and all-encompassing faith that *God has reigned and will reign again*. At other times, when it is some aspect of Jewish culture that is his theme, some educational institution about to be founded, or some contribution to Yiddish letters that has just been made, the mode of *Mogen Avoth* comes to the fore – 'the shield of ancestry' – the sense of Jewish continuity, the development of our cultural heritage, the one increasing purpose of our presence upon this earth. Again, when he chooses favoured subjects, the essence of Jewish music, some new cantata, some recently-discovered version of an old folk-song, is it not the mood of *Ahava Raba* – of the great love – which informs his work?

What are Rabinovitch's themes? Nothing Jewish, of course, is foreign to him. All is grist to his mill; whatever is of importance or of significance in Jewish life is the worthy object of his comment. Nonetheless, throughout the decades there have appeared certain emphases, certain interests which dominated, without ousting, other competitive subjects. In this wise, it may be said of him, as it has been said of artists of the brush, that his career has been characterized by a progression of favourite colours. The rose-period, which heralds his first entry into journalism, is devoted to *belles-lettres* and the theatre; that is followed by a sort of blue-and-white interregnum devoted to the national and spiritual motifs as they centre about Jewish organizational and ideological life; and finally, a brown-period, marked by the rise of antisemitism, international, national, and provincial, thrusts Rabinovitch into weekly polemic with Arcand *et al.* Throughout these years, moreover, there flashed, in a special number, in a festival issue, in an essay published in one of the literary magazines, and above all, in the manuscript of his book on Jewish music, the rainbow-colours of his creative work on music, the entire spectrum fused in one.

In a word, Rabinovitch is both a versatile commentator and an accomplished stylist. Many of the essays and columns which he has written are, of course, of an ephemeral nature; such, alas, is the unhappy lot of all journalists – they must wait for history to bring perspective to their necessarily one-dimensional work; but many, a very great number of Rabinovitch's essays, are of lasting worth and merit. A selection from his columns of the last number of decades, would constitute to our mind, not only a kaleidoscopic view of the developing Jewish community, but also a date by date revelation of an interesting and genial personality. Even divorced from theme and subject-matter, they could stand on their own feet, as literary creations of enduring value. Those of our community who are interested in the written word expertly shaped, interested in that continuity of our culture of which Rabinovitch is an indubitable link, owe it – to themselves – to make this suggestion – the publication of I.R.'s essays – an early reality.

For ourselves, we join with the many who have extended to him their congratulations and best wishes. After all, Rabinovitch is, to judge by the vigour of his style, in the very prime of his life; only in the *midst* of his career; if life begins at forty, not even *bar-mitzva*. The community that trusts him, the multitude of readers who think through him, and his friends who cherish him, all join in wishing him many, many more years of fruitful and constructive endeavour – the fiftieth birthday is only an arbitrary musical pause, to heighten and emphasize the ever-developing symphony.

On the Writing of Obituaries   4 May 1945

One of the more unpleasant tasks of the editorial scribe is the duty, sanctioned by immemorial custom, of noting in his periodic pronouncements, the regretted passing of the distinguished. The reader somehow seems to expect his editor to be in continual contact with the morgue thence to issue both notification of, and lament for, the importantly deceased. It is for this reason that the discussion of the most world-shaping events is in this column sometimes interrupted to permit its writer to publicly mourn the passing of sage, or seer, or statesman, suddenly snatched from the scene. It is a task which is often prompted by sincerity, and always, of course, impelled by a respect for the conventional decencies.

But we never enjoy it. If the subject of our threnody happens to be one because of whose death we feel a real sense of personal or communal loss, naturally the writing of the obituary is no merry-making performance; and if the mourned is a lesser dignitary, or a man not entirely *integer vitae*, but propriety and the *de mortuis nil nisi bonum* slogan demand funereal benediction, our task, too, is not a gift of felicity. As for those wretches who are quite properly better placed under the earth than upon it – and they, too, sometimes, die – of them we never publicly comment. It would be unseemly; one is better advised to receive the news of their reward in silence.

But not so of the two knaves who perished this most happy, happy week. At last an obituary that one can unequivocally enjoy; at last a carcass that it is a pleasure to behold. For five long years we waited for this day of jubilee, sharing our expectation with millions of our fellowmen, and now it is arrived. This is the day, as said Holy Writ, for which we hoped; and to us, the fortunate before whose eyes justice is at length vindicated, to us it has been vouchsafed.

Reflections on V-E Day   11 May 1945

Not with surprising suddenness did it come; it did not come – as in the dark days we had hoped it would – as a miraculous flash on a radio, a startling announcement lifting us from the depths of despair. By instalments, with forewarnings, parcelled in rumours, it finally arrived, and even then was only quasi-official: *the Nazis had surrendered, unconditionally.* Indeed, but a week earlier, President Truman himself had had to take to the microphone to squelch a premature report of peace, to issue a negative proclamation; moreover when the final tidings were brought, they came not from the lips of authoritative statesman, or general-on-the-spot, but from the despatch of a Mr. Kennedy, who scooped the world on the world's most momentous news.

And yet, despite these prognostications and warnings, how few were prepared for the reception of this news of the half-peace! How difficult it was to articulate the proper response! So much hope, so much day-in-day-out longing was wrapped up in the coming of this announcement, – this, the day for which we had hoped! – that thoughts stumbled over one another; and the mind was confusion, and the heart a bursting inexpression. Us the moment found on St. James Street: inglorious place. In an instant the street was a bedlam of joy, the tall buildings smiled with hundreds of faces, the paper that streamed from the windows was itself an extended and ubiquitous smile. Everybody said unrememberable things; it wasn't really speech; it was ejaculation, brimful and jubilant. Girls danced, soldiers were borne up on shoulders. People danced in the streets; even those who walked alone glowed with an inner illumination.

And we could not help reflecting upon the great kindness which had been vouchsafed to all of us to be permitted to behold this day. Five years ago – let it be frankly admitted – we saw about us only darkness palpable. The great trek which we had made through history seemed about to come to an end. The enemy appeared invincible, and to us Jews, implacable. A Haman had arisen who meant to obliterate our people, to destroy us, beyond remnant, and beyond memory. For the time being, his ravages were confined to Europe, but his intentions were never concealed – he meant to make the whole world the scene of his totalitarian iniquity. Every Jew felt the Nazi tentacle stretch out to reach him, personally. Until the last Jew was cremated, Hitler, we knew, would feel that his task had not been done. Surely, in all our troubled history no such threat had ever been lifted against us.

Now, as the radio blared forth its news, and as these people danced in the streets, they knew not how musically it sounded, or how worthily they danced. Both of us had been saved, we, in our mortal skins, and they, in their immortal souls. For the menace was levelled against them, too; had the fiend emerged victorious, these dancers, these joyous celebrants would themselves have become, in due course, cogs in the Nazi machine, and soon, all too soon, the mimic shadows of their masters. From that fate, they had been saved.

As for myself, now in the hour of triumph, we could take the Nazi propaganda against us, and make it into a crown, even as we had made the Yellow Badge the shield and ensign of nobility. In their cunning they had, in the hour when speech was still theirs, shouted across the world that this was a 'Jewish War'; that, save in the sense that none had suffered in it as much as Jews, it never was; but this peace, truly, symbolically, this peace was a Jewish peace. The arch-enemy of our people had fallen into the dust, miserable and ignominious; the murder he had planned was only partially accomplished; his grand scale of slaughter had been frustrated. Whence could one summon the voice, and whence the hallelujah, that could utter adequate thanksgiving for that this thing did come to pass?

How often, in the past, have we as a people boasted of the ordeals and martyrdoms which we have survived! Antiochus, Pharaoh, Haman, Torquemada, Chmelnitzki – these were names which marked the danger-points of our survival. We had outlived them, and their wicked intention; and ever thereafter, their appellations were like a pendent of grim bloodstones which we wore upon the throat of our history. Sometimes, indeed, as the élan vital effervesced in us, as with emancipation new strength came to us, we made out of these names a playground for humour, a field for our wit. Pharaoh outlived was a comic character; Ahasuerus outlived was a drunkard and fool; and Chmelnitzki only an adjective for antiquity. But when the whole might of the German Reich was mustered against us, and all the genius of organization, and all the inventions of science directed towards our annihilation, we thought, in our despair, that here was the foe unconquerable. But the Lord has triumphed, and for His innocents intervened:

The Lord hath broken the staff of the wicked,
The sceptre of the rulers
That smote the peoples in wrath
With an incessant stroke,
That ruled the nations in anger,
With a persecution that none restrained.
The whole earth is at rest, and is quiet.

How art thou fallen from heaven
O Lucifer, son of the morning!
How art thou cut down to the ground
That didst cast lots over the nations!
And thou saidst in thy heart:
I will ascend into Heaven,
Above the stars of God
Will I exalt my throne ...

Yet thou shalt be brought down to the nether-world,
To the uttermost parts of the pit.

I wondered what place Hitler and his doings would now occupy in our folk-lore. I thought about the past years, and the words *blitzkrieg, lebensraum, festung Europa* – portentous terms! – and how henceforth they would sound in the vocabulary of civilized man. But of one thing I was certain – these words and their kindred would never form part of our humour.

For while the bombs were silent, and while the bombast sounded, we could not help but think upon our missing. Conservative estimates place the number of our martyred at five million; only the months to come will reveal the actual figure. To that must be added the tally of those thousands who willingly made the supreme sacrifice; to the list of martyrs, the roll of the heroes. The victory had come not merely by wishing for it; its price had been paid in blood. Many a home to-day, I thought, cannot understand these peals of triumph, this jubilation – for a son, a brother, a father, is not returning; and on the mantelpiece there stands only a photograph ... Multiply the tragedy by thousands, and victory – sweet victory – wears black.

Nor can one at this moment banish from thought also the memory of these 'other missing ones' – the Fuehrer, Ley, Goebbels, the whole crew of unspeakable malefactors who seem to have disappeared. Who knows – to emerge another day?

Yes, we have survived; but as we take count of our numbers and take stock of our conditions, we discover that we have survived, bleeding and maimed. We are less by one quarter of our population. The poison that has been brewed in Nuremberg still spreads its fetid odour across the face of Europe; much still remains to be done before victory is translated from its military language into a living and meaningful reality. In the meantime, for the great blessing, the supreme boon, gratitude and thanksgiving. For the day, *dayenu*; for the rest, He who has led us thus far, will lead us still.

Crimes and Punishment   25 May 1945

Review of M.H. Myerson, *Germany's War Crimes and Punishment* (Toronto:
Macmillan Company of Canada 1944)

Ordinary honest folk who in recent weeks have had the dubious privilege of
beholding with their own eyes – on film and in newspaper – the pictorial
representation of both the techniques and the effects of Nazi barbarism, have,
we have noted, reacted very simply to these grim spectacles. They have said:
Surely these things which have been shown to us, and which hitherto we
deemed unbelievable, constitute crimes, unqualified and heinous. Their authors
ought to be punished. Here were no subtle distinctions, no sophistical
qualifications. Crimes had been committed, the *corpores delicti* lay there in
their thousands, obviously the criminals should be brought to justice.

To us, such a reaction, though simple, is infinitely healthier than the
heavy legalistic disquisitions with which jurists are wont to sickly o'er the pale
cast of thought, when they touch this subject. Such a reaction indicates that the
spectator aches for another's pain, and is not arrogant with that false piety of the
lawyer which would be fitting only if they had come to investigate the
unwarranted slaughter of a trainload of cattle in transit. The relatives of the
murdered, they say, may not have it in their hearts to see the situation in its
proper perspective; we, however – endowed with doctrine, and bearing codes, –
we can rise above such human handicaps. Accordingly, they apply to a given
situation, not the throbbing reactions of men, but the sterile immovability of
automatons. They are the slot-machines of justice; throw in a problem, press
down a maxim, and out comes a judgment of Solomon.

Three are the maxims which the jurists of international law bring to the
subject of punishment of war-criminals, three blindfolds triply to emphasize the
classical image of Justice. First, devised apparently for the protection of prime
war-mongers, stands the rule that the head of the state is not personally
responsible for the acts which he perpetrates in that capacity. This rule, it is to be
noted, is a corollary of the doctrine of national sovereignty, a doctrine which
appears more and more outmoded as people move towards Wendell Willkie's
concept of 'One World.' From this sweet premise, therefore, it would follow
that Adolf Hitler, if still alive and to be caught, might be deemed, – by the
international lawyers – innocent as the undriven snow. What he did, although
perhaps reprehensible, was an exercise of his sovereign power – hence, not
amenable to the sanctions of international law. Indeed, it was on this very
doctrine that learned memoranda were submitted, by learned counsel, to the
Lloyd George Cabinet to dissuade it from prosecuting William Hohenzollern.

The next metal-vest worn by war-criminals, and armoured by lawyers, is the theory that the subject can not be held personally responsible for orders that he is fulfilling. Rule One exonerates the arch-criminal; Rule Two exculpates his henchmen. And both rules, taken at their face-value, and not treated as comic paragraphs in a macabre code, serve to whitewash, or at least to render immune from punishment, an entire nation banded together for the exercise of 'sovereign crime.'

But, it will be suggested, these laws were invented by men; can not men change them? A third doctrine leaps to the rescue of the first two: criminal law cannot be made retroactive. It is unjust to provide punishment today for an act which yesterday, when it was done, was unpunishable. All the palpable iniquities perpetrated by the German Reich during the last five years were perpetrated at a time when no new international code had as yet been enunciated. Any rules that may be now devised can apply only to the future; wherefore, again the criminals go scot free.

It can be seen from this very skimpy outline of the problems inherent in this subject that Mr. Myerson – who is a lawyer, but happily not of the type previously adverted to – undertook no simple task when he set to discussing these questions of 'individual and collective criminality.' Confining himself within the bounds of legal analysis, Mr. Myerson has nonetheless been able to rid himself of the conceptual petrifactions which in legal circles, usually weigh down and hinder a free exposition of the subject. While it is true that at times Mr. Myerson's vocabulary assumes a passionate intensity which belies the reputation for coolness which his profession enjoys, as a Jew, and kin of the victims whose cause he pleads, he is hardly to be taken to task for not displaying equanimity before corpses. Indeed, it is to the great credit of this book, that from it there emerges not only the initialled outlines of a law degree, but the full figure of a human personality applying his intelligence to a vital human problem.

It is no doubt because of this quality that the book is so highly readable. There have been, the reader will readily conceive, other books – ponderous tomes – which have devoted themselves to an exposition of these aspects of international law; Mr. Myerson's has the double merit, first, of examining these doctrines in the light of the hitherto inconceivable crimes of this war, and second, of examining it with a minimum reference to legal shibboleths, and a maximum reference to the human passion for justice.

Mr. Myerson's book, it is to be noted, was written before the news of Maidanek, Oswiecim, and the other hell-holes of the Nazi gehenna. Subsequent revelations indeed, have served only to emphasize its general theses, its impatience with the quibbles and quiddities which, as he illustrates, made a travesty of the Leipzig trials. The appearance of the book now is of the utmost timeliness. v-e Day has brought into the hands of the Allied forces a host of well-known criminals. At this very writing, the remaining fugitives are still being sought. When these men are brought to trial, what criteria will be applied in determining their guilt or innocence? This is a question of vital importance, not only, forsooth, to the accused themselves, but to the man on the street, to the millions who have endured untold sacrifice as members of the great military posse engaged in rounding up these criminals. Certainly the future peace of the world depends in large measure upon the justice which is to be meted out to the Hitler gang. Mr. Myerson's book constitutes an intelligent man's guide to a consideration of the legal and human aspects of this subject. It should be widely read.

Rescue or Kidnapping?   29 June 1945

The protest which has just been broadcast by the Chief Rabbi of England, complaining about the forced conversion of Jewish child refugees all over the European continent, is one which will receive the full-hearted endorsation of all those who are sincerely concerned about the survival of our people. The bald statement of the Rabbi's cause for protest constitutes in itself a shocking revelation of what has been transpiring with the remnants of Israel. According to this indictment – and there is no reason to doubt its foundation in fact – thousands of Jewish children who, during the Nazi occupations, were spirited away into Christian homes and Christian religious institutions, are now not being returned to the community of their people, but are being adopted into the Christian faith.

It ought to be stated forthwith that those families which dared, under the threat of the Nazi taskmaster, to give sanctuary to orphaned Jewish children are owed by us a tremendous debt of gratitude. Their act was a tribute both to their courage and their Christianity. Certainly, it is because of them that thousands of our flesh and blood were saved from the lime pits and crematoria and preserved among the living. The heart wells forth with a profound sense of indebtedness at the recollection of these charities.

But, surely, a different complexion is put upon the entire transaction when subsequent events would lead one to believe that it was not merely the rescue of physical bodies that was intended, but also the kidnapping of souls. The guardians of these children have accepted a trust from the deceased martyrs of German terror; surely it was never part of that trust that the children should be deemed, though alive, as lost to the congregation of Israel.

We have heard it argued, somewhat cynically, that individually these children will be better off, in a prejudice infested Europe, if they were brought up as Christians. Such an argument, of course, is not a compliment but an insult to European Christianity. It would be a bitter wrong, indeed, if we prepared ourselves in advance to consider Europe forever doomed to the antisemitic virus. Indeed, if the argument is valid for children now under duress, it should be equally valid for all of European Jewry – a counsel of wholesale conversion.

The truth is that European Jewry has already been sufficiently (*sic*) decimated by murder, without the additional losses to be heaped upon us by a system of spiritual kidnapping. Those who posed as our friends in the hour of our need now, by adopting this policy of non-restitution of our children, do join our mortal enemies. The original gesture may have been intended as a kiss of consolation; the final embrace can be considered only as the embrace of death. Certainly European Jewry did not suffer and survive savage cruelty only to be liquidated by a dubious kindness.

The Secret Weapon of the Supermen
3 August 1945

The description of the attitude and morale of the Nazi supermen, now awaiting trial, does indeed make disgusting reading. From all accounts it would appear that the 'blond beasts' presently caged in their wired Valhallas do possess none of the noble and heroic qualities which they so arrogantly boasted in the happier days when they were the authors of their self-descriptions. Fat Goering, it is reported, is now nothing more than so much avoirdupois of cowardice; he sweats; he mumbles; his jelly shivers with fear and excess weight. Even his adjutants regard him with contempt: was this the face that launched a thousand ships, and burned the topless towers of London town?

Nor does Ley present a happier spectacle. It is understandable, not only because all bullies are essentially poltroons, but because the bravado of Robert Ley never did issue from the depths of his being, but rather from the depths of beer-casks. The courage of alcohol, it is apparent, is not on the menu for war-criminals. And even Julius Streicher is now a changed man. The man who never walked, but stalked; who never issued from this home save he be booted, and possessed of a furious riding-whip, now crawls and whines before his captors. Even his ideology has suffered a prison-change. Streicher is now of the opinion – he openly admitted it to his interviewers – that Jews may be permitted to live!

Ah, what a low, slimy, obsequious crew this is. Criminal and boastful in their heyday, no courage, no dignity, follows them as their night approaches, as their shadows grow smaller. The myth of the superman is completely exploded. The doctrine of the élite is now seen to be what it always was – a thing invented by a group of wilful gangsters to maintain themselves in power. How resplendent they once looked in their polished leather and bemedalled uniforms, how like turkey-cocks did they strut upon the stage, and none was like to them! Now the secret was revealed: what the regimented masses of Hitler Europe worshipped and followed for a decade were not men, but mere uniforms. The uniforms gone, the straw which stuffed them now appears.

The Jews of Europe
3 August 1945

For the past six years, while the press was full of a detailed description of the methods adopted by the Nazi extermination squads to encompass the destruction of European Jewry, while the Nazis themselves openly flaunted the murder-blueprints they had prepared, and while reporters standing upon the abandoned scenes of Gestapo atrocity sent accounts of the number of containers of human ashes they had discovered in the macabre buildings, the quantity of gold torn from the teeth of Jews about to be cremated, while all this was being attested, both as to place and as to time, as to method and as to result, Jews, and all civilized beings, secretly entertained a hope, a wish, a concealed but cherished incredulity. It can't be as bad as it's described! Inhuman monstrosity could not possibly go to such lengths! True, the villages and cities redeemed from the hands of the fleeing Germans were invariably empty of Jews. Perhaps, ran the secret hope, they have fled into the woods, they have changed their names, they are being concealed by friendly peasants ... Come the end of the war in Europe, and they will reveal themselves.

The hope was doomed to frustration. The Nazi program for Jewish annihilation was by no means over-estimated. If Jews survive in that continent today, it is simply due to the fact that Himmler was hard pressed for time. Certainly within the months which were allowed to him, he could boast of no mean record of 'production.' Truly the calamity which has befallen the Jewries of Europe is without parallel in our history; not the persecutions of Torquemada, not the havoc of the Crusades, not the pogroms of Chmelnitzki, nor those, at a later date, of Petlura and Deniken, have taken so great a toll of Jewish life as have the camps, the 'medical institutes,' the crematoria of the Third Reich. In but a little while, and the entire black program of Hitler would have been executed; indeed, thousands of Jews were burned, poisoned, slaughtered in the very last days of the war, by Nazi officials fighting against time and discovery; but even as it is, the figures reveal a sombre achievement in the perishing of Jews. Not all the mortalities are in, of course; many were murdered in secret, and no intelligence of them has yet been received; and many areas of Jewish habitation are, for various reasons, still inaccessible either to the investigator or the relief-worker.

But the figures which we already have are as eloquent and tragic as an *El Moleh Rachmim*. Through the offices of the United Jewish Refugee and War Relief Agencies, we are able to refer the reader to a table of statistics to be found elsewhere on this page.

It will be seen forthwith that the estimates of Jewish losses have been very conservative, indeed. Approximately four million Jews have been destroyed during the half decade of the Hitler madness. These figures, moreover, clearly attest to the fact that in proportion to the total Jewish population, our people has suffered casualties greater than that of any other. One quarter of our race has been annihilated. We are now, populationally speaking, in the condition in which we were during the last century. A generation, and more, has been wiped out.

That such a thing could come to pass in the twentieth century and in a world presumably civilized is a subject for the meditation of those political potentates who have been entrusted with the task of making the recurrence of such events impossible. For ourselves, we would like to dwell upon the fate of the million who survive. The conditions under which they persist in life are of course, well known; shattered in health, their morale broken, they do still oft-times find themselves in an environment where Nazi practices still linger on. That each one of these victims of Nazism is entitled to the fullest aid that we can bring to them is but an elementary imperative of philanthropy. Common humanity is satisfied with no less.

But there is yet another aspect under which the million who survive ought to be regarded – that is, as a totality, as the means for the maintenance and continuation of our people. Succour brought to these, therefore, is not an act of charity; it is an act of national reconstruction. It is under this aspect, too, that the value of the survivors, as a national asset, is accentuated by the very fact that they constitute so minimal a remnant of so large an entity.

To make possible the proper functioning of this million of Jews in their essential role as agents of Jewish continuity, a number of prerequisites are imperatively urgent. In the first place, there must be no stinting in the amount of economic relief which the free Jewries of the world ought to accord to them. It is no exaggeration to state that these masses of people are absolutely penniless. Before one can even think of the wider implications of rehabilitation, it is necessary to grant them the wherewithal to keep body and soul together.

It is also necessary to obtain for them, through proper representation, the milieu in which their mere survival may transform itself into constructive living. When one realizes the statelessness which many, and the disabilities which all of these suffer, one realizes at once that an International Bill of Rights is a *sine qua non* for the proper rescuing of this remnant of Israel. And no Bill of Rights for Jews is complete which does not grant to all Jews who desire it the right to enter a Homeland of their own. It is only through such means that the Jewish people may somewhat recover from the havoc which has been wrought against it.

The Post-War Period Begins   17 August 1945

At last the great ordeal which the world has endured for the past six years has come to an end. Though the fighting citizens of the United Nations, convinced, as they had to be, in the eventual triumph of right over might, ever foresaw precisely such a culmination to the epic of the forties, the fact does remain that many a time and often even the hardiest of spirits stood troubled and concerned over the outcome. Now the issue has been resolved. The organized iniquity which the Fascist powers had meant to impose upon the world has been frustrated; the arch conspirators of the scheme against world peace and world civilization lie ground in the dust; mankind can again resume the paths of peace and progress. Indeed, there has been something schematic, and as if predetermined, about the collapse of the Fascist powers; one by one they fell before the outraged might of the United Nations, first Italy, then Germany, the apex of the triangle, and now Japan.

No electrocardiogram has yet been invented which can measure the exultation of the world's heart to-day, both at the news of victory, and at the prospect of the days of peace to come. Yet this jubilee is not without its bitterness, a bitterness evoked by the untold sacrifice, the universal misery, which had to be expended to win – not yet a better world – but merely its potentiality. No one can fail to think to-day, even amidst the sound of sirens and the snow of festive paper, that there are families throughout the countries of the United Nations which do sit, grateful for their country's victory, but bereaved with the personal loss of one who made the supreme sacrifice and whom they shall see no more. No one can fail, even as the account is made of the rewards of victory, to remember, in addition to the heroes who fell on the field of battle, the countless thousands who perished as helpless victims to the madness which raged over Europe for half a decade. Certainly these reflections, anguished and bitter as they are, would be but vain lip service and an empty remembrance if they were not accompanied by the determination of all to see to it that such things shall not be again.

For if we will it, there may be ushered in, not a mere calendar continuation of time past, but definitely a new era. Nor do we mean the era of the atomic bomb. The world would do well to forget about the ingenious instrument of destruction, and devote its God-inspired minds to endeavour more constructive. Certainly the past five years have shown that the capacity of human intelligence is practically limitless; projects unheard of, indeed projects unsurmised in the past, were executed for the purpose of slaughter; sums hitherto inconceivable were spent to this end. Might it not now be right and wise that the same energy, the same expense, the same genius be now applied to projects which might add to the world's total happiness?

We have no doubt but that all of the United Nations are profoundly thankful that the dirty business of war is now over, and that they now may concentrate their attention upon undertakings progressive and civilized. There is not one of the United Nations which does not possess to-day some blueprint indicating the intended architecture of its self-fulfilment. The thought that predominates everywhere is *Rebuild*. All of the victorious peoples, although perhaps ignorant of the precise agenda for to-morrow, know at least that *they now have a to-morrow*.

All the peoples, all – except Jewry. We, who as a result of the activities of the common enemy of mankind suffered to a greater extent than any other race or nation. One quarter of our total population has been destroyed – no other combatant has suffered such casualties. One million and a half of our sons marched side by side with the embattled legions of democracy against the foe. But whereas all our co-belligerents know that a certain territory is now to be theirs, that their citizens, wherever they may be found, shall now be free from hurt or molestation, no such guarantee is enjoyed by Jewry. Touching our own country, the potentates of the world's destiny stand silent, if embarrassed. Touching the right of Jews in various European countries, one is often in doubt as to whether the Nazis were really defeated. Nor is it as if Jewry stands awaiting the disposition of conquered territory; it is the freedom of access to a land which is its own, by right of historic due and by sanction of international declaration, that it expects. And as yet all is silence, or, at best, ambiguity.

It is for this reason that we find it necessary, upon the very day of triumph, to recall some of those principles and promises which the leaders of the United Nations saw fit to enunciate during those dark days of trial and tribulation. We do not speak of the Atlantic Charter which specifically declared the rights of all peoples; we refer rather to definite utterance and precise commitment. The White Paper was always understood as a piece of expediency; it was, indeed, the last vestige of the appeasement policy of Chamberlain; and certainly there is no reason for expediency now. Prime Minister Winston Churchill, together with the late lamented President Roosevelt, declared more than once that at the termination of hostilities the suffering and the aspirations of the Jewish people would be borne in mind. It remains now for this remembrance to be converted into real and fruitful action.

One of the leading thoughts about which the ideology of the last war rotated was the concept of the inter-relation of all the peoples of the world. This idea was made most popular by Ernest Hemingway's revival of John Donne's sermon about the tolling of the bell. It tolled for all, was the gist of that paragraph. No man was an island unto himself. The same is true of nations. Peace cannot be assured piecemeal; justice and discrimination are contradictory terms. Certainly it would be a frustration of all the hopes which have swelled in the hearts of men during these trying years, if, after the tumult and the shouting, the same iniquity would prevail thereafter as before. Certainly it would be a travesty of the war objectives, if after the suffering and tragedy which all have endured, some should now emerge, re-established, re-habilitated, vindicated, and one should continue to be The Forgotten People.

The *Patria*   31 August 1945

Several days ago, there were returned to the shores of Palestine the thirteen hundred survivors of the *Patria* who, after languishing for five years in the concentration camps of the island of Mauritius, in the Indian Ocean, were at long last 'repatriated' to the land from whose haven they were so ruthlessly snatched. And thus ended a bitter odyssey; a tale of wandering, pursuit, and tribulation such as has not been matched even in the cruel annals of this war. Hunted by the hounds of the Reich eager for Jewish blood, several thousand Jewish refugees, from various parts of the European gehenna, finally managed to get a ship which would take them to Palestine and to sanctuary. We pass over in silence the heartbreaks and disappointments which these people had to endure before they could, out of the tens of thousands of Jews who entertained similar aspirations, finally obtain passage on this ship of 'hope and reconstruction.' Finally the *Patria* arrived at its destination, the port of Haifa; in the distance one saw the outline of the blessed land. Here no Gestapo could reach them, here they might build their lives anew; was this not the Promised Land? But the hopeful 'immigrants into their own Homeland' counted without officialdom. There was a White Paper, and the refugees could not be permitted to remain. They might return to the fire of Europe, or stay on the waters of the Mediterranean, but upon the soil, hallowed by their ancestors, they could not land.

As the 'immigrants' found themselves thus suspended between violent exit and prohibited entry, the *Patria* stood at anchor in the harbor. Then, for some unknown reason, the ship exploded. Many lives were lost. The whole thing had the character of a nightmare, – flight, violence, poverty, absence of distinction, and finally even the absence of immobility – an explosion.

Nightmarish, too, was the irony which grinned sadistically from the tale – to have escaped, after many trials, the savagery of Hitler, to come to the very shores of sanctuary, and then to be stopped and blown up!

But the nightmare is not ended. There were survivors, thirteen hundred of them, still left alive, to struggle, even as in some mad dream, with White Paper. Here officialdom extended its right hand – its left was busy issuing communiqués about justice, four freedoms, ten commandments, fourteen points, etc. – its right hand to push the survivors away from the shores towards which they were struggling. Bureaucracy decided that for others to want to live was a misdemeanor, and to want to live in one's own Homeland, a crime. The thirteen hundred were therefore interned in a concentration camp on the island of Mauritius. Their wanderings had resulted, not in changing their condition from slavery to freedom, but only in changing their climate from north temperate to torrid.

Now after five years they are returned to their original destination. In the meantime, six thousand five hundred years of Jewish life have been destroyed – the equivalent of the murder of one hundred complete lives. Is this not a story of Sodom, a Gomorrah tale? Is it not made all the more horrible in that the deed was perpetrated against the helpless and the already afflicted, perpetrated in the name of law, and perpetrated by people whose status is presumably that of 'guardians'?

As frequently happens, restitution – the heart finally softening to let my people go – only emphasizes the heinousness of the repented crime. Moreover, repentance has come only with regard to the passengers of the *Patria*; there are, however, tens of thousands of such potential passengers, refugees caught and held in the labor-camps of Europe – for them the White Paper still stands as a flaming sword – not ordered by God – between their plight and their redemption. Will the saga of the *Patria* be a lesson for those who thus far, in the name of an expediency ever as unprincipled as now unnecessary, have stopped their ears to the cries which issue from the homeless, the dispossessed, the uprooted? Certainly nothing could bring home the iniquity of the White Paper policy as the appearance, upon the newspaper columns, of these thirteen hundred ghosts, recently emerged from an incarceration to which they were doomed, not by enemies, but by friends.

The Judicial Process   19 October 1945

For centuries the British judicial process, with its untold number of protections designed to safeguard the rights of the individual, has justly enjoyed a reputation of pre-eminent excellence. This reputation was recently further enhanced by incidents of contemporary history, and in particular by the contrast afforded by the respective trials of Pierre Laval and 'Lord Haw-Haw.' That both of these men were reprehensible knaves is not a subject for debate; we would wish to place no one in the dilemma of having to choose between them. The treacheries of both, indeed, were matters of public knowledge, and insofar as democratic opinion was concerned, it did not have to wait for courtroom revelations to come to its conclusions. In England, fortunately, mass opinion, subject to innumerable prejudices and countless pieces of misinformation, is not a substitute for the judgment of the court.

Accordingly, Alfred Joyce was given a trial. He was supplied with the best counsel. His most technical objections were given serious consideration. All the safeguards of British justice were his to invoke. Found guilty, no one could deny that he had been given a fair trial. Found guilty, no one could mistake the convict for a martyr. How differently, however, things proceeded in the case of Laval. We do not – let it be stated forthwith – weep for him, nor mourn him. Our layman's reactions make it impossible for us to ignore Laval's treatment of Jews under the Nazi occupation. But we do regret that French justice failed to achieve the same end within the proper framework of the impartial trial. Laval, doubtlessly, got his just deserts; but in many quarters the manner of his conviction has served to endow him with a halo of martyrdom. It is a contrast – this between the trial of Lord Haw-Haw and Laval – which serves to prove that the British system is not only more just, but also wiser and more expedient.

The trial at Belsen, we note, is also being carried on, by British judges, in the same spirit. There are, we know, many who are impatient with the tender considerations, the long-drawn out tolerance which is being manifested by the Bench towards the accused. 'They should have died ere this' – that seems to be the general mood of the public reading, day in, day out, of the atrocities perpetrated by the monsters in the dock. And if a trial were not involved, we would heartily subscribe to such a stand. No one, indeed, would have seen anything wrong if the Belsen bandits had been summarily shot immediately upon capture; but since they have been put before a tribunal, let the trial proceed according to all the rules. The fact is, of course, that it is not only Belsen which is on trial, but all of Germany.

We can well understand, therefore, the attitude of the presiding judge who at a given moment, when the spectators burst into laughter at the evidence which was given by the accused, threatened to clear the court. He wanted to maintain the judicial dignity, and did not want the spectators to act as a judge. After all, even a giggle is a judgment. We think the judge was right, although we do sympathize with the spectators. For ourselves, we can hardly see how it was possible to refrain from laughter when one listened to the ogres picturing themselves as innocent babes.

But sometimes, alas, even Homer nods, and even a British judge goes sleepy. For at another point in the proceedings, a British defense lawyer, no doubt overcome by the exuberance of his own generosity – or perhaps expressing the thoughts of the unconscious – referred to the victims of the Belsen holocaust as 'the scum of the European ghettoes.' We believe that such a remark was uncalled for by the defense lawyer's duty, and was a gratuitous insult cast upon the memory of the innocent martyrs of German savagery. That the judge, so meticulous in all respects, so careful to observe the judicial amenities, so sensitive to the impaired dignity of the court, should have permitted this piece of heartless vituperation to pass without reprimand is unforgiveable. It nullifies his previous scrupulosities. For the essence of the judicial process is to be fair – fair to both the accused and the complainant. And at Belsen it is the shining martyrs of the European ghettoes who are the complainants.

Le Canada and 'This Hatred' 16 November 1945

We were, we must admit, both astonished and shocked to read in the Tuesday issue of *Le Canada*, distinguished organ of Quebec liberalism, an article which for its malice and hysteria, could easily have found a place in the columns of Julius Streicher's unlamented *Stuermer*. The incongruity of the thing, moreover, was further enhanced by the fact that this piece of clumsy and venomous race-baiting appeared – of all places – on the women's page of that journal, a page usually reserved for questions of cooking and coiffure. This time however, Mlle. Odette Oligny decided to use her boudoir-cuisine space as a forum to discuss no less a subject than the origin of hatred in general, and of the hatred of Jews in particular.

The result was a *pot-pourri* unpalatable in the extreme. According to Odette's little ode on race-relations, the Jews are hated – she loves the use of this word – in the course of a half-column she applies it to Jews about a score of times, relinquishing it only for the sake of the word *détestés* – the Jews are hated because they refuse to assimilate. Mlle. Oligny does not define what she means by assimilation, but she does give an example – how familiar this technique is – of a Jew whom she does not hate. This particular person apparently recommended himself to her affection, first because he turned Catholic, and secondly, because he was killed in battle. Using this piece of personal reminiscence as a criterion we must come to the conclusion that for Miss Oligny an acceptable Jew is one who has changed his faith and is moreover no longer alive.

In taking up this question of assimilation Mlle. Oligny – for the sake of French manhood we imagine she is a mademoiselle – seems entirely oblivious, not only of the fact that the paper in which she is published is presumably a liberal one, but also a French-Canadian one. She seems, indeed, to be utterly unaware of the fact that the most rabid baiters of French Canada, use precisely this argument of non-assimilation against the citizens of the Province of Quebec. When, then, is assimilation a proper philosophy of life and when is it not? Does Mlle. Oligny's kitchen really permit of no variety, but is everything evoked according to a uniform and reiterated menu?

But Mlle. Oligny is not content to discuss her problem on the high plane of ethnic relations. At her sixth paragraph, she loses her scientific composure, and begins to write in a style which is reminiscent of nothing so much as of the billingsgate of uneducated women quarreling across their balconies. The Jew is unsocial, he has no civic spirit, there is a *'malédiction à eux attachée'*; he monopolizes the sidewalks, he shakes carpets in the open, etc., etc. Any talented apache woman could supplement this fishmarket catalogue – and she wouldn't think of calling it journalism!

After descending to this niveau of argument, this hysterical woman apparently does not realize how ridiculous she appears, even according to her own premises, when she writes: *'Ils sont d'un égocentrisme qui nous blesse, nous qui avons toujours, dans nos relations avec le prochain, la crainte de déplaire.'* 'They ... the Jews ... manifest a selfishness which wounds us, us who in our relations with our neighbors, are always so careful not to displease ...'

We do not, of course, intend to argue with Mlle. Oligny. Hers is not our idea of a standard of polemic; moreover, Mlle. Oligny appears, time and again, to be arguing with herself. Indeed, fearful lest her journalistic self will lose out against her better self, she has recourse, in her last paragraph, to sentiments so shrill and unbalanced that they can be construed only as a sort of helpless self-justification. 'The Jews,' she says, much in the tone of that quarreling *commère* above referred to, 'are hated everywhere. The Moslem spits at the passage of a Jew. And look what happened to them recently. *Le monde entier ne peut se tromper.* The whole world can't be wrong!' So why shouldn't Odette, the assimilating, get in on the world-movement?

It is to be stated that on the day following the publication of this the case-history of Odette Oligny, the management of *Le Canada* – its liberal-minded editor, Mr. Turcotte, has been away for some time thus giving the mouse a chance to play – repudiated Mlle. Oligny's sentiments, saying that those were but an expression of her personal opinion. It does not seem like a convincing excuse. If the author of the column were Julius Streicher himself, would *Le Canada* also expect to clear its conscience by saying that these were Julius's own prejudices? *Le Canada*, in its apology, if it is intended as apology, makes reference to favorable articles about Jews that it printed. We must admit that it does not seem much of a defence to us for a newspaper to state that it does not spread its Jew-baiting all over the journal, but reserves it only for a special department ...

Exodus and Numbers   4 January 1946

The Palestine Administration, it would appear from recent events in the Holy Land, is having a difficult time not only with the numerous White Papers which clutter up its files, but also with the volumes of the Bible which, after all, remain the final authority on the destiny of Eretz Israel. Moreover, the reconciling of the texts of Holy Writ appears much more difficult than the reconciling of the various White Papers; these latter, as is well known, are couched in language so delightfully ambiguous that it is possible from their total number to extract either yea or nay, as the spirit moveth. Not so with Scripture. Here language is explicit; even the ingenuity of the Foreign Office cannot adequately cope with it.

It is quite clear, for example, that the Balfour Declaration was intended as a sort of new *Genesis* for the Jewish people. Here, in its Homeland, Israel, after many wanderings and vicissitudes was at last to be reborn. Upon the ancient theme, a variation was to be played; and that glorious contribution to world civilization which Jewry upon its own soil had once made, would, in the spirit of the times, now be repeated.

It was equally clear that to accomplish this laudable end *Numbers* were required. That was the way it was of yore; that was the way it would be again. Nor were the numbers lacking. All over Europe there are thousands who clamor to be permitted to participate in the new renaissance. At least two volumes of Holy Writ were thus accounted for.

Unfortunately, the book of *Leviticus* was not now exactly of the same text as in days gone by. The Levites who now served at the Temple apparently knew not Joseph; they appeared to be on more intimate terms with Abdullah.

Here, then, was an impasse. The recalcitrant Civil Service, the Levitical Foreign Office found the modern version of the Bible impossible to produce. With that ingenuity, however, which has always stood them in good stead, they invented a new version of another biblic tome: *Exodus*. Only this time, instead of it being an exodus from Africa into Palestine, it is, in the form of deportations to Eritrea, an exodus from Palestine to Africa.

It is a sorry text which is now being written in Palestine by the descendants of Cromwell's bible-loving folk. Only one source of consolation is there in this nightmare of latter-day exegesis: *Deuteronomy*, the last word, is not yet written.

The Pleas Begin   8 February 1946

Throughout the six years of this war, people who remembered the experience of the last warned us that all the animosity which was then being directed against the barbarian enemy would not last, that inevitably, after hostilities ceased, the sentimentalists – sentimental about the aggressor but not about his victim – would again find their voices, and that there would rise in the land the cry of a perverted magnanimity: Let bygones be bygones. We did not believe these prognostications. The misdeeds of the Nazis, we felt, were *sui generis*; the world had not seen their like before; and the world would not soon forget them. Only a proto-fascist, we thought, would dare lift his voice in their defence, or plead for clemency on behalf of the war criminals.

We were wrong; and we have been proved wrong sooner than we expected. The Nuerenberg trials, as everybody knows, are still proceeding. The horrible record of Nazi iniquity has, after weeks of description, not yet been exhausted; indeed, yesterday the Russians announced the discovery of a mass grave – contents, 100,000 corpses – not previously known. And yet, at the very moment that these macabre indictments are being read, the state of Uruguay made so bold as to ask the United Nations to rule out the death penalty for Hermann Goering and other top Nazi war lords, and to limit their maximum punishment to life imprisonment!

Nor was this outrageous suggestion – outrageous when one remembers the millions, the millions of human beings, every whit as good as any of these 'war lords' whom they wantonly murdered – unaccompanied by the necessary pseudo-humanitarian window-dressing. For the Uruguayan resolution, presented on orders from the Montevideo Government, argued that public execution of the Nuerenberg defendants would be a 'demoralizing spectacle,' and would be apt to create world-wide sympathy for them. It furthermore claimed that life-imprisonment is the severest penalty compatible with democratic respect for human life.

We doubt whether it is necessary to argue with such a resolution. Apparently its framers never thought of the demoralizing effects which the adoption of their resolution would have before the people of Europe who would see that banditry may be committed with impunity, if only it is committed by the heads of states. The Uruguayans, moreover, entertain unfounded fears if they are alarmed at the prospect that Goering's death may put all the world in mourning. Even the Germans, according to general report, seem indifferent where they are not enthusiastic about Hermann's present plight.

But it is the last quiddity of the Uruguayan logic which really takes the prize. It is in the name of democracy that the lives of these its bitterest enemies are to be spared. Was ever a stranger plea heard? For originality, it is matched only by the plea of the parricide who asked for the clemency of the court on the ground that he was an orphan!

But this South American suggestion ought not, really, to be judged by the standards of public morality. It only appears to belong to that realm; actually, it is nothing more nor less than a political move. We do not know who inspired this démarche, but a number of possibilities suggest themselves. In the first place, it well may be that what we hear is the voice of Uruguay, but that actually the speaker is Argentina, not a member of the United Nations. The accused at Nuerenberg, as is well known, have many friends in that republic; and it is not impossible that they have paid that such a service might be rendered them.

It is also not inconceivable that some of the members of the United Nations, foreseeing a possible role for Goering et al., at some future time, would like to preserve them intact for such a contingency. Whatever the motivation, there is no doubt but that this impertinent and callous resolution will be vigorously resisted. To adopt it would be to dance wantonly upon the graves of those whom these murderers martyred, to sanction this abolition of law and justice, and to flaunt the justified desires of the people of Europe. And, on the other hand, is not the Uruguayan resolution, somewhat premature? Are then the delegates so certain that the accused are going to be found guilty? Everything is possible; we didn't think the Uruguayan resolution possible; but there it is. But perhaps the South American sentimentalists wanted, in any event, guilty or not, to give the poor helpless accused at Nuerenberg some peace of mind, some assurance that come what may, their skins would not be used to make lampshades.

Arms, and the Spy   22 February 1946

Until the day before yesterday, most Canadians thought that espionage and international intrigue were occupations which were practised only in Oppenheim novels, and then confined only to European capitals, and such places as Monte Carlo. Certainly one never imagined that Canada, with its wide open spaces, and its candid population, were a fit or repaying milieu for this questionable activity. The last time, to our recollection, that spies were spoken about in our Dominion was when they were mentioned, and fascinatingly described, by one of our Governors-General, the late Lord Tweedsmuir. But he, too, created them for fiction, for fiction and for export to Hollywood.

The announcement of Prime Minister King, however, points up the wide gulf that lies between literature and life. The gentleman who, in chapter six, appears romantic, courageous and intriguing, loses all of these qualities if we find him rifling through our own desks. The revelation by the Prime Minister that the government was in the process of rounding up a gang of conspirators who intended to hand out their country's defensive secrets to a foreign power, has both alarmed and incensed the Canadian public. At this writing, the details of this conspiracy consist mainly of a spate of rumors and surmises. A Royal Commission is presently in session studying the evidence which the R.C.M.P. is bringing them, and an interim report, it is said, will be issued shortly.

No doubt Canadians should be flattered (sic) at this turn of events; we are now, quite evidently, worth spying upon. Until yesterday we were left strictly alone; it seemed we knew nothing which anybody might envy us. We were, even at most self-confident, only a Middle Power. But now we are being treated, to our extreme annoyance, like a Great One.

We are not pleased. Mr. Joseph E. Davies, former American Ambassador to the Soviet Union, may very well point out, with a pseudo-judicial impartiality, that espionage is quite the international thing; nonetheless, we do not like it; and we like even less the thought that some Canadians might lend themselves to be the catspaws of a foreign state. When it is reflected that these characters held places of confidence which made important information available to them, their role is seen for the treachery that it is.

The identity of these worthies has not yet been disclosed. We have no doubt but that when it is disclosed, and their guilt established, punishment will follow, swift and exemplary. There is nothing, in the hierarchy of man, which is lower than a traitor, and the less of these creatures we have at large, the cleaner the Canadian air will be, and the safer Canadians will feel.

The United Palestine Appeal   22 March 1946

The United Palestine Appeal which, opening in Montreal this week-end, is being launched at a time of grave decision in Jewish life, will evoke from the local community, we are certain, a response commensurate with the importance and the urgency of the needs it is called to meet. Certainly at no time in our post-exilic history has the necessity of a Jewish homeland been so tragically apparent, at no time before have so many individual lives, and indeed the entire destiny of a people, hung upon the fate of Palestine, as to-day. Six million Jews ruthlessly murdered – one third of a nation has been cruelly lopped away. As for thousands of survivors, not in the miasmic European continent, scene of their ordeal, cemetery of their near ones and dear ones – not there can they find a home. It is only to Palestine that they look for sanctuary and a new life; and it is only to the English-speaking Jews of the world that they turn for a voice and a hand on their behalf.

Our readers are no doubt familiar with that macabre spirit, so dear to would-be protectors of Jewry, which consists of looking for new territories, other than Palestine, for the resettlement of our people. It is a geographical pastime to which even the noblest succumb, as witness the case of the late Israel Zangwill. But the sport did not perish with Zangwill, and even to-day one sees men of good-will, and men of ill-will, suggesting that the Jews betake themselves anywhere, anywhere, but not to Eretz Israel. One announces that Biro-Bidjan, which receives no non-Russian immigrants, is the earthly Paradise, and another announces that in distant Australia he has discovered 'free' land. The torridly-inclined advocate San Domingo, or better still, Madagascar. We will not speak ill of the territories, since it was the good Lord who created all of the earth, and the fulness thereof. But somehow all of these projects invariably meet with two stumbling blocks: in the first place, Jews don't care to go there; and, in the second, if they do, they are not permitted entrance. In the final analysis the geographic sport remains academic, educational but not edifying.

It is, indeed, ironical, bitterly ironical; the world is so big, but for Israel, even an Israel considerably shrunk, there is no room. Islands on the Pacific, we note, are to be bombed into non-existence, by way of atomic experimentation. Ungava – we do not envy nor desire Ungava – we cite it merely as an example of *lebensraum* – Ungava, an area larger than Palestine, is being leased to a private company. But Israel, as Byron earlier observed, has no resting-place.

For many years, Jewry looked to others for aid in obtaining its legitimate rights in Palestine. That that is not everywhere the attitude to-day is not due to any whimsy on the part of Jewish thinking. Time, and the events of time, have amply exemplified and justified that dictum of the Fathers: *If I am not for myself, then who is for me?*

One of the most constructive principles which the Yishuv has introduced in the life of Palestine, none will deny, is the principle of self-help. It is a principle at once national and ethical; it declares that in the building of Eretz Israel, Jews ought to rely, as much as they can, upon the labor of their own hands. Thus it eliminates that exploitation which one usually associates with the colonization of a country; and thus, too, one fashions a spirit of self-reliance, of self-confidence, and of self-respect.

This principle of self-help, we feel, is as applicable in the Diaspora as it is in the Yishuv; and in the Diaspora self-help takes the form of support to the United Palestine Appeal. For let no Jew imagine that when he makes his contribution to the national fund, he is merely indulging himself in a self-gratifying philanthropy, but is himself remote from, and untouched by the achievements of these funds. The existence of a Jewish Homeland, of personal and vital significance to the refugee to-day, is of no smaller significance to the more fortunate sections of Jewry who, from the knowledge that in that eastern land there is a throbbing, real, authentic Jewish life, must perforce take on a new dignity and pride.

But the past record of Canadian Jewry indicates that we are preaching to the converted. The achievements of our people in this Dominion with regard to the up-building of Palestine are second to none. We have no doubt but that in the light of the increased needs of the hour and the accentuated urgencies of the contemporary situation, that record will be maintained, maintained and surpassed.

The Herrenvolk   3 May 1946

One of the most charming (*sic*) quiddities of the Nazi ideology – in the day when it still masqueraded as an ideology – was the self-flattering doctrine that the German people constituted a national élite, that what came out of Berlin was the salt of the earth and the cream of society, that, in a word, all the Fritzes and the Gretels, by mere birth and existence, showed to the world the example of an herrenvolk. The theory, moreover, had a corollary; if every ordinary German was by his sole nativity, *ipso facto*, a man of honor, the leaders of that nation were, of course, the most honorable of the most honorable.

It was a doctrine, no doubt, which helped to bolster up the natural inferiority complex from which all Prussians apparently suffer. Its historical origin, it would appear, dates back to the chivalric concepts of the Middle Ages; then the knight in armor, the *ritter, le chevalier sans peur et sans reproche*, was the world's *beau idéal*. Ignoring the fact that this knighthood flowered only upon the dung of an oppressive society, fertilized by well-spread and heavy layers of serfdom, the theoreticians conceived of the whole of the Third Reich as being all of knightliness made. As for serfs, they were to be sought among the lesser breeds beyond the frontiers. The citizens of Germania, however, were to be deemed pure *herrenvolk*, and its leaders the elect of the chosen of the élite.

The whole world, except the deluded dupes in Hitleria, understood of course that this invention was nothing more than another method of massaging the national body into a sense of vigor, and towards a feeling of superiority. The result of the war, we feel, did much towards dissipating that feeling. But it is at Nuerenberg that the German people is being given an opportunity to see their cornered leaders in their true knightliness.

Herrenvolk, indeed! The world has not seen a crew more snivelling, more cowardly, more obsequious, than the honorable paladins who are presently testifying before their judges. All, without exception, hide behind the corpse of Hitler. Not a one has risen to attempt to justify his doctrines, to face his accusers boldly, but all whimper, and crawl, and throw the blame on an unlamented Fuehrer. Hjalmar Schacht, for example – that wing-collared creature – to imitate a cherub in reverse – poses as if he were innocence personified. He didn't approve of Hitler's doctrines, he was against them, they were wicked; but he did nothing; on the contrary, he and his associates profited tremendously from the machinations of the man whom he always recognized, he says, as a monster. And Streicher – what a true knight this pervert turns out to be! He loved the Jews; he burned the synagogue in Nuerenberg only because he didn't like its style of architecture. One does not know at which to be more nauseated – at the effrontery of these men, at their wickedness, or at their cowardice.

Nor are the deviations from the high standards of honor typical of the herrenvolk the result of the pressure of a trial. Even in the halcyon days of power, these heroes in shining armor were no more honorable. Has any state trial ever revealed intrigues more disgusting than those which Goering engineered to prove von Fritsch a homosexual, or von Blomberg the latter-day husband of an early-day prostitute? Indeed, for us, to whom the entire trial has been a piece of misguided unrealism, it was only at this stage that the thing became realistic. Here, it became clear, as ever it could be made clear, that the judges stood face to face, not with political offenders, not with the champions of some recognizable ideology, but with a gang of underworld characters – dope-addicts, perverts, pornographists, prostitutes, cuckolds, pick-pockets, and garroteurs. Behold the herrenvolk!

An Anniversary

10 May 1946

This week the democratic world, we gathered from newspaper spacefillers, did casually note – it would be wrong to say *celebrated* – the first anniversary of the conclusion of the Second World War. The newspaper issues of last year were duly photostated and republished; the reader was made to recall the fact that a year ago today Germany surrendered. Such an evocation of a still fresh triumph might have been followed, one thought, by songs of praise and paragraphs of general optimism. Alas, no journalists could bring themselves to the expected literary ecstasies. There was chronology and no comment; the *yahrzeit* – and the rest was silence.

It was not surprising, this absence of commemorative hallelujahs. For if some intrepid panegyrist had indeed, been prompted to use the day for jubilation, surely he would have had to find some reason, some cause, some area of sunshine or some locus of happiness to give substance to his projected rhapsody. Such causes and reasons, it would appear, are conspicuously absent from the contemporary scene. After one year of peace, after a resounding victory which laid the universal enemy low, the world still is beset by problems of tremendous difficulty. The brave new world of the future, to which all men of goodwill looked forward, even as they were involved in the smoke and haze of battle, still is a thing of the future, as unimminent as ever. Not even the debris of the past has been cleared; and we refer to the destruction of human relations as much as to the rubble of European architecture.

For a moment, last summer, at San Francisco, it did seem as if a beginning had been made. A new world charter had been enunciated, brimful of the loftiest principles, all reiterating the dominance of right over might. The Big Four appeared in solemn comradeship embraced. The 'little millions' could look forward to the prospect of a world where at least the bane of war might be eliminated.

Came the atomic bomb. Geographically, it fell on Hiroshima; factually, there is not a spot on the face of the earth where its implications did not resound. At a stroke, the world's planning was shifted from the domain of ethics back to the domain of power. The focus of the protagonists had changed from 1945; but the atmosphere of tension bore a striking and uncomfortable similarity to things as they too long had been.

With a shocking awareness, the ordinary citizen, that man of the street who never seems to go home, realized that a year had passed after victory, and not a step had yet been taken to fashion the peace treaties. With even greater shock, he realized the reason for delay: the victors were struggling among themselves. And suddenly there appeared in the public prints statement after statement praising the virtues of peace. Why should one have to praise peace in a world which had just endured six years of horrible war – unless the hounds of war were again heard barking in the distance?

No wonder, therefore, that the editorial writers and the pulpiteers and the radio announcers contented themselves merely with signalizing the advent of the anniversary, that – and nothing more. The hallelujahs they had doubtlessly planned, choked in their throats.

If that was the case with regard to one who surveyed the world in general upon this v-e day, how much more is it the case of him who looks upon the Jewish scene and recalls that a year has passed since Hitler and his works were destroyed. Jews, of course, did not have to wait an entire year to come to this gloomy conclusion. As soon as victory revealed what had happened behind the German screen, it was clear that, no matter who may have won the war, Jewry had lost it. Six million Jews – more than a third of a nation – were not there to celebrate the dubious victory. No reparations could bring them, and all they stood for, back to life again. The survivors in Europe, too, were but slightly better off than those whom they had survived – the distinction was between motionless and animated corpses.

And now, a year having passed, a year in which the survivors had been liberated (*sic*) and had begun to cherish hopes of a new life, – and they were still in the same concentration camps from which they had been liberated! One is not surprised to learn that the DP's indulged in no celebration this year. The truth is that the date of the original V-E day was premature; peace has yet to come to the world.

The Labor Party, Mr. Bevin, and Palestine   14 June 1946

The Labor Party of Britain, which is presently holding its convention at Bournemouth, this year as in years past again took up the Palestine question. But how different things were now from what they were of yore! In days gone by, when the Labor Party stood out in the wilderness of opposition, it was the time-honored custom of these conventions to pass annually, with great éclat and with practically unanimous approbation, a resolution calling for the immediate revocation of the White Paper and for increased immigration into Eretz Israel. At one convention, indeed, a gallant minority, led by Mr. Hugh Dalton, went to the point of recommending that the Arab population of Palestine be transplanted to other territory, and that Palestine be established as a Jewish State. It is significant that Zionists at the time repudiated the necessity of such a procedure. In any event, until recently the Labor Party set itself up and was regarded as the great champion of Jewish aspirations for a Homeland.

But that was when the Party was in opposition and resolutions cost no money. What a change coming to power has effected in the *ideology* of the Labor leaders. Thus we read that this year, not only is there no Palestine resolution such as was run off the typewriters last year, but that a proposed recommendation calling for lifting of restrictions on Jewish immigration and land acquisition in Palestine was withdrawn.

Instead, Mr. Bevin came to the convention to outline his foreign policy. We do not intend here to comment on the tale of his troubles with the Russians; it is his plaint about Palestine which here interests us. Said he: 'If we put

100,000 Jews in Palestine to-morrow, I would have to put another division of British troops there. I am not prepared to do it.' Like the traditional Tory of ancient days, Mr. Bevin pictures his role as that of the keeper of the peace; the truth is that the so-called danger of the situation is being grossly exaggerated. Witnesses of the Jewish Agency testifying before the Commission clearly stated, particularly Mr. Ben-Gurion, that for their part the British troops could leave now, and that if they were being kept in Palestine, it was for other reasons which had nothing to do with keeping the Arab-Jewish peace. The clear fact is that as long as Jews have arms, there is no danger of rioting. Rioting in Palestine takes place, as it did in 1922, 1929, 1936, when the Jews are unarmed.

In any event, the problem of an extra British division need not trouble Mr. Bevin too much inasmuch as the Americans have indicated, as reported elsewhere in this journal, their willingness to consider military and financial support, if necessary.

Mr. Bevin, with that uncouth and unfortunate technique of his, then went on to advise: 'I must say to the Jews and the Arabs: Please put your guns away. Don't blow up the British Tommy who is quite innocent in this business. You are creating another phase of the anti-Semitic feeling in the British Army.'

We quite agree that the British Tommy is entirely innocent in this business. Guilty are those, including Mr. Bevin, who have sent those good soldiers, who are entitled, after many battles, in Europe and Africa, to go back to their well-earned welcome in Yorkshire and elsewhere, sent these soldiers to stand on guard, not against spies, or Nazis, or fascists, but against poor helpless refugees seeking sanctuary in their own home. Tommy is doing his duty, but he didn't seek out that duty; that gallant function was provided for him by Mr. Bevin and his comrades of the Colonial Office.

As for the reference to anti-Semitism, Mr. Bevin is getting to be quite an expert on this subject. We still recall that typical remark – but typical of whom? – made by Mr. Bevin when after the cessation of hostilities and the uncovering of the plight of Jews in Hitler's concentration camps, Jews suggested that something should be done about the situation. Mr. Bevin then said that Jews should not try to queue up at the front of the line – as if Hitler had not already queued them up right there, and as if the wretch coming out of Belsen was seeking some special privilege in asking for food and shelter. And now Mr. Bevin talks about anti-Semitism in the British Army. What Mr. Bevin is suggesting, of course, is that if the Yishuv acquiesces, and abandons its European brothers to their unhappy fate, then perhaps, Colonel So-and-So may learn not to dislike Jews as actively as heretofore. The truth is that Mr. Bevin is slandering the British Army, for it must be a very weak group indeed, which can be moved to racial phobias simply because the policies it is called upon to execute are being opposed.

Mr. Bevin then went on with some palaver about ethical principles, and an opportunity for Jewish statesmanship – if the Jews would keep their mouths shut, they would be great statesmen (quite obviously, not all great statesmen take this advice) – and more of the same. Then he really let the cat out of the bag. 'You cannot deal,' he said, 'with the Palestine Arabs alone. Bound up with this is the great problem of Egypt. The policy in Egypt is not quite Churchillian. I don't believe in absolutely exclusive racial states. You cannot sort the world out that way.'

In other words, the fate of Palestine, by Bevin's admission, is being made a pawn on the general chessboard of colonial politics. This, certainly, is a frank confession that all the talk of ideology was but pure window dressing, and that Bevin's principal *considerants* are those of what he believes to be power-politics. This would be all very well, and quite shrewd, were it not that Mr. Bevin seems to forget that by law Palestine is *not* part of his chessboard. It is a mandate. It is held in trust. The relationship of Britain to Palestine is that of a guardian to his ward; and no guardian, unless he would be prosecuted, would state that his ward's property must be considered as part of the general private property of the guardian. The Balfour Declaration, which is clear and specific, makes no mention of Egypt. The truth is that Jews have conceived of Palestine as a place to go to 'out of the land of Egypt,' not a place to be tied up to the destinies of Egypt.

In true statesman-like (*sic*) fashion, Mr. Bevin took pains to butter up his harsh negations with some general and indefinite hopes. 'There never was a greater chance in the history of mankind to solve this problem. I say to the Arabs and Jews, theirs is a great territory.' (Thanks.) 'I beg of them not to push their particular points of view.'

We wonder what Mr. Bevin's reaction would be, if Mr. Molotov addressed him as follows: 'There never was a greater chance in the history of mankind to solve this problem. I say to the British their Empire is a great territory. I beg of them not to push their particular point of view.'

It was, however, in his concluding remarks that Bevin really manifested his mentality. Disturbed by the force with which American Jewry has been pressing the Zionist cause, and the sympathy with which this agitation is being received in important circles, Mr. Bevin sought to malign the American supporters, and to insinuate low and improper motives for their attitude. 'The agitation in the United States and particularly in New York for 100,000 Jews to be put into Palestine – and I do not want the Americans to misunderstand me – is because they do not want too many of them in New York.' One wonders at the psychology, and the intelligence, of a man who could make a remark like that. What Mr. Bevin is saying is that American pro-Zionism is motivated by anti-Semitism! And, of course, Bevin is a fighter against anti-Semitism wherever it appears. At the same time, Mr. Bevin declares that eventually he hopes the Jews will have a state in Palestine. Is his hope, too, motivated in the same way as that of the Americans?

It is, indeed, disheartening to watch the contortions through which a man who is wrestling with his conscience must need go. Bevin seeking to tailor humanitarian ideology to British expediency certainly has undertaken a task beyond his humble capacities.

The Disappearing Mufti   14 June 1946

At another time, and under other circumstances, the tale of the disappearing Mufti – now he is here, now he is not – could no doubt have been treated as but another one of those comic opera adventures with which Levantine potentates so often regale the Parisian *monde*, or, if you prefer the truly oriental, as a sort of diminuendo addition to the *Arabian Nights' Entertainment*. Certainly one would be inclined – on happier occasion – to smile at the spectacle of two mighty empires, the British and the French, both solemnly agreeing – with M. Bidault's *personal* undertaking, if you don't mind – to keep a down-at-heels adventurer confined to a certain area, and then seeing the said adventurer, despite Paris Sureté and Scotland Yard, suddenly popping up, like an enchanted snake, in the bazaars of Damascus. Certainly one would have been justified in hailing this Haj Ammin as no Husseini, but rather as the reincarnate and irrepressible Houdini himself, and certainly one could have made something for the gaiety of nations out of the Anglo-French butterfingers.

But things being as they are, this is no laughing matter at all, at all. The whole world knows that the Mufti is not exactly a dove of peace, that wherever he goes the paths are not strewn with olive-branches, but that, on the contrary, riot and rebellion follow in his wake. For the last twenty years, his life has been a book, open, lurid, and ugly. His part in the riots of 1922 was of such distinction (*sic*) that the British even then found it necessary to exile him from the locus of his incendiarism. In 1929, he was no less pyromaniac; throughout the thirties, he was in constant contact with Fascist elements, financing his movement of banditti with funds generously supplied by the late unlamented Benito Mussolini; and finally, when the war broke out, Haj Ammin al Husseini made the pilgrimage which he no doubt then considered the most important in his life – to Mecca which was in Nuerenberg. Both from Bari, Italy, and Berlin, Germany, the Mufti conducted, by air-wave, his propaganda among the Arabs, crying from Marconi's Minaret for the destruction of the British, and the French, and all that to them appertained. Nor did this holy one forget the Jews.

Upon reliable authority, namely that of a witness in the Nuerenberg trials, it is reported that the ingenious plan for the liquidation of European Jewry – through starvation, disease, slavery, and murder – was first suggested by the magnanimous Mufti himself, who thus hoped to solve his Zionist problem at Maidanek and Oswiecim.

The point we wish to make, and, as the French say, *ça saute aux yeux*, is that if anybody in the dock at Nuerenberg is a war-criminal, so is the Mufti. He ought never to have been held merely in hospitable custody, as he has been since v-e day; he ought to have been arrested, and put on trial together with the rest of the herrenvolk. However, the powers, for reasons best known to themselves, thought otherwise. Good. But certainly, once he was so generously detained, so big-heartedly absolved from standing trial, he ought at least to have been *detained*.

We are at a loss to fathom the inscrutable, and this loss, apparently, is shared by everybody involved, except the Mufti. The French say, they don't know how it happened. Apparently, they just looked around one day, and he was gone. How he went, who supplied him with the necessary transportation, how this transportation was able to leave France without French officialdom knowing of it, these remain questions unanswered. Everybody, it would seem, was busy counting the election results, so nobody could pay attention to the foreigner. Perhaps France has enough *étrangers* as it is, and they were glad to see him go.

Nobody, too, has arisen to explain how come the Mufti flew in a British airplane, how come he wasn't stopped in the course of his flight, how come the radar machines on the Palestine coast, which are so vigilant to trap wretched refugees, couldn't detect the approach of the great one's chariot. All is in doubt and confusion. The French say to the British: Did you see him go? And the British answer: Did you?

All is in doubt, but one thing is certain: Somebody has taken somebody for a ride. And we mean this more than literally. Could it be that the French, chafing under the recollection of how they lost Syria, and believing that in this loss the British were somehow responsible, decided to pay the debt by releasing the precious vulture to ravage Palestine? Or can it be that the British themselves, in their attempt to curry Arab favor, have decided to add another gift to the plentiful *baksheesh* already handed out – a volatile gift, the Mufti? Or is it some realpolitiker's notion that the presence of the Husseini in Damascus may somehow immunize the local denizens against the Moscow flirtations? Who knows?

Nobody even knows what route or what vehicle the new Mohammed took, let alone who aided and abetted him. It is said that he left by plane, but nobody saw him. The pilot has not yet been identified. Perhaps he mounted El Burak? Perhaps he disguised himself as a d.p. – after all, he's a semite, too – and made his way westward as the first of the hundred thousand? Perhaps he was smuggled out of the country by parcel post, like that other treasure, the crown jewels of Hesse? Who knows? There is none to say either yea or nay.

Certainly the guardians who were supposed to guard the Mufti, stand by, ignorant, they say, of how it was done. They look embarrassed, like *shlemiels*; although with them, too, one may pose the Shakespearean problem: Was Hamlet mad, or only feigning madness? It's the first we hear of it, they say, when the reporters came to them to ask for a statement on the disappearance of the Mufti.

But in Palestine, it appears, the news spread faster. It is true that the Palestine Government has placed a ban upon any radio or newspaper mention of the Mufti; this, however, has not prevented the beggars of Jerusalem announcing that 'He' had arrived in Syria and to-morrow would be in Palestine. The beggars know it, but the Colonial Office sent an inquiry to the Quai d'Orsay ...

We must state that the entire incident is of a cheap and transparent cunning; to expect anyone to believe that the Mufti escaped, and was not merely let go, is to impose outrageously upon the naiveté of people. No doubt one will never know, unless the arrangers fall out, how the Husseini managed his *tour de force*; but the reason why he was let loose, we feel certain, will not be long in manifesting itself.

In Defence of the Atom 21 June 1946

We are quite well aware of the fact that the atom, with its chain reactions, its pleading protons and nimble neutrons, hardly requires benefit of counsel; it can, as the Yiddish proverb has it, 'maintain its own little city.' The truth is that the last thing we would like to meet up with on a dark night in a secluded lane is an atom on the rampage. Nonetheless, amidst all the slander and vituperation which is being flung upon the poor heaven-crested atom, which, after all, through all the millenia and up to this date has kept its peace, a word should be spoken in its favor.

Certainly there are enough ministers, moralists, and people who do not possess the recently discovered atomic know-how, to throw up their hands in horror at the unbottled genie to cover the case for presentation thoroughly enough. Thus, we find Mr. Ilya Ehrenburg, a distinguished and witty novelist, also among those who speak of the new nuclear physics as if it were the invention of the devil. Arriving in Montreal, Mr. Ehrenburg complimented this province as being the locale of two great cultures, English and French; then, to give an acrid zest to his compliment he added – 'two great cultures working in harmony together to produce – an atomic bomb.' The irony, we feel, would have come with better grace if it came from the representative of a culture which had already discovered the atomic secrets but in the interests of morality had decided to abandon them. As it is we read that new prizes are being offered to Russian scientists so as to stimulate them to greater effort in their atomic researches, researches which are being carried on simultaneously with those devoted to the highly moral objectives (sic) of the death-ray.

But it is only the invidious comparisons in Mr. Ehrenburg's comments that we resent. We are at one with him in his disapproval of the fact that to date these great revolutionary discoveries in the great science of the atom are being applied solely to destructive ends. Certainly that is an abuse of the scientific discipline; but it is not the first abuse of this kind. Gunpowder, as we know, has been applied to many industrial and constructive purposes; it is a force; it depends only upon the people who inhabit this planet whether this force is used for good or for evil.

The same is true of the principles of atomic physics. These principles, authorities upon the subject have indicated, may well be used to revolutionize the forms and procedures of practical life. If properly applied, they well may provide all of laboring mankind with millions of inanimate slaves, doing the work which hitherto had to be done with the sweat of one's brow, providing that leisure which all philosophies recognize as the first prerequisite of the highly civilized life. Instead, the best minds are now engaged in discovering how these principles may be annexed to cause bigger and better and more annihilating explosions. Is this, we ask, the fault of the poor atom, which never demanded to be shocked out of its orbit, which, until a war brought pryers into its secrecy, was content to cohere to its peaceful fellow-atoms, and not mix into the misguided affairs of men.

Let us not put the blame upon *things*, but upon *men*. To do otherwise is to revive that comical mediaeval doctrine of deodand, which declared that if a man murdered his fellow with an axe, the axe was taken out of circulation, and made forfeit to the church, deodand, given to God. The Lord can dispense with such gifts. It is the human heart, to paraphrase Scripture, which is the Lord's most acceptable offering; it is man, if you prefer later quotations, who is, as Marx said, the root. From him it is that the evil, or the good, of atomic physics stems. But the thing is man. Here it is that science and knowledge and learning are singularly behind the need; here it is that the great discovery – that which will bring trust where distrust now is, comradeship where rivalry now prevails – still has to be made. Blame not therefore, the atom, but blame that cosmos which, at war with itself, so arrogantly calls itself Man.

A Fitting Memorial   28 June 1946

A number of Jewish organizations, we are informed, are giving thought to the necessity of erecting some fitting memorial to the memory of the millions of Jews who perished at the hands of the Nazis, either as helpless victims or in the various armies of resistance. We doubt whether there breathes a Jew who fails to understand the motivation behind this desire. Certainly, there springs in the heart of everyone a natural compulsion to do something which would eternalize, as much as mortal man can eternalize, the heroism and martyrdom of our millions, on the one hand, and on the other the memory of the great European aberration.

But such a monument, whatever the form it takes, need not necessarily be, we feel, located on the European continent itself. That continent already has a sufficient number of such monuments, erected by the monsters themselves. The crematoria of Oswiecim and Maidanek, we understand, are to be solicitously preserved as memorials; that is as it should be; let the historian of the future, travelling through Europe in some super-enlightened century to come, halt before these grim structures, and let his own eyes behold the noble edifices which the twentieth century protectors of *Kultur* erected to illustrate their philosophy. No, Europe already has enough memorials of the holocaust, ruined villages, destroyed cities, mass graves.

The true locus for such a monument, we think, would be in the Jewish Homeland. There we would be sure, at least, that it would be regarded with veneration, and not scrawled over at dawn with intransigent swastikas, the work of the secret mourners of Hitler. There, too, the monument would evoke more than merely the sad memories of the past; it would also emphasize a happier present and point to a more fruitful future. Indeed, if monuments there must be, let them be in our own territory, seen by eyes that cherish the things and people they stand for, cared for by a posterity that understands and values the message they bring.

If monuments need be – frankly, we think that the noblest commemoration of those who died *al kiddush ha-shem* would be the Jewish National Homeland itself. Not that we are one of those who particularly enjoys the archaeological and memorial uses of Eretz Israel; on the contrary; but we do think that the best way to commemorate the dangers through which the six million lived is to build a land where no such dangers are. Then we could appropriate for us the famous epitaph of Sir Christopher Wren, writ in St. Paul's Cathedral: 'You who would see his monument, look about you.' Similarly could we say: 'If you would know whether we have learned the lessons of Europe, look about you here, and behold what we have done in the land of our forefathers.'

When Is Kidnapping Legal?   5 July 1946

It could hardly be believed. That Jewry which for the past generation had so trustingly placed its faith in the pledged word of England could hardly believe its eyes, as it read, with mounting indignation, of the uncalled for and arrogant measures which the Palestine Administration – itself recognized by the same document which recognized the Jewish Agency – had taken, out of both impotence and a sense of guilt, against that Agency, and, indeed, against the entire Yishuv. Without a scintilla of proof, without even a charge known to any code of law, to have laid hands upon the members of the Jewish Agency – this was something that not even the most malicious slanderer of Albion would ever have dared to imagine – and this had come to pass. It was not without pertinence, therefore, that many, watching the antics of the myrmidons who now lord it over the Holy Land, asked: Is this really Naomi? Are these the true heirs and executors of the late Lord Balfour, of the late Lloyd George? Is there really no relationship between the official statements of the Foreign Office, and the officious practise of its agents? Or is it permitted to a few latter-day bureaucrats, dressed in their little brief authority, to betray, to pervert, to soil the bond and honor of Britain?

The sudden and sensational arrests which took place in Palestine last week-end, must, of course, be considered in their context. Their context, Mr. J.V. Shaw, the Secretary of the Palestine Administration has said, is the terror which certain minor elements of the Yishuv have practised during the past number of months. We will not pause to point out that even the terror has a context of its own – namely, the desperation born of the cruel prohibition which forbids the brothers, sisters, and parents of Palestine inhabitants to come into their own land to their own kith and kin. We do not wish to appear, even indirectly, as justifying acts which are as foreign to the temperament of our people as to its philosophy. But in what manner, by what reasoning, are the members of the Jewish Agency, who have consistently condemned and repudiated the Sternists and the Irgun Zvai, to be held responsible for the deeds of their political opponents? Because they didn't suppress them? But that is the duty of the Palestine Administration, which is there presumably to maintain law and order – and it is only a spurious law and order which is maintained by the indiscriminate arrest of all.

There is, however, a context, in which the raids of Mr. Shaw can be more readily understood – that is, the anti-Zionist, and very frequently, anti-Semitic attitude of the Palestine bureaucrats. Insofar as the personnel of the Administration is concerned, this attitude is born mainly out of a sense of annoyance at the Jews who refuse to act with that same submissiveness which the procurators have learned to expect from all other 'natives' in colonial possessions. (The procurators, for their part, refuse to realize that Palestine is not a colonial *possession*.) Hence a series of provocations of which the arrest of the Agency is but the most recent.

We cite the provocation at random. When a raid was perpetrated upon a Jewish colony several weeks ago, signs were left, reading: Streicher was right. Bigger and better crematoria ... When the King's birthday was celebrated in Jerusalem, Major Glubb's Transjordanians were transported to the Holy City to take part in the parade; members of the Jewish Legion were at first prohibited from participating, and then, granted only a grudging token representation – this, in spite of the fact that Jews fought in all the armies against Fascism, and the Arabs, everywhere, when they were not treacherous, were indifferent ... When a Jewish delegation sought an interview with the Commissioner of a Northern District in Palestine, he turned them from the door ... When ...

But it is unnecessary to continue, for all of these calculated discourtesies are overshadowed by the great injury – the White Paper – the division of Palestine into Jewish ghettos and Arabs estates, and the heartless refusal, against all legal and humanitarian considerations, to give sanctuary to the refugees in the only place where they have a right to expect it.

The text of the context, however, is not complete. While the arrest of the members of the Jewish Agency is being planned – and the plan was announced on the radio of the Jewish Underground several weeks ago; none would believe it – the Mufti, who by all standards deserves to be in Nuerenberg, is mysteriously permitted to escape, and unmysteriously to receive sanctuary in Egypt. Such a series of events closely points to systematic design conceived and intended to intimidate the Yishuv and to destroy the very basis for a Jewish National Home.

We cannot overlook, too, as indicative of both the animus and policy which dictated the Government's kidnapping of the Agency members, the details of its execution. With a malice reminiscent of the Roman procurators – where is the Roman Empire? – the raids were set for the Sabbath, and Rabbi Fishman, who refused to break his Sabbath by sitting in a jeep considerably supplied by the military, was compelled by force to be taken for his ride.

Some more context: The orders which Mr. Shaw and his legions were executing presumably emanated from Bevin's Government. One can now understand Mr. Bevin's appeal for more soldiers in Palestine. That Government, it will be remembered by those whose memory extends prior to the British elections, was supposed to be a Labor Government. Yet it is a Labor

Government which sends its gendarmerie to dynamite open the doors of the Histadruth Headquarters – fellow-members of the World trade unions, and a workers' organization.

One seeks the why and the wherefore. One seeks them in disquisitions on ethics, in analyses of law. It is a vain search. These are the wrong books, the wrong texts. Explanation, if any, for these strange acts can come only from an understanding of the international imperatives by which the British Government, in despite of all previous commitments, finds itself compelled to act. The end-purpose is the liquidation of the Jewish National Home. Such an entity does not seem to fit in with the *present* plans of the Administration. One cannot, however, cancel a pledged word, just like that. Tradition says that when you want to do that you have to invoke some noble word, some all-embracing grandiloquence to cover up the design. That word, Mr. Shaw has already used. He is doing what he is doing to prevent 'anarchy.' He maintains curfews over entire cities for days on end to prevent anarchy. He wishes to disarm the Haganah – to prevent anarchy – to introduce the unanarchic conditions of 1929, and 1936. He puts under arrest thousands at a time – to prevent anarchy. One is entitled to wonder whether Mr. Shaw has not culled his definition of anarchy from a dictionary of antonyms.

For the truth is that the procedures of the p.a., whatever their ostensible purpose may be, are specifically designed to bring about within the Jewish body politic in Eretz Israel, precisely that anarchic fission and despair against which the Government with so much piety and self-righteousness has set its face. The arrest of the Agency members is more than a gesture of appeasement to the Arabs; it is an abject genuflection, a low surrendering salaam. Its purpose is, first, to divide the Yishuv itself into two groups; it will be noted that the technique of arrests was not the same in the case of all of the members of the Agency; and second, to demonstrate such arbitrary naked force against the Yishuv as will drive even its more moderate elements to intransigence. This accomplished, the patient would then be ready for that complete pharmacopoeia of repression which the doctors in Government House are so anxious to prescribe. Should that alone not suffice to make the Balfour Declaration a chapter out of the past, there are always the Arabs that one can let loose – provided all the arms caches have been discovered and confiscated.

We know that many of our readers who know Englishmen different from those who now sit in power will find it difficult to give credence to this picture of a cool, cruel, and calculated scheme to nullify even the status quo of the Jewish Homeland, to exsanguinate the already anaemic, to outblanch the White Paper. Yet the speeches of Mr. Bevin, and particularly the unhappy conversations between Mr. Bevin and Mr. Molotov, only throw into relief this picture we would rather not look upon. The Arabs are now in the happy position of being courted by the two Great Powers. Russia, it has been observed, has been no shy peasant in its flirtations with Islam. Tito, Russia's mouthpiece, withdrew his demand for the indictment of the Mufti as a war criminal. And Britain, in the passion of this courtship, is ready to capitulate, holus-bolus, to the Arabs. The net result is that once more upon the stage of history, the Jews are being offered up as scapegoat – this time by friends.

When it is remembered that these friends are people who, in the integrity of their Socialist principles, never make a sentence without invoking justice, equality, and freedom as witnesses to their high ideals, the situation seems even more incredible still. But it isn't. A great Englishman who knew whereof he spoke, once very pertinently said: Power corrupts; absolute power corrupts absolutely. Recent events in Palestine stand as vivid examples of this text. The party which a year ago, at its Labor Conventions, and in its official statements, stood out as the knight on the white horse ready to defend the oppressed and rejected, has come to power; with what results, all who read, may see.

The Attempt on the House of David   26 July 1946

For the outrageous perpetration of the group of irresponsible terrorists who, at a critical moment in the history of the Yishuv, took it into their heads, with a tragically misplaced bravado, to bomb, causing great loss of life, the King David Hotel, headquarters of the British Administration in Palestine, there can be nothing but unqualified condemnation. Such acts run counter to the entire tradition of our people; they are as wicked as they are stupid; and taking place at a time when negotiations were going on as to the fate of the one hundred thousand, they demonstrate an unspeakable callousness and indifference, not only towards the fate of the innocent persons who happened to find themselves in the hotel, but also towards the fate of thousands whose position this act has still further jeopardized. If an antisemite – if one of General Anders' colonels, now reputedly active in Palestine, had desired to embarrass our people, he could not have done more cunningly than arrange just such a tragedy as occurred in Jerusalem.

Indeed, we strongly feel that there were not a few of our refined crypto-Jew-baiters and diehard imperialists who were waiting for just such an incident to be able to cover their designs against a Jewish Homeland with an air of outraged righteousness and piety. For them, this act of the Irgun Zvai has constituted an 'opening to the mouth of Satan'; an opportunity to damn indiscriminately the whole enterprise of Zionism. The truth is that Jewish Palestine is no more responsible for these acts of violence than is Protestant Toronto for the acts of those of its citizens who happen to run amok.

It is true that a White Paper – our readers will excuse us for the use of this word – has just been concocted which seeks, with a most unconvincing and indeed pitiable ingenuity, to associate the Haganah with some of the enterprises of the Irgun Zvai. This White Paper is a piece of apologetics intended to explain why the Palestine Administration found it necessary to pogromize the Jewish Agency, kidnap its membership, and in general raid the Palestine Yishuv. The excuse is presumably an intercepted telegram from Moshe Shertok to Bernard Joseph in which the former, among general information as to the European itinerary of David Ben-Gurion, requests the latter to 'congratulate Chil on the birth of a new daughter.' It is this *Mazel Tov* which is interpreted by the genial authors of the White Paper as constituting a coded encouragement of isolated acts of sabotage. Unfortunately, for the paper-writers, they do not indicate how they arrive at their equation; we cannot but feel, however, that whoever these detectives were, they missed their vocation; civil servants who identify births of daughters with acts of sabotage could not but have done well as humorists.

The Haganah, as its name and its record indicate, is a self-defense organization. In its entire history, it has never once committed an act of aggression. It is with ironical reflection upon the nature of colonial administrators, that we recall that but a short time ago, as Rommel stood before the gates of Cairo, secretly beckoned by the Mufti's Arab collaborators, the Haganah was the recipient of gallant compliments from one British general after the other. No one said the Haganah was a secret organization, then; the British knew about it, the British relied upon it. It is only now, as the appeasement policy of Chamberlain takes on a new lease of life under the artificial respirations of Mr. Bevin, that the attempt is made to identify the Haganah with lawlessness.

The attempt, of course, is not motivated merely by venom and malice; there is method to the calumny; the object is to vilify the Jewish Agency, and then, by unilateral decision to put an end to it. It is for this reason, in addition to our natural shock at the wanton killing of fifty people, including, be it noted, a number of Jews, that the adventurism of the Irgun Zvai is to be severely reprobated.

One last word about the use of force in connection with the Palestine problem. We are against it. We are against it when it is used by the desperate elements of the Yishuv; we are also against it when it is used by the powers that be to prevent the entry into their Homeland of the wretched and the dispossessed of the ghettos of Europe. It is with a cynical inappropriateness that those who use radar to trap the hapless refugee at last approaching his sanctuary, and then haul him off to a concentration camp in the desert, speak so devoutly against the use of 'force' – their lips know not what their hands are doing.

Literature at Latrun   30 August 1946

It is not surprising, in the light of the completely unprincipled motives which to-day dictate international affairs, that the Agency prisoners who now find themselves in a concentration camp at Latrun should have betaken themselves, no doubt as a legal means of escape, to the writing of pure literature. It is reported, for example, that Moishe Shertok, in an attempt to while away the hours which the Government has expropriated from him, is writing a book – on Hebrew grammar! David Remez, on the other hand, has betaken himself to a field equally innocuous, and has just sent on to the *Davar*, an article – on archaeology!

Doubtless, both Shertok and Remez would have preferred to send out of the camp writing which put in its proper perspective the activities of their gaolers. Unfortunately, turnkeys, from time immemorial, have not been able to find anything *belles* in such *lettres*. Bernard Joseph, who is also in durance vile, it is to be noted, is not participating in the activities at all. His specialty is law; and *that* subject, as treated by their prisoner, would certainly be most unexportable from Latrun.

So Shertok writes on grammar. We can understand the satisfaction this subject must afford him. Here, for happy relief, is a field where right is right and wrong is wrong. Here, no white papers, no parliamentary notes, can prevent the adjective – the Jewish people – from agreeing with its substantive – the Jewish land. A solecism here is a solecism, and not a political necessity. And accent and emphasis are so fixed that not even tanks and cannon can alter them.

We have not had the advantage of seeing Remez's article on archaeology and so we do not know precisely with what subjects it deals. In all likelihood, David Remez, as all archaeologists, discusses remains – the remains of the various conquerors who came to Eretz Israel and whose bones left in the soil of the land, serve only to facilitate the date-setting of historians and researchers. From Latrun, that would be indeed a fitting subject. As the Talmud says, for the wise a *Remez* is sufficient.

The New Year   25 September 1946

Every consideration of the potentialities of the New Year, every attempt to pierce by logic and analysis, beyond the veil of the future – and at the Holiday

Season such an undertaking is a sore temptation – must, we think, necessarily involve, as a first condition, a consideration of what the French are pleased to call 'the actualities of the contemporary scene.' It is a dismal prerequisite. For upon the contemporary scene there is very little, indeed, which could tend to buoy up the spirit, or arouse the optimism, of the beholder.

For after six years of arduous warfare, warfare which significantly enough was accompanied and inspirited by solemn declarations of lofty purpose, many of the principles for which a self-sacrificing humanity fought still remain honoured in the breach rather than in the observance. More than a year has passed since the unequivocal defeat of the enemy, yet it would be wrong, grievously wrong, to say that upon the face of the earth peace reigns. The truth is, in fact, that not only is Peace itself still an objective concealed somewhere beyond the horizon, but even the peace-treaties – which are in themselves much less than peace itself – remain to be written.

It cannot be denied, of course, that now and again these statesmen whom destiny has called to play a role in the decisive years, occasionally recall that peace has yet to be redacted, but every time they do so recall, alas, they seem only to accentuate new causes of strife between new belligerents. Everywhere, in fact, people are getting the impression, an impression so forceful that it is no longer described in hushed whispers, but in bold open statement, that what is actually going on today at the diplomatic green tables is not the fashioning of peace but the re-alignment of allies for a third great world conflict.

Perhaps one of the principal causes for this universal suspicion and mutual fear is the existence of that new death's head at the council-table, namely, the atomic bomb. Our readers no doubt will recall with what enthusiasm its macabre performance was greeted when it first demonstrated how a war could be shortened and tens of thousands of United Nations' lives saved; today, however, that same saving device is regarded with mixed feelings. Those who own and control it, of course, deem it a democratic asset, a guarantee of security, a shield for the righteous; and those who covet it denigrate its invention and by every means possible seek to nullify the military disadvantage under which they labour. And it is the last phrase which is the key to the situation: the nations of the world, and particularly the Big Powers are not thinking in terms of social and human co-operation, but rather in terms of military advantage and disadvantage. Such thinking, of course, reveals intentions which bode no good for the future.

This is serious, deadly serious; but the cancer runs even deeper still. It runs to the very heart of the problem where it reveals a complete absence of morality in international relations. Now, this, to the student of history, should not be particularly surprising; the conduct of international affairs has never been distinguished by piety; but certainly after the high resolve of the past decade, after the vociferous condemnations of Hitler's realpolitik, after the apocalypse of the Atlantic Charter and the revelation of the Four Freedoms, one had a right to expect something loftier than the cynical perversions, the straight-faced double-talk, the unashamed jockeying for position which now characterizes the friendly (sic) negotiations between states.

Perhaps the most telling aspect of the contemporary a-morality – we will be pardoned, we trust, for choosing our examples close at home – is the callous and gallant fashion in which the Jewish victims of Nazism have been forgotten. One would have imagined – and in a moral world one would have had a right so to imagine – that the European conscience, the Christian conscience, would have been so plagued by the memory of what had been done to Jewry – six million cruelly, wantonly, murdered in a kind of murder for which a new word, so diabolic was its plan, had to be coined, namely, genocide, the murder of a race – that it would have sought every means to make amends. True, the dead can not be revived; but surely something should have prompted that conscience to do aught for the survivors. Indeed, many were the occasions, as the battle was actually going on, when responsible leaders of states, shocked at the outrages committed against European Jewry, solemnly promised that our ordeal would not be forgotten, and that, when peace shone again, measures would be taken to prevent their repetition.

Alas, promises, no matter how sacred, made during the course of a war, are no more than weapons of war. The miserable plight in which the remnant of Israel finds itself to-day tragically attests either the cynicism or the amnesia of statesmen. As one beholds the survivors wandering upon the face of Europe in search of sanctuary, and every sanctuary closed, – the quarry of pogromchiks, the inmates of concentration camps, the hunted, the harried, the deported – one is at a loss to distinguish 1946 from 1943. It is no wonder that in so many quarters of Jewry there is spreading a feeling of defeatism, a contagion of hopelessness. In some countries, indeed, Jews are flying from the burden of their ancestry towards the embrace of the Church; and in other places, all reaction is being reduced to the stolidity, the numbness, the unconcern of those who, *not* entering here, have abandoned hope.

For in the past, when upon the annual occasions the editorialist made his retrospect of the vanished months, and beheld, in one country after another, Israel encompassed by darkness, invariably, for consolation's sake, he focussed upon the attention of his readers the ray which shone from Palestine. Today, unfortunately, even that ray is dimmed by dark counsel and darker event. The hope of a Homeland in Palestine, a hope which through the unhappy years, sustained thousands, is being diminished, distorted, thwarted, and thwarted by those very friends who once were most vociferous in its defense. It is not with reluctance that we bid farewell to the year which now joins and emphasizes its predecessors in the Exile.

And of the future? Only this: hopelessness and despair are not the way of

Israel. If that had been our way, surely we would long ere this have joined the extinct Carthaginian, the Assyrian who is no more. Surely it was not to vanish in some Mediterranean port, to disappear in the dust of the European highways, that we braved and survived the many who have risen against us. New Year, new events; let us hope that those which come towards us will be happier than those which recede, be it forever, into the past.

The Nuremberg Trial
4 October 1946

At last, after a leisurely year of probing the obvious and investigating the notorious, the learned jurists who sat in judgment over the Nazi war criminals have arrived, inevitably, at the foregone conclusion. The henchmen of Hitler, the court found, were guilty. We doubt very much whether this procrastinated verdict came to the world this fateful Monday as anything but a judicial confirmation of the already universally known; certainly there was nothing apocalyptic about the revelation that Goering is a bandit and Streicher a murderer. Insofar as those condemned to death are concerned, therefore, the entire trial was an act of supererogation; they should have died ere this; it is a pity that no penalty that may now be inflicted can be in any way commensurate with the heinous crimes these monsters have perpetrated. One would almost have wished, indeed, that science had discovered some resurrective process if only for the purpose of re-inflicting the death penalty upon the unspeakable creatures in the Nuremberg dock. For there, then, a summary justice, executed within a week after their capture would have provided a much more salutary lesson than the somewhat ambiguous and falsely discriminating verdict as it now issues.

The argument that the condemned ones had to go through this marathon trial, not because their guilt was at any time in doubt, but because it was necessary to enunciate by example the principle upon which they were tried, is quite a fallacious one. Either that principle existed before the trial, and therefore did not now require such lengthy exemplification, or it didn't exist before the trial, and then the entire proceedings are impugnable. The truth, of course, is that the acts of the condemned men which shocked the moral sense of the world were not, as the court would wish to indicate, those involving 'aggressive war' – some of the judges, indeed, represent powers which have extended their domains precisely by such aggressive wars – but because these men conceived entirely new objectives in war, such as race murder, enslavement of populations, attack upon civilians, the withholding of quarter, – in fact, all the nefarious corollaries that flow from the concept of total war.

But not all of the verdict of the scholars and gentlemen who sat highest in that room in Nuremberg was as foreseeable as the conclusion to which we have just adverted. Some of the accused, against whom the prosecution had brought evidence as damning as that which was sending others to the gallows, were sentenced only to imprisonment. Others – *mirabile dictu!* – were acquitted.

It is this aspect of the verdict, arrived at after twelve months of consideration and deliberation, which has most astonished the world. Hess, for example, is held to be sane and therefore responsible for his acts. By what subtle distinction, therefore, is his life preserved – the life of Hitler's first paladin and earliest cell-mate – while the just sentence is visited upon the others? The same difficulty arises in the case of others sentenced to imprisonment of varying durations. Either these men were not involved at all in the conspiracy to which the judges referred, and should have been acquitted, forsooth, or they were, and then their responsibility surely extended as far as that of Goering. Why is Jodl who executed Hitler's will upon land to be hanged, and Raeder, who implemented that will on the high seas only to be imprisoned for life? How does one justify the fact that Baldur von Schirach who *personally* was responsible for the murder of hundreds of Viennese Jews, sees his life spared? Certainly it is difficult in this erratic maze of penalties to find some single principle to which they all adhere.

Even more inscrutable is the reasoning which prompted the judges, over the dissent of the Russians, to exonerate, if not honourably, at least safely, Dr. Hjalmar Schacht, Franz von Papen, and Fritzsche. Surely if Konstantin von Neurath who was a minor diplomat is found guilty, for thus sharing in the conspiracy for war, von Papen, a major diplomat, and the schemer who more than any other one man is responsible for Hitler's achievement of the chancellorship, deserved at least a like fate? Surely if Albert Speer who used his engineering talents (and slave labour) for Hitler's purposes is to be incarcerated, Hjalmar Schacht who masterminded the entire German economy ought to share his imprisonment?

It is in vain one will seek for some legal or penological principle as motivating the distinctions which have been drawn between the one murderer and the other. One cannot resist, in fact, the temptation of suspecting that principles other than those of the laws of evidence prompted the unfounded and unexpected clemencies. One hesitates to be cynical about so sacrosanct an institution as a court of justice, particularly when that tribunal has so conscientiously taken twelve months to rush towards judgment, – recent events on the world scene, however, are not without their effect upon the editorial temper – but the strong distinctions which have been made smell very strongly of the odour of expediency. It may even be, in fact, that the very length of the trial was prompted not so much by the Solomonic riddle with which the judges were presented, as by the necessity to keep the judicial arm in harmony with the political one.

Can it be that the common factor which has saved the lives of so many of the accused – some of them, of course, it was impossible to exculpate; a tribunal which exonerated Goering, for example, would deserve itself to be hanged – can it be that that common factor is the possible future use of the accused? Can it be that Papen and Schacht are acquitted because they may yet be allowed to use their undoubted knowledge and talents to play a convenient role in European politics?

Is it possible that not the comparative innocence, but the future potentialities of a youth leader like Baldur von Schirach, a builder like Albert Speer, military leaders like Doenitz and Raeder, exempted these worthies from the penalties they so honestly earned in the company of their less fortunate peers? Can it be, in fact, that in the list of the spared and acquitted, one may read the names of some future German cabinet?

These are disturbing thoughts; one would like to evoke them merely to banish them, but it is impossible. The crippled and broken survivors of Hitler's 'conspiracy,' stand up in tragic amazement as their persecutors go free; the millions of dead, of course, are luckier; they have been spared the witnessing of the last indignity.

A Reply to Dr. I.M. Rabinowitch   16 October 1946

A week ago Monday, but two days after his Day of Atonement, Dr. I.M. Rabinowitch delivered before the Canadian Club, whose chairman took pains not to associate the club with the opinions of its speaker, an oration sensationally titled: *The Menace of Political Zionism*. When the announcement of this address was first made, there were many, it must be stated, who were at a loss to understand the relation of this speaker to this subject; for while Dr. Rabinowitch was regarded as an expert on diabetes, a scholar in metabolism, and a master of chemical warfare, no one had hitherto suspected him of being an authority on politics, or Zionism, or menaces, and still less on matters pertaining to Jewry. Nor was the fact of the doctor's Jewish extraction sufficient to explain this addition to his repertoire of lectures, for throughout the years that Dr. Rabinowitch had resided in Montreal, it was known, his association in Jewish activity and his relation to Jewish institutions of welfare, religious, educational or philanthropic, had been minimal, if not totally negative. Certainly he was the last person one whould have thought of in connection with a representative statement on anything Jewish.

The speech itself, however, soon cleared up the mystery, for what the doctor actually did therein was to confuse his roles to launch against his own people an onslaught of chemical warfare, noxious with concoctions all of his own invention. The vials of vilification which he let loose against the large masses of Jewry in general, and against its rabbis and spiritual leaders in particular – men whom he named by name, and soiled with epithet – made one wonder whether one was before a forum of discussion or in an experimental laboratory; one could imagine only that by this strategy the doctor hoped to stifle his victims into silence. One need hardly say that this toxic rhetoric has failed of its purpose.

The entire address of Dr. Rabinowitch, in fact, may be considered as an attempt on his part to see into how many fields of knowledge – outside his own department of medicine – he could, at one week's notice, intrude. His qualifications as an expert on the general topic of political Zionism have already been indicated; but the address itself bristled with still more specialties; for in about forty minutes of talk the doctor also posed as lawyer, national biographer, statistician, Talmudist, geographer, censor, expert on civics, and, finally, theologian.

First, the doctor looked at law – international law. Calling for the immediate reorganization or dismissal of the Jewish Agency for Palestine, Doctor Rabinowitch invoked Article 4 of the Mandate which states that the purpose of the Jewish Agency is to advise and co-operate with the administration in Palestine – I quote the doctor allegedly quoting the Mandate – 'on matters pertaining to Jewry.' Reference to the actual text of the Mandate discloses a shocking fact – the doctor has amputated his quotation, and has omitted therefrom just those words which, had he quoted them, would out of his own mouth have contradicted and undermined the entire content and purport of his speech. For Article 4 does not speak about the Jewish Agency co-operating on something as vague as matters pertaining to Jewry. It speaks, and I quote verbatim the words the doctor spirited away, it speaks of co-operating – and this the Agency is, has been, and always will be ready to do, – 'co-operating in such economic, social, and other matters as may affect the *establishment of the Jewish National Home.'* Why did Dr. Rabinowitch cut out, hide away, and cover up that which was an essential part of his quotation – the duty of the Mandatary and the Agency to co-operate in the establishment of a national home? Is it fair, is it honorable to come before men of good will, eager to learn the facts, and know the documents, and so to distort and excise what is of the essence? And discovering the doctor in the midst of such a procedure, what is one to think of those protestations of piety and that verbiage on ethics with which he padded out his address? Particularly when it will be seen, as it will be shown, that other quotations adorning the doctor's text have been similarly fractured and similarly re-set?

Abandoning the realm of jurisprudence, the doctor on a holiday – a Roman holiday – then betook himself to national biography. His manner had not improved. Theodor Herzl, whose memory is revered wherever Jews foregather, he termed – even the dead were not safe from his anatomizing – a renegade Jew. His remarks on Moses Hess I have traced, through the borrowed idiom of his language, to the article on that subject in the Jewish Encyclopedia, and here again one discovers that Dr. Rabinowitch has juggled and paraphrased to suit his own purpose. The article, for example, describes this nineteenth century writer as a socialist; seeing that the Labor Government in England whose cause he was espousing is also socialist, Dr. Rabinowitch couldn't use that designation as a term of insult, wherefore he looked through the rest of the article and found a reference to the dissemination of the so-called anarchistic doctrines of Proudhon, also a socialist; in Rabinowitch's speech Hess emerges – threatening though dead – an anarchist! The same biographical style is applied to the blackening of the reputations, among others, of David Ben-Gurion, Chairman of the Jewish Agency, and Dr. Stephen Wise, a great and good man. It is to be noted that some of these vituperations the doctor omitted – whether through repentance, or oversight, or just his general habit of deletion, I do not know – from his spoken speech; the published version, however, preserves the gems.

Doctor Rabinowitch also imagined himself a geographer, a geographer in search of a place of sanctuary for the hundreds of thousands of homeless Jews whose plight so tortured his soul. Standing, therefore, in the comfort of the Windsor Hotel, he turned before him, did this stationary explorer, the globe of the world, and pointed to countries which, but for those Zionists, might have received large numbers of Jews. He mentioned the Argentine. But one still has to hear from Señor Juan Peron. He spoke of an offer on the part of Australia to permit a mass immigration of refugees. The offer is mythical; it still has to issue from the federal government of that country. He suggested French Guiana, no doubt because the penal colonies of that area are soon to be cleared out. He suggested other places; the suggestions were all one-sided; the governments of those places still had to open their triple-barred gates. Finally, Dr. Rabinowitch went through the gesture of making an appeal to President Truman to take into the United States the total number of Jewish displaced persons in Europe. It is significant that the doctor studiously avoided making a plea, or even mentioning the possibility, that Canada might admit to refuge some of his afflicted brethren.

The conclusion of these geographic wanderings, of course, still found the doctor standing at the microphone of the Canadian Club, and his agonized co-religionists still stranded on the highways and byways of Europe.

Nonetheless, Palestine, where a Jewish Homeland had been sanctioned by His Majesty's Government in the Balfour Declaration, in the form of a mandate which received international recognition through the fifty-two nations of the League, including Canada and the United States – Palestine as a home for his suffering people, he dismissed, I use his typical phrase, he dismissed at once. A quick decision! There did not seem to be, in the speech of the doctor, an awareness of the fact that had it not been for the accident of his father's transatlantic crossing, he, too, like almost anybody on this continent, might have been a European 'displaced person.'

In the course of his remarks, Dr. Rabinowitch also dabbled in statistics. His object, apparently, was to prove that the majority of the Jewish people were not in sympathy with political Zionism. The method of his proof was simplicity itself. Taking the total Jewish population of the world, he subtracted therefrom the registered memberships of the Zionist organizations, – and *voilà!* – the rest were against or indifferent to Zionism! It is as if one were to arrive at the number of Canadians in the land by confining the census solely to the membership of clubs in Canada! It is to be hoped that the doctor does not take his blood-counts with the same arithmetic as he takes count of his people. For what are the facts? The Roper Poll in the United States recently showed that eighty per cent of the Jews in that country supported Zionism, ten per cent were doubtful and ten opposed; in Canada the percentage of support is even higher; and insofar as the Jewish displaced persons in Europe are concerned, ninety-five per cent of them, in a poll carried out under UNRRA auspices expressed not merely an ideological support but a profound, and under the circumstances, a pathetic hope that they themselves might at last, in Palestine, end their wanderings.

May I suggest an even simpler arithmetic to demonstrate whether Dr. Rabinowitch's speech represented, as he said it did, the vast majority of the Jewish people. It is this: I challenge the doctor to indicate or name, throughout the Dominion of Canada, not fifty thousand, not ten thousand, not a thousand, but one single Jew who shares his opinions and his attitude! The fact is that the doctor, as a Jew, is so erratic in his views that he represents the crank extreme of eccentricity, and were it not for the auspices under which he spoke, the wide dissemination which his remarks received, and the danger that many attribute to the ventures of the politico the authority of the medico, we would not feel ourselves constrained to answer him at all.

The doctor's vocational hobbies, however, are not at an end. Dr. Rabinowitch also presumed to include in his talk a lecture to Jews who were Zionists touching their civic duty. With the quotations from the Talmud which he cited in this connection we find no fault; they are the maxims which have moulded Jewish behavior and made for good citizenship long before the doctor ever discovered them. It is the utterly superfluous repetition of these maxims – thus implying that they needed repeating – which constitutes an unpardonable slur on the loyalty and civic pride of Canadian Jewry. Canadian Jewry whose sons rallied to the flag of their country in numbers far beyond their proportion to the population, needs no lessons in patriotism; and least of all from Dr.

Rabinowitch. Indeed, from the loyalty which the doctor has displayed to the group into which he was born, one may well surmise his general capacity for this virtue.

The doctor's versatility is not yet exhausted. He is also a censor, and it was in this role that he fell upon the issues of *The Canadian Jewish Chronicle*, the oldest Anglo-Jewish publication in the Dominion, a journal consistently devoted, since its establishment in 1897, to the expression of representative Jewish opinion and the promotion of good Canadian citizenship. Here, however, the doctor's technique of quotation showed some dubious progress; he no longer quoted partial phrases; he now snatched out of their sentences single isolated words. Innuendos, too, he allegedly found, directed against the Attlee Government. May I say that here for once the doctor is indulging in understatement; the present Palestinian policy of the Government the *Chronicle* has condemned, not by innuendo, but by declaration forthright, open, and unconcealed. In this the *Chronicle* has gone no farther than Mr. Winston Churchill who castigated as the worst kind of appeasement the White Paper of 1939, and done no more than other Canadian publications which have condemned, without restraint, the domestic policies of the Attlee Government. As a matter of verifiable fact, the general content of the editorials and of other articles in this journal has consisted, when discussing the subject, of references to British constitutional documents, including the Balfour Declaration, on Palestine, and of reminders to the present Labor Government of the Labor Party's unequivocal, and until yesterday unbroken support of the Zionist cause.

The doctor's shock, obviously must arise from some other cause. Certainly Dr. Rabinowitch does not begin to understand either the British constitution or the British character if he imagines that reasoned editorial disagreement with the policy of a government is something to be suppressed. For our part it is to be noted that while the White Paper of 1939, prohibiting the entry of Jews into Palestine, and restricting the purchase of land by Jews in that country, a restriction which no longer exists even in lands previously under German domination, while that document caused great grief, and indeed loss of life, the Zionist Organization and Palestine Jewry, throughout the years of the war, postponed discussion upon this vital question, and threw itself into the great struggle which more than a year ago ended in victory. One million Jews fought in the armies of the democratic countries, and Palestine Jewish youth, under the direction of British generals, issued into Africa, Syria, the countries of the Mediterranean to win glory for themselves and the flag under which they fought. Then came the peace. The peace revealed the tragic plight of European Jewry, diminished by six million of its kith and kin, broken and shattered, without sanctuary or refuge. Then, and not until then, was the question of the White Paper re-opened. Does Dr. Rabinowitch, whose soul is so tortured for his brethren, consider it an offence on my part, on anybody's part, Jew or Gentile, to have reminded the world of these sacrifices and sufferings, and to have pleaded, with those in authority, for the visas that meant survival?

From the doctor's speech, and his intonation of it, it appeared that he considered my offence particularly heinous in that I had expressed these things in English. I must admit myself at a loss to understand his point. Is one to deduce that the King's English must not be used for the expression of opinions contrary to those entertained by the government in office? One must weep, therefore, for the leader of His Majesty's Loyal Opposition who thus is smitten dumb. Or is it to be inferred that if the editorials had been written in Yiddish and had therefore remained uncommunicable to those to whom they were addressed, that, then, it would have been alright with the doctor? Certainly such an attitude throws considerable light upon Dr. Rabinowitch's concepts of sincerity and frankness; these, however, are not our concepts; we adopt in English in *The Canadian Jewish Chronicle* precisely the same attitude as we articulate in Yiddish in the pages of *The Jewish Daily Eagle*.

From journalism – and gentlemen of the press will appreciate the contiguity – the doctor elevated himself to theology, and here he came to the main gist of his address. It consisted of two propositions: (a) The banner of the Jew, he said, was something called Sinaism and not Zionism, and (b) Zionism, he alleged, was detrimental to the interests of the British Empire.

Touching the first it may be stated that the religion called Sinaism is purely a nonce-thing, invented by the doctor for the occasion, a religion, however, having a total membership of one, Dr. Rabinowitch. How the doctor performs his religious rituals in this creed must, I regret to say, remain inscrutable; in his address the doctor declared himself to be a member of a synagogue in Toronto – where he hasn't lived these thirty years. And even if by Sinaism the doctor meant only that part of Judaism which is incorporated in the Ten Commandments given at Sinai, he is again not the proper man to speak about it, inasmuch as his very address contravened at least two of these Commandments, that pertaining to the honour due to one's forefathers, and that pertaining to the giving of false testimony.

But in fact there is no Sinaism, there is Judaism, and in all Judaic writing the love of Zion – geographic Zion – is a cardinal principle. It is true that the doctor sought to give the impression that the Talmud – the Talmud! – was anti-Zionist. It is absurd in a discussion of such issues, at this time, and before any but a theological forum, to enter upon a quotation-contest, but the interests of truth demand that it be pointed out that the particular quote to which Dr. Rabinowitch referred was garbled from its context – he quoted a third of a thought – and that if his Talmudic erudition is as great as he would have us believe then he has willfully ignored a host of statements on the subject all attesting to the uniform and passionately pro-Zionist stand of the Talmudic teachers. I refer the doctor to a partial list of these which he may find in this week's issue of *The Canadian Jewish Chronicle.** But really it is superfluous to go to the Talmud when the Bible itself is explicit on the subject. Every Sunday school child knows Psalm 137, where it is written, of a geographic and not eschatological Zion: If I forget thee, O Jersualem, may my right hand forget its cunning. The next verse is even more to the point: If I remember thee not, may my tongue cleave to the roof of my mouth.

As false, and malicious to boot, was Dr. Rabinowitch's second proposition – that political Zionism is against the interests of the Empire. One did not know – as one listened to the doctor holding forth on the human wreckage left in the wake of war, and then watched him painting those who sought to come into the land promised to them, as threats to the Empire – whether to laugh or weep. Now, let me make myself abundantly clear: If Dr. Rabinowitch had confined his condemnation to that small band of terrorists in Palestine who against all our traditions and all our interests have acted so as to besmirch our name, he would have been repeating only that which has been felt and stated by every responsible Jew and every responsible Jewish organization. Terror is not the way of the Jewish people; our doctrine, our credo, our Torah repudiates and condemns it; and our own history, in which for two thousand years we have invariably, without exception, always been on the receiving end of terror, has but emphasized that belief. If an antisemite – we said in the *Chronicle* of July 26th about the acts of terror – if an antisemite had desired to embarrass our people, he could not have done more cunningly than arrange just such a tragedy as occurred in the King David Hotel.

But all of Jewry, surely, ought not to be held hostage for the deeds of a few hundred irresponsible youths, driven by an agony and despair the extent of which only God knows, to acts from which all their co-religionists recoil with horror.

Such an indictment, however, would not have made a sensational address. All who speak well of Zion, all who seek to enter it, all – said Dr. Rabinowitch – all are conspirators against the Empire. It is surprising, since this is his thesis, that he did not call for the expulsion of the Jewish settlement already in the land. To what ridiculous conclusion are we led by his logic! If what he says is true, then Lord Balfour who issued the famous declaration which bears his name, Lloyd George, one of Zion's staunchest friends, and Lord Tweedsmuir once Governor-General of Canada, all proponents of political Zionism, all were traitors to Empire. Loyal is only I.M. Rabinowitch. One has but to recall the

**Yerushalmi, Shekolim,* chapter three; *Gittin,* p. 8b; *Kiddushin,* p. 31b; *Pirkei d'Reb Eliezer,* chapter 5; *Sanhedrin,* p. 102; p. 94; *Megillah,* p. 25; etc.

events of the last seven years to see things in their proper perspective – England fighting for her very future in the Middle East – and what happens? Egypt awaiting with indifference the arrival of Rommel, remains neutral; Iraq is treacherous and makes an uprising; the Arabs in Palestine see an opportunity and send their leader, the Mufti, to Berlin – only Palestine Jewry rallies to the cause, transforms the land itself into an arsenal of the Middle East, and sends its sons to all the battlefields, in Asia, in Europe, and in Africa, where as the gallant Field Marshal Montgomery has declared, they helped to turn the tide of battle at El Alamein.

Certainly Dr. Rabinowitch has rendered a grave disservice to his people. Nor has he, in his speech, advanced the interests of Empire. Whether he has rendered a service to himself only he knows. This, however, everybody knows – a responsible man ought to think twice before launching into lectures on a subject where his speech can only display his ignorance, or his malice, or both. Nor is this to question the doctor's right to the freedom of speech, but freedom of speech does not mean, as an eminent jurist has said, that a man has a right to rush into a crowded theatre and shout 'Fire!' where no fire is. To the doctor therefore, who is a collector of quotations, I offer yet another; it is from Plato's *Republic*. Said the philosopher: 'More will be accomplished, and better, and with more ease, if every man does what he is best fitted to do, and nothing else.'

Dr. Rabinowitch may well take this to heart. His stimulants and soporifics, certainly, could be used to better advantage in his practice of medicine. As for political Zionists they are firm in the faith that the differences which now exist between the Mandatary and the Agency are purely temporary; that the better counsel which characterized British policy heretofore will yet prevail; and that it is merely a matter of time – but oh, let not that time be too long! – merely a matter of time before the British tradition with regard to Palestine, as stated by Lord Balfour, will be re-established. On that day, the role of Dr. Rabinowitch will appear even clearer than it does today.

The Nobel Prize   29 November 1946

Every year, as wisdom is translated from the Scandinavian, the world awaits with bated breath the announcement of the Nobel awards. Accorded to those who 'in the preceding year have most contributed to the benefit of mankind' – whether through distinguished effort in literature, in science, or in the works of peace – the Nobel prizes have ever been deemed, and for the most part justly deemed, the *ne plus ultra* of international approval, the supreme accolade of world appreciation.

This year, as the season of the Nobel harvest came round, and as one reflected upon the present case and future prospects of world peace, one had a right to wonder, first, whether the peace prize would be awarded at all, and second, if awarded, upon what basis the choice would be made. Should it be granted to Mr. Winston Churchill for having achieved peace through victory over the Nazis? But Mr. Churchill, according to Comrade Stalin, was a warmonger. Should it, then go, to Comrade Stalin? Comrade Stalin's veto at U.N., it was felt in many quarters, was as much a military weapon as the atomic bomb. Perhaps Gandhi? The Mohammedans in India would hardly approve. The truth was, of course, that the hushed military manoeuvres which are now the constant strategy of international affairs seemed quietly to heckle any choice of the Nobel committee, even in the very act of its contemplation.

Nonetheless, the prize has been announced; and, like peace itself, it is split in two. The choices of the Scandinavian selectors, moreover, clearly show that they too, arrived at their decision not without serious misgivings. For the prize has gone to two oldsters, one 81, and the other 79, Mr. John Raleigh Mott, and Miss Emily Greene Balch. Mr. Mott's efforts on behalf of peace, moreover, can only by stretching a point be considered as part of current affairs; it was way back during the last war that he headed the Y.M.C.A. canteen and prisoner-of-war work; and since that time has been distinguished mainly for keeping his own peace. It is true that he is also known as the grand old man of Protestant world unity; we doubt very much, however, whether it was his labour in this field which earned him the present tribute; after all, Germany is a predominantly Protestant country, and it is hardly to be imagined that Germany's actions during the past decade resulted from a spirit of Christian fraternity. Mr. Mott is also somewhat hard of hearing; this, of course, is often an asset to a peacemaker; unfortunately, it is not unique enough to justify a Nobel award.

Miss Balch, too, has toiled in the vineyard of peace. She helped found the Women's International League for Peace and Freedom at the Hague in 1915, she served on Henry Ford's abortive peace mission in 1916, and she lost her Wellesley professorship for pacifism. A career on behalf of peace – but hardly a successful career.

And this, perhaps provides the key to this year's choice. For the first time in its history, the Nobel Prize committee has demonstrated that it has a sense of humour, for certainly it is not otherwise than as irony that one can accept this designation of two quixotic failures as the recipients of the Nobel peace prize. It is as if the Swedes, who remained neutral during the recent hostilities, were saying to the world: Behold, here is the composite picture of your two octogenarians, one deaf, the other asthmatic, and both in their most serious efforts equally discredited – behold the champions of your peace!

Peace, it's wonderful! But literature is even more so. Here the Swedes really went out of their way to play a practical joke upon all those who delude themselves with the belief that 'poets are legislators' and writers the moulders of the human mind. For the winner this year is a man called Hesse. Ever hear of him? No, not Rudolph! That would be too much, although that, too, would have its pertinent irony. Hermann Hesse, of whom the secretary of the Swedish Academy – with what relevancy to literary standards it is difficult to establish, said: '...One of those who first eluded German suppression of free opinion.' By this the secretary meant that Hesse ran away from Germany and became a Swiss citizen. Emigration thus becomes an aesthetic quality. It is, however, when one realizes that Hesse fled from William Hohenzollern, and not from the Nazis, – he has been a Swiss citizen for more than twenty years – that even this apologia – the writer as fighter for liberty – is exploded. The Committee, it would appear, must have been sitting in front of a 1918 calendar. The only other assumption that can explain this otherwise inscrutable choice is the theory that the award was given for national rather than personal considerations – a gesture from neutral Sweden to neutral Switzerland. If this was the kind of thinking that went on among the Scandinavian selectors, then they really muffed their chance. For a national gesture they could have made, a gesture which would, in some small measure, have served as an atonement – a fruitless atonement – but an atonement for the great crime which Christian Europe has perpetrated against a small people. Certainly thought might have been given to the question of an award to a Jew *qua* Jew – to, let us say, any one of a half dozen Palestinian writers whose literary stature is certainly as high as that of Herr Hesse. In this manner, something might have been done to alleviate the propaganda which has not only resulted in the murder of six million Jews, but also in the degradation of the very status of the Jew in Europe. Such an award would have been an act of consolation, a declaration of sympathy, and a judgment of reintegration emanating from one of the most respected tribunals of the civilized world.

Instead, the Nobel Prize committee chose, for the object of its condolence, a German, and a German, moreover, of merits unknown.

The prizes awarded in science, too, were not without their symbolic significance. In the first place, it is to be noted that no experts in atomic physics received, this year, as they have in the past, the annual tribute. In this respect, the committeemen were no doubt acting as the continuing conscience of the late Alfred Nobel, who in the past established the prizes as a sort of penance for his discovery of dynamite. It would have been callous, indeed, now to award the penitential offerings to the inventors of a super-dynamite. Besides, what would Miss Emily Greene Balch think?

In physics the prize went to Professor Percy Williams Bridgeman, who had proved that nearly all substances change profoundly if squeezed hard enough. An important discovery; and one not without its uses in international relations.

Finally we must note that one of the prizes in chemistry went to Dr. Wendell Meredith Stanley who found 'a Thing which acted like an inanimate chemical, and also like a living, growing organism.' The virus which causes the 'mosaic disease' in tobacco plants, it can spread from plant to plant, multiplying within the living cell, apparently living itself. Tricked into a test-tube, it quiets down, the 'living' molecules stacking together into protein crystals. But within this seemingly dead chemical, the spirit of life remains. When injected into a tobacco plant, its molecules awake, and become deadly germs again.

The zombies of biology. Life-in-death. Death-in-life. The perfect fauna of an atomic age!

The Japanese Deportations   6 December 1946

The Japanese deportations which were ordered some time ago and which were stayed to allow for an appeal upon the constitutionality of the orders to the highest court in the Empire, the Privy Council, are about to be set in motion again. The learned lords, basing their judgment solely upon legal *considerants*, have ruled the orders *intra vires*. *Dura lex, sed lex.*

The Privy Council, of course, is not accustomed, nor is it permitted, to go outside the scope of law to seek among the dicta of morality, lights whereby to illuminate its judgment. This, however, should not prevent the Canadian Government from now re-considering, in the calmer post-war light, both the effect of its orders upon many innocent Japanese, – wives and children – and the international and moral implications of the orders. For most people, indeed, will find it difficult to evaluate these Japanese deportations otherwise than as legislation and decisions based upon unworthy considerations of race and colour. The fact is that the naturalized members of other enemy nations, as for example naturalized Germans, have not been subjected to such discriminatory legislation, nor to such wholesale expulsions. The only distinction, moreover, which can be made between the Canadianized members of a militarist foe and those of a fascist regime is that the ones are yellow and the others are white – a simple and unashamed distinction of colour which ought to play no part in the law-making of our country.

Certainly legislation based upon such premises constitutes a most dangerous precedent in Canadian life. Distinctions of colour are akin to distinctions of race; distinctions of creed are not far removed; the movement set afoot by such legislative tendencies is toward discord and not toward unity. The unity of Canada has always been based upon a formula as simple as it is worthy – a union of peoples, who, having different pasts, dedicate themselves to an identical future. Racial legislation tends to break down that unity, to shatter, break, and parcel it off into those constituent elements which only after much effort and great progress were coalesced in the entity known as Canada.

This, of course, is not to be construed as a defence of those Japanese, who albeit naturalized, still declared themselves loyal to the country's enemy. But not all of those who are to be deported are suffering that fate because of a personal responsibility; most, indeed, are victims of the notion of group responsibility, a notion which is not far removed from the punishment of hostages.

Witnesses of Jehovah   13 December 1946

Mr. Duplessis' recent demonstration of power arbitrarily exercised is such as will leave all citizens, and particularly those belonging to minority groups in the province, with a justifiable feeling of insecurity touching their civil rights. Certainly we have no axe to grind on behalf of the Witnesses of Jehovah; we deem, in fact, their alleged association with Jehovah a usurpation of our own ancestral prerogatives; we consider their method of proselytizing as objectionable as their doctrines, and their doctrines as questionable as their all too violent denigrations of other people's creeds; but, believing all these things about the over-testifying witnesses, we still do not know of any law or principle which would justify an Attorney-General in visiting punishment – in the form of a cancellation of a license – upon a sympathizer of the Witnesses who exercised the ordinary and right of putting up bail for them.

As we understand the law, anybody can put up bail for anybody charged with any bailable offense any number of times – provided his bail is sufficient to assure the appearance of the accused. It is an act which – since it eliminates the possibility of imprisonment before condemnation – facilitates the administration of justice, rather than hinders it. The nature of the offense involved is irrelevant; bail has been put up for the purpose of temporarily liberating bank-bandits; but no one has, therefore, impugned the honesty, or the moral standing, of the bondsman.

It is true that the possession of a liquor license is not a right, but a privilege. Not everybody can get a liquor license. Certain prerequisites, not clearly enunciated in the law, seem to be required. Whatever these are, Mr. Roncarelli did appear to have them, inasmuch as he did for some time enjoy the possession of a license. This being so, the Attorney-General, having given, the Attorney-General, like divinity itself, could take away. It is not therefore, the cancellation of Roncarelli's license which is the shocking element in this affair; it is the reason given for that cancellation.

The reason, put boldly, is that Mr. Roncarelli, supporting a religious movement of which the Attorney-General disapproves, forfeits rights and privileges which otherwise he might have continued to enjoy in peace. This reason strikes at the very principle of freedom of religion; and *pro tanto* jeopardizes the rights of all groups who worship in a manner different from that sanctioned by Mr. Duplessis. Indeed, this reason, if accepted, would jeopardize, in other parts of Canada, the position of Mr. Duplessis' own co-religionists; and would, before long, revive in this country those sectarian quarrels which, fortunately, have for many years played no part in our national life.

Moreover, Mr. Duplessis has supplied the Witnesses with more publicity in one week than they have been able to obtain in a year of door-bell ringings.

Science and Savagery   10 January 1947

Others before us have noted the rather disappointing fact that culture and humanity are not necessarily kindred concepts, and that, indeed, it may often happen that they bear a relation to each other which only the mathematics of inverse proportions can adequately express. The atomic bomb is not without justice adduced as a case in point. Here, in atomic physics, was a field of knowledge whose secrets were hitherto deemed unreachable; nonetheless, in the fullness of time, the mind of man, broadening out from explosive to explosive – the arduous and ardorous ingenuity of the human mind nonetheless did reach the field, turned it, and ploughed it. A mighty achievement! The last accolade to the wizardry of the scientific genius! But – and here indeed is the moral crux of the problem – but to what purpose used? Not – as yet, – for the harnessing of power to lighten the burdens of mankind, to increase civilized leisure, to make possible a better distribution of the benisons of Nature – but for destructions and annihilations, man-made cataclysm perpetrated upon a scale hitherto unknown!

It is a contrast which must at once induce a sense of humility touching the vaunted progress of civilization, and an inevitable scepticism touching the teleologies of scientific research. Moreover, as if the atomic bomb were not sufficient in itself to point up this antithesis between culture and civilization, between the uranium formula and the golden rule, there is offered for the contemplation of moralists an even more macabre example, an example afforded by the scientific (*sic*) debris uncovered in enemy country.

That throughout the years of the war, the Nazis were engaged in a systematic plan of murder is to-day not any longer deemed the revelation of a war secret. The laboratories in which their plans were executed – concentration camps, so-called hospitals, and crematoria – are still standing; the apparatus of execution is still there, and may be examined. But while, until yesterday, everybody thought – because so Adolf Hitler had indicated both in his speeches and in his writings – that these mass slaughters were designed to achieve for the German people *lebensraum* by killing off inconvenient populations – to-day it is maintained, particularly by lawyers defending those Nazi murderers who at last are brought to book, that all of these deaths were purely scientific – nothing malicious about them – just the result of necessary experiments carried out in an attempt to make discoveries which would eventually benefit the billions of mankind. Sacrificed for such a lofty purpose, what significance do the lives of a mere six million have? Why, if the experiments had proved successful – if some sensational cures to the world's plagues had been found – why, the world, far from criticizing these deplorable deaths, might have stood up to bless the German doctors and butchers!

Nothing, of course, is said in this argument about the fact that the deceased, offered upon the altar of science, were unwilling victims, and still less, of the fact that no Nazis were thus operated upon for the greater glory of science. Discovered records, it must be admitted, do show that a number of the murdered were done in to the accompaniment of much pseudo-scientific jargon, that human beings were vivisected and the process attributed not to sadism but simply to anatomical research, and that all deaths were recorded as due to heart-failure.

It is precisely with reference to these slaughters, performed to the accompaniment of medical incantations and headsman's-pantomime, that the macabre moral question about which we spoke has arisen. It would appear that in British medical circles quite a debate is raging about the question: Should these scientific post-mortem reports be published, or should they not? If anything useful lies in those abattoir records, should they be used or not?

The Lancet, a distinguished medical journal, it appears, has already refused to publish 'detailed reports of lethal experiments performed by Germans' which have come into its hands because 'none of these has seemed to us to be worth the publicity and the tests were generally ill-conceived and ill-conducted.' The magazine continues: 'However, supposing facts of real value to medicine were still to emerge from the records of the experiments, should they be published or not? Those who favor publication say that the crime has already been committed and that their duty, both to the victims and their surviving friends is to see that all possible advantage is gained from their suffering so that they shall not wholly have suffered in vain. Those who would refuse argue that the crime has already been committed and that we should make ourselves accessories to the fact if we were to profit in any way.'

Already a professor in the department of entomology (this has to do, significantly enough, with insects) at the London School of Hygiene (!) and Tropical Medicine, one Dr. Kenneth Mallanky, has demonstrated the superiority of his intelligence by declaring that the reasons given against publication were nothing more than 'pernicious sentimentality.'

It is to be wondered whether the hard-boiled Dr. Mallanky and those practitioners who side with him do fully realize the implications of their attitude. We do not refer merely to the revival of the mediaeval doctrine of deodand – the doctrine whereby the instrument which effected a murder was confiscated, 'given to God' – which here undergoes a scientific transformation: 'their suffering made sacred by science, so that they shall not wholly have suffered in vain.' But do these thirsters-after-knowledge, these picker-uppers of learning's crumbs, fully appreciate the fact that by their attitude they tend to give a sort of *ex post facto* justification to the heinous crimes which now happily provide them with hunting-ground. Is it now to be an accepted principle in medical research that every time a gang of banditti run amok, a scientific commission is to be sent to study their techniques – provided they have been educated enough and methodical enough to keep records? Truly the only light which medical investigation could throw upon the activities at Belsen would be diagnostic – diagnostic of the Krafft-Ebing personalities who established and ran those places – and that diagnostic has already been made *ad nauseam*. As for the discovery, among the bloody records, of cures beneficial to mankind, – merely to indicate such a hope is to manifest a singular scientific obtuseness as to what went on in the camps, and indeed, to seek by indirection to convert cannibalism into a study of vitamins.

Of course this debate would never have ensued, even in medical circles, professionally a most argumentative clan, were it not for a fact which by now must be abundantly clear: divorce between scientific and human values. A passion for facts, a mania for discovery, – these by themselves certainly do not constitute the scientific spirit, they merely manifest the existence of minds voraciously curious and not very different, in essence, from the minds of crossword puzzle workers. It is when such curiosity is joined to a proper view of humanity, to a philosophy of man's relation to man, that the merely inquisitive rises to the truly scientific. To postulate otherwise is to declare that scientists are instruments and not persons, to proclaim an adding machine a scientist. No; we do not admire the man who dissects his mother, nor him, either, who compiles learned reports – to prove, scientifically, the human capacity for suffering, – about the unwilling death-throes of his brother.

Chisels and the Man ...   10 January 1947

A NOTE ON THE SCULPTURE OF OCCASION

It is particularly after a war that the sculptors, a tribe that in the flat days of peace is usually found lugubrious over its unpatronized lot, do really come into their own. Then it is, as the laurel wreaths are fixed upon the heads of the returning victors, that the sculptor, lifting up his eyes from his sorry contemplations, suddenly discovers that through the dust and smoke of battle everything has taken on proportions heroic. What but a short untrumpeted while ago was dully civic and pedestrian is now transformed, metamorphosed, made triumphantly equestrian; who yesterday left for the wars, a meek bank-clerk liberated from behind a wicket, now stalks back, a hero and bemedalled; where yesterday stooped a politico, – in spectacles, – with papers, – competent but uninspiring, there now rises a conqueror, erect and masterful, his sword back in its *portfolio*, and his heel (rubber) set upon the neck of the vanquished.

The guild of the stone-cutters, of course, is not slow, – since their interests are involved – to realize that these, certainly, are meet subjects and fit themes for the immortality of granite. Certainly when the contemporary has been made historic, and the ephemeral rendered epic, certainly then, the day of the warrior must be followed by that of the artist. A boom – gloat the sculptors – a boom surely is now indicated. Will there not be memorials to erect, cenotaphs to hollow, arches to arch? Shall our own not unheroic days be different from those of the Caesars, gloriously commemorated in stone?

It would appear that the sculptors, having taken counsel with themselves, have decided to put these questions to the test. They began, naturally enough – a good rule in everything save architecture – from the top. Whereupon were presented, with a strange simultaneity, two projects – one for the erection in England of a monument to the memory of the late President Roosevelt, and the other for the erection upon the cliffs of Dover of a tribute in stone to the living Churchill. Why the third member of the Potsdam triumvirate has thus far been ignored by the hatchetmen remains inscrutable; perhaps a mustache is a hard thing to sculpt. We wouldn't know. Perhaps the sculptors – fellow-travellers? – wished to experiment upon the lesser two-thirds before they betook themselves to the final supreme Thirdissimo of Potsdam.

If this last was their motivation, we fear greatly that the Moscow commission will not be forthcoming. The two statues – thus far exemplified by photographed statuettes – are far, very far, from constituting an auspicious beginning to a campaign for post-war sculpture. To judge by the evidence to date submitted, our age, doubtless has had its Alexanders; its Praxiteles is still to be discovered.

Let us consider – for rejection's sake – the proposed statue of President Roosevelt by Sir William Reid Dick. Here, with an utter disregard of historic truth, the artist has represented the great President, not in a sitting position, as for the last decade of his life he lived, and laboured, and had his being, but erect and standing. As a concession to the paralysis from which Roosevelt suffered and to which he publicly referred when he spoke of 'the ten pounds of steel upon his lower legs,' Sir William shows the President wearing a cane. A hero with a cane! A jaunty man-about-town hero! One is tempted to look for the *boutonnière*. The resemblance to the President, in actual elementary facial characteristics seems also to be missing; as one examines the photograph of the sculpture more closely, one realizes why: the President, cane and all, has been made to look like George M. Cohan! This is not the Happy Warrior; this is a Yankee Doodle Dandy!

The apologists for Sir William's statuary of course explain that the artist did so erect his subject that he might appear, as was fitting under the circumstances, the more dominating. It is, then, only as one stands that one dominates? Emperors seated upon their thrones – do they, sedentary, abjure their imperial prerogatives? Does the hero of an equestrian statue *stand* upon his saddle? Is it not obvious that the conquest of a man sitting, 'weighed down by ten pounds of steel,' is at least *pro tanto* greater than that of him who bustles and runs around?

> O, abler did he work, the sculptor of Voltaire
> Who showed the great one, leaning from his chair ...

No; Roosevelt deserved better of his chisellers. Even his raiment they have maligned; the jacket obviously belongs to the wardrobe of Theodore, not Franklin; and the trousers – let it be said simply that they are not presidential. Remembering that it was as he sat for his portrait that the president was taken with his last fatal stroke, one begins to suspect an artistic conspiracy whose effects are intended to reach even beyond the grave.

For Mr. Churchill an even more ludicrous memorial is proposed. The octogenarian inspiration of an eccentric millionaire, one Charles Davis of Cape Cod, it proposes an 80-foot statue of the protagonist holding a mammoth cigar over his head like the Statue of Liberty torch, the whole, cigar and Prime Minister, mounted on a 100-foot-high pedestal. A model thereof prepared by a New Hampshire sculptor, Viggo Brandt-Erickson, lies duly photographed before us. The first impression that one gets is that Mr. Churchill, – like Napoleon not a tall man – is here reduced to proportions even lesser than those which nature has accorded him. The optical illusion, of course, is easily understandable; when the pedestal is 100 ft. high, the person pedestalled, to look full-size, let alone heroic, – must be done on a scale which will give him certainly more than the hundred feet which lie beneath his soles. Here, however, Mr. Churchill is given a height equal to four-fifths of his threshold. Moreover, this effigied homunculus – where is the Churchillian resolve, the firm indomitable will? – is endowed with an expression of benignity verging upon blandness. Not so would we remember the mightiest spirit of our day! Of the illuminated and illuminating cigar, – as if Churchill, in admiral's weeds, were some Ulysses ready in comic warfare to blind his Polyphemus – we shall say only that it is so pretty a thought that it were better to reserve its implementation for the memory of another prime-ministerial symbol – the burning bowl of Baldwin's pipe.

As we descend the one hundred and eighty feet of this erection, we descry – yet another ingenuity – four carven creatures crawling on the plinth. At first it is difficult to tell what exactly these animalcules are. But – of course! Bulldogs! Four of them! And all four of them showing the marks of an austerity diet.

Why the artist has cast the British Lion into the outer dark, and has preferred to show domestic animals escorting the Prime Minister upon his foreign affairs, will have to remain as unfathomed as are the many other idiosyncrasies of the artistic mind. This, however, must be stated: the artist meant well. What he meant is indicated, with an originality of sermon equalled only by his originality in stone, in the raised inscription at the foot of the pedestal: *Never was so much owed by so many to one man.* Mr. Churchill could not have said it better …

It is, however, from the Mayor of Dover, to whom the project was offered, that there has come the *ne plus ultra* of appreciation and criticism. Said he: 'We agree that a memorial to Churchill might be a good thing, but something more modest and utilitarian would be preferable.' The tradition of Dover – impervious Dover – still lives.

The Talmud Torah Campaign   17 January 1947

No one will gainsay but that the period through which we are presently passing is fraught with the greatest significance for the future of our people. We are here not speaking of the tragic fact that our world population has been so cruelly cut down through the murder of six million of our kith and kin; not even the best established of educational institutions can do aught to bring them back to life. Nor are we adverting to the fact that the years to come must be those which will, which must serve to establish the status of the Jewish people among the peoples of the world; that is a matter which lies within the province of Jewish politics rather than Jewish education. We are referring, rather, to that grave peril – as grave as any which we face – which lies in the possible – may the Lord forfend it! – the possible discontinuity of our cultural tradition.

For Hitler's outrages, though they reached physically only European Jewry, struck and maimed the entire Jewish people. The loss of lives – are they not recorded in the ash-containers of Maidanek, in the mass graves of Belsen?

Unrecorded, and equally inestimable is the great tragedy which all of Israel also suffered in the loss of the cultural institutions of Europe. Here in eastern Europe there existed not only a compact Jewry, but a Jewry which through religious practise and intellectual interest and cultural creativeness stood as the great continuation of a tradition which went back to Sura and Pumbeditha. With the destruction of that Jewry, a great, an important, a vital link in that chain was broken.

The paramount question of Jewish culture to-day is: Shall that hiatus be permitted to remain, or shall North American Jewry, free, vigorous, and conscious of its responsibilities both to the past and the future, step in and fill up the breach? Shall we resign ourself to the existence of this cultural vacuum, or shall American Jewry now play the role which both position and duty impose upon it?

These questions, we know, are purely rhetorical. No self-respecting Jew could possibly contemplate that spiritual suicide which must follow, as the night follows the day, from an indifference to these issues. *Yisroel chai v'kayom* – despite the annihilations and the ravages, Israel exists and persists. Even our enemies are beginning to believe that we are an eternal people. Such seems our destiny. But whether we are also a People of the Book is not merely a matter of destiny, but of will; and that will is best manifested, both in our own personal respect for the treasures of our heritage, and in the support which we give to our cultural institutions. Such a key institution is the Talmud Torah. Here come the sucklings of the kindergarten – upon whom, as the Talmud says, the worlds are poised – and the students of the parochial schools, and the graduates in the High Schools, to imbibe from the inexhaustible fountains of our culture. It is here that they are born Jews; here that they first catch hold of those strands which must forever knit them to their past, and here that they forge those minds and those wills of which their people to-day so grievously stand in need.

The World's Conscience

24 January 1947

Our readers have no doubt observed how orators, when they wish to make a particularly pathetic point, almost invariably appeal for sympathy, corroboration, and support, to some ineffable arbiter known as the world's conscience. The implication of course, is that while all other systems of justice may be fallible or corrupt, here is a judicial instance, an ethical barometer which is sensitive to the slightest shadings of right and wrong, here, from the world's conscience, there must ineluctably issue the response for which the persecuted and the downtrodden so agonizedly languish.

It is with regret that we are beginning to be led to the conclusion that this *argumentum ad conscientiam mundi* is no more than a rhetorical device, an empty gesture, an appeal in which even the appellant has no faith. It is, in fact, an *argumentum in vacuo;* for whereas it may be stated although with some latitude that all humans have consciences, it cannot so positively be asserted that the world is possessed of one. As soon as the conscience is distributed among the many, alas, it ceases to exist even among the few. The public conscience is a conscience so dissipated that its component parts, infinitesimally divided among the commonalty, lose all ethical vigour, and subsist in the general mind only as an impotent figure of speech.

Nothing, we believe, illustrates the mythicality of this conscience better than its lack of efficient response to the anguished problem of the European D.P.'s. The very name which has been affixed to this category of unfortunates reveals, we think, the callousness of the world's conscience (*sic*) to it. They are not described as the refugees, or the persecuted, or the victims; they are dubbed with a nomenclature unemotional and innocuous – displaced persons – as if their tragedy consisted merely in the fact that they were on tour, away from home, the victims of an error in railway shunting; and, as if even this were too passionate a designation, that name is further reduced to the skeletal impersonality of its initials, D.P.'s. Scientific dehumanization of a problem, certainly, could go no further.

Well, it is now almost two years that these tragic initials – these majuscules deemed minuscules – have been liberated – that was the word the headlines shouted – and still they are, – to fall in with the universal understatement, – as displaced as ever. One would have imagined that by now the so sensitive world's conscience, broken and racked by its concern over the fate of thousands of human beings, would have collapsed – a neuralgic wreck; collapsed, or done something about it. Imagining so, one imagines mere imaginings; the world's conscience is to-day as uncollapsed as ever; the non-existent is not subject either to disease or death.

We did say that a divided conscience, though functionless as a moral agent, still subsists as a figure of speech; it was doubtless under this aspect that a Gallup poll was recently taken on the question: *Do you think that the problem of the 600,000 Jewish people who have lost their homes and are looking for a new land in which to settle – do you think this problem should be left to the Jewish refugees themselves to solve, or do you think it should be handled by the countries of the United Nations?*

We leave uncommented the rather leading nature of the question; the imagination of the catechist seems to have been a limited one; more than two alternatives he could not conceive; and even these ... But no matter. Let public opinion speak.

Of the said public opinion, it must first be reported, 21% declared that it had none. Either because it hadn't given the matter any thought – Am I my brother's keeper? – or having given thought, still returned empty of an answer, one out of five of the individuals interrogated rendered that safest and most conscienceless of verdicts: *Ignoramus: We don't know.* Of the knowers, 57% felt that the problem should be solved by the United Nations. It is not indicated that the respondents were aware of the fatuousness of their reply; to hand the matter over to the United Nations – we judge only by the way the United Nations in convention assembled have acted to date – is to hand it over to that algebraic world's conscience of which we spoke; in a word, to assure the *status quo*; the displaced remain displaced. At best, it is a case of everybody's responsibility; at worst, it is an invitation to make out of the 600,000, pawns of an international chess.

A third category rendered a somewhat enigmatic reply. These 22% urged that the problem 'should be solved by the refugees themselves.' What can this sphinx-like utterance mean? Does it mean that the D.P.'s have no right to look to the world for a solution; it's their problem, let them solve it? Given the circumstances, that is not a reply, but a taunt. The D.P.'s by themselves cannot solve the problem of their next meal, let alone that of their permanent sanctuary. The reply then must mean that a referendum having been taken as to where the refugees would like to go, that place should be opened to them. That, we are informed, has already been done; the D.P.'s, however, are still where they were; apparently this solution is not one which can be achieved 'by themselves.'

The questionnaire of Mr. Gallup, in justice to Mr. Gallup must it be stated, was further broken down. It included also the question direct: *Have you yourself any ideas as to how the problem should be solved?* This put the exponents of the world's conscience right on their mettle, with the result that – 47% had no reply. Two per cent declared definitely that the problem could not be solved; the 600,000 presumably were to be left, like Mohammed's coffin, hanging in mid-air. One per cent felt that they could settle in the United States; another one per cent suggested settlement in Empire countries. It is clear that even the man on the street knows that for the man in the camp not all the doors are open. Two per cent – and only two per cent – urged that they return to their original countries. Three per cent suggested that the D.P.'s might be used to colonize the empty parts of the world; the said empty parts, however, were not geographically designated. Ten per cent, – obviously cynics – replied that the United Nations could solve the problem, *if the nations would co-operate.* Lest the reader imagine that we have set out to prove the questionees were of another Sodom and Gomorrah among whom there was not a single righteous man, let it be stated that ten per cent felt that the refugees were entitled to a land of their own, preferably Palestine.

Another twelve per cent gave what are described as 'miscellaneous answers.' We are thus left with a balance of twelve per cent. These were all too articulate. The Gallup tabulation, heading their wisdom 'anti-Jewish,' gives examples of how this area of the world's conscience reacted to the plight of the 600,000 hapless survivors of Hitlerism. Said they, in tones so unambiguous that the poll-taker was never at a loss as to which column should embrace their answer: *Let the Jews solve it themselves.* Another's was really a devastating retort: *Let the Arabs settle it.* This, too, is unambiguous. In the same group, a third, apparently withholding – lest it be spurned, – his Solomonic solution, said: *Jews will never be satisfied.*

No doubt the ubiquitous Man of Mars will condemn himself of naiveté as he asks, in the context of these questions and these answers, about the much vaunted culture and humanity and religion of Western civilization. Certainly he will find it difficult to understand this callousness towards the earliest and latest victims of fascism as he recalls the noble utterances, made but a few years ago, about liberation and human rights, and the sacred values. As for the world's conscience ...

England and the Bible 14 February 1947

There is no doubt but that that sympathy which British statesmen have until recently extended to Jewish national aspirations in Palestine owed much of its driving force to the fact that ever since the Authorized Version the English people have been a people brought up on the Bible. Until almost the end of the nineteenth century there was not a piece of literature published on the British Isles which did not manifest, in a hundred places, the impress of that great book. Whether we consider the soldiers of the Cromwellian armies who went forth into battle chanting the Psalms of King David, or the Royalists whose entire philosophy touching the tenure of kings was motivated by Old Testament doctrine, or the great masters of English writing, not the least of whom was Milton, who revealed again and again the idiom of a translated Hebrew, everywhere, in English life, we encounter the influence of the thought and diction of the divine masterpiece. Truly, it may be said, that second only to the Jews, the British have been a people of the book.

That the study of the Bible in England has declined is a fact, we think, which requires no extensive substantiation. It is almost everywhere apparent. Except from the pulpit, the language of the Bible is but rarely heard. Our authors go for their allusions and their evocations, not to the writings of Isaiah, but tractates of the latter-day psychologists and folk-lorists. That there was a time when Manasseh-ben-Israel (1648) could approach Oliver Cromwell and argue with him for the admission of Jews into England because – so ran Manasseh's argument – because Cromwell believing that the Messiah would come only when the Jews were everywhere dispersed, it remained only for him to make that dispersion ubiquitous by allowing Jews also into England, such an argument appears incredible to us. It is an incredulity which must vanish before a knowledge of how in England, for centuries, homiletics and politics were intermingled. Indeed, we have often felt that a great deal of the contemporary impatience with Milton stems principally from the fact that readers have lost the biblic key to his Paradise.

If this decline in bible-reading and bible-study has had deleterious effect upon English literature, its effects upon British politics particularly with regard to the Jewish question, we submit, has been no less deleterious. Mr. Bevin, we fear, has not read in the same books, as Mr. Balfour. That spirit which motivated so many British statesmen – a spirit which moved them to seek to implement prophecy via foreign policy – is, it would seem, one to which Mr. Bevin, denizen of Transport House not Bible House, is singularly immune. An eighteenth-century foreign minister, even a nineteenth-century one, we feel, would have thought twice before he sought to imitate Pharaoh by refusing to let the people go.

It is regrettable that a book unread should cause such havoc. We, however, who have read it, and indeed live by it, shall not, we think, wait for the non-readers to catch up on their neglected education.

The Feast of Passover   4 April 1947

Throughout the past decade, as we stood engaged in a life-and-death struggle with the most implacable foe ever to rise up against our people, conviction in his inevitable defeat and doom never forsook us. It could not be otherwise; we already had in the history books, quite a crew of barbarian megalomaniacs who had set themselves the same dastardly objective, only to end up as derisive foot notes at the conclusion of the chapter; and there was no reason why Hitler should not suffer the fate of Pharaoh or of Haman. (As it turned out, he did suffer the same fate, but with a variation: while Haman perished on the gallows upon air, and Pharaoh in water, the Fuehrer met his end in fire.)

Together with this ineluctable conviction, we entertained the hope that when at last salvation would be granted, the entire history of the Hitlerian period would constitute a paradigm not less impressive than that of the exodus from Egypt. Indeed, we did believe that the time would come when at our annual celebrations we would use the events of this last epic, instead of the pharaonic one, as basis for song and moral. Out of the saga of these last years, we felt, would henceforward be forged our tradition of freedom; where, in the past, we remembered the oppression of the Nile and the triumph of the Red Sea, we would in the future recall the agonies of the Rhine and the redemption of the Jordan. What the new Haggadah would lose in antiquity, it would gain from the vividness of recent events and from the colossal scale of the threat which had been brought to nought.

Alas, our hopes were premature. The old Haggadah still remains the better narrative of liberation. The contemporary nightmare, moreover, is not yet ready for commemoration; it is still going on. For while it is true that Hitler and all his immediate minions have gone to the dust they have so rightfully inherited, their legacy is by no means dissipated. Antisemitism still remains an ugly factor in present-day European politics.

The chief glory of the Haggadah, we need hardly say, is the fact that it records the passage of a people from bondage to freedom; and from that freedom, to great constructive achievement. In the present instance, we have reached only the stage where the Pharaoh and his sorcerers are doomed; but complete liberation, let alone entry into the area of constructive endeavour, still remains as remote as ever. Two years after the Nazi debacle, two years after the proclamation of the four freedoms and the multitudinous charters, there still are to be counted thousands of survivors of the Fascist persecution in durance vile confined. The concentration camps have been accorded a different, a more lenient personnel; but the inmates remain the same. These camps may not be on German territory; but they are German in reminiscence and effect. It is as if, to evoke the parallel of the Haggadah – as if the geography, instead of the inhabitants, of Egypt had pursued and captured our ancestors. The stakes of the barbed wire have changed; the barbed wire remains the same.

There is yet another distinction between the two chapters which sets the first above the second; the refugees from Egypt had a destination which they had but to reach to enter. The D.P.'s of to-day also have a destination; the *terminus ad quem* has been unanimously agreed upon; it is Palestine; but when after many new vicissitudes and ordeals, they finally reach this point, they find the nautical seraphim, with swinging swords, barring the way into their home.

No; we will build our hopes and our actions rather upon the formula provided by the scholars of Bnai-Brak, who engaged in the narration of the miracles of the exodus – until the dawn arrived. Hence our faith that the promise of the Promised Land must be fulfilled; hence our faith in the immortality of our people. Though the butchers and the murderers heap high, peak upon peak, our mortal remains: hence our conviction that the destination indicated of yore must in the fullness of time be reached. It is true that difficulties may beset our way; it is true that there may be much wandering in the desert; but the end of the story is pre-ordained. For us, only to hasten that conclusion.

Hamlet without Hamlet 9 May 1947

No one who has followed the proceedings of the United Nations, now assembled in deliberation over the Palestine question, could have failed to be struck by the unreal, almost nightmarish character of the goings-on at Flushing Meadows. The whole thing in fact has thus far given the impression of some fantastic play, staged by a mad director, the actors coming upon the stage each to steal the lines of the other; and, to heap unreality upon unreality, there is the unmistakable implication that even this absurd performance is, by the consent of the participants, of a significance even less than that of a rehearsal.

Let us enumerate the macabre details. Almost two weeks have passed and the great issue – one upon which the basic principles of the United Nations are staked, has not yet come under substantive discussion. Thus far, all the battles have been about procedure, that is to say, not about the actual pros and cons of the case, but about the question as to who shall appear before what, and when. We had occasion to point out in our editorial comment of a week ago how fatal it was to the reputation of UNO as a chamber of justice that one of the most interested parties in the dispute could not even appear before the full assembly. Since that time the existence of that lacuna has dawned also upon the consciences of some of the UNO members, and the week's lobbying and manoeuvres have been devoted to finding some compromise whereby the Jewish case might be heard before a political committee instead of before the full house.

This state of affairs appeared so outlandish that even the Moslem member for India took occasion to say that the session without Jewish representatives reminded him of 'the play of *Hamlet* without Hamlet.'

The palaver at Flushing Meadows, moreover, suffers also from the fundamental defect that it is not even a play; nor yet a rehearsal. The best denouement that can issue from the debates is the appointment of a commission to study the Palestine problem. Another commission! Obviously, the objective is not further enlightenment, but only further delay. The United Nations organization is being used, first as a platform for anti-Zionist propaganda, and second, as an instrument of procrastination.

Even as a play – the real drama, the drama of a nation betrayed, is taking place off-stage – it is a singularly mad performance. Nobody speaks the lines you would expect from them. The suggestion that the Jews should be heard before the full session issues – from Peron's Argentina! The counter suggestion that the Arabs' status should be allowed to countervail such permission, comes – from Truman's America. And the strongest protestations of sympathy for the Zionist cause are made by the representatives of Soviet Russia, where Zionism is a criminal offense, being considered an ideology auxiliary to British imperialism. The place is full of ventriloquists!

As often happens in a performance in which the actors exchange their parts, going even so far as to *ad lib* as the spirit moves them, many a profound truth receives unconscious utterance. In this fashion the Arab who charged the Americans with 'adding petrol to the Palestinian fire,' spoke more wisely than he knew. The speaker thought he was coining a metaphor; actually he was articulating a literal truth. Petrol – the scramble for Arabian oil – has more than any other single factor bedevilled the humanitarian thinking of the American State Department. The delegates at the session, however, very conveniently took the Arab interjection as but another example of oriental luxuriance of language.

The Octogenarian   4 July 1947

Perhaps this is too venerable a designation to apply to the sprightly youngster who attained his mere fourscore years this first of July; in the history of a nation, after all, a thousand years are but as yesterday, as a watch of the night when it is past, – and eighty years, the mere twinkling of an eye; the calendar fact, however, is indubitable: Canada as a Dominion is now eighty years old.

The stripling, it must be admitted, has not done badly for himself. He has come up in the world. While he has not yet taken over the full legacy which the late Sir Wilfrid Laurier so generously bequeathed – the twentieth century, he said, belongs to Canada – he has stepped forward to play his part in the affairs of men. But yesterday a farmer boy exercising his youth in the northern prairies, he is to-day acknowledged a Middle Power. He has acquired new skills; his estate is full of machines and patents and processes. He has acquired a wider outlook; he has long ago stepped out of his hyperborean seclusion. And, unlike most octogenarians, his chief activity to-day is not reminiscence. He looks forward; there is much to do; and he means to do it.

He has grown. Some of his juvenile clothes no longer fit. That heirloom suit, for example, the b.n.a. special, – there are places where it shows constricted, tight at the elbows, curved on the lapels. It makes the big boy look gawky; and it inhibits his movements. A good tailoring job is called for, not a Bond Street performance, no, but something which will produce a garment sturdy and wearable.

No doubt that, too, will take place with time. Meanwhile, the octogenarian youth keeps striding on; he has destinations to reach. Good luck to him!

Two Kinds of Justice

That justice is not always impartially blind, that occasionally she does play bo-peep from behind her bandage so as to catch a glimpse of the identity of the accused and temper her judgment accordingly, is an observation which has not waited for this column to be stated. Both philosophers and jurisconsults have noted that justice often changes with the degrees of geographic latitude. What is considered a high crime and misdemeanour in northern countries is often a virtue to be practised in southern ones; and *vice versa*. Of course these distinctions have always had reference to *different* systems of justice prevailing in different lands; when, in a single system of law there appears this elasticity, then one is face to face, not with the vagaries of local custom, but with the shrewd conveniences and calculated expediencies of men who are judges only in name.

We cite a striking instance. Recently a number of young Jewish political offenders were involved in a jail break at Acre; three of them were recaptured, and, on the day when the United Nations Palestine Commission came to the Holy Land, they were sentenced to death. Since that time, hope was expressed in many quarters that this sentence, imposed upon youths of an average age of twenty for an offense which was purely political, would, out of clemency and as a gesture towards pacification, be commuted. News is now received that the general in charge of British occupation troops in Palestine, has instead confirmed. There is still hope that perhaps the High Commissioner, who has the last word, may yet save the youngsters from execution.

Thus far, therefore, it would appear that *dura lex, sed lex*; the young men contravened a law which had a capital sanction, and they must pay the penalty.

But having looked upon this dismal picture, now look on this. In Italy Marshal Kesselring, together with some other Nazi butchers, had after dire trial, been sentenced to death for wanton murder committed upon Italian civilians, and in particular for the callous slaughter of hostages chosen at random, a slaughter now notorious as the blood bath of the Ardeatine caves. There were many who felt, indeed, that it was regrettable that Kesselring had only one life with which to pay for these atrocities. After all, hundreds of non-combatant innocents had been killed; and a penalty was being exacted from only a few.

But justice, as we have already indicated, is also among those things which suffer a sea-change. North of the Mediterranean it is one thing; east of it, another – although in both directions administered by British generals. News has now been issued that the general in charge of such matters has commuted to life imprisonment the death sentence imposed upon Kesselring and others. That mercy which could not be invoked in favour of young boys, charged with jail breaking, Jewish victims of Nazi savagery – that mercy bursts forth with loving kindness for the Nazi mass-murderer!

We know that it is often impossible for justice to achieve the absolute of fairness. Bias often intrudes, and strange elements – prejudice, expediency, professional soldiers' *esprit de corps* – often fall surreptitiously upon one side of the scales and weigh it down. These things do occur. But certainly they ought never to occur so as to effect so shocking a contrast as that illustrated by the case of the carnage which was forgiven and the escapade which was punished by death.

Dr. Magnes and the Bi-National State   18 July 1947

There is not a man in Jewry, we believe, who will gainsay the pre-eminence as a spiritual figure which Dr. Judah L. Magnes enjoys in contemporary Jewish life. Chancellor of the Hebrew University from the days of its inception, world Jewry has consistently regarded him as the intellectual mentor of Palestine youth and the right trusty keeper of Jewish cultural treasure. The outstanding facts of his biography – the forlorn hopes he has entertained, the lost causes he has espoused, the unpopular convictions he has held, – these have further endeared him to the lovers of the quixotic; and there is not a Jew who secretly does not admire the perennial battler of windmills. The tribute, indeed, which was recently poured upon Dr. Magnes upon the occasion of his seventieth birthday was but a confirmation of the manner in which his co-religionists, while vigorously disagreeing with his tenets, continue to cherish the gallantry and the idealism of their sole and only votary.

Among the unrealistic elements with which Dr. Magnes has made roseate his view of the situation in Palestine is his firm and undeviating espousal of the cause of a bi-national state, as Arab as it is Jewish, as Jewish as it is Arab. Let it be said forthwith that this credo of the Chancellor's springs from a general optimism about the nature of man and an incapacity, shared with the prophets of old, to distinguish between things as they are and things as they should be. It is this same temper of his mind which explains the Doctor's intransigent pacifism during the first World War. Now no one will quarrel either with Dr. Magnes or the Bible when it is asserted that the living-together of brothers (or cousins) is a thing good and seemly to behold. Unfortunately this picture of fraternal harmony is conceived oftener as a desideratum than as a reality. In the case of Palestine, as Dr. Magnes's testimony before the international commission made clear, the realization of the picture would entail a constant juggling with ethnographic figures; a revision, from time to time of majority and minority positions; and above all, a good-will on the part of all those concerned, to achieve the parity without which bi-nationalism is a nonsense if not an outright injustice.

And it is precisely here that Dr. Magnes's doctrine is subjected to its nullifying test. Throughout the years in which he has preached his gospel of mutuality, he has recruited from the ranks of the Arabs not one convert. The Arab world does not have a Dr. Magnes, let alone followers of this morally magnetic way of life. It is a doctrine, therefore, which cannot but be regarded as academic, existing *in vacuo*, fit discussion theme for the *stoa* of the Hebrew University, but having no relation at all to the realities of the much vexed Palestine situation.

Exodus 1947   25 July 1947

Those who fondly believe that the ubiquitous urge of Jewish refugees from Europe to Palestine is a stimulated and artificial trend received yet another shock to their wiseacre smugness when they read this week of the arrival near the coasts of the Holy Land of another shipload of displaced persons, this time to the number of forty-five hundred. The 'artificial stimulation' must indeed be irresistible if it can persuade almost five thousand people to leave the European paradise, to brave the dangers of the sea and to risk the hospitality of Cyprus. But of course no one seriously believes that this pathetic *drang nach osten* is motivated either by a longing for a Mediterranean cruise or by a cantankerous desire to make things difficult.

The name which the refugees gave to their ship indicates the spirit in which the voyage from Marseilles was undertaken. *Exodus 1947*: the parallel is clear: the refugees are repeating, this time over a wilderness of water, the trek once performed by their ancestors forsaking Egypt. The Europe of Hitler, certainly, was for Jewry a greater bondage than the Egypt of the pharaohs. The choice of the name of a book out of the Pentateuch has further implications: what is intended is not only an exodus out of the lands of slavery, but also a genesis, a renascence of a people.

Unfortunately the present rulers of Palestine confine their bible-reading to Sundays. Insisting – by virtue of a factitious White Paper – that Jews were aliens to Palestine, the keepers of the gates decided once again to slam these gates in the face of the returning exiles. Once again the might of the British Navy was directed to the capture of a shipload of unarmed Jewish refugees and once again that navy, whose annals record some of the most glorious of British exploits was compelled, on the order of Mr. Bevin, to descend to the hunting down of the helpless and the dispossessed. An Englishman concerned over both the traditions of the Navy and his national reputation for fair play, must be at a loss, we feel, to know which of the two aspects of the situation he ought to resent more: the interception of innocent persons seeking national sanctuary, or the fact that the navy is used for such inglorious purpose.

It is true, of course, that the self-righteous executors of this policy justify themselves on the ground that they are maintaining 'law and order.' The law they speak of, they conveniently forget, is an arbitrary one, one of their own making, a law which did not exist prior to 1939. It is a law, moreover, which runs counter to the over-riding commitment of the Balfour Declaration; it is a law which was never sanctioned by the only power which could possibly sanction it: the League of Nations. In other words, this law is a gross illegality. Certainly if there is anything illegal in the attempt of Jews to return to Palestine, it is in the efforts designed to frustrate that attempt.

The latest exploit of the Mediterranean pond-catchers introduces, moreover, a new wrinkle into this international game of hide-and-seek. Whereas in the past it was the custom to send 'illegal immigrants' to be incarcerated at Cyprus (the island which the Jew Disraeli had with so much foresight brought into the Empire), the present 'flotsam' is to be rejected back into the past whence it issued. The argument of the proponents of the new ejection-technique is that, apparently, imprisonment at Cyprus is not a sufficient deterrent; return to the 'European paradise' may be. We think that the geniuses who have invented this new punishment err seriously as to its effects: incarceration in Cyprus may or may not end in arrival at Palestine; return to Europe certainly will.

Irgun, and the Reign of Terror   8 August 1947

There is no doubt but that the latest exploit of the pseudo-patriots of the Irgun – the cold-blooded murder of the two innocent British sergeants, captured, so ran their cynical 'argot,' as 'hostages' – has left world Jewry fevered with horror and revulsion. It could not be otherwise; these abominations malign the character of our people; throughout our long and minutely-recorded history one will look in vain to find its like. Sergeants Paice and Martin were not only not guilty of any crime; they were declared by Irgun definition and broadcast personally to be free from any imputed crime. They were simply soldiers doing their duty. Certainly they were not responsible for the White Paper; certainly it was not they who had had anything to do with formulating the policy which has just condemned forty-five hundred homeless Jews to an indeterminate sentence as flotsam of the Mediterranean. By members of a race which has been scapegoated for centuries, Paice and Martin were captured, held and murdered, – as scapegoats. The mere recounting of the details of this dastardly deed fills us with horror. That perpetrators of such a monstrous crime could be found in our midst! This is not the Jewish underground; this is a Jewish underworld.

It is not for the sake of metaphor but by design that we apply this epithet to these Palestinian Apaches. It may well be that the Irgun has exploited the neuroses of the survivors of Maidanek and Oswiecim to recruit to its ranks a number of misguided, emotionally-upset, but honest youths; the leadership, however, makes display of all the tactics of the ruthless 'gang' and all the techniques of the marginal racket. Its kidnappings of Jew and Briton, holding the one for money-ransom and the other for political ransom; its ambushes; its indiscriminate bomb-throwings (the 'pineapple' wrapped in a flag); its hold-ups of banks and merchants, regardless, of course, of race or creed; its slaughter of innocents, a bloody toll which includes as many Jews as Britons, – all this runs true to a pattern made notorious in metropolitan slums, European and American. Its abuse of the verbiage of patriotism is also of a piece: the bravoes of the Chicago South Side, too, called their blackmail – 'protection.' And finally, there is the unmistakable give-away: the conscienceless irresponsibility which has characterized and characterizes the Irgun tactic. Never a thought is given to the consequences, let alone the unspeakable immoralness, of the criminal heroics – to the effect which they may have upon the fate of the Zionist ideal, an ideal whose entire strength lies in its moral claims; to the corruption which this small leaven may work in the Jewish entity; or to the repercussions in other parts of the world.

If an antisemite had desired in one single act to level a most telling blow against Jewry, he could not have improved upon the method of the Irgun madness. Already have the subterranean Mosleyites, the aestivating fascists, grasped the opportunity to put in motion a hue and cry against Jews in British cities thousands of miles away from the scene and perpetrators of the reprehensible *nefas*. Nonetheless, Menachem Beigin and his henchmen, fatuous in their Hasmonean delusion, sit in their hideouts, proud of their past, and planning a future more hideous still.

Such is the character of the lethal and parasitic gangsterism which has attached itself to the Jewish body, and seeks to identify itself with that body. The suspicion which we have articulated in these columns in the past, when, week-in week-out, we have sought to analyze the true character of the Irgun muscle-men, we must, with ever greater pertinence, repeat once more: it is not otherwise than that into the ranks of Irgun, and above all into its leadership, there have insinuated themselves agents-provocateurs eager to fish in the muddied waters of the Jordan.

Either that, or the people are insane; or both. Otherwise it is totally incomprehensible; for from whom could the Irgunists have learned this morality? From their fathers conning the Torah, day and night, the Torah which prescribes the rules of good behaviour even towards the laboring cattle in the field? From their mothers, the pious matriarchs in Israel? Or have they taken their German persecutors for their instructors?

The answer is that Menachem Beigin considers himself above the inhibitions of his silly devout forefathers. He is a realpolitiker; he mouths military palaver. He is wise in his own conceit. He does not see that the day he threatened reprisals there was rejoicing among the St. John Philbys of the Near East. They had them: if they backed down from their threat, they were discredited; if they fulfilled it, all Jewry would be discredited. The Irgun chose the latter alternative.

The syllogism which ninety-nine per cent of Jewry saw while only the premises were enunciated is now complete to its ghastly conclusion. The Irgun is an enemy of Israel. The tactics of Irgun constitute a conspiracy against Jewry. Whether these tactics and this policy are impelled by knavery or stupidity is all one – the result is the same: the parasite seeks to destroy the body it lives on.

Nor is this fact a revelation which has ensued as a result of recent events. From the inception of the current troubles, the Jewish Agency, the body recognized to speak on behalf of Jewry in matters of Zionism, has repeatedly and unequivocally condemned the free-lance irresponsibilities of Irgun. The Irgun – which represents nobody but its minor-minority self – has, on the other hand, directed against the Agency, and against the majority of Jewry, such abuse as makes clear its isolated locus. It has dubbed the members of the Agency, Vicheyites, collaborationists, ghetto-Jews.

We believe that the time has come – is indeed past due – when this abomination must be cleansed from our midst. This is a minority which must be nullified. We have not come this long way, through trial and tribulation, building brick upon brick and stone upon stone, to see all our work and hopes shattered by the irresponsible Gorboduc play-acting of those for whom Zionism is only a *mise-en-scène* for their histrionic neuroses.

The New Judaea   5 December 1947

It is not in the staid and restrained vocabulary of the editorial column that one can adequately describe the great wave of joy which swept over world Jewry as there was brought to it the news that the United Nations had at last sanctioned the establishment of a Jewish state in Palestine. The theme is rather a subject for poetic treatment – an epic of two thousand years of wandering and homelessness brought to an end, if not as yet *de facto*, at least *de jure*; a drama in which the great wrong which the world had perpetrated, – either through positive act or unconcerned acquiescence, – against a helpless people is now, in the penultimate act, in some measure righted.

It was a decision momentous both for its actors and its beneficiaries. To-day, at least thirty-three of the nations of the world rest in somewhat easier conscience. That feeling of guilt which from time to time allowed itself to be expressed through the voices of 'the saintly of the world's peoples' is alleviated. The United Nations have done a great service – in the first instance – to their own peace of mind.

For the United Nations Organization, as such, the Palestine problem, too, has afforded a signal opportunity, – at last an occasion for constructive policy. After a history, marked since its San Francisco inception, by futile discussion and frustrative vetoes, it was finally given to UNO still to prove its international usefulness. Here was an instance to prove that UNO could at once spread justice and advance world peace. UNO adopted the partition decision, moreover, at a moment when it could easily have evaded its responsibility; the last-minute device for procrastination which the Arab delegates sought to invoke may perhaps have held out its temptation; it is to the memorable credit of the thirty-three nations that they spurned the easy cunctatory path, and did rather, seriously and with solemnity, pursue their Solomonic decision. They had had enough of delays; two thousand years were altogether too much.

Salutary though the decision may have been to the nations which made it, it was even more so to the psyche of the Jewish people. That crying injustice, the anomalous situation of statelessness, had been ended. Biblical prophecy and age-old aspiration were about to be fulfilled. A path was cleared toward Zion.

Yet the feelings of Jewry were not altogether those of unmixed joy and jubilee. Gratitude to those who had made this day possible; regret for those who, by a cruel fate, had not survived to see this day; solemn awareness of the many challenges which still lay ahead – all of these emotions passed upon the mind to share it with the prevailing hosanna mood. Certainly Canadian Jews felt with pride that in the laying of the foundation stones for the New Judaea, Canadian statesmen – Ilsley and Pearson – had played a distinguished and memorable role. Certainly Jews everywhere could not but reflect that if this international decision had been made but a decade ago, several millions of souls might have been snatched from the burning; and certainly no Jew was under any illusion as to the difficulties which still loomed ahead.

One has but to state what actually happened at Lake Success to realize both the greatness and the limitations of the UN decision. The United Nations have by that vote *permitted* the creation of a Jewish state; they have not created it. That creation can be achieved only by the Jews. A potentiality has been released; the actuality yet remains to be accomplished.

There is every reason to believe that it will be accomplished. Already there are in Palestine over 700,000 Jews, enjoying a sound economic life, a community strong and determined to build its own future. For the creation of that more-than-nucleus not a little credit is due to the British Mandatory Power which first issued the Balfour Declaration, and which, though it refrained from voting on the present issue, still deserves the place in the Golden Book which the Jewish people have justly assigned to it. More will come; and all are implacably determined that now, with their interrupted history reintegrated again, it shall not again suffer interruption.

It is true that as we write these lines the Arab world appears to be much agitated. Enjoying six seats at Lake Success, the Arab delegation has clearly demonstrated that it is ready to support the world organization – as long as that organization advances its own interests; and that otherwise, it is minded to exercise a veto of its own, namely, the veto of the Jehad. The extraordinary benefits which the Arab world has won through victories not theirs are ignored; the vast territories they dominate are ignored; the disproportionate voice they exercise at UN is ignored; it is the parcel of a parcel of land in Palestine, allocated for a Jewish state and sanctuary which to-day, in Arab eyes, constitutes the great injustice!

Gandhi's Fast   16 January 1948

As if to illustrate the strange inexplicable powers that in the East can be evoked like some *djinn* out of his imprisonment, there is brought before the attention of the world the latest of Mahatma Gandhi's gestures. As in the past, it is again the threat of a fast unto death which the Mahatma directs against those whom he would persuade; but unlike his abnegations heretofore, the present fast is aimed not at the British Raj but against the people he presumably liberated from the British subjection.

In a drab world, a world in which international gestures are made on a pedestrian level, – *give me this and I'll give you that; stop me here and I'll stop you there* – this technique, – *if you won't do the right, I'll stop eating* – comes trailing clouds of glory. The Western mind finds it difficult to pierce through the nature of such a threat; the Western world understands only a threat in which starvation is the likely portion of the instructed, not of the instructor. Is it conceivable that at the next session of UN, when M. Molotov exercises his usual veto, is it conceivable that General Marshall will counter-attack with a fast unto death; and – assuming the inconceivable to have come to pass and General Marshall regularly missing up on his meals, is it further to be imagined that such a strategy is likely to bring Molotov to his knees: For God's sake, General, you haven't touched a bite of food since last Sunday; in Lenin's name, eat something!

Much as one is prepared for all contingencies in current politics, this is a scene, we greatly fear, which is not likely to take place. The fact is that the very opposite is taking place; Marshall's weapon is not fasting, but feeding. To feed another, to be sure, is to achieve a certain moral altitude; but that altitude, of course, comes nowhere near the Himalayas of a fast in the public interest.

Beyond doubt one must not jump to conclusions; it still remains to be seen whether the population of India is truly sensitive to Gandhi's lenten politics, whether the Mahatma's fasting can stop that civil war the folly of which so much shed blood has hitherto failed to demonstrate. For the moment, however, the very attempt to use this weapon of the fast opens magic windows upon concepts not dreamed of in western philosophy.

The Death of Gandhi 6 February 1948

That in the death of Gandhi, not only India, but the whole world, has suffered an irreparable loss is a truism so obvious that it seems almost an insult to his memory to utter it. For the spirituality of his thinking, for the prophetic character of his personality, and for the almost other-worldly saintliness of his career, he knew no equal. Nor does there appear anywhere upon the horizon an individual who might be mistaken for his successor. His death has truly left a gap; from the world there has been removed a great and goodly treasure.

Such a removal, of course, was foreordained. Although the memory of the Mahatma bids well to become immortal, the Mahatma himself – and this indeed was his greatness – was mere mortal, even as you and I. Even without the assassin's bullet, he would in time have proceeded on to his next incarnation – but that his exit should be as it was, that we never imagined. We thought it possible, and in the light of contemporary Indian affairs, quite likely, that Gandhi should breathe his last at the end of some significant fast, that, completing the pattern of his life, he should expire in the midst of some grand moral gesture, some inspiring act of self-immolation. But that there should be found in India any one, and least of all, a Hindu, who should wish harm to this saint and seer – that went beyond our wildest surmises.

The whole narrative of this fateful incident, in truth, strikes us with that thrilling esoteric impact which we associate with those moving parables which from time to time, come to us from the East. Here, on the one hand, is the Mahatma, a saint who throughout all the days of his life preached peace, a statesman, it is true, who led resistances, but resistances that were ever passive, a prototype upon earth of the nature dubbed angelic, – and there, on the other hand, was the unrepentant lurking figure of Brute Force. We had hoped that the example of the Mahatma's life had proved, like the music of Orpheus, sufficient to silence the roarings of the beasts of the field. Upon the man, we felt, not even the most savage would dare lay hands. Alas, one saintly example is not enough; the same world which held Gandhi also held his assassin; and there was not room for both; and it was the Mahatma who had to go.

In the last five years, the world has witnessed the singular deaths of many of the mighty. The horrible passing of Mussolini, tied topsy-turvy like a swine to the rafter of a butcher's stall, is an image, flashed from our newspapers, which many still carry with them. The departure of the abominable unmentionable of Third Reich, vanishing in flame, was, by premeditated stage-direction, also intended to be impressive. But these creatures – and we pray a thousand pardons from the ashes of the Mahatma for the blasphemy of this association – lived like beasts, and died like animals. Gandhi lived a saint, and died a martyr. Certainly our generation will not soon look upon his like again.

In Memoriam: Leib Yaffe   19 March 1948

There is not a single casualty arising out of the war in Palestine which does not come home to Jews everywhere bringing with it a sense of both personal loss and great dramatic tragedy – personal loss, because with every hero fallen in the fight the entire people is by that much diminished, and great dramatic tragedy because the victims of Arab sniping are for the most part Jews who but recently in Palestine, after terrible ordeals and wanderings, began to live. These, certainly, are not mere newspaper deaths; they are family bereavements.

To the loss of no recent casualty does this more poignantly apply than to that of the revered Leib Yaffe who a week ago in the Jewish Agency building, fell victim to an Arab dynamite blast. His name had been known to millions of Jews throughout the world; his passionate loyalty to the cause which he had adopted from earliest youth and to which he dedicated his life's energies, – and in the end, his life's blood – was proverbial throughout the Diaspora. Wherever the Jewish National Fund sent forth its emissaries to collect the self-imposed tribute for the national renascence, there the spirit, the moving force of Leib Yaffe was felt.

And his was more than merely an administrative power. Leib Yaffe was a poet. Some of his lyrics still quicken the heart of the forlorn wanderers in exile. Alas, Leib Yaffe did not write as much as his talents warranted; instead, he transferred his poetic intensity, his inspired insights and his sense of order and exaltation, into his work on behalf of Zionism. His sincerity was infectious; during his sojourn in our own country which he visited on behalf of the J.N.F., thousands got to know this unassuming man who brought everywhere the inspiring afterglow of the Old Guard and the moving prospect of the new life.

Leib Yaffe was entitled to be present at the inauguration of the Jewish State to make the benediction: *Shehechianu*. Unfortunately, the assassins laid him low as he was officiating in the very temple itself. Like a soldier, Leib Yaffe died at his post of duty. Perhaps this is the way he would have wished it; if he was not destined to be present at *Geulah*, this is the way he would have wished it. Like another, he looked into, and laboured for, the Promised Land; but to him entry was not vouchsafed. The poet, the martyr, the hero, made one. Jewry mourns him.

Life and Eternity   2 April 1948

Lawyers with hopeless cases, entangled diplomats, spouses flagrant with delict, confidence men, and in general all those who have need of a verbal technique whereby guilt may be made to shine like piety beneath a halo, could do worse in their desperation than to study the article called 'Easter in Palestine' which appears in this week's issue of *Life*. For there they will find exemplified, in large type and all on one page, enough gestures of innocence, sufficient pantomime of sanctity, to annul even in the direst of straits. Written by that composite editorial genius recently described in the pages of *Time*, the disquisition does corroborate *Time's* co-operative boast: the talent for hypocrisy displayed in every paragraph is surely beyond the gift of any single writer. An entire crew, obviously, was massing to accomplish the Pecksniffian *tour de force*.

For *tour de force* it is; to bless and curse simultaneously, to be both Balaam and his ass, – this, of necessity, involved a *tour de force*. The task which the incorporatored authors of the editorial put before themselves was, in fact, nothing less than the harmonization of *Life* and death. On the one hand, they earnestly desired – oh so earnestly – to intone – with benefit of research workers – a *kaddish* for Jewish aspiration in Palestine; on the other hand, they also desired those of their best friends who were Jews to remain, if no longer Jews, their best friends still. *Que faire?* Advance the heartless thesis, and cover it up with a feigned moderation, flattery and fawning, references to the Easter season and quotations from the Hebrew.

This, therefore, they proceeded to do. Objective – to make it appear that the nullification of the United Nations policy was really in the best interests of the Jews themselves. The reversal on the partition question with the consequent closing of the doors of Palestine really constituted a great favour to the DP's still languishing, more than two years after the end of the war, in the scattered concentration camps of Europe. The organization of a people into a state was, after all, not such a wonderful asset; it involved the possession, among other things – and we quote – 'of a president, a navy, and a gallows.' (A fine comment upon Mr. Luce's concept of Americanism! A fine comment, too, upon contemporary politics, this joining in one breath, of a president and a gallows!) Moreover, narrow nationalism was to be reprehended, and Jews would do well to heed Dr. Magnes, who, like Mahatma Gandhi, was against it. (Only broad nationalism – namely, imperialism, was to be encouraged.) Again, it was a shame that Jews – several thousand of them – were getting killed because of the 'evil and unworkable partition decision,' a decision which was the result of 'ignorant goodwill.'

Nor are the writers oblivious to the achievements which have already been accomplished in Palestine. In their third paragraph they absolutely go wild with generous gestures of appreciation for every pilgrim who ever set foot upon Holy Land. The Jews, for what they did (six lines of it); the British; and even some Arabs, 'lowly Arabs who often sheltered hunted Jews,' elsewhere described as 'embittered and frightened' as compared to 'Arabs exultant and ungenerous,' and also forward-looking Arabs of distinction like Fawzi el Husseini, a cousin of the Mufti, subsequently murdered – all come in for commencement prizes awarded by the very impartial principal behind the editorial.

Even the six million slaughtered in Europe are sympathetically mentioned.

Could you want anything fairer? If this isn't philosemitism, what is? The answer, of course, is that this indeed is philosemitism, but philosemitism used as a tactical device in an anti-Zionist campaign. After the caresses and the compliments of the opening paragraphs are over, the editorial proceeds to make the suggestion it was ashamed to make without benefit of embracings; after the pawing, the mauling.

Accordingly, the editorial suggests a new American policy in Palestine. 'The British should be induced by the u.s. to postpone their departure from Palestine, to throw themselves energetically into the task of maintaining law and order, of suppressing both Arab and Zionist terrorists. In this they should have responsible support from the u.s. Government. This might mean a few u.s. troops; it must mean u.s. dollars. Our interests would justify the contribution.'

Thus suddenly does the writer who was hitherto so cunning, begin to feign naiveté. A child knows that a Government cannot commit itself 'with a few troops'; this is not an oil company whose liability may be limited. If the few troops are in danger, more must be sent, more and more, until the situation is in hand. This means military intervention; if so, what happens to the principal reason advanced for the reversal of the partition decision – namely that it involved precisely such a military commitment? The answer is unconsciously given by the editorialist, – under the new set-up, '*our* interests would justify the contribution.' A colony is about to be acquired, a colony, oil-terrain, and battleground.

But, of course, a nice term must be found to cover up the uncouthnesses of the scheme. It *is* found. 'The trusteeship proposal of the u.s. should get before the u.n. General Assembly as soon as possible … u.n. votes are available for a sound decision now that the u.s. has a clear head on the matter.' Naiveté is now followed by cynicism. The u.n. General Assembly, it is innocently admitted, is but a u.s. machine, like a Tammany caucus. When you wish, u.n. is world opinion; when you wish, u.s. opinion is u.n.

But the brazen pay-off is yet to come. 'Pressure should be brought *a*) on the Zionists to abandon the idea of a sovereign Zionist state in any part of Palestine, and *b*) on the Arabs to abandon the idea of such a state in Palestine as could in any way oppress the Jewish population.' The editorialist apparently hopes that it will not occur to the reader to suggest that perhaps *a* and *b* should be reversed; that perhaps it would be greater justice if the Arabs, who already have six sovereign states would abandon the idea, not of their additional state in Palestine, but the idea of thwarting the one very narrow state promised to the Jews. As for a state which by constitution is allegedly prevented from oppressing its Jewish minority, this really cannot be considered as more than a taunt and an irony. Pre-war Poland had a constitution which was designed to protect minorities. The Assyrians in Transjordania were once a minority in an Arab country; they, and their problem, have both been liquidated. The plight of the Jews in Yemen is another instance of the felicity of a minority under Arab rule. Ah, but there will be a 'benevolent trusteeship.' Yes, but that 'benevolent trusteeship' no doubt will again argue that it cannot antagonize the Arab world; and besides, 'it's an internal matter.'

Having relieved himself of this statesmanlike solution, the editorialist, it seems, still felt one problem buzzing, like Titus' gnat, unresolved through his brain. What is going to happen to the thousands of DP's? Here, too, he is generous. Congress should immediately adopt the Stratton Bill. 'This would admit in the next four years 400,000 European DP's, 80% of whom are Catholics and Protestants.' Eighty percent of whom are Catholics and Protestants – this is the solution to the problem of the Jewish DP's excluded from Palestine!

The truth is that the entire editorial is a typical example of the new imperialism preached by Mr. Luce. Fundamentally, it is Hearst journalism, written by Harvard graduates. If it were honest and forthright, frankly confessing its von Clausewitz mentality, it would not be half as objectionable as it is veiled in its seven modest veils. Even its peroration nauseates with its hypocrisy. 'To all in the land that is holy to Christians let us say in the words of the Arabic-speaking Semites, "Salaam Aleikum", and in the words of Hebrew-speaking Semites, "Shalom Aleichem". Both mean the same: "Peace be with you".'

We know well what peace this solution – which is dissolution – means. It is a peace which does not pass understanding. It is the peace of the cemetery.

But of the Eternal People, *Life* still has much to learn.

The Capture of Haifa   29 April 1948

For two thousand years all headlines, and even lesser news reports, relating to Jews, have been singularly unepical. We say unepical, and not unheroic; for of heroism – that kind of heroism in which the heroes go forth to battle but always fall – there have been far too many instances. Even as late as 1943, world Jewry was solemnly thrilled by the report of the valiant defense of the ghetto of Warsaw, a defense in which a mass of starved and poorly-armed Jews for weeks stood against the might and terror of the ruthless organized forces of the Third Reich. It was, of course, from the beginning a doomed undertaking; at no time was victory the objective of the Warsaw uprising; the objective was much simpler and much more heroic: it was the desire of the despairing 'to give a good account of themselves.' They did.

The uprising, however, remained – by definition – quixotic. Its only reward was heroic memory.

The other twenty centuries of Jewish history in the diaspora were also signalized by gestures great and inspiring, but still gestures of futility. Until recently this aspect of our exilic chronicles was practically an obsession with our historians. He who reads Graetz touching the activities of our ancestors throughout the centuries of the Christian era must come to but one conclusion: our ancestors were engaged either in literature or in suffering. When they weren't being persecuted, they were writing commentaries upon Holy Writ; when they weren't writing such commentaries, it was because they were being persecuted. The badge of the tribe was either the sufferance mentioned by Shakespeare, or the frontispieces produced by the Soncino press.

Not at this late date would we speak scornfully of either the literary and religious values produced during these centuries or of the tremendous piety which welled up from secular martyrdom. We do think, however, that of these things we have produced more than our share. The time has arrived for a new kind of achievement.

The capture of Haifa was a symbol of that kind of achievement. For the first time in centuries, one read of Jews taking a city. With that announcement the walls of the ghetto crumbled, the Talmudic hump straightened out; a salutary transformation in the national psyche was asserted. Again Mount Carmel looked down upon a breed worthy of the Maccabaeans.

Ordinarily the enunciation of moral rights and the taking of a city are concepts which are incompatibly opposed. The moral and the militarist, it is said, do not go together. Here where might came to supplement, and not to combat, right, the exception was at last illustrated.

The capture of Haifa, moreover, is important for more than merely its inspirational value. While the bolstering up of national morale is always a laudable objective, it was not to supply a gratifying headline that Haifa was taken. The move, in fact, was of the utmost tactical significance. Haifa is a port, – the only good port on the Palestinian coast. Haifa is the end of the life-line which joins European Jewry to Palestine Jewry. Haifa contains more than merely its recorded population; Haifa contains, – now in realizable potentiality – also the hitherto floating population of the concentration camps of Europe. Haifa means the open door, and the re-enforced hand. Haifa means that the vast internee population of Cyprus now has where to go.

Altogether, this chapter is one which is most satisfying. It proves that the courage and energy of our people are not at an ebb, and it proves that that people is being led by a wise generalship. It augurs well for the future. The prayer of the day is: That Providence stay with us, and that our energy suffer no decrease.

The New Jewish State 14 May 1948

Conceived two thousand years ago on that same day the long agony of exile and dispersion began, – throughout the centuries nurtured in the very body and beneath the heart of the people, – borne, through suffering, with patience, – in its own blood sustained, – the Jewish State is at long last about to enter into life. The ticking of all the clocks of Jewry herald its approach, proclaim its imminence. Unless another Joshua again make the sun to stand still in Ashkalon, the unaltered circuits of the heavens, the mere passage of time, renders its birth inevitable. The dream of centuries is about to be fulfilled, the dark night breaks, and on the horizon is kindled a new dawn.

For before the Sabbath which approaches will be over, the Jewish State will be a *fait accompli*, and that *neshama yesaira*, that saving additional soul which ever enters with the Sabbath will this time enter but not pass. As the Friday following the Ides of May – the day when the British mandate legally terminates and the unrevoked resolution of the United Nations touching partition automatically comes into force – as that day is folded back upon the calendar of the past, a new state – yet a state most ancient – rejoins the comity of nations.

It is a theme for rhapsody. How many hopes this theme fulfils, how many frustrations it frustrates, – these are accounts which are kept in records beyond mortal reach, subject to surmisal, not scrutiny. Clearly one descries only the general contour of the shadows which break – the hideous forms of nightmares which, having haunted the exile, now vanish forever. The Arch of Titus, and all of the suffering it evokes, is now reduced to but masonry and monument; its humiliation and its ordeal are nullified; the Tower of David now over-arches the Arch. The memory of Spain, too, breaks upon the mind, by contrast accentuating the joy of this hour. The bear-dance of the Vistula fades into vagueness, it is the *hora* which is now the measure. And all the bitter recollections of the Rhine and the Donau, the ghetto shuffle and the hunched back, the rheum spat upon the Rialto and the stones thrown at Frankfurt-am-Main, the days of sufferance and the nights of flame and horror, all sent vanishing into oblivion, as by a dreamer at last rousing himself from his tossed and tortured bed to look out upon a bright new day, full of birds and sunshine.

Another spectre, too, is laid. It is the spectre, so vividly described by Leo Pinsker, the spectre of a people – our people in European exile – 'a ghost among the nations.' The prophecy and the exhortation of his book are at last fulfilled: auto-emancipation is the day's slogan. The ghost has doffed his ghostliness, and is now in his own land, is clothed with flesh, like a man stands up, and calls his body his own!

But not all the departed, even in the exaltation of this moment, suffer so easy a forgetting. Six million there stand, encircling the Jewish State, silent witnesses to its necessity. In spirit they have issued from the furnaces of Maidanek and Oswiecim, bearing both a message and a reproach: *If this had been, we would be! Since this was not, we are not!*

That reproach will never be justified again.

For a Jewish State is born, a sovereign body enjoying in its own domain the rights of sovereignty. Jewish history is again – *Jewish* history; the long hiatus of the exile bridged, the past rushes forward to embrace the future. There stand, therefore, as sponsors of the new Eretz Israel more than simply the cabinet about to be announced; all who through the generations laboured for Zion, or for Zion sighed, all rejoice in the hour of *geulah*, and all receive the charter of deliverance, even as all Israel – of all generations – stood before Sinai accepting Torah. Yet are there some who for their exemplary devotion and outstanding works should in this time of fulfilment be named by name: it is an inspiring roll-call, beginning with Rabbi Zadoc who for the sake of Jerusalem fasted himself to a shadow, and remembering a millenium later Rabbi Yehuda Halevi, blissfully perished on sacred soil, and the untold *paytanim* on whose lips the hope of Zion was never silent, and the Chovevei Zion, cherished in their name as in their being, and the incomparable prince, Benyamin-Zev Herzl who died fifty years too soon. There are not many states which begin with such cabinets!

A new Jewish State is born. Though it stems from the past, it looks to the future. No one aware of the antecedents and the composition of the Yishuv but must entertain hopes not utterly fantastic for the emergence of a new kind of culture from Eretz Israel. Here the West meets the East; here the East has come around full-circle. Who will gainsay, that there is in the New Jewish State the possibility for the creation of a way of life which will be an amalgam of the best of the Orient and the best of the Occident – the efficiency of Europe joined to the spirituality of Asia? Time was when there came out of Zion a light whereby the whole world was illumined; the fruitfulness and the resource of our people are by no means exhausted; what was may be again. It is a small state? No matter; that other whereof the prophets spoke and the seers saw was not a big state, either.

The proclamation of a Jewish State attests to yet another salvation. It attests to the fact that at long last Jewry has regained its voice. The plea of Jewry no longer has to be uttered by ventriloquy through agents and intercessors. Granted, as to it there must be granted, a seat in the councils of the world, Jewry may now speak as party and not as petitioner, in its own voice and not through advocates. A nation that was stifled dumb has won back its speech!

It has also won back its stature. No more the gypsy taunt, the nomad jeer! No more the fictitious minority right, nor the farce of 'tolerance' which in its own pious name betrays its double standards. And no more the protective coloration of 'the helots of the Mosaic persuasion'!

Born also is The New Jew. The hero of the epic is the Yishuv. Only because the Yishuv showed itself as of the fibre of the Maccabees does the wondrous thing come to pass:

> O who is this, rising from the Sharon, bearing a basket of grapes, vaunting the golden apples? And who is he, that other one, following the plough, breaking the soil, as hard as the heart of Pharaoh?
>
> If this be a Jew, where is the crook of his spine; and the quiver of lip, where?
> Behold his knees are not callous through kneeling; he is proud, he is erect.
> There is in his eyes no fear, in his mind no memory of faggots.
> His hump he has left in Ashkinaz; in Sphorad his maimed limb; beyond the seas his terror he has abandoned.
> He has said to the sun, Thou art my father that gives me strength; and to the cloud, Thou art my mother suckling me thy milk.
> The sign of his father is on his brow, and the breath of his mother renders him fragrant. No legion affrights him, no flame in the dark, no sword in the sun.

For a thousand shall come upon him, and a thousand be carried away.

A son has returned to her that bore him; at her hearth he grows comely; he is goodly to behold.

Behind the bony cage there beats the bird of joy; within the golden cup is wine that overflows.

'The Dangers of Divided Loyalty'

28 May 1948

Among the subtler techniques of denigration none is as difficult to combat as that which takes the form of pseudo-friendly advice, the brotherly tip-off counselling its victim to refrain from doing impolitically just that which the victim has no intention of doing at all. With this device, the slanderer is able both to eat his cake and treasure it still; in attributing to his victim motives that victim does not entertain, he satisfies his malice; in defending the victim from the implications of his very own suggestion, he preserves intact his role as friend and mentor. The victim, moreover, finds himself – as he is intended to find himself – in a position where he cannot complain; for to his complaints the answer stands ready: 'I did not say that you did such a thing; I said only that you might do such and such a thing; all may err; – and, friend that I am, I warned you against it.' Could anything be more decent?

It nonetheless remains a fact that it is considered discourteous to warn, even in the most amiable of terms, a judge against the temptation of theft or a journalist against prejudice or venality. Obviously there are cases where the proffering of counsel must be deemed, not only superogatory, but downright insulting. Such a case, we regret to say, is provided by the editorial which appeared in the May twenty-first issue of *The Montreal Daily Star*.

Hanging its sermon upon a text gleaned from an advertisement published by the United Zionist Council on the occasion of the proclamation of a Jewish State in Palestine, the editorial proceeds to deliver its lesson on 'The Dangers of Divided Loyalty.' To prove that loyalty is in such schismatic peril, the editorial quotes the opening paragraph of the ad:

'We have decided, relying upon the authority of the Zionist movement and the support of the entire Jewish people, that upon the termination of the mandatory regime there shall be an end of foreign rule in Palestine and that the governing body of the Jewish State come into being.'

'This is not,' continues the editorial, 'a copy of the proclamation issued in Tel Aviv and signed by Ben-Gurion and other Palestinian leaders.' The editor is right; it is not. Ben-Gurion's proclamation was published in *The Montreal Daily Star* on May fourteenth, and the language is not the same, though the sentiments are identical. 'The *We* in the advertisement,' the editor now goes on, by a very primitive process of elimination, to conclude, 'is the United Zionist Council of Canada and it points to the confusion of thought of many Jews outside Palestine as to their relations with the state of Israel.'

Now if any confusion of thought is pointed to it is the confusion of thought in the editor's mind. How could he possibly have made peace with his reasoning mind to attribute to the United Zionist Council of Canada, statements such as 'with the support of the *entire* Jewish people'; or, subsequently in the statement 'we turn to the Arabs in the Jewish state and to *our neighbours in adjacent territory*'; or, 'We are *here* to build in peace'; and more, and more. The entire statement, both in its language and in the distinct typography in which it was set by the *Montreal Star* linotype man (more perspicacious than his editor) proclaim it to be a quotation, and certainly not the first person plural utterance of the United Zionist Council of Canada.

The fact is that it *is* a quotation. The text of the quoted paragraph is the text of a resolution adopted by *the Jewish Agency in Jerusalem*, at a meeting held prior to the official proclamation by Ben-Gurion.

But the editor, it appears, was not entirely unaware of the absurd conclusions to which his misconstruing was leading him. Said he: 'The wording of the local proclamation assumes the Zionist Council's right to proclaim something and give it the force of law, to bring the state of Israel into existence by a fiat issued in Canada. This, clearly, was not in the minds of Canadian Jews, even of members of the Zionist Council. They labor under no such delusions.' So the editor did know better! Then why didn't he make that clear in the first paragraph? Because if he had there would have been no occasion for a lecture on loyalty!

Canadian Jewry repudiates such lectures and sends them back to authors who obviously seem to stand in greater need of instruction on how to be loyal to fellow-Canadians. Canadian Jewry in its loyalty to country cedes to no one; that loyalty has been amply demonstrated both in peace and in war, and requires no fortifying through editorial comment. It is true that Canadian Jewry is passionately concerned about the fate of its co-religionists overseas, and in particular, about the fate of Jewry in Palestine; but such interest and concern is not treasonable. There is, in fact, hardly an ethnic group in this Dominion which does not admit to sentimental and emotional attachments to places and things located beyond the seas. No one impugns the love which a Canadian of Irish extraction has for things Irish as disaffectionate to our country. Mr. Ferguson's fondness for heather is not in any way to be construed as an overt act of treason against the maple leaf. That the *Canadien* has a soft spot for France beyond the Atlantic casts no shadow upon his oath of allegiance. Nonetheless, we have yet to read in *The Montreal Daily Star* disquisitions on divided loyalty addressed either to Irish- or Scotch- or French-Canadians on the occasion of St.

Patrick's, or St. Andrew's, or St. Denis' day. Such disquisitions, indeed, would be as inappropriate in those cases and on those days as they were on May twenty-first.

Canadian Jewry considers itself to be, and is – Canadian. It is 100% Canadian, and that Canadianism nothing can divide or diminish, not even the insidious substractions in kindly editorials attempted.

Unnecessary Polemic ...   16 July 1948

Written for some inscrutable reason and sent to us for reasons even more inscrutable, there has of late come to our desk quite a number of books and pamphlets, all written by rabbis, and all concerned either with the historicity of Christ or with the authenticity of the New Testament version of the famous Trial of Jesus. We must confess ourselves at a loss to understand why these things should still be the subject of polemic and discussion at this late date. Can it be that the rabbinate is no longer attracted by the *pilpul* of the Tosfoth thus to forego their proper field to transgress into debate which is doomed at the outset to be barren and futile? Is it possible that the good matrons of Israel do no more repair to the rabbi's house with their problems and *sha'aloth*, and that therefore the *Responsum* is vanishing from our midst as a form of theological literature? Or is it that the success of the many best-sellers touching the life of Jesus has stirred and moved these authors into fields which otherwise they would not think of entering?

We do not know the motive, but there they are before us, all the fruitless tracts, the sterile dialectics. Whom do they seek to convince? The Jew? The Jewish attitude is a foregone conclusion. The Christian? His attitude is a conclusion equally foregone. Time was when these debates, whether on the printed page, or through the spoken word, were forced upon our ancestors; indeed, it was considered quite a sport during the Middle Ages to compel a rabbi to argue with a priest, it being always understood that the priest would win. But now when no such compulsion exists, what *is* the point of these arguments and refutations? Certainly they are at best useless, and at worst creative of ill-will. Dialectically, they perpetrate the error of the false premise: they assume that one chooses one's religion after a process of ratiocination, they assume that a man keeps an open mind on these subjects until he comes to the age of discretion, that then he is confronted with three syllogisms, a Jewish, a Christian, and a Mohammedan, and that, exercising his wisdom, he makes choice of one of the three. It is only upon such a premise that one can see any sense in meeting faith with arguments. The manner in which one acquires one's religion, of course, is far otherwise; it is imposed by inheritance, fostered by environment, and strengthened by factors which have very little to do with the principles of logic. He does not begin to understand the faith that moves mountains who believes that he can measure or controvert it by the technique of Aristotle.

No, let every man go in peace and by the light of his own conscience. Gentlemen do not argue about religious convictions.

And into the Scandinavian   24 September 1948

Throughout the ages, amidst varying cultures and civilizations, the Jewish people, by dint of its dedication to things literary, and particularly, to writ holy, has justly earned itself the title of the People of the Book. No doubt the most persuasive example of the ubiquity of its literature, and of its identification with works of the mind and the spirit, is the Bible, the great inspiring classic – if so technical a designation may be given to it – which has been translated into all the known languages of the world. To think within the ambit of his own culture, and to be translated into all the tongues, including – as the copyright lawyers say – the Scandinavian, has ever been the goal which the truly typical Jewish author has set before himself.

With the proclamation of a Jewish state in Palestine one had reason to look forward to a period of developing culture in which the People of the Book, at long last liberated from those obstructions to creative endeavour which were not the least of the laws of the Diaspora, would now even more effectively continue along the path of its spiritual traditions. One had reason, indeed, to believe that the word of God would again come out of Zion, again to find its echo in the remotest corners of the world.

That the majority in the Yishuv entertained and entertains such hopes is beyond question. Achad Ha'am's ideal of cultural Zionism is today – precisely because of the victory of political Zionism – stronger and more real than it ever was before. The Yishuv languishes for the time when it may in peace be permitted to fashion in the twentieth century a culture worthy of the biblic and prophetic culture which still inspires it.

The first and foremost tenet of that culture was, is, and ever shall be the ineluctable pricelessness of human life. Man, being created in the image of God, is himself a part of divinity; and until he has lost, through disgrace or degeneration, that trait essential to his being, his life is as sacred as Deity itself.

It is this tenet which the members of the Stern Gang, in assassinating Count Folke Bernadotte as he walked unarmed through the streets of Jerusalem, reviled and blasphemed. Invoking that scoundrel's refuge – patriotism – they murdered an innocent man, and sullied the name and reputation of an entire people. Where our ancestors spoke of the sanctity of life, they have corruptly introduced death and murder, and – with this latest of their international victims – translated their iniquitous concept into the Scandinavian.

That the wrong which the Sternists – be they Sternists, or Fatherland Front members (note the fascist appellation) – have done cries to high heaven is not debatable. Bernadotte was a peacemaker; and he was met by stealthy war. Bernadotte was a Swede – and the gratitude which Jews remembering Swedish sanctuary during the Hitler persecutions owed was changed, by persons calling themselves Jews, into treachery and ambuscade. Bernadotte was a mediator and representative of the United Nations – the impartiality which should have protected him was riddled by bullets. Bernadotte was unarmed, unprotected – but murderers know no gallantry. It is true, as the Sternists state, that Bernadotte was warned not to come to Jerusalem; but this is an aggravation, not an exculpation; the warning merely shows premeditation. It is true that Bernadotte's suggestions were in many respects unacceptable to the Jews; but Bernadotte was not bound to make acceptable suggestions; he was bound only to recommend as his conscience dictated. That the man who held his conferences at Rhodes was no Colossus is irrelevant; honest error is not punishable by death.

We have no doubt but that the Sternists repudiate reproaches such as these, posed as they are upon effete (*sic*) moral laws. But even according to their own standards of expediency, the murder of Count Bernadotte was, insofar as Jewish interests are concerned, an act of criminal stupidity. It served nobody but the enemies of Israel. It did not, it will not, alter the course of history. It blemishes the Jewish name, it handicaps the Jewish position before the United Nations. It affords succour and consolation to the Arab High Committee. Indeed, the more one dwells upon the various factors of this incident the more one is inclined to question even the motives – the pseudo-patriotic motives – of the Sternist leadership. For whom are they really working? Whose is the Power which stands behind their strategy? Who is it that is so desirous of keeping the Palestinian pot boiling?

The only gratifying element in this melancholy incident – and minor gratification it is – is the fact that the Israeli Government has now been roused to take vigorous measures against these traitors, arrayed in the blue and white. Proclaiming both the Sternists and the Irgun illegal organizations, the Palestine police forces are doing all in their power to round up Stern members and to ferret out the murderers of Bernadotte. It is an act which all Jewry everywhere will applaud; Jewry has recoiled with horror and revulsion from the execrable dastardly un-Jewish deed.

That the private armies and free-lance gangs of the Yishuv constituted a grave danger to Israel has long ago been foreseen. Recent events serve only to point up that peril. No state can afford to have in its midst agencies or cabals or juntas or bands which presume to exercise a law of their own; the State of Israel, young and making its first steps, even less than others. The slogan of the day in Palestine should be – and all reports indicate that it is: *Ecrasez l'infâme* – crush the unspeakable abomination.

A Lady with a Lamp   8 October 1948

> A Lady with a Lamp shall stand
> In the great history of the land,
> A noble type of good,
> Heroic womanhood.

Such, in part, was the tribute which Henry Wadsworth Longfellow paid to the sainted Florence Nightingale. Her self-dedication during the Crimean War to the health and welfare of the fighting man, the nursing service she organized, the weary days and sleepless nights she spent in bringing solace and healing to men wounded in battle – these, and the general nobility of her character, were things of beauty which no poet, and least of all a poet of a country where the best in womanhood is worshipped as it is worshipped and adored in the United States, could possibly pass by, overlooked and unsung. To this day, wherever the noble is cherished and the gentle appreciated, the memory of that nineteenth-century angel, moving with her light through the dark watches of the hospital ward, allaying fever there, easing agony here, – that memory shines on, is made vivid, is made golden, in the recollection of the Lady with a Lamp.

Our generation, too, has produced its Lady with a Lamp – Ilse Koch, Mistress of Buchenwald. She, too, 'stands in the great history of her land ... a type.' She, too, was possessed of a lamp, many lamps; and she, in addition, was more artistically souled than poor Florence Nightingale; she fitted her lamps with lampshades. And thereby hangs a tale.

For the lampshades affected by Ilse Koch, Mistress of Buchenwald, were not ordinary lampshades. They were neither of paper, nor of cloth, nor even of silk; they were lampshades of parchment, real parchment, – *human* parchment. Wife of the overlord of the inferno of Buchenwald, it was the custom of the fastidious Frau Koch from time to time to select from among the hapless inmates of her concentration camp, victims for immediate killing. Contrary to what has been unfairly imputed against her, she did not select them arbitrarily. Every one of her victims was guilty of the same offence – *he had a lampshadable skin.*

For the edification of the innocent to whom this crime is unknown it should further be explained that Frau Koch, like some of the most distinguished of European art-collectors, was ever on the *qui vive* for some new skin which might be flayed, dried, and treated, to furnish a shade for her numerous lamps. With this end in view she had developed an entirely new set of rules for lampshading, an aesthetic, indeed, which took into consideration not merely the exigencies of geometry and the dictates of design – any tyro could do that – but also the qualifications – age, texture, condition, etc. – of her *raw materials*. To Ilse Koch must go the credit of having discovered the human skin's paramount adaptability to lampshading.

But Ilse Koch's creative experimentation did not stop with this discovery. She was one of those pioneer spirits who follow a revolutionary premise through to its practical conclusions. Thus she early realized – and upon that realization, acted – that the skins of men who had been tattoo'd would, if converted into lampshades, throw a most lovely light. The skins of men, on the other hand, whose bodies had been scarred by the whip, while they might afford some interesting if haphazard designs, left, from the point of view of permanence, much to be desired; for these lampshades often cracked.

Here is not the place to enter into an analysis of Frau Koch's art – of her essays with sutures as a basis for the abstract; of the trial she made, for the sake of lampshade fringes, with bearded skins; or of the lampshade leg she dressed up in human flesh. Here it is sufficient to note that the German historian of the future, when he comes to record the various art-movements which flourished in the twentieth century, will have to point with pride to the originality and courage of the achievement of Ilse Koch. At that time there will not be, it is true, the museum of *objets d'art* which Frau Koch managed to collect during her brief artistic career; the lampshade of the man with smallpox will be but a legend of pointillism; the lampshade slitted with eye holes but a memory of the functional; and the lampshade with the anterior rib-structure but a reported instance of the X-ray made theme of art – but *the lampshades will live*.

Unfortunately there are very few artistic practises which are not subject to controversy. When the American armies overran Germany, Frau Koch was arrested, tried, and through an act of leniency sentenced to life imprisonment. Thus was her act repudiated – on the wholly irrelevant issue of human life. The Americans, who apparently had no appreciation of the finer things, recoiled in horror before what they considered a monstrous, an unspeakable iniquity.

That was in 1945. Now, in 1948, a change seems to have taken place in the lampshade standards of the Army. According to a recent release, Ilse Koch's sentence of life imprisonment has been commuted to four years, and since the lady with a lamp has already served three, she is due for liberation next spring. It is a decision which has baffled the understanding of all men endowed with hearts that feel and minds that remember. What, it is asked, what possibly could have prompted this act of outrageous clemency? While American soldiers who committed the heinous offence of having failed to sir their officers still languish in prison, the Monstress of Buchenwald is to be let out on parole; where is the sense of proportion? What possible motive could there be for this diminution of sentence; was it discovered that an error was made, that Frau Koch fashioned herself only four and not twenty lampshades; and therefore the penalty is reduced *pro tanto*? Or has there been some miracle in the Occupied Zone, and Koch's victims are now resurrected? Or – and this is the *or* paramount – or can it be that the members of the Judge Advocate General's Staff have themselves been converted to new standards of art?

The American people, and indeed the world at large, is entitled to an explanation. Considered on its face, the commutation is second in abominableness only to the crimes charged against Ilse Koch. By it, a most distorted construction is placed upon American justice. We cannot conceive of any possible explanation; but whatever it is, it ought to be made public. Certainly to the case of the Lady with the Lampshade there ought to be applied Goethe's dying injunction: More light! More light!

Religion in Palestine   19 November 1948

Intercession by the anti-Zionists with every other Great Power having failed, they now seek to intercede with God. Hence the spate of pharisaic scripture recently released onto the printing presses all purporting to prove that in the Holy Land the heathen rage. Vicariously through the eyes of his employees, Mr. Luce sheds weekly tears for that the six hundred and thirteen *mitzvoth* of Holy Writ in the Holy Land allegedly go unobserved; the tycoons of the oil companies, it is rumoured, have taken to a study of the *Shulchan Aruch* to discover what thingumjig of the iota gets broken by the stiff-necked ones of Israel; and foreign correspondents in Palestine, it is reported, are trying for a look at Ben-Gurion's biceps to see whether there are signs of two sets of *tfillin*. The news that the Israel army has banned the wearing of beards is held by these defenders of the faith as a sure indication that the sacred lore of the ancestors has been repudiated by the descendants.

Since most of the critics don't believe their criticism, it seems superfluous to point out that the State of Israel is not a theocracy; that in Palestine, as in all civilized countries, there is a separation of state from synagogue; and that one of the first principles of the new Jewish State, as it was of the United States, is freedom of religion. Freedom of religion – not freedom from religion; indeed, the rebuilding of the Jewish State constitutes in itself the greatest act of faith that has been witnessed in generations.

As for the petty deviations from the strict and rigorous – such as this matter of beards – they will be found in most cases to have been motivated by considerations which transcend the mere act of piety. The rebuilding of a people, after all, outweighs the behest of custom and ceremony. One recalls in this connection what is related of one of the Chassidic rabbis, incarcerated with twelve hundred of his disciples, in a German concentration camp. The dietary laws of these camps are well-known; the Chassidim at first lived upon the dry crust of bread and the gulps of water, but then as hunger drove them they were forced to surrender to the non-kosher morsel which their tormentors tauntingly flung to them. Rather than starve, hundreds ate. The rabbi was well aware of what was going on, but, considering that the sustenance of human life is higher than the observance of dietary law, he said nothing. Came then to him one of the ultra-pious, and cried out, 'Rabbi, rabbi, a thousand Jews eat non-kosher meat!' 'It cannot be!' replied the rabbi. 'That which sustains a thousand Jews in their hour of need is kosherest of the kosher!'

Canadian Recognition of Israel
26 November 1948

It is a long time now that a number of governments have looked upon the State of Israel and, induced into a wilful blindness, have failed to recognize it. The proclamation of May the fifteenth they seemed to consider as but a false echo, and the governmental apparatus actually functioning in the Holy Land as but an eastern mirage. The movement of Jewish troops both to the north and the south, vivid and real to the forces which opposed them, appeared to these myopic governments as but optical illusions.

When one suffers from an eye disease, a remedy may be found; one goes to an eye-specialist. But when one suffers from a derangement not of the eye but of the psyche, when the eye is in all respects faultless and unblemished and yet its owner persists in not seeing what the whole world beholds – then it is to a psychiatrist, or at least a psychologist, that one must have recourse.

And it is this which leads us to the truth about the failure on the part of a number of states to recognize the State of Israel. For that state is a fact, incontrovertible, palpable, a vigorous reality as its immediate opponents in all things, save formal admission, attest; it exists, moreover, not only *de facto*; it exists *de jure*, for it is upon a legal decision of the United Nations that it came into being. And yet there is this voluntary blindness. Why?

In a good number of cases, that blindness, that non-recognition, is due simply to ill-will: one refuses to admit the existence of that which one does not like. One escapes from the fact by denying its reality. The fact, Berkeleyan philosophy notwithstanding, still persists. In other cases, non-recognition is a formula for delay, a bargaining instrument. The idea is that if that which does not exist – namely, the Israeli State, – will make certain concessions, as to territory, for example, – then its existence will be admitted. It were a comical situation, were it not also fraught with elements of the gravest import; for, reduced to simplicity, it means that the existence of the State of Israel will not be admitted unless it consents to a decrease in territory, that is to say, a lesser existence.

The delay in Canadian recognition of the Israeli State is, we think, not attributable to either of the attitudes indicated above; to what it is attributable we do not know. We know only that it has been a delay too long pursued, and that in the case of Canada, which played a determining role in the U.N. solution, it has been a glaring, an incomprehensible *non sequitur*. It is all the more gratifying, therefore, now to see that Mr. Lester Pearson, to whom the Palestine problem is not altogether unfamiliar, is coming around to a point of view which augurs well for the future. In a statement made before a session of a United Nations committee, Mr. Pearson made it his basic premise that the State of Israel was a fact. It is an important admission. One cannot, if one has regard to one's reputation, persist indefinitely in not recognizing the consequences of an admitted fact.

Declaration of Human Rights   17 December 1948

The text of the U.N. Declaration of Human Rights, recently published in full in the public prints, is, though couched in simple language, difficult to understand. The worthy objectives it enunciates, though hitherto beyond human practise, are of course not beyond human comprehension. In democratic countries most of these objectives are quite properly deemed truisms. The statement that all men should be given equal opportunities and that everybody should be nice to everybody else is clear, clear as glass, like glass may be seen through, and like glass cannot be got through without injury.

What we do not understand is, first, with what kind of a conscience did some of the subscribing nations underwrite its articles, and second, what practical effect issues from these signatures. Are the injunctions of these articles now part of international law? If so, what is the penalty for their inobservance, and where is the instrument for their enforcement? Are they mere desiderata? If so, why should the United Nations intrude upon the jurisdiction which properly belongs to a church synod?

'All human beings,' says Article 1, 'should act towards one another in a spirit of brotherhood.' Is this *should* mandatory, or is it merely hortatory? Is this legislation? Or just piety? Certainly the framers of the article afford no very fine example of their own doctrine. The only brotherhood some of the members of u.n. have hitherto displayed has been that of Cain and Abel.

'No one shall be subjected to arbitrary arrest, detention, or exile.' Did Vishinsky, the prosecutor of 1936, really read this, before he instructed the Russian delegate to sign? Or the article (No. 10) which follows, calling for 'independent and impartial trials'?

'Everyone,' says Article 11, 'charged with a penal offence has the right to be presumed innocent until proved guilty.' With what mental reservations did the French delegate, in whose country, we are given to understand, the opposite rule prevails, put his signature to that one?

'Everyone has the right to leave any country, including his own, – and to return to his country.' Russians, too?

'Everyone has the right of equal access to public service in his country.' Everyone – including American negroes?

Surely this document must be a declaration of the United Nations of Mars. It doesn't seem to have any pertinence here. For centuries one had hoped for such international legislation; it has come; but instead of appearing like a just achievement in idealism, it has all the characteristics of a cynical practical joke.

Pharaoh in Reverse   7 January 1949

One of the most entertaining of techniques used in the moving picture industry is that one in which the movie operator suddenly decides to reverse the progress of the film. Thus is the diver, half-way down from his board to the water, made to soar gracefully backwards until he is again poised in his original springing stance; thus, too, in a scene of battle, is the pursuing host suddenly made to flee with back-running haste, a sort of goose-step turned inside out.

We find these erratic transformations extremely fascinating. They satisfy in us, first, the desire for surprise; and then, the longing for the comic. There is also in these unexpected apparitions something supernatural, a defiance of the laws of gravity, a taunt at the Newtonian.

Something of the same sort of pleasure is ours, we must admit, as we consider the recent change in fortune which the Egyptian invaders of Palestine are reported to be suffering. With what bravado, with what a flashing of scimitars, with what pharaonic arrogance these first ventured upon their Jehad! The conquest of Palestine was to be but a matter of a day; the new Jewish State was to be stifled even before it was born. Then it was that one watched the Egyptian hosts traversing the desert, entering the Holy Land, and in some places, proceeding even as far as the eastern Negev.

Came suddenly the movie operator in the shape of the Jewish Army, and began setting into reverse the vaunted Egyptian military progress. This for King Farouk was a most unexpected turn of events; so unexpected, in fact, that his prime minister was called upon to pay for it with his life. The world was then regaled by the spectacle of 'the Egyptian exodus' – Egyptians being made to flee from territory not their own – and by the pathetic cries of a latter-day Pharaoh: Let my people stay!

The whole incident would have been nothing more than another occasion for the Gaiety of Nations did not the 'high sources' and 'reliable informants' and 'unnamed correspondents' begin to bedevil the situation. These worthies, moved by a hunger for news and no doubt also inspired by those whose interests they would serve, began to circulate in the world press a series of lurid statements all to the effect that Israel was invading Egypt! The truth is that all that was happening was a re-invasion of Egypt by its own soldiers, for whom the Palestine climate had been made most inclement. All the State of Israel was doing was preserving the integrity of its own frontiers. This the Egyptians very well knew; but harrassed by a public opinion in their own country, a public opinion the Government itself fomented, they decided to repeat the ancient technique – the thief crying: 'Stop, thief!'

The latest *canard* had also a deeper purpose. Discovering that the pan-Arabic movement was unable to cope with a resurgent Zion – this pan-Arabism was from the beginning an eastern mirage, the invention of a group of feudal lords and political careerists – the Egyptians now seek to embroil more powerful forces in the conflict. There is a treaty providing for British aid in the event that Egypt is attacked. British aid is now most heartily desired; hence, the invented invasion.

It is to be doubted whether the shrewd minds of the British Foreign Office will be duped – unless they wish to be duped – by a trick which even a Cairo tourist-guide would not condescend to perpetrate. It would be, indeed, a supremely bitter irony that the Government which once issued the Balfour Declaration should thirty years later find itself in hostile opposition to the Jewish Homeland. We forebear to dwell upon the dangers to *world* peace inherent in the démarche which those whom the gods would destroy now seek to perpetrate.

The Dangers of Success

I will be forgiven, I hope, for venturing to write now, at the very height and intoxication of Zionist success, what it would never have occurred to me to say during the long years of hope, and the frustration of hope, which constituted the sad sober prelude to our great consummation. Recently, however, there have been advanced certain philosophic views which make the issuance of a caveat imperative.

I refer particularly to the notions fostered by that crew of chauvinists who, under the justifiable afflatus of the Israel renascence, have dared to propound the doctrine they so scientifically and so callously dub: 'the negation of the Diaspora.' According to this doctrine only those Jews who will forthwith wend their way to the State of Israel there to establish themselves among the citizens of the land, only they, and they alone, shall henceforth be counted as of the congregation; the others, the stiff-necked others – seeing that they persist in remaining in the Diaspora – shall be considered as lost to Jewry, if not immediately then in a generation – their ultimate perdition, it is but a matter of time. The most obvious corollary of this theorem is that cis-Atlantic Judaism is proleptically calculated as at zero; two categories of Jew are established – the Israeli and the non-Israeli; and non-Israeli is equated with non-Jew.

A more wicked or more pernicious doctrine it is impossible to conceive. It seeks to achieve with a theoretical dictum what all the tyrants of all the ages failed to achieve with fire and sword, namely, the nullification of Diaspora Jewry. It seeks to set up in the very bosom of Jewry a permanent, an unreasoned, a purely doctrinaire discord – to foment an abominable class distinction between *aretz* and *chutz l'aretz*; and to establish what was hitherto unknown to our thinking – an aristocracy of residence. The grave, the fatal error of the Bundists who thought to build themselves a home out of the *galuth*, is here equated, though reversed; the *galuth* is sufficiently exilic without the necessity of being banished also out of the community of Israel.

Nor do I dwell upon the basic ingratitude of these negators, of their wilful and inexplicably arrogant disregard of the fact that it was Diaspora Jewry which made Israeli Jewry possible; it was not done for gratitude, and hence this argument is an irrelevancy; but one must, indeed, pause to wonder at the stupidity of so-called national philosophers to whom a pose is so dear that they fail to see that in striking it they leave themselves (and their pose!) in a most vulnerable position. Why, we can conceive of a situation in which – there being no Diaspora Jewry – it were well for the State of Israel to create it! For not all domains follow the same rules of growth; sometimes it is the host which comes first, and the colonies after; and sometimes the process is reversed.

It is true that 'the negators' can adduce many texts – including some from my own writings – to prove how superior *aretz* is to *chutz l'aretz* – but such texts are essential to the culture of a people in exile. It is through such texts that it lives until the day of the reintegration. But once reintegrated – such texts are but literature.

The *primum mobile* is neither land nor language; it is people. It is the folk – and all of it, everywhere – which is of the essence. Domicile, status, speech, etc., these are but adjectival; the substance is *Amcho* – thy people.

What the time demands is not a negation of the Diaspora, but the affirmation of a total Jewry.

The truth is that this new philosophy cannot really be understood in terms of simple ratiocination; it is built not upon syllogisms but upon psychological reactions. It is in its own way, a nouveau-riche philosophy; as such, it negates its own past.

We would not pause so seriously upon this paltry doctrine were it not for the fact that it is symptomatic of a general attitude, characterized by numerous variations, and, both in the general and the particular, extremely dangerous to the future of our people.

The establishment of the State of Israel, for which every decent Jew has worked and prayed, is a great blessing. It must be protected, therefore, all the more vigilantly, not only against its enemies, but also from its misguided friends.

The perils which on this score beset it are not difficult to foresee. Some of them have already made themselves manifest. The people of Israel must be warned, first of all, against the sin of insularity. There are many parallels to be drawn between the Hebrew Renascence and the Irish one; but one parallel must be carefully avoided; the Yishuv must not become *Sinn Fein* – 'ourselves alone' is not a proper slogan for those who cherish a concern for '*klal Yisroel.*'

Equally to be eschewed is that xenophobia which often takes hold both of those who feel uncertain of themselves, and those who walk proud in the consciousness of some recent great achievement. Xenophobia is in general an attitude alien to our spirit; and two thousand years of experience of it should have conditioned us forever against its emulation. Xenophobia directed against one's own – this is the very golden calf of abominations.

One hears much of the value of back-to-the-land movements. They have, of course, their reward. They give one the sense of indigenousness; they supply a feeling of solidarity; they call back, for a people long bereft of them, the wonderful and fundamental simplicities of nature. But they have their risks – not the least of which is a flight from culture as from something involved, artificial, sophisticate. One need not labour the point; one has but to consider the peasant and his standards, let us say in cultured France, to be horrified at the prospect of its repetition in Eretz. These dangers may not be imminent; when one counts the number of books published annually in Palestine, the number of its libraries, its readers, etc., one may assure oneself that it is not for the *immediate* future that one fears; but these readers are not peasants – they are only intellectuals who want to be.

The conduct of a state brings a sense of responsibility. That is good; what one worries about is the bureaucrat's oversize sense of responsibility; that sense which causes him to dictate to the citizens his goings and comings, his labour and his rest (Blue Sabbaths!), his reading and his entertainment (censorship), etc.

The impulse behind the establishment of a State of Israel was the desire – to be *mit leiten gleich*. It was a worthy ambition, but now should be amended – to be even as others are, *but with a difference*.

The New Haggadah   13 April 1949

In anticipation of the Passover Seder we have been examining, these past several days, a variety of Haggadahs which have come within our ken, issued, as their frontispieces announce, either by proud publisher or insistent organization to meet the needs of the sacred annual ritual. Some, we found, were ornate, resplendent with a multiplicity of colours, curlicued and illuminated; others were of a sad and sober mien, as if printed to be read to the poverty of *matzoth*, their letters somewhat indistinct, their woodcuts faded and blurred. Some were fortified with hard resounding decorated covers; others, coverless and limp and like brochures just issued by Moses.

They differed, moreover, not only in format but also in content; it is true that all of them boasted the Four Questions and the Ten Plagues, and the other renowned pieces, but here and there (in some of them), deviations had been allowed to intrude. For one thing, they differed in translation, – in some instances, the Englishing was fine, polished, literary; in others the translations asked for translations of their own. The compilers of some of the Haggadahs, moreover, could not resist the temptation to use this text to advance their own pet notions; liberties were taken; classic sections were omitted, and in their place one found doctrines and dicta – such as those in praise of democracy – not contemplated by, let us say, the Haggadah of Rashi.

It was all very confusing, but not altogether unedifying. It shows that this text enjoys a popularity which far exceeds that of any other in the whole field of Hebrew liturgy. This may be due to the fact that this is a liturgy for use in the home, not to add, for use with *kneidlach*; whatever the reason, its familiar eminence is undisputed.

We are loath, therefore, to make the suggestion which we are about to advance. It is not intended in any way to diminish either from the sanctity or the favour which the Haggadah has hitherto enjoyed. All we have in mind is – not its supplanting, forsooth! – but its extension. The redemption from Egypt, we concede, constitutes an undying memory in our tradition. Without it, the rest would not have been. Without it we would have been remembered, if remembered at all, as but pyramidal cement, a human subservience to Pithom and to Rameses. That saga, indelibly inscribed upon the tablets of our memory, can never be effaced.

But there is another Haggadah which clamours to be written, to be compiled even as was compiled the Haggadah which now lies before us. It is the Haggadah of these our recent years. Here, too, there was trial and suffering and at last promise and redemption, here, too, the tyrant and his thwarting, the exodus and its consummation. What a wonderful anthology, sacred and secular, there is to be gathered from the scriptures of those our latter days! Calls from behind barbed wire, battle-cry from ghetto, defiance to despots, liberation and the long trek home! For one pharaoh, many; for ten plagues, thousands; and a contemporary *Hallel* all of hallelujahs compact!

It is true that this new Haggadah would require an editor of talent, indeed of genius; but genius has not vanished out of Israel. Certainly his material is ready to hand; it requires but the trained and discriminating eye to seek it out and from much literature to select that which is of the true note authentic.

When should it be read? We do not wish to multiply holidays in a calendar already very red-lettered with days of rescue and salvation; nor would we wish to prolong the hebdomadal Passover to extend right into the month of Iyar, but the fifth day of that month (date of the proclamation of the State of Israel) would, we think, be a day most apt and fitting for such a recital. If such a suggestion does not recommend itself to the proper authorities on these matters, then perhaps the Passover eves would be the right occasions for the anthological reminiscence we have in mind.

It is a subject upon which hasty decision is highly undesirable. For in addition to the text of this contemplated new Haggadah there are also a host of ritual details to be decided upon. Shall the youngest of the house ask the same Four Questions, or shall another set be substituted? The answer, of course, will remain the same: it was the Lord who redeemed us. What is to be the latter-day equivalent of *matzo*? Or of *moror*? Shall there be invoked also a new Rabbi Yehuda to make mnemonics out of the plagues? Shall the same psalms be read as of the *Hallel*, or shall Psalm 137 also be added to the text?

The language of the new Haggadah must be Hebrew – that goes without saying; but what shall its vocabulary be? Primitive and poetic, or up-to-date and scientific? What allusion is there among the Prophets to the atomic age? Shall the vanquished enemy be named by name? Or shall his unspeakableness be kept from out the canon of Hebrew diction?

We have not any ready answers to all these questions. Such answers are in any case impossible – not possible until one sees the new Haggadah in its proper conspectus and in its entirety. For the moment it is enough that the question be mooted; that, too, is a kind of Haggadah.

What this latter-day requires is a duplication of the old Bnai-Brak – those worthies whose merit is recorded for that they stood one night so engaged in the narrative of the exodus from Egypt that they perceived not that dawn had risen and the time for morning service had arrived.

In our day, too, the dawn has risen. And the time for another service arrived.

Of Hebrew Names   22 April 1949

There is nothing in contemporary events which is as symbolic of the direction which Jewish history is taking as the custom, now prevalent in Israel, of changing one's name. One day it is the jargoning nomenclature of the *Galuth* which in its thousand versions is recorded at the ports of entry; the next day from these ports into the very heart of the country there issue entire hosts bearing names such as these two millenia have not been heard in Jewry, names racy of the soil, of Holy Writ odorous, and in the true Hebrew accent couched.

It is as if a whole people, having been unjustly charged and unjustly pursued, had at last succeeded in reaching its sanctuary, and there, doffing its many foreign aliases, had again assumed the real and authentic name of its nativity. It is as if the communities of the concentration camps, having felt the Dark Angel hovering by, had followed ancient tradition and had changed – so as to confuse and confound this angel and his mission – the appellations that he read upon his sinister roll. It is as if an entire nation had disappeared beyond the eastern horizon, and in their stead there had sprung up a new race indigenous.

It is altogether a good, an inspired movement, this of sloughing off the Exile together with its curious tags of call. Most of the names thus dropped in the Mediterranean were, in any event, of an uncomplimentary origin; Jewish surnames were unknown to the early centuries; our ancestors contented themselves with patronymics. It was only in the Diaspora that there rose up kings, greedy for taxes and therefore zealous with the census, who sent out their agents to number and name the heads of Israel. These agents were by no means friendly souls; to console themselves for having to deal with Jews they soon converted the taking of the census into a sport. Did the Jew not reply promptly with his surname, he was there and then christened with a name entirely of the census-taker's inspiration. Hence there suddenly appeared in Israel the families of Drachenblut, Groberklotz, Gotlos, Singmirwas, Geldshrank, – a roll-call of names of a most unpalatable connotation. It is true that in time the owners of these names modified them somewhat so that the original insult was lost in metathesis; but the original cruel jest was there for all to read and know. Nor was it the Germans alone who practised this uncouth baptism; the Russian scene, too, had its Kasokis (cock-eyed), its Shkrabs (old shoe), its Mertvoys (corpse). These names were, in fact, but verbal equivalents of the Jewish badge. It is good that they and all their memories be left in permanent quarantine at Haifa.

The movement for name-changing in Israel, moreover, is not confined to any class or group. It embraces the entire nation. Moishe Shertok is no longer called Shertok; he is Sharett – a servant, a name which recalls the papal epithet: servant of the servants of God ... The Israeli Ambassador to the United States, once yclept Epstein, is now Elath. Rabbi Berlin, too, hastened to abandon his surname of unsavoury memory; it is as Bar-Ilan that he and his generations shall forever appear in the congregation of Israel. Professor Harry Torczyner, Professor of Hebrew Philology at the Hebrew University, did not, it appears, have an easy time with his name; being a philologist, however, he was able to fathom the secret of its derivation. He is now Tur-Sinai (Mt. Sinai).

Nor is it merely a desire to get rid of the practical jokes played upon them centuries ago which prompts the changing of names. There is also manifest here a powerful incentive to begin anew, to start from the place where one was interrupted, to leave no memory of hiatus. There is something, indeed, which is grand and Adamic about this attitude, – as if the world were again at its first day, and the ritual of giving names to persons, places, and things, freshly performed.

It is with such gestures that the Diaspora is truly nullified – this is the *Shlilat ha-galuth* – the negation of the exile, against which no exception can be taken. How much sounder and more dignified it is than that spirit which moves certain generous but unthinking people to go out upon campaigns to build institutions in Israel which will not only be the counterpart of similar institutions in the Diaspora, but which will even bear their names. Should such a movement catch on, one may well expect the State of Israel to be dotted and pimpled with such a multitude of memorials – the synagogue of Brest-Litovsk, the Paris school, the Pinsk technicum, etc. – that the country will look like some levantine reduction of Europe. Indeed, in Montreal several weeks ago a synagogue no longer in use was sold, and the well-meaning directors have suggested that the proceeds of the sale go to establish a synagogue in Palestine to be known as *Beth Hamidrash Hagodol d'Notre Dame*. D'Notre Dame! Of our lady!

Such incongruities, of course, are unthinkable. They would make out of the Jewish Homeland but a dark carbon copy of the Diaspora. Among the reasons adduced in the Haggadah for the redemption of Israel from Egypt is the fact that they kept their original Hebraic names. History played pranks on our nomenclature, endowing us with a babel of appellatives, but now that redemption has indeed come, the old virtue, certainly, should again be resumed.

Of Jewish Culture

The establishment of the Israeli State, it can be seen by even the most superficial of observers, presents not only a challenge but a great opportunity to culture. It was Bialik who pointed out in a classic lecture on the subject that exilic Jewish culture, although it had the most extaordinary achievements to its credit, suffered nonetheless from certain very apparent deficiencies. The principal deficit that Bialik found in Diaspora culture was that too often it founded itself on foreign traditions; it made its contribution to an entity already established by others; it added, improved, ornamented, but it did not found. This was so, said Bialik, because the ambience in which Diaspora culture flourished, was an alien one; the premises belonged to others, no matter how excellent the Jewish contribution was.

Although we do not entirely agree with this viewpoint, it has, it must be admitted, a great deal of truth in it. That truth, moreover, can now manifest itself creatively in Palestine. Here the ambience is certainly Jewish; and here tradition is at its very centre. All that is now required for the development of an authentic Hebrew culture is, as the cynics say, – talent. Of this the Jewish people has never suffered a dearth.

Nor will the flourishing of an Israeli culture be without its effect upon the life and thought of Jews everywhere. That, too, must now thrive as it never throve before. The mere fact that Jewish existence has now achieved a national status and dignity cannot be without its influence even upon the culture of those who have another sovereign allegiance. And it is precisely here that the true flowering of Jewish culture is possible. A culture which is confined to but one area tends to become restricted and insular; a culture which is everywhere planted tends to become diffuse and diluted. Neither the one nor the other are consummations greatly to be desired. But with Israel hewing straitly to the line, following directly in the path of ancient tradition, and with world Jewry thinking in larger cosmopolitan terms, our culture is very likely to acquire a completeness and wholeness it never enjoyed before. At once placed solidly in the ground and yet looking with eager eyes upon the world, surely it may inherit the best qualities of both Diaspora and Israeli culture.

Notebook of a Journey

Date of Departure – July 31st. Destination – Israel.
In how many ways, in how many varied and lingering ways, is the full implication and force of this so-unexcited time-table brevity to be made clear? For certainly as it stands now, cold, staid, typographical on a printed page, not a millionth of the emotion it evokes, can issue therefrom. Shouldn't one pause over these equations, turn them – like ben Bag Bag was wont to do to the texts of Holy Writ – about and about – to note them, to spy them, to see them, and in all their aspects to comprehend?
Thus:
Reportorial. On the 31st day of July, 1949, at 7 p.m., subject prepared to board at La Guardia Airfield a TWA plane, destination, Lydda, Israel. He had with him not more than sixty-six pounds avoirdupois of baggage, a coat flung over his arm, and upon his person various documents of importance. Subject appeared to be calm, the only sign of excitement being a repeated rubbing of his nosetip with the knucklepoint of his forefinger. It must, of course, be stated that his blood pressure was not taken, nor his heartbeats counted.
Rhetorical. Who can describe, what master of language can communicate the emotions which must thrill the heart of a Jew, scion of sixty generations of exiles, when at last, after two millenia of tribal banishment, he turns again his face in expectation of a return, albeit temporary, to the ancestral soil? Has the vocabulary for such a description yet been invented? Has the pen writing of the theme been fashioned, or its wielder born? What is the name of the Angel who could inspire such speech – speech that must be more a fluttering of wings than an articulation human – speech of joy and hope, elation and dear sweet reunion? Et cetera.
Sentimental. At last, at long last, to see with one's own eyes the primal hearth, the original home! The dream of a lifetime about to be fulfilled! Surely one should make ready, like Moses, to look from the heights of the plane upon the Promised Land, like Yehuda Halevi, to descend and press one's lips against the sacred soil, and –
Ironic. And in due time to return back into Babylon!
Satiric. Another tourist to Israel! As if there weren't enough of these D.P.'s (delicate pilgrims) already arrived, like gay locusts, to eat into the rations and the patience of the land! Goggle-eyed bores, wrong-reasoned enthusiasts, garrulous manics, cautious critics, picture-takers, autograph-hunters, interview-seekers – did we think, after Samson, to be rid of the Philistines? Behold them arriving again, each with his camera and letters

of introduction (all addressed to Ben-Gurion), pausing at the very shore of the land to go *tsk-tsk* and *ai-ai*. Is this the company I join?

Poetic. Fares a Jew to Palestine,
    Gets a form to fill in,
    Only baggage he declares —
    Tallis and his *tfillin.*

Biblic. And it came to pass that the word was spoken unto Abraham, saying, Get thee out of thy country, and from thy kindred, and from thy father's house, which is in Tur-Malca, that is to say, Montreal.

And go thee forth to thy kinsmen and thy kinsmen's country, to the house of thy father's father, which in these latter days, has been builded again.

And I will shew thee a land ...

Mishnaic. On the day of the redemption and at the time of the rebuilding of Erez Israel, what is the benediction to be uttered? The benediction of *shehechianu*. Rav says: The benediction prescribed for the appearance of a monarch, or wise man. Samuel says: The benediction of the Tishbite.

Talmudic. 'The benediction of the Tishbite' — what is it? It is a benediction not yet composed, the Tishbite Elijah will compose it. Said R. Chiya in the name of Rabbi Samuel: Israel has never yet been reconstructed, — how then is one to know the form prescribed for such occasion? Let the time come, and let the heart tell.

'*Shehechianu*' — for that is the essence. The land of Israel exists for the survival of Israel, Israel exists for the maintenance of the land of Israel. The men of the East add: For the maintenance of the Torah of Israel.

'A monarch or wise man' — In the academy of Rehovoth, one reads: Weizmann.

Cabbalistic. When the years were ripened and the years fulfilled, then was there fashioned Aught from Naught. Out of the furnace there issued smoke, out of the smoke a people descended. Sambation raged, but Sambation was crossed, the desert swirled, but the desert was sand.

Then truly was it *ma'aseh breshith*, a work of creation, the which to behold there flew in the skies many chariots — *ma'aseh merkavah*.

The plain unvarnished fact. I'm going to Israel!!!

July 13: Have begun my tour of the consulates, and am discovering that 'the earth is the Lord's and the fulness thereof' is only a manner of speaking. The fact is that heavy and plunked over the various territories of the earth's surface, there sit, like Buddhas, a number of jealously possessive individuals. They are all gentlemen, polite, courteous, but implacable. If you wish to pass through their domains, you must pay the toll. It may be true that you do not intend to sojourn in the land, that all you desire is the right of transit – nonetheless, your visa, please.

Utopia: a visaless world. Everyman can go everywhere anytime.

Utopia in abeyance, was delighted, and not annoyed that I stood in need also of an Israeli visa. The Israelis, too, are jealously possessive – and a good thing. Hold visa No. 9, issued by the Israeli consul at Montreal. Klein – nine – sign. Fine.

There is, apparently, a hierarchy in visas. To pass through Belgium costs only $1.50; France, however, will not grant the same privilege for a cent less than $1.89. Italy feels that its scenery is worth $6.00 per month to look at. Israel, a stickler for religious detail, will not admit the tourist save upon payment of a full *minyan* (10) of dollars.

No doubt a political conclusion can be drawn from the graph of this list of charges. The more financially sound the country, the cheaper the visa. It is a twentieth century miracle that Israel, this state of one year, can already afford to reduce its charge to the abovementioned figure – a most acceptable tithing.

Relished a sort of anticipatory pleasure upon walking into each of the consulates. In virtue of the internationally accepted doctrine of extraterritoriality, each consulate is deemed to be, by legal fiction, a part of its own soil. The French consulate on Stanley Street didn't look like France, but it was French territory nonetheless.

By the same token, the Israeli consul had for his ambience, a bit of Erez Israel. A wonderful transplantation. One almost was tempted to plant an orange-tree in the consulate – if it observed international law, it should grow.

And yet not so strange. What more natural than that in a city in which saints meet at every street-corner there should also be a parcel of Holy Land.

July 15: It is not easy to get to see Jerusalem. You've got to suffer first. Hence, the inoculations. Old liturgies contain prayers beseeching the Lord to protect the traveller from 'wild beasts that lie in wait.' These beasts, to judge by the number of immunizations required, though reduced in size, are as terrible as of yore. Germs. Viruses. Microbes. The old maps, when they wished to warn the wanderer against a forest fearful of passage, inscribed thereon *Hic sunt leones*. Over my atlas there is one continuous warning – Here are germs.

Have, accordingly, been scarified against smallpox, punctured against typhus, pierced for tetanus, injected for typhoid, and needled with cholera. Wounds and bruises, says Isaiah, and putrefying sores, they have not been closed, neither bound up, neither mollified with ointment.

Am, however, a healthy and immune pin-cushion. Let them come on, the 'small deer' that lie in wait.

Am beset by various advisers. Three categories.

(a) *Itinerary Makers*. They know where to go, where not to go, what to see, what to overlook. Out of the vast experience of the single tour made two decades ago, it is simple for them to act as long-distance cicerones to the sights and marvels of Europe, Asia, and Africa.

(b) *Warners*. I should have gotten an injection against their infectious hypochondria. Watch the food! Don't drink water! Don't drink wine! Beware – the prices! Caution – pickpockets! Eschew the guided tour! And, of course, for propaganda, the grain of salt. For further traits, see Numbers 13:32.

(c) *Prophets*. Mine is presumably a tour of investigation, but to listen to these my counsellors, all my conclusions are ready to hand here in Montreal. These gentlemen know exactly what is going on in the Ministry for Foreign Affairs; in what stage of prefabrication the prefabricated houses are; in what way Bernard Joseph's austerity program is superior to that of Pharaoh's Joseph; etc. etc.

Palestine, one of the gloomy ones says, will at best become the department store of the Middle East. Is that, he asks, a destiny?

We didn't do so bad, I reply, running a circulating library for two thousand years. And with only one book.

19 August 1949

July 31: Have always considered Bialik's 'El Hatzipor' a poem unworthy of the great master. These maudlin accents, this easy apostrophe, – a *Yeshiva bochur* discoursing seriously with a fowl! – all this ever seemed strange to me issuing from lips which I had learned to associate with mighty malediction and prophetic thunder.

> Greetings! Peace to you, returning
> Lovely bird, unto my window
> From a warmer clime!
> How my soul for songs was yearning
> When my dwelling you deserted
> In the winter-time.

The translation – Jessie Sampter's – is pedestrian, and the poem really deserved no better. It is one of Bialik's earliest and shows everywhere the influence of the Romantic Movement in European literature. (Compare Lord Byron's conversation with the Atlantic Ocean, the one in which he permits it to roll on, deep and dark-blue, roll!) The sentiments issue heavily, certainly didactically, from one who was, more than the author of 'The *Mathmid*,' the *mathmid* himself. Often its coyness is embarrassing. '*El Hatzipor*' deserves its fate – an elementary poem for primary text-books.

Readers will recall how in this particular poem, Bialik avails himself of the appearance of the bird – how typical it is that the species of the bird is never indicated – such a degree of naturalism was way beyond the ornithological scope of a Talmud student – to invite it to bring his regards and greetings to the Holy Land. Unless one is ready to concede *everything* to poetic license the situation is terribly *invraisemblable*. So heavy a freight for so small a creature! So strange a creature – was it a carrier-pigeon? – for so fruitless a mission! The whole thing appears to be what it should not – an imitative gesture, a striking of attitude, mimicked but not really felt.

There is, however, a bird – neither dodo nor roc – which would indeed have evoked Bialik's true manner and made his apostrophe something grand and apocalyptic. It is the bird I now mount, the TWA Constellation, of mighty wingspread, gargantuan multi-auricled heart, and cavernous maw palatial. This is the bird with which to send a message, its destination Lydda, Israel.

> Does your singing bring me greeting
> From the land, its glens and valleys,
> Mountain height and cleft?
> Has her God compassioned Zion?
> Is she still to graves deserted,
> Only ruins left?
>
> Falls the dew like pearls on Hermon,
> From its snowy heights descending,
> Tearlike does it fall?
> How fare Jordan's shining waters,
> How the hills and how the hillocks
> And the mountains all?

This, surely – pulsating, throbbing, high in the empyrean – is the bird that Bialik should have addressed.

Cannot resist continuous wonder at the marvel of our levitation. So much metal, material, and human freight, and the thing not only roars into the air – it stays there. Should, of course, be accustomed to the phenomenon, but am not. This is due, no doubt, first to my extraordinary respect for the law of gravity, second, to the fact that it is I who am sitting on top of the phenomenon, and third, to my natural desire so to continue to do.

Recall the *Machzor's* praise of Deity: *Toileh eretz al blimah.* Syllabically translated: *He hangs the world on withoutwhat.*

Let him who is abashed by details, trammelled and tangled in the thousand minuscule particularities of daily living, mount in a plane if he would win for himself again the wide perspective, the unconfined horizon, the very vistas of interstellar space. It is a sovereign remedy, this rising above the clouds, for all those beset by the multifarious agenda of our pavlov-civilization.

For here on the heights – not among the clouds – that is a locus universally in bad repute – trivialities cease to exist. The prospect is the prospect of the eagle, and the view is the view of the Martian man. Great forests appear no better than moss-covered rocks, and the widest river a cartographer's line. Only the most fundamental of the laws of Nature retain their pertinence, the motion of the planets, and the notorious 32 feet per second per second.

And even these are modified. Crossing the Atlantic we are in continual competition with the sun. The golden ball is batted forward; we return. The very passage of time is nullified.

But that this is the year 1949 – I cannot forget. In our own day – a messianic year. It bears all the indicia foretold as typical of the Great Advent. There is, first of all, the *chibut hakever* – the trundling of Jewry's cadavers, in unsanctified soil interred, through the earth's surface into Holy Land. No one will gainsay but that the transportation of the thousands of relicts of the concentration camps exemplifies this miracle in most realistic fashion.

There is also, as with me, the miracle of *kvitzas haderech* – the road condensed – the path to Jerusalem made a journey of two days instead of a forty years' wandering.

Where the 'wine preserved' is hid, and where the roast leviathan – those other felicities concomitant with the Messianic – has, alas, not yet been revealed.

1949 – *Annus Mirabilis*. The year subsequent to achievement. In all our exilic history, there has been no forty-nine as golden as this! Consider –

1849 – The year subsequent to the turbulent European revolutions. All men were soon again to be equal, and everyone soon to be endowed with a Constitution. Illusion and mirage! How soon the darkness, broken only by the lightning flash, returned to swallow up again, village and town, ghetto and slum.

1749 – Feudalism still rampant, and the Jew still battered from pillar to post. Refuges? Either the ivory towers of mysticism or the daedalean labyrinth of Talmudic legalism.

1649 – The year after Sabbatai Zvi declared himself False Messiah!

The year after Manasseh ben Israel thought to persuade Oliver Cromwell to permit the Jews entry into England. A strange argumentation, his! Seeing that the Messiah was not to come until Israel had been thoroughly dispersed to all the corners of the world, and seeing that that dispersion, save for England, was complete, and seeing that Oliver presumably adhered to this belief, it well behooved the Protector to open the doors of Britain, finalize the Diaspora, and thus hasten the Advent! Cromwell, caressing his wart, got lost in a brown study.

And 1649 – the year after the horrible pogroms perpetrated by Chmelnitzki – Jew and dog hanged from the one gibbet!

1549 – 1449 – 1349 – it is a progressive lapsing back into an ever-thickening darkness, with only here and there a flash, with its very appearance vanishing.

Only 1949 – problems and all – seems to shine with constant light. Or so, at least, it does here, in the supra-global heights.

26 August 1949

August 1st: From the Marine Airport, over New York harbour at about midnight – an edifying spectacle. Gotham and its tentacle piers floating beneath us, resplendent in its neon jewelry – fake ruby, emerald, tawdry topaz, sapphire synthetic. Considering our objective, a fitting point of departure – 'look on this picture, and then on this.'

The passengers are all Jewish (with one exception – a German-speaking Viennese returning to see her parents) – and most of them are set for Lydda. Ours is a mode of pilgrimage contemplated neither by the *Tannaim* nor by Chaucer. The only element required by tradition is the aeronautic power – x number of messianic horses.

From time to time we are fed. This is a labour not only for our hostess but also for the three or four orthodox passengers who find it difficult to reconcile themselves to the TWA menu. The compromise is always the same – eggs.

O, ungrateful tradition of our folk, annually to take hen and rooster to circle over the head, scapefowl for our sins! These deserved a happier fate, a worthier meed. Orthodox Jewry should build a statue to the hen, – in position hen accouchant – for that this bird it was that throughout the centuries of strange cuisines and alien hospitality rescued it from the hard alternative – non-kosher or starvation. Thus was every laying a laying-on of hands, and every egg a golden one!

Our first stop is at Shannon, Eire. The Israel-conscious passengers feel a warm bond of sympathy with the local people. They did it, too.

After a stop of about an hour during which we partake of much Irish courtesy but little food, listen to the Gaelic coming throaty from the loudspeaker – the girl making the plane announcements must be in constant expectation of a movie-director, her enunciation – 'Mr. Horowitz at the wicket!' is so intimate, confidential, mysterious – and hearkening to the policeman bemoaning the fate of Ulster – we proceed to Paris.

A pretty sight – the coast of France, with its land neatly parcelled off into squares, rhomboids, parallelograms, all of varying shades of green, and all pointillated with trees, singly, in clumps, in forests. A natural beginning for abstract art.

At the Paris airport engage in conversation with airport employees. Returned soldiers, and both bitter about post-war France. Was it worth while? Would it have been worse under the Germans? Yes, they would not have had liberty, but, economically – ? Detect covert sympathy for Pétain. Fear greatly that it is the American weather – together with much of its bad manners – which, passing through this station, creates the unconcealed hopeless what's-the-use resentment.

Exempla gratia: One of our passengers had bought a bottle of Chanel No. 5 – is it really Chanel No. 5? – how beautifully she would smell in the Bronx! – and the station vendor had quoted her so many francs to the dollar – the government rate. Doesn't she run over to my friend, the returned poilu, and ask him: And how much do you offer?

'Dair eez no bleck macket hiar!' he replied, curtly, very curtly. '*Ces Américaines, elles pensent que toute est vendable, même notre âme!*'

He permitted himself this liberty, because, after all, I was a Canadian. (It would happen time and again that as a Canadian I would receive special treatment, of one kind or another – treatment, on the one hand, which assumed that Canada was a forty-ninth state of the u.s., and treatment on the other hand (rare) which assumed that the u.s. was an eleventh province of the Dominion.)

Back in the plane – it is now evening – and on our way to Zurich. The Zurich airport filled me with nostalgia for the Laurentians. Mostly it is a memory of free fresh odour; didn't see much except the spick-and-span pinewood concession – tempting liquors, gayly wrapped chocolates – and twelve red umbrellas to escort the passengers from plane to rest-room – Swiss efficiency!

In the dead of night – Rome. Here meet up with both Rabbi Zambrowski and the Italian lire. The Rabbi, hearing that among my baggage were *tfillin*, greets me like a prodigal brother. Bethinking himself, however, he inquires as to whether I had the *tfillin* examined for faults and nullities. I repudiate the question. Does not the Rabbi know that such a one as I would pray in two pair of *tfillin*, Rashi's and Rabbenu Tam's?

Nonetheless, I didn't see any of the orthodox gentry don their phylacteries in the plane.

Wonder what would have happened among the TWA personnel if someone suddenly had started saying *Shachrit*! Somebody could have; we had a *minyan*.

Dawn, Tuesday: The Mediterranean – it deserves its reputation. And now the coast of Israel, brown, dry (it is the rainless season), with gentle declivities, and bounded land, and habitations. Beatific vision!

Lydda: As the plane descends upon the airfield at Lydda, I am not without recollections of the first time I had heard this name. In my student days, while conning the pages of the Tractate *Baba Bathra*. Then it was that my twelve-year-old mind encountered that of the shrewd 'merchants of Ludd' – the *tagrai Ludd* – who made quite a business out of manipulating percentages.

How changed, how altered is the personnel that now stands behind the customs wickets – everywhere courtesy, efficiency, despatch! And if you reply in Hebrew, why, that is the equivalent of seven inoculation certificates. Enter the land! And fill ye it with hope who enter here!

It is true that some of my American companions are somewhat testy at the slight delay – examination of passport, medical papers, luggage. After working one term in the u.s.a. they had expected that at least Moishe Sharett, if not David Ben-Gurion, would have come down to meet them and take them, each and every one, on a personal tour. They had laboured for a Jewish State, but hadn't realized, apparently, that this involved also customs regulations.

The men at the gate, however, are polite and patient. Is it not written that the worthies of Ludd were renowned for wisdom?

Mrs. Judith Beilin having arranged for a taxi to take me to Jerusalem – right into the Holy of Holies! – I proceed with the chauffeur, a talkative sabra. He points out the town of Ludd, formerly Arab, now occupied entirely by the new immigrants. A dispiriting spectacle – these are not houses, but blocks of stone, four walls and a roof, *succoth* in cement.

Here and there – tents. The tents have addresses!

We pass the site of a British camp. There will be many such. The British went through this country with Caesar's *Gallic Wars* for a *vade mecum*.

The hamlet of Maror – here once were Arabs. I make a joke, *Maror*, I say, is bitter. My sabra-friend enjoys it, a Passover delight.

The whole area is barren. Thorns, and no vegetation. A sycamore. Exsanguinated rock.

As we detour to avoid a destroyed bridge, the sabra announces that we are crossing Palestine's Burma road. It is almost with a professional pride that he makes this announcement – the heroism was that of chauffeurs. Foch's battle of the taxis was nothing compared to this.

On the road – Jews at work. New immigrants, a motley company. Young men, old men with beards, men with *payoth*, men bare to the waist, men in caps, hats, galabiehs. The sun beats down cruelly, but these men are at work on an artery. The road, everyone now knows, is also a weapon.

We leave the flatland, and approach and enter the hills of Judaea.

And now, in the distance, setting a thousand versicles beating through my heart – the heights of Jerusalem!

2 September 1949

Telaviviana:

1. In the hotel rooms, *mezuzoth* on every door.
2. Almost all of Tel Aviv seems to live out-doors, in the side-walk cafés. Telavivians will sit for hours sipping their *gazoz*, watching the passing throngs. To be a spectator is also a role.

This custom is the result of two factors: (a) the European tradition, (b) the housing shortage. I have a wife and two children, says a Telavivian to me, and we have but one room. Shall I spend my entire evening in that hot cubicle? His case is typical.

Hence the crowds sitting, walking, filling the streets. Tel Aviv looks like one grand Poalei Zion meeting.

3. This country is very fertile. Never saw so many barbershops.
4. The signs of Bernard Joseph's austerity are ubiquitous. No meats four days a week. Everything controlled, many things rationed. The Hebrew name for the pull-your-belt-in plan is *tzena*; the wags call the Minister – Tzenator Joseph.

Returned to Israel like a prodigal son, I had expected the fatted calf. There wasn't even a piece of veal.

But it's worth it. The people complain, but only jokingly. My fellow-Montrealer has saved the country from profiteering, the black market, and iniquity. After the Road of the Heroes, and the Negev, this is a small sacrifice, indeed.

Laughter and pride is there in Israel; there is not a belch from Dan to Beersheba.

5. The ingenuity of our folk is not exhausted. Nothing bears more telling witness to this than the imaginativeness with which commercial and industrial objects are named. An insurance company is called *Sneh* – after the bush which burned, but was not consumed. *Klipah* – a word hitherto confined to Cabbalistic treatise, signifying the gross as distinct from the ethereal, is now attributed to garbage – *nid klipah* – a nest of garbage. An ice-cream organization puns its way to custom – *kortov*, a drop, is fissioned *kor-tov*, cold and good. A talkie is *kolnoa* – sound and motion. This is also the name borne by *Screen Magazine*. *Screen Magazine* – in the language of Isaiah!

6. To judge by the names of the streets of Tel Aviv, this is the most intellectual city in the world. No squares named for ward-heelers, no streets immortalizing politicos and rentiers.

For the directory of Tel Aviv is a dictionary of national biography. Arlosoroff, Alcharizi, Herzl, Rambam, Rabbi Akiba, Baalshemtov, Graetz, Frug, Frishman, Yehoash, Smolenskin, Pinsker, Obadiah, Molkho, Micha,

Yehuda Halevi, – you can't cross an intersection but you traverse the memory of Jewish worthies, ancient and modern.

To walk through Tel Aviv is to have studied Jewish history.

7. Ben-Gurion, affectionately referred to as B.G., not only makes the laws, he appears also to set the style in male coiffeur. Must have noted about a dozen men in cafés and parks and elsewhere, with hair blanched – that is a prerequisite – combed fuzzy, tufted, and electrified.

Trees of Palestine: The cypress. It is difficult to understand why this tree has been appropriated, in so many places, for funeral purposes. Here it stands, if alone, like an index finger pointing heavenwards, – if in a line, like a group of sentinels, protective and on guard.

The eucalyptus – the water-souse, an Australian auxiliary to the reconquest of the land. Carrying water in its thousand pouches, it is the kangaroo of trees.

The palm – a one-armed headwaiter stalking over his guests.

The tamarisk – Abraham's tree, a pleasant shade.

The olive – the tree arthritic.

Wanted to see children in their natural habitat – went to the Tel Aviv Zoo. Despite the pedantic nomenclature attached to the cages, everything here throbs with an authentic and contemporaneous reality. The Bible and my childhood came to life. Behold them, the jackal and the hyena, – hitherto to me but metaphors of the prophets – dozing in a cage. The leopard and the lion and the eagle and the bear – what would the poets of the Scriptures have done without them? Upon an artificial elevation, wild goats right out of the *Canticum Canticorum*.

Nor does this zoo cater only to the grand, the solitary, the austere. The monkeys with continually embarrassed pink, very pink buttocks, make a great hit. So does the marabou, amorphous, mystical, circling ever in a round.

And for beauty – the golden pheasant, the sulphur-crested cockatoo. The soft-eyed gazelle – every glance is the beginning of a shy idyllic love affair.

These creatures have Hebrew names. The people is again returning, from ghetto, slum and camp, to an adamic intimacy – *And he called them by their names* – with Nature.

What a far cry from the urban commentaries of Rashi who did never come across the name of a bird or beast in Holy Writ but he had to make some indirect acknowledgement of unfamiliarity: X, he would say, is a *kind* of animal, Y a *kind* of bird. What bird? What animal?

Yet the experience of the zoo not altogether happy. Always, in the background, an uncomfortable parallel. I had seen it before. Only yesterday. At the camps.

There, too – confinement. There, too – signs announcing that the creatures had enough to eat, and, please, nothing further should be thrown to them. And there, too, names and registrations, appellations Hebrew and Latin and of the many tongues of the ferocious wide Diaspora.

Above all these my brothers Dov and Zev and Aryeh, now called for lions and for bears and for the stag – now all of an animal docility, homeless but domesticate. And my sisters these, some surely with faces shrewd and calculating – in the forest one yearns – and some to shame the soft-eyed gazelle for its brazenness.

What a decade! That which should have been free – caged; and that which should have been caged – the human vulpine – allowed to roam, predatory and voracious.

The pedant in me recalls that zoo is Greek for 'life,' and the Jew remembers that respect for life is of the first of the commandments.

Ten Don'ts for American Tourists:

1. Don't act as if it were you who, at a chicken-dinner in Pittsburgh, redeemed and conquered this land. Your help was appreciated, but it was merely help, that is to say, an auxiliary and not a principal force.

2. Don't stop to tell 'the natives' how you could do such and such a thing so much better in the U.S.

3. Not everybody likes to be photographed. The 'inmates,' as you call them, of refugee camps may have lost everything; they still possess, thank God, their sense of dignity, and do not wish to be treated like specimens and exhibits.

4. For goodness' sake, remember this is a State, and therefore, a conglomerate of various groups. Do not expect everyone to wear *payoth*, observe the Sabbath, and pray thrice daily, while you an American pursue your ways untrammeled by religious inhibitions. The State of Israel was not designed to be a monastery, offering up its many-voiced liturgy for the salvation of your materialistic soul.

5. Do not hail the waitress, as if she were a slave, and you a gentleman of the deep south. She is probably a graduate from Heidelberg, and could tell you a thing or two – in seven languages.

6. American currency is esteemed, but not everything is calculated in exchange values.

7. So there is no Coca Cola in the land. So what?

8. Shed your preconceived notions about the exotic. This is a modern state. Arabs, it is true, are very picturesque, so are rags, – but there are worthier things to note than a darkie on a donkey.

9. Every American is important and should be given a welcome – by the people. Moishe Sharett, however, is too busy. His concept of 'foreign affairs' does not include the entertainment of American Jews.

10. Remember, the State of Israel is but a little over a year old. It is a precious infant. Naturally, it cannot as yet compete with the aged Bronx.

One Don't for Israelis:

1. Please remember that the American Jewish tourist is *also a Jew*. He is in the country only because he is interested in the future of Israel. It's not his fault if he didn't have to go through the ordeals you went through.

Met Choneh, sunning himself in front of the Histadruth building. Who is Choneh? Who knows not Choneh knows not the clown and jester of the national renaissance. His witticisms are bandied throughout Jewry, his carefully designed insults have touched and humanized the great. No Zionist Congress was ever complete without him. Coarse of feature and heavy of build, gat-toothed and leather-skinned, it is not those which render him unique in Israel. It is his feet. They are huge, splayed, long as the Jewish exile. Primo Carnera would hide his bootsies in his presence. They are the feet of a wanderer – some day Jewry should put them at least in a discreet corner of its coat-of-arms.

Well, these feet were extended before the door of 113 Allenby Street, ready to trip up the bumptious functionaries who briefcase in hand kept entering the Histadruth building. Mr. Choneh stopped with his big toe.

His wanderings are done, he tells me. At last he has come to his resting place. He doesn't know why he deserved it – Moishe Rabbenu did not get into the Promised Land, and he, Choneh with the big feet, did! He proceeds to describe Weizmann's inauguration – the hush, the thrill, the breaking emotion. Everything, he says, wept.

He lifts the portcullis of his lip to smile his gat-toothed smile. A wonderful State, he says – with a wonderful hierarchy. First Weizmann, then Sharett, then Choneh, and only thereafter Ben-Gurion.

They say Ben-Gurion is proud. Can't be, he says. Look – and he snatches out of his pocket a snapshot – David Ben-Gurion and Choneh!

Choneh has lost weight since I last saw him a number of years ago in Montreal. It's nothing, he says, I feel healthier.

You hear, he says, a member of the Knesseth the other day asked me why I don't work. Imagine – for sixty-three years I haven't worked, and now in my old age spoil a career!

Choneh bids me convey his regards to our mutual friend Hirsh Wolofsky. Let him come to Israel, he says, Choneh will make him a name in the land.

9 September 1949

The Return:
Deafened by the wheels and pistons of the occidental civilization wherein I dwell

and have my precarious being, I had not heard, I had not caught, the sound of the Messiah's footsteps, – only from time to time – this little indeed had happened – I had thought that there had come to me from afar the tramping of multitudinous feet and the hiss and rustle of desert sands.

Nor did I recognize it for what it was, the blast of the Messiah's ram's-horn. Blast of ram's-horn it may have been, but what I had descried was only – O bitter and all-inclusive *only*! – a loud bleating of sheep, prolonged and unendurable, of sheep led in their six millions to slaughter and to silence. It was not, surely, a sound of jubilee and annunciation.

The cadavers and corpses of Jewry deceased, rolling and striving through subterranean passage, through catacomb and underground, directed all to rise a resurrection on the heights of Carmel, on the hillocks of the Negev, on the mountains of Gilboa – the whole as precisely foretold – of this I had heard only rumour and report. Mine eyes had not beheld it.

The signs and wonders of the Apocalypse of my day had passed me by.

They had been to me items in a newspaper, exclamations from a radio, strange tidings of ecstatic emissaries come from the East to stir me with the terror of Arabian nights, and move me with the trembling of an Israeli dawn. But what it had actually meant, what it had really portended, not I, nor any distant spectator, remote eavesdropper, could possibly conceive or imagine.

The *chevlai yemoth hamoshiach* – the sweat and agony of the Coming, of the Return – this too had been beyond the comprehension of all who had stood from afar, of all who had not marched or travelled or stalked the blood-soaked roads of Palestine.

For them, for us of the West, this renaissance which we had mistaken for an act of charity, had been a conception without ecstasy, a gestation without clumsiness, a parturition without pain. Its real character had escaped us. We had been omitted.

But to-day with my own eyes I was witness to his return. I saw him come, I saw him enter, I heard him welcomed.

This grace this day vouchsafed to me, wonderful and moving as it was in its visitation, had already earlier to me been heralded. I had arrived in Jerusalem on the second of August, which is to say, on the seventh day of Ab. I had timed my arrival so as to be present at the event announced to take place on the fourth of August, which is to say, the ninth day of Ab, day of memorial for the destruction of the Temples. It would have been indeed an apt conjuncture. It would have been a coincidence such as had found favour in the eyes of the Talmudists who in their vision of the fitness of things had seen the Messiah as being born on this ninth day of Ab.

But something had happened, something had failed to happen. The event was postponed to the tenth of August, that is to say, to a day during the Week of Consolation. It did not take place. The event – delayed not one day, nor one week, but two score and five years – finally transpired. And I witnessed it.

The mortal remains of Benjamin Zeev Herzl now lie in state in the Knesseth Circle in the city of Tel Aviv, Israel. To-morrow they shall be brought to their last, their much-desired resting place in Beit Vegan, an eminence upon the outskirts of Jerusalem. They have been disinterred from the cemetery at Vienna, where so short a time ago the goose-stepping monsters of our age, lorded it over our people, and they have been brought in an El Al plane to Lydda, air-port in Israel, thence convoyed to Tel Aviv, metropolis in Israel, and to-morrow are to be taken to Jerusalem, Israel's capital.

The mausoleum in which he is destined at length to rest was the first of the holy places I saw in the Holy Land. I saw it by moonlight, and the happening thereof was thus. After two nights and a day without sleep in the transmigrating plane, I came to Jerusalem at about noon of the second of August. I was hungry for the sights and visions and revelations of the land of my pilgrimage, I would have hurried from shrine to shrine to partake of their halidom – was loth to waste a moment lest I overlook some miracle, ancient or modern, – O that I might swallow it all with my eyes, at once, and forever! But the flesh is weak, and – tell it not in Gath! – I fell asleep. My very first day in Israel – and I fell asleep! I had waited forty years for this, for this I had journeyed thousands of miles, and when at last I had come to sojourn a while in this my spiritual oasis, – I fell asleep! My fathers before me, men of fasts and vigils, yes, and here my brothers contemporary, heroes of sieges and forced marches, were made, surely, of sterner stuff.

I slept; and when Major A. Friedgut came to the Eden Hotel – aggravation of the offence: to slumber in Eden! – at three o'clock in the afternoon, he found me dead to the world, dead to all things sacred *and* profane. He had thought to accomplish a rousing; he found he was challenged by a resurrection. He desisted, and left me to my dreamless slumber. He returned at seven, and woke me.

So passed my first afternoon in Jerusalem. It was shameful. And yet, as I was later to discover, it was symbolically, mystically right. This is a land of awakening; the appreciation of that awakening ought properly to be preluded by a sleep. I had certainly preluded it.

It was twilight, and we drove through the New City and through the outskirts of Jerusalem. Below us lay the Old City, its roofs, its towers, its domes, still in the hands of the enemy. In the distance we descried the buildings of the Hebrew University, access to which had been made impossible by the enemy. In another direction there extended the vista to the Dead Sea; the enemy still held it. As we passed through areas of bullet-pocked buildings, through streets still tangled with barbed-wire, the Major pointed out to me scene after fighting scene; here seven had been killed, here a little victory had been won, here one alone defended, surrounded and against odds.

These scenes, these memories were a fitting introduction to the place where we finally stopped and lingered – site of the tomb of Herzl, still under construction. A great full moon shone in the heaven, not a romantic moon, not a moon such as those overgrown oranges imagined by writers of love-lyrics, but a moon sublime, a great bronze gong waiting to be struck.

The site was upon an eminence, a mountain-top, Judaea's topmost mountain, and it commanded the entire panorama. As yet it was a cenotaph, an empty sepulchre awaiting its guest. Soon, in but a fortnight, it would be the royal though sombre couch of him who, amidst the tatters and rags of his people, had preserved the dream of his people's inalienable majesty. In his life-time, and after, that dream had been broken and nightmared; he himself, at the age of forty, had died, a broken-hearted man, a pillar shattered; and now, on the heights of Beit Vegan, the pillars of the mausoleum rose in posthumous vindication and embrace.

We stood in silence upon that height, our thoughts grappling with justice and history.

I thought of tombs and resurrections. I thought of Rachel's tomb, Rachel lamenting her children's bitter fate, and of her tomb still in enemy hands. I thought also of that other sepulchre, emptied on the third day, and of how much good and how much evil it had brought to the world. I thought of them all, the many tombs and cairns with which this country was covered and of how the memory of the saints and sages whom they hid had kindled the minds of men for generations. Yet all of these tombs, instead of being merely mementos of death, had been somehow, had been above all, signposts for life. Surely in this land always had there come out of the lion's fell – sweetness, and out of the very tomb – life and light.

And now Tel Aviv is greeting its mentor and true architect. Three days ago a delegation had left for Vienna to disinter the relics of the Herzl family and to bring them to Altneuland. The plane bearing this cherished freight has now returned. It brought with it the prince of Israel and his kin; it brought also, in his coffin enclosed, a scroll issued by the Jewish worthies of his native city explaining the circumstances under which the transfer of the bones of Herzl was made from Vienna, 'barracks of the Xth legion, destroyers of Jerusalem, to the State which saw his dream fulfilled.' Alas, this finely phrased scroll was pre-pared, not by the worthies of Vienna, but by a member of the Israeli delegation; the leaders of the Viennese community, most of whom had been 'concentrated' in Theresienstadt, knew no Hebrew, and only with difficulty signed their names in that script.

But the composition of the escort atones for these tragic diminutions. Standing watch over the body of Herzl is David Remez, he of the felicitous name, who represents the Government of Israel; with him is Izhak Gruenbaum, valiant fighter for Zion; the Army of Israel, *Giborai Yisroel*, is there in the person of Aluf Yosef Avidoar; there are the uniforms of the infantry and the artillery, the navy and the airforce; and holding the plane up, as if with their breath, the congregated masses of Jewry watching from the shores of Israel. Over Haifa a fighter escort rose to meet the incoming air-craft; it circled thrice; and below in the harbour, the guns of the Israeli navy fired their salvo.

And now Tel Aviv in its tens of thousands greets the last of the *oylim*, who was the first. There are no salvos here, no shouting, no, and no mourning, but only a still small voice, uttering many languages, the languages of the *Galuth* giving the greeting of redemption. This is not a funeral but a reintegration, there is no sadness; this is not a triumph – O that it had been that the man had come alive, bearing with honour his four-score and five years! – not a triumph, but a vindication; there is everywhere solemnity and the knowledge that right has come into its own; there are tears, but pride, not softness shed them; there is, above all, thanksgiving.

One of the last of the *oylim*! But a week ago I had seen a camp of fifteen thousand new immigrants, dwelling in tents, living in the open, their bag and baggage unpacked and scattered in heaps, in corners, and the immigrants themselves, refugees of a decade of homelessness, waiting, waiting. To this camp they had come from many parts, from different countries; they spoke varying tongues, they had customs unlike; and I thought as I beheld this debris, material and human, this wreckage of hearts once warm and domestic, that a great wind, a furious tempest it had been that had taken them, whirling and swirling aloft in the ether, them and their children and their pitiable impedimenta, a pell-mell confusion, Ashkenazi and Sephardi, of refined and uncouth, from the five continents and the seven seas, and had carried them helpless in its hold, through the air, suspended and afraid, at last to drop them, in confusion pell-mell, here upon the coast of Haifa. No wonder, then, that the thousands who had known this experience now stood to welcome the latest flotsam of the air, the latest of the storm-tossed *oylim*, to welcome and to offer up their silent thanks to the man who had been signator of all their passports, the author of the Idea that had become their Home.

To-morrow the cortege of cars will wend its way to Jerusalem over the road which this past year won itself its new, its immortal name – the Road of Heroes. I should have liked to be of that cortege and to have followed the coffin to its destined terminus, but other Jewries call me, in the ghettoes of Europe and in the mellahs of Morocco there are other *oylim* to be visited.

Hail, and farewell, then, O Prince of Israel! May the earth rest lightly, now at last, upon your bones! The wanderings are over, and over even the temporary sojourn in Austrian soil. You have deserved well of your people, and at length you have been granted what even to Moses was not granted – to rest, a king of the kings of Israel and Judah, in the Promised Land! You are yourself the fulfilment of Ezekiel's prophecy – have not the bones come to life? is not a new breath breathed into the body of this people?

Rest well, rest easy, O Seer of Visions, Master of Fulfilments! To the high places of Israel are you lifted up to dwell in the heart and pinnacle of Hierosolyma the Splendid, Jerusalem the New! The hills of Judaea kneel before you, the plains lie prostrate before your coming! For all of us, and in especial for my generation you dreamed a dream, it was a truth, and now you lie in its midst. Farewell, Majesty and Master of my days! I go, your word upon my lips ...

I shall not be to-morrow night upon the eminence of Beit Vegan. Whether the moon will shine upon it as it did that first night, I do not know. I know only that the great bronze gong has sounded.

16 September 1949

In Casablanca, which is of the Sultanate of Morocco, which is a Protectorate of the Republic of France, which is of the civilized world, – there is a mellah. The word, not being current in the vocabularies of the West, it should be explained; described, described in its utter and abysmal unspeakableness, it cannot be. A mellah, then, is a ghetto – not a metaphorical ghetto: the neighborhood which is the result of Jewish gregariousness, but a literal ghetto, a ghetto established, a ghetto by law ordained. It is true that in Casablanca the gates of this ghetto have been thrown open; it is no longer the prison which its Arab architects designed it to be; but, since its denizens have not the means – the paltry means – to issue from the stench and ordure of its narrow alleys and waterless habitations, a place of confinement it still remains.

I visited the mellah of Casablanca. Perhaps 'visit' is not the proper verb; it was not a social call I was making; indeed, as it turned out, it was an ordeal which I had invited. But I had heard so much of the exodus of the Moroccan Jews into Israel; some, in fact, I had met in the D.P. camps at Marseilles; an evening with them I had spent at Ain Hakerem, outside Jerusalem, speaking an Hebrew so peppered with French it would have warmed the heart of Rashi, – that now I desired to see them in their habitat, their un-natural habitat.

I expected, of course, to see things colourful, oriental, exotic – did not the guidebook enjoin all visitors to journey to the mellah for that it was *très pittoresque?* – but sights such as afflicted my eyes I had never in my wildest imaginings anticipated. It was a sunny day, yet cool; before us, as we stepped out of the Ambassador Hotel, there extended the pleasant palm-sentinelled esplanades of Casa; behind, the Atlantic lay calm and blue, a scarf flung from the Americas. The streets we traversed were comely streets, wide and handsome, with good-looking store-fronts, here and there a monument to French military prowess, and, breaking the skyline, several tall buildings, symbol of Casablanca's modernity. Then, suddenly, across a boulevard upon which there fronted a most up-to-date hotel, suddenly, behind wooden walls such as those upon which posters are posted, we came upon, we entered, we slid into the mellah.

And it was, indeed, a sliding, – a literal sliding, for the narrow lanes were thick with slime and offal, and an emotional sliding, for in a moment we knew that the twentieth century was behind us – in the hotel across the boulevard? – behind us, and we were descending into the sixteenth, fifteenth, twelfth, eleventh centuries. The streets, narrow and mounting, descending and serpentine, pullulated with creatures shaped in the image of man. Everywhere poverty wore its hundred costumes, more varied, surely, than the wardrobes of the rich – tatters of red and tatters of yellow, rags shredded and rags pieced, patched, and holes showing the swarthy skin – the badge of our common humanity. House leaned upon house, but most of the people seemed to dwell in the open, the tailor sitting, his feet under him, upon the cobblestones; the housewife caressing a vegetable; the aged and the blind – upon so sunny a day so many blind! – reclining against a wall, waiting for to-morrow against a wall to recline. Up and down the streets – a water-carrier, of whom I noted only the picturesqueness, not the social importance.

As we made our way with difficulty through the congested thoroughfares, avoiding a body here, evading a donkey there, we were everywhere beset – by hands! Wherever we turned – hands! It was, in truth, like one of those drawings of Gustave Doré's in which the despair of the Inferno rises from the depths in a foam and clamour of hands, hands snatching at straw, at air, at anything. It was a population all of beggars compact! This – this was the civic gesture – the outstretched palm, the five-fingered plea!

Over the protests of my guide, who informed me that if I began there was no end to this thing, I distributed the largess of some Morrocan pennies, and made to go on my way. I could not go on my way, for there before me, at my feet was this poor creature, blessing me with all the blessings which the richness of his imagination and the poverty of his state commanded, salaaming before me, hitting his forehead thrice to the ground – an oriental obeisance. Pity seared my heart, and embarrassment; I had not realized the meaning of his abasements until they were over, and a human, a Jew, had to me all unworthy bowed down.

I hastened on my way; it is a figure of speech, this hastening. For through the streets of the mellah one does not hasten – in these narrow confines twenty-five thousand Jews live and have their being. One battles one's way through this mess of suspended animation, through these outstretched palms of petition. All the time, of course, one must be careful of one's footstep; there is commerce – yes, commerce – and the refuse of commerce in the streets. Here, behind this veil of flies is a butcher; he has one piece of liver to sell; he stands before it, fanning it; the flies are his only customers. Yonder, his competitor does better; he sells tripe. Fish are for sale to-day, too, and through their own fishiness proclaim it. Upon the cobbles of the street, everywhere, the marks of trade – a gut, a fish too rotten, green leaves, and signs of the donkey's passage.

Yet the commodities are but the emphasis of poverty, not its negation. They are mementos of food, not food, tokens of the great lack which everywhere gnaws at the hungry maw of the mellah of Casablanca. Have not the civil authorities of this great city some solution to the crying and shameful problem? They have – a slogan and a policy. *Supprimer la mendicité* – abolish the art of begging. Not poverty, not sordidness, congestion, dirt, not these are to be abolished, but begging. It hurts the self-pride of the worthies of Casablanca, it makes a bad impression upon the tourists – *supprimer la mendicité*.

But hunger is greater than slogans or policies. Behold a beggar-woman, at high noon, in the open street. She is one of a company of beggars, yet she is unique. Not unique in that she is blind and deaf, there are many such; not even unique in that she has an assistant, blindness compels such organization; but unique in the place in which she lives. She has no home, but here, at the side of a home, there is a kennel. In it her assistant places her, and withdraws, as circumstances require.

Très pittoresque. Surely, I say to myself, this cannot be reality. Some magician out of the Arabian Nights' Entertainments must have ensorcelled me, me in the comfort of the Ambassador Hotel, to bring me, by some malicious open sesame, into this lurid nightmare. It is August of the year 1949, and these scenes do not belong to that date! This is Casablanca, possession of a republic which proclaimed equality and fraternity, and these relationships, this mendicancy surely, is not of that picture. Not otherwise but I dream, or I imagine, or some Hollywood producers are setting a set for some historic film, very picturesque. It can't be real.

It is. You have but to breathe to know that it is. The stench!

23 September 1949

The odour of the centuries hovers over the mellah, and will not dissipate. Not all the breezes of the Atlantic blowing nearby have yet effected its purification. It is an odour palpable and ubiquitous. Escaping therefrom there is not; flight into a side-alley but changes the intensity, not the nature thereof. It is an odour of nuances, an odour, also, of thick heavy undertones. Only occasionally – as when upon the air there are wafted some few motes of the pulver of spices (what are these spices of the mellah for? To spice hunger? To disguise the fetid?), only then is there subtlety for the nostrils; all otherwise is reek and miasma. The fish-heads scattered beneath the booths give off their peculiar smell; the viands, too, send up their intimations of ptomaine; there is a touch of the rancidity of dairies; garbage and refuse steam mephitic at one's feet. Through this fanfare of stenches, it is only the very sensitive who can distinguish the contribution of the dead cat, putrescent in the sun. Yet it is not a composition without a theme – again and again, in the intervals between the abatement of one rankness and the rise of another, there is sensed, with a revulsion insufferable, the major offensiveness. It is that of ordure and dregs. There is no water in the mellah. There is no system of sanitation. The mellah's alleys are its cloaca. Decades of digestion raise their disgust through the streets. It is a nethermost ring of the inferno through which we walk, shattering in its grossness, destructive of all thought and reaction save those of nausea and pity.

One turned aside to be for a while sick against a wall.

After recovery, there comes the reflection horrible: for thousands this is no temporary ordeal, but their constant element! Across the boulevard from the mellah there are sumptuous hotels, with hot and cold running water, gallons and gallons of it, and here – for the lack of a pipe and drains and the most primitive provisions for cleanliness these are the abominations of most emetic hell. One is set to wondering whether all this, even under the enlightened French Government, is not the result of design rather than of helplessness, – the desire to establish, so that the exploited may be content, a helotry even more exploited than they, – the desire to maintain the triple hierarchy: the bureaucracy of the colonial metropole; the illusory sub-élite of the Arab medina; the untouchables of the mellah!

It is true that the new rulers of Morocco have had to cope with the ingrained prejudices of the local population. For centuries under their Moslem masters, the Jews of Morocco have been deprived, not only of civil, but of ordinary human rights. No Jew was allowed to walk on the sidewalk as an Arab passed; no Jew was permitted to ride so noble an animal as a horse; no Jew could testify against his Arab opponent. Even the clothes which the Moroccan Jews wore was determined as to its colour by their oppressors – black, not white. To this day, despite their common swarthiness, one can distinguish Jew from Arab by mere glance at his headgear: a black skullcap is a Jew. Nor were these discriminations imposed from above; they constituted then, as in some measure, they still constitute now, part and parcel of the fabric of Moslem thought. In many quarters when a Moslem feels constrained to bring the word Jew into his conversation, he apologizes therefor, – as if it were a piece of pornography.

It cannot be stated that things have changed much since the days of these despotic discriminations. The present rulers have yet to bring their national emancipation to their 'protégés.' The France of Chanel No. 5 is not the France of the Mellah No. 1.

As we continued upon our staggering course through Casablanca's slum of slums, many were the questions which rose in the mind, as if they were internal fumes to harmonize with the odours all about us. What, we wondered, what did the leaders of western civilization, Messrs. Roosevelt and Churchill, when *they* were last here to bring to the world the evangel of the four freedoms, what did they think of the mellah of Casablanca? Did they get around to it? Or did they prefer to live in the pure empyrean of their lofty aspirations, removed from and undistracted by the grosser imperatives of the mellah? Did they really consider these twenty-five thousand human beings as so many irrelevancies, foreign to their declarations of human rights?

No one knows the explicit answer to these questions. The fact, however, that in the year 1949, the mellah, like some disease, still rages unabated, is answer sufficient.

Another question which presented itself as one trod gingerly amidst this population, was: Are these really Jews? It was not their complexion – it is but dark, not black – which prompted the query – it was their attitude. Not elsewhere had I encountered such resignation, such mystical acquiescence in the hard decrees of fate. I soon realized, however, that my experience had been confined to western Jewries; this made a double-fold difference. In the first place, democracy, no matter how limited, brings to all who find themselves within its circumference, a desire for progress, change, advancement. To speak of the concepts of democracy as one speaks of the Jews of Casablanca is, of course, to speak of concepts stranger to each other. And in the second place – the vital difference – the Jews of Morocco are, like the culture (sic) in the midst of which they live, fatalists. How, I asked my guide in my naiveté, how do they continue to endure this life? Has not their wretchedness reached the breaking point?

'By no means,' answered the local citizen who had kindly consented to escort me through the harrowing hell. 'By no means. It never can reach it. They have a philosophy. Ask them and they will answer you: Katoob! It is written. It is written that the one should be a prince and the other a pauper. There is nothing to do about it. It is the will of God.'

Katoob! It is written. I would have preferred to have seen the document.

They are dark – Regard me not, say the Canticles, for that I am black, for the sun hath burned me – they are dark, and they are Jews. Not upstart Jews, nor converted ones, but Jews, the descendants of the Hebrew hidalgos and dons of the Golden Age of Spain. Once their forefathers were indeed princes, that now are paupers. Once the cities of Morocco and Fez and Tetuan were renowned in Jewry, – seats of learning, and birthplaces of scholars remembered. Now their progeny is reduced to begging, and their children the victims of unnecessary disease and early death. There are no real statistics in Casablanca, but from the registers of births and the records of the synagogues it can be gleaned that only half the numbers of young Jews who are circumcised reach the age of Bar-Mitzva. Trachoma takes its toll, blinding and killing; ringworm of the scalp brings to the youth of the ghetto itches and scabs and baldness; tuberculosis is its annihilating pestilence. Yet the sires of these were once the flower and glory of our people.

Casablanca, I was told, was, in its treatment of Jews, not unique. The plight of Jews in the interior, who eke out their living through work for poor Arab farmers – the serfs of serfs – is even worse. I didn't go down to see them. I had seen enough in Casa, and as for the rural status of Moslem's Jewry, it was enough for one to know that the synagogues of the villages consisted of a hut where the *Ner Tomid* was some tallow stuck in a beer-bottle.

30 September 1949

From such lofty estate – scions of some of the noblest of our genealogies – have fallen the Jews of the mellahs of North Africa. Reduced to-day to an almost incredible primitiveness, they are the untouchables of their society. It were indeed a picture of dark African despair were it not for the new trends, new movements, which, like some fresh salubrious breezes, have begun to agitate the flower of Moroccan youth.

For the tale of the establishment of a Jewish State has come to them, young and old alike, as if it were a market-rumour of the coming of a personal Messiah. The old, exhausted and forespent, are content to continue their sitting in the cobbled alleys of the mellah, waiting for the Messiah to come riding into their midst upon his white donkey; the young would go out to meet him. One evening at Ain Hakerem, near Jerusalem, I sat with some of these Casablancans, they were a fine lot, who despite their lonesomeness for *auld lang syne* (Baudelaire would have called it *la nostalgie de la boue*) were heart and soul and song for the new land. Others I encountered at the penultimate place, at Marseilles, where confined in camps they were receiving preparation to fit them for their new life in Israel.

Here, at Marseilles, on the *Côte d'Azur* – the sea and the sea's foam, the sky and its clouds, both made Israeli flags for them – I saw them as they really are, as God made them before the Arab tyrant unmade. It is true that vestiges of their sub-level upbringing still remained: little Moroccan children, when first given soap, do in their ignorance of its uses, cut it up and try to eat it; the same, when provided with beds to sleep in, run to lie *under* them, upon the hard floor, their accustomed couch. But gradually lifted up to the standard of the civilization of which they have been forcibly deprived – fatalists are fatalists about getting accustomed to good things, too – they stand forth from yesterday's disabilities and rags, a virile and splendiferous youth. Many are handsome with a handsomeness unknown to the denizens of the European ghettoes; they regain, by mere transplantation, their Sephardi dignity, and once entered into an Israeli community they are – save for their personal distinction – indistinguishable from the generality of Jewdom.

It is true that some of the Moroccan emigrants in Israel have turned out to be problem children. Certainly they cannot compare, either in ideology or in know-how, to the *chalutzim* of the earlier *aliyoth* or the refugees of the later. Moreover, many of their mellah habits, difficult to abandon, do not belong in the new Jewish State. But these are defects which must be regarded as merely temporary, they will vanish with time; reconstructed Israel will its Israelis reconstruct.

The Yemenites

Some day the whole story – Operation Magic Carpet – will be written, and the world will learn of one of the most exciting and elevating chapters in the tale of the ingathering of Israel. It will tell of the depressed plight of the Jewry of Yemen, of its dwelling in that land for centuries – it is one of the oldest Jewries in the world – of the abominable devices which its oppressors practised upon it, of its hearing of the news of the establishment of the State of Israel, of the JDC come to the camp outside Aden whither the Yemenites had by stealthy marches fled, of their transportation in planes – an eight hours' journey over the Arabian desert – and of their final arrival in Holy Land.

It is indeed a beatific vision to see these Yemenites descend from the JDC plane upon the sacred soil. Years of oppression have dwindled them in size; a plane which should hold forty persons carries about one hundred Yemenites; they issue, the little dark men, from the magic carpet which was their transport (in more than one sense) and fall to the ground, and kiss it. This is for them a great fulfilment – answer to prayers, inauguration of a great new age. They rise from their embrace of the dust of their languishing, and turn to their guide, and ask: Where lives here the Messiah?

It is such emotions that the Yemenites bring to their new sanctuary. Everything for them in this difficult land is therefore easy, acceptable, and most pleasing. They in their very smallness are Israel's labourers, its stevedores, its warehousemen, its newsies; they do not complain for the sweat that runs down their faces: it is as the dew of Hermon. Tel Aviv has small miniature elevators; it is the Yemenites who operate them; they are the only ones who can turn about in them. To Jews who in Yemen were not permitted to dwell in houses higher than the single story, this occupation is not merely a trade; it is a consummation.

If the Moroccans are handsome, the Yemenites are beautiful. For they have a delicacy, a refinement of feature, a lightness of movement not elsewhere seen in the land. They all look like paintings of the east; as they walk down in the streets, the Bible comes alive.

Indeed, one of the first sights I beheld in Tel Aviv was the Yemenite Jew walking one Sabbath morning his way to the synagogue, his wife at his side. He was arrayed in white, colour prohibited to him in Yemen, and he paced his way to the Holy House with dignity, a prince about to enter his palace. At his side, his wife, like a princess, pride and piety in her face commingled. The Yemenite walked, not as if he trod upon a place which had given him sanctuary, but upon his ancestral heritage; and upon his countenance there was a look which assumed that the years of exile had not been, and that this, the year 1949, was but the year after the reign of King Solomon.

If you would see vividly the continuity of Israel, go see the Yemenite on his way to his worship in the land of his desire.

7 October 1949

Safed
Though Safed is counted as of the cities of the State of Israel, it is really of a realm all its own; it is of this world – otherworldly. It is true that with the arrival of the new immigrants from the European camps there have been introduced into the old cabbalistic atmosphere, which endues this townlet as with a *tallis*, some strange incongruous modern elements – a stone's throw from the Synagogue of the Great Ari there is a shop which announces its wares as *chic* – right in the very centre of mysticism, women's cosmetics are in windows wantonly displayed – but these things are as nothing. The total ambience nullifies them. Clouds of history rest upon this mountain; cumuli of cabbala float in its sky. The knick-knacks and quiddities of twentieth-century merchandising are as if they were not.

Nowhere, not even in Jerusalem the Holy, is the heavy mood of religion as pervasive as it is in this – one of God's minor metropolises. The heart of the Galilee, it beats among its altitudes; it is an eminence in a landscape from of old designed and intended for divine communings. One has but to pass through this country – its sultry valleys, its cool mountains – one has but to pierce this shimmering atmosphere – an atmosphere of such fabric made it appear but a veil flung upon earth to hide the Lord's countenance from mortal sight – one has but to breath the alternating airs of wrathful heat and coolth compassionate – to catch a glimpse of the wherefore of this country's abundance of prophets, seers, and mystics. It was not an empty boast that the Cabbalists uttered when they declared, in language unusually forthright: 'Whoever lives in Safed has an advantage over him who dwells elsewhere in Palestine – Safed is auspicious for probing the deepest mysteries of the Torah.'

For Safed was ever a place of illuminations, illuminations not only such as those which light up in the soul, but illuminations also literal, conflagrative. Here in ancient time, when the calendar was as yet a mystery from the uninitiate concealed, it was Safed which announced to the land its new moons and its feasts; here upon the hills round about were kindled those vast beacons whose fires proclaimed to the length and breadth of the country that the Academy was announcing as pending a holy day, or a waxing of the moon as imminent. Thus for the fires and constellations of the heavens, Safed set upon earth its own fires and constellations. And so, thereafter, has it continued.

Is not Safed, indeed, the burying place of the author of Time's brightest illumination – the Zohar? Is not Rabbi Simon ben Yochai – he who spake with angels and out of such conversations fashioned his Brightness – is he not Safed's halidom, the special sanctum of its pilgrimages? Let the scoffers scoff who proclaim the Zohar a forgery, and Rabbi Simon ben Yochai as the forger's *nom-de-plume* – holy thoughts ever provoked the tauntings of the profane – but Safed knows its own.

Its own – What noble and inspiring names there are which are forever bound to Safed's name! That of Rabbi Joseph Caro – he who with wisdom carpentered for all Israel its *Shulchan Aruch*, its *Prepared Table*; and that of Rabbbi Isaac Luria, known as Adonenu Rabbi Izhak, initialled ARI, which is to say, in holy speech, the Lion. I did make a pilgrimage to the synagogue in Safed, dubbed the Synagogue of the Ari. It is no magnificent edifice, bursting with wealth of prelacy; it is a humble house; a place of worship such as one finds in the poorer quarters of Jewry. It was high noon when I entered it, I had expected to find it deserted; instead I intruded upon a scene which , I suspected, had been static against that background for centuries. The young boy, no more than eleven, holding his heavy tome, the Tractate *Baba Kama*, might have been there as of the sixteenth century, forever unaging in the study of the Torah which is Life; and the old venerable sage, bearded like antiquity itself, conning his own sacred book – a book of piety – I took as a sort of proleptic figure, an image of the boy an era hence. Surely they were not of this world; history with its many chariots might pass them by; the boy stood rapt in the analysis of some complicated Tosfoth, the old man engaged in seeking blear-eyed to peer behind the mysteries of the *Pamalyah shel Malah*. They were not only not of Israel, they were not even of this globe, but transcendent with immortal longings, seraphic with nostalgia for the Shechinah.

It was a vision not without its contagion, even upon one immunized by western scepticism and twentieth-century hard-boiledness. I issued from the cool shadowed synagogue into the bright sun of Safed, and then took my way along Safed's tortuous streets, its cool stepped alleys. It was noon, and the street was empty, but suddenly there murmured through my head an old and cherished melody, – the melody of *L'cho doidi*, the song of Sabbath greeting. It was here, here in Safed, that Rabbi Solomon Halevi Alkabez, from the very darkness of the sixteenth century, composed its words of hope and consolation. The day was not the Sabbath; the memory of music had come unsolicited, through association's twin compulsion. It was a felicitous memory, for it worked in me also recollection of my departed father – may he rest in a Paradise of eternal Zohar! – with whom, as a boy, I had faithfully gone to the synagogue every Friday night, and sang, in antiphony, the sweet stanzas of *L'cho doidi*. Then I had thought them to be a poem in praise of the Sabbath, the Sabbath royal as opposed to the week-days servile and profane. But now the words regained their original significance; now, indeed, to me came from the rebuilt places of Israel, its colonies and its cities, the words of Rabbi Solomon Halevi Alkabez, uttered in the darkness of his century, at once a prophecy and its fulfilment:

> O site most kingly, O royal sanctum,
> Arise, go forth, from among your ruins!
> Enough your sitting in the vale of sorrow!
> The Lord has readied His compassion.
>
> Bestir you from your dust; array you
> By grace of David, son of Jesse
> In this my people's beauteous garment!
> My soul, it knows redemption nearing.
>
> Arise! Arise! Arise and waken!
> For it has come at length, the dawning!
> Lift up your voice your song to utter.
> For on you is revealed God's glory.

I returned to the bus which had brought me to the sanctuary of Safed. As we left its precincts, the chauffeur pointed out to us in the distance a high hill whose top rock-formation had by nature been hollowed out into the shape of a seat. 'That,' said the chauffeur, 'is called by the Cabbalists *Messiah's Throne*. It is not known,' added the member of the transport co-operative, 'whether Ben-Gurion will take his seat upon it, or no.'

14 October 1949

It manifests itself everywhere in Israel. People of the most cynical temperaments speak of miracles as if these had become natural phenomena. You would say indeed that when the Lord returned the captivity to Zion, they were as dreamers. Yemenites issued out of the inferno of the Crater at Aden and professors graduate of the most distinguished universities of Europe, both alike have made the word 'miracle' as commonplace in their conversations as 'Good day.'

Yet this credulity, if so you would please to term it, is not surprising. Most of the inhabitants of Israel have themselves been witness to one of the most outstanding miracles of our time – the same era which saw them in danger of complete annihilation found them also citizens of the first Jewish state in two thousand years of troubled history. For them in truth it was as if the furnace of fire had been providentially opened and they had walked out into the cool open air; for them in truth it is as if the graves had been uncovered and they had issued therefrom alive.

To this miracle of the brands plucked from the burning there is added the miracle of David slaying Goliath. During the recent war, all the odds were against the Israelis; by all military calculations, they should have lost. Against forty million Arabs incited towards a jehad, they were but 750,000. Against the cabal and conspiracy of a Pan-Arabism involving Egypt, Syria, Lebanon, Yemen, and Transjordan, they were but sole and alone, and struggling to be born. And against the accumulated arsenals of the Moslem states, the Haganah opposed but smuggled arms and emergency equipment. Yet the Israelis won.

To me the secretary of the Jewish Agency ventured an explanation. The Jews, he said, won for two reasons – a natural one, and a miraculous one. The natural reason was that God was on the side of the Israelis, as was to be expected … The miraculous one was that Jews, after two millenia of *sholom aleichem* pacifism, had learned to shoot, and to shoot straight …

A similar obsession with the marvellous I encountered in the very precincts of the Israeli Foreign Office. Here one would expect hardness and not sentimentality, mathematical calculations and not pious naivetés; the personnel of the Foreign Office comes largely from what may be termed the Holy Land equivalent of Missouri. Yet here, too, one of the diplomats of the new state permitted himself to say that 'if in the Foreign Office we did not believe in miracles – we would not be realists …'

One of the wits of Tel Aviv went so far as to affirm that in the very interests of economy, miracles were to be expected. 'If the Lord,' said he, 'can get by with a miracle, why should he incur additional expenses?'

These were quotations, I must admit, which struck me as propaganda slogans rather than realistic estimates. I could appreciate the readiness which prompted them, yet I felt that they were explanations much too easy. I could not understand them. It was only when I went through the land itself that I began to see the *physical* vestiges of these recent miracles.

I stood in Jaffa. Once this city had a population of 80,000 Arabs. There were none there now, none to speak of. The city was largely inhabited by recent arrivals. The mere military gesture of the Haganah had caused these Arabs to flee in panic. Jaffa, I remembered, was the place where the whale swallowed Jonah. Now, I realized, Jonah had swallowed the whale.

I stood outside the ramparts of Acre. They were formidable walls, yawning moats, threatening battlements. This was the city which the great Napoleon had besieged; here he had waited for the city to surrender, and hence he had gone empty-handed away. But the Haganah took Acre in three days.

I was at Haifa, and beheld the ruins of the Arab section. All about me there extended the plains of Zebulun, scene of the mighty exploits of Deborah. The accents of her song echoed again through my mind: *They fought from heaven;*

the stars in their courses fought against Sisera ... The river of Kishon swept them away, that ancient river, the river Kishon ... O my soul, thou hast trodden down strength.

I journeyed to Beth Eshel, which is beyond Beersheba, and named after Abraham's tamarisk. There I examined the underground dugouts in which the heroes of the Negev withstood the siege of the invading Arabs. By all military prognostications, they should have been crushed and buried in the catacombs. They weren't; they issued victorious, flaunting their new-grown beards.

Also in Safed, city of miracles, I received report of the miraculous. Two thousand Jews had overcome twelve thousand Arabs. The fighting had taken place during a thunderstorm, one of those heavy turbulent tempests which frequently rage over the mountains of Galilee. Lightning flashed. Rumbled the thunder. In the morning the Arabs were gone. A rumour had spread through their camp that the Jews had use of the atomic bomb! Sinai's thunder become Safed's!

All this, I said in my disbelieving occidentalism, all this is very well; but really, really I would give a portion of my share in the world to come – my share in this world would not be very tempting – if I could get some reason which would rest upon foundations other than miraculous.

Such an explication I finally obtained. It came from the most realistic of the vocations of Israel – the taxi-driver's. These are people who go everywhere, they see everybody; acceleration is their second nature. Said my cicerone on the road from Tel Aviv to Haifa: We won because we had no alternative. *Ain brairah.* The Arabs could always go back to where they came from – to Egypt, to Transjordan. The Israelis could only go back – to the sea! There was no alternative. We had to win. Desperation was our general!

It was realism that my chauffeur was selling me, but a realism which belonged to the realm of the supernatural. It might be grimly comforting to be led by General Desperation, but that General did not always win. Yes, even when couched in pseudo-realistic language, the twentieth century superstition of the land betrayed itself. It betrayed itself in the speech of the European newcomers; in the speech of the Yemenites its revelation was no betrayal but a basic premise. To them current history was a truly biblic ingathering. Indeed they could conceive of it in no other fashion. For theirs was a tale told of the Arabian Nights – did not the JDC dub its Yemenite activities as Operation Magic Carpet? – a tale of the old marvellous genre in which a people, yea even the Jews of Yemen, are lifted up in the air upon a carpet fashioned of aluminum, lifted up out of the twelfth century and from a remoteness of fourteen hundred air-miles from Israel, and dropped, after a passage of but eight hours' duration, right into the midst of the world's newest republic, right into the heart of the twentieth century!

What is the diminutive of miracles? For these are but minor wonders compared to the greatest wonder of the age – the fact that precisely at that moment in history when European Jewry stood under threat of complete annihilation, at that moment it is that the State of Israel is established! 'Behold I will open your graves,' said the prophet, 'and cause you to come out of your graves!' That prophecy is fulfilled. Out of the very darkness, illumination came forth.

In Hebrew the same consonants NS spell both the word for miracle and the word for banner. It is a happy coincidence. The miraculous is, indeed, Israel's contemporary banner.

21 October 1949

They call it *shlilath ha-galuth*, the negation of the Diaspora. The protagonists of this philosophy, if philosophy it can be termed, – it is more an emotional state than a reasoned system of thinking – maintain that now, the State of Israel being established, Jewry in the Diaspora is doomed – whether by the fierce hug of anti-semitism or the uxorious embrace of assimilation, doomed to disappear. From the Diaspora, therefore, no new Jewish cultural contributions are to be expected; its days are numbered; it lives on borrowed time; all devotion, accordingly, must go to Israel alone.

I had thought before I came to Israel that these most unpalatable prognostications were the special sport of but a few diehard chauvinists, the obsession of bitter and disillusioned Jews seeking in the prospect of the Israeli future a revenge against their memories of the Diaspora past. It was not long before I found that this kind of thinking was popular even with people who did not pose as philosophers. The native-born youth, for example, is in some measure already infected with it.

These young men – in Israel they are known as *sabras*, which is Hebrew for cactus; the epithet is designed to let all and sundry know that they are not to be sat upon – are Jews such as have not appeared in Jewry since the iron days of the Sadducees. They have known no other land but Palestine; the sense of alienation is foreign to them. They are singularly free of that schizophrenia which befalls so many of the denizens of the Diaspora; they lack the minority-complex, and the anxieties which go with it. The victories of the recent months, moreover, have heightened their self-assurance; they are, and they know themselves to be, a race of conquerors.

The advent of the new immigrants into the country has not lessened but rather increased their belief in their certainties. The spectacle of the human wreckage, the debris of Europe, launched on their shores – their own kith and kin broken in the ordeal – rises before them as a lesson in the felicity of being native-born. For them *galuth*-Jew is a term evocative of many concepts, all objectionable. They do not share the sentimentality which so many generations of self-pity have worked up in the heart of Israel; they are hard, tough, like characters in a Hemingway novel. They scorn the sophistication of the Diaspora, – what uses did it bring? Theirs is the soil and the intimate contact with the primitive, the fundamental. They are disillusioned with the large humanitarianism which so many preachers preached, and which in the end proved to be both a sermon and a stone. In their loyalties they are tribal; in their psychology, stiff-necked.

They are a phenomenon new in Israel – a race apart. Sixty generations of Jewry have not seen their like. Peasants zealous in their peasantry, they are the nearest yet which Jews have come to the habits and attitudes of the gentiles. One tells in Tel Aviv the anecdote of the little Yiddish girl, recently arrived in the land, who lived next door to some sabra children. One day she returned from her play with one of these children, weeping. 'Mother,' she sobbed, 'the Hebrew *shiksa* struck me!'

All the characteristics of the sabra are understandable; many are to be rejoiced in; but some few cannot but be recognized as an undesirably extreme reaction from the evils of the past. Pride is sinful and arrogance unseemly; both of these the sabra too often displays. In the sabra magazines there occur time and again the antonyms 'we' and 'they' – and by the uncomplimented 'they' the sabra means the recent arrival, or what is worse, the miserable creature still languishing in Diaspora darkness. This 'we' – *anachnu* – is, of course, not a new thing in nationalist assertiveness, it is the *nous autres* of the Gaul, the *sinn fein* of the Gael. It is the pronoun of inhospitality, xenophobia's first person plural. I was not very surprised, therefore, when I came across a magazine, published and managed by sabras, in which these referred to themselves not as Israelis, but as Canaanites! More aboriginal than the aborigines! It was, indeed, an appellation which exemplified at once both their own sense of belonging, and their sense of 'their' not belonging.

Altogether this new phenomenon is not an unmixed blessing. It is gratifying to encounter at this late date this new dynamism in Jewish life, so refreshing a contrast to the passivity which has marked our chronicles throughout the exilic centuries. At the same time the new attitude constitutes an unpleasant negation of some of the highest standards established by our culture – learning is no longer to be cherished as the *summum bonum*, peace is not always the highest desideratum, softness of heart not always to be regarded a virtue.

I am inclined to believe that the sabra mentality is but a transitional manifestation. It is a reaction arising from the tragic experience of recent times. It does not spring from the natural thought ways of our folk, but surges up only as answer to contemporary history. It is Israel's retort to Europe. But when that retort will no longer seem as important as it does to-day, when Israel begins to live its own life and not, as now, a life conditioned by the European preface, then the sabra, too, will return to the cherished traditions of our civilization. To be a Canaanite is no great objective; the true objective is to be an Israeli, in the natural significance of the term – that is to say, a member of that people which gave to the world whatever of humanism it possesses, gave to the world whatever of divinity it aspired to. Such concepts once rose out of the Palestinian soil, even more indigenous than cactus, – and may do so once again.

28 October 1949

Political Parties in Israel

I didn't journey to the State of Israel to study its political parties, and these notes are not by any means intended as the authoritative pronouncement (after less than a month of observation) upon its political trends and alignments. Yet nowhere, I imagine, are the people so politically conscious as in the new State of Israel. From the minor capitalist who happened to be my room-mate in the Eden Hotel in Jerusalem (he was on vacation from his business in Haifa) to the very world-peace-minded waitress in Tel Aviv who served me the austerity meal followed by a generous dessert of Marxist polemic, everybody, but everybody, seems to think that in him or her Ben-Gurion has overlooked a counsellor of the shrewdest political perspicacity.

This assertive self-confidence, it must be admitted, is not entirely unwarranted. The quotient of average political intelligence in Israel is very high; the Israelis, having gone to one of two schools of political education, have been in both apt retentive pupils. Graduating from either the universities or the DP camps of Europe, the implications of politics have necessarily engaged their attention with more than a merely academic relevance. Even those without benefit of formal school education have not escaped political instruction; *they*, like that wretched victim in Kafka's *Penal Colony*, learned it writ large, and annotated, upon their very own persons. These latter are like those recalcitrant Russian soldiers of the First World War of whom Lenin once asserted that they had actually voted for peace. When confronted with the fact that no peace-vote had been taken when these so prematurely withdrew themselves from hostilities, Lenin replied: They voted all right but instead of voting with their hands, they voted with their feet. Of the tens of thousands of Jewish refugees who survived the camps of Europe it can likewise be said that their political education, as the political expression of the Russians, was largely concentrated upon their feet. Persecution is also a political school; flight, too, is a peripatetic academy; escape is the post-graduate course.

Moreover, Israel is to-day a country in which politics, in the best sense of the term, is woven through the very warp and woof of life. It does not exist, as in so many other places, in a departmentalized vacuum, reaching the people only at times of election and franchise. Politics is a day-to-day phenomenon. It does not exist, as in most of the Middle Eastern countries, only upon the top levels. It exists in all ways for all always.

Considered under its most genial aspect, politics provides the most constant topic of both public and private humour. Politicos have replaced mothers-in-law as the most usual target for satire. Yet satire, perhaps, is not the correct word; for the barbs are almost always coated with the honey of affection, and the point of the joke very frequently not the fact that the man is a politician, but an Israel politician in an Israeli State, that is to say, a person who can never be altogether unacceptable.

Naturally the austerity regulations have brought their spate of anecdotes. The old one about the man who, having saved from drowning the Minister Dov Joseph, desired to remain incognito follows the recognizable pattern. *Tzena* is the Hebrew for austerity (it is a word etymologically related to the word for chastity) and gives rise to frequent allusion to Tzenator Joseph. The new élite of bureaucrats, too, does not pass without comment; *pakid* is Hebrew for 'official' – the bitter ones console themselves by referring to the *Kiryah* (the Government Offices) as Pakidistan. But the laugh which follows these witticisms is a mingled laugh, – it is only in part a laughing at the humour of the anecdote; for the rest it is a gaiety at the thought that there is a Government to laugh at.

Even the most cursory acquaintance with Israeli life soon provides the impression that its politics are of the essence, and not, as so frequently elsewhere, merely marginal. Insofar as the settlements are concerned, their very raison d'être is political; but even in the cities there is not an activity or an attitude which is not motivated by some political philosophy.

My room-mate in Eden is a case in point, a case, moreover, which illustrates not only the politics but also the psychology of contemporary Israel. It did not take me long to discover that my partner was a Revisionist, a secret sympathizer of the extreme Right elements in the land. I withheld from him both my identity and my mission; he knew only my name and the fact – startling to him – that someone from the allegedly assimilated wilds of Canada still spoke Yiddish and smattered Hebrew. Accordingly he regaled me with a heavy bill of indictments directed against what he called the doctrinaire regime of Ben-Gurion. He disapproved of its politics, he abhorred its economics, he sneered at its foreign policy. I contradicted him only sufficiently to keep him going, – not mildly, because I desired to hear his entire story, but not vigorously, because we were to sleep in the same room. I underestimated his zeal, however; he didn't require any prodding; he continued accusative way into the night.

Already he was beginning to repeat himself. I had learned all I had wanted to learn from him, and I was tired. But I couldn't find any way to halt him. Finally, in somnolent desperation, I began to agree with him. This was my mistake. For no sooner did I express that exhausted agreement, but he volte-faced, and launched into one of the most eloquent defences of the Ben-Gurion Government that I had ever heard. This was the leadership which had made possible the declaration of the State Israel, it had had both vision and courage, it was doing very well, indeed. What did I expect of a state but one year in existence? What others had taken centuries to do, Ben-Gurion had accomplished in twelve months, etc. etc.

He certainly was the most chameleon antagonist I had ever had. Wearied and bewildered, I at last surrendered. I wanted to tell him that his second opinions had been mine all the time, but I resisted the temptation; I didn't wish to fling him into the ranks of the Revisionists once more. 'Good night,' I said. 'Good night,' he answered, 'we will continue our discussion at breakfast to-morrow.'

11 November 1949

The fact that during the recent elections twenty-one different political parties contended for the Israeli franchise has evoked, in certain quarters, sage and knowing comments concerning Jewry's natural tendency towards disunity. There is only one thing about which two Jews will agree, assert these wiseacres, and that is what the third Jew should give to charity. Witness – the example of the election. Israel's political habits might have been modeled either on the American or Russian example, two-party system or one-party regime – and instead, eschewing this easy alternative between East and West, veered simultaneously in all the directions of the compass. This, these commentators maintain, is a symptom of Jewish individuality, the result of an absence of the experience of communal discipline throughout all the centuries of the Diaspora.

These strictures are difficult to understand. It is difficult to understand how one expected, in a state but recently established and in a culture in process of formation, that there should ensue a condition of voluntary uniformity not known in any but totalitarian states, a sort of latter-day miracle of *na'aseh v'nishma*. The true marvel of the elections is not that there were twenty-one party-names on the electoral list; the true marvel is that there were not more. Whether one tabulates by countries of origin, variety of interest, or degrees of education, the roster certainly should have run to more than this single score-plus-one parties. Indeed, if the designations of the scoffers at Jewish unity were sound, if Israelis are truly as individually self-assertive as their premise would indicate, there should have been as many parties as there were voters. The apparent multiplicity, moreover, was really an optical illusion; many of the parties were nothing more than isolated banners with a single follower – the candidates who bore them.

What should be noted about these parties and has hitherto escaped notice is that all of them rotated about some political or religious outlook, and not upon a country of origin. Our readers are no doubt familiar with the tendency which Jews manifest upon coming to a new country of congregating in *landsman-schaften*. The Russians form Russian societies, the Roumanians Roumanian; societies are even formed about provincial nostalgias: Bukoviner, Volhyner, etc.; in many instances, about a single town or hamlet. None of this backward-glancing kind of political organization has taken place in Israel. One starts from scratch. It is the children of Israel who live in Israel, not outlandish family compacts. The German Jews may have common interests; but their interests are not common because they have issued out of Germany. The clannishness of the *gubernias* is unknown to Israeli politics. It is *klal Yisroel* which divides itself according to political outlook, and not immigrant *Yisroel*.

I had occasion one Sabbath to take in a full view and audience of the major Israeli political parties. It began one Friday night when I attended a Communist meeting. Though the speakers were vigorous and indeed bellicose, not even their Hebrew could make their arguments sound novel to me. For the speeches were no different from Communist speeches delivered at that same moment in Paris, or Rome, or New York, or Montreal. The Communist party line is always a polyglot version of a ventriloquist original. In Tel Aviv, too, I heard about the iniquity of the Marshall Plan, the provocativeness of the Atlantic Pact, the conspiracy of the warmongers, and the eternally pacific intentions of the Soviet Union. The atomic bomb, of course, was an especial target of the speakers' wrath. For the purpose of giving the meeting a local pertinence there was the usual exploitation of current difficulties – housing, unemptied camps, etc.

On the Sabbath morn I attended, for a while, a synagogue service. I include mention of this here for this was the equivalent of a Mizrachi meeting. The orthodox parties in Israel have this advantage over all other parties: they do not have to think up their platform. It is already there, a table prepared, *Shulchan Aruch*. Nor does this table stand only in the synagogue: the orthodox elements have brought it into the Knesseth itself, and because the Coalition Government of Ben-Gurion cannot maintain itself in power without the support of the Mizrachi, Ben-Gurion himself must eat from that table, and make his legislative benediction. The result is that the developing law of Israel is mosaic in more than one sense: it is, first of all, mosaic in that wherever possible the skullcap supporters of the Government insist on observance of the decrees of Moses; it is mosaic also, in that in the attempt to make these decrees conform to modern concepts, the original legislation is often chipped, and broken and put together again, much after the fashion of Byzantine art.

There was also, that same morning a meeting of Mapai, B.G.'s party. This wasn't as interesting as the others inasmuch as it consisted largely of apologetics. Ben-Gurion a week earlier had declared in the Knesseth, under the stimulus of his own rhetoric, that only the members of his party had fought and won the battle for Israeli independence; the thing was so palpably an exaggeration, to say the least, that it not only created a furore of resentment throughout the land – Israel's multifarious newspapers broke out in a rash of indignation and cartoon – but even B.G.'s supporters felt that he had overshot his mark. Hence the meeting of apologia. Its main thesis was that even Homer nods.

The Freedom Party (Revisionist), too, had its Sabbath service that day. It took place in a theatre, packed to the rafters. The main topic of discussion was the Prime Minister's recent suggestion that he was ready to allow the return into Israel of one hundred thousand refugee Arabs. The speakers were against this move. They charged the Government with making this gesture largely for the purpose of impressing the United States with their humanitarianism. 'Look for whom they would preen themselves,' exclaimed the orator, 'for that world which stood with arms akimbo while six million of our brothers were sent to their burning deaths!' This, as could be expected, made a strong impression; encouraged, the speaker went further and insisted that these Arabs, having originally come from Syria and Transjordan, were not really refugees at all, – they were expatriates! Many in the audience were Yemenite Jews and it was to them that the speaker's Arabophobia largely appealed. This was understandable; the Yemenites had upon their own bodies and persons learned the meaning of Moslem oppression.

Between the sniping of the Communists, led by Moishe Sneh, on the one hand, and the cannonading of the metamorphosed Irgun on the other, Ben-Gurion runs his middle course. The Communists, articulate far beyond their strength (they attracted only 3% of the votes and won only four seats), keep attacking the Government for its alleged flirtations with capital; the Irgun and other Right elements assail it for the opposite reason – its allegedly passionate socialism, its cool platonic attitude towards free enterprise. The truth is that like all coalition governments, Ben-Gurion's pursues a policy of compromise, tempered by a remembrance of past principles. The result is one of the finest examples of the welfare state. His is no easy task; the road he must go is Jonathan's: 'And between the passage by which Jonathan sought to go, there was a sharp rock on the one side, and a sharp rock on the other side; and the name of the one was *Bozez*, and the name of the other *Seneh*.' 1 Samuel 14:4.

25 November 1949

Cultural Note
It is doubtful whether in contemporary Israeli literature anything has yet appeared which deserves inclusion in the canon of the immortal and the universal. Masterpieces are not created by proclamation. A culture is not decreed. Much as I would desire to possess and show off scriptures of the first

year of the Israeli State, the whole to illustrate how independence overnight evokes genius, such *chefs d'oeuvre*, I am afraid, did not come within my ken. The verses of Nathan Alterman, about whom I shall have occasion to write at greater length, though typical of the period of struggle and victory, are not of the type of literature I have in mind. Alterman's verses, as he himself seems to insist as he preludes them with newspaper quotations, are but an inspired kind of journalism; he is a columnist in rhyme; his lines remain quotable as long as his occasions remain referable. The poet of sweep and majesty whom I sought I did not find. The nearest claimant for that throne is Uri Zvi Greenberg; but he, after all, cannot be considered typical of the new Israel; too closely identified with one extreme political view, a writer, moreover, with a past (the designation is not intended as derogatory), he can hardly qualify as the product of the gesture of May 14, 1948.

I did encounter a type of literature which was representative of the new Israel and that was the series of books consisting of 'Letters from the Front.' These were volumes, almost all written by very young men, all serious, all reporting, in epistolary form, the author's adventures in battle. Their tone was, for such literature, unique. The accents of the professional soldier were entirely lacking. Not the picaresque was emphasized, but the ideological. Here and there a certain pacifism of the conscience intruded; the dominant theme, however, was – reconquest of the heritage. It was this awareness, in fact, which explained the plethora of biblical reference; not a salient was spoken of, but its military history in the time of the Judges and the Kings was proudly recalled.

Though firm-footed and self-assured, it is not a literature without pathos. Again and again the letter is marred by the laconic reports that such and such a one has made the supreme sacrifice. The pathos is accentuated when one notes that in many cases the fallen heroes are indicated as having died in the fifteenth, or sixteenth, or seventeenth year of their lives. Others are further characterized as old classmates, or young men from neighboring colonies, or D.P.'s but recently arrived.

Yet, engrossing and tragic though these works be, they are to be regarded as materials for the future historian rather than as literature of the first order. At best they are Chronicles upon a reduced scale, Lamentations in a minor key; missing is the apocalyptic flash one so yearningly desired.

No, the time for book-culture has apparently not yet arrived. But culture upon a less elevated plane seems everywhere in ferment. Upon the very streets and signposts of Tel Aviv, one sees the creative energies of the Israelis in perhaps prosaic but nonetheless effective manifestation. This is a good thing, and not a bad. It shows that the language, for example, is not the monopoly of an élite, but common property, that it is the whole Yishuv which is participating in the revitalization of Hebrew culture, and not some select academy of greybeards and pedants. Thus culture falls into the proper category –that of daily necessity, and not of occasional and sumptuary luxury.

In no field is this more apparent than that of commerce. That commerce should be a vehicle for linguistic renascence is in itself a paradox, but that it should at this moment be one of the most far-reaching vehicles is passing strange indeed. It testifies both to the nexus between the new culture and the old, and to the constant fertility of the Jewish imagination. It was, for example, to me as satisfying as the reading of a witty poem when I noted that a well known brand of Israeli boloney was being advertised as *Bashan* – a just tribute to its magnum size, for was not Bashan a territory which produced giants, including its huge monarch, Og, King of Bashan? An insurance company incorporated under the name of *Sneh* – the bush that Moses beheld which burned but was never consumed – surely this was a nomenclature in the direct traditional line. A dry cleaner called his firm *Kesheth*, the rainbow, symbol of the cessation of floods.

The amalgamation of the old and the new was everywhere in evidence. I was in Israel on the eve of Tisha b'Av; the Book of Lamentations I heard intoned – on the radio. On another occasion it was a page of the Talmud which came over the same station – a reading of a *blatt Gemora* not contemplated by the Gaon of Vilna.

On the news-stands a multiplicity of journals, informative, political, artistic, and of sport. Accounts of football games couched in the new adaptive Hebrew were altogether *mirabile dictu* – the Hellenic Hebraized. From the movie magazines Lana Turner smiled, the sub-title of her photograph writ in the language of Isaiah; the magazine itself was called *Kolnoa* – the moving voice.

I had often wondered how, when the day eventually would come, how would be tied together the broken strands of the Judaic tradition. So many centuries had elapsed, so much had seemed forgotten – I thought it an almost impossible task to bind together yesterday's *relictae* with the currencies of to-day. It has proved not an impossible but only a difficult task. To that difficulty, the eager creative zeal of the Yishuv has been more than equal.

9 December 1949

Rome: The Statue of Moses
My schedule called for my presence in Rome for but a few days and so I had to exercise a difficult choice in determining what sites and monuments I desired particularly to visit. Of most of the landmarks of this historic metropolis it may be said that they can be seen, and even appreciated, quite adequately from afar; from any of the hills of this seven-crowned city one can descry with ease the familiar postcard contours – the jig-saw indentations of the broken arches of the Colosseum, the equestrian statues mounted upon their several eminences, the ubiquitous spires pointing so many fingers to heaven, and the grand, the magnificent, the perorating dome of the Basilica of St. Peter. As for the relics of

paganism, the shattered monuments of the Caesars, the most fleeting ride through the city sees them sufficiently displayed; more only a pedant would desire. (Had I had the time, I assuredly would have been that pedant.)

Because Rome and Jerusalem were an antithesis established from of yore; because had not Jerusalem been holy, Rome would not have been sacred, I sought out especially those of Rome's treasures which spoke to me with an Hebraic accent. Foremost among these was the statue of Moses, carved by Michelangelo. I had seen photographs shadowing the noble outlines, the glorious beard, the commanding presence of the greatest of the prophets as limned by the greatest of the sculptors; and I longed to look upon the original. There echoed through my mind, moreover, a description of this masterpiece that I had encountered in James Joyce's *Ulysses*, and there attributed to Seymour Bushe, a most polished period from one of the most eminent of practitioners before the Irish Bar. It spoke of Michelangelo's Moses as 'that stony effigy in frozen music, horned and terrible, of the human form divine, that eternal symbol of wisdom and prophecy which, if aught that the imagination or the hand of sculptor has wrought in marble of soultransfigured and of soultransfiguring deserves to live, deserves to live ...' Such gorgeous and orotund prose I found irresistible.

I also felt some affinity for the man who from the remote past and across the centuries had posed for this portrait.

In the Basilica of St. Pietro in Vincoli I stood before the celebrated statue. It is all that it is said to be. It is worthy of its subject – though its subject brought to the world the prohibition against graven images. The Moses that Michelangelo imagined, imagined him seated as on a throne with the tablets of the law under his right arm, is a Moses of unsurpassable majesty and holiness. The fingers of that right hand hold between their interstices the pendent curls and waves of a beard of glory; the aged Moses looks forward into the future, and his countenance is the countenance of a man who has stood on the mount and now looks out upon the plain ... He is a mighty man, greatly-proportioned, a vanquisher of Egyptians; a man of thews and sinews, a broad-wristed man, perhaps a sculptor himself, – did he not carve out on stone the Tablets of the Law? Michelangelo has carved him with strokes all of superlatives. The statue – this is just – dominates the Basilica.

I stood for many moments of admiration before this marvellous artifact. If grandeur could be communicated through stone, this assuredly communicated it. Nor had the Great Master, in his obvious adulation of his subject, forgotten that he was human. I scanned the statue, inch by inspired inch, from head to toe, my eyes coming at last to rest upon the great toe of the prophet's right foot. The toe-nail was broken – true sign of the desert-refugee, the wanderer of the wilderness!

Only one disappointing feature did I find in the statue –Michelangelo, and

Michelangelo's teachers knew no Hebrew. Holy Writ when speaking of Moses describes the rays of light – *karnai or* – shooting from his forehead. Unfortunately the word *karnai* may also be rendered 'horns'; Michelangelo, thus misreading, has affixed horns of stone rising from the forefront of the Mosaic head. The result is that some critics find themselves compelled to refer to 'the goat-like Moses'; but it is regrettable that a personality should be judged by its dandruff.

It was altogether a transfiguring experience. For a moment I was saddened at the existence of the Second Commandment which had deprived us of the potentiality of similar achievement. I was consoled only by the reflection that Michelangelos are not born every day, and that one Moses for Jerusalem and one Michelangelo for Rome was a division which eminently suited me.

My secular pilgrimage to S. Pietro in Vincoli was not without its humorous denouement. As I made my way out of the church, I paused, in the company of my cicerone, at the stand at its entrance where postcards, rosaries, and other sacred mementoes were being sold. On the table there stood a number of little statuettes of Moses, fashioned in alabaster. I was praising Michelangelo's handiwork to my guide when the vendor of sanctities interrupted me to draw my attention to the aforementioned white carvings of a miniature Moses. 'Cheap,' he said, 'look just like the one in the church.'

'I'll buy,' I replied, intending amiable refusal, 'I'll buy if you'll show me Michelangelo's signature on the statuettes.'

The merchant looked at me in disgust. '*Der parshoin,*' he said turning to my Italian guide who appeared to understand him perfectly, '*zicht metzios!*'

16 December 1949

The Arch of Titus

Despite the passing of the centuries, no Jew can go through imperial Rome without feeling a sense of bitterness at the recollection that much of the grandeur which he beholds was built upon the servitude of his ancestors. The vast Colosseum which to-day still stands, a mighty relic of a mighty past, engaged the labour, not of the Roman proletariat, but of the captive slaves brought from Palestine. Forty thousand Jews groaned beneath the taskmaster's lash so that these arches might rise – and be for a Roman wonder centuries later! It was not for nothing that in Talmudic literature the Rome of the Caesars is almost invariably taken as the type and exemplar of The Enemy. Too often in its history did Rome's generals and Rome's procurators issue forth against obstinate Judaea to take the land 'for a spoil' and its sons for captives.

Perhaps the most blatant memorial to this relationship between Rome and Jerusalem is the notorious Arch of Titus. Erected by a grateful Senate, it commemorates the infamous Emperor's triumphs over the Jews. 'It consists of a single arcade adorned with sculptured crowns and tympans; three bas-reliefs adorn the passage of the arcade. One, on the Colosseum side, shows Titus, crowned by Victory, standing upright in a car drawn by four horses and conducted by a female personifying the city of Rome. The second represents Roman soldiers without weapons, crowned with laurels, and carrying the spoils of the Temple of Jerusalem. These spoils are: two tablets fastened on staffs, the seven-branched candle-stick, and the golden table upon which are the golden trumpets. The third bas-relief under the vault, exhibits Titus sitting on an eagle, as he appears on the medals struck to consecrate his apotheosis ...' Thus, the *Jewish Encyclopedia*.

Up the *Via Sacra* I made my way; all about me there stood erect, or leaned, or lay in the mud, the pillars of the pagan temples of Rome, – the temple of Julius Caesar, the temple of Castor and Pollux, the temple of Vesta, – the emperors were gone, and the gods banished; and I stood at last before the unspeakable arch. A custom it has been among certain of my co-religionists to pilgrimage to the spot of this abomination, to stand before it, and mightily to spit thereon. Though in my heart I did not disapprove of the discourtesy of this gesture, it struck me rather as feeble – a pitiable return for the blow delivered by the Destroyer. I had not come that day to this monument to indulge in the empty consolation of expectoration.

Mindful of a tradition sedulously kept by the Jews of Rome not ever to permit themselves to walk under the arch – bitter enough it was that their ancestors at lance-point and *sub jugum* had had to cross beneath this yoke of stone – I scanned the monument from a disrespecting distance. I walked about it and about, but my heart being a drum and not a trumpet, Jericho's miracle was not repeated. The Arch of Titus stood, adamant.

I forewent the pleasure of looking at the face of Titus imaged on the vault. I could not do so saving I stood under it. Moreover, I knew that face only too well; often in the history books I had looked, as a boy, at the loose dissolute slobbering lineaments of that countenance, as if I had wished to memorize them against the case when I should meet the destroyer alone, young hero of my race, avenge my people's wrong ...

But my eyes did dwell upon the other bas-reliefs, regarding them askance. I looked at Titus, imperial in his chariot, and smiled to think of his end, as the rabbis report it, of the gnat which entered through an orifice of his face into his brain, and there kept buzzing, buzzing, buzzing ... until the Emperor went mad, and died. Was it the agony of guilt, that the Rabbis in their parable suggested? I think not. Look again at Titus's hangman's face, and you will see no shadow there of conscience or remorse. The parable comes rather to teach us how in the end the titanic are confounded even by the trivial.

It was the other bas-relief, however, which kept me fascinated as by the wand of a wicked wizard. I looked upon the laurelled legionnaires of Rome carrying away into captivity the most sacred trophies of my people; the seven-branched candelabrum, lifted arrogantly in the air, burned seven wounds in my eyes; the two tablets, so wantonly transported – I would have seen them shattered, as Moses did his tablets shatter; and the trumpets – out of the very stone they sounded, not as of yore, the sound of jubilee, but the broken murmur, the tragic *shvarim*, of wandering and exile. The soldiers bearing the table of the shewbread led the ungodly procession.

Had I come to Rome first, that is, before I had visited Israel, I would have been utterly shattered by this spectacle, these sculptural taunts, this gloating in stone. I would myself have been brought to the humiliation of my forefathers, slaves in Titus' triumphal march.

But I had come to this place after having beheld the renaissance of Israel. The captive spell which held me bound and mortified was dissipated by this recollection; the Arch of Titus, from being a taunt, was suddenly metamorphosed into an irony, an irony directed against itself. The bas-relief did not mean any longer that which its sculptors had meant it to be. History had made its own annotation; it was an annotation which nullified the text.

For as against the table of the shewbread which the centurions so proudly carried, a new table, a table prepared, a *Shulchan Aruch*, had been set before an entire generation. They who in camps and behind barbed wire had fed, when they had fed, out of cans and upon leavings, now sat at their own festive board, in their own land, eating the fruits thereof.

The seven-branched candelabrum, too, brought its contrast and antonym – the new light that had shone up in Israel at the very moment of Israel's greatest darkness. And truly for the trumpets silenced, new *shofroth* were sounding throughout the length and breadth of the land.

The Arch of Titus, there, were as if it were not. It had become, at best, an ironic anachronism. History had rendered null and void its orgulous boasting, Titus crowing from the grave had at last been smothered. As I turned to walk away from this hump of arrogance, it seemed as if it had ceased to be, as if it had crumbled to dust, as if it were no more than a mirage upon the Roman horizon.

23 December 1949

Of sundry and diverse things and places

The sole and solitary rose growing in the only garden of Beth Eshel in the desert. Red in the face with defiance against the surrounding wilderness ... At Haifa, the little cups of Turkish ... The Yemenite newsboy shouting, Idiot! Idiot! Peddling the daily *Yediot* ... The waterworks in the Negev with all the machine-parts identified in Hebrew. *Lachatz*, said the device on a circular face. The word had always meant to me *oppression*, as in the Haggadah: *lachatz asher haim loichatzim oisom*. Now it owned to a new and happier meaning:

water pressure ... The wild whirling pressure of life at Tel Aviv's most congested intersection at the Mograbi. A constantly improvised hora ... Haifa and
its hierarchical geography: waterfront, middle mount, and topmost height ...

The invasion of the Mediterranean by the Coca Cola Company. Almost
like a crusade, a jehad in favour of a new religion. Not Episcopalian, Cocacolian
... The sumptuous tombstones in the Jewish cemetery at Casablanca ... The way
the rich live ... The Casablanca heat – the hotel pillows sweat ... The Atlas
mountains seen from a plane. Not so impressive: mighty Atlas become a pigmy
hunchback ... Tunis, dinner at the Belvedere, guest of Monsieur Ghez, most
charming of hosts, and brilliant conversationalist to boot. Develops existential-
ist explanation of Jewish history. Plays with antithesis between sedentary and
ambulatory anxieties. Contrasts the Incarnation of the Jew with the de-
incarnation of the Jewish people ... Tunis, like getting lost on a Hollywood set
... The Tunisian ghetto: only place in North Africa I heard Yiddish speech.
From European refugees – for them the *haura* a sanctuary! ...

Jerusalem, the lovely stone of its mansions. A debt to Sir Ronald Storrs,
who had insisted under British regime that all Jerusalmite houses be built out of
the stone of the country. Excellent Judaean quarrying. Result – Arab snipers
frustrated by solidity of Jewish residences. House after house – pockmarked.
The New City has had its infantile disease ... *Mea Shearim* – the hundred gates.
An understatement. The most tortuous labrinthine winding area of all my
peregrinations. The Underground's underground. But really not a part of Israel
– a part of Eastern Europe. Hebrew is tabu, too holy for week-day use. The little
yeshiva boys with great big calves' eyes, and long black garments, and
serpentine side-curls. Faces like a page of Gemara: centre, text; on the left a
payah of Rashi, on the right a *payah* of Tosfoth ... And the odour – not of
sanctity ...

Tiberias, the most idyllic environs of this land of idylls ... Every Hebrew
poet has a rendez-vous with Tiberias ... Lake of the bluest blue, sunk lower than
the Mediterranean, at once a dimple and a beauty-spot ... Sat on the terrace,
eating almonds, watching its boats ... Kinnereth – is the word derived from
kinnor, a harp? Like David's, it plays of itself ...

The printing plant of *Davar*, at Tel Aviv. Most modern in all Jewry.
Proud of its working locale – air, sunshine, and coolth ... Saw for first time
pointillated type, every letter varied by each of the vowels ... A centre of Israeli
public opinion; in the beginning was the *Logos*, the *Davar* ...

Beersheba ... Full of old biblic association, still the most biblic city in the
land. An outpost in the desert, reminiscent of the milieu usually occupied by the
French Foreign Legion ... Heat – of desert intensity. It can curdle the brain ...
The horses in Israel seemed to be small, but the flies at Beersheba are like horses.
No wonder the ancient pagans worshipped Baalzebub – god of flies. The
creatures are very impressive ... Another corollary of heat – the ubiquitous
odour of ammonia ...

At Beersheba, in company of Beduin, sat on a camel to be photographed ... The camel is the most ill-mannered of all beasts. As I sat, warrior-like, at his hump, he turned his muzzle: Who's this? Most disconcerting. Camel peculiar also in motion, going step by step, nodding acquiescence. The yesman of the desert ...

The strange painter in Paris, M. Kislakoff ... Paints only at night, by electric light, or in the streets by automobile headlight ... Gets most wonderful phosphorescent effects. Does not paint by day at all. The owl's talent. Do not know whether he's Jewish, but his talent is certainly symbolic of that of contemporary Jewry, rising from moment of greatest darkness to flash illumination across the Israeli canvass ...

The Etruscan tombs in the Roman campagna. An almost forgotten culture, its language unknown, its mores only suspected, its persistence into modern life but funereal. Yet older than Romulus and the Caesars. The culture of my ancestors had a happier fate; it lives ...

Saw more Arabs in Marseilles than in Israel. Entire areas swarthy and sinister with them ... Altogether a sinister city – apart from the main street, Rue de la Canebière, every street an alley and ominous ... The flotsam and jetsam of the world comes to this port ... Excited at my first sight of Senegalese, face scarred with concentric circles, and tattoo'd ...

Shannon, waiting for plane to take me back home. Delayed two days. Much conversation with TWA officials and local folk. Irish very much like Jews. Some day someone should write a volume of parallels, not only the parallels of psychology but also those of national struggle ... Feel warmly to Shannon, here someone possessed a copy of A.J.M. Smith's *Book of Canadian Poetry*, and knew my work. That's how I got out of the country faster ...

If I Forget Thee, O Jerusalem ...   25 November 1949

It has been noted before that very frequently the resounding cause of patriotism is invoked for purposes which cannot be stated above a whisper; it is equally true that almost as often holiness itself is the cause behind which lurk considerations far removed from sanctity. This reflection is prompted by the great to-do which is presently being made in the councils of the United Nations, the whole presumably motivated by a desire to preserve the halidom of Jerusalem.

That same concern was not always a dominating factor in the thinking of the saints of Lake Success. We recall that when Abdullah's Arab Legion kept bombarding the Holy City, reducing to rubble one synagogue after another, damaging shrine after shrine, there was no great uproar at UN. The most sacred site in the world was being shelled mercilessly, the Israeli delegate to the United

Nations kept imploring some kind of intervention, – but the mighty ones, who to-day are altogether with piety vibrant, did not a thing to bring about an end to the murder and desecration.

We recall, too, that during the war in Israel, report after report emphasized with what meticulous concern the Israelis were careful to preserve all sacred places which came within their military jurisdiction. The city of Nazareth, captured by forces led by Ben Dunkelman, of Toronto, affords a classic example of this solicitude. No group in the world, not even a body of guardian angels, could have watched over the shrines and churches of this city with greater devotion than did the members of the Haganah. Indeed, in the whole history of Israel in recent times there is not a single instance where a sacrilegious imputation has been or could be made against the Israelis.

These facts are well known. The indifference of the Arabs to the sanctity of Christian shrines is no secret. The record of the Haganah is open to all. Nonetheless, the syndics and trustees who now agitate themselves at Lake Success act as if they were in momentary expectation of blasphemies to be perpetrated by Jews in a city which to them constitutes the first holiness.

The truth is that they are political, and not religious considerations, which for most of the parties impel the heat and direction of the debate. If the considerations were only religious, then the Israeli solution would have been accepted: internationalize the holy places, leave secular Jerusalem alone. It is because the struggle is a struggle for territory, in this world, that several of the powers have suggested internationalization of the entire city. It is as if the cathedral of Notre Dame being subject of controversy, one were to suggest that Paris be internationalized.

That the Roman Catholic Church should adopt its attitude is understandable. Here the considerations are indubitably religious and the debate in a sphere not mundane. Its policy is one with which one cannot argue; one may agree or not agree, and that is all. But it should certainly give this church reason to pause when it realizes that upon this matter it has arrived at exactly the same conclusion as that of the Soviet Union.

For their part, the Israelis will not stand by as the attempt is made to internationalize the whole of Jerusalem, to convert the Holy City into another Danzig, another Trieste. Jerusalem is an integral part of the State of Israel; this cannot be refuted without refuting the Bible. Without Jerusalem, the state is without its proper capital; it is headless; the Israelis have not struggled thus far to give birth to a monster.

One cannot foretell, at this juncture, what is likely to be the outcome of this unseemly lobbying with Jerusalem. One recalls only that but two years ago one lobbied in the same fashion with the whole of Palestine. One recalls also that the Scriptures have some very serious things to say about those who toy with the City of David.

Uncle Tom's Cabin   9 December 1949

The city of Dresden, which is in the Province of Ontario, is distinguished in history – we doubt whether otherwise it would be noted – as the last resting place of the negro who stood for Harriet Beecher Stowe's portrait of Uncle Tom. In the early days of the American slave trade Dresden was, in fact, a Canadian terminus for the underground of negro escapees. Even to-day this city has a considerable negro population, descended from those refugees who, pursued by bloodhounds biped and quadruped, made their way, after many perils, to the land of their liberty.

Throughout the following decades Canada has been to the children of these self-emancipated slaves truly a land of liberty, and, until yesterday, a land of equality. Last week that constitutional right of equality was taken from them.

What happened constitutes not a story of which Canadians may be proud. Some of the Dresden merchants, it appears, began to refuse to permit negroes to enter their establishments. This applied particularly to certain restaurants which somehow had caught, all the way from the deep South, a Jim Crow infection. The City Fathers of Dresden found themselves embarrassed by this situation; they sought therefore to settle the matter in a 'democratic' way – they called for a plebiscite. It didn't occur to them, apparently, that their method of liquidating this problem constituted a fine irony at the expense of democracy itself – a plebiscite of Canadians enjoying equal rights to decide whether equal rights should be enjoyed by all Canadians!

The citizens of Dresden, moreover, were not only oblivious to the ironic implications of the choice put before them; they went further, they made their choice in such a manner as to accentuate the irony. They voted in overwhelming numbers in favour of anti-negro discrimination and against the doctrine of equality.

These are the bold facts of the inequity which was perpetrated on Canadian soil. It comes, – at a time when Canadian statesmen are eloquently perorating about a Canadian Bill of Rights – like a loud belly laugh in lieu of applause. It constitutes a sad and saddening step backward. The Dresdenites cannot with their plebiscites introduce again the venerable institution of slavery, but one of its defining characteristics they have, indeed, resurrected from the dismal past – the 'principle' of inequality. Uncle Tom has his cabin again. It is significant that these accommodations were provided by a city whose name is evocative of things German.

Of Reynard the Fuchs

No one of our generation, certainly, can complain of the dullness of contemporary life. Not a day passes but we are regaled with tales lurid, harrowing, and intriguing to such a degree that they pass invention; only the fertility of history, it is clear, can encompass them; and nowhere is this more true than in the field of international affairs.

Had some romancer of tales of international espionage devised a plot which had as its central mystery the existence of a spy at the very hearth of the White House, such a one would have been summarily dismissed as an incompetent purveyor of the implausible, a writer with no real understanding of secret service precaution, a dilettante who allowed his nightmares to do the work of his imagination. Yet the trial of Alger Hiss revealed that such a state of affairs did actually exist. Similarly, had some dramatist attempted to give verisimilitude to the story of Canadian espionage, before *that* broke, he would have been hooted from the stage, if not as a war-monger then at any rate as a scenarist of B-pictures. Yet the facts of the Canadian spying have long since passed from the jactitation of controversy to the acceptance of truism.

The most startling of the revelations, however, seems to have been left to but yesterday. Its timing was dramatic in the extreme. Hardly had the possibility of a hydrogen bomb been announced but it was also announced that even that invention might no longer be a secret – one Fuchs, privy at the highest level to the esoterics of the atomic bomb *and* its corollaries, was being charged in England with having revealed to the Russians the most important of his confidences. It was because of him, it was being alleged, that the Russians had been able to make their atomic bomb, and because of him that they might yet fashion a hydrogen bomb.

The man at the moment stands merely indicted; and he has not yet been convicted; we refrain therefore from comment on his case beyond a simple expression of shock universally entertained. What does strike us in this whole melodrama of espionage and counter-espionage is not just the dexterity of its plot but the ingenuity of the mysterious arbiter who chooses its principal *dramatis personae*. What name could be more fitting for a villain and perjurer than *Hiss*? In what better guise could the sweet-scented hypocrite parade than in the guise of a *Rose*? Secrets and hiding places – how are they better suggested than by *Chambers*? Has this activity a driving force – let *Carr* be its name. And now the final flourish, the last brush and curlicue – the arch-spy, the core at the centre, he is called *Fuchs*.

The Confessions 24 February 1950

The manner in which the Russians manage to extort confessions from their victims still remains the riddle of the Kremlin sphinx. Many theories have been advanced to explain this strange self-incriminating passion which the Russians have somehow learned to induce in the bosoms of their accused ones; almost all of them have had something to say about either the nature of the Russian soul which presumably is infatuated with self-mortification, or the consequences of the Marxian dialectic which apparently leads to a confusion between concepts and their antonyms, that is to say, between innocence and guilt.

As long as 'the confessors' were Slavs, these explanations, while far from convincing, seemed at least pertinent. It was a *Marche Slave*, and therefore subject to its own musical rules. The situation, however, has changed with the intrusion of the recent so-called confession by the American, Vogeler, in Budapest. Here was a *Hungarian Rhapsody* played after the manner of an American 'blues.' The Slavic explanation was no longer valid.

Perhaps the Soviets, though enjoying an invention strictly Muscovite, have developed some way of transplanting it into all languages, – as yet, however, not the Scandinavian. There must be some musical adept – a psychological Shostakovitch – who is able to arrange this confessional music to suit all times, occasions, and countries. The essence of these compositions, we understand, is antiphonal: question and answer; and out of these antiphonies the self-indictment ultimately ensues. For ourselves, we are content to remain ignorant of these procedures. Let others abide the questions. We thank God we don't have to.

The Books but Not the People 22 September 1950

There is at present on the premises of the headquarters of The Canadian Jewish Congress a variegated collection of Jewish and Hebrew books, awaiting distribution to libraries, synagogues, and community centres, the mere examination of which would move the hardest of hearts. For it is part of the printed residuum of a destroyed European Jewry. As thick as the leaves in Vallombrosa's vale were the books which the barbarian hordes of Germany had garnered from the cultural institutions of the communities they slaughtered, garnered to preserve them for the future as the hideous relictae of this tribe they had caused to perish from the earth; many they put to profane earthly use, as wrapping for parcels, as kindling; with others they established libraries to illustrate 'the barbarism of the Jews,' libraries that at long last were rescued from their hands.

And these books, some of them several centuries old, all of them once the proud and cherished possession of persons, now dust, or institutions, now ruins of a world passed by, are now to become part of the cultural apparatus of Canadian Jewry. The great bibliothecal tradition of our people, having suffered the terrible interruption and sundering of recent years, is thus to have some manner of continuation in our own country.

Yet, as one rummages among these ancient tomes, so many of them with their fly-leaves inscribed with the names of near dear departed kin, so many brilliant with marginalia – some stifled reader's frantic explication to the future, others, again, novels, thumbed and wept over by the simple and humble of years gone by, – bitter, indeed, is the sense of inheritance. A thousand times better would it have been if these books had been consumed in some mad auto-da-fé and their owners issued unscathed from the threat of cremation! As it is, the people of the book perished in their millions; the books survived.

And there they lie, the eloquent witnesses both of a people's martyrdom and a people's high purpose. Truly might it be said that it was because of these books, because of the spiritual message in them contained – anathema to the destroyer – the people were hated, attacked, and cut down! And as truly may it be said that it was because of these books, the faith that lies in them, the eternity with which they are pregnant, the people, as a people, survived!

The page is burned, but the letters fly out of the flame to live, to combine, to live again!

The Notorious Restrictive Clause   1 December 1950

Some time ago, Mr. Bernard Wolf, of London, Ontario, bought from a Mrs. Noble a property located at a summer resort poetically called Beach o' Pines. The deeds to that property, however, contained a clause restrictive of its sale; the original sons of Beach o' Pines had covenanted between themselves that for a period of at least a generation no part of the summer resort was to be sold to Jews and such-like. Mr. Wolf is a Jew. Mr. Wolf sought, therefore, a judicial decision to determine whether in this free Canadian democracy segregating and ghettoizing clauses of the type described were legal.

The fact that the case finally was brought up by Mr. Wolf to the Supreme Court of Canada, indicates how the petitioner fared in the lower tribunals. Highly respectful of the sacrosanct principles of contractual liberty and the rights of property, they had held that Mr. Wolf, being a Jew, was barred from the acquisition of the aforesaid property. Such was principle: even if one of the twelve apostles (Jews all) had sought to intrude upon this breach of felicity, he, too, would have found himself confronted by the whirling sword of the excluding clause.

It is with gratification and pride that we now report that the highest court of the land has just issued a decision declaring the said clause illegal and of no effect. To this judgment there was the dissenting voice of but one judge of the Supreme Court; the majority decision was rendered by the great jurist who had already made himself famous for the broad democratic and liberal views which confirm his judgment, the Honourable Mr. Justice Rand. There is no doubt but that this decision marks a milestone in the history of the Canadian democracy. It gives the deathblow once and for all to these infamous private attempts to thwart and distort the public will, – attempts such as the one made at Beach o' Pines to introduce into Canada, under the very protection of the Canadian law, a system of ghettos and reservations such as would do honour to the spirit of Nuremberg. It is true that the particular case in issue had to do only with a summer resort, a place of luxury; but if the principles of the restrictive clause were valid there, it would be valid also on the main streets of any one of our cities.

The Supreme Court decision serves also as an additional weapon in our battle against Communism, which rejoices in the manifestations of prejudice, manifestations which it is not slow to use for its own purposes.

To felicitate the Supreme Court would be an impertinence; in the august realm where it moves and has its being, it is beyond felicitation. We content ourselves simply in expressing our pride in the wisdom and justice of our highest tribunal. To Mr. Wolf, however, who carried on a valiant uphill battle, not merely for his private right, but above all for the principle involved, our sincerest congratulations. It remains only to add that the Canadian Jewish Congress, keenly interested on behalf of all of Canadian Jewry in the outcome of this issue, stood by Mr. Wolf throughout all the stages of this history-making case.

The Hurried Amnesties   9 February 1951

What is the strongest weapon in the arsenal of a fighting people? The belief that it is in the right. The conviction that its cause is the cause of justice. It is upon this premise that one says that right is might. It is this fact which endows a people both with the defensive and aggressive spirit. Morality it is which builds morale.

Indeed, it would be fatal to a combatant state to announce publicly that its war objectives were in no way related to right and wrong, but were merely a part of the game of power politics. Such an admission would deprive it not only of the goodwill of neutrals, always an important military asset, but would even go to undermine its own fighting forces. Only mercenaries fight in the armies which divest themselves of the banner of righteousness; soldiers must have an ideal.

It is unfortunate that these incontrovertible truths do not seem to play much of a role in the councils of the occupying forces in Germany. During the past couple of weeks there have been announced a series of pardons and amnesties granted to Nazi war criminals duly convicted. The clement gaolers who so generously have flung open the gates of Landsberg prison seem to be of the opinion that all may now be forgiven since most is now forgotten.

We are not by nature of revengeful and vindictive spirit. There is, however, a point whereat clemency itself becomes vindictiveness – a vindictiveness directed both against the victims of the criminals, and the officers and soldiers sent to bring those criminals to the bar of justice. Faith is not kept with the men who fell on the various battlefields of Europe if the villains against whom they were sent not only survive them, but survive them amnestied and exonerated.

We understand very well the motivation behind these releases. It is thought, by those who have arranged these things, that thus crafty politics is played; that thus one wins the love and affection, if not the reformation, of the criminals. The granters of amnesty really believe that they are pulling off a shrewd political coup; that although what they are doing may be cynical, it is cynicism directed towards a good end. But cynicism when carried to an extreme, even in politics, often turns out to be naiveté. Not only does the criminal fail to become an ally; his very freedom alienates the tried and the true who through his parole have been bitterly deceived.

Take for example the case of Krupp. He has not only been released; most of his property has been restored to him. He issues a free man and a rich man. Yet the crime for which he was convicted is one of the most heinous in the calendar. To him was brought home the guilt of having used in his various enterprises, slave corps numbering millions, the captured, the imprisoned, the submerged population of Europe. In his own person Krupp did not have enough lives to be able to atone for the untold misery he brought to hundreds of thousands driven into his peonage. And now, less than five years after his conviction, he is free and a tycoon.

What do the authorities who are responsible for this sort of thing really think their own people are? How is the ordinary soldier to be sure that the next knave who is pointed out for his military wrath will not, in due course, after the casualties and the amputations, be duly amnestied?

We do not pause to condemn these amnesties as wicked. Their wickedness cries to heaven. We pause only to point out the abysmal stupidity which prompts them. For actions like these make us vulnerable, in the ideological war, to the attack of our opponents (who, be it noted, are playing, have indeed introduced, this shameful game), and serve to weaken our sense of righteousness, without which there is no strength at all, without which all other strength is futile.

Education in Israel   23 February 1951

We do not wish to enter at this point into a discussion of the relative merits of the contending arguments which have recently brought about another governmental crisis in Israel. The details of the conflict have not been made public. All that is known is that the presumable issue on which the coalition broke was that of education. We know also that these frequent crises are not in the best interests of the Jewish State. They not only create confusion abroad, hinder and complicate the efforts for support of the various agencies and funds, but they also leave Israel itself in that condition of disunion which constitutes always a serious temptation to the enemies who surround it.

What we do wish to comment on, however, is this entire question of education in Israel. As is well known, at the present moment, the schools in Israel are being run, each group by its own particular sponsors and supporters. There proliferates through the land, therefore, a multitude of institutions of learning, each indoctrinating its students with either the inherited creeds or pet ideologies of its trustees. Thus the Labour group jealously watches over its preparatory schools, and sees to it that its pupils imbibe Socialism together with their alphabets. The Orthodox group, too, is not content merely to communicate to its disciples the value and the utility of the three R's; it must also inculcate the 613 *mitzvoth*, and that over-all 614th *mitzva* which holds that those who do not abide by the 613 are not truly of the congregation of Israel. We pass over in silence the minor sects and coteries, each with its own special ideological nuance, to which it must perforce dedicate all the paraphernalia and authority of a separate school system.

The result of such a disjunctive system of education is obvious. What is being builded among the youth of Israel today is not a nation, but a congeries of schisms. From kindergarten age on, the thought of one group is being set up against the other. A generation hence there is thus bound to appear in Israel not a single people moulded by the same educational ideas, but a repetition of the division of the elders, a duplication of the quarrelling antipathies which mark the present scene.

The basic question, of course, is : What does the Jewish State as a state signify? Does it signify the establishment of a twentieth-century sovereignty, characterized by twentieth-century features, or is it to be merely a belated continuation of Jewish history as of 70 B.C. ? Is the Jewish State a means to shape an ideology, or is it the instrument to build a nation?

The answers to these questions must determine the character of the Israeli educational system. Not even Ben-Gurion will maintain that the supreme significance of the State of Israel lies in its possibilities as a crucible for social experiment; and not even Rabbi Maimon will hold that Jewish history must remain static, petrified, as of before the Diaspora – like a moving picture suddenly turned into a silent still.

The answer, indeed, is so obvious that we are at a loss, at this distance, to understand the resistance which prompts all other solutions except the right one. The answer is a *national* school system – a system of elementary and primary schools, supported out of taxes, and run by the government, not along the lines of the political convictions of the government of the day, but according to the standard of national schools in all modern countries. The aim of this school system would be to teach its students to read and write, to appreciate and cherish its national literature, in all its aspects, religious and secular, to communicate the basic truths of science, to cultivate appreciation of art. In this primary school system, there should be no place for the teaching of politics or economics; what should be taught in their stead is civics – thus, and thus only, can there be developed a sense of nationality, a feeling of solidarity, embracing all the classes, embracing all the varied groups, Sephardic and Ashkenazic, European and Yemenite, which go to make up the Israeli entity. Israel is a modern state; as such its state is separate from its synagogue. In a modern state, the teaching of religion is free; it is not, however, a duty incumbent upon the national school system.

Is all this to say that in Israel there is to grow up a generation deprived of a religious education, bereft of political or economic knowledge? By no means. Economics may justly be taught in the secondary schools. As for religion, it should be in Israel what we Jews insist it should be elsewhere – an extra-curricular discipline and chosen by each family for its children according to its own religious persuasion.

Thus will there issue from the schools of Israel, year after year, the annual crop of Israelis, sharing the same national ideals, cherishing the same school memories, endowed with the same store of elementary knowledge. At this point, but only at this point, each may continue in the direction in which either he or his parents incline.

To do otherwise would be to place the State of Israel under an extraordinary handicap. It will be again to cover the face of the Holy Land with retreats and hermitages – this time, political ones. It would be to nullify the true, the essential, the over-all purpose of The Ingathering. It would also mean setting up a wall of misunderstanding between the Jewry of Israel and the Jewries of the rest of the world, whose support is dedicated to the building of the Jewish people, not the fostering of a latter-day clericalism, or the encouragement of political experiment.

It was thought at one time that this issue, seeing the dangers which threatened from without, could be indefinitely postponed. The present, it was said, was no time for a *Kulturkampf* in Israel. It would have been well if other things had been avoided. But these recurrent crises show that it cannot be avoided. It must be solved. And the solution is one – and one only. To insist upon an imposed clericalism would be to turn back the clock. To insist upon special political indoctrination would be altogether to take the face off the clock. Only a national school system can at once show the right time and preserve the features of the Israeli face.

Varieties of Genocide   2 March 1951

It is an error to imagine that the perpetration of the crime of genocide is a new thing in 'human' history. Typical always of barbaric ages, it has often manifested itself also in ages deemed civilized. Thus it was that the Phoenicians disappeared; thus the Assyrians perished. What in our time was startling was that this type of mass-murder should have persisted into the twentieth century; here, given the advantages of science and the efficiencies of organization, the thing became more ruthless than ever: an extermination which in ancient times would have taken generations, and even then never have been completely thorough, in our own day could be accomplished with comparative despatch. Hitler's liquidation of the six million is the classic bitter case in point; given but a little more time, and his performance in genocide would have been complete.

This phenomenon is one so horrible to contemplate that the years following the war saw the leaders of all nations, greater and lesser, engaged in framing international law which would make genocide the most heinous of crimes. Nor was this motivated solely by a high sense of morality; practical self-defensive considerations played no inconsiderable part; with the invention of instruments of destruction proceeding ever more furiously from day to day, no people was assured immunity against the crime of genocide. To-morrow some neighbour, indeed, might discover the single weapon which with one single outburst might bring to it a total irrecoverable annihilation.

There are, moreover, – as Mr. Chaim Greenberg points out in an extremely illuminating article in *Der Yiddisher Kempfer* – various kinds of genocide. There is, first of all, the type to which we have adverted – the physical extermination of an 'undesirable' people. There is, and it is here that Mr.

Greenberg makes pause, also a spiritual genocide, – a subtler form of murder in which the body remains extant and 'only' its principal characteristics, its features of identity, are eliminated.

In an open letter addressed to the Soviet Ambassador in the United States, Mr. Greenberg directs against the Soviet Union specifically this charge of having perpetrated and continuing to perpetrate against its Jewish population the crime of spiritual and cultural genocide. The writer takes note of the fact that Russia has used as one of its principal boosts for export its legislation against antisemitism; he is not, and we think justly, impressed. For a state to vaunt the fact that it does not countenance murder and mayhem is no particular credit.

It is then that Mr. Greenberg adduces the devastating facts concerning the organized system of assimilation, indeed, of agglutination which now prevails in Russia. There, Zionism is still a counter-revolutionary crime, and thence no Jews are permitted to emigrate to Israel. Moreover, the proud propaganda that one once heard about the flourishing of Yiddish literature in the Union has been silenced; instead, one reads in the Soviet press characterizations of Jews as 'nomad beggars' and 'homeless cosmopolites.' There is not a Yiddish journal published in Russia. As for Biro-Bidjan, once advanced as the great rival to Palestine, the true exemplar of an autonomous Jewish republic, that, too, is gone. Even the sign-post has been removed from its solitary abandoned station.

Once Russian Jewry constituted a great and fruitful element of the Jewish totality. Russian Jewry in the nineteenth century constituted the main fortress of Jewish culture, not to speak of a principal source of population. Between that Jewry and the Jewries of the rest of the world there prevailed continual exchange of thought and influence. Now all that is gone. The Kremlin has intervened. Russian Jewry is hermetically sealed against its brothers abroad. And in its own confinement is doomed to cultural disappearance.

Where are the Yiddish writers who were but a short time ago the pride and boast of Russia? Many are the inquiries which have been made touching this matter; never has an answer come forth.

Genocide is a terrible crime; its terror is not decreased when it spares the body and 'only' kills the soul.

The Feast of Purim   16 March 1951

We have noted concerning ourselves that during the past number of years the reading of the Book of Esther which recounts the plot and the downfall of Haman, has recaptured for us again some of that fine literary grace, that easy consolatory pleasure, that fairy-tale conviction that all will eventually end well, which this adventurous tale brought to us in the days of our childhood. We say, the past number of years, – it wasn't so in the early forties. Then, as the war raged, and as the decimation of our people continued apace, the Book of Esther seemed to us like a taunt, an irony: the classic Haman was discomfited, but the real and actual one continued to thrive; the Jews of Shushan were rescued at the last hour, but those of Oswiecim continued to go down to the pit. We thought, indeed, that at last the pattern of Jewish salvation had been confounded, that contemporary event had rendered the story of Haman obsolete, and that a time would come when the version which would be read, if any remained to read, would tell of an ending altogether different.

We thank God that in His good time He at length repeated before our eyes and for the benefit of this generation the miracle and wonder first flashed from Persia. If the latter-day Haman was not brought to the gibbet, he did, at any rate bring himself to an ignominious end. Our own people, moreover, were not only rescued, though not without wounds, but achieved also a consummation they hitherto had not dared to entertain, except in their most flattering dreams – the establishment of the State of Israel.

That is why this book has regained for us, last year and the year before, some of its pristine charm and aptness. It has again returned to the canon of our hearts. We had been too impatient for the required *dénouement*; yet that unfolding, though long in coming, came.

We have, however, one disappointment to record. The Roll of Esther, it will be recalled, tells how all those who followed Haman, including his ten sons, met the same gallows fate. This part of the pattern, unfortunately, has not been repeated. But last week amnesty was granted to a number of Hitler's convicted followers. Yet perhaps, this too is in fulfilment of the original story: is it not written of Ahasuerus, the original occupying power, that he was as stupid as they make them?

The Pit and the Pendulum   6 April 1951

Our readers are no doubt familiar with that macabre tale of horror and impending death in which that master of the horrific, Edgar Allan Poe, described, as only he could describe, the ordeal of the pendulum and the pit. We had occasion recently to re-read this masterpiece of terror and were again made victim of Poe's dantesque verbal hypnotism. Only this time – for the first time – we descried in the passages and paragraphs of the inquisitional narrative a parable for our times.

For those who have gratefully forgotten the agonizing details of this story of protracted torture, it may be edifying, perhaps, to recall, in brief and without benefit of Poe's special delight in excruciating his readers, some of its action and argument. The tale, written in the first person, tells of the sufferings and the reflections which one condemned by the Inquisition endures in his cell immediately after he has been convicted. The narrator is at pains to indicate that what he is about to describe is a process of *moral* torture; at no time is he subjected to real violence; he is subjected only to the threat, the most cathartic threat, of *imminent* violence, imminent annihilation.

He is taken to this cell, and is left in utter darkness. Full of fears and terrors, he is most anxious to study the contours and size of his cell; he crawls along its length and width and arrives at an approximate notion thereof. Suddenly in the darkness he stumbles; he feels his chin pressed against the slimy floor, but his legs – his legs, he realizes are dangling over space! Carefully, very carefully he turns until his face is where his legs were; a foetid miasma assaults his nostrils; he is hovering over the brink of a pit! He drops a pebble into the pit and after a while, hears its reverberation echoing through his cell. What terrors lie below – terrors of torture and annihilation– inflame his fancy with new, and even more horrible, imaginings.

He is now afraid to move. He fevers, he faints, he swoons. Suddenly a thin ray of light flashes in his cell. He is being watched! He finds at hand some food and water. He drinks, the water has apparently been drugged. He falls into a profound sleep.

When he wakes, he finds himself tied to a very low bed. He can move, but only sufficiently to reach down for some food at the side of the bed. It is, however, as he gazes upward that he realizes that a new torture has been prepared for him. Over him there swings a heavily weighted pendulum. Its base is a large curved crescent blade. It swings right, it swings left; and with every motion sideways it descends imperceptibly, imperceptibly but relentlessly ever lower. The narrator realizes that when in time – how long a time he does not know – it will descend to striking level, its crescent scimitar will beyond doubt cleave him in twain across the breastbone. In the meantime, it continues to descend, and with every lowering the *hissing* of the blade becomes more audible, more ominous. In his terror, the victim seeks devices of escape. But he is tied down firmly, and cannot move – except for his right hand. In the meantime, rats, a swarm of rats, despoil his food, and even climb over his person, his face, his lips.

The method of escape suggests itself. With his partially free hand, he smears across his chest and the ropes binding it – the locus of impending cleavage – some of the fats and remnants of his food. Immediately the rats are upon it. They nibble, they bite, they eat away the rope. The pendulum is now within a millimetre of his body. In one frantic effort, skilfully accomplished, the man slides his body off the bed to evade – in the nick of time! – the ferocious scimitar.

But now it is made clear that every move of the victim has been watched. The unseen tormentor knows himself frustrated. The last device of destruction is now set in operation. The walls begin to throw off a terrific heat. They turn fiery red. The heat impels the victim away, ever away, and always towards the brink of the yawning pit. And more! The walls themselves are moveable, and they move! The square room is being constricted into a lozenge! The fall into the pit is almost inevitable.

It is at this point of intolerable suspense that Poe concludes the story with the arrival in Toledo of the liberating French army.

Who can read this tale, the mere product of imagination, without feeling that in our own day it has been experienced, it has been witnessed, in ineluctable reality? Who can tremble over its tortures without at the same time sensing that these tortures have been visited, in our day upon our own people? Its dilemmas – are they not the dilemmas with which vast numbers of our people have been confronted?

Let us consider them, one by one, these insufferable episodes of Poe's man-made inferno. The pit: has it not been this same pit which in Europe yawned annihilation to our European brothers? Maimed and broken, did not the body of that Jewry hover over the brink, convinced that in a moment it would be totally engulfed within the depths of that all-encompassing, reverberating chaos? From that edge and precipice it was saved, and see! a new ordeal in another area reveals itself. Deadlines swing back and forth over the heads of a million Jews who lie shackled and fettered on Moslem boards. It is a scimitar which hisses over them, and they must escape or be carved to death! It is a pendulum which swings over them, second by second, counting the instants of survival that yet remain, indicating the moment of destruction that must soon, so soon descend.

Fortunately there are rats upon the scene. Even from the hand of the manipulator of the pendulum release can be bought – even as to-day it is being bought in bitter and urgent ransom of the despoiled of Iraq and of Yemen.

But one cannot rely forever on the operation of these temporary salvations. Soon, sooner than we expect, the walls themselves may begin to move, exerting pressure once again towards the notorious annihilating pit.

Is it necessary further to point a moral?

Joseph and His Brethren   20 April 1951

The usual versions of the Exodus from Egypt focus attention upon the careers of Moses and Aaron, the one as the great prototype, the other as the eloquent spokesman, of Jewish emancipation. Such is the tale as told in Holy Writ, and such as recounted in the Haggadah.

There is, however, another character in the *dramatis personae* of the epic of Mizraim who, to our mind, affords also the pattern of recurrent history. It is Joseph whose adventuresome career it was that first brought the children of Israel into what was destined to become for them a land of bondage and persecution. His is a career difficult to unravel, it has its high points and its low, it speaks of the heights of power, it speaks of the depths of the pit – one would almost say, as Thomas Mann has at great length said, that what we read of is not the biography of one man, but the telescoped biographies of several men. Certainly we can descry, as we seek to draw a parallel between the misery and grandeur of the life of Joseph and the misery and grandeur of our own contemporary scene, at least two aspects of this myriad personality.

First, of the Joseph who knew affliction, and the bitterness of affliction. We find him, at the very outset of the narrative, wearing a coat of many colours. One would have thought that this gay raiment would have brought him immediate happiness, – it served only to arouse the envy and hatred of his brethren. Jewry of the unhappy lands of the Dispersion, too, was arrayed in vestments many-hued: of the hieratic style of the Egyptian exile; the flashing colours of the Babylonian sojourn; the bright vogues and flourishes of the Persian; the candid habiliment of the Greek; the striped raiment of the Islamic diaspora; the dyes and pigments of the several European badges. A coat of many colours – and how much hatred and envy ensued therefrom.

There was yet another cause in Joseph's character which made for hatred. He was a dreamer. He spoke not of the actual, but of the possible. His dreams – does he not later say it explicitly: *It is not in me; God shall give Pharaoh an answer of peace* – are intimations of the divine. This is a thing even more heinous than the gaudy robe. This is the crime that the world of brothers has never forgiven the Jews – they brought them God. Therefore is it written: *They hated him yet the more for his dreams and his words.*

And finally he commits the unpardonable offense. He is oblivious of hatred; he forgives. As he wanders in the vale of Hebron, a man asks him, saying, What seekest thou? And he answers: *I seek my brethren!*

This, of course, is too much. Such goodness is an affront. The brothers, therefore conspire: *Let us cast him into some pit, and we will say, Some evil beast hath devoured him, and we shall see what will become of his dreams.* Thus is he flung into that waterless pit, and then sold to a company of Ishmailites bearing spices and balms and myrrh. It is as if to say, at the very moment of crime, that Joseph is one of these and, too, giveth off a good odour.

To prove to their father Jacob that his son had indeed met with mischance at the claws of beasts, his coat of many colours is stained in the blood of a goat. The blood of a goat! Was it possible to indicate more clearly Joseph's role as scapegoat?

So much for the Joseph of the unhappy days. The incidents of his life are like nothing so much as like parables of the plight of Jewry in the lands of oppression.

Comes, then, the Joseph who dwells in a land whose Pharaoh holds him dear. He is an economist and knows how to make the fat pay for the lean. He is an authority upon life's material essentials, and understands well the dreams of butler and of baker. He has come a long way from the pit. Almost has he forgotten his brothers who themselves now are dwelling in a land of famine, and know now some of the first Joseph's hardship and anguish.

We doubt whether we have to draw a chart to demonstrate who is the latter-day exemplar of this affluent Joseph. The description fits in almost all its details the condition of the Jewries in the lands of freedom and democracy. Its metaphors are the literalisms of the American-Jewish situation.

And what, according to Scripture, is and should be the relationship between this Joseph of the heights and his brothers in hunger? After long separation, Joseph at last makes himself known to them. He gives them food, and returns to them the price of purchase. He knows that without his help his father's tribe shall not persist. *God sent me,* says Joseph of the court of Pharaoh to his weeping brothers, *to preserve you a posterity in the earth and to save your lives by a great deliverance.*

The function and duty of American and Canadian Jewry could not have been better expressed. Its role is, indeed, to preserve a posterity in the earth for all our people and to save the lives of those who still in bondage lie by a great deliverance.

The reward? The reward is expressly articulated by Jacob on his death-bed. He blesses his sons, and Joseph (now a composite – the one Joseph of both rich and poor, the Joseph reconciled) he blesses thus: *Joseph is a fruitful bough, even a fruitful bough by a well; whose branches run over.*

Blessed is the tree that grows by its well, even as the Israelis flourish by theirs! And blessed are the branches that run over, even as do those that give fruit and shade to American soil!

The Council for Judaism, Inc.   27 April 1951

We must confess that, with the establishment of the State of Israel, we had expected never again to hear from the unspeakable junta of clerics and pseudo-Jews which, with typical bad taste, had organized its Judaism into a commercial compact and had dedicated itself to the 'sale' of the *taryag* behests and prohibitions as if they were so many items in Lessing Rosenwald's Sears-Roebuck catalogue. When during the past number of months we had ceased to be assailed by their hissings and gnashings of teeth, we had thought that the incorporators of Judaism had disappeared forever, had skulked back into the darkness whence they had emerged and had there so eaten out their hearts that in due course the venom had destroyed them.

For certainly these miserable crawlers and fawners had had good reason for mortification. For half a decade, as the tens of thousands of the persecuted of European, African, and Asiatic Jewry sought sanctuary in their Homeland, and as the Yishuv itself stood embattled in defense of the elementary right of brotherly asylum, these puffed plutocrats and their venal ministers had sought, discovered, and made use of every means, first, to dissociate themselves from their own blood, and then, to make certain that that blood continued to seethe and spill in its accustomed cauldron of misery. To these despicable purposes, moreover, they were moved by reasons as shameful as they were callous. They wished in their prosperity to sever themselves from kinsmen who languished in penury and destitution. They wished, because of the good fortune which was theirs in having reached a free country there to win material wealth, to be separated forever from the incubus of a persecuted Jewry. Sensing the ignominy of the considerations which impelled them, they sought to conceal their meanness by covering it up with a flag – they didn't want their patriotism to be impugned, they feared the double-talk of double loyalty, they owed it to the country of their adoption studiously to ignore the country of their ultimate origin. And this folderol of hypocrisy, these contemptible counsels of smugness, this long-distance xenophobia directed against their own flesh and blood, they dubbed – Judaism! It was not surprising that they should have thought it fitting that this Judaism should be incorporated – a corporation is legally distinguished from a person in that the former has no soul.

It cannot be denied but that during the years of Zionist aspiration and struggle, this cabal, vociferously articulate and powerfully placed, caused our people many moments of anxiety. But worse than the anxiety – subsequent event showed that it was unwarranted – was the shame. That from our own midst, and in the very hour of our deepest suffering, such-like should arise! It appears that we underestimated the intelligence of the non-Jews: they, too, saw the members of the Council for Judaism for what they were; they, too, recognized behind the pious features and the patriotic gestures, the unmistakable cast of the Semitized countenance of Benedict Arnold. It was the Council which was left a voice crying in the wilderness for the wilderness.

Then came silence. It seemed that the *fait accompli* had taught the Council what moral imperatives had been unable to teach. That seeming, it now appears, was an illusion. The Council, dead, will not remain buried; but a week ago it rose again to croak its sepulchral croakings and to spread abroad once more its odour of corruption and decay.

The State of Israel, despite the maledictions of the incorporated Balaams, is a reality; let us seek to undermine it. There issued, therefore, from Chicago, headquarters of another Syndicate, a new refrain from the old keenings and cursings. After belabouring the United Jewish Appeal for that, forsooth, it is robbing the impoverished millionaires of their own local institutions (never in the history of America have so many institutional buildings been erected; psychologists speak of an 'edifice-complex'), the head and front of the chartered pandemonium betook himself to the question of bonds. Said Lessing J. Rosenwald, whom the newspapers described as a Philadelphia philanthropist, meaning, no doubt, something akin to a Philadelphia lawyer: 'The whole face of American Jewry and Judaism is being changed to implement an Israel national policy. We are witness to-day of the spectacle of American Jews being mobilized as salesmen for Israeli bonds.'

For shame! The emissaries of Juan Peron may seek to float loans in the United States – that, Lessing Rosenwald regards as legitimate finance; a million of yesterday's refugees ask to sell bonds which will make possible for them an honorable and productive future – that is treason! Cartels, monopolies, chain-stores, far flung imperial department houses – these may come to the public soliciting help in the cause of profit – not a whimper from Rosenwald, on the contrary, the broad smile of pleasure; a reborn people requests aid – to be compensated for, with interest – in its march towards economic independence – that is an assault upon the integrity of American Jewry!

The thesis, indeed, is not merely ridiculous, it is insane. Consider it: it is treasonable for Jews to sell bonds for Israel to Americans; this – when the American Government itself is extending to the new State loans of gigantic proportions! It cannot be otherwise than that Truman has become a Zionist traitor to American Jewry!

But enough of this eavesdropping upon the moribund delirium of the fevers of discomfiture. What we hear from these chambers of Judaism, Inc. are the dying gasps, the incoherent death-rattles of men being slowly – too slowly – mortified to death. Already the hippocratic signs are upon them, the pinched nose, the glazed eye, the mouth that fogs no mirror. Soon they will be of the past, remembered, if remembered at all, with execration and disgust.

What! No Drama?   4 May 1951

We must confess ourselves unable to conceal our impatience with those people who seek to explain the diminishing graph of Zionist responsiveness by alleging that the situation in Israel to-day is not as 'dramatic' as it was in 1948. We doubt whether these apologists are fully aware of the implications of their thesis, whether they realize how base a slander they thus level against a folk from of yore dubbed the 'compassionate.'

For if the fact is indeed so, if it indeed is true that American Jewry will not respond to the appeal of the harrowed and persecuted unless that appeal is dressed in some acceptable dramatic form, then American Jewry is but the caricature of what it is purported to be. These apologetics, whether their authors realize it or no, put into the mouth of the American Jew alternatives such as these: *You want contributions, ask me like Sarah Bernhardt! You wish me to believe in the helplessness of your plight, make like King Lear! Surely you do not expect me to respond, if all you tell me is that someone far away is hungry; show me a moving x-ray (in technicolor) of an empty stomach! Only if the Aristotelian ingredients for tragedy are provided, only then will I suffer the necessary catharsis! You speak of the State of Israel daily being created – but where are the parades? You tell us of persecution in Moselm countries – but we don't hear the agony; bring us a talkie!*

But to put down in black and white these callous alternatives is to show how grossly American Jewry is being calumniated. No Jew thinks like that.

Moreover, the real truth of the matter is that the situation in Israel to-day, beset as it is by insidious economic pressures from all sides, is more dramatic, more menacing than ever before. Look but on this picture, and on this:

An army goes forth to meet in battle its enemy. The opposing hosts face each other. Military intelligence on both sides gives to each an approximate idea of the strength of the other. The battle is imminent, and each army has a good idea of what to expect. Even the military surprises are imaginable, that is to say, they may be unknown, but are not mysterious. The contest will be joined, the struggle will ensue, and the decision will be determined through the operation, as yet untried, of factors well-known. The spectacle is heroic, is dramatic. This is the scene in 1948.

But how much more dramatic – dramatic with unseen yet palpable menace – is the encounter to-day, – which is no encounter – which is the encounter of ambush. An army, after many forced marches and engagements with the enemy, at last finds itself in an open clearing. That clearing, however, is surrounded on all sides by wooded terrain. Everything is deathly still. No shots are fired, no enemy movement is heard. Yet the very silence is alarming. Throughout the army there runs the conviction that eyes are peering from beyond the trees, that guns are levelled, that the entire scene is one of lethal camouflage. If it be true that melodies unheard are sweeter than those heard, even truer it is that the foe unseen is a threat more serious than the foe noted, observed, measured, and prepared for.

And this last picture is an exact description, in military terms, of the economic ambuscade which lies in wait about a financially-embattled Israel.

Yet even for those of little imagination, who see the heroic only in the raised rifle, and the dramatic only in the open clash, even for those it would be wrong to say that the events of 1948 have altogether passed. Even at this moment the northern frontiers of Israel are being defended by military means. The skirmishes in the Huleh, the invasions and the retaliations – you may consider them as either the echoes of 1948, or the opening detonations of 1952 – whichever you hold them to be, all is not quiet – or if quiet, menacingly quiet – on the Israeli front.

Shevuoth   8 June 1951

With the celebration of the Feast of Weeks there flashes again before Jewry, as before the world, the recollection of that great event, lost in the remoteness of time, glorious and fearsome with the lightnings of Sinai, which gave to western civilization its ten basic imperatives. Neither historians, nor archaeologists, nor theologians, have been able to fix with precision the exact year in which that grand epiphany – the granting of Torah – took place; what there is of record is the anniversary date and month of that transfiguring occurrence, a date calculated as seven times seven days from the celebration of the Passover. That, however, has been sufficient; from that time on, year in, year out, our people have celebrated, with joy and verdant festivity, this world-shaking, world-making event.

We do not wish to pause to-day upon the intimate connection, established by Holy Writ, between the Passover, a feast of freedom, and the Pentecost, a feast of The Law. He must be dull and blind, indeed, who does not see nor appreciate the ineluctable relationship between these two fundamental concepts. The Law cannot be given to slaves; it can only be given to free men. Civilization and mass servitude are incompatible notions; only there can civilization prevail where freedom reigns, where men have choice, where man can say *Yea* and *Nay* to the *Thou-shalts* and the *Thou-shalt-nots*. And this the Scriptures bring to us with a parable from the calendar which confirms with a mystical mathematics – seven times seven – the connection between that which passed over and that which in due time came to pass.

But that nexus is only half of the story. The other half is that which asserts, through the annual celebration of this holy day, the necessity for the recurrence of the event in our own time. Even as it is an injunction of the Rabbis that all Jews, of all the generations, present and to come, must regard themselves as having been personally a part of the exodus from Egypt, so must all – Jews and non-Jews alike – regard themselves as having personally glimpsed the lightning of Sinai and heard its shattering thunder.

For the Decalogue – that set of fundamental rules of *human* behaviour –

cannot be taken for granted, but must be continually re-stated in action and practise. Again and again, throughout the ages, there must be heard the echo of that immediate responsive cry uttered by the children of Israel at the foot of the mountain: *We will do, and we will hearken!* It was Isaac Rosenberg, the English poet, who thus wrote about the universal and pervasive influence of those thunderblasts in the desert when the mountain was 'altogether on a smoke':

> Moses, from whose loins I sprung,
> Lit by a lamp in his blood
> Ten immutable rules, a moon
> For mutable lampless men.
>
> The blond, the bronze, the ruddy,
> With the same heaving blood,
> Keep tide to the moon of Moses.

Alas, it is to-day a very erratic tide, governed by a mad moon, whose waxings and whose wanings confound Copernicus, setting all awry and out of joint. The tribute that is paid to the Decalogue is purely verbal; in action men do as is right in their own eyes. We say 'men' in their plurality and mean nations; individual man does, within the limits of his human weakness, observe the ten behests – were it not so, one man would swallow his fellow. But nations – here there is the need for a reassertion of the elementary precepts of morality. For it is one of the strange phenomena of human psychology that there are things which a man would not think of doing, would be ashamed to do in his private personal relations, which become to him, once he is robed in the robes of political office, not only permissible, but virtues; positive acts of patriotism. X, a man, would not dream of putting his hand in another's pocket; X, a Secretary of State, finds nothing wrong, finds all commendable in the act of unilateral annexation of others' territory. Y, the man, would not hurt the fly crawling on the wall; that same Y, a generalissimo, views with indifference, if not elation, the slaughter of thousands. This is not because he has suddenly become, in his new role, a man corrupt and iniquitous; it is, on the contrary, because he suddenly feels himself an instrument of virtue and patriotism that he now hallows what otherwise he would consider profane, that he now sacrifices himself and his ideals of integrity upon the altar of statecraft. Far from believing himself to be a breaker of the Commandments, he deems himself altruist and victim.

Oh, for a new Sinai, one specially set and ordained for nations, not individuals! A Sinai in which the threat of the lightnings and the menace of the thunders is directed chiefly against the makers of policy, the office-holders, of all nations, all enjoined to obey or suffer the full penalty of divine sanction!

And yet, as one reflects upon it, one sees the wish fulfilled. Is not the atomic weapon, mushrooming out, as it does, into an inverted mountain, such a new Sinai? And does not this new Sinai announce that he who disobeys – he himself, and not only others – will be swallowed up in condign punishment? It had been better, of course, if this new Sinai had been one persuasive with the speech of divinity, and not with the terror of its diabolism evoking submission; but such as it is, perhaps it may yet serve – by its very outrageousness – to preserve the world from outrage.

The Shadow of the Mushroom   15 June 1951

To-day, the world itself is in process of fission. Although the seismic break has not yet taken place, everywhere one senses, one is already able to identify, the tensions and strains which prelude some vast cataclysmic upheaval. In some quarters, it is believed that this global earthquake is inevitable, is part of the natural (*sic*) course of history; in others it is hoped that somehow, some way – by alleviating a stress here, by establishing a counter-balance there – the calamity may be avoided; everywhere, however – whether among those who approach this horrific anxiety head-on, or among those who would only tangentially skirt it – this is the pervasive engrossing obsession of our age.

It is the age which has been called atomic. A weapon has given its name to an era. How barbarous a nomenclature this is may be realized if we subject other earlier stages of history, each with its own civilizing glory, to similar designation, dubbing the Renaissance the gunpowder age, naming the age of The Fathers the bow-and-arrow era, characterizing the nineteenth century, known as the century of Liberalism, as the century of the Maxim gun! Surely there must be something ripe-rotten in a mentality so shaken by the death-wish, the death-fear, that it calls the age of its most recent progress by name lethal, a name vibrating with the imminence of agonized moribundity, a name that is not so much a name as an encompassing, shattering, intimation of deformity and death.

Yet the fact remains that all of us live under the shadow of the mushroom – that monstrous growth that first poisonously flowered over Bikini. It might have been a plant of life; certainly it bespoke the release of forces and energies which, if properly channelled, had introduced for mankind a golden saturnian age of comparative leisure and unremitting joyous cultivation of the soul. But the time and the occasion of its sprouting decided otherwise; the temptation to eat from that tree 'and be as gods' proved irresistible; we have eaten from it, and the result has been far from the precedent established in Eden: the knowledge of good and evil has been withheld.

The subconscious, instead, has been made a whispering gallery, ominous and sibilant, in which an unacknowledged Nietzscheanism stalks, mumbling about realms that lie beyond good and evil.

Over international affairs, the radiations, hardly the radiance, of atomic weapons cast a lurid light. As two great powers stand poised one against the other, it is as if the horizons themselves – East and West – glared hostility. As, in the light of the new science geo-political, the maps get drawn and the targets identified, it is as if the earth itself, the very soil had become – in some mad latter-day version of the old Greek myth – itself combatant. And as that fatal elixir, uranium, comes more and more to engage the covetousness and ingenuity of mankind, it is not otherwise than that a forty-ninth element, monstrous in its very impersonality, has stalked upon the scene, to destroy and cannibalize the other forty-eight. Global the terrain, the instruments are global. The earth itself is at once fortress and catapult.

Were the conflict one in which only weapons were involved, it were a thing as simple as the contests of the forest. The superior weapon naturally achieves superiority; the battle is to the strong, the weak perish or slink away, the jungle – following its heartless Darwinian course – continues to pullulate its strong and its weak, the feeding and the fodder. On humanity's plateau, however, there are complications. Frowning morality steps in to confuse, if not to confound, the combatants. The good clean jungle fight gets corrupted by Queensberry rules cunningly devised by the weak; the conscience paralyzes the arm. What to do?

To forestall the collapsing of the struggle through the treacherous inertia induced by ethics, only one counsel recommends itself – to make mortality itself a combatant, to turn the ethical into an auxiliary force.

One has only to read the propaganda, or listen to the broadcasts, disseminated from East to West and from West to East, to assure oneself that this is precisely the technique that is in operation to-day. It is a war of the antonyms: Light against Darkness, Good against Evil, Liberty vs. Slavery. The bewildering irony of the thing is that both opponents use the same antonyms.

It were simple, under such circumstances, to beplague both houses and mentally to levitate to some serene altitude high above the battle; it were simple – long ago; not now. Now there are no altitudes immune, no invulnerable ivory towers, no sanctuaries. All is engaged; engaged are all.

Involved, necessarily involved, only one course of action is open to Everyman – and that is to seek to discover, as far as is possible, which of the two parties is using 'the big words that make us so unhappy' in their actual and real significations, and which is using the noble vocabulary only to mask designs ignoble. It is not an easy task; semantics has been developed into a black art; falsehood has acquired technical facilities not dreamed of by the most brazen of history's liars; and it is difficult to pierce beyond the benignancies and the grandiloquences to descry the countenance mean, small, craftily narrowed.

For the classic dictum of our century is Hitler's: The bigger the lie, the sooner and the more universally will it be believed. And to this, the barbarization of the mind, there conspire the very instruments of culture. World-girdling air-waves grasp the sounded untruth and hoop it, as it were, circumambient about the earth. Newspapers, that but yesterday dealt in village gossip, may now corrupt with a single infection millions of readers. And already there looms on the shimmering horizon the latest of the prevaricators, the television set, preparing its optical illusions.

In such a setting, indeed, there can be no little lies. All lies, even the slightest, even the whitest, must become, through generous currency, lies big, lies gigantical, lies epidemic.

When it is recalled that the falsehoods of our day stem not from sources complicated and abstruse, but rather from the misconstruction of concepts simple in themselves, concepts which a shrewd propaganda seeks to subtilize and render dialectical, then it is seen how urgently imperative it is to return to a consideration of the fundamentals; to weigh once more the basic premises of our mores; to investigate, not *beyond* good and evil, but *within* them, and to extract from such research some trove of knowledge touching the nature and the implications of these so menacing words.

Peace with Germany   13 July 1951

We suppose that eventually it had to come. The state of quasi-hostility between the United Nations and the former Reich could not, in the very nature of things, continue for an eternity. No doubt the present relationship of tension between East and West hastened the formal forgiving and forgetting. We must confess, nevertheless, that we could not read the reports of peace and reconciliation without a good measure of distaste and disgust. When, moreover, these declarations were accompanied, as in some instances they were, by promise of new-born love and affection, embraces, kisses on both cheeks, and long-held warmly-grasped handclasps, the spectacle struck us, we must admit, as somewhat obscene.

Perhaps international necessity called for a peace to be struck with the heirs of Nazidom at the present time. Certainly there is no one who imagines that it is with a changed and reformed Germany that formal relations are now being instituted. From all sides, indeed, there come reports of diehard fascism, of recrudescent Nazism, of a Reich repentant only of its defeat. Only a desperate expediency can justify, if anything at all can justify, this much too early re-admission of the bandit polity into the comity of nations. But what does raise the gorge, what does sicken with its unseemliness, is the easy conscience with which all of this is being accomplished – nowhere is there any evidence of a wrestling with the spirit, the casualties of a great holocaust are as if they were not, utterly forgotten is the thunder and nemesis promised in the mighty utterances of Churchill and Roosevelt – all that one does see is but a dry as dust emotionless printed announcement in official gazettes that henceforward the years 1939–1945, and all their tragedy, are to be blotted out from the recollections of the new friends.

And that's all there's to it. One must, indeed, pause in wonder at the magic trickling from the pens of statesmen who with a mere scrawl can thus change memories freighted with anguish and nightmare into a clean candid *tabula rasa* where bygones so happily fade, vanish, leaving only the combined benign Cheshire grins of the signatories! The keener, therefore, is one's regret, that the same magic must fail to effect a resurrection of the hundreds of thousands slain on battlefields, the millions martyred in camps and crematoria, must fail to bring a healing to the monstrous multitudes crippled and maimed, must fail, in a word, to bring about the only kind of reintegration that would have pertinence and value!

We shall now see the German foreign office send forth its emissaries to the various United Nations, *herren* immaculately dressed, gentlemen soft-voiced and full of quotations from Goethe, diplomats making nice distinctions between the 'true' Germany which they represent and that optical illusion which for a decade managed somehow, despite its unreality, to create so much misery in the world – a brood of cooing doves all busily engaged in seeking help to rebuild again a fourth German Reich – Prussian might and power – the old Juggernaut this time again, as last time, temporarily turned East.

During the last war, we heard again and again, the promise that the penalty of the criminal Reich would be such that that type of crime would be effectively discouraged from recurring. It is to be surmised that what is now taking place was the kind of punishment envisaged – dire thunder from the bench, grim utterance in the sentence, and then an easy, expeditious ticket-of-leave!

Surveying the scene after the Kishineff massacre, the late immortal Chaim Nachman Bialik could not but be impressed by the shining aftermath of that pogrom, the indifference both of nature and the world to the abomination, the signs of which still lay before the eyes, and wrote, in words that are most relevant to the same before us, of that spectacle, forestaste and minuscule miniature of the pogrom colossal which our new ally perpetrated:

Pause not upon this havoc; go thy way.
The perfumes will be wafted from the acacia bud, –
And half its blossoms will be feathers,
Whose smell is the smell of blood.

Unto thy nostrils this strange incense they will bring.
Banish thy loathing – all the beauty of the spring,
The thousand golden arrows of the sun
Will bid thy melancholy to be gone;

The seven-fold rays of broken glass
Will bid thy sorrows pass;
For God called up the slaughter and the spring together –
The slayer slew, the blossoms burst, and it was sunny weather!

The Arab Refugees   21 September 1951

Timed to coincide with the Arab-Israel discussions now taking place under the auspices of the UN in Paris, discussions which are being conducted as through a screen – the Arabs refuse to sit at one table with those from whom they are now imploring concessions – certain elements of the American and British press have begun a campaign designed to elicit public sympathy for the Arab refugees. With such philanthropic motivation, taken in and by itself, we have no quarrel. None better than our people can understand what it means to be homeless and uprooted. We, too, would like to see the encamped thousands of Palestinian expatriates, deluded into abandoning their homes, given sanctuary and reintegration – provided such reintegration is undertaken within the perspective proper to the circumstances.

Kindness and humanitarianism are commendable qualities; but, here, let the facts be put straight. Not a single Palestinian Arab was ever expelled from the country by Jews! The flight of the Arabs was never the result of an imposed banishment; it was to be, so thought the 'refugees,' no more than a strategic withdrawal, a retirement from the area of battle, maintained until such time as the invading forces drove the Israelis into the sea; then, then the 'refugees' were to return to inherit the lands and the possessions of their enemies; and problems, international and personal, would be solved.

That things didn't turn out quite as planned was not due to the kindness and humanitarianism of the refugees. Civilians, they had decided to fulfil a military role; the battle went against them; wherefore they doff their martial hardihood, and plead as citizens expatriate.

It is not to be overlooked that there were great numbers of Palestinian Arabs who did not join in the conspiratorial evacuation. They remained, peaceful, in Palestine. With what result? With the result that not one has been molested, that all enjoy their full civil and religious rights, that their representatives sit in the Knesseth, and that their way of life is maintained in its fullest integrity.

It is to be noted furthermore that the Israeli Government, as its spokesmen have frequently declared, is not opposed on principle to the return of the refugees. It is, and always has been, ready to discuss this matter; but only as part of a total settlement. Certainly it is unthinkable that while Egypt insists on its rights of belligerency against Israel, despite the truce, as evidenced by its continuing Suez Canal blockade, and while the Arab countries persist in their economic boycott and speak openly of a 'second round,' that at such a time Israel should allow into the country – the enemy's soldiers! The fear is often expressed that these returning Arabs might some day constitute a 'fifth column'; that well may be; but at the moment their role is even more menacing: they are combatants, defeated it is true, but combatants ready and eager to continue the combat.

Their leader? The Mufti! It is enlightening, therefore, to see what proposals for repatriation issue from that pre-eminent source. The Mufti's plan, indeed, was presented at Paris. It was simply this: that the Arab refugees be returned to Israel and settled the length of its frontiers!

Could anything be more transparent? Arab leadership is not so much interested in their repatriation, as in placing them at the doors of the country, a static vanguard for the invaders! Naturally the Israeli Government has rejected this plan out of hand; it can think of more reliable gatekeepers.

Nor is the Mufti alone in his view touching the uses of the Arab refugees. All of the Arab leaders have repeatedly shed crocodile tears for lo! their poor relations; and all have persisted in leaving them were they are. And these leaders were, in the truest sense of the word, the very authors of the Arab misfortune; they it was who induced the panic, persuaded the reluctant, held forth promise of glory and booty! Yet not one Arab country has granted these refugees rights to citizenship! Even to their sustenance in the camps they have been indifferent; the refugees are being fed out of the funds of the United Nations.

What an eloquent contrast this affords to the manner in which affluent Jews come to the rescue of Jewry in destitution!

Thus far, indeed, all that one has heard at the Paris Conference is Arab demand. To give these demands a favorable ambience, it was, of course, desirable that the proper mood of pity and compassion be created. But ever and always the object is political. Thus, the Arabs were not slow in advancing yet another project: that Transjordan be afforded access to the port of Haifa! It seems that it is not sufficient for ultimate Arab purpose that the returned Arab refugees cordon the country in its length; there must also be a corridor through its width!

Surely these are not the requests of neighbours; they are of the cunning of antagonists.

And amidst all of these requests and petitions, not a word in suggestion of quid pro quo. The city of Jerusalem – must it still continue to be partitioned, half of it in the hands of the invader? Must the Hebrew University still remain inaccessible to those who established it and through it brought so much good to the people of the country, regardless of tribe? Must the Huleh region still remain debated ground? And Gaza – now occupied by Egyptians – is it of the land, or some isle in the sea? Above all, is it peace or war?

The Israelis want peace; but they want a reciprocal peace. They are tired of making all the concessions, and receiving in return – the casuistical speech of Syrian and Egyptian announcing unilateral truces. They see clearly that all this propaganda about the Arab D.P.'s is no more than a lachrymose cascade flung forward to conceal the military machinations of the Arab leaders. Settle the refugees? Yes, but settle the problem – all of it; not by piecemeal instalments, not by one-sided concessions, but by total resolution leading to permanent peace.

The first thing that is necessary is goodwill. This, the Arabs have yet to display. Certainly negotiations in which each party speaks to a third party for relay to the other, as the Arabs insist on doing (the discourtesy one may overlook, one cannot overlook the intransigence it demonstrates), are not very promising of success.

Buber's Prize   21 December 1951

The Goethe Prize – it is reported – which is awarded annually for the furthering of a 'supra-national outlook' will go this year to Dr. Martin Buber, professor of social philosophy at the Hebrew University of Jerusalem.

Now, here is a problem. There is no doubt but that no one better merits such a prize than Dr. Buber. Metaphysician of a philosophy of religion which, though grounded in Torah, assuredly transcends outlooks more national – Buber's main concern is with the I-Thou relationship, the relationship between God and man – Buber assuredly deserves this accolade. Being a philosopher, one therefore by vocation as unwealthy as Diogenes, he is in a position, no doubt, also to make use of the cash value of the prize – the material phenomenon of the spiritual noumenon.

But should he accept it? We hesitate to give advice to a philosopher, all we can indicate is what would pass through our mind were we tendered so flattering a distinction. That this is a distinction of the highest – an award coupled with the great name of Goethe – is beyond question. That there is a possibility that the gentlemen of Hamburg who selected Buber's name were sincere in their tribute is also conceivable. But is it fitting – six years after the holocaust – that the professor at the Hebrew University should accept honors from their people?

We realize, of course, that it is most unphilosophical to harbor a grudge. Certainly a philosopher of religion should take cognizance of a contrite heart. But then, to raise this issue is to confuse, rather than to clarify, thought on the subject. Is the prize being awarded because the German people wish to make a gesture? If so, the prize has nothing to do with Dr. Buber himself, but is being directed to the Jewish people. What that people's decision would be is not in doubt. That people would certainly reject a supra-national prize resulting from infra-national behaviour. Then, perhaps, the prize has nothing to do with contritions and regret. If so, Dr. Buber should certainly reject it.

Certainly it would be a disservice to our people, at the time when the Germans have not yet done anything to atone or compensate for the heinous crimes against millions of our kinsmen, for the philosopher of Chassidism, the exponent of our Creed, to enter into ceremonial and courtly relations with people who have probably saved the prize money from the sale of gold teeth extracted from Jewish crematoria victims. Here, too, Buber's philosophy is pertinent and receives a mundane interpretation; it is the 'You-They' philosophy; remember who you are, remember who 'they' are.

German Reparations 18 January 1952

Is it right for the State of Israel to accept on behalf of the surviving victims of Nazism, most of whom are now citizens, and in many instances, also charges within its borders, the offer of reparations recently made by Chancellor Adenauer? That is the question which is now agitating Jewish public opinion; and it is not a question easy to resolve. That Jew would indeed be bereft of all sensitivity who did not find it distasteful to think of negotiating, or having any truck or traffic, with the heirs and assigns of the butchers of but seven years ago. How great is the temptation to say: The hands of these people are still stained with blood; though those hands hold millions, we refuse to go within their reach! They have murdered six million of our kinsmen; they have pillaged and robbed us; – let them remain gorged with that blood and that plunder, the abomination of mankind, and to us, excommunicate and anathema; we shall not step within the four cubits of their ambience!

And had the Israeli Government, or the Jewish Agency, decided to indulge in such a gesture, its motivation, its prompting, would have been readily understood. Unfortunately, most of the important problems in life bewilder with alternatives more complex than that which beckons between black and white. The Lord in his wisdom placed in the affairs of men, as He set up in the heavens, a rainbow of selection; between black and white there are many gradations.

One recalls, in connection with these hard alternatives, the opening scene of *Cyrano de Bergerac*, by Rostand. Cyrano, it appears, is displeased with what is going on on the stage; even as we, surveying the world scene, Cyrano cares neither for its actors nor its action. Exercising the terror of his reputation and the power of his personality, he intimidates the actors into leaving the stage; and when they do, he flings to them, as compensation for their loss, his purse of gold! But later in the same scene, he is compelled to borrow money from a companion. 'You threw them all you had?' this companion queries incredulously. 'Yes – *quel geste!* What a gesture that was!' 'Yes,' replies his interlocutor, '*mais quelle sottise* – and what a stupidity!'

The fact is that much as the Israeli Government would prefer to reject any offer of reparations, it is not, either from a practical or moral viewpoint, in a position to indulge in such a luxury. It cannot afford it, practically, because the only purpose which reparations would serve would be to alleviate some of the continuing distress to which European Jews, now in Israel, were brought by the Hitler regime. The resources of the State, as is well known, are limited; to refuse alleviation would mean, at worst, to grant charter for the continuance of the Nazi havoc. At best, it would mean that American Jewry would be compelled, *pro tanto*, to come to the rescue; in other words, American Jewry would be called upon to pay German reparations!

Nor is this gesture possible morally. For what, in the long run, would such a gesture effect? It would effect an immunity for robbers. (There is no question here of 'paying' for the six million murdered ones; not all the gold, or diamonds, or uranium, of the world could compensate for that so grievous loss.) But refusal of reparations would mean that Jewish property illegally confiscated remains confiscated: the plunderer is not punished – he is *rewarded* by being allowed to retain his booty!

And yet – having presented some of the arguments *pro* and *con* – one is at a loss to know how one would have voted had one been a member of the Israeli Knesseth. The very fact that that vote evoked a large objecting minority indicates that this is not one of those easy problems that one can readily solve by syllogism, by theorem, by arithmetic. For in this matter there moves a systole and diastole of conviction – they are the movements of the heart – which now say *Yea* and now assert a most recalcitrant *Nay*.

In any event, it is a matter which the Israelis have a right to settle by the ordinary democratic process, without threat or intimidation from intransigent groups. The attempt made by the leaders of Herut to utilize an easily aroused hysteria to menace the members of the Knesseth as they sat in deliberation was deserving of the severest censure and of the most active suppression. It was in itself a fascist phenomenon. It would be a sorry day for Israel, indeed, when, under the guise of reprehending all that to fascism appertaineth, a wilful group succeeded in indulging with impunity in fascist tactics and blackmail.

Without the Prince of Denmark   1 February 1952

It has been reported – and subsequently modified, if not denied outright – for the which concession we are extremely grateful – that somewhere in the ranks of Mapam there is being circulated for the edification of its youngsters a book of readings from the Bible. This is a sensation in itself: Mapam, an extremely leftist but gratifyingly small party, is hardly the party that one would associate with Holy Writ. Here, however, comes the rub: these readings (from the Bible!) sedulously, meticulously, most cautiously, avoid all mention of God ...

The world's wonders never cease.

We have not been privileged to examine this ingenious text. We can only ponder in bewilderment at this singular *tour de force*. How, indeed, was it achieved? Is there an asterisk placed everywhere where the name of Deity would ordinarily occur, or is it only a blank space? How, we would like to know, is the very first verse of the very first chapter of Genesis handled? Does it read: In the beginning the heaven and earth were created by You Know Who? Or is the reference invariably made, in the spirit of the *Sneh* (both the biblical and the contemporary one), to I-Am-That-I-Am? And what do the poor sucklings of the kindergarten say about all this darkness and allusiveness, the new Marxian mystery, this latter-day tabu?

We are at a loss for answers. What we can't figure out is why these mute blasphemers should have found it necessary at all to feed their infants on biblical pabulum? Is it because the rest of Israel, in this new Messianic age, is returning with greater and still greater fervour to the ancient sources, the original fountains of inspiration, that the Mapamniks fear lest their progeny be left out of things? If so, why the deletion from the Decalogue of four of its commandments and the passing over of all mention of Providence?

When Premier Ben-Gurion came to power, he anticipated no doubt all manner of difficulty. Certainly he could have foreseen that the orthodox elements would exercise whatever power they had to bring religious influence to bear upon the daily official life of Israel. It is to the great credit of the Israeli Premier that he has met such demands wherever possible. Indeed, it often seems to us that Mr. Ben-Gurion is much more religiously minded than the religious bloc itself; for that bloc strives earnestly to make God a cabinet minister, with a small portfolio, while B.G. sees Him as controlling an Upper House whose providential legislation manifests itself in the social ideals of the new State.

But how Ben-Gurion is to cope with lunacies such as have provoked this column is beyond us. Fortunately, the thing is so unique as to be sensational. But how – sensational! Imagine it – a Bible without God! If one had gone out of one's way to stretch absurdity to its absurdest, one could not have better (*sic*) achieved one's purpose. Until yesterday, when one wished to speak of that which was at once empty and ridiculous, one spoke of *Hamlet* without the Prince of Denmark. But the Bible without the King of Kings ...

Truly, those whom   would destroy, He first makes insane!

Israel and Germany   6 June 1952

There can be nothing but admiration for the attitude adopted by the Government of the State of Israel with regard to the contract of peace recently effected between Germany and the civilized world. Ordinary people all over the world, indeed, watched with astonishment as the German Reich, but seven years ago proclaimed arch-criminal, and during the past seven years making but the feeblest gestures of contrition, was once again embraced by its former enemies, embraced and welcomed back to the fold like some dear, though erring, brother. The spectacle was certainly not one which was calculated to evoke in the unsophisticated an extraordinary admiration for the implacable righteousness of statesmen. Aspects about this transaction there were which could not but prompt disgust.

Indeed, as we scanned the smiling photographs of the representatives of the high contracting parties – Acheson's furry grin, Adenauer's cadaverous charm – we could not but recall the dying prophecy of Adolf Hitler: Whoever wins, Germany cannot lose. Had one not watched the preparation of this mésalliance through all the obscene stages of the recent courtship, the thing, as it actually occurred, would have been utterly incredible, something to be dismissed as an optical illusion. Imagine it! The barbarian hordes of yesterday hailed as the gallant comrades of to-morrow! The unspeakable enemy converted overnight into honourable associate!

As if to point up the unnaturalness of this political act of miscegenation, the Germans themselves provided the focus of a side-play. For as the details of the alliance were being arranged – the amount of the dowry, the respective duties of the consorts – Frau Funk, wife of Walter Funk former director of Nazi finances, now confined to Spandau Fortress, was busily engaged in circulating a petition requesting amnesty for the un-executed murderers at Spandau. To this end she was enlisting the support of numerous denazified (*sic*) politicians, all of whom agreed that Rudolph Hess, Karl Doenitz, Baron Konstantin von Neurath, Albert Speer, Baldur von Schirach, and Erich Raeder should immediately be set at liberty.

We do not think that it is necessary at this point to tell our readers who these men of blood are. It was an arrant miscarriage of justice that they were not executed together with the other monsters of Nazism. But to ask that they be freed after an incarceration of less than seven years – men who hold-up a drug-store have gotten more – that were impossible were it not for the new political climate in Germany, and elsewhere.

Audacious, therefore, as was Frau Funk's intervention, it was not altogether illogical. If it is right that one forgive the thousands of ordinary Nazis because they may be tomorrow's useful soldiers and sailors, it is, *a fortiori*, right that one forgive the leaders, generals, and admirals, of the soldiers and sailors. If the argument of expediency is valid in the one instance, it is even more valid in the case of a minister of finance, like Funk, a great production genius (taskmaster of millions of slaves) like Albert Speer, a commander of the navy, like Karl Doenitz. Why, if it were possible to resurrect the noble Goering, or reconstitute out of his ashes, the peerless Fuehrer, why ...

Justly does the Government of Israel, which speaks not only for many thousands of the survivors of the Nazi gehenna, but also for the six million of its victims, turn from the whole transaction with revulsion and deep distaste. Its consuls and representatives in German territory, serving their function under the occupation, are to be withdrawn; its signature certainly is not to appear upon this premature act of oblivion, this cynical act of reconciliation.

A Fable   8 August 1952

The warfare among the beasts of the forest, unceasing and bloody, was taking its toll. One day it was a hare that fell prey to superior guile, the next day a fox that fell victim to superior force. The wolf was beaten by the bear, the bear was mauled by the tiger, the tiger devoured by the lion.

Nobody felt safe. And everywhere the complaint was the same – the inequalities of combat. The denizens of the forest were not evenly matched. In most conflicts, the outcome was a foregone conclusion. It was not only not sporting, it was fatal.

And indeed, was the porcupine with his puny quills a match for the pachydermatose monster who laid him low? Could the elephant with his ferocious tusks be dared by the small, furred, toothless midgets? Of what avail the majestic antlers of the stag against the fang and claws of the brigand wolf? And how could one cope with the lion, supple and daring, mighty of paw, carnivorous?

Meanwhile, as these questions – snorted, howled, roared, bellowed – were rhetorically advanced, contention continued. The population of the forest was being systematically decimated.

'And by ourselves!' said the fox.

Making use of his natural persuasiveness – something about united rations – the fox convoked, under a declaration of temporary truce, a general assembly of all the beasts of the domain. As the lion stood by, sullen and suspicious, the fox presided over the meeting and began by explaining its purpose.

It was not that anyone entertained any thought of outlawing war; that – in a jungle – was unthinkable. (Sighs of relief. Roars of applause. Groans of despair.) Not he would ever be the one to move for the degeneration of the noble animal species. The qualities of resourcefulness, bravery, self-sacrifice, engendered by war, ought ever to be kept alive in the race – even if it did mean the death of some individual members of that race. These would not have died in vain. (Belches.) But things had come to such a pass that war was no longer a true test of courage. Why? Because the combatants were not equal!

Could it be said that the struggle between his humble self and, let us say, meaning no offense, a tiger – was a fair fight? A fair fight was one in which both champions went forward to the fray similarly and equally armed. Was it just to oppose the feeble horns of the goat against the crushing, tearing, overwhelming ponderosity – the example was random – of a bear?

No; the truth of this fact everyone, at one time or another, had felt, either in his own person or through his kith and kin. What was now needed was an inter-animal convention, a supra-bestial agreement laying down the rules of war, a pact which would outlaw –

Dozens of ears stood cocked. Now, at last, a solution!

' – which would outlaw,' the fox continued deliberately, 'the use of paws, claws, horns, antlers, tusks – '

Here the fox was interrupted by a squirrel gesturing towards a skunk and shouting: 'Chemical warfare, too?'

'Everything, except one thing, one weapon.' He paused for effect. 'Intelligence.'

The din which greeted this announcement was surely not intended as applause. 'A wise guy!' ... 'A smart aleck.' ... 'Everybody's weapon – but his own!' ... 'How foxy can you get!'

'Ask him how and with what he ate that chicken last night? ... Intelligence!'

But the assembled delegates did not wait for answers to their jarring questions. 'Give up my claws!' cried the wolf with indignation. 'I'll give it up alright! Right into the deer's throat!'

'Without tusks!' snorted the elephant. 'Good. How about this? Is this legal?' And he squashed with his foot a bear that was raising its paw to strike down a jackal that was going for a field-mouse.

The fox, however, was a born parliamentarian. Rowdy audiences disturbed him not at all. 'All those in favour of my motion,' he said, 'please signify by raising the right hand.' ...

At this, so menacing a forest of paws, claws, tusks, even fangs – all moving forward towards the chair – bristled in the air that the fox forthwith climbed a tree and asked for a leave of absence.

But the meeting did not disperse. It was now converted into a melee, a free-for-all. Everybody was howling at the same time; above the noise the lion's roar could be heard.

Then – suddenly – a shot was heard!

A great silence fell upon all the beasts. They knew what this meant – something more powerful than anything they had was approaching. Those two-legged things were in the vicinity. They were as if paralyzed.

Descending from his tree-limb, the fox again took the chair. 'I have,' he said, 'a new motion to put forward. Did you hear that noise? Do you know what it is? It's a bomb, an at-him bomb, and the him is us! I tell you it is a weapon the most shameful, the most uncivilized, the most anti-jungle, ever yet invented! I call for a formal vote against it. Better, I ask our friend, the bear, to pass around the peace petition.'

Oh, what a scratching and a scrawling was there, with claw and tusk and tooth!

The meeting then adjourned, the delegates withdrawing each to his own pursuit, the wolf to claw at the two-legged one's lamb, the fox to steal his chickens, and the bear to raid his honey.

Of Armorial Bearings   15 August 1952

A suggestion has been made in Israel, its author preferring to remain anonymous, that a Herald's College be established and that coats of arms be devised for the country's notabilities. – (News report)

We must confess that the item adduced above evoked in us a set of mingled feelings. Our first reaction was one of excited approval; some new colour, we felt, would thus be introduced into the drabness of life; how rich and fascinating would shine the shields of Yemenite, Moroccan, Bokharan Jew! Other peoples, moreover, indulged in such self-flattery, why not the Israelis?

We recalled indeed, our experiences and our reactions, when we had first encountered the gorgeous shields of chivalry.

We resented, as if they were oblique allusions to a personal degradation, Europe's proud crests and scutcheons. As we moved through the renowned capitals of that continent, these arrogant blazonings, that were to us not other than usurpations, seemed to be deriding us, detractive, jeering. It was as if beneath every scroll there ran the orgulous device: *We are of the elect. Who crawls there below?* On public monument, over sculptured gate, and even on the tapestries of chairs antique, the fatuous emblems proclaimed their own pre-eminence, while their every curling line curled, as it were, a nose at us, over-weening and disdainful. We walked amidst a taunting of shields, a heckling of banners. Everywhere Europe's aristocracy trumpeted itself heraldic, noble.

Yet how upstart this aristocracy was, how unworthily won! When the ancestors of these who now arrayed themselves in vert and gules and azure – the comparison was irresistible – still ran naked through the forests, barbarians bedaubed with the juice of roots, bloodied of the boar, *our* ancestors had already discovered the living God, and had built Him a temple, and had established before Him a ritual, lofty, spiritual, pure. From Him it was, from that Liege Lord, King of kings, that they held their patents of nobility, from Him than whom is no higher sovereignty, and not from some uncouth robber-chief, his hand stained with slaughter, with his knife dubbing his henchmen gentle, bidding each rise, though besotted, Sir Knight, Sir Knight.

We thought, then, of the oldest and the most serene of insignia, those worn by the High Priest, priest of priests, on the Day of Atonement, sabbath of sabbaths, while ministering in the innermost sanctum, the holy of holies. We thought of those things made for beauty and for glory, the resplendent ephod and the jewelled breastplate. Twelve were its precious stones for the twelve incomparable sons, twelve gems for twelve tribes, twelve constellations shining from the sacred ephod on the most sacred of the twelve months! Armorial bearings of a holy militancy, they were now no longer valid, they were obsolete, but across the centuries and over the din of the thundering chariots, one could still hear, in the midst of those mystic pauses that sometimes come to hush the world's turbulence, the pious tintinnabulation of the bells and pomegranates of the High Priest, moving, as in a trance, alone, within the secret sanctuary, – sounds faint and delicate, like the last death-breaths of saints, so immaterial they will not fog a glass.

Heirs of a heraldry such as this, the charges and figures of the beauty of holiness, what need was there to go rummaging among the charters and designs of a newcome self-appointed aristocracy? What did the Earl Marshal, what did the Kings at Arms, propound that deserved to be emulated? One had only to scan the devices with which they adorned the fields of their escutcheons to discover where their hearts lay, what their standards were, what symbols they deemed flattering. Argent, a dragon proper, tail nowed – was that not a wonderful mirror to flash before the sprigs and imps of an honoured house, model to be imitated, in all its monstrous features, right down to its knotted, arrow'd tail? Gules, a boar's head proper couped – now there was a right good standard to bring distinction and eminence to those who vaunted it! Or the gryphon, abortion of two kingdoms; or the wivern, spawn of a foul miscegenation; or the eagle displayed, its talons flashed.

These be the paragons, these the gods that win their worship – not a one but he is furr'd, or tusked, or claw'd, or sheer monster appalling, all creatures of prey, hunters, tearers, devourers. But where is imaged the seraph on a shield? Is there to be found anywhere among these quarterings, designed to set before their bearers an exalting sign, the figure of the cherubim rampant regardant? Do not all these scutcheons proclaim everywhere the virtue of the untamed beast, the hunger and power of the swooping bird? Ah, but they must have swords! Then why is that angel, he of the turning sword, unknown to the herald's office?

No, there is nothing here to imitate or transcribe. Moreover, the day is long since past for such ill-conceived snobberies. The Israeli who dreams to-day of such hierarchical distinctions simply does not understand the spirit of the times. Not only are the badges and ensigns of mediaevalism to-day pathetic anachronisms, but even those sacred emblems, in the contemplation of which we did, a moment ago, so smugly indulge our spirit, even these have passed, have vanished, are potent only as memories. There is but one device to-day, shape it as you will, that lifts and honours – the forked Chinese ideogram, symbol of man. It is no mean symbol, seeing that it is also *effigo Dei*; and he who lives up to the pretensions of such a coat of arms is, indeed, of the true nobility.

The Day of Atonement   26 September 1952

Nothing so succinctly, and yet so eloquently, expresses the spirit which should move the faithful on the day of Yom Kippur as that pithy, and seemingly dogmatic, assertion which in bold black type dominates, and through cantorial rendition, informs with pathos the High Holiday Services. 'Fasting, prayers, and alms,' says the rubric, 'annul the severity of the judgment.'

It seems like but another pious dictum invented by theologians to bend the spirit towards contrition and reform. Yet how psychologically shrewd, how true, how deep, this triple counsel is! For these three attitudes designed to soften the judgment of the Recording Angels must inevitably effect a spiritual transformation which goes beyond the mere gesture of their performance.

Though the triple code appears to enjoin acts that are but formal in their nature, such acts cannot honestly be performed unless preceded by that *sine qua non* of religious observance – a change of heart.

For what is fasting? Not a mere mortification of the flesh, not simply a one-day dietary experiment, but a lesson, impressed upon the very bloodstream itself, a lesson to set up in the midst of that which is closest to man – his own body – the wrangling contrast between the material and the spiritual. What soul is there that has not at one time or another longed to rise to the status of the angels, untainted by food, force of all grossness? It is, of course, for the body of man shackled by creature needs, an impossible ambition. Let there be taken, then, a tentative step in that direction; let there be accomplished a partial foretaste (see how even in one's longing towards things spiritual the images of the material creep in, so caught is one in the mesh of flesh!), a foretaste of freedom from animal needs, – for fasting is a kind of inner ablution, a preparation, a conditioning of the spirit. It does not mean, this abnegation of a single day, that the world is rejected; it means only – only! – that for a space the heart of man looks, catches a glimpse of, 'the pure serene.'

And prayers? Is it to be imagined that He who is omniscient must wait the articulation of prayers before He may know the heart's desire? To utter prayers in such a spirit is to blaspheme. He who knows all knows the hunger of His petitioners while yet they think themselves sated. No, the saying of prayers is of the things invented for man, not for God. To pray is to talk to one's self; to probe one's longings so as to discover whether they be worthy; to take an accounting of the soul; prayer is a spiritual exercise. Like fasting, it is a preparatory office.

And it is at this point that the votary turns from things divine to things human, and through things human serves the divine. Alms – it is an oriental word, and not without its objectionable, because patronizing, connotations. Some other word ought to be found to translate the original *zdakah*, which has in it at once undertones of justice – *zedek* – and overtones of saintliness – *zadik*. What is enjoined indeed, is a thing simple to understand, difficult, perhaps, to perform, namely, that we do right one by the other. For certainly the most spiritual – and the most practical – way of serving the Maker is so to act that all one's actions show that all bodies our Maker has made are as our own body dear, that all persons are one humanity.

To what may this thing be likened? To a subject who came before his king, and said: 'Majesty, I would serve you. Do but tell me how.' To which the king replied: 'I stand not in the need of any man's service. If you would serve, serve the subjects of my kingdom. You shall thus serve me.'

The Case of Regina O'Hara   21 November 1952

We gather from *American Judaism*, the official organ of Reform Judaism on this continent, that theological circles are now bending all their scholastic talents towards the solving of the weighty canonical problem presented by the case of Regina O'Hara. Regina O'Hara, a convert to Judaism, is intent, it appears, upon applying for admission to the Hebrew Union College Jewish Institute of Religion to study for the rabbinate. Arise, then, two large questions. *Quaere*: May a female officiate as rabbi? And *quaere*: Is it possible for an O'Hara to have the true Mosaic vocation?

This is, indeed, a knotty problem. If we venture an opinion upon it, that opinion must be taken as that of a simple layman, bereft of authority either to bind or to loosen. For we have conferred neither with the local Council of Orthodox Rabbis nor with Rabbi Stern, both of which bodies no doubt can muster chapter and verse to support their inevitably contradictory conclusions. The remarks which follow must be construed, then, as mere passing commentary. The destiny of Regina O'Hara must surely await higher disposition.

There are, of course, a number of difficulties which, as the French say, 'leap into the eyes.' Is it really possible for a girl, not from Minsk but from Mayo, to determine from an inspection of its innards whether a chicken is kosher or not? To the gentiles, can the liver bring light? Will she really feel at home instructing *shochtim* touching silk of the kine? How about her liturgic brogue – Ashkenazic or Sephardic?

Nonetheless we cannot resist the assertion, advanced by ourselves as by an *amicus curiae*, that the granting of spiritual authority to a woman is not without precedent in our religious annals. Thus was Miriam filled with the spirit; thus was Deborah made a vessel for words inspired; and thus – to leap the centuries – did the daughter of Rashi suffer a laying on of hands. Of this last female mentor it is reported that she taught the lesson to her father's disciples while standing behind a curtain. Modesty had perforce to be preserved. Even if the same sensitivities prevail to-day as prevailed in the eleventh century, this should be no bar to the Reverend Regina O'Hara's religious functions; her sermons would easily be delivered from behind a screened pulpit – *vox*, as it were, *et praeterea nihil*.

It is the O'Hara, both the name itself and its intimations of gentility, – to judge from inhospitable opinions already expressed – that appear to constitute for this special calling an impediment more serious than sex. And here, too, we are all for a leniency of interpretation. The name, surely, should be deemed no handicap; one has but to go through the pages of the Talmud to encounter – not, forsooth, Irish names – but names equally as foreign to the pristine Hebrew nomenclature. Moreover, O'Hara, as it happens, has a singularly Hebraic resonance; we would not be surprised if some Dublin scholar were to come forward with proof that the name is derived, not from the Gaelic, but from the Hebrew, from the Hebrew verb *horoh*, perhaps; in any event, this objection is easily dismissed. If there may be rabbis whose first names are Montmorency, we may have *rebbitzins* whose surnames are O'Hara.

As for Miss O'Hara's antecedents, there is no law in our corpus of jurisprudence which excludes the convert from spiritual leadership. One of the translations of the Bible that makes authority – the Targum Onkelos – is reputed to be that of a convert. We are at a loss to see anything incongruous, let alone prohibited, in an epistle from the Hibernians to the Hebrews. If, as is generally conceded, a sermon is rendered the more attractive the more English there is put upon it, why should a bit of Irish, a touch of high serious blarney, a cadence of Synge-song, be considered tabu? *Abie's Irish Rose*, the records show, ran for weeks and weeks. The combination is a natural.

There is, finally, the question of reciprocity. We have not the statistics at hand, but Jewry, it seems to us, has given more than one Father Greenberg to the Christian Churches. A pulpiteering O'Hara may well be considered a *quid pro quo*, a mutual exchange *do ut des*. We think this is the point of those good-will meetings frequently arranged for the purpose of cementing better relations between the faiths. How wonderful, how truly harmonious, it would be if at such a meeting a Cohen represented the Christians, an O'Hara the Jews!

Yes, we are altogether in favour of Miss O'Hara's admission to the Jewish Institute of Religion. It may be that by the time she completes her course, she may no longer be interested in the rabbinate as a profession; it may be that through marriage she may become a *rebbitzin*, as it were, by *ricochet*; whatever the times may bring, we certainly would not bar her way with xenophobic restrictions. The O'Hara, all technicalities notwithstanding, has our vote. Confident are we that with her convert's zeal and natural eloquence, Rabbina O'Hara, like Father O'Flynn in the song, would make drakes of them all.

The Golems of Prague   28 November 1952

The wonderful legend, floated abroad from 'the seacoast of Bohemia,' which tells how Rabbi Jacob Loew, in the hour of his people's need, fashioned upon the banks and out of the mud of the Moldau river, a *golem*, an automaton, which would do his inspired bidding, is one of the brightest fables to issue out of the darkness of Jewish diaspora history. One pauses, as one recalls the details of this great adventure in Cabbala, to wonder about the precise articulation of the tetragrammaton, the four-lettered name of God, which the audacious rabbin used to effect his miracle; one follows the adventures of this golem, the clod suddenly become defender of the faith; and at length, after his many vicissitudes, and particularly at the dénouement of the tale when everything goes wrong (a golem is only a golem), one realizes that an artifact, a mere mechanical man, is no substitute for the truly human in the image of God created. A legend, it is also a parable, vibrating with multitudinous significances touching our human condition; its moral is ineluctable – the man who would fashion a human out of a clod of earth is doomed to defeat; for this creator, he is himself but earthly clod.

He is a kind of Hebrew Faust, this Rabbi Jacob Loew of Prague, and his example has ever since inflamed the imagination of many spirits unhappily cabin'd within the four close walls of human potentiality. Frankenstein is of this golem's lineage, and so, too, in a latter day, are Karel Čapek's Bohemian robots. However, with the passage of time and time's perennial frustrations, the challenge of the golem was abandoned as a *tour de force*, it was conceded, now impossible of accomplishment. The world turned its back upon these mediaeval monstrosities; the report of their fashioning was dismissed as mere legendary; the world gave itself over to science.

But the pendulum swings back – and with a vengeance. For that ancient city of Prague, still echoing with the lumbering heavy footsteps of the man Friday who was Rabbi Jacob Loew's, is once again a scene for magical performances. This time there is not but one golem who strides upon the stage – there are fourteen! For fourteen are they who taking their stand within Czechoslovakia's Soviet high court, now do imitate the antics and gestures of that aboriginal citizen, the golem: they ventriloquize, even as he did; they make pantomime, as once he did. There is, of course, a difference. Rabbi Loew's golem was a benign creation.

Never, in our wildest imaginings, did we conceive the possibility that the day would come when Joseph Stalin would seek, even in a perverted way, to imitate the example of Jacob Loew. Yet it has happened. The fourteen accused, now standing trial in Prague, daily mimic the attitudes of their model. The mysterious puppet-master pulls the unseen strings – surely there is no tetragrammaton involved here – and the puppets, all fourteen of them, sound forth from their own reverberant hollowness the expected chorus of guttural guiltys. The Zohar glows again, with Marxist commentary.

Since this is the technique – a technique torn from the tradition – it is not surprising that the great majority of the accused are Jews. For this is an anti-Jewish trial that is taking place a stone's throw from the antique venerable synagogue in the attic of which there still remain hidden – so it is reported – the curious talismans of Rabbi Loew. The faded abracadabra shines once more.

Naturally enough, the indictments resound with charge of Titoism and Trotskyism, ignominiously crowned by Zionism. It is not the mere *minyan* that stands in the dock that is on trial; the prosecution hopes to convict – and this prosecution's hopes are always fulfilled – an entire movement, an ideology, a people's aspiration.

It is for this reason that this judicial show – this Loew's Circuit – is so menacingly meaningful to world Jewry. For the Czech trials, though obviously useful to the regime as a political cathartic, signify more than a simple, though violent, changing of the guard. They constitute the opening cannonade in a campaign against Jewry in general, and Israel in particular. The polity which once boasted that its was the only domain on the face of the earth where Antisemitism was a criminal offense has itself launched upon a career of racist criminality. It is no accident that most of the accused are Jews; this is the result of a designed process of selection; it is no accident that in Soviet Russia itself Jews have been eliminated from all positions of influence, and Judaism itself – such of it as remained – reduced to the condition of a crypto-culture. Apparently the makers of Soviet policy, cynical as ever, have realized that central Europe, after Hitlerism, is still covered with vestiges of the Ice Age; it seeks, accordingly, to exploit that asset at the same time as it pursues its own international machinations. The onslaught upon Zionism and the State of Israel is simply a variation upon the Czarist Russian theme: the threat to-day, presumably, is not from the Elders of Zion; it is from its youngsters. That the day should have come when Junkers and Zionism could be straight-facedly advanced as related concepts! But propaganda maketh all.

Purge trials are not new things within the Soviet orbit. By now, they are 'wine of the country.' As long as they were directed against purely home-bred talent, they remained, easily, matters of indifference to us. Our sympathy for the humans caught in the net was always alleviated by the recollection that they were Communists themselves, that is to say, net-flingers who had suffered a mishap. But these trials strike us where we live. They sound all the rumblings of a vast antisemitic prelude. They glower at the precariously located State of Israel. And they bode no good for the two and a half million Jews whom the Soviets hold in fee.

But one consoling factor emerges. It is now made clear to our own western brand of Antisemites that Communism and Zionism are, to put it mildly, antipathetic. How much good this will do, we do not know; the local Antisemite, in danger of being deprived of his so cherished phobia, will no doubt assert that this antipathy announced as existing between Communism and Zionism is itself a piece of Communist (or Zionist) propaganda. For though the incorrigible receive, they are not edified by, correction.

The Feast of Chanukah 12 December 1952

All of the holidays of the Hebrew calendar commemorate the occasions of some divine intervention. Whether it be the saga of Passover or the tale of Purim, in both one discerns the unseen hand of God. Our festivals, for the most part, are mementos of martyrdom and miracle, bondage and redemption, ordeal and wonder. Even the Book of Esther, which makes no mention of God's name, remains, nevertheless, preeminently a religious tract, the record of an adventure in which mysteriously-inspired dreams work the harassment and final discomfiture of the enemy. The same is true of the accounts which provide authority for all our other feast-days and fast-days; they all owe their origin to some sensational incident, some outstanding event, in which the human actors were but the passive instruments wherewith angels and heavenly ministers accomplished their gratifying but most inscrutable designs. The protagonist, if such a term may be applied in this connection, was always God; humans were merely the agonists.

The sole exception in this red-letter list is the long war associated with the name of the Hasmoneans. Here, too, of course, the Hand is ever a divine Hand (in the Book of Maccabees no arrow is ever twanged from the bow but tribute is paid to the Lord of Hosts); the voices that are heard upon the historic stage, however, are the voices of men, of warriors, of champions. These voices proclaim, as did the voice of the aged Mattathias: *Who is for God – to me!* That memorable call, however, that stirring gesture, comes down through the centuries, not with sacerdotal mellifluousness but with fierce bellicosity, it is a war-cry, not an intonation, that we hear. The Book of Maccabees has its prayers, but they are prayers before and after onset. The centre of attention is battle.

Not that the story of Chanukah is bereft of the elements of the miraculous. The tale of Hannah and her seven sons belongs, in spirit and in act, to the chronicle of the cruse of oil, which the soldiers found in the Temple, and which should have fed fire but for one day and did in fact feed it for eight – this is a Hasmonean anecdote which has consistently stirred the racial imagination, answering, as it does, man's insatiable appetite for miracle, the desire that never passes for the passing strange.

But the holiday itself is a military holiday. Its record, in the very opening sentence, makes allusion to a great military leader, 'Alexander the Macedonian, the son of Philip, who came out of the land of Chittim, and smote Darius.' So much for gentile prowess; the story then rushes *in medias res,* to concern itself with Antiochus Epiphanes (God made manifest) and his provocations against the Jews. 'He entered presumptuously into the sanctuary, and took the golden altar, and the candlestick of the light, and all that pertained thereto, and the table of the shewbread, and the cups to pour withal, and the bowls, and the golden censers, and the veil, and the crowns, and the adorning of gold which was on the face of the temple, and he scaled it all off.' Swine were sacrificed upon the altar; the sanctuary itself became 'a place to lie in wait in.' No wonder that 'every bridegroom took up lamentation, she that sat in the marriage chamber was in heaviness, great mourning was upon Israel.'

Such the *casus belli*, then rose up in those days Mattathias, of Modin, who, zealous for the law, did unto the swine-sacrificers 'even as Phineas did unto Zimri, the son of Salu.' Five sons he had, of whom Judah was the bravest and most cunning; Maccabaeus he was called, from *Makab*, a hammer. The hammer smote. The dying testament of the old Mattathias was itself as an army with banners ('Be not afraid of the words of a sinful man; for his glory shall be dung and worms') and they moved against the Syrian hosts. Appolonius was slain, his sword taken; a great victory was had at Bethhoron; another at Mizpeh; Georgias and his legions were routed, the hindmost falling by the sword; at Akrabathine the children of Esau were smitten with a great slaughter. Timotheus, leader of the Ammonities, was pursued and 'possession was got of Jazer and the villages thereof'; met again by the brook near Carnaim (The Horns), he was again defeated. Chapter after Maccabean chapter is thus devoted to a recounting of the military exploits which marked the war against Hellenism.

The Book of Maccabees, indeed, affords the only example in our annals which may be considered as a parallel to Caesar's *Gallic Wars*, with this distinction, of course, that the Maccabeans fought a war of resistance and liberation while the Romans conducted a war of conquest and subjection. Yet despite the glory of the Hasmonean triumphs, the martial spirit in Jewry throughout the centuries was hardly stirred. While the Book of Esther is accorded the distinction of public recital on Purim, the Books of the Maccabees remain among the Apocrypha. Save by scholars, they are never read. To the mass of Jewry, it is as if they were not. A Chanukah *dreidel*, that spinning memorial thingumajig; pancakes; candles and candelabrum, – these exhaust the paraphernalia of Chanukah celebration. Of the many devices used by the Maccabees in their open battles and sudden skirmishes against the enemy – of their concealment in caves and their sallies of surprise – of pitched encounter and Fabian evasion – of these matters there is not much talk in Jewry.

Now we do not counsel a sudden transformation of the habits and outlook of the people whose greeting is: Peace. The fact remains, however, the changed times evoke changed *mores*. Already there prevails in Israel a system of conscription which brings to the colours, in one field or another, a vast proportion of the population, male and female. Such a standing army is not to be nourished with contemporary slogans alone; the recollection of ancient virtue, the glorification of recent exploit, in a word, martial tradition – this is at least as important to officers as their mess, as important to rank and file – since it, too, is a weapon – as their armament. One way of fostering such a tradition is by holding up before the people the scrolls, not only of their idylls, like the Book of Ruth, nor of their moralities, like the Book of Jonah, nor of their salvations, like the Book of Esther, but also of their courage and self-help, like the Books of the Maccabees. We move, accordingly, for the re-instatement of these Books into the canon and corpus of living, remembered, and quoted literature. Such a reading, certainly, would constitute a fitting ceremony for the celebration of that which occurred 'early in the morning, on the five and twentieth day of the ninth month, which is the month of Kislev.'

Stalin Purges Doctors! 16 January 1953

It may be that an attempt to peer through the interstices of the Iron Curtain, even with the telescopic help of the Associated Press, is of necessity an exercise in frustration; it may be that what one distantly diagnoses as symptoms are no more than shadows evanescent, describable for an instant and then destined to disappear; it may indeed be that the sinister deductions recently drawn from what appeared to be manoeuvres distinctly anti-Jewish did do grave injustice to honest Stalin's right good innocent intentions. For the sake of the more than two million Jews whom he holds as hostage, we sincerely hope so. Yet much as wishful thinking would seek to induce belief that the new Slavic anti-semitism is limited in its scope and incidence, that these prisoners' docks crammed with Jewish accused are accidents, a temporary aberration of the law of averages, and that Prague's freighted gallows are but mirages of the mind, we cannot banish the suspicion, we cannot at all dispel the fear that these judicial unfoldings and these journalistic revelations constitute the opening moves of some vast, calculated and callous design against the liberties, such as they are, and the persons of the Jewries of Soviet Russia and its satellites.

For all seems to move here as in some madly-prompted yet cleverly conceived drama, the brainchild of some sick, cynical playwright whose idiosyncrasy it is to think of his work as being subject to but a single presentation, the actors perishing with the *première*. Its overture was provided by that chorus of eleven who, having elocuted, by way of prologue, their inspired and prepared confessions, were from the stage drawn upward by the rising curtain. Their exit was a dangle of feet, a histrionic assumption which opened to the audience the prospect of the play proper.

What the theme of the play is to be, what course it will take, its development, its peripeteia, its climax and denouement, – these are matters still carefully concealed behind the inscrutable countenance of the Kremlin's master. Premonitions as to what is likely soon to take place upon the stage, however, do throw a numbness over the heart. One recalls the past triumphs of this impresario, and the blood runs cold. One remembers his remark to Dzerjinski in 1923 – this playwright showed early promise – and the grim and gory already vibrates behind the curtain. 'To choose the victim,' he had then said, 'to choose the victim and carefully prepare the blow, to have one's glass of tea, and then go to bed, confident in the assurance that all will be duly executed – there is nothing sweeter in the world.' Zinoviev, who made the study of Stalin a life-work, albeit thankless, understood his subject well. 'If we die suddenly,' he wrote in a letter put aside for post-mortem reading, 'let it be known that it is the work of Stalin.'

The dramatic works of Stalin, insofar as their general skill and tenor is concerned, are not difficult to estimate. Only motives, methods, and *dramatis personae* remain to be revealed. As to the last, a hint has been given; identities, indeed, have been provided. But a few days ago, *Pravda*, converting itself into a playsheet for the latest production of the master-spirit, published the names of nine physicians who, it is clearly indicated, are shortly to appear before the judicial footlights, charged with murder, treason, deviation, and spying, not to mention malpractice. These doctors, variously described as therapeutists and neuro-pathologists, six of them Jews, were assigned, it appears, to look after the health and well-being of leading Soviet politicians, including the man who once stood in relation of heir-apparent to Stalin, one Zhdanov. But these Jewish doctors, so runs the *Pravda* story, instead of curing, killed. Were these fatalities the result of faulty diagnosis, an error in the prescription, a numb palpation or a deaf percussion? No. Confessions made by the accused, says *Pravda*, and *Pravda* means Truth, indicate that the wicked physicians had sold themselves to foreign powers, were conspiring against the State, and had wilfully destroyed the personages entrusted to their care.

Certainly the props are all here; there is no doubt but that a stage-trial is in the making. Already one can see the accused, robed in medical white, denouncing themselves guilty of every crime in both the code and the pharmacopoeia. Frantically will the physicians seek to heal themselves. Healing, however, will come only when they have taken their own medicine. Forewarned, their attitude is foreseen, themselves foredoomed.

But it is precisely there where the farcical indictments and travestied verdicts end, that the significance of this drama begins. Obviously the planned purge is but a point of departure; the question is: departure in which direction? Are the charges but the upshot of some internal intrigue that now explodes in public, an intrigue in which the participants *happened* to be Jews? Or is this all a set-up, a phony pharmaceutical concoction, now being well-shaken before use by the innocent primed masses? What does it purport? The charge of assassination by prescription is not a new one in Communist Russia's judicial annals. One of the accused in the purge of the thirties, if we remember correctly, was declared to have medicated Gorki to death. Is the contemplated purge similar in its intent with that of the precedent purges? Or is some new and ominous international policy heralded in the proceedings?

Thus far we see only the beginnings of the first act of the dramaturgist's latest opus. We see the four corners of the stage, each corner representing a Russified European capital. Four persons are upon the stage; they talk into telephones, their excited jabber is Polish, German, Czech, and deep Russian, and the burden of their simultaneous speech is the (sic) Jewish peril. The word Zhid keeps constantly recurring, as it were a ceaseless expectoration. The voice of the German rises above the others; indeed, when the others falter in their anathemas, the German temporarily forsakes his own conversation – it can wait, he has an understanding auditor – obligingly to prompt his colleagues. As the four monologues proceed, a picture is flashed upon the wall of their joint office; it shows Molotov smiling to smiling Ribbentrop. Their slogan follows: Antisemitism is a matter of taste. At this phenomenon, the four speakers cut short their Judaeophobia, click down their receivers, rise and stand to attention, flinging forward their arms in salute to the smiling comrades. The salute is a composite gesture: arm extended, the palm is alternately opened for heiling, and fist-clenched for healing. The curtain falls, and a stage-hand, obviously a Jew, rushing forward to his duties, is pinned to the floor.

It is a curiously ambiguous opening scene. It looks like farce; it may bode tragedy.

Soviet Antisemitism:
The Beginning of the End   6 February 1953

There can be no doubt but that Stalin, forging a codicil to Marx's will, intends to make Antisemitism an integral part of Soviet policy. This intention of his, indeed, has been long elaborating; for the past number of years its signs and portents have been many. It is true that there was at one time a halcyon period in which the Soviet Union held it up as its proudest boast that its legislation was unique among the legislations of the world in that its statutes, and of all jurisprudence only its statutes, declared Antisemitism a criminal offence; but that was a long time ago, and 'besides, the lady is dead.' For this very enlightened law appears now to have been abrogated through desuetude; certainly if it had not been thus abrogated, the entire Politburo would to-day have been holding its sessions in the fortress of St. Peter and St. Paul.

Whether it was progressive degeneration of conscience, or a noticeable worsening in the State of the Soviet Union, which called forth the Jew to play the role of scapegoat, it is difficult to say. The advancing shadows of the present policy, however, were early to be descried. The doctrine of cultural autonomy went by the board; Biro-Bidjan was liquidated; Jewish writers and artists disappeared one by one, from the sight of men. Enquiries made at the Soviet Embassies abroad were all made in vain; there was no intelligence forthcoming. But the disfranchisements and liquidations were but the prelude; soon the prologue was to swell forth, in Czechoslovakia, in Poland, and in the other satellite countries, with ominous premonitions of the sinister major theme. With the menacing cacophony recently raised in the Moscow press, that theme has been explicitly declared. The Soviet Union, holding as hostages within its own borders 2,000,000 Jews, and 500,000 more in occupied countries, is launched upon a policy of outright Antisemitism.

Aye, what a fall was there! This regime, which once presumed to solicit the heart of mankind with a message of hope for the downtrodden, heritage for the dispossessed, freedom for the enslaved – how has it turned now, not only from the practise of its preachments, but from its very preachments and protestations! The slogans are now seen to be but mere shibboleths; the promises were no more than cunning and hypocrisy. For the Soviet Union has declared itself a failure with regard to the very first test which a civilized polity must pass – its treatment of its Jews. Behind the lofty declaration and the enunciated high ideals there was hollowness and inner bankruptcy.

What, one asks in this thirty-sixth year of the Soviet Union, has brought about this shameful reversal, this cynical volte-face, this negation of the negations of iniquity? The answer, it seems to us, is to be found in a consideration of the basic premises upon which this system of government was founded. There it is laid down that all human action is motivated by interests invariably material; that spiritual impulse is an illusion; that religion is an opiate; and that only through a manipulation of greed and creature comfort can human beings be governed. The elements of all of these syllogisms lead but to one conclusion – the apotheosis of power.

Force, then, is the constant determinant, power – both the means and the end. Whatever tends to increase the power of the state, that is a positive good; whatever diminishes from it, an evil. The individual? He is ever and always but mere accessory. As for a minority, it consists of but a number of individuals. Against the Jews, there may or may not be a feeling of articulate malice; it makes no difference; if strategy requires that they be sacrificed, sacrificed they must be.

For what is there to inhibit this fierce and callous attitude? Conscience? That is a quality of the spirit, and therefore not in the Marxist book. The fear of God? God, by Soviet definition, is a dispenser of opium. A categorical imperative? There is only one imperative in Russia, and that issues from the Kremlin.

Power corrupts; absolute power corrupts absolutely! This is a truth which may well serve as an index to the nature of Soviet Government. It is a truth, moreover, which leads one to suspect that the Soviet attack upon the Jews, despite its origin as political expediency, is not altogether free from specific animosity. For though power deny conscience, conscience is what it fears, and though it revile the spiritual, in its heart it is uneasy about what the spiritual, if sufficiently roused, may accomplish. In his fulminations against Jewry, it was in particular against the Judaeo-Christian tradition, a tradition which emphasizes qualities spiritual, a tradition which hates Power's cynical sneering worldlings, that Hitler most bitterly inveighed. Not armies nor armaments did he seem to fear, but 'the still small voice.' At the end, that still small voice was thunder and annihilation.

Mystique is a word at which the power-proud curl the lip. In their despite, there *is*, however, a mystique of survival. Wickedness only seems to prosper; it flourishes, and then goes down to dust. Though all men mortal be, man's spirit is immortal. For a while stifled, quenched it cannot be. From the deepest of pits, from the depths of misery, ever it rises resurgent. That, indeed, is the burden of the Judaeo-Christian tradition. Our own people's story has illustrated it again and again. The Egyptians rose up to destroy us; they are no more. The glory of Pharaoh is past; those who dwell in his palaces dance with savages. Haman is but a name, a mere aspirate, an expulsion of the breath of disgust. The Assyrians came like wolves; they are departed. Hitler in fire was consumed. All of these heard with hate our teaching, and would destroy us. Themselves they were destroyed. Israel exists, persists.

Is it the company of the Hamans and Hitlers that Stalin would now join?

The Decline and Fall of the Gibbons   15 May 1953

It was in astonishment and with a sense of the waning of the great administrative virtues which in times past served so admirably to build across the continents of the globe both the *imperium Britannicum* and the *pax Britannica*, that we read of Mr. Oliver Lyttleton's recent démarche with the baboons of Gambia. Colonial Secretary Lyttleton, as his record up to date has amply demonstrated, is a proconsul in the great tradition; it is all the more surprising that in his dealings with the apes of that West African colony he showed himself diminished of his usual perspicacity and judgment.

'When I was in Gambia last year,' said the Colonial Secretary, addressing the House of Commons, 'I found there was some danger that the baboons might take over the administration of some parts of the protectorate from the Colonial service.' We do not know how startled honourable members were at this disclosure of rising peril, a peril, moreover, which for once did not issue from the Communists. Mr. Lyttleton, however, allayed perturbation. 'I am happy to state,' he added, triumphantly, 'that the danger of a change in administration now has been averted.'

Without intending any disrespect to the inspired bureaucrats who have governed, and govern, the renowned polity of Gambia, we refuse to share, we must confess, Mr. Lyttleton's sense of triumph. His action, we feel, runs counter to the first and most fundamental principles of British Colonial administration. It has ever been the glory of British governance abroad that it meticulously respected native customs and beliefs, that it sought not ever to uproot these ancestral ways, no matter how outlandish they might seem to western eyes, that it refrained, both through decency and as a matter of policy, from imposing its own way of life upon the populations brought under its rule. To the indigenous, no indignity; for the autochthonous, autonomy: such have always been the basic precepts enjoined upon the magistracy of the colonial domain. We hold that there could not possibly be anything more native in Gambia than its baboons, chimpanzees, gibbons, apes, marmosets, lemurs, gorillas, and orangutans, in their various tribes and septs. Mr. Lyttleton's suppression of the movement towards self-government among the baboons cannot be otherwise considered, therefore, than as an unwarranted deviation from accepted practise, as an act of gross discrimination, as an espousing, in fact, of the very noxious principles of *apartheid* which Mr. Lyttleton affects elsewhere so indignantly to reprehend.

There are, moreover, other considerations, considerations over and above those which inhere in the tradition of colonial regulation, which should have impelled Mr. Lyttleton towards a more understanding attitude towards the *risorgimento* of the baboons. The most obvious of these is the incontrovertible moral and physical superiority of these petitioning citizens. That the baboon is a creature naturally law-abiding is one of the truisms of sociology; about the only law that he has ever been known to disregard is the law of Malthus. Except in the fiction of Edgar Allan Poe, there is no record anywhere of indictable offenses having been committed by any of this pacific folk. One weakness they do have, an irresistible inclination towards mimicry, but even this takes on the properties of a vice only when the baboon is brought in too close a proximity with the human. Untouched, untinged, untainted by civilization, they are the true 'mintage of man, come fresh from the Maker'; all that came afterwards was devolution; they are the pristine humans, what followed was merely human-oid. It was an arrogance to have determined that in those hairy bosoms the urge toward self-determination ought not to be permitted to stir.

For not only as an individual, but also as a social animal – the term is not to be taken literally, but as the Aristotelian metaphor which it is – the baboon is beyond reproach. Are there any recorded wars that are imputable to him? Have the marmosets ever been known to assault the lemurs? Ignorant of arrows, blameless for gunpowder, and certainly innocent of the atomic bomb, the baboon is the true Horatian exemplar: *integer vitae, scelerisque purus.* He is, in this latter day, humanity exhumed, the adam whom no apple touched. He may, perhaps, when face to face with a human, be moved to mayhem, but who, who even of the other breeds, can regard his own caricature with equanimity? It is true that the gorilla has provided a synonym for ferocity; but it is not monkeys, but humans, the superior houyhnhnms, who make the synonyms. Besides, where are there more gorillas – in darkest Africa or among the bright lights of that other continent?

No, Mr. Lyttleton did not 'avert a danger,' he missed an opportunity. He missed the opportunity of turning back the clock and ushering in history's first refulgent dawn, he missed the opportunity of setting in motion once again the climb upward from the abyss of evolution. Had he seen the possibilities which lay in the establishment of a baboonocracy, had he understood the aspirations of these latest radicals from Gambia, had he granted their petition and established their polity, a new era might have been launched and the chronicles of the future might have henceforward counted time as of AWOL – After Wonderful Oliver Lyttleton. All this he might have achieved; some movie-operator showing the film of an avalanche, he might have reversed the process, have made resurgent the landslide, and initiated mankind's second and greater period, the period of devolution. But the operator was asleep at the machine; the great challenge thundered, and Lyttleton answered only with his name.

When will there be such another opportunity? It took the baboons centuries before they condescended to knock upon the doors of Whitehall; they were turned away. They would be our benefactors, and we turned them away. It may now be centuries before they will deign to condescend again. In the meantime, down the helminthic spirals of evolution, we rush to our doom. The baboons, they are in safe arbour.

Her Majesty Queen Elizabeth, Long May She Reign!   29 May 1953

'...Touching her magnanimity, her majesty, her estate royal, there was neither Alexander, nor Galba the Emperor, nor any that might be compared with her ... This is she that useth the marigold for her flower, which at the rising of the sun openeth her leaves, and at the setting shutteth them, referring all her actions and endeavours to Him that ruleth the sun. This is that Caesar that first bound the crocodile to the palm tree, bridling those that sought to rein her. This is that good pelican that, to feed her people, spareth not to rend her person. Behold, in this glass, in all gifts of the body, in all graces of the mind, in all perfection of either, a woman, a queen ... To talk of her court were, after the setting out of the sun, to tell a tale of a shadow; but this I say, that all offices there are looked to with great care, that virtue is embraced of all, vice hated, religion increased, manners reformed; that whoso seeth the place there will think it rather a church for divine service than a court for princes' delight.'

Thus, in a courtier's hyperboles, did the gallant John Lyly write of the reign and rule of the first Elizabeth. The course of constitutional change has somewhat attenuated the pertinence of such description to the rule of a modern monarch, – to the rule but not the reign. The epithets which the master and first inventor of euphuism applied to the royal person and regal bearing of the first Elizabeth are certainly still of service to portray the lineaments and character of our own gracious Queen, Elizabeth, second of that name, whose formal coronation, to take place on the second of June, is so eagerly awaited by a loyal and jubilant Commonwealth.

Unerringly did the great Elizabethan, speaking of the royal court as 'a church for divine service' touch upon the true source and origin of royal power. Here, in the holiness and awe with which the royal prerogative is exercised, here, indeed, lies the key to that divinity which hedges kings. We would not in these times evoke once more a controversial, and now irrelevant, doctrine; we would, however, assert, even as the entire coronation ritual, in all its stages and proceedings, asserts, that royalty is a vocation in the service of God, that the Orb and the Scepter are not simply curial but also religious symbols, and that the highest grace that issues from the Throne is the grace which the Throne itself derives from the King of kings.

Our Queen is queen over all her subjects, gentile and Jew alike. Jews, however, whether present at the actual ceremony of coronation, or reading about it in the journals, or watching its august unfolding upon the television screens, will not be able to resist, we are sure, the feeling, the ancestral racial recollection, the conviction that they are witnessing a rite which harks back to the days of the Bible. The very liturgy of the crowning will be all compact of biblic phrase; the Throne itself will be founded on a stone reputed to have served the second King of Israel; the rite of the anointing will echo the sanctifying speech in old Judaea heard. Certainly all Jews fixing eyes upon this spectacle must be moved to utter the benediction, prescribed for such occasion, praising Him who 'apportioneth of His glory to a mortal.'

Moreover, it is in Westminster Abbey, that hallowed fane of kings, that shrine of British sanctity, that the ceremony is to be held. Here there will be gathered together the lords spiritual and temporal, princes of the blood and commoners of distinction, emissaries from foreign realms and representatives of the Queen's far-flung domains, all constituting, not a mere concourse of people witnessing a pageant, but a convocation, a congregation participating in a sublime and solemn sacrament. And here, amidst these sacred observances and in this religious mood, those 'queen-becoming graces,' that Shakespeare numbered, 'as justice, verity, temperance, stableness, bounty, perseverance, mercy, lowliness, devotion, patience, courage, fortitude,' will fall upon the shoulders of our Monarch, her robe most royal.

Thus, and not otherwise, by the grace of God and not through the mere operation of succession, is to be ushered in the promise and forecast of the second Elizabethan era. Elizabeth – it is a name to conjure with! Out of its four syllables there rise up, as from an incantation, the vantage and the splendour of a great, a memorable age, casting across the centuries its inspiring pattern and simulacrum. It is a name that augurs well. Omens, however, are from God; to men is it given to endow omens with their meaning. Here it is that challenge radiates from the Throne to the Queen's subjects and liegemen. Which of them shall emulate Raleigh and Drake and Shakespeare, forsooth, even as the Queen herself is Gloriana of our day? How shall this thing be composed? The prayers of an entire realm are raised in petition, beseeching Him from whom all good flows that He grant to our Queen long life and happiness and grant to her subjects the impulse and the power to render her name a name of glory and a word of blessing.

Herzl and Bialik   10 July 1953

Joined in their lives by a shared interest – their common dedication to the ideal of a renascent Israel – Herzl and Bialik, each an incomparable leader in his chosen vocation, are posthumously joined also, in the national memory, through the anniversaries of their passing. It was the month of Tammuz, – 'Tammuz yearly wounded' – which marked the ending of both careers, of Herzl in 1904, of Bialik in 1934.

There is no record of any intimate collaboration between these two leaders of the Zionist movement. Each appeared to cultivate only his own garden; their paths crossed, if at all, only on the broad highway which led to the ultimate destination. Yet their temperaments singularly complemented one another. Herzl, the man of affairs, the practical Zionist, the negotiator and statesman was at heart really a poet. One has only to refer to his diaries, to his feuilletons, to his Congress addresses, to encounter, again and again, the flaring and burst of the poetic spark. His great masterpiece, *Altneuland*, was so palpably poetic in its thesis that it was greeted at once as both inspired prophecy and empty fancy – the common fate of all such works. History, it is true, has converted the Herzlian poem into a prose reality; but this in no way detracts from the original conception; it goes to prove only that History is, after all, the greater bard.

At the same time, as Herzl infringed on Bialik's domain, Bialik showed not a small awareness of the practicalities of Herzl's realm. For Bialik, poet, lord of language, rhymer and shaper of a nation's dream, ever entertained a great admiration, which he did not seek to conceal, for the practical and pragmatic. He held that the fertilization of a tract of land in Israel was much more important to Jewish destiny at the initial stage than the composition of some florid verbal epic. For many years, when he lived in Tel Aviv, he abandoned his muse and devoted himself almost exclusively to the development of that city's communal life. The *Oneg Shabbat* which he instituted soon became a regular feature of Tel Aviv's cultural being, and served, not only to sanctify the Sabbath, but also to cast a holiday aura upon the remembering week-days. His very poems, particularly those written upon occasions of crisis in Jewish life, were, though prophetic in tone, political in purport. Bialik a statesman unheeded, Herzl a poet *manqué*, the two titans of the Hebrew renascence, merge, under analysis, into a single colossal figure.

The influence which they exerted in their lifetime is still quick in our midst. Since their passing, their successors, as well as their contemporaries, appear as mere epigones. No other individual, no other illustrious twin, has equalled their scope and reach. After forty-nine years in the case of the one, after nineteen years in the case of the other, the vacuum which they left still gapes its emptiness. But Jewry is not a people forgetful; each year as the lethal Tammuz comes around, the ache of loss is once again renewed, renewed and suffered, suffered and alleviated only by a sense of gratitude for that to a people that needed them, they were, in the hour of need, divinely vouchsafed.

Statistics for Heaven   7 August 1953

Angels, Principalities, Powers and Dominations, rejoice – for you are indeed believed in! According to a study which has been pursued in the United States for the last eight months, the preliminary conclusions of which have just been issued by Father Paul Bussard of the *Catholic Digest*, fully ninety-nine per cent of the American people believe in the existence of God and almost seventy per cent go so far as to postulate the hereafter of a heaven. What were the techniques and devices adopted in the canvassing of this galumphant poll, we do not know; no doubt it was through the classical method mentioned in the Book of Job – from going to and fro in the earth and from walking up and down in it – that these statistics were culled; whatever the method, the results, we feel certain, must have prompted loud and incessant hallelujahs in the heavenly spheres. God had at last been endorsed by the American public.

It should be noted, lest the nature both of the report and of our comments be misconstrued, that though the results are given in the name of Father Bussard, investigation was not confined to the Catholic confessional. This gratifying approbation of the Godhead issues from the members of all sects and creeds – they are the American people as a whole who do, as is in fact asserted on their sacred coinage, put their trust in God. The ninety-nine per cent who commend the Lord commend Him without distinction as to race, colour, or creed. At the Heavenly Throne this news must have been received as millennial.

Though the report was doubtlessly intended A.M.G.D. – for the greater glory of God – it is possible that the celestial jubilation may have been somewhat diminished after a breakdown of the figures. For of the ninety-nine per cent who affirmed their faith in the existence of God, two per cent wavered, suffered a backsliding, declared they were not sure, asserting, however, that they liked to think that He exists. The two per cent are not further identified; it is clear that they are of those Voltairean spirits who hold that if God had not existed, He would have had to be invented. Further reference to them is subsumed under the statistics of Hell.

Distinctions as to sex and social status, as revealed by the report, are equally illuminating. Women, it is seen, justify by faith their characterization as angels; the number of non-believers among them amounts to less than one-half per cent. Those fed on print, on the other hand, justify their characterization as devils; college graduates contribute four per cent atheists. No account, it appears, was taken of the relative potency of faith, day or night; Young's dictum: 'By night an atheist half believes in God,' remains, therefore, still unverified.

As for a life after death, seventy-seven per cent, it is computed, entertain immortal longings, but of these, only seventy-two per cent allow their eschatology to lead them to a belief in a Heaven where the good are eternally rewarded. When it comes to Hell, however, the suspension of disbelief grows stiff-necked and recalcitrant; for a mere fifty-eight per cent, it would seem, have reconciled themselves to the possibility of the existence of this place of retribution, and even these – what an epiphany we have here of the human soul! – think of it largely as an abiding place for others; only twelve per cent (not thirteen; thirteen, for the religious, is a lucky number) admit the likelihood that they themselves might have to go to Gehenna.

As for the concept of Deity, the predominant notion – held by seventy-nine per cent of adults – is of 'a loving Father who looks after us.' This is indeed the orthodox theorem, its corollary the Brotherhood of Man; but here, when read together with the other answers of the interrogated, their theological naivetés, and their unashamed materialism, it seems rather to approach the Indian's idea of the President of the United States: Great White Father. (The report is silent touching the Father's complexion, both as imagined in the northern states and as insisted upon in the southern.) Moreover, the admission of more than fifty per cent of the answerers to the effect that their principal devotion and duty is 'to get ahead' – ahead meaning anything but hereafter – must lead one to wonder whether this report's Father-idea is not to be modified by the Kinsey Report's Oedipus complex.

What we have given here is a summary of the first consolidated summary. Further enlightenment about the creed-habits of the American is yet to be furnished. We note with a sense of thankfulness that the pollsters did not call upon their informants to pass judgment upon the divine rule of the universe; they asked them simply to state whether they believed in God or no; they refrained from asking the age-old question, first put by Jeremiah, who, however, had no patent thereto: wherefore doth the way of the wicked prosper? wherefore are all they happy that deal very treacherously? God knows to what esoterica from the horse's mouth we might then have been treated; for small graces, therefore, much gratitude.

There is a spectacle in the affairs of men that, presenting itself from time to time upon the human stage, must ever evoke in the beholder feelings of revulsion, indignation, righteous wrath. This is the spectacle which ensues when an arrogant spirit, dictator, plutocrat, or merely domestic tyrant, decides in his circle to play God. The heavens thunder. But there is yet another spectacle, not heinous at all, no more than pathetic, which, too, provokes the skies. This is the spectacle of pygmy mortals seeking to measure and weigh deity. Here, however, the sound is not the sound of thunder. It is laughter that is heard from Olympus.

Sir Wilfrid Laurier 16 October 1953

Canadian Jewry is most happy to join in the tributes of ceremony which this week, on the occasion of the unveiling of a statue of Sir Wilfrid Laurier, were lavished, and justly lavished, upon the memory of that immortal statesman. It will indeed rejoice all to know that now, at last, there may be encountered, in our pantheon of metropolitan monuments, the cherished figure of that beloved man; that the stranger, eager to make acquaintance with the shapers of our history, and the native son, desirous to stand in the auspicious company of our departed great, both may now, in the delphic grove of Dominion Square, look upon the image of one whose like our chronicles have not since known; and that thus the reproachful lacuna of the decade has at long last been gloriously filled.

Sculpted by Emile Brunet, twenty-six years ago, the statue, raised up in our city's most central square, now stands upon its rightful pedestal. It faces the figure of another great Canadian, Sir John A. Macdonald, and, to the contemporary observer, it is as if these two titans of our formative history, rivals and opponents in their lifetime, now stood forever communing – now that the hurly-burly of the House of Commons was over and done – about the one dream, the dream of Canadian destiny, which, high above racial difference, high above party platform, both men held and shared in common.

The figure of Sir Wilfrid modelled by the sculptor is no exercise in modernistic distortion; it is the well-known figure, the figure that has become almost a cliché of the Canadian imagination. It could not be otherwise: Canadians want to remember Laurier exactly as they knew him; and there he is – his hands clasped in the pose that preludes a peroration; his parliamentarian's coat hanging draped and dignifying from square-set shoulders, of notarial collar; his countenance firm yet paternal, of a Roman sincerity; and, crowning the secular head, the famous aureole of white hair. We dubbed this cast cliché; but it is symbol, rather – the part and features of one man taken by his people to be – so indelible is his mark upon his times – the personification of some of its finest ideals, its noblest attitudes.

Would you know how deeply cherished is the memory of this man, how deeply set in the hearts of his countrymen? Go to the homes of the humble, to the three-room dwellings in our industrial suburbs, to the farmhouses of the *habitant*, and there behold, upon the same walls where there glow the coloured prints of the Sacred Heart, the treasured photograph, cut from some Sunday supplement of *La Presse*, of the dear, unforgettable Sir Wilfrid! Would you learn how ineradicably impressed is this man's influence upon the thought and policy, yes, of our own day? Go to the pages of Hansard, yesterday's, to-day's and there encounter, in passage upon passage, echoes of the principles Laurier first espoused, record of views Laurier first adopted! For the man now rates more than mere Prime Minister; he belongs now to the mythology of statesmanship; in his own domain like fabulous Paul Bunyan, a creation outside of history, broods over history; is legendary in that his biography is not self-sufficient but is a channel through which there flow the anonymous aspirations, the unpatented hopes, the intermingled blended tendencies of an entire nation!

Consider the varied principles which, though not written into our Constitution, are now part and parcel of Canadian thought. Of almost all, Laurier was either author, or renovator, or most eloquent exponent and advocate. The position of Canada in the British Commonwealth of Nations? There is not an orator, mounted on the hustings to enlarge upon this theme, who can succeed in going beyond Laurier's shimmering descriptions of that galaxy of nations! Is it Canadian-American friendship that is the glowing discourse? Again it is Laurier, the statesman whose career of leadership, ironically enough, stumbled precisely over the issue of reciprocity, who is the first publicly to note those four thousand miles of undefended frontier – that staple conjuration of good neighbourliness. Is it Canadian unity? Here, once more, it is the bilingual skill and the ambidextrous phrasing of Sir Wilfrid Laurier which supply the classic utterance for this basic creed.

But it was not only from the tenets which he held that there ensued Laurier's greatness; Laurier was more than a random doctrinarian, asseverating the desirability of the cardinal virtues; he was, above all, a personality, a man of vision, one who rose above the narrow confines of colonialism to conceive nationhood, one who crossed the limiting threshold of his own century to look into the farthermost decades of the next and to see that it, the twentieth century, was of Canadian birthright, was Canadian patrimony.

In the heart of Canadian Jewry this man of the transcending vision occupies a special place, for it is to him, and to his policy, that an entire generation of Jews owed their welcome to the Dominion. He it was who, foreseeing the great potentialities of our country and its consequent need of further population, stood sponsor to the influx of new Canadians which marked the opening years of our century. To these shores, then, there came our fathers, in flight from the oppressive regimes of Eastern Europe, seeking a new life in a new land. Of that land they knew but little, they knew only that it was a land of freedom. Of that land's leaders they knew none, save only – his face having been caught on some newspaper or railway circular – that saintly man, Laurier. Crossing in the steerage of the great Atlantic ships, in their mind's eye they saw, if directed to the Port of New York, the rising Statue of Liberty; and they saw, if directed to the Port of Halifax, the father-image of Sir Wilfrid Laurier. Come to Canadian soil, they knew release, sanctuary, promise. Rasputin and his terrors were now behind them. The future might yet be bright, even laureate, at least free. And when, later, they beheld Laurier riding in a chauffeur'd automobile through the Jewish district, Jewish communal leaders at his side, they knew the man to whom they owed their debt, and their hearts went out to him with gratitude and affection.

All honour to his memory!

The Changing Middle East 13 November 1953

Ask any Occidental, Englishman or American, what it is, apart from the occasional motive of self-interest, that has so often won his unreasoning sympathy for the Arab cause, and he will be, we think, at a loss for an answer.

True, he will at first venture some reply, but so venturing he will soon discover that all these big, glib words which one summons up to bolster another people's national struggle, such as liberty, progress, self-determination, here have no pertinence at all, here issue forth only as unintended ironies. For to talk of freedom as being enjoyed by the oppressed masses of Arabia is outrageously to belie the fact; to speak of progress as being advanced by reactionary effendi and bigoted mufti is to speak nonsense; and to raise the cry of self-determination touching domains ruled by tyrannical monarchs or self-seeking oligarchies is to pervert the meanings, and corrupt the uses, of language.

What, then, is it that so moves the Westerner to feel some spiritual affinity, some secret predilection, for the aspirations of Arabia? It is romance! They are the prancing chargers, the flowing robes, the curved scimitars, that have so inflamed his imagination. Dwelling among things mechanical and man-made, his heart yearns for the freedom of the desert, the kinship with nature; and he would fain identify himself with those who are vouchsafed the privilege. Living a life pedestrian, he longs for the equestrian, – the sheik, mounted on his pure Arabian steed, brandishing the rifle of victory, crying the name of Allah. He cannot be as they? Why, then, he will at least espouse their cause and be vicarious sheik.

Responsible for these feelings are two books – the Bible and, *l'havdil hevdalim*, The Arabian Nights. In the first they are the illustrations, the coloured frontispieces, which have served to implant in the heart of the Western child those images of romance, not untouched with holiness, those mystic evocations of the East which all the years of adulthood will not eradicate. But the worthies of the Bible, it may be objected, were Jews! Not quite, comes the response of the romantic, they were Hebrews, a race extinct; the Jews wear business suits. It is the Arabs who still go arrayed like Solomon in all his glory, the Arabs who have never doffed the biblic vesture! Thus does it come about, by a singular twist of sartorial circumstance, that in the quarrel between Jew and Arab, western sympathy so often goes to the Moslem in longs rather than to the Hebrew in shorts.

The Arabian Nights' Entertainments are a factor even more potent to effect this psychic transformation. Here are tales which speak to the heart's longing for the remote, the faraway, here are occasions of poetic justice, magic incantations, sudden intercessions of deity, – the passing strange and the enduring true; they come, these narratives, as balms from the East, they introduce into lives drab and commonplace surpassing elements of wonder; they breed a belief in souls beset by trouble that he may appear again, Haroun-al-Raschid, in his poncho concealed, to right injustice and lift up the fallen. And the worthies of this book, are they not to be found walking the streets of Damascus, praying at the Mosque of Omar, at the gates in Amman, on pilgrimage to Mecca?

Nothing, indeed, is so confirmative of the existence of this nostalgia in the bosoms of the most staid Americans as the flourishing of the Shriners' Club with their colourful paraphernalia and their eastern nomenclature. Nor are the sentiments confined to the babbitry seeking escape from the routines of Main Street; the makers of public opinion, writers in the public prints, men in whom one had expected a more sophisticated attitude to public affairs, these, too, succumb to the magic spell. Take the reports of the passing of King Ibn Saud of Arabia. In all of them he is, of course, dubbed 'fabulous,' key-word to the notices obituary. His stature as a monarch is given with an innocence most primitive; he was a 'six-foot-four-inch ruler' (there were giants in those days). It is not stated of him that he found an Arabia of sand and left an Arabia of glass, no, but it is reported that, potentate, he sired at least 150 sons upon not less than 200 wives. As though they were the proverbs of some weary Koheleth at the end of his days looking back upon that which in his life was most enduring and satisfying, his dicta are quoted. 'Three things have I loved, perfume, women and prayer' – it is a saying which has all the soul-stirring ingredients, ladies and liturgy and lotions, that combination of the sensuous and the spiritual which one has been conditioned to expect from the philosophers of Bagdad. The King's use of even modern gadgets takes up, in the romantic content of these necrologies, an antique flavour; his favorite pastime is said to have been motoring (Magic Carpet), the telephone (Open Sesame), and the radio (Message of the Djinns). His wealth is extolled.

One senses in these reports, moreover, a feeling that with the death of Ibn Saud an era has passed, and that now the fabulous begins to cede to the factual. Already in the reign of the deceased monarch, the odour of petroleum dominated over the odour of the jasmine. Often it seemed to have been a moot question in the calculations of Ibn Saud, which was more important, the pilgrimage to Mecca or the interview with Aramco (Arabian American Oil Co.). With Ibn Saud now departed to his heaven of houris, much of the glamour of his kingdom is gone; remain now the hard facts of commercial exploitation of natural resource, the realistic struggle between clique and clan, the social climb and the family feud. The veil has been torn away.

Nor is it only in Saudi Arabia that this has occurred. The murder of the late King Abdullah, too, removed from the eastern pageant a mythical figure. What has since transpired in Jordan, the struggle between the sons, the interdiction of the one and the crowning of the other, this has smacked more of a *cause célèbre* reportable in the *Daily Mirror* than of a conspiracy out of the Arabian Nights. On a lower plane, perhaps, stood ex-King Farouk; the romance that hovered about him, if that is the right verb, was Gallic rather than Nilotic; but, he, too, no longer sits in the seat of power, his realm a prosaic republic.

The Arabian Nights giving way before the memorandum of agreement between the party of the first part and the party of the second, perhaps now the

West will adopt a more realistic attitude to the Middle East and its politics. The Arabs, too, it will be realized, wear business suits; the Arabs, too, like the West, keep their mysticism and their money in separate treasuries. A new perspective should now issue, a perspective which sees that while royalty may be romantic, royalties are very realistic indeed.

Where the Cap Fits
20 November 1953

The Honourable George Drew, leader of Her Majesty's Loyal Opposition, who but a short while ago was bent on decreasing the cost of government by millions of dollars and who was prevented from fulfilling this laudable intention by the ungrateful vote of the Canadian electorate, has seized, nonetheless, his first opportunity to add to the wealth and mintage of our land: he has coined a phrase. Inveighing in the House of Commons against the nationalizing policy of the St. Laurent administration, particularly as it affects traffic by air, Mr. Drew delivered himself of an epigram. He pronounced Liberalism to be but 'Socialism in a silk hat.' While the lid does not appear by this blast to have been blown off the intended legislation, nor Mr. St. Laurent himself bowled over, the phrase has been most enthusiastically received by all the outraged and mad hatters of the free enterprise press.

It is, indeed, a most stimulating epithet, and opens the way for a more thorough categorizing, hood, snood, and tricorn, of the varied tilts and slants of political science. The debate on the speech from the Throne, we feel, might well have been pursued along the line suggested by Mr. Drew. Thus it might have been retorted by Mr. St. Laurent, had he had the same experience as Mr. Truman, that if Liberalism is 'Socialism in a silk hat,' Conservatism may well be styled, in the spirit of his perennial [...] sub-amendment, to point out that top hats, including the socialistic ones allegedly worn by the Liberals, are usually collapsible, and that, in any event, both the Liberals and the Conservatives were tarred with the same tarbush.

The lesser parties and interests, too, need not have remained uncovered. The mayor of Montreal being absent from the House of Commons, the House must needs stay hoodless, but a ten-gallon hat for the temperance advocates, a derby for the horsey set, a skull-cap for the ministerial assistants, a panama for the St. Lawrence waterway proponents, and, for the so-called Canadian saboteurs of the McCarthy commission, right good curly astrakhans, – all these, for the edification of the House, might well have been conjured up. Not to have been forgotten, too, was Mr. Solon Low, who, we imagine, would helmet all their houses.

Talking through a hat, Mr. Drew, we think, has started something. Whether he has provided a theme for a Canadian *Of Thee I Sing* or a thesis for some prospective Ph.D., we do not know. It does not matter. It is a good thing, for all purposes, for a contemplation of politics to begin, paradoxically, from the top. A haberdashery interpretation of history, a study in the dialectics of headgear – this we have not yet had. It cries to be done, and might be some professor's crowning achievement. Should it ever be undertaken, we offer, from T.S. Eliot, an epigraph: *There I saw one I knew, and stopped him, crying, 'Stetson!'*

Would such a study lead to some new conclusions concerning the nature of politics? We doubt it. But the route should prove interesting. One may well end up with the old Adam, but, consider the number of people – and hats – one may meet on the way!

Gibraltar and Suez   5 February 1954

Many of our readers will no doubt recall the days when the late Benito Mussolini, *Duce* on a balcony, was wont to inflame the Roman populace with demands, imperially enunciated, imperiously insisted upon, for 'Corsica! Tunisia! Africa!' Though the sawdust Caesar was eventually overturned under a meat-hook, his example, it would appear, still inspires emulation in the minds of certain temeritous and amnesiac statesmen. One of these is Francisco Franco, who, having displayed during the years of the last war a most remarkable caution, a most un-Castilian sense of discretion, now finds further self-restraint intolerable and has launched forth on a dream of Spanish expansion.

There is no question but that this new bravado has been prompted in the bosom of *El Caudillo* by his very successful arrangements with the American Government for the establishment of air-bases within his domain and for the various other emoluments that went therewith. He feels important. The great general who for so long was a dubious neutral on the world scene is now promoted; he is a dubious ally. Glorious Spain, which once presided over a partition of the known world and relapsed into a fifth-rate obscurity, is again a power to be reckoned with. If the Italian peninsula represents a boot sunk into the Mediterranean, and to-day an empty boot, the Iberian peninsula – so must run Franco's thought – represents a firm footing in that inland sea. But the Iberian foot aches. It suffers from a corn. That corn is Gibraltar.

Franco, accordingly, would redeem, in a campaign combined of politics and pedicure, the Spanish toe from its aching, its British accretion. It is true that after more than two hundred years, the Rock might well have become as callous'd as its name; such a diagnosis, however, underestimates the sensitivity of the hidalgo organism. It was bad enough when, despite Hitler's encouragements, prudence counselled an ignoring of the Gibraltar bunion, but now, after so many years of peace, after the American blood transfusions, and after the announcement that the British Queen is about to visit the fortress, really, it is unendurable!

Not, of course, unendurable enough to prompt ultimatums and to start cannon booming – Franco is Franco, and not Don Quixote – but unendurable enough to set off the small squibs of Madrid journalism, the loud charivari of Spain's university adolescence. The Spanish dictator even took a fling at a little diplomatic note, a kind of writ of pacific revendication, addressed to the British Government – the which the Foreign Office duly and rightly non-suited. Case dismissed; Gibraltar remains British. Franco, it is clear, is no Moses; he strikes at the Rock, but no water flows. Churchill is not liquidating.

Yet, though the entire affair has the qualities of some comic Spanish opera, the campaign of peripheral intrigue which Franco is conducting simultaneously with his presumably central demand for Gibraltar, the subversive activities of his agents in the Moslem capitals, his fomentation of Moroccan rebellion against France, his strange unorthodox pose as a protector of Islam – these are fraught with the greatest danger to the peace of the Mediterranean littoral. Certainly it must be more than a coincidence that precisely at the same time as the Madrid mob was shouting itself hoarse with demands for Gibraltar, the Egyptian junta was stepping up its campaign for the ousting of Britain from the Suez, and these two points, Gibraltar and Suez, it cannot be gainsaid, are not simply targets for prestige, they are two vital salients of the Empire; they are the two jugulars of the Mediterranean. (That one of the jugulars is to be found near the Gibraltar bunion should not cause undue surprise; such is the anatomy of politics, it makes strange head-fellows.) It is quite obvious that Franco's manoeuvre with regard to Gibraltar was designed largely to satisfy the passions of Spanish chauvinism, to give his people, who for decades have not had much to agitate their pride, something to get excited about, a little orgy of irredentism, the euphoria which comes from an inexpensively valorous gesture. A very tyro in politics knows that a foreign grievance is almost as good as a domestic reform. But the danger lies not in the first small sip of bellicosity, it lies in the headiness which that sip brings on, which prompts further draughts, and which leads finally to that typical infirmity of the dictatorial mind – intoxication by the feeling of power.

The Franco press, of course, builds its case for Gibraltar upon the fact of earlier possession. This is not to be denied. The fortress that is soon to be visited by Queen Elizabeth came under British control in 1704 during the reign of another queen, Queen Anne. But if the states, governments, sovereignties and dominations that prevail in the world to-day had to be re-arranged so as to conform, in territory and frontier, to their pristine appearance upon the face of the earth, this could be undertaken only at the cost of permanent eruption and convulsion, a perennial martyrdom of man. Instances there are where such changes, confined to given localities, are indeed justified. It would be, however, a strange distortion of justice which so altered the complexion of the map as to seat the last remaining fascist leader in Europe astride the Straits of Gibraltar! For Franco does not languish for those two square miles so as to increase the arable extent of his territory. He wants them for power, he wants them so as to be able to exercise an unwarrantable control over the comings and goings of what he, too, would like to dub *Nostrum Mare*. Has Spain suffered damage by this diminution? By no means. Spain is the only country in Europe which has not been attacked, still less invaded, in over a century and a quarter. The last time it was invaded, by Napoleon during the Peninsular War, they were the occupants of Gibraltar, the British, who expelled the foe.

No, Gibraltar itself is not really in danger from the Falangists. One may make assurance doubly sure, of course, by permanently settling some of the anti-British demonstrators on the Rock itself: it is a tradition that as long as Gibraltar retains its quota of monkeys, Gibraltar remains British. The danger is from Franco's frequent pilgrimages to the political shrines of Islam. It would be well if the Americans, to whom Franco must be so beholden, would include among the memoranda of their agreement some enforceable stipulations forbidding, not only his poaching upon impregnable Rock, but also his fishing in muddied waters.

Israel Abolishes
Capital Punishment　　　　　　26 February 1954

It will be, no doubt, an occasion for surprise to those who have always affected to find some ineluctable association between the *lex talionis* ('an eye for an eye') and the Hebraic spirit to learn that that spirit, exercising itself for the first time in two thousand years of history through the channel of its own sovereignty, has impelled the abolition of the grossest instance of retaliatory law, the law of capital punishment. By a vote of 61 to 33, polled in the Knesseth which is the Israeli Parliament, death penalty for murder has been deleted from the statutes. The final prerogative over life is returned to Providence.

Some will wonder, perhaps, how it was possible, in a state in which the traditions of Talmudic law still continue to hold sway, that a latter-day generation should take it upon itself to nullify, with a single ballot, the entire tractate of *Sanhedrin*, its provisions for the incidence of the death penalty, its detailed directions for the four modes of executing it. But to entertain such a wonder is to have misunderstood the spirit which motivated the seventy-one judges who comprised that antique court, the Sanhedrin. True it is that the old law fashioned a particularized and involved jurisprudence touching capital offenses, but these very provisos, conditions, qualifications, were, in fact, no more than a subtle hedging of the law, a kind of jurisprudential antitoxin against its ultimate implementation. So much so was this the case that once when the Sanhedrin, after a seventy year period of acquittals and extenuations, did find itself compelled to have an accused executed, that Sanhedrin was ever thereafter known and referred to as the *Sanhedrin katlonith* – the lethal Sanhedrin.

For though God, in one of his aspects is described as a severe and jealous god, visiting the iniquity of the fathers upon the children unto the third and fourth generations (He is, in the same tradition, also *el rachum v'chanun* – a God of compassion and lovingkindness), though severity is the attribute which the prophets, with their gruff voices, have most frequently assigned to the God of Israel, with the people of Israel severity seems always to have run against the grain. Hence the so-called sophistries and casuistries of the Talmudists, designed, not as general opinion has it, to heap stricture upon stricture, onus upon fardel, but rather to cause 'to pass over the severity of the decree.' Indeed, almost all the jurisprudences of the world show instances where laws draconian have been alleviated, by annotation and commentary, to a legislation humanly more tolerable.

It is in this sense, therefore, that the new Israeli legislation on capital punishment, far from constituting a *volte-face* in Jewish tradition, is rather a consummation thereof. It now renders explicit what was ever implicit – a reluctance on the part of the Sanhedrin to sit in final and irrevocable judgment over their fellows.

It is to be noted too, in support of what has been said above, that the vote in the Knesseth cut across party lines. The law was not the special project of the fabian Mapai nor the particular taboo of the orthodox Mizrachi. They were temperaments that voted, not party manifestos. Whence, then, came the opposition? Well, unanimity has never been a Jewish characteristic. Moreover, the present constitution of the Knesseth is essentially a cosmopolitan one, with representatives of Sephardic origin steeped in the oriental tradition and representatives of Ashkenazic origin influenced by the concepts of western civilization. The severity, and indeed the arbitrariness, of oriental law is proverbial, particularly under regimes of absolute monarchy. As recently as last week, the disclosures published in the French press concerning the modes of punishment adopted by the ex-Sultan of Morocco, 'made scandal.' As for the rigors of western civilization, one recalls the cry of the shipwrecked sailor, sighting shore and noting upon that shore a gibbet erected: 'At last a civilized country!'

It should be pointed out, lest a false impression be given, that the death penalty has not been altogether banished from the laws of Israel. It still continues as the punishment reserved for persons convicted of murder under the Nazi war criminal law. The distinction is well made; for while murder which is the result of passion, or aberration (the Talmud wisely says that no man sins unless temporarily beset by stupidity), while such killing may be spared the supreme penalty, murder, cool and calculated, such as the Nazis planned and executed, murder the result of cunning applied in the interest of *lebensraum*, deserves no alleviation of punishment. Such murder, indeed, is part and parcel of the greatest crime of all, the abomination of recent invention, the ultimate *nefas*, the crime of genocide. It is their humanity which impelled the Israelis to abolish capital punishment; and the exception they make, they make, too, because they are human.

There is yet another point of view from which this piece of legislation must be regarded, and that is the example it affords to the Middle East. It is not to be expected, of course, that Israel's Arab neighbours, seeing the draft of the new law, will forthwith enact similar legislation in their own domains. The standards of justice which prevail in Moslem countries, the rigors which must be invoked by the ruling class to cast their fear upon, and maintain their power over, their impoverished and oppressed subjects make such clemencies impossible. What the Arab Solons might well do, however, is abolish some of the truly mediaeval laws which still have force, and are daily executed, at the 'Gates of Justice.' Indeed when one contrasts the progressive and forward-looking legislation of the State of Israel with Moslem statutes which, in some places, still condone the traffic in slaves, and in others visit upon the convicted thief the barbaric penalty of hand-lopping, it is seen to be much more than a mere propagandistic cliché. These are reforms, however, which are unlikely to take place in Moslem lands. There, it appears, life is held to be the cheapest of commodities. Did not the King of Saudi Arabia recently declare that he would willingly sacrifice ten million Arab lives (more than twenty times the Arab population in Palestine when at its maximum) to settle his quarrel with Israel? The value *he* places on life, the lives of his own people, may thus be easily deduced. Surely this is a case of 'look on this picture and on this, the counter presentiment of two brothers.'

Has Anybody Here Seen Kelly?   19 March 1954

Seen Kelly? Here? In the *Jewish Chronicle*? ... Well, what's so incredible about that? But look at the calendar and see there a contiguity that parallels, but exactly, like a *haman-tasch* garnished with shamrock, the query that somehow has burst upon this page – see there the festival of Purim following within twenty-four hours upon the celebration of the Irishmen's St. Patrick's day! Exegetes, perhaps, may try to establish some esoteric connection between these two vernal days; they may point out that in the Book of Esther the curtains in the palace of Ahasueros (O'Hasueros?) were, among other colours, also green; that the story takes place in the city of Sheehy-Shaun; that its time is the month of O'Dare; and that its central action revolves about the destruction of Haman and ten lesser snakes. But such far-fetchednesses are really superfluous. The spiritual affinity between the Jews and the Irish, noted heretofore and often, is proverbial.

We have often thought that this affinity might be investigated, upon a scale more promising than that of *Abie's Irish Rose*, in a study of the similarities between the Irish Nationalist and the Zionist movement. Certainly there is much here to challenge the erudition and perspicacity of some candidate for a doctorate, the said doctorate to be granted, of course, by both the Jerusalem and Dublin Universities. We can imagine it even now, the thesis and its subdivisions: the Jews, a Chosen People, the Irish, all king's sons; the grandeur of the days of Solomon, the glory of the days of Brian Boru; invasion, expulsion, persecution; the Irish and the Jewish Pales of Settlement, studies in ostracism; the Celtic Revival and the Hebrew Renascence; the respective struggles, culminating in *Eire* and *Yisroel*; notes on the constitutions of the two states (drafts for both proposed by Dr. Hans Kohn); *Sinn Fein* and *Irgun*; partition, Irish, Israeli; etc., etc. Caveat: the subject of *orange* production in Israel to be avoided as too citric for parallels.

But that isn't what we wanted to find out when we put the question. It appears, from a recently published letter addressed to Mr. Hanley, that there was a street in Ahuntsic ward called Kelly, and that its name has been changed to Bourassa. Bourassa too, is a good name, but there already is a street of that name, and the elimination of the Ahuntsic Kelly leaves Montreal's thorough-faredom Kellyless. We agree with Mr. Hanley that this is quite inequitable. We think, however, that the situation may be remedied. There is, we understand, a new square soon to be laid out in our metropolis. Good! It will no doubt have four sides. Let one of them, we respectfully suggest, be named Cartier, or any other French-Canadian name; let it be faced across the street by Churchill or Shakespeare or any other English name; between them and at right angles to each, let Kelly stand! The fourth side? Why, there it is right and proper that facing Kelly there stand Cohen! ... *Concordia salus* ...

Einstein: His Eternal Verities

and His Relative Conveniences   19 November 1954

It would appear that it is not only Homer who occasionally grows drowsy and nods. Even the genial mathematical Merlin of our generation, the incomparable Einstein, it would seem, is prone to fly off at an unorthodox tangent and deviate into a much too facile common sense. Thus, in his latest expostulation, the great scientist, wearied beyond patience by the ignorant interferences which some American politicos are wont to visit upon the otherwise tranquil investigations of science, expressed himself as regretting that he had ever chosen the vocation of scientist and as wishing, earnestly and retroactively, that he had become a plumber instead.

It must be said that the mood which prompted this *cri du cœur*, this *cri de guerre*, is not at all incomprehensible. Ever since the politicians, those prime pragmatists, perceived that science, even pure mathematics, had uses which went beyond the mere quenching of a thirst for knowledge, the lot of the scientist has not been an enviable one. Gone were the days when the rapt stargazer was to be regarded as but another innocuous simpleton intruded upon the *dramatis personae* of life. Henceforward, every time Euclid would look, as Edna Millay once expressed it, 'on beauty bare,' he would inevitably be surrounded by a host of *voyeurs*; henceforward every time a new equation would be conceived, it would be examined, not only for scientific legitimacy, but also for political adoption. With the advances made in atomic physics, and the devastating uses to which that branch of knowledge might be put, the milieu in which scientists operated became a milieu of stifling, and sometimes explosive, discomfort. The harassments to which scientists have been subjected by investigators such as McCarthy are notorious. It is no wonder that Einstein, who, as scientist, is preeminently a man of patience, seeing himself intolerably molested in what should have been the calm atmosphere of his study, the pure serene of his laboratory, at last lost his patience, and longed for the sealed and secret cubicles where the maestros of plumbing freely and profitably ply their art.

Hinc illae lachrymae ... and yet, it seems to us, that the Master, in so flying off the handle, abandoned the very fundamentals of his own theories, – sought, in a world where all things are, by definition, relative, the maintenance of absolutes, insisted, in a cosmos ruled by quanta that are invariably discontinuous, a continuity in the most fickle of all things, human behaviour. Certainly the much quoted limerick may now be changed to pay tribute

To the grand old scholar, most bright,
Whose speed was much faster than light,

Who set out one day
In a relative way
And returned on the previous night.

It is interesting to surmise what impelled Einstein to make choice of plumbing as the most desirable alternate to a career of frustrated science. It is true that the plumbing profession is a notoriously well paid one, but we doubt very much whether it was the profit motive which evoked the Einsteinian nostalgia. Ordinarily when a scientist becomes disappointed in his science, it is to theology that he turns:

There was an old fellow of Trinity
Who solved the square root of infinity,
But it gave him such fidgets
To count up the digits,
He chucked maths and took up divinity ...

but plumbing! The only hypothesis we can advance is the suggestion that despite Einstein's unconscious rebellion against the labour and discoveries of a life-time, his *principia* still were with him, even in the very act of making choice of an alternative. One has but to recall his three dominating enunciations touching universal law to perceive that even in the field of plumbing they are not without relevance. These assert, first, the harmony of all natural behaviour ... second, the non-existence of absolutes, of any stationary frames of reference in the universe ... and third, the truth that movements can be described only in relation to each other.

We do not know whether, since he expressed his plumbing longings a week ago, Einstein still feels the same way. For those longings, it is to be noted, have been at least theoretically satisfied; Mr. Stephen M. Bailey, business-manager of Local 130 of the Plumbers' Union, hearing of Einstein's secret ambitions, has since proffered him honorary membership. We do hope, however, that the scientist, who is also a philosopher, has since availed himself of the opportunities of second thought to refer, not to his scientific dicta, but to his ethical principles, for a solution to his psychological dilemma. There in his own writings, he will find the

one law, one element,
And one far-off divine event
To which the whole creation moves.

It is a law and an element which reduces all slings and slurs to the infinitesimally trivial, which renders nugatory the outrages of politicians; which re-establishes right vision and true perspective; which gives the final accolade to the theory of relativity, for it insists, above all, upon the sense of proportion. It is thus that Einstein has expressed this law. 'My religion,' he has said, 'consists of a humble admiration of the illimitable superior spirit who reveals himself in the slight details we are able to perceive with our frail and feeble minds. That deeply emotional conviction of the presence of a superior reasoning power which is revealed in the incomprehensible universe, forms my idea of God.'

Gaza and Good Neighborhood   11 March 1955

'Which of the states of the earth,' it might well be asked now upon any one of the current quiz progams, 'is the most aggressive, war-mongering, and bellicose of those which to-day threaten the world's peace? ... Some clues: it breathes brimstone on its borders; it experiments atomically in the interior. It is hated on all its frontiers; it is advisedly barred from all contact with its neighbours. It repeatedly keeps calling for peace; it consistently keeps preparing for war. Now, which is it?'

Had this question been put forward a fortnight ago, there would have been no doubt whatsoever as to the right answer. The specifications would have fitted four-square with the belligerent tirade, smoking with fire, steaming with hydrogen, in which M. Molotov had just made public Russia's Pacific intentions. But that is all changed now. To judge from the recent *démarches* of jittery diplomats and from the newspaper headlines reporting the 'sense of outrage' felt by certain UN representatives, another people has ousted the Soviet Union from its position of pre-eminent militancy, a new war-like Power has arisen to trouble our global harmony. That Power is – tell it not in Gath, publish it not in Ashkelon, for both are too close to Gaza – that Power is the bristling, rampaging, imperialist State of Israel!

It were laughable, this black-letter journalistic indignation over Israel's alleged bellicosity, were it not at the same time so serious in its effects upon the general public opinion. Look whom the diplomats and editorial-writers have chosen to depict in the role of combative aggressor! A state but seven years old, old enough to be designated *enfant*, but hardly old enough, even by the most cynical assessment, to entertain impulses *terrible*; a state the population of which is composed largely of people who, survivors of the most heinous attempt at genocide in the history of mankind, have come as refugees to this land, that is to say, as people who desire above all else at long last to know peace; a state, moreover, builded by a nation which, for the past two thousand years, has suffered, not merely studied, the meaning of persecution; such it is, this state, and such they are, this nation, this people, who are now grimly caricatured so as to be made to appear as the imminent ravagers of the Middle East, the Genghis Cohens of the twentieth century! ...

Whence came this strange colossascope view of the State of Israel as the myrmidon monster militant? Ironical it is that it should have been an incident at Gaza, a place which for the past number of years has served as but an Egyptian military forward-point, a dagger aimed at Israel, that should have been used as the occasion to endow the proponents of the policy of *Havlagah* (restraint) with so belligerent and, to use the epithet of one of the diplomatic pronouncements, so 'brutal' a new look. It is not denied that Israelis attacked the military encampment at Gaza; but this was but the most recent event in a long series of provocations, raids, and ambushes perpetrated by the Egyptians during the past several months. For public and international opinion to focus isolated attention on the attack upon Gaza, while ignoring the chain of causality which provoked it, and would have provoked even in the land of Uz, Job's dwelling place, is for public opinion itself to indulge in an ambush against the good name of Israel.

For surely no just appreciation of the relation between Israel and its neighbours can be achieved by separating what happened at Gaza from all that went before. On the very night preceding the day of the Israeli attack, Egyptians had effected an ambush and opened fire upon Jews across the border. These hit-and-run assaults, perpetrated not only by Egypt but also by Israel's other Moslem neighbours, have become, indeed, almost a weekly institution. Between September 1 and January 31, the UN Mixed Armistice Commission has, upon thirty-five different occasions, felt itself bound to censure Egypt for truce violations ranging from theft of livestock to murder of men.

The reprimands, however, have fallen upon deaf ears, and the appeals which accompanied them, recoiled against hard hearts. Hostility to Israel was, and has remained, the dominant policy of the Egyptian Government, a government which has found it to be an excellent cover for inefficiency elsewhere, a veritable pyramid under which might be buried and embalmed its do-nothing programme with regard to its own internal social and economic urgencies.

Not the single day at Gaza but the policy adopted by Egypt and the other members of the Arab League during the past five years is the true pointer to the rights and wrongs of this case. It is a policy which has already resulted, and this at a time presumably of truce, in the killing of hundreds of Israelis, killing effected far from the limelight of UN indignation, killings that evoked, at best, but unresurrective regrets and uninhibiting censures. It is a policy which, finding ambush on the Israeli frontier not sufficiently effective, tried it out also in a Cairo courtroom, under the judicial presidence of a brigadier, when two more Jews were with impunity liquidated. The attempted prohibiting of Israeli passage through the Suez Canal and the seizure of Israeli ships upon these waters is another aspect of the aggrieved innocence of Mizraim.

Nor have the Egyptians kept their intransigence secret. Openly, brazenly, in scornful defiance of the same UN jurisdiction where they now so loudly proclaim themselves wantonly attacked, they have announced their unrelenting hatred of the new State, their implacable determination to destroy it. Time and again have the Israelis appealed to Arab leaders for the institution of negotiations which would put an end to uneasy truce and usher in permanent peace. All such appeals have been either ignored or insultingly repudiated. The Arab League, in fact, has no other *raison d'être* than the planning of an ambush, from all four sides, against the State of Israel.

When, moreover, the Israelis note that the Western Powers, now in session as judges over Israel's action, proceed with their supplying of arms to the Arab countries, presumably as a condition of a Middle Eastern compact against Communism, a compact from which Israel is, upon the insistence of the Arabs, excluded, and note that these same Powers willfully ignore the threat to the new State, then, surely, it cannot be surprising that they should want to keep their fingers trigger'd and their powder dry. Only then when the leaders of the West will have made clear why they are compacting with the Arab states to isolate Israel will they be in a position to sit in judgment over the desperate efforts which a small State, naturally defendable by neither mountains nor rivers, defendable solely by the strength of its spirit, is making to protect itself.

Sir Winston Churchill   15 April 1955

Several have been the occasions when the career of Sir Winston Churchill has been considered as having reached either nadir or zenith, and the man himself deemed ready for the pages of history, headline or footnote. So was it in 1905 when the scion of Marlborough, defecting from the Tories, championed 'the people against the peers'; so was it when, during the first World War, the daring of Gallipoli miscarried; so was it again, during the regimes of Baldwin and Chamberlain, when Churchill's was but a voice crying in the wilderness; so was it even at the hour of greatest victory when, to use the words of Churchill, 'all our enemies having surrendered or being about to do so, I was immediately dismissed by the British electorate.' On each of these occasions, whether of climactic victory or eclipsing defeat, friends regretted, and foes exulted over, 'Winnie's imminent disappearance from British politics,' and after each of these occasions the undaunted warrior came back stronger than ever. The defeats, over which he was taunted, turned into victories, the victories, for which he was resented, turned into triumphs.

But a short while ago the whole of the British Empire, indeed all of the Western world, joined in the celebration of Sir Winston's eightieth birthday. It was a moment when the highlights of the man's career, though ceremonially repeated and applauded, required no emphasis; they were universally known, they were already part of the tradition of the age; what required emphasis, so agile and vigorous was the Prime Minister in his responses, was the fact that he was octogenarian. To-day, retired from the helm of affairs, his well-wishers hold out to him, as an honourable addition to his already varied and colourful wardrobe, the mantle of 'the Grand Old Man' of British statesmanship. It is an habiliment, one can be sure, which he will carry with a sprightliness and flair to be envied by much younger men; nor is his return to a leading position in the councils, not only of his own people, but of the world, for which precedent has been set by the much austerer Gladstone, absolutely to be excluded.

The world, indeed, should take comfort from the fact that the man who, in the dark and oppressive days of the war, spoke to it from the eminence of parliamentary leadership, may now parley with it from the summit. For he whose career has stridden forward from the spacious days of Queen Victoria to the constricted world of the atomic age still has much to contribute, by way of counsel born of experience and perspicacity, to these our own so greatly troubled times. The world is already deeply indebted to him; his courage, the peculiar nature of which it is to be tempered by adversity itself, stands example for emulation, unprecedented, peerless; his slogans, mightier than an army with banners, still resound in the hearts of all lovers of freedom; his personality, titanic in action, remains, despite his withdrawal from the stage, a cherished and living image, which no office, no matter how exalted, can heighten, nor the numbered decade dim.

Certainly Jewry knows in him a friend whose understanding of our problems is gratefully remembered, whose championship of our cause was ever a tower of strength. Nor is it difficult to discover whence came that understanding. English, and not Latin or Greek, as Churchill has said, constituted the major study of his youth; and that English, as is revealed in almost everything he has uttered or written, stems from the Bible. So assiduous, indeed, was his study of the Book that very early in his career, he wrote for the *Morning Post*, a criticism, based on military *expertise* (his own vocation), of Joshua's conduct of the siege of Jericho! We doubt whether he would be as severe in his strictures of the biblic general to-day as he was then; he has himself demonstrated how trumpets (his own slogans) and encirclement (his own strategy) have combined to fell walls, those of *Festung Europa*, more formidable than Jericho's.

But it is not in the role of a constant reader that Churchill has demonstrated his sympathy and friendship for the oppressed of Jewry. One of the most stalwart champions of the Balfour Declaration, he was and remains one of the best friends Zionism ever had. It is true that the White Paper of 1922 which diminished the territory of Palestine by establishing the state of

Transjordan bears his name, but that document, dictated as it was by the exigencies of British politics, is not entirely to be laid at his door; indeed, reliable authority – no less than Dr. Weizmann's – has it that it was Sir Herbert Samuel who author'd that Solomonic disposition. What was indubitably Churchill's was the principle which it enunciated, namely, that the Jews were in Palestine of right and not on sufferance. His consistent attitude, indeed, is summarized in the reply which he made when he was criticized for having given an irrigation concession in Palestine to Phineas Rutenberg. Said he: 'It is hard enough in all conscience to make a new Zion, but if, over the portals of the new Jerusalem you are going to inscribe the legend, "No Israelites need apply," I hope the House will permit me in future to confine my attention exclusively to Irish matters.'

He would not carry through a policy of discrimination against Jews. Such a policy, as conducted with maximum efficiency and malevolence by Hitler, was not the least of the factors which aroused his wrath, as, during the years of appeasement, he launched forth phillipic after phillipic against that nefarious regime. He took issue, too, in one of the most brilliant addresses of his career, with another of the appeasing Chamberlain's policies, that which, at the moment of greatest need, limited Jewish immigration into Palestine.

For these, and many other instances, Jewry is grateful, and, at this juncture, joins with the world in paying tribute to the great octogenarian. To these it adds its special benediction, the traditional benediction which deems no life lived to the full unless it number, in health and achievement, years one hundred and twenty.

Albert Einstein   22 April 1955

To few men is it given to enter history while they are still preoccupied with biography, and rare, indeed, is that genius who while engaged in his daily mundane tasks, sees his name made synonymous with cosmic fact. Such a one was the late Albert Einstein. They were not many who understood his esoteric theories; his basic assumptions concerning the structure of the world came to most as but an inscrutable kind of music of the spheres; few stood equal to his equations; yet all sensed by instinct, and many realized from the pragmatic uses to which his mystical hypotheses were put, that here was the scientific titan, the mathematical Merlin, who, more than any one, had contributed towards the transformation of our time and age.

Einstein was, first of all, a mathematician. The world is wont to regard its professional mathematicians as a breed apart, a type of individual sundered from the realities of life, one who lives in the company of Platonic essences and

Kantian categories, one who, to modify one image from Aristophanes, is so rapt in his contemplation of the orbits that he is forgetful of the very spectacles on his nose. The world stood in amazement, therefore, when it realized that it was precisely from such a one that there had issued a formula which not only explicated, with comparative simplicity, a vast number of natural phenomena, – if that had been all, it still could have been ignored, as being purely academic – but a formula whence there was ultimately to be conjured forth the greatest medium of power, atomic power, ever to have come within the reach of man.

Certainly Einstein had here afforded the sublime example of the efficacy of mathematics, mathematics which begins in minuteness and ends in magnificence. There are many, we know, who believe that this world might have been a better place to live in had Einstein had the inspiration to fail to discover the divine formula which led to the infernal machine, but Einstein, it must be pointed out, was pre-eminently a scientist, that is to say, one dedicated to the search for Truth. It is interesting in this connection to read how the first seminal hypothesis, later to foliate out into the gigantic Tree of Einsteinian Knowledge, early presented itself to the great scientist. What would happen, the sage wondered one day at the beginning of this century, what would happen were he able to imprison a ray of light?

We are not able to trace the steps by which this first surmisal touching the nature of light ultimately led to the brilliant illumination which issued from his pen. What we do wish to emphasize is Einstein's preoccupation with light – with light, not with destroying fire or corrosive flame. Einstein was not looking for atomic bombs; he was studying light. The sun, the source of all light, and the starry heavens above, these were to him, as they had been to Kant, the bright counterpart of the conscience within.

It is not surprising, therefore, to find that Einstein, far from being the customary pedant over his signs and symbols bent, left his study and his laboratory, and went forth, again and again, to champion just causes, to vindicate great truths. His was one of the mightiest voices to speak out against the abomination of Hitlerism. Though he was, in a sense transcending the concepts of civic naturalization, a citizen of the world, indeed, a voyager of the planets, he did not forget the people from whom he sprang, and was one of the most steadfast protagonists of Zionism. Freedom everywhere found in him its champion; as recently as a year ago the old warrior asserted again the right of men, everywhere, to pursue the search for truth and knowledge, unmolested.

It is not to be imagined that because great scientific discoveries had been vouchsafed him, Einstein's was one of those spirits arrogant in their achievement and in their trust in the mind's unaided endeavour. Einstein was a humble man; humble in his relations with his fellows, and humble in his concept of his own place in the universe. 'The most beautiful and most profound emotion we can experience,' said the master of matter, its substance and nature, 'is the sensation of the mystical. It is the power of all true science. He to whom this sensation is a stranger, who can no longer wonder and stand rapt in awe, is as good as dead. To know that what is impenetrable to us really exists, manifesting itself as the highest wisdom and the most radiant beauty which our dull faculties can comprehend only in their most primitive forms – this knowledge, this feeling is at the centre of true religiousness.'

The unequalled surrealist scientist who sought to fathom the secrets of the planets has himself now passed into the Great Beyond. Was his sojourn upon this globe of a benign or of a malign influence? The answer to that question will be found, we think, not in the intrinsicality of his achievement, but in the uses to which those who now inherit his vast estate of knowledge will put it. It is, as he would perhaps have said himself, a matter of relativity, relativity which he once explained in simple apologue. 'When you sit with a nice girl for two hours,' he said, 'you think its only a minute. But when you sit on a hot stove for a minute, you think it's two hours. That's relativity.' The research which finally exploded into atomic power is in similar case. If men will use it for the purpose of launching against each other those instruments of total and horrific destruction which Einstein's formula made possible, then, indeed, it were a moot question whether coming ages, if coming ages there be, would rise up to call him blessed; but if men will use it, as nuclear power may be used, for the purposes of peace, for the diminution of human labour, for the production of such abundance, as would automatically eliminate all contests of partition, then, surely, an age must come when Einstein's name will be not only honoured as that of a man who wrested from nature its secrets, but revered as that of a man who with a mere formula – 'one law, one element, and one far-off divine event to which the whole creation moves' – heralded human happiness.

The Power of the Slogan   6 May 1955

Until but recently the relationship which prevailed at any given time between any given number of nations could be described as belonging to one of three categories: they were either at peace, or at war, or in a state of truce. In the first, they exchanged commodities and, sometimes, ideas; in the second, they exchanged bullets; in the third, they exchanged protests.

Within the last decade, however, a fourth category has been added to the parlance of international behaviour. This is the state which is universally and aptly referred to as that of 'the cold war.' The cold war, of course, is not a status recognized by the law of nations; no diplomat would make use of the term; but no statesman, on the other hand, could make his way through the maze of international affairs without thinking it. Though not a proper theme for a foreign office *démarche*, it is nonetheless, a reality; though describing neither a nexus nor a schism between nations, it exists and is palpable as a kind of pervasive temperature, a mood that tends to harden into a mode, a climate of politics in which all the changes and exchanges are given in terms of subzeros. The cold war, indeed, differs from shooting war only in that while the latter is an actual state of storm the former is still but a type of weather.

Like the weather, the cold war is a topic of general conversation; but unlike the weather, only one party seems to be doing anything about it. It is the Russian Communist leadership, indeed, which appears to have studied and made a science out of the art of refrigerating hostility.

The first thing which the Kremlin quite obviously has realized in the pursuit of this new study is that peace has its *weapons* as well as war. The objectives of its foreign policy, as the Yalta papers have amply demonstrated, remain always the same – the enhancement of power and influence preferably with, but if necessary, without extension of territory. To reach this objective, there is one strategy to be followed in time of war, another in time of cold war; and both strategies – we speak here not of military strategy directed against positions in the field but of psychological strategy directed against men – have one purpose: to weaken the morale of the opposing nation.

In war this is achieved by a propaganda designed to proclaim Russian cannons as being pacifist in their very manufacture. Its army, it is announced, does not advance to conquer; it marches forward to rescue. Under the bombardment of such slogans the will of the enemy, it is hoped, may be broken. Doubts seeded in the mind of the fighting soldier, it is recognized, are the most effective instruments of sabotage.

It is the application of the slogan as a weapon for use in the cold war that marks Russia's present conduct of its foreign affairs. At the very same time that the diplomats of East and West meet in frigid negotiation, the propaganda agencies of Moscow are busy inventing and broadcasting slogans shrewdly intended to appeal to the inherent decencies of the large masses whom they would fain 'keep on ice' until the day came for their final melting in the Marxist pot.

Examples of these slogans are not far to seek. It was Stalin who, in the very midst of an aggressive *realpolitik*, coined the phrase 'peace-loving nations.' Thus was there conjured up, in the place of the Russian eagle, an image intended for international distribution – the Russian dove of peace fluttering benevolently over as yet unincorporated satellites. There is no Gallup poll to count the number of people who were taken in by this *canard* in dove's plumage; certainly China seems to have succumbed to the pidgin propaganda. And the West? The West announced, through the mouth of Mr. Dulles, a policy of 'massive retaliation'! A good slogan, perhaps – but the wrong time! A slogan to be used in time of actual explosive war – as Churchill used it when London was being bombed – but hardly a banner to settle the shivers of a cold war!

As corollary to Stalin's meaningless adjective there followed Molotov's insubstantial substantive: 'peaceful co-existence.' This, too, as those who pause to consider must conclude, is not true description, but only slogan. What it describes is a juxtaposition of hostilities, a stay of antagonisms, a petrifaction of the *status quo*. This would be all to the good were it not known that at the same time as this highly palatable and effectively paralyzing slogan is being distributed, the constants of Russian foreign policy – enhancement and extension – continue unrelentingly in operation. And with what does the West meet the challenge? With reports, made part of foreign policy speeches, touching advances in the manufacture of atom and hydrogen bombs! The Russians, too, have these; year by year their military budgets are successively increased; their whole economy is geared to war; but these facts, these statistics, are not turned into slogans; they are not publicized, they only slip through. Certainly, in Moscow, the right hand, which holds the gun, does know what the left hand, which holds the pamphlet, is doing – but between the two, since one is really in aid of the bellicose other, there is a real and realist co-existence!

From a Position of Strength   10 June 1955

When, at the drawing up of the Treaty of Versailles, the late President Wilson insisted, over the opposition of statesmen more conventional in habit and more cynical in thought, upon the recognition of the principle of 'open covenants openly arrived at,' he did no more than at last bring to the attention of his colleagues the fact of the presence behind the diplomatic table of that new but unaccredited censor of negotiations, the invisible spectator, the eavesdropper with the power of veto, the Common Man. It was at this point that the twentieth century constructively passed into the heritage of that ubiquitous but still straitened legatee. Up to this time, the fate of domains and nations invariably had been determined by a few chosen aristocrats, met in hushed chambers, where with ceremonious formality, they addressed each other concerning the contending interests of their respective élites, all the time discoursing in a jargon which added the inscrutability of enigma to the secrecy of procedure. All here was protocol, and private profit. Henceforth, however, a new element was to make itself felt in international discussion; though the hieratic techniques and petrified etiquette of the old diplomacy were, in appreciable measure, to persist even into our own day, a new component was now sensed as present in the council chamber – public opinion. The plenipotentiaries were no longer able to act solely according to the dictates of narrow interest and elastic conscience; now they had to take into consideration also the reactions of a vast mass of anonymous populace that stood attentive and vigilant over all negotiation and that brought to these high matters of state no other protocol than its sense of right and wrong.

Diplomatic negotiation, accordingly, altered in character. It ceased to be a mere contest of lawyers, solely a chess-game of strategists; it became an arena of struggle, where, amidst the usual ambiguous greetings – handshake or wrestling-hold? – the principles of good and evil were also to be described as grappling for mastery. Though the agenda might speak of position and territory as being the main objects in dispute, always there was an additional prize for which the contenders fought – the sanction of conscience, the heart and goodwill of humanity.

It is in the light of this incontrovertible transformation that one finds it difficult to appreciate either the pertinence or the effectiveness of some of the statements of policy which have recently issued from the United States State Department. That famous 'parley at the summit,' for so long Sir Winston Churchill's elusive Everest, seems at last about to be taking place, either in Geneva, no doubt desired of the West as having once been the seat of the League of Nations, or in Vienna, no doubt preferred of the Russians as having recently been the scene of what they obviously regard as an exemplary philanthropy, and in preparation for this event the Americans have taken pains to announce, again and again, that they intend 'to negotiate from a position of strength.'

This is, we believe, a slogan which, far from advancing the American cause, can only serve to unmake friends and alienate people, a catch-word destined to catch nothing, destined only to trip up its authors. Whom is this 'negotiation from a position of strength' designed to impress? The Russians? They are, no doubt, already sufficiently impressed; if they were not, there would be no negotiations at all. Nobody, in truth, negotiates with an antagonist who moves from a position of weakness; against such a one, one issues ultimatums. Negotiation takes place only between opponents, who, respecting each other's strength, transact their differences by a process of bargaining in which the purpose of the participants is either to transform immediate concession into later advantage or purchase the security of the essential at the price of the incidental. This the Russians know; they do not have to be informed of the might of America. Is it, then, for home-consumption that this vaunting slogan was devised? But here, too, it is supererogatory. The American people have a right to take it for granted that their government, elected for that purpose, has seen to it that its strength is adequate to all challenge.

Perhaps, then, it is for the neutrals that this phrase of magic potency was concocted? But surely Mr. Dulles must know that it is precisely on the part of these neutrals, these non-atomic states, these little powers, these marginal sovereignties, that there exists the strongest resentment against any flaunting of American force. Force operates to conquer, not to win over. The State Department does itself a grave injustice, indeed, when it so gratuitously misrepresents its Government as a self-conscious titan, a giant lumbering into the council chamber there to assert the prerogatives of size.

Not size, but proportion, is what makes civilization; and in human relations it is morality which provides the sense of proportion. Not from a position of strength, not from such a position only, but from a position of right does the Western cause have its best chances of success. Seasoned diplomats, we suspect, may sneer at the artlessness of such a standard; but is it not a greater naiveté for them to reject from the quiver that very arrow – the sense of right and wrong – the mere feather of which is more persuasive than the point? In convincing language, with compelling fact, let the theory and the practice of our principles be set forth. Let our antagonists understand us, and the world overhear. Let it be shown that wherever the West has brought its influence to bear, life, languishing, has been revived, – life, suppressed, has begun to flourish, – life, empty and dully reiterative, has taken on new meaning. The contrasts and the antonyms are there, ready for exposition. We move according to the recognized moral doctrines of our participating democracies; they pursue but the doctrinaire. We join with nations in democratic international council; they seek but to multiply heliotropic satellites. We negotiate from a contention for right; they seek but to move the left. We offer aid and know-how to our neighbors; they offer but existence, partial and hyphenated. We seek to open the light of the world to undeveloped countries; they ring down iron curtains. Though these antitheses, of course, are not matter for expatiation at Geneva or at Vienna, they ought properly to form part of those announcements in which our strength has been so unduly emphasized. Thus, indeed, may we, with that very conviction of right which we seem to disdain to promulgate, confront and confound our antagonists, inspire and fortify our supporters, persuade and actuate neutrals.

In Praise of the Diaspora (An Undelivered Memorial Address)   9 January–27 February 1953

To mark, to mourn, and to pay tribute to the memory of a world and a life that has passed, – it is for such sombre rite that this assembly, come from the congregations and tabernacles and booths of Israel, has gathered here this day in concourse pious and solemn. It is no mere personal bereavement, the sudden cutting-down of a household, that, engaging our sympathy and fellow-feeling, draws us forth from our homes to share the heavy sigh and shed the consoling tear. Discountenanced and abashed at heyday's high noon, it is alone that the widow mourns beneath the unpillar'd roof; the orphan'd, in a sorrow they misdeem shame, hide from the sight of men. Nor is it the passing of some great prince in Israel, early snatched from power and the throne, that has elicited the homage of this multitude. Oppressive and sad as is such calamity, it nonetheless but symbolizes the implacable course of mortality, which alike strikes down both pauper and prince; at the very moment that its loss prostrates, it holds up for us as a parable its instance of the common human plight, into which the Angel of Death intrudes himself with black impartiality, bidding the one prince go, and the prince his brother rise in his stead. Such exequies mark but the transition from reign to reign; we would speak rather of the going and the coming of an era.

Nor is it the six million of our kith and kin, heroes and martyrs perished for the Sanctification of the Name, whom we seek, in anguish and lamentation, once more to bring to remembrance. Is there anywhere a Jeremiah with tongue so bitter and heart so clenched that his words would not issue feeble, inadequate, mocking, in the face of an annihilation so widespread and so wanton? Who is there who can descry, amidst the impalpables of the human spirit, the true measure of this vast anonymous loss? Who can weigh the genius that has been stifled, the goodness that was snuffed out before it could act, or even speak, the thousands upon thousands of the humble and the obscure whose sole desire was but to be permitted to utter the benediction for breath in-taken, and whose breathing was made cyanide and death? The air of Europe is freighted with their ash; the winds of Europe blow four ways murder; invisible, uncountable, but ever inescapable, the sifted and scattered *corpus delicti* floats gruesome under the European sky. The blue of oblivion is not its blue. Who, then, can value and assess that tragic dust, the pollen that did never bloom? Here, certainly, memorials and threnodies would be but empty ceremony, not only futile to assuage the heart, but in their very insufficiency, compressing and agonizing the heart still more. The thunderblast is not to be answered with a sigh. There is, indeed, no voice to utter such catastrophe; wailing is vain, and clamour almost obscene. Only in the stillnesses of the night, only in the forums of the heart, can *its* memorials be held.

No, not these are the causes which have prompted our convocation. Not so as to note the demise of some exalted personage, nor yet to bemoan misfortune dire and nation-wide have we assembled here. Here are we assembled rather to speak to the honour of a way of life; to applaud, not a man, but an idea; to extol, though in a full awareness of its shackling strictures, a condition, a state of being; to glorify – insofar as glory from the fact itself will issue – to glorify a period in our history which, far from hitherto having been considered glorious, has too often been deemed squalid and ignoble.

The Diaspora is dead! That condition of fate, that dictate of Providence, that cabal of the heathen – various are the ascriptions – that destiny under which Jews seemed millenially condemned to remain wanderers upon the face of the earth, abiding in inhospitality in lands not their own, subject to another's will, beholden to another's favour, labouring for another's gain, that inscrutable Necessity designated the Dispersion, that, said the proclamation, was no more. *The Diaspora is dead!* Henceforward, should Jews continue in lands now no longer justly called lands of exile, theirs would be an act of choice, a voluntary disposition, an embracing of an allegiance and not any more a mere submission to subjection. *The Diaspora is dead!* What a sense of long-delayed vindication throbbed through Jewry as the news from Tel Aviv, that fateful May fourteenth, announced Israel reborn, and announced, by way of corollary and natural consequence, the final dissolution of the *Galuth*! The cauchemar was lifted. Evaporated exilic memory! The grim break that, with a chasm twenty centuries wide, had split asunder our history, was being closed. About to be renewed again, – the line of Hebrew succession. The sun smiled, and the miasmic vapours of exile seemed to lift, scatter, dissipate. The Diaspora was dead. – Nobody was inclined to mourn.

To mourn? At the very moment that the Diaspora-idea waned and was about to vanish, denigration, hitherto smothered in the mumbled curse or in sufferance dismissed, came to articulate and violent expression. Heaped upon it were the unuttered maledictions of the centuries. This it was, cried the refugee, and the philosopher, and the new nationalist joining together in vituperative chorus, this Diaspora it was that brought Death into our world and all our woe! From it our humiliation; through it our agony; in it, the long emptiness of our days. Nothing do we owe it, least of all grateful remembrance. If today we are diminished in spirit and soul from the stature which after the lapse of the frustrated centuries should rightfully have been ours, it is this long baneful interlude which is the cause and origin of such diminution. Better were it that that day had perished wherein was born the Diaspora! Better that darkness and the shadow of death had stained it! Far from mourning it, we despise it, we abhor its memory, we would raze it from recollection, keep it secret from our children, bury it in the desert places of the mind, there where no thought ever passes ...

The justness of the execrations, levelled against the Diaspora and all that it commanded, only a most wilful obduracy would dare to confute. His must be a bold, a temeritous spirit, who would blind his eye and dull his ear and close his heart to the sufferings, endured and remembered, that stir up such full-mouthed imprecation. He speaks false who proclaims these oaths ill-prompted. For to take issue with these condemnations, to argue against their obloquy, to dismiss these anathemas as but the froth and anger of impetuous emotion, is in servility to disassociate one's self from the common tribulation, treacherously to sever one's self from the racial ordeal, – is, indeed, to stand on freedom's promontory and declare the rage and welter of the surge below, not only not to be, but never to have been at all.

And what, in truth, are the recollections of the Diaspora that should now, now that the Diaspora is no more, be cherished and held dear? What are they? Is it the yellow badge that we should now treat as fetish beloved – that badge that throughout the mediaeval centuries foul-flashed the degrading of our name, flashed it lower than the lowliest of villains, baser than bar sinister the basest? Is this the medal of our Diaspora glory, this shield of ordure, these peddler's piebald tatters? Or are they the dark ghettoes, the stifling alleys and slammed sundown gates that should shine in our memory cities of splendour and renown? Whither should our nostalgias wander? To the *Judengasse*? To the *Juiverie*? Or to the *Judacaria* of rich Venice? Prisons and humiliations – are these the treasures that are to be garnered for a cherishing? Or shall it be the Diaspora's customs that shall forever hold captive our imagination, the special rights and privileges we enjoyed thereunder, the *sui generis* distinction which there was ours? Shall we, then, add new festivals to our calendar, and ordain set days for the commemoration of these patents and charters, – a day perennially to be marked by the dancing of the bear-dance, even as our forefathers, in bearskins, in pitiable bearish fawning were compelled to dance it before boisterous Polish baron and his tittering dame; and another day for the running of the race with trollops, after the manner and genial custom of old Rome; and yet another, a day of faggots and great bonfires, to vivify the air once more with memory of holocaust and holiday? Are these the testimonials which we should save and honour? Or are they other choices we would exercise for symbol and memento? Oh the choices, they are many! Device of degradation; technique of tribute; pillage and plunder; baptisms and burnings; scourgings, expropriations, indignity, injury, expulsion. No, they are not to be blamed for whom the word Diaspora, like some cabbalist's furious incantation, conjures up vision of incubus and succubus, the exsanguinating nightmare, and the shattering demon that stalks by night.

Yet having said, in gross disparagement, these things, not all has been said. The picture that has been presented is painted altogether black, and therefore is no picture at all; much to the merit of the Diaspora is omitted; it is a prosecutor's indictment, and not an impartial exposition, that has been heard.

It is no wonder. A man's spirit is loath to be discovered among those who, in the hour of deliverance, remember with longing the fish of Egypt, Egypt's cucumbers and melons, its onions and its leeks. It would not be condemned of a slavish nature; it would not have it said that so low had it fallen, so debased and degenerate had it become, that, even in freedom's hour, it spoke in praise of the prison's comfort and the music of its chains. Therefore would it keep silent, and while inwardly pondering the Diaspora's merits, stifle its speech, standing mute as to those merits for decorum's sake.

The inhibition, moreover, works upon this spirit that would speak and yet dare not, with a restrictiveness the greater in that its utterance would be likely to fly in the face of Israel's accomplished sovereignty. There it rises, the State of Israel, the fulfilment of a millennial dream, a present help, the vindication of the past, the future's promise, the very antonym and negation of the Diaspora! To this end, the generations strove; for this the saints prayed, the martyrs died; to make this thing to come to pass, patience and perseverance and intelligence and devotion joined in implacable compact, suffered rebuff and braved adversity, and ceased not from their purpose until the healing of the centuries, if not as yet their crown and triumph, seemed assured. The day dawned, and Jerusalem, that sat solitary, rose from her widowhood and ruins. The ways of Zion mourned no more. David's dynasty and the Maccabaean sword were brought home again. *Yisroel chai v'kayom*: Israel existed, persisted!

And shall one now in the face and presence of such consummation speak of the Diaspora – the shame this State was meant to cover? Is it not blasphemy to befoul the risen altar with mention of the abomination? Is not a word of praise to the one, insult most vile, though oblique, against the other? Hard and bitter was our lot when they that carried us away captive required of us a song, and they that wasted us required of us mirth, saying, Sing us one of the songs of Zion. How shall we sing, we asked in our anguish, the Lord's song in a strange land? Yes, that were an agony! But would it not be an agony the greater, both an agony and disgrace, were we, now that the Lord's land is founded on its base again, now, now, were we now, in retrospective infatuation, to sing the songs of the strange lands that mocked us and reviled us?

True as all of these denunciations are, they are not the whole truth. Seldom, if ever, is the truth one-sided. Truth, oftenest, is a composite, a series of gradations, a harmony in which *yea* and *nay* echo one another, a melody the dominant notes of which are always attenuated through undertone and overtone, proviso and reservation. A sore affliction was the Diaspora, yet was there in it much of good, much that remained for a permanence, much that helped to shape us as we are.

And to speak good of it rather than evil, that is our present purpose. Therefore have we pondered upon it, turned it in the mind about and about, considered its colour, weighed its worth, sought its very ambiguities to unravel; and thus pondering, there ensued in the mind a transformation. From an idea, from a mere concept of time, a vague cold image of space, the Diaspora changed, it subsumed bone, it took on flesh, it became – a person! *Galuth*! Uncle Galuth! One who had been real and warm and human, and was no more, – my deceased kinsman, he who had walked a stony, tortuous road, had known men and cities, had embraced, had wrestled the world, and, at length, giving up the ghost, had left – a name!

Indeed, I saw, as in a dream, my uncle's coffin upon its catafalque. I was, it seemed, in the great domed synagogue in Jerusalem; I recognized those pews, I knew that pulpit from before. Keeping a watch about the coffin, four bearded men, holding psalters, stood at its four corners. Four tall candles flickered there; transfixed in my dream, I beheld their tallow dripping drop by drop, dripping as if to prove their white uprightness an illusion. A wreath of last year's Succoth plants – the myrtles withered and the palm-leaves reversed – was set atop this coffin that was to be my uncle's lasting tabernacle. No sword flashed through my dream, but a staff there was, a wanderer's staff, which lay prone and slant upon the prayershawl that, with pendules tasseling its sides, draped the sombre casket.

I looked closer at this casket to note it made of pinewood and clapboard, and I thought it a most humble habiliment in which my uncle now was to go his long way home. Then, as if to answer my thought, I heard it whispered among the pallbearers that these rough planks were there, not for a humbling but for an exaltation, for they were of the wood taken from a table upon which a good man had once fed the poor.

I stood thus in my dream when suddenly the voice of the cantor was lifted in lament. *El Moleh Rachmim* – O Lord, Full of Compassion, – his syllables, his words, were a shivering levitation to raise the soul of the departed one, higher and yet still higher, mounting, ascending, soaring, until at last it seemed that I heard, as one hears the encounter of winds, I heard the coming-together of the soul and the sweet Shechinah's wings!

Now did the pallbearers bear the coffin out-of-doors to its carriage, a vehicle such as that upon which the bearded hawkers of our race, in ghetto-lane and side-street slum, are wont to display their wares. As I looked upon the vast congregation of people that darkened the streets, even as I was noting the order, the precedence, the symbols of the funeral solemnities, the hieratic march began – a strange procession – for everywhere Pomp and Pathos, like mourners, brothers though of differing temperaments, seemed to lean one upon the other, sharing bereavement.

Twelve men, advancing in paced spaced march, drew the carriage forward. No cannon boomed its defunctive salute as the dead march started on its way. At first only a shuffling of feet was heard, and a universal sighing; and then, ten quartets of fiddlers, with frantic bows and trembling fingers, began their sobbing strains. How shall I describe that music, how communicate the language of those strings that, as it were a soft rain in a sad dream, at once struck and caressed the earth? It was a sound such as I had never heard before, a concord one had not thought possible – ineffable dipthongs: men weeping, angels greeting.

The procession moved along its way. What a host of personage was there! How richly did the dream array them! Princes of the blood, in alien Roman togas still superb ... diplomats – did one not mark the features Abarbanel? – of the royal court of Spain ... rabbins and cabbalists, pensive, of premeditated gait ... the Duke of Naxos ... portly, dignified, men of influence, the *Hof-Juden* ... my Lord Rothschild ... barons Hungarian, German, French, the touch of the accolade still upon them ... and now in modern dress, the business-suited tycoons ... Nobel Prize winners ... a Polish revolutionary ... artists, writers, scribes, exegetes, scientists ... alone, apart, flanking the ranked marchers, the pseudo-messiahs ...and bringing up the rear, those men of gaiety, hushed now and subdued, Shaika Feifer, Motka Chabad, Hershel of Ostropol.

An endless anonymous train followed, an undistinguished press of people, an amorphous mass, the far-flung scattering of the race. Yet were there some who, though still bereft of identity, seemed to rise above their namelessness; thus did I count twelve aliases, eight that assuredly were *noms-de-plume*, and blessed incognitos thirty-six.

And now the names again were known, the celebrated not of our faith who had come to these obsequies either through an impulse of sympathy or in a spirit of contrition. Thus did I know and recognize three abdicated monarchs, some ousted presidents, some exiled philosophers. These wore black bands upon their sleeves, and on their bands an understanding heart. And hearts lately come to understanding were those of the distinguished who followed – by their costumes did one know them, Crusader, Mussulman, Inquisitor.

We had reached the cemetery gates. Here eight sabras lifted the coffin from its bier, and carried it forward, halting seven times before they came to the open yawning pit, seven stances to mark the seven vanities whereof Koheleth preached. Upon that solemn field was now a great concourse gathered, all bereft, all mourners, all preparing themselves for the rite of *kriah* – the garment rent in token of great loss. As the rabbi officiating spoke the Hebrew words prelusive of the rite, all, all as with one gesture, withdrew from their pockets – the passports they had held in foreign lands! And they tore them apart, and they praised the Lord who giveth and taketh away, and they flung the shreds to the four winds.

Slowly the coffin descended the grave. I heard the falling of the clods, and heard the voice of the cantor intoning the twenty-sixth psalm: *Gather not my soul with sinners, nor my life with bloody men, in whose hands is mischief ...* Alas, the mischief had been done, my uncle was no longer among the living. The voice of the cantor broke, a murmur and whimper of mourners filled the air, groans of men and suspiration of women, rising and falling. Many dispersed, some lingered about the grave, women clung to the ground. And here the dream faded, became insubstantial, an unshadowed grey, its last vision a vanishing blurred glimpse of a female mourner, weeping, sobbing, tearing at the grass of tombstones.

It is, then, as of some favourite uncle that one cherishes the recollection of the Diaspora, an uncle one surely never thought of as sad Wandering Jew, – unhappy and alone; an uncle whom one saw rather as the family's most colourful son, eager and adventuresome, – a kinsman widely travelled, easy of manner, his luggage rich with mysterious souvenir, the very world's map lined and frontier'd on the palm of his hand; and himself, himself full of anecdote, reminiscence, fancy, the sorcery of far-off places brought on his lips to make strange and exotic a long winter's evening. How wonderful the trophies he had garnered, the personages he had known, the events, the scenes, that he had burst upon! Always would one treasure his memory as that of some daring explorer, an informal raconteur, retailer and embellisher of high autobiography, *the* philosopher peripatetic, twirling the geographic globe, darting a finger hither and yon: *Here were lions ... Here anthropophagi most ravenous ... Here desert where we ate mirage, and were sustained ... Sambation here ...*

For the magnetism of his personality was irresistible. To lie at ease in Zion, plucking the vine and fig-tree, is, of course, a thing not to be despised. Yet is it a thing confined. After a little, ensues monotony, the deadly pall of iteration. For in Zion, though that Zion embrace both sides of the Jordan, the landscape hardly alters; there are either the hills about Kinnereth or the wells of the Negev, the rock of Judaea or the salts of the Dead Sea – variations that always do return identical. It is, indeed, as if one were forever to circle Jericho, and Jericho not fall. Even *aliyot*, the goings-up to Jerusalem, effect but little change. For whether the land be called Canaan, or Philistia, or Israel – it is but circumference to the one unchanging centre, Zion.

But this my kinsman set his sights abroad, and thence brought back new vision, new insight, the lore of far horizons. Yes, Egypt was an ordeal, and one would gladly forget its fleshpots, but were not the Egyptians parted from more than their mere jewels? Was there not carried across the Red Sea a knowledge unknown to the Patriarchs? The rituals of dying that the Pharaohs taught, lesson of tomb, preachment of pyramid, – sermons in stones! – were not these things also an enlightenment to daily living? The mind, too, is a Nile, and has its alluvium: not negative entirely was the experience of Mizraim. Some there are, indeed, who say that the very notion of the One God was by Moses borrowed from the Egyptian priest. It is a surmisal; the borrowings were general: *Speak now in the ears of the people, and let every man borrow of his neighbour, and every woman of her neighbour, jewels of silver and jewels of gold.* But be that as it may, surely the Decalogue was an adventure of the Diaspora. Is it, then, among the mountains of Judaea that Sinai rears its height?

The journeyings of the *Galuth* were many, and not one without its reward. Whence issues, in our lore, the belief in a World to Come? In vain will one search through the Holy Book; *sheol* one may find there, and the pit, but not a syllable of either the recompense or the retribution of the life beyond. Among the Medes and the Persians, it was, that to this our adventurer then first was shown a glimpse of what lies behind – a world where this world is judged and given its reward. Thus was rounded out the total theological view, eschatology bringing to the hollow concave of mere mundane life the glorious convexity of the hereafter.

In Babylon he sojourned a space among the hanging gardens, and there did add, not to the Law and the Prophets, but to his own skills interpretative, discovering how best to treat and handle Holy Writ, how to extract from the single verse, by dint of thirteen hermeneutic rules, its subtlest savours and its deepest meaning. Some feign to look upon the Talmudic procedures as but exercises in hair-splitting, a kind of pious prestidigitation, but none can deny that the effect of those Amoraic casuistries, those Tannaitic disciplines, left marks indelible upon the traveller's mind.

And shall not a word be said about the great enterprise of the Masoretes, the punctators who gave our consonants their vowels? Were it not for these the *Nakdanim*, the scrolls carried out of Israel had been but a hissing, a gargle, an astonishment, our verbs all in the wrong mood, our substantives adhering to possessives not their own, the whole a Babel's frustrative discord. From them it was that the Diaspora learned where in the Scriptures to place the pause, where to linger in cantillatory tremolo, where the pendulous *kometz* to the flat *patach* gave way, and where, at last, the sacred sentence was to come to rest. Chapters they named, and the portion of the week, and gave to the treasure of Sinai an order, a sequence, a set tradition.

The peregrinations continue, and now it is Greece, old Hellas, that proffers its artifacts and the techniques of its gymnasia and the mysterious view of Plato's cave, Greece that to this new adept would teach the full life, expertise in both body and soul; but he passes on; and suddenly is in Andalusian Spain, a collector of poetry and spices, in love upon this western strand with the fragrances of the East; it was a short sojourn; then followed France, paradise of the exegetes, Rashi and his scions, the nimble jugglers of the Word. Who like they could set the texts on end, joining a phrase from Exodus to Deuteronomy's location to bring forth some new, some hitherto unsuspected beatific vision? The impetuous wanderer did not rest, but traversed Europe, its length and its breadth, acquiring in Germany a language, and in the Slav domains a way of life, a Council of the Four Lands. Are they not still heard in our imagination, the mascots of the Diaspora, the little goat that at the cradle stood, the golden parrot that from far-away countries brought its ambiguous tidings?

Let us, then, – if we would know wherein the Diaspora hath deserved our loves – let us take inventory of our kinsman's estate. Let us make catalogue of the tokens with which we were remembered, let us deliberate upon each of the things bequeathed, not, surely, so as to assay and value them, but to probe their deeper symbolical meaning, to surmise from his legacy, as it were a rebus, the affection he sends us from beyond the grave. Let us consider this patrimony, its worth, its significance.

Let us, moreover, come to this inheritance, not like hungry and avaricious legatees covetous of lands and tenements; for that way lies frustration; but as kinsmen eager to hear, for its wisdom, counsel, and worldly knowledge, their kinsman's last inspired testament. For they are his insights and his experience, the adventure of his life and its lessons, that we would take for heritage, not his earthly possessions. For of earthly possessions he had none, or but few; it is a seizin to be scorned; neither principalities nor counties were of his estate; though he traversed the continents, no acre ever was unmortgaged his, no asset but was pledged. It is in search of tokens that we break the seals affixed, tokens, objects of reverence, talismans, things dear to us because they once were his, and are to-day still eloquent of his mode and custom.

'The will! Let us stay and hear the will.'

This was no Caesar, lord of imperial munificence, but a humble man, a disposer of knick-knacks, kickshaws, keepsake, souvenir, relic. But he, too,

> hath left you all his walks,
> His private arbours and new-planted orchards
> On this side Tiber; he hath left them you
> And to your heirs for ever; common pleasures
> To walk abroad and recreate yourselves.

'And recreate yourselves' – there is the will, its secret virtue, its specific for survival. Recreation as the consequence of walking abroad – that is the Diaspora's message. It is a message which issues out of every item of the inventory, each the memento of some lesson, each now entered into the apparatus of our culture. A multitude of these bequests we pass over in silence; they were but the impedimenta of our travels, the adherent barnacles of a long voyaging. Such are the recipes of the exilic diet, their spices, their condiments the menu of geography – these may or may not be taken for a remembrance. Such are the auxiliary customs borrowed of the heathen, the peasant's superstition, the etiquette adopted of the manor's lord, – these were for a day; beyond that day they are mere sentiments and habit. But other units and parts are there in that catalogue that are, indeed, legacy to be striven for, things perhaps valueless in themselves, certainly things outside the realm of commerce, but things we would not willingly let fall; they are ours; and as they in his lifetime served the testator, may yet serve his heirs.

Item, a globe. The earth, and if not the fulness thereof, at least its length and breadth, its beauty, variety, extent. This globe, our going to and fro in the earth, our walking up and down in it, this it was that preserved our people from shackling insularity, that saved us from the narrow fate of Philistia. We would not be taken as insulting over the trials and ordeals of the Dispersion, but had we remained these centuries confined between the Jordan and the Middle Sea, who knows but how we might have fallen to the low estate of *fellahin*, day-labourers of the limited horizon, a tribe sealed off from the rush and progress of the world? History passing us by like some strange argosy descried off the Palestinian coast? Who knows but what some universal catastrophe, bursting across these frontiers, had annihilated us all, put us forever with Carthage and Assyria, and into archaeology beyond recall translated us? Windows to the world did the Diaspora fling open, too often, alas, by way of defenestration, yet did they bring new light. Thus were we spared rusticity; snatched from the centre, we learned circumference. Nor ever completely cosmopolite, for never was Zion altogether forgotten, the Dispersion saved us from the yokel's fate. It was a fulfilment, then, this Dispersion, and not a crude scattering, the Grand Tour designed to teach abroad what could not be learned at home, the arc penultimate to the completed circle.

How mightily now does this heritage conduce to the colour and the vigour of the Return! For the Ingathering enters the land, not like the dead of the wilderness, not like some host that has slept these twenty centuries, and now roused, remembers as last waking thought the Roman agony, the rest a blank; it enters it, rather, with continuing knowledge and memory undimmed, its experience augmented, its recollection unbroken; the continents and the centuries make up its customs-declaration. This is no press of nomads come back to early pasture, no tribe of aborigines from foray returned as aboriginal as they issued; this is a global people that now resumes its home! Behold, the floors of that home, they are carpeted with many strands, its walls, they are tapestried with the skills and weavings of the far-flung world! To Israel, microcosm, cosmos is brought, the knowledge of the world! Thus at that place where other peoples end, this one again begins!

We continue through our kinsman's inventory ... *Item*, a polyglot library. It is the accumulation of the centuries, a work picked up here, a rare edition there, manuscript, incunabulum, early printing, recent masterpiece – the composite index of a continuing Jewish creativity. Upon the long secular journey, these, indeed, were viaticum. Headed *Judaica*, the catalogue spans the continents and almost confounds all tongues. Recording the works enduring a single culture, it shifts from language to language; now as it holds up with pride, indeed, with veneration, the great corpus of Talmudic learning, it speaks Aramaic; now, as it leaps forward from Babylon and in a later day conjures up the name of Maimonides and his school, Arabic are its accents; and now, with a deeper love, with memories the years have not yet dimmed, it is in Yiddish that it speaks.

Nor do these three exhaust the versatility of its utterance. Upon all the tongues of Europe the Jewish genius played as upon instruments orchestral. Would you seek to discover the earliest examples of French speech, go not to the authors accredited of that mighty literature; go, rather, to the Jewish vintner of

Troyes, Rashi, that incomparable exegete, for it is in his annotations to the sacred Scriptures that you will find them, French verbs, French nouns, – those illuminating *la'azim* – so early shaped, so early recorded, that in comparison Villon's are the very neologisms of modernity. With pride the catalogue remembers them; remembers, too, the songs of the Jewish troubadour, Susskind von Trimberg; and the true Castilian of the ragman of Cordova, Anton de Montora; and Leone Ebreo's fine Italian hand, penning *Love's Dialogues*; essays of Montaigne, lyric of Heine, Mendelssohn translation; Disraeli's epigrams and Proust's untiring contemplation of his soul. Even the snippet from the Jew Caecilius of Calacte, dicta touching *The Sublime*, made famous by Longinus, is recorded:

'Sublimity is the echo of greatness of soul. This is illustrated from the legislator of the Jews, no ordinary man, who wrote in the opening words of his Laws: "God said, Let there be light, – and there was light".'

The catalogue seems endless. All the languages are mustered to its roll. Is there anywhere among the cultures of the nations of this earth a legacy to compare to this – a culture, a tradition, a view of life, that under so many protean guises still adheres to its one increasing purpose; a literature which, though single in its quest – the relation of man to God: all other things are but commentary – changes its speech from century to century; a lore encyclopedic the several chapters of which are couched in differing scripts and vocabularies? All other peoples have persisted in the monotony of their ancestral speech; only to the Diaspora was there granted, over and above the *lingua franca* of its Hebrew, the gift of tongues.

These, then, were the polylingual adventures of the soul in search of healing. Nor was the health of the body neglected. As we unfix the seals of our estate, it is an unique cabinet of medicine, item by item, that is opened to our gaze. Here is a tradition, a skill, an inspired efficacy, that remained constant throughout the years of the exile. Its greatest achievement was from Sinai – the Sabbath rest – a prophylaxis than which there is none more preservative. But the Diaspora, too, ceased not from its preoccupation with the thousand afflictions which beset the human frame. From Maimonides' *Treatise on Poisons and their Antidotes* to Freud's excursions into the realm of the subconscious, the physician's was almost a vocation national.

Its successes were many: they have been admirably indicated by Dr. Lukatchevsky, a non-Jewish medical man, who, in the following paragraph seeks to depict the quandary of a conscientious anti-Semite (Nazi or Communist) who refuses to avail himself of any remedy invented by Jews: –

'A Nazi who has venereal disease must not allow himself to be cured by Salvarsan, because it is the discovery of the Jew Ehrlich. He must not even take steps to find out whether he has this ugly disease, because the Wasserman reaction which is used for the purpose is the discovery of a Jew. A Nazi who has heart disease must not use digitalin, the medical use of which was discovered by the Jew Ludwig Traube. If he has tooth-ache he will not use cocaine, or he will be benefitting by the work of a Jew, Carl Koller. Typhoid must not be treated, or he will have to benefit by the discoveries of the Jews Widal and Weill. If he has diabetes he must not use insulin, because its invention was made possible by the research work of the Jew Minkowsky. If he has a headache, he must shun pyramidon and antipyrin (Spiro and Filehne). Anti-semites who have convulsions must put up with them, for it was a Jew, Oscar Liebreich, who thought of chloral-hydrate. The same with psychic ailments: Freud is the father of psycho-analysis. Antisemitic doctors must jettison all discoveries and improvements by the Nobel Prizemen Politzer, Barang, and Otto Warburg; the dermatologists Jadassohn, Bruno Bloch, Unna, the neurologists Mendel, Oppenheim, Kronecker, Benedikt, the lung specialist Fraenkel; the surgeon Israel, etc. etc.'

Nor are they things merely ponderable, computable, palpable, that are of our kinsman's estate. Perhaps the greatest, the most precious of all his bequests is the inspiriting example of his life. Here, indeed, may we find instance upon edifying instance of the challenge accepted and resolved, of principle espoused and vindicated, of angels wrestled, embraced, of demons down'd, of suffering endured in silent triumph – an entire curriculum of guidance that may in our own perplexities stand us in good stead. There is no problem which we may possibly encounter that the Diaspora has not already taught us how, encountering, to counter. This history, this biography, that we have too often held to be squalid, mean, depressing and depressed, is, in truth, full of rich and ennobling example; at every turn therein we meet, beneath the anguished chronicle, with what is seen to be pattern and standard of behaviour for similar occasion contrived; everywhere, whether in the dignity with which the yellow Venetian hat is borne, or in the defiance with which the final *Sh'ma* upon the burning faggots is proclaimed, everywhere is there asserted and exemplified the unsuppressable power of the human spirit.

It is not simply that our kinsman beneath these buffetings endured in life. It is that he endured and did not pay the price of abjuration. Ingenious in devices, supple towards circumstance, he learned the art – to use a mediaeval phrasing – the art of making the accidents subservient to the substance. He became a master in accommodation. He sacrificed the incidental, and saved event and outcome. Is there anything, indeed, more protean than the Diaspora, changing with the meridians, adaptive to clime and time, mobile but not unstable, mutable, volatile, almost mercurial, yet ever beneath all its transmogrifications constant to its purpose, undenting adamant with regard to the first principle of its religion and faith? Let a vivid, though otherwise insignificant, conjuration illustrate this matter: the costumes that throughout the wandering ages our people donned. Leaf the pages of some book on the subject and you will see how the flowing garments of our Hebrew forebears give way, with the investiture of changing time, to the Greek chiton, and the Roman toga, to gaberdine of ghetto and the court-Jew's lace and ruffs, to quasi-clerical caftan, to frock-coat of the Exchange and simple business suit of latter days: the wardrobe of almost all recorded history; and then descry, behind this variegated apparel, the ineluctable Jewish countenance which, despite exotic garb and habiliment archaic, remains unchanged, unchanging. It is a talent acquired, this, of the adaptive skill; it was our kinsman's talent. He bequeathes it to us through the precedents of his life; he transmits it to us through the stream of his blood. It is no small inheritance.

His is, moreover, a will with a codicil, a codicil that summarizes, as it were, the whole tenor of his testament. It is a codicil that teaches us how to meet, face, and nullify adversity. For what is the unvarying pattern of the existence we have been describing, so precarious at times and yet so permanent? It is the pattern of survival. The greatest of the talents of the Diaspora was its talent for survival. Many were the oppressors who rose up to destroy us, who raised the murderer's hand against us, who thought to go stamping on the Diaspora's graves; themselves they are no more:

> It is not necessary to name names,
> But it may serve anon,
> Now to evoke from darkness some dark fames,
> Evoke
> Armada'd Spain, that gilded jettison;
> And Russia's last descended Romanov
> Descending a dark staircase
> To a dank cellar at Ekaterinoslov;
> Evoke
> The glory that was Babylon that now is gloom;
> And Egypt, Egypt scarcely now recalled
> By that lone star that sentries Pharaoh's tomb;
> And Carthage, sounded on sand, by water walled;
> And Greece – O broken marble! –
> And disinterred unresurrected Rome.

The Diaspora knew them all, suffered them, endured them, survived them. They blew against us, as though they were some evil pestilential wind; we bent, the wind passed. The wind passed; we remained. What had seemed so fearful and menacing, turned out to have been but a disturbance in the air. Their decrees, their edicts, their draconian hate persisted only in their obituaries. Time, and our resilience, had reduced them to their size –

The dwarf dictators, the diminutive dukes,
The heads of straw,
Th' imperial plumes of eagles covering rooks!

The Diaspora is dead. Our kinsman has gone to his eternal rest. We will remember him. In every gesture that we make, in every thought we think, manner of thought and mode of gesture both hereditary, we shall erect him memorials; we are his walking monuments. In us, beyond survival, his talent for survival persists. Not as hitherto shall we gloss over the acta of his life, suppressing the dark passage here, deleting the ignominious chapter there; neither ignominy nor darkness was there in him, but dignity and pride unquenchable, the fire that might be stifled but never snuffed quite out; not as hitherto shall we speak in hushed whispers about the denigration, the humiliations, the oppressions, that were visited upon him; they were for a test and a trial; trial and test he sustained. Now rather is he vindicated; at the hour of his death he is seen in the true light, exemplar, model, inspiration. We shall remember him. In the hour of prosperity his memory shall be to us as a warning; and in the hour of adversity that same memory shall be strength impregnable. Our kinsman has passed on, but no, he is not dead, is with us still. He has but suffered a time-change. His body we have lowered into the grave, but his spirit, now in our own lives made more free, now summoned to tasks easier than any of those he has already vanquished, now for constructiveness and not simply for survival 'bound in the bond of the living' – his spirit shall prevail!

Textual Emendations

is so strongly] is strongly p 5, l 15
Even in] Even of p 7, l 31
own heritage] won heritage p 13, l 32
him] them p 18, l 28
Herzl inspired the] *sic, maybe*: Herzl was inspired by the p 19, l 33
doomed] deemed p 22, l 40
have] has p 23, l 27
those] these p 24, l 18
will have and] will and p 24, l 34
source of his] source his p 25, l 10
is a ten] is ten p 32, l 3
oneself with] oneself that p 35, l 1
were perpetrated] was perpetrated p 35, l 14
Do] Does p 36, l 1
science] service p 40, l 36
Zionism] Zionist p 42, l 39
despair, pessimism] despair; saninism p 49, l 6
have] has p 51, l 35
has] have p 59, l 20
and each] and that each p 59, l 21
holocaust of stupendous] holocaust stupendous p 60, l 21
spirit only] *sic, maybe*: spirit but only p 67, l 1
mutually] naturally p 67, l 34
word] world p 68, l 1
of refuge] or refuge p 68, l 27
pseudo-Demon] *sic, maybe*: pseudo-Damon p 69, l 37
human] hounding p 71, l 24
say] any p 74, l 16
out] our p 76, l 24
give up the] give the p 78, l 6

two] true p 80, l 14
is inherent] is as inherent p 82, l 11
couched] coached p 85, l 7
not only to] not to p 85, l 25
if as] if what p 87, l 11
glebe] globe p 88, l 30
Samuel Bronfman] Editorial Comment p 92, l 1
significant as what] significant to what p 95, l 17
filled] fitted p 97, l 24
Shaw] Stalin p 101, l 36
any time] by time p 101, l 37
Cabinet] Cohort p 102, l 14
their] there p 103, l 35
and looking] and looks p 104, l 15
Alas] Also p 106, l 5
has] *sic, maybe*: have p 107, l 28
Or] Oh p 107, l 37
apart] apparent p 112, l 30
talk] talk and parlor [*maybe*: talk and palaver *or* talk and parley] p 113, l 15
his] its p 115, l 20
heathenry] heatheresy p 115, l 21
verities] veritas p 119, l 10
summaries] summons p 120, l 15
those] these p 127, l 10
which has] which it has p 127, l 35
that though all] that all p 131, l 2
is no doubt] is doubt p 132, l 34
those] these p 135, l 26
had] has p 135, l 27
not at a] not a p 140, l 41
their] that p 141, l 16
shackled] shattered p 142, l 34
the part] this part p 143, l 8
sea-chanty] sea-chanting p 144, l 4
ceasure] *sic, maybe*: caesura p 144, l 12
Modern] *sic, maybe*: Madame p 144, l 35
coda] code p 145, l 32
masses] mass p 153, l 12
retired] retire p 153, l 14
reach] reaches p 154, l 39
have perhaps] has perhaps p 157, l 28
and materialism of the West] and West p 159, l 31

assemblies] assembly p 166, l 29
concerns] concern p 167, l 2
organizations] organization p 167, l 35
faithful] fateful p 168, l 5
banquet] bouquet p 169, l 37
in the second] on the second p 171, l 11
those subjects] these subjects p 171, l 20
enmity] minority p 180, l 8
shreds] *sic, maybe*: shards p 181, l 20
form it may] from it we may p 181, l 40
weak] work p 183, l 22
perpetrating] perpetuating p 187, l 12
where] whom p 189, l 37
was available] were available p 190, l 18
tortuous] torturous p 190, l 27
annals] annual p 190, l 31
reflects, one has] reflects / that p 191, l 37
objectives] objection p 192, l 4
evidenced] widened p 193, l 20
Jewry there] Jewry that there p 193, l 27
when] where p 196, l 3
when] why p 199, l 2
truly deformed, […] Calf!] truly deformed, / Calf! [*maybe*: truly a
    deformed Calf!] p 203, l 33
are second] are of second p 206, l 7
detracting] *sic, maybe*: distracting p 206, l 28
Whitehall whom] Whitehall to whom p 207, l 10
Kenya] Kenga p 207, l 35
of *der*] of the *der* p 211, l 10
rigorous] vigorous p 211, l 22
one which] one in which p 211, l 31
patently] potently p 212, l 19
eastern] western p 213, l 8
clear] clearly p 213, l 16
much of the] much, the p 218, l 23
dissemination,] discrimination; p 219, l 22
evidenced] widened p 219, l 35
that their] their their p 220, l 3
work goes] work must be made goes p 220, l 10
wares] wars p 220, l 17
Cromwell's] Cornwall's p 221, l 6
run] men p 226, l 6

murderers] murders p 226, l 16
wife-murderer] wife-murder p 226, l 20
certainly] certainty p 226, l 23
ages] age p 227, l 36
reverberation] revelation p 227, l 41
discussion] decision p 228, l 27
mirrored] memoired p 228, l 36
dispersion] depression p 229, l 17
pure] pace p 230, l 10
mores] moves p 230, l 11
prosecution] persecution p 230, l 30
consummation] *sic, maybe*: consolation p 232, l 24
are] on p 234, l 16
demand] demands p 235, l 29
effervesced] effervescence p 237, l 27
Three are] There are p 239, l 25
program] progrom p 243, l 23
events] event p 244, l 18
often] after p 245, l 10
both at the] both the p 245, l 20
expended] expanded p 245, l 23
see] are p 245, l 28
their] these p 246, l 22
silent, if] *sic, maybe*: silent, as if p 246, l 24
historic due] historic to p 246, l 28
of knightliness] of the knightliness p 257, l 33
snivelling] shrivelling p 258, l 5
even] ever p 259, l 30
were] ever p 259, l 31
back] look p 260, l 6
is his plaint] is plaint p 260, l 37
need] *sic, maybe*: needs p 263, l 4
Burak] Barak p 264, l 42
of a culture] of culture p 266, l 3
had] has p 266, l 21
annexed] anisked p 266, l 24
century] country p 267, l 16
lived] live p 267, l 35
his] this p 267, l 37
belligerents] belligerencies p 274, l 18
had] have p 283, l 11
perspective] prospective p 285, l 1

science] service p 285, l 34
first eluded German] first to elude German p 287, l 6
afoot] apart p 288, l 35
pasts] posts p 288, l 37
forfeits] he forfeits p 290, l 1
benisons] tensions p 290, l 24
induce a] induce with a p 290, l 27
last] least p 291, l 5
we should] we should not p 291, l 37
learning's] burning's p 292, l 8
life] live p 295, l 28
adverting] advertising p 295, l 29
establish the status] establish to status p 295, l 30
as the Talmud] as Talmud p 296, l 23
some] come p 296, l 32
instance] *sic, maybe*: instrument p 296, l 34
word] world p 297, l 23
world's] world p 297, l 29
questionees] questioners p 298, l 38
destination] distinction p 301, l 29
destination] distinction p 301, l 30
about] almost p 302, l 13
literal] liberal p 303, l 8
farmer] former p 303, l 23
seemly] seemingly p 305, l 35
conscienceless] consciousless p 308, l 21
latter] later p 309, l 13
while only] lith noly p 309, l 14
last] least p 310, l 12
nations] nation p 310, l 23
is it] it is p 311, l 35
have proceeded] have been proceeded p 312, l 26
Alas] Also p 313, l 6
many] may p 313, l 12
tragedy] loss p 313, l 23
Alas,] Also p 313, l 37
sufficient] sufficiently p 314, l 20
boast] boost p 314, l 23
incorporatored] *sic, maybe*: incorporated p 314, l 29
Luce's] Leed's p 315, l 8
unworkable] unavoidable p 315, l 14
indeed is philosemitism] indeed philosemitism p 315, l 29

interests] interest p 316, l 6
argue] augur p 316, l 31
four] few p 316, l 37
proclaim it] *sic, maybe*: proclaims itself p 322, l 13
Is it] It is p 323, l 16
dialectics] diabetics p 323, l 23
far] for p 324, l 1
cultural] cultured p 324, l 27
did not, it] did, it p 325, l 26
Proclaiming] Declaiming p 325, l 37
murderers] murders p 325, l 39
affected] *sic, maybe*: effected p 326, l 29
an act] of act p 327, l 33
decrease] decree p 330, l 7
perpetrate] perpetuate p 332, l 34
perpetrate] perpetuate p 332, l 39
those] *sic, maybe*: these p 336, l 15
editor] edition p 336, l 19
exilic] exotic p 339, l 6
excellent] activist p 339, l 13
must] most p 340, l 20
that in a] that a p 342, l 25
alas] also p 345, l 25
Mirabilis] *Mirakilis* [K] p 345, l 27
Refuges?] Refugee? [K] p 345, l 35
warm] ward [K] p 346, l 34
don] close [K] p 347, l 36
galabiehs] galabrihs p 348, l 36
klipah] *Klepoh* p 349, l 30
heavy of build] heavy build [K] p 352, l 11
dream had] dream and p 355, l 10
these] *sic, maybe*: there p 360, l 11
then] them p 360, l 27
therefor] therefore p 360, l 30
numbers] members p 361, l 35
ambience] ambrino p 364, l 15
float] floats p 364, l 17
altitudes] attitudes p 364, l 21
appear] *sic, maybe*: appears p 364, l 24
opposed to the] opposed the p 365, l 42
century, at] century, were at p 366, l 3
your] you p 366, l 7
on] in p 373, l 20

bellicose] billicon p 374, l 15
was] were p 374, l 23
sweep] swap [K] p 376, l 8
These] There p 376, l 16
marred] mawed p 376, l 25
has] have p 376, l 26
elevated] elected p 376, l 36
see] say p 380, l 38
imputation] importation p 384, l 12
while] which p 387, l 10
enterprises, slave] enterprises of slave p 390, l 33
building of the] building the p 393, l 2
as the Yishuv] as Yishuv p 400, l 8
technicolor] *technical* p 402, l 11
foe unseen] foe is unseen p 402, l 39
channelled] challenged p 405, l 32
that type] the type p 408, l 27
abomination,] abomination of p 408, l 34
people, at] people if, at p 412, l 15
was at once] was once p 415, l 10
Albert Speer] Walter Speer p 416, l 19
not sporting] sporting p 416, l 35
force] *sic, maybe*: free p 421, l 9
this is the] it is this p 423, l 19
puppet-master] puppet monster p 424, l 33
then] *sic, maybe*: there p 427, l 8
whose] where p 427, l 38
the changed] *sic, maybe*: that changed p 427, l 38
recent] *sic, maybe*: ancient p 428, l 1
charge] change p 430, l 1
boast] boost p 430, l 31
theme] there p 431, l 11
There] Then p 431, l 28
inhibit] inherit p 431, l 40
waning] warning p 432, l 29
now] never p 433, l 7
fane] fame p 435, l 40
endow] endure p 436, l 15
works] work p 437, l 2
no patent] a patent p 439, l 16
going] giving p 440, l 43
birthright, was] birthright, won p 441, l 14
chargers] charges p 444, l 12

administration] administrator p 444, l 13
tilts and slants] tilts one slants p 444, l 20
Thus] This p 444, l 22
head-fellows] *sic, maybe*: bed-fellows p 446, l 28
changes] charges p 447, l 4
steeped] stuped p 448, l 33
it is] is p 449, l 25
Boru] Bone p 450, l 18
where] when p 451, l 29
where] when p 451, l 33
frames] forms p 452, l 21
of the diplomatic] of diplomatic p 454, l 9
coined] cursed p 460, l 35
rite] rites [K] p 463, l 33
fellow-feeling] fellow-feelings [K] p 463, l 36
its] an [K] p 464, l 8
theirs] this [K] p 465, l 7
closed. About to be renewed again, – the] closed about to be renewed again
        the [K] p 465, l 14
joining] journeying [K] p 465, l 22
our] over [K] p 465, l 23
Better that darkness and the shadow of death had stained it] Let darkness and the
        shadow of death stain it [K] p 465, l 29
they] *sic, maybe*: there p 466, l 25
existed, persisted] exists, and persists [K] p 467, l 13
the shame] that shame [K] p 467, l 15
were we now] we were now [K] p 467, l 23
denunciations] documentations [K] p 467, l 25
undertone and overtone] undertones and overtones [K] p 467, l 28
pews] Jews [K] p 468, l 1
personage] personages [K] p 468, l 40
marchers] marches [K] p 469, l 6
gaiety] quality [K] p 469, l 7
murmur] mourner [K] p 469, l 34
effect] affect p 470, l 19
then] *sic, maybe*: there p 470, l 40
tremolo] tremols p 471, l 17
he] that [K] p 471, l 40
snippet] snipper p 474, l 10
undenting] *sic, maybe*: unbending p 475, l 39
time-change] time-charge p 477, l 19

Notes

Klein's writing is replete with references and allusions to historical and literary persons and events, with quotations from many sources, principally biblical and Shakespearian, and with foreign expressions drawn from many languages but chiefly Yiddish and Hebrew. The notes below attempt to aid the reader by supplying sources, translations, and brief commentary where the context of the article itself does not adequately provide such information.

Deciding what to note and how much to note has not been easy. Names such as William Blake, Adam Smith, and T.S. Eliot familiar to academically oriented readers might well be unknown to others; references to such persons as Rashi, Herzl, and Bialik that are obvious to most Jewish readers will not be as clear to non-Jewish readers. Quotations have been noted, but phrases from familiar quotations, or lines that echo familiar quotations – and there are, literally, hundreds of these – have not always been noted. Such references are provided just often enough to give the reader a sense of Klein's style, or an awareness of his ability to draw on many cultures, often simultaneously. For the most part the distinction between what had to be noted and what did not is clear, but there remains a considerable grey area where the editors simply have had to exercise their judgment. Similarly, with translations of foreign words and phrases the principle followed has been to translate all foreign expressions, but again there is a grey area where foreign words, such as 'laissez-faire,' might be regarded as sufficiently anglicized as to be part of the common language. Here, too, personal judgment has been used.

In order to keep the text itself uncluttered, notes are placed here at the end of the volume and no footnote symbols have been given in the text, except in one instance where Klein's own footnote has been reproduced.

Because of the great number of references and foreign terms, and the frequency with which some are repeated, an explanatory note is provided only when these names or words first appear. The inconvenience which may result from this policy will be diminished by the alphabetical glossary of some of the more important Hebrew and Yiddish terms.

NOVEMBER 1928

pilgrims of eternity: Shelley, 'Adonais' xxx

Achad Ha'am (1856–1927): pen name ('one of the people') of Asher Ginsberg,
    Russian-born Hebrew essayist, scholar, and editor, proponent of
    'cultural Zionism'

out of Zion: Isaiah 2:3

'*luftmensch*': a person 'up in the air,' without a definite occupation

'*nullum ... ornavit*': Samuel Johnson's epitaph on Goldsmith, in Boswell's
    Life III 82

'they made me the keeper ...': Song of Songs 1:6

Young Judaea: North American Zionist youth organization

Mogen Dovid: 'shield of David,' six-pointed star, symbol of Jewish
    identification

MARCH 1929

Eretz Israel (Erez Israel): 'Land of Israel,' originally a biblical name, used as
    the official Hebrew designation of the area of Palestine governed by the
    British mandate after World War I until 1948

Kennesseth Hagadola: 'Great Assembly,' supreme Jewish legislative assem-
    bly during the Second Temple period (538 BC–70 AD)

Sopheric Age: age of the *sopherim*, the 'Scribes,' scholars from the Second
    Temple period

Ecclesiasticus: a book of the Apocrypha; not a person, unless Klein had in
    mind Ecclesiastes

Josephus: first-century Hellenist-Jewish historian; *Contra Apion* was
    among his last works

Rabba and Abbaya: early fourth-century Babylonian *amoraim*, scholars of the
    post-Mishnaic period (c200–500 AD); their agreements and disagree-
    ments constitute a major element of the Talmud

Pumbeditha: site of one of the leading Jewish academies in Babylonia dur-
    ing the Amoraic period (c200–500 AD)

Maimonides: Moses Maimonides (1135–1204), Spanish-Jewish religious
    philosopher and legal scholar, author of *Guide for the Perplexed*

Yeshiva bocher (pl. -im): *Yeshiva*-lad; *Yeshiva* – a Jewish Talmudic academy

teg: days; *es'n teg*–'to eat days,' the practice of poor *Yeshiva* students to
    eat as regular guests at certain homes on given days of the week

NOVEMBER 1929

Haggadic: variant English spelling of Aggadic, pertaining to the *Aggadah*,
    those sections of the Talmud and Midrash containing homiletic
    expositions, stories, maxims, and folklore, as opposed to strictly legal
    material. The reference to keeping the language is to be found in *Mid-
    rash Rabba, b'Midbar Rabba* 13.

Mizraim: Egypt

Ladino: a Judaeo-Spanish dialect

Koheleth: Ecclesiastes, the title of the biblical book, and also its narrator, according to Jewish tradition, Solomon

'Sholem Aleichem': Peace unto you

DECEMBER 1929

power of Esau: Genesis 27:22

the wolf and the sheep: Isaiah 2:4, 11:6–8

Bar Cochba: leader of the second-century revolt in Judaea against Rome

Akiba (Akiva) (c50–135 AD): one of the most important of the *tannaim* (scholars who preceded the *amoraim*), supporter of Bar Cochba, martyred by the Romans for teaching the Torah in defiance of their edict

Deborah: judge and prophetess during the period of the Judges; her name in Hebrew means 'bee.'

Esther: heroine of the Book of Esther; bride of Ahasuerus

Ahasuerus: Persian king who was initially duped by Haman to further his plot – see Book of Esther; in Jewish folklore, the archetypal foolish monarch

Haman: son of Hamdatha the Agagite; according to the Book of Esther, an official in the court of Ahasuerus and author of an unsuccessful plot to murder all the Jews in the realm

Judith: heroine of the Apocryphal Book of Judith, beheaded Holofernes, an Assyrian general in Nebuchadnezzar's army

Hannah ... seven sons: legendary religious martyrs associated with the story of Chanukah

Antiochus: Antiochus Epiphanes, Seleucid monarch of Syria from 175 to 164 BC, remembered for his brutal attempts at forced Hellenization of the Jews in Palestine

Hasmoneans: a priestly family that led the Jewish revolt against the Seleucid kingdom, culminating in the conquest of Jerusalem by Judah Maccabee and his brothers in 164 BC; their victory is commemorated in the holiday of Chanukah

Mattathias: father of Judah Maccabee, first leader of the uprising of the Hasmoneans

Shma: the Jewish proclamation of monotheism, beginning with the words Shma Yisroel ... 'Hear, O Israel: The Lord our God is one Lord' (Deuteronomy 6:4), recited frequently in prayers, at times of crisis, and also on one's deathbed

Haganah: 'defence,' the name of the clandestine military defence organization of the Jews in Palestine, 1920–48

Joseph Trumpeldor (1880–1920): Russian-Jewish soldier killed in an Arab attack on the Jewish settlement of Tel Hai; became a famous symbol for the cause of armed defence

the recent massacre: the Arab riots of August 1929, in which many Jews
   were killed in Hebron, Safed, and Jerusalem. See also Klein's poems
   from this period, 'Greeting on This Day' and 'Sonnet in Time of
   Affliction.'
Yishuv: 'settlement,' more specifically the Jewish community settled in
   Palestine during the pre-State period
'How good ...': Psalms 133:1, here misattributed to Solomon instead of
   David

JANUARY 1930
Herzl: Theodor Herzl (1860–1904), father of political Zionism and founder of
   the World Zionist Organization
Sabbathai-Zebi (Shabtai-Zevi) (1626–76): self-proclaimed Jewish Messiah,
   attracted a considerable following in the 1660s, causing widespread
   religious and social disruptions in most of the Jewish communities of
   Europe and Asia
Judenstrasse: Jews' Street
'Console ye ...': Isaiah 40:1
gematria: the interpretation of Hebrew words according to the numerical
   value of their letters, used as a method of finding the hidden
   meanings of biblical or other texts
Shofar (pl. Shofroth): ram's horn sounded on the High Holydays, at the
   proclamation of great national events, and to be sounded at the coming
   of the Messiah
Ephraitic Messiah: Messiah ben Joseph – messianic figure descended from the
   tribe of Ephraim, who is supposed to precede the Davidic Messiah,
   and who is destined to die in combat with the enemies of God and Israel
Leopold Zunz (1794–1886): German-Jewish scholar and historian
Leviathan: a fabulous sea animal reserved as food for the righteous in the
   hereafter
Chaluz (Chalutz, pl. -im): pioneer, more specifically the immigrants who
   cultivated the land of Israel before it became a state
Emek Jezreel: Jezreel Valley

MAY 1931
But My Own Garden: Song of Songs 1:6
Disraeli: Benjamin Disraeli (1804–81), Jewish-born author and politician,
   Prime Minister of England 1868, 1874–80
Heine: Heinrich Heine (1797–1856), Jewish-born German poet

JUNE 1931
a cornerstone: Psalms 118:22
Don Joseph: probably refers to Joseph Nasi, Duke of Naxos, who rose to
   high position in the Turkish Empire in the sixteenth century

Ibn Nagdela: eleventh-century poet and statesman, vizier of the King of
 Granada

Beaconsfield: Disraeli

Dreyfus: Alfred Dreyfus, French-Jewish army officer convicted on forged
 evidence of treason in 1895 and later exonerated; his case aroused
 scenes of antisemitism which Herzl witnessed as a journalist

'Hep Hep': a derogatory rallying cry against Jews, common in Germany

Sokolow: Nahum Sokolow (1861–1936), Polish-born Hebrew writer and
 Zionist leader

the *Judenstaat*: *Der Judenstaat, The Jewish State* (1896)

Baron de Hirsch: Maurice de Hirsch (1831–96), outstanding Jewish
 philanthropist who distinguished himself in projects of Jewish resettlement and training

Zaddikim (sing. *Zaddik*): saintly persons

siddurim: daily prayerbooks

Chovevei Zion: 'Lovers of Zion,' an early Zionist movement founded in
 Russia in the 1880s

Neue Freie Presse: Vienna newspaper for which Herzl wrote

Israel Zangwill (1864–1926): Anglo-Jewish author, proponent of Territor-
 ialism, a movement dedicated to the creation of a Jewish territory in any
 country, not necessarily Palestine. *King of the Schnorrers* (1894) and
 Dreamers of the Ghetto (1898) are among his better-known works of
 fiction. Klein's quotation here, from the latter, is slightly inaccurate.

Susskind von Trimberg: mediaeval Jewish troubadour, the subject of Klein's
 short story 'The Meed of the Minnesinger'

MAY 1932

Golus: variant pronunciation of *Galuth*, exile, Diaspora

Blow, bugles ...: Rupert Brooke, 'The Dead' III

minyan: a group of ten male adults, the minimum required for communal
 prayer

8 JULY 1932

two professional mudslingers: Adrien Arcand, the Canadian Fascist leader,
 editor of three antisemitic French weeklies; and Joseph Ménard, his
 publisher

katzenjammer kids: a pair of shrewd, playfully malicious young characters
 in a popular comic strip in the 1920s and 1930s

Louis-Joseph Papineau (1786–1871): French-Canadian leader under whom
 legislation was enacted in 1832 giving full civil rights to Jews, including
 the right to hold public office

sans cœur et sans approche: playing on the usual description of knightly
 virtue, *sans peur et sans reproche*, 'fearless and irreproachable'

fetor Judaicus: 'offensive Jewish odour'

Protocols of the Elders of Zion: antisemitic forgery dating from the turn of
the twentieth century, purporting to show the existence of an international Jewish cabal bent on world power; became notorious worldwide

Lindbergh's baby: the two-year-old son of American aviator Charles
Lindbergh, kidnapped and murdered in March 1932

apple of Sodom: fruit of corruption referred to by Josephus as a fruit,
attractive in appearance, which dissolves into smoke and ashes when
plucked

9 JULY 1937

Balfour! Thou Shouldst be Living at This Hour: This editorial, signed by
Klein, was prefaced by the following statement: 'While the publisher of
this journal agrees with most of the arguments of this editorial, still,
because of its conclusions it can not be taken as the editorial policy of this
paper but as purely the personal opinions of the undersigned. The
journal's policy will be enunciated in next week's issue.' The title of this
editorial echoes the opening line of William Wordsworth's famous
sonnet 'London, 1802': 'Milton! thou shouldst be living at this hour.'

the Royal Commission: the Peel Commission, set up to investigate the
causes of Arab riots in Palestine, recommended partitioning the
territory into a Jewish state, an Arab state, and a British mandatory
enclave. Its recommendations were not implemented.

Jewish Agency: an international non-governmental body, centred in Jerusalem, executive of the World Zionist Organization

from Dan to Beersheba: 1 Samuel 3:20 (and elsewhere)

Emir Abdullah: king of Transjordan

like Gaul: Julius Caesar, *De Bello Gallico*, I, 1

Churchill White Paper: 1922 policy statement, drafted by then colonial secretary Winston Churchill, which provided a restrictive interpretation of
the Balfour Declaration and set limits on Jewish immigration to Palestine

Nachtasyl: shelter for the night, temporary lodging – Nordau's phrase
regarding the Uganda proposal

Remember Uganda!: an allusion to the British offer made to Herzl and
the Zionists in 1903 to make part of Uganda available for Jewish
colonization. After many long and bitter debates, the offer was declined.

18 NOVEMBER 1938

happenings in Germany: the events of *Kristallnacht*, 9–10 November

Goering: Hermann Goering, German Nazi leader, one of Hitler's most loyal
supporters, prime architect of the Nazi police state, the air force, and
the wartime economy

vae victis: 'woe to the vanquished,' Livy, *History* v

al kdushas hashem (*al kiddush ha-shem*): ' for the sanctification of God's name,' an expression often used in connection with acts of religious martyrdom

2 DECEMBER 1938
Le Devoir: a French Montreal daily newspaper

16 DECEMBER 1938
his advice: that German Jews should 'refuse to be expelled or to submit to discriminating treatment'

23 DECEMBER 1938
Chanukah: eight-day celebration commemorating the victory of Judah Maccabee over the Syrian king Antiochus Epiphanes and the subsequent rededication of the Temple in 164 BC

dreidlach: four-sided spinning tops used for games of chance on Chanukah

'sorrow's crown ...': Tennyson, 'Locksley Hall' l. 75

gelt: 'money'; Chanukah *gelt* – gifts to children on Chanukah

23 DECEMBER 1938
Admirable Crichton: the assertive butler in James Barrie's play *The Admirable Crichton*

Ben-Gurion: David Ben-Gurion (1886–1973), leader of the struggle for Jewish independence in Palestine, first prime minister of the State of Israel

30 DECEMBER 1938
King Carol: ruler of Rumania from 1930 to 1940

10 FEBRUARY 1939
War: The Evolution of a Menagerie. See Klein's poem 'A Song of Degrees' (Psalm v in *Poems*) on this theme.

24 FEBRUARY 1939
Camillien Houde: mayor of Montreal almost continuously from 1928 to 1954. On 7 February 1939, addressing a Young Business Men's Club at the YMCA, he declared that in the event of a war between England and Italy, French-Canadian sympathies would favour Italy: 'The French Canadians are Fascists, not by name, but by blood.' Houde was interned from 1940 to 1944 for his open defiance of the National Registration Act.

Sir Wilfrid Laurier: Liberal prime minister of Canada from 1896 to 1911

heroes of '37: the *patriote* rebels of 1837 in Lower Canada who fought for
    self-government and against British colonial rule
le petit gars de Ste Marie: the little guy from Ste Marie
Mazzini, Garibaldi, Matteotti: Italian nineteenth- and twentieth-century
    patriots
Dickens: *The Pickwick Papers*, ch. 8

10 MARCH 1939
'The wicked ...': Psalms 1:4, 2:4
Baruch Zuckerman: American Labour Zionist leader
Zohar: 'Splendour' or 'Illumination,' the main text of the Jewish mystical
    tradition, written in the form of a commentary on the Bible

17 MARCH 1939
Steel: 'Stalin' in Russian means 'steel.'

26 MAY 1939
White Paper: the MacDonald White Paper, 17 May 1939
another Munich ... the umbrella: a reference to Prime Minister Neville
    Chamberlain's 1938 Munich agreement with Hitler. Chamberlain's um-
    brella became the symbol of his appeasement policy.
'green and pleasant land ...': William Blake, preface to *Milton*
shel rosh and *shel yad*: 'for the head' and 'for the hand' – phrases used in
    reference to phylacteries, one worn on the head, the other on the arm
    and hand
Malcolm MacDonald's venture: Malcolm MacDonald, Colonial Secretary in
    the Chamberlain government, son of Ramsay MacDonald
MacDonald letter: a 1931 letter to Weizmann from Prime Minister Ramsay
    MacDonald which was meant to nullify the anti-Zionist implications
    of the 1930 Passfield White Paper
'my father did chastise': 1 Kings 12:11
hinc illae lachrymae: 'hence these tears'; Terence, *Andria* I, 1
finis coronat opus: 'the ending crowns the work'
famous letter: letter from Arthur Balfour to Lord Rothschild, 2 November
    1917 – the Balfour Declaration
Balfour Declaration: pledge by the British government 2 November 1917 to
    establish a Jewish National Homeland in Palestine
Weizmann: Chaim Weizmann (1874–1952), distinguished scientist and
    statesman, president of the World Zionist Organization (1920–30,
    1935–46), first president of the State of Israel
Torah: the Pentateuch or Five Books of Moses, transmitted by God to
    Moses on Mount Sinai; by extension it has come to include all tradition-
    al Jewish religious teaching

26 MAY 1939
Bulls of Bashan: Amos 4:1, Psalms 22:13

9 JUNE 1939
'Luftmenschen' and 'Wassermenschen': 'air people' and 'water people'
'The waters have risen ... ': Psalms 69:1
a flaming sword: Genesis 3:24
a similar ship: the ss St Louis. See 16 June 1939.
The Ancient Mariner: S.T. Coleridge, 'The Rime of the Ancient Mariner'
après nous, le déluge: 'after us, the deluge,' attributed to Madame Pompa-
    dour, favourite of Louis xv

14 JULY 1939
Jewish Territorial Movement: a 1903 breakaway group from the Zionist Or-
    ganization which, under Israel Zangwill's leadership, aimed at estab-
    lishing autonomous Jewish settlements in places not limited to the land
    of Israel
'Yom Yisroel': 'the ocean of Israel,' playing on the phrase Om Yisroel, 'the
    nation of Israel'
'Yom Yisroel Chai!': playing on the phrase Om Yisroel Chai, 'the nation of
    Israel lives'

8 SEPTEMBER 1939
schrecklichkeit: 'frightfulness,' 'terror'

25 AUGUST 1939
Tovarisch: Comrade

22 SEPTEMBER 1939
Berchtesgaden: a town in the Bavarian Alps, site of Hitler's country retreat
Maginot line: French line of fortifications along the eastern border from Swit-
    zerland to Belgium

3 NOVEMBER 1939
November tenth: Kristallnacht – a night of smashing, burning, and looting
    by Nazis of synagogues and Jewish shops. See Klein's editorial for 18
    November 1938.
von Fritsch: Werner von Fritsch, commander-in-chief of the German army,
    unsympathetic to Nazism, dismissed by Hitler in 1938, killed in ac-
    tion 1939
Molotov: Vyacheslav Molotov, Soviet leader, foreign minister 1939–49,
    deputy premier 1941–57

19 JANUARY 1940
Bouchard: Paul Bouchard, Quebec fascist and separatist, admirer of Mussolini,
    director of the weekly *La Nation*

23 FEBRUARY 1940
magic casements ... forlorn: reference to John Keats' 'Ode to a Nightingale'

15 MARCH 1940
Freiheit: American-Yiddish daily newspaper, founded in 1922 by the Jewish
    section of the American Communist party
Yeshiva-bochur of Hebron: reference to the massacre of rabbinic students,
    among others, during the rioting in Hebron. See Klein's poem,
    'Greeting on This Day.'
shamas: synagogue sexton

22 MARCH 1940
their rendez-vous: Hitler and Mussolini met on 18 March to discuss Italy's
    involvement in the Nazi offensive.
Count Ciano: Italian fascist leader, foreign minister 1936–43
von Ribbentrop: Joachim von Ribbentrop, Nazi foreign minister 1938–45
Sumner Welles: American undersecretary of state; had discussions with
    Hitler in early March

10 MAY 1940
Anders: Wladyslaw Anders, commander of Polish forces in the Middle East
    and Italy during World War II
Haller: Jozef Haller, Polish soldier whose army after World War I slaughtered
    many Jews in Poland; a minister in the Polish Government-in-Exile
    1939–43
Beck ... Smigly-Ridz: Polish foreign minister and marshal, respectively,
    before the Nazi invasion
Plus ça change, plus ça reste la même chose: 'the more things change, the
    more they remain the same'

7 JUNE 1940
a fat Cassius: echoing Shakespeare, *Julius Caesar* I.ii

2 AUGUST 1940
Chaim Zhitlovsky (1865–1943): Jewish intellectual and writer
Max Nordau (1849–1927): writer and social critic, associated with Herzl in
    founding the World Zionist Organization

9 AUGUST 1940
Vladimir Jabotinsky (1880–1940): Zionist activist, soldier, orator, co-founder

of the Jewish Legion in World War I, founder and leader of the
Revisionist Movement

Haboker: Tel Aviv daily Hebrew newspaper

Razviet: Russian-language Zionist weekly, organ of the Revisionists, Berlin
1921–33, Paris 1933–4

Chaim Nachman Bialik (1873–1934): major Jewish poet, essayist, and editor,
influential shaper of modern Hebrew culture

Nansen passport: visa issued by the League of Nations to stateless persons

'aye, but a man's reach ...': Robert Browning, 'Andrea del Sarto'

Is it not fine ...: Elinor Wylie, 'Hughie at the Inn'

6 SEPTEMBER 1940

Vichy: seat of government of unoccupied France 1940–4

Pétain: Henri Philippe Pétain, marshal of France and chief of state of
unoccupied France 1940–4

poilu: French front line soldier

Laval: Pierre Laval, premier of unoccupied France, leading collaborator in
the Vichy regime with the Nazis

20 SEPTEMBER 1940

Dieu me pardonnera ... : 'God will pardon me, that's his calling'

Urim and Thummim: objects worn on the breastplate of the Jewish high
priest, used as oracular media to divine the will of God

27 SEPTEMBER 1940

New Zionist Organization: breakaway organization of Revisionist Zionists

1 NOVEMBER 1940

The mountains look ... : Byron, *Don Juan* III, 86

Drang Nach Osten: 'thrust to the east,' basis of German foreign policy from
Bismarck's time on

For freedom's battle ... ': Byron, 'The Giaour' ll. 123–5

15 NOVEMBER 1940

l'shabair eth ha-ozen: 'to shatter the ear,' to express something in a way
that can be easily understood

mene, mene, tekel, upharsin: Daniel 5: 25–8

Deus sive Natura: 'God or Nature,' Spinoza's phrase

Belial: one of the fallen angels described by Milton (*Paradise Lost* II, 109) as
being 'in act more graceful and humane'

15 NOVEMBER 1940

General Metaxas: Prime Minister of Greece 1936–40

17 JANUARY 1941

Canadian Jewish Congress: national organization founded in 1919 to assist East European Jewry; reactivated in the thirties to deal with Nazism and the refugee problem. Klein was involved with the Congress as a speechwriter for its president, Samuel Bronfman, in the forties and fifties.

I. Rabinovitch: Israel Rabinovitch, editor of the Montreal Yiddish daily *Kanader Adler* (*Canadian Jewish Eagle*)

I.I. Segal (1896–1954): sometimes referred to as J.I. Segal (Jacob Isaac), noted Montreal Yiddish poet, friend of Klein

Amcho: 'your own people'; common folk; Jews

sefer yetzirah: 'Book of Creation,' an early cabbalistic work stressing cosmology and the symbolism of letters and numbers

Baal Shem Tov: 'Master of the Good Name,' Israel ben Eliezer Baal Shem Tov (c 1700–60), founder of Chassidism in the eighteenth century

Litvacks: Lithuanians. The Lithuanian Jews were often represented (by neighbouring Jewish communities) as sharpwitted and pedantic.

31 JANUARY 1941

Voelkischer Beobachter: Berlin daily newspaper owned by the Nazis

gauleiter: Nazi district governor; typically, the arrogant henchman

Streicher: Julius Streicher (1895–1946), Nazi politician and journalist, anti-semitic agitator, editor of *Der Stuermer*

Quislings: Vidkun Quisling (1887–1945), Norwegian fascist, served as puppet prime minister during Nazi occupation of Norway

Rosenberg: Alfred Rosenberg (1893–1946), Nazi leader and writer, editor of *Voelkischer Beobachter*

14 FEBRUARY 1941

Ossa upon Pelion: mountains in Greece, mentioned in Homer, *The Odyssey* XI

Wavell: British field marshal, in command of British forces in Middle East and North Africa in early years of World War II

'Knock ... ': Matthew 7:7

'Those pagod things ... ': Byron, 'Ode to Napoleon'

'Sail on, O ship ... ': Longfellow, 'The Building of the Ship'

Invictus: poem by W.E. Henley written in 1875

28 FEBRUARY 1941

'Don Juan': III, 41

sour grapes: Ezekiel 18:2

the Canticum: Song of Songs 2:12

The moan of doves ... : Tennyson, 'The Princess' VII, 202–3

7 MARCH 1941
Samuel Bronfman: prominent Montreal industrialist and philanthropist; head
     of Seagram's; president of the Canadian Jewish Congress, 1939–62;
     employed Klein as writer and public relations counsel
Whither thou goest ... : Ruth 1:16–17

4 APRIL 1941
Schoen: beautiful, good, noble

11 APRIL 1941
Haggadah: the 'telling' – a narrative of the exodus from Egypt, presented
     through a set form of benedictions, prayers, homilies, and psalms,
     recited at the family meal on the night of Passover
'darkness palpable': 'the palpable obscure' (*Paradise Lost* II, 406)
Judenrein: 'clean of Jews,' in Nazi terminology, the condition of a locality
     from which all Jews have been eliminated
Pithom and Ramses: the two treasury cities which, according to the Bible,
     the Israelites were forced to build for Pharaoh (Exodus 1:11)
'lest they multiply ... ': Exodus 1:10

9 MAY 1941
'the sons of Belial ...': *Paradise Lost* I, 501–2
Schuschnigg: Kurt von Schuschnigg, Austrian chancellor from 1934 until
     the Nazi occupation in 1938; imprisoned by the Germans
Beneš: Eduard Beneš, president of Czechoslovakia from 1935 until the Nazi
     occupation in 1938, and again 1945–8

27 JUNE 1941
declared war: Germany invaded Russia on 22 June.
der alle beide stinken: Heine, 'dass sie alle beide stinken,' that they both stink

27 JUNE 1941
Peccavimus: 'we have sinned'
Lindbergh ... Wheeler ... Ford: all prominent Americans who advocated isola-
     tionism and who were regarded, for the most part, as reactionary,
     even pro-German

8 AUGUST 1941
Arma virumque cano: 'Arms and the man I sing' – opening words of
     Virgil's *Aeneid*; *canis* is Latin for 'dog.'

15 AUGUST 1941
d'Annunzio: Gabriele d'Annunzio (1863–1938), a decadent fin-de-siècle

Italian poet who became violently patriotic and was honoured by Mussolini's fascist regime

'agenbite of inwit': 'remorse of conscience'

5 SEPTEMBER 1941

Sic Semper Tyrannis: 'Thus always to tyrants'

the de facto law: Talmud, *Gittin* 10b

'a hand may still ...': Job 2:5

19 SEPTEMBER 1941

High Holy Days: Rosh Hashanah (the New Year) and Yom Kippur (Day of Atonement), holiest days of the Jewish year

Machzor: festival prayer book

26 SEPTEMBER 1941

'Lone Eagle': Charles Lindbergh, American aviator, an isolationist and outspoken opponent of American intervention in World War II before Pearl Harbor

Gerald P. Nye: American senator, among the leaders of the America First Committee, a pressure group that opposed aid to the Allies in the early forties

10 OCTOBER 1941

Rudolf Hess: high-ranking Nazi leader, had flown solo to Scotland on 10 May apparently under the delusion that he could arrange a peace with England; held as war prisoner

Yom Kippur: Day of Atonement, solemn fast day observed on the tenth of Tishri (September-October), preceded by 'ten days of penitence' starting on Rosh Hashanah

31 OCTOBER 1941

casus belli: 'act that precipitates war'

lebensraum: 'living space'

blitzkrieg: 'lightning war'

donnerwetter: 'thunderstorm'; used as a cursing exclamation in German

14 NOVEMBER 1941

Titus: Flavius Vespasianus Titus, Roman legion commander in Judaea who besieged and captured Jerusalem in 70 AD, emperor of Rome 79–81 AD

5 DECEMBER 1941

Tennyson: in 'Hands All Round' –'That man's the best Cosmopolite/Who loves his native country best'

Yehuda Halevi: c1075–1141, poet and philosopher. See Klein's poem
  'Yehuda Halevi, His Pilgrimage.'
auch Juden: 'also Jews' – phrase used by assimilated Jews
bauch Juden: 'stomach Jews' – Jews by virtue of their cuisine

12 DECEMBER 1941
Marlowe: *The Jew of Malta* IV.i
tzitzith: tassels or fringes of thread on the four corners of prayer shawls and
  garments worn by religious Jewish males
Ost-Juden: 'Eastern Jews,' who were often looked down upon by the more
  assimilated and more prosperous Jews of Western Europe
goy (pl. *goyim*): 'non-Jew'
hof-Jude: 'court Jew,' a type of Jew who served in European courts (from
  the seventeenth century on) as financial administrator, often representing Jewish interests as well, but isolated from the main body of Jewry
  by virtue of his privileged position
De minimis non curat lex: 'the law is not concerned with trifles'
Brandeis: Louis Brandeis (1856–1941), jurist and prominent American Zionist, first Jew to be appointed to the United States Supreme Court
lovely and pleasant ... : 2 Samuel 1:23
marranos: Jews who hid or denied their Jewishness to escape persecution;
  applied originally to Spanish Jews who were forced to convert to Christianity but who practised Judaism secretly
Stephen Wise (1874–1949): American rabbi and Zionist leader

12 DECEMBER 1941
dastardly attack: reference to Japanese attack on Pearl Harbor on 7 December
conflict of Gog and Magog: the battle preceding the coming of the Messiah.
  See Ezekiel 38–9.

2 JANUARY 1942
tzelem-elohim: the 'divine image' in which man was created
'reasons Reason does not have': Pascal, *Pensées* 277
al kiddush ha-shem: 'for the sanctification of God's name'
to thy tents, O Israel!: 1 Kings 12:16
comfort ye ... : Isaiah 40:1
man does not live by bread alone: Deuteronomy 8:3
Shulchan Aruch: Jewish code of laws compiled and systematized by Joseph
  Karo in the sixteenth century

23 JANUARY 1942
Agudath Israel: Jewish orthodox religious movement and political party

27 FEBRUARY 1942
Antonescu: Ion Antonescu, premier of Rumania 1940–4
Shechita: slaughtering; usually refers to kosher slaughtering

13 MARCH 1942
Hamaniacs: reference to Haman, arch-enemy of the Jews, Book of Esther
Yeshiva (pl. *Yeshivas* or *Yeshivoth*): Jewish school for religious study; a
    Talmudic academy
'doth sit solitary ... ': Lamentations 1:1–2
Tosafoth: famous commentary on the Talmud written during the twelfth to
    fourteenth centuries by Jewish scholars in France and Germany
Talmud: a compendium of discussions of Jewish law and practice by genera-
    tions of scholars in various academies from the third century to the
    end of the fifth. Together with the Bible, it constitutes the basis of
    Jewish law and learning.
Mr. Suchachevsky: Zvi Hirsch Suchachevsky who, along with Rabbi Simcha
    Garber, was one of Klein's early Talmud tutors
Rashi: Hebrew acronym for Rabbi Solomon ben Isaac (1040–1105), one of the
    most authoritative commentators on the Bible and Talmud; born and
    lived in Troyes, France
Kidushin, or *Baba Bathra* or *Chulin*: tractates of the Talmud
Haskala: 'Enlightenment,' a movement for spreading modern European
    culture among Jews, started in the late eighteenth century
Yiddische Wissenschaft: the 'scientific' study of Judaism by subjecting it to
    modern critical methods of research
herrenvolk: 'master race'

27 MARCH 1942
Bourassa: Henri Bourassa (1868–1952), journalist and politician, leading
    French-Canadian nationalist
A Bas la Conscription: 'Down with conscription'
A Bas les Juifs: 'Down with the Jews'

1 APRIL 1942
cinque-spotted mole: Shakespeare, *Cymbeline* II.ii
Mayer-bal-haness: 'Mayer the miracle worker,' a legendary rabbi whose tomb
    near Tiberias is a famous shrine
the Talmudic one: Rabbi Mayer, second-century *tanna*, played a decisive part
    in the development of the Mishna, the earliest basic codification of
    Jewish law
Mayer ha-golah: 'beacon unto the exile,' a term of praise applied to illustri-
    ous Diaspora Jews

bracha: benediction
Abou-ben-Adam: Leigh Hunt, 'Abou Ben Adhem' ('may his tribe increase')

24 APRIL 1942
Beethoven's Ninth: Klein presumably had in mind the Fifth
Sir Stafford Cripps: a leading figure in the British Labour party, special envoy
    to India in 1942

8 MAY 1942
Zend-Avesta: the Zoroastrian Scriptures

22 MAY 1942
Shevuoth: Pentecost, festival celebrated on sixth of Sivan (May-June),
    seven weeks after Passover, in commemoration of the giving of the
    Torah at Mount Sinai
Shas: acronym for *shisha sedarim*, the 'six orders' of the Mishna; refers
    basically to the complete Talmud
Rabbi Yochanan ben Zakkai: one of the most important sages of the last
    decade of the Second Temple period, obtained permission from Titus to
    found an academy at Yavneh after the Temple was destroyed in 70 AD
Sura and Pumbeditha: sites of two of the leading academies of Babylonian
    Jewry, founded in the 3rd century AD, where many of the discussions
    in the Talmud occurred
pilpulistic hair-splitting: *pilpul* – a method of Talmudic study involving
    sharp dialectical argumentation, 'logic chopping'

12 JUNE 1942
yahrzeit: anniversary of a person's death
Chevra Kadisha: a fellowship for carrying out the Jewish burial rites
chibut hakever: purgatorial suffering
Kaddish: a type of 'Magnificat' in Jewish liturgy, one form of which is recited,
    following a death, by the closest male kin, usually a son
Cohanim: priests; any descendants of the biblical priestly family of Aaron
Rosh Hashanah: Jewish New Year, first and second days of Tishri (September-
    October)
Borden's Elsie: a cow, featured in advertisements of Borden's Dairy

19 JUNE 1942
Heydrich: Reinhard Heydrich, deputy chief of the Gestapo, was living in
    Prague in 1942. A bomb was hurled at him on 29 May and he died on 4
    June.
Sodom: a place of corruption and evil (Genesis 18:20–19:28)

Hohenzollern: German royal family; William II, last emperor of Germany, abdicated in 1919.

17 JULY 1942
Emile Zola: French novelist whose 1898 open letter, *J'accuse!*, accusing the French army and government of framing Alfred Dreyfus, led to the latter's ultimate vindication

14 AUGUST 1942
on this picture and on this: Shakespeare, *Hamlet* III.iv. Klein's phrase 'counter presentiment,' which occurs elsewhere in his writing, is a garbled echo of the Shakespearean phrase 'counterfeit presentment.'

28 AUGUST 1942
cheshbon hanefesh: spiritual self-examination and self-appraisal
mitzva (pl. *mitzvoth*): religious commandment, good deed; usually but not necessarily in connection with biblical or rabbinic teachings
'The Tishbite will answer ... ': an expression used in the Talmud to close unresolved arguments; the solution will be provided by the prophet Elijah (the Tishbite), ie, in the days of the Messiah
galuth: 'exile,' 'Diaspora'
Shmoneh Esra: central daily prayer consisting of eighteen benedictions, including a prayer for the return to Zion
Mordecai M. Kaplan (b1881): American rabbi, founder of the Reconstructionist movement, an offshoot of Conservative Judaism, which tries to adapt Judaism to modern naturalist and rationalist ideas

4 SEPTEMBER 1942
Mr. Ilsley: J.L. Ilsley, Canadian minister of finance during World War II

11 SEPTEMBER 1942
Nihil Judaicum ... : 'Nothing Jewish is alien to me,' playing on Terence's 'I am a man; nothing human is alien to me' in *Heauton Timoroumenos* I.i
Vaad Ho'ir: 'city council,' Jewish community council, chiefly for religious affairs
Kashruth: Jewish dietary laws
landsmanshaften: societies of persons who emigrated from the same region
Je suis tout ... Je suis partout: 'I am all ... I am everywhere'
chai: the number eighteen expressed in letters which also form the word 'living' or 'alive' – hence a mystically significant number

20 NOVEMBER 1942
Sinn Fein: 'ourselves alone,' the Irish nationalist slogan and party name

11 DECEMBER 1942
Jean Drapeau: later to become mayor of Montreal

22 JANUARY 1943
Wendell Willkie: 1940 American Republican presidential candidate, identified
    with the 'One World' concept of international co-operation
ding an sich: 'the thing itself' (a famous Kantian term)

5 FEBRUARY 1943
'into the dark backward ... ': Shakespeare, *The Tempest* I.ii
Rommel: Erwin Rommel, commander of the German forces in Africa

5 MARCH 1943
Sir Norman Angell: journalist and author, winner of the 1933 Nobel peace
    prize
Sir William Beveridge: British economist, author of the Beveridge Plan for
    social security
Viscount Halifax: British ambassador to the United States

5 MARCH 1943
I.R.: Israel Rabinovitch, editor of the *Kanader Adler*, Montreal

5 MARCH 1943
'On a little brown pony ... ': 'Into the Town of Chelm,' from Klein's *Hath
    Not a Jew ...*
aim b'Yisroel: 'a mother in Israel,' used in reference to the great cities and
    settlements of Jews throughout history. See 2 Samuel 20:19.
Exterminationskolonnen: Klein evidently means extermination camps.
The time is out of joint ... : Shakespeare, *Hamlet* I.v

23 APRIL 1943
Bermuda Conference: Anglo-American conference on refugees held in Ber-
    muda 19–30 April; produced no practical results
Passover: seven-day spring festival starting on the 15th of Nisan (March-
    April) commemorating the exodus from Egypt
open-and-shut covenants: echoing the first of Woodrow Wilson's Fourteen
    Points – 'open covenants of peace openly arrived at'

21 MAY 1943
ghetto was liquidated: fighting ended on 16 May

18 JUNE 1943
dis aliter visum: 'the gods thought otherwise,' Virgil, *Aeneid* II, 428
Keats: in 'Ode to a Nightingale' – 'Do I wake or sleep?'
four freedoms: enunciated by Roosevelt in 1941 – freedom of speech, of religion, from want, and from fear

9 JULY 1943
Lessing Rosenwald: American Jewish merchant and philanthropist, at one time chairman of Sears, Roebuck & Company; founder of the anti-Zionist American Council for Judaism in 1943
Jerome Frank: See Klein's article of 12 December 1941.
'What's Hecuba to him ... ': Shakespeare, *Hamlet* II.ii

13 OCTOBER 1943
Succoth: Tabernacles, seven-day festival beginning on the 15th of Tishri (September-October)
'every man under his vine ... ': 1 Kings 4:25
olim meminisse juvabit: 'it will be pleasant to remember these things in after times,' Virgil, *Aeneid* I, 283–4

26 NOVEMBER 1943
Oswald Mosley: leader of British fascists in the thirties, interned 1940
the *Struma* and the *Patria*: ships carrying refugees without permits to Palestine. See Klein's editorials for 27 February 1942 and 31 August 1945.

24 DECEMBER 1943
'the bourne from which ... ': Shakespeare, *Hamlet* III.i
'He dipt into the future ... ': Tennyson, 'Locksley Hall' ll. 119–20
untermensch: 'lower or inferior person,' opposite of *ubermensch*, idealized 'superman' of the Nazis
circumcision of hearts: Jeremiah 4:4, Ezekiel 44:7
'faultily faultless ... ': Tennyson, *Maud* I.ii

7 JANUARY 1944
Rabbi Levi Yitschok of Berditchev (c1740–1810): famous early Chassidic rabbi, stressed joy and fervent prayer, pleaded the cause of the Jews in singing his prayers, remembered for his dramatic summonsing of

God to judgment for allowing the suffering of the Jews. See Klein's poem 'Reb Levi Yitschok Talks to God.'

tallis: 'prayer shawl'

tfillin: 'phylacteries'

Rebono shel Olam: 'Lord of the Universe,' often used colloquially in addressing God

'O, how is she become ... ': echoing Lamentations 1:1–2

a Thou-song: from Klein's English rendering of Levi Yitschok's Yiddish '*A Dudele*'

Pamalyah shel maalah: heavenly court, ministering angels

shabbos-goy: a non-Jew who performs for Jews tasks forbidden to them on the Sabbath, such as kindling a fire

Ne'ilah: concluding service on the Day of Atonement

21 JANUARY 1944

Beth: 'house of'

shochet: ritual slaughterer

Taryag: the number 613 expressed in letters, ie, 613 commandments of the Torah

'So many good years him ... ': playing on a Yiddish expression which means roughly: 'May he have as many good years as good deeds he has performed'

Havelock Ellis (1859–1939): British essayist and scientist, noted for his studies in the psychology of sex

28 JANUARY 1944

Pierre van Paassen (1895–1968): Dutch-born journalist and author, ardent pro-Zionist

au dessus de la bataille: 'above the battle'

Lukes and Keith-Roachs: senior officials in the Palestine administration at the time of the Hebron massacre; both were regarded as pro-Arab

Yeats: 'The Second Coming'

3 MARCH 1944

Jude: Jew

For there they that carried us away ... : Psalms 137:3–4

'who sink their blood ... ': from Klein's translation, 'The Chastisement of God'

10 MARCH 1944

Purim: festival on the 14th of Adar (February-March) commemorating the deliverance of the Jews in Persia from Haman's plot to kill them, as narrated in the Book of Esther

megillah: 'scroll,' ie, the Scroll or Book of Esther, recited on Purim

gragers: 'rattles' or other noisemakers used to drown out the name of Haman whenever he is mentioned in the public reading of the Book of Esther on Purim

Hitlertaschen: playing on *hamantaschen*, three-cornered tarts named after Haman and served on Purim

fast of Esther: on the 13th of Adar, the day before Purim

7 APRIL 1944

Goshen: region of ancient Egypt inhabited by the Israelites from the time of Joseph until the exodus

b'mhairo b'yomainu: 'speedily, in our days'

5 MAY 1944

Endeks: right-wing Polish political party, the force behind much Polish antisemitism in first half of the twentieth century

Seyss-Inquart: chancellor of Austria after the German occupation

'*Der Tag*': 'The Day'

19 MAY 1944

Sir Herbert Samuel: English Liberal leader, a Jew, first British high commissioner to Palestine, 1920–5

16 JUNE 1944

'the foxes, the little foxes ... ': Song of Songs 2:15

paying back to Normandy: reference to William the Conqueror's invasion of England from Normandy in 1066

'cursed will be that man ... ': Joshua 6:26

'Ye shall not shout ... ': Joshua 6:10

23 JUNE 1944

'Of Lowly Things': This piece is listed by Klein under the heading 'stories' in his index to the contents of his personal files. It may have been intended for ultimate use in a larger work of fiction, such as his unfinished novel 'The Golem.'

17 NOVEMBER 1944

volkstum: nationality; possibly Klein meant 'volksstamm' – tribe or race –

but probably he mistakenly used 'volkstum' to mean mass or popular assembly
Balaam: Numbers 22:5–24:25

24 NOVEMBER 1944
Lord Moyne: British deputy minister of state in the Middle East, assassinated 6 November 1944
lien de droit: just claim, logical (inherent) connection
Stern group: militant Jewish extremist faction in Palestine led by Abraham Stern in the 1940s

8 DECEMBER 1944
Shmaryahu Levin (1867–1935): Zionist leader, writer, and lecturer

29 DECEMBER 1944
Clear-it-with-Sidney: Sidney Hillman (1887–1946), outstanding American labour leader, Jewish confidant of Roosevelt and chief labour advisor

16 MARCH 1945
shiva: seven days of mourning following burial of a close relative

27 APRIL 1945
masterly work on Jewish music: *Muzik bei Yidden*, published in Yiddish in 1940, was translated into English by Klein and appeared in instalments in *The Canadian Jewish Chronicle*. The translation was augmented and published in book form in 1952 under the title *Of Jewish Music, Ancient and Modern*.
'opes his oyster': Shakespeare, *The Merry Wives of Windsor* II.ii
Yoshaiv Rosh: 'chairman'
Imperator Rex: 'Imperial Majesty'
pour épater le bourgeois: 'to shock the bourgeois'
bar-mitzva: the attainment of religious and legal maturity by Jewish males at the age of thirteen

4 MAY 1945
integer vitae: 'of upright life,' Horace, *Odes* I, 22
de mortuis ... : 'of the dead, nothing but good'
two knaves who perished: Mussolini was executed by Italian partisans on 28 April; Hitler committed suicide on 30 April.
This is the day ...: Lamentations 2:16

11 MAY 1945

Torquemada: Tomas de Torquemada, first head of the Spanish Inquisition
in the fifteenth century

Chmelnitzki: Bogdan Chmelnitzki, leader of peasant revolt against Polish
rule in the Ukraine in 1648 which resulted in the destruction of hundreds of Jewish communities

The Lord hath broken: Isaiah 14: 5–6, 12–13, 15

festung Europa: 'fortress Europe'

Ley: Robert Ley, Nazi leader, noted for antisemitism, head of Labour Front
from 1933

dayenu: 'it were enough for us,' the refrain of a Passover song enumerating
all of God's deeds for the Jews in the exodus from Egypt

25 MAY 1945

corpores delicti: 'bodies of the crime,' the victims' corpses

sickly o'er the pale cast of thought: Shakespeare, *Hamlet* III.i. This is a
good example of Klein's tendency to quote inexactly from memory or to
echo and modify, for his own purpose, a quotation.

Leipzig trials: trials of Germans accused of war crimes in World War I

3 AUGUST 1945

Petlura and Denikin: Semion Petlura, Ukrainian nationalist leader, and
Anton Denikin, Czarist 'White Army' general, both responsible for
widespread pogroms in the Ukraine in 1919–20, in which over a quarter
of a million Jews were killed

El Moleh Rachmim: 'Lord, Full of Compassion,' opening words of a prayer for
the dead

on this page: of the *Chronicle*; statistics not reprinted here

19 OCTOBER 1945

'Lord Haw-Haw': William Joyce (erroneously named Alfred by Klein),
British traitor, broadcast propaganda and threats against England from
Germany throughout the war

4 JANUARY 1946

who knew not Joseph: Exodus 1:8

8 FEBRUARY 1946

skins ... lampshades: reference to Ilse Koch, infamous wife of German
concentration camp commander, who made lampshades from skins of
camp inmates

22 FEBRUARY 1946
Oppenheim novels: E. Phillips Oppenheim (1866–1946), British novelist of
    espionage and diplomatic intrigue
Lord Tweedsmuir: John Buchan (1875–1940), statesman and writer of adven-
    ture stories, Governor-General of Canada from 1935 until his death
    in 1940
announcement of Prime Minister King: a royal commission was appointed
    on 5 February 1946 to report on the Soviet-Canadian spy ring that had
    been exposed in September 1945 when Igor Gouzenko defected from
    the Russian embassy in Ottawa. Klein wrote an unpublished novel about
    the Gouzenko affair shortly after. See below, 10 February 1950.

22 MARCH 1946
Biro-Bidjan: region of eastern Russia established by the Soviets as the 'Jewish
    Autonomous Region' in the thirties, began to decline as a Jewish
    centre in the late forties as a result of the Stalinist policy to suppress all
    Jewish activities in the USSR
Byron: 'Oh! Weep for Those'
If I am not for myself ... : Ethics of the Fathers I, 14

3 MAY 1946
von Blomberg: Werner von Blomberg, minister of war in Hitler's cabinet
    1933–8

10 MAY 1946
at San Francisco: the founding of the United Nations Organization
DP: displaced person, used to describe people who had been driven out of
    their homes as a result of Nazi decrees and World War II

14 JUNE 1946
Mr. Bevin: Ernest Bevin, British labour leader, Labour government's for-
    eign secretary 1945–51
Mufti: Haj Amin Al-Husseini, Palestinian nationalist leader, mufti of Jeru-
    salem
M. Bidault: the French premier
ça saute aux yeux: 'it leaps to the eyes,' it is clearly evident
El Burak: fabulous animal on which Mohammed is said to have ascended to
    heaven
shlemiel: unlucky habitual bungler

21 JUNE 1946
Ilya Ehrenburg: Soviet journalist and writer

5 JULY 1946
Is this really Naomi?: Ruth 1:19
Irgun Zvai (Irgun): short for Irgun Zvai Leumi, 'National Military Organiza-
    tion,' a Jewish underground organization founded in Palestine in
    1931, an activist breakaway group from the Haganah
Major Glubb: Sir John Glubb, British soldier, commander of the Arab Legion in
    Transjordan
Histadruth: 'Federation,' ie, the Labour Federation
P.A.: Palestine Administration
Power corrupts: Lord Acton. See letter in *Life of Mandell Creighton* (1904) I,
    372.

26 JULY 1946
Moshe Shertok: Zionist leader and statesman, known by his post-1948 adop-
    ted name, Moshe Sharett; foreign minister of Israel 1948, prime
    minister 1954–5
Bernard Joseph: Israeli political leader and lawyer, originally from Canada;
    military governor of Jerusalem during the siege of 1948; member of
    parliament 1949–65; minister in various posts, including supply and
    rationing 1949–50
Mazel Tov: 'Good fortune,' a customary form of congratulatory greeting

30 AUGUST 1946
David Remez: labour leader and later cabinet minister; also linguist and writer
Davar: Tel Aviv daily newspaper affiliated with the labour movement
Remez: 'hint'

4 OCTOBER 1946
Jodl: Alfred Jodl, chief of staff of the German army
Raeder: Erich Raeder, commander-in-chief of the German navy
von Schirach: Baldur von Schirach, gauleiter in Vienna 1940–5
von Papen: Franz von Papen, chancellor of Germany 1931–2, ambassador to
    Turkey 1939–45
Fritzsche: Hans Fritzsche, official in the Propaganda Ministry
Speer: Albert Speer, minister for Armament and War Production
Doenitz: Karl Doenitz, German naval commander

16 OCTOBER 1946
Juan Peron: President of Argentina
UNRRA: United Nations Relief and Rehabilitation Administration

6 DECEMBER 1946
intra vires: 'within the jurisdiction of the law'
Dura lex, sed lex: 'a hard law, but the law'

13 DECEMBER 1946
Mr. Duplessis: Maurice Duplessis, premier of Quebec 1936–9, 1944–59

10 JANUARY 1947
third member: Stalin
Cohan: George M. Cohan (1878–1942), American playwright and lyricist,
    writer of musical comedies

17 JANUARY 1947
Yisroel chai v'kayom: 'Israel is alive and enduring'
sucklings of the kindergarten ... upon whom worlds are poised: Talmud,
    Shabbat 119b

24 JANUARY 1947
argumentum ad conscientiam mundi: 'an argument appealing to the world's
    conscience'

4 JULY 1947
BNA: British North America Act, passed by British Parliament in 1867 to
    embody the resolutions on which the confederation of the Dominion
    of Canada was founded

11 JULY 1947
Ardeatine caves: sites of Nazi massacre of Italian civilians in March 1944

18 JULY 1947
living together of brothers: Psalms 133:1

8 AUGUST 1947
nefas: 'crime,' sin
Menachem Beigin (Begin): commander of the Irgun 1943–8, founder of the
    right-wing Herut party in 1948, elected prime minister of Israel in 1977
St. John Philby: British author and explorer in Arabia, advisor to kings Abdul-
    lah and Saud
Gorboduc play-acting: *Gorboduc*, a sixteenth-century play filled with violence

5 DECEMBER 1947
United Nations ... : On 29 November the UN voted 33 to 13 in favour of
    partitioning Palestine into a Jewish and an Arab state.

Ilsley and Pearson: Cabinet ministers in Prime Minister King's Liberal government

Jehad: Moslem holy war

16 JANUARY 1948
General Marshall: George Marshall, American secretary of state 1947–9, originator of the Marshall Aid Plan for post-war reconstruction of Europe

6 FEBRUARY 1948
death of Gandhi: assassinated by a Hindu fanatic on 30 January

19 MARCH 1948
JNF: Jewish National Fund, branch of the Jewish Agency responsible for purchasing and restoring land in Palestine and Israel

Shehechianu: 'Who hath kept us alive,' a benediction to mark a novel, happy occasion

Geulah: 'redemption,' deliverance

2 APRIL 1948
Mr. Luce: Henry Luce, publisher of Time and Life

Titus' gnat: alluding to the Jewish legend that, in punishment for blaspheming God, the Roman emperor Titus was killed by a gnat which entered through his nostril and fed on his brain for seven years, growing to the size of a small bird. Talmud, Gittin 66b

29 APRIL 1948
Graetz: Heinrich Graetz (1817–91), Jewish historian and scholar

badge of the tribe: Shakespeare, The Merchant of Venice I.iii

Soncino press: Jewish press founded in Italy in the fifteenth century, existing to this day

Mount Carmel: a ridge on whose slopes Haifa is built

14 MAY 1948
sun ... in Ashkalon: Joshua 10:12; the correct reference is to Ajalon.

Sabbath which approaches: 15 May; the State of Israel came into being at 4 pm on Friday the 14th.

Arch of Titus: Roman arch commemorating the conquest of Jerusalem by Titus in 70 AD

hora: circular group dance popular in Israel

Leo Pinsker: Russian forerunner of Zionism, author of Autoemancipation, 1882

all Israel – of all generations – stood ... : *Midrash Rabba,* Exodus 28:6
Rabbi Zadoc: first-century *tanna.* See Talmud, *Gittin* 56a.
paytanim: composers of Hebrew liturgical poems from the 5th century on
    through the Middle Ages
O who is this ... : taken from Klein's early poem, 'Greeting on This Day'
Ashkinaz: Germany
Sphorad: Spain

16 JULY 1948
sha'aloth: legal questions addressed to a rabbi
Responsum: written reply to a question in Jewish law

24 SEPTEMBER 1948
Folke Bernadotte: Swedish stateman, UN-appointed mediator in the Arab-
    Israeli conflict, assassinated 17 September apparently by Jewish extrem-
    ists who opposed the territorial exchanges his peace plans entailed

19 NOVEMBER 1948
Chassidim: literally 'righteous men'; pietists, a sect of Jewish mystics founded
    in eastern Europe about 1750, in opposition to formalistic Judaism
    and ritual laxity. The term now is generally used to designate the fol-
    lowers of the Chassidic movement, which emphasizes ecstacy in prayer
    and charismatic leadership as well as religious learning.

17 DECEMBER 1948
Vishinsky: prosecutor in the Russian purge trials in the 1930s

7 JANUARY 1949
King Farouk: ruler of Egypt 1937–52

18 MARCH 1949
aretz and *chutz l'aretz*: 'the land' and 'outside the land,' ie, Israel and the
    Diaspora
Bundists: Jewish socialists devoted to Yiddish language and secular national-
    ism, and opposed to Zionism
primum mobile: 'prime mover'
klal Yisroel: 'the totality of Israel,' the whole community of the Jewish
    people
mit leiten gleich: 'on a par with others'

13 APRIL 1949
Seder: order of ceremonies observed in Jewish homes on the night of Pass-
    over, when the Haggadah is recited

matzoth (plural of *matzo*): specially prepared unleavened bread eaten during the week of Passover

Four Questions: a part of the Haggadah in which the youngest child present asks four questions relating to 'why this night is different from all other nights'

Ten Plagues: a part of the Haggadah in which the plagues inflicted on Egypt are enumerated

kneidlach: soup balls made of matzo meal

Hallel: Psalms 113–18 as a unit in Jewish liturgy expressing thanksgiving and joy for divine redemption, recited on the three Pilgrim Festivals and on other days of special rejoicing

moror: bitter herbs eaten at the Passover Seder, to symbolize the bitterness of the Egyptian enslavement

Rabbi Yehuda ... mnemonics: reference to passage in the Haggadah recited on Passover eve

Bnai-Brak: Klein means 'the old sages of Bnai-Brak,' mentioned in the Haggadah.

22 APRIL 1949

Drachenblut: dragon blood; Groberklotz: boorish clod; Gotlos: Godless; Singmirwas: sing me something; Geldshrank: money chest

Beth Hamidrash Hagodol: the Great Synagogue

12 AUGUST 1949

Notebook of a Journey: published in seventeen weekly instalments from August to December 1949, but here grouped in a series. Klein's other editorials during this period follow separately, resuming on 16 September.

ben Bag Bag: first-century *tanna*

Get thee out ... : Genesis 12:1

Tur Malca: a literal translation of Montreal ('Mount Royal') in Aramaic

Mishnaic: Klein is imitating the terse legal style of the Mishna. The reference to Rav and Samuel is technically anachronistic – they are sages in the Talmud, not the Mishna.

the Tishbite: Elijah the prophet, associated in legend with the eventual coming of the Messiah as precursor and active partner

Talmudic: The Talmud analyzes and comments upon the Mishna, just as Klein comments here on his own earlier phrases.

academy of Rehovoth: ie, the Weizmann Institute of Science

Sambation (Sambatyon): legendary river across which part of the ten 'lost tribes' of Israel were exiled by the Assyrians; according to legend it rages constantly except on the Sabbath, and so cannot be crossed.

ma'aseh breshith: the 'deed (or account) of creation' (of the world) – one of the central concerns of early Jewish mysticism

ma'aseh merkavah: the mystical-prophetic account of the 'chariot throne,' based on Ezekiel 1:1–28

13 JULY 1949
'the earth is the Lord's ... ': Psalms 24:1
saints ... every street corner: Many of Montreal's streets are named after Catholic saints.

15 JULY 1949
Hic sunt leones: 'Here are lions'
Wounds and bruises ... : Isaiah 1:6

19 AUGUST 1949
'*El Hatzipor*': 'To the Bird'
Byron: 'Childe Harold's Pilgrimage' IV, 179
'The *Mathmid*': a famous poem by Bialik. A *mathmid* is a *Yeshiva* student who studies the Talmud exclusively day and night.
invraisemblable: 'improbable'
no forty-niner as golden: probably an allusion to the great California gold rush of 1849

26 AUGUST 1949
Tannaim (sing. *Tanna*): rabbinic teachers of the Mishnaic period, from about the first to the early third century
scapefowl: alluding to the ritual during the week preceding Yom Kippur, wherein the punishment for one's sins is, as it were, transferred to the fowl. See Klein's poem 'Plumaged Proxy.'
'*Ces Américaines ... *': 'These Americans, they think everything is for sale, even our soul!'
Rabbi Zambrowski: Canadian religious-Zionist leader
two pair of *tfillin*: Because of a difference of opinion between Rashi and his grandson Rabbenu Tam on the exact arrangement of the contents of the phylacteries, a small number of punctilious Jews follow both opinions by having two different sets of phylacteries.
Schachrit: the morning prayer service
Baba Bathra: a tractate of the Talmud
sabra: native-born Israeli, named after the 'prickly pear'
succoth: 'tabernacles,' 'booths,' temporary huts erected for the festival of Succoth when, for seven days, religious Jews 'dwell' or have their meals in them
payoth: 'earlocks,' which very religious Jews leave uncut

2 SEPTEMBER 1949

Mezuzoth: pl. of *mezuza*, parchment scroll of the biblical verses proclaiming
  monotheism, stored in small cases and traditionally affixed to doorposts
  in Jewish homes

gazoz: 'carbonated drink'

Poalei Zion: Labour Zionists

nid klipah: *klipah* means 'shell' or 'husk'; *nid*, or anything resembling it
  cannot possibly be the word Klein wanted here – *nid* is in fact French
  for 'nest'

Dov, Zev, Aryeh: Hebrew names meaning Bear, Wolf, Lion

Choneh: nickname of Elchanan Mozdof (1886–1966), an eccentric Polish-born
  American Jew, deeply committed to Zionism and Jewish labour causes,
  and having no fixed occupation, who was a very witty self-appointed
  critic of persons and policies in Jewish public affairs

Carnera: Primo Carnera, Italian boxer, briefly heavyweight world champion,
  noted for his size more than for his skill

Moishe Rabbenu: Moses our teacher

the Knesseth: the Israeli Parliament

Hirsh Wolofsky: publisher of *The Canadian Jewish Chronicle*

9 SEPTEMBER 1949

chevlai yemoth hamoshiach: sufferings and tribulations preceding the coming of the Messiah

Messiah as being born on this ninth day of Ab: Jerusalem Talmud, *Berachoth*
  2:4

tenth of August: the event was repeatedly postponed until 16 August. By
  then Klein had to be in Tel Aviv to prepare for his departure from
  Israel. This entire section must have been written in Tel Aviv on the
  16th. The description here of the first night in Jerusalem is a flashback
  filling in part of the gap between Klein's arrival in Jerualem on the 2nd
  and his notes on 'Telaviviana.' Between the 2nd and the 16th he was
  touring various parts of the country and probably was too preoccupied to
  do any writing.

Friedgut: formerly from western Canada, an acquaintance of Klein's through
  Jewish organizational activities

lion's fell: Judges 14:8–14

Giborai Yisroel: 'mighty heroes of Israel'

Aluf: brigadier-general

oylim: immigrants to Israel

Ashkenazi: pertaining to the central and east European community and culture of Diaspora Jewry

Sephardi: pertaining to the Spanish community and culture of Diaspora

Jewry, including the descendants of the Jews expelled from Spain in
1492, who settled mainly along the Mediterranean coast of Europe,
North Africa, and in Holland and England
bones come to life: Ezekiel 37:1–14

23 SEPTEMBER 1949
Regard me not ... : Song of Songs 1:6
Ner Tomid: a light which burns perpetually in front of the Torah ark in the
synagogue

30 SEPTEMBER 1949
la nostalgie de la boue: 'homesickness for the gutter'
aliyoth: waves of immigration to Israel

7 OCTOBER 1949
Isaac Luria: foremost sixteenth-century cabbalist
Baba Kama: a tractate of the Talmud
Shechinah: 'the Divine Presence'
L'cho doidi: 'Come, my friend,' a Friday night hymn, greeting the arrival of
the Sabbath

14 OCTOBER 1949
when the Lord returned the captivity ... : Psalms 126:1
brands plucked from the burning: Zechariah 3:2
They fought ... : Judges 5:20–1
Ain brairah: 'There is no alternative'
'Behold I will open ... ': Ezekiel 37:12

21 OCTOBER 1949
Sadducees: Jewish aristocratic sect, 2nd century BC to 1st century AD, opposed to Pharisees
shiksa: gentile girl

11 NOVEMBER 1949
na'aseh v'nishma: 'we will do, and be obedient' (Exodus 24:7)
gubernias: Russian provinces
Mizrachi: a religious-Zionist party
Mapai: the Israeli Labour party

25 NOVEMBER 1949
Tisha b'Av: ninth of Ab, a day of mourning and fasting, commemorating the
destruction of the Temple in Jerusalem

blatt Gemora: 'a page of Talmud'
Gaon of Vilna: eighteenth-century Talmudic scholar, generally considered
    to be one of the most authoritative rabbis in Europe

9 DECEMBER 1949
Der parshoin zicht metzios!: 'This "gentleman" is looking for bargains!'
    (in Yiddish)

16 DECEMBER 1949
sub jugum: 'under the yoke'
shvarim: a broken note sounded on the ram's horn

23 DECEMBER 1949
Yediot: *Yediot Ach'ronot*, a Tel Aviv Hebrew daily newspaper
lachatz asher haim loichatzim oisom: 'the oppression wherewith they oppress
    them,' Exodus 3:9
haura: probably a reference to the Arabic name for the Jewish quarter of
    Tunis
Mea Shearim: an ultra-orthodox neighbourhood of Jerusalem whose name
    means 'a hundred gates'
Gemara: Talmud
Davar: the 'word,' a Tel Aviv daily newspaper affiliated with the labour
    movement

10 FEBRUARY 1950
Had some romancer ... : In 1946, Klein had written but failed to get pub-
    lished a novel, 'That Walks Like a Man,' on the Gouzenko spy dis-
    closures. In a letter, Klein stated that his imagination was captured by
    the 'whole melodrama of espionage and counter-espionage.'
Alger Hiss: American State Department official convicted in 1950 in a trial
    involving the passing of secret documents to Whittaker Chambers, an
    editor of *Time* and in 1938 a communist espionage agent
Fuchs: Klaus Fuchs, German-born British scientist convicted in 1950 of dis-
    closing nuclear secrets to the Russians
Rose ... Carr: Fred Rose and Sam Carr, two of the Canadians in the spy
    ring revealed by Igor Gouzenko in 1946

24 FEBRUARY 1950
The Confessions: See Klein's unpublished story from this period, 'Letter from
    Afar.'

22 SEPTEMBER 1950
Vallambrosa's vale: Milton, *Paradise Lost* I, 303
letters fly out … : reference to the martyrdom of Rabbi Hananya ben
   Teradyon, who, when burned wrapped in a Torah scroll by the Romans,
   cried out: 'I see parchment burning, while the letters of the Torah
   soar upward.' Talmud, *Avodah Zorah* 18a

9 FEBRUARY 1951
Krupp: Alfred Krupp, inheritor of the Krupp armament factories, sentenced
   in 1947 to twelve years' imprisonment

23 FEBRUARY 1951
70 BC: Klein evidently had in mind 70 AD, the year of the destruction of the
   Second Temple
Rabbi Maimon: religious-Zionist leader, minister of religions in the first
   Israeli government
Kulturkampf: 'ideological struggle'

20 APRIL 1951
Joseph and His Brethren: See also Klein's essay 'The Bible's Archetypical
   Poet,' *Canadian Jewish Chronicle* 6, 13, and 20 March 1953. Biblical
   quotations here are from Genesis 37, 45, and 49.

27 APRIL 1951
Council for Judaism: anti-Zionist American-Jewish organization founded
   by Lessing Rosenwald in 1943. See above, 9 July 1943.

4 MAY 1951
Sarah Bernhardt (1845–1923): famed French-Jewish actress
Look but on this picture … : Shakespeare, *Hamlet* III.iv
melodies unheard: John Keats, 'Ode on a Grecian Urn'

8 JUNE 1951
'all Jews of all generations … must regard themselves … ': Talmud, *Pesachim*
   116b
We will do and we will hearken: Exodus 24:7

13 JULY 1951
Kishineff massacre: a particularly violent massacre of Jews in 1903 instigated
   by Russian authorities
Pause not … : from Klein's translation of Bialik's 'In the City of Slaughter'

18 JANUARY 1952
Herut: a right-wing Israeli political party

1 FEBRUARY 1952
Sneh: 'bush'; allusion both to the burning bush encountered by Moses in the wilderness, and to Moshe Sneh, leader of Israel's Communist party

6 JUNE 1952
Acheson: Dean Acheson, United States Secretary of State 1949–53
Adenauer: Konrad Adenauer, Chancellor of West Germany 1949–63

15 AUGUST 1952
ephod: breastplate worn by the high priest in the ancient Temple service
effigo Dei: 'in the image of God'

26 SEPTEMBER 1952
zdakah: 'almsgiving,' 'charity'

21 NOVEMBER 1952
silk of the kine: a name given to Ireland (a term Klein may have taken from Chapter 1 of Joyce's *Ulysses*)
amicus curiae: 'a friend of the court' – an impartial advisor
vox et praeterea nihil: 'a voice and nothing more'
horoh: 'to teach' or 'to be pregnant' – probably only the first meaning was intended; they would be spelled differently in Hebrew, but Klein's pronunciation makes them homonyms
rebbitzin: 'rabbi's wife'; here used more loosely in the sense of 'female rabbi'
Synge-song: J.M. Synge (1871–1909), Irish playwright and poet
do ut des: 'I give (to you) so that you may give (to me)'

28 NOVEMBER 1952
Loew's Circuit: a chain of American theatres featuring movies and other popular entertainment

12 DECEMBER 1952
'Alexander the Macedonian ... ': this and the following quotes are from 1 Maccabees 1 and 2

16 JANUARY 1953
Zhid: Jew
Molotov ... Ribbentrop: an allusion to the Nazi-Soviet pact of 1939

6 FEBRUARY 1953
'besides, the lady is dead': Marlowe, *The Jew of Malta* – 'besides, the
    wench is dead'
'the still small voice': 1 Kings 19:12

15 MAY 1953
risorgimento: 'renaissance'; revival of energy or spirit
law of Malthus: formulated by the Reverend Thomas Malthus (1766–1834)
    relating to population growth
integer vitae, scelerisque purus: 'of upright life, from frailties free'

29 MAY 1953
'Touching her magnanimity ... ': John Lyly (c1554–1606) *Euphues and His
    England*
divinity which hedges kings: Shakespeare, *Hamlet* IV.v
'justice, verity ... ': Shakespeare, *Macbeth* IV.iii

10 JULY 1953
'Tammuz yearly wounded': Tammuz, a Mesopotamian vegetation god typical
    of a dying-rising deity. Tammuz is also a Hebrew month (June-July)
    containing an important fast commemorating the breaching of the Tem-
    ple Walls by Titus and earlier by Nebuchadnezzar.
Oneg Shabbat: 'Sabbath enjoyment,' or 'entertainment,' reception held on
    Sabbath, devoted to study, singing, and refreshments

7 AUGUST 1953
Young: Edward Young (1683–1765), *Night Thoughts* V, 177
'wherefore doth the way ... ': Jeremiah 12:1

13 NOVEMBER 1953
l'havdil hevdalim: an expression that in effect means 'excuse the comparison'

20 NOVEMBER 1953
George Drew: leader of the Progressive Conservative party 1948–56
Solon Low: leader of the Social Credit party 1944–60
T.S. Eliot: 'The Wasteland' l. 69

19 MARCH 1954
This editorial may have been written by Klein as a witty exercise in 'Purim-
    Torah,' a traditional parody of a rabbinic sermon or of Talmudic
    exegesis, indulged in on the joyous festival of Purim.

haman-tasch: small three-cornered tart, a traditional Purim food, named after Haman

Sheehy-Shaun: ie, Shushan. See Book of Esther.

O'Dare: ie, Adar, Hebrew month (February-March)

Brian Boru: c940–1014, high king of Ireland

Hans Kohn: presumably Klein meant Leo Kohn (1894–1961), Israeli scholar and diplomat and constitutional expert, and not Hans Kohn (1891–1971), American historian

Concordia salus: 'Hail, Goddess Concord,' motto of the city of Montreal

19 NOVEMBER 1954
one law, one element ... : Tennyson, *In Memoriam*, conclusion

9 MAY 1955
Yalta papers: reference to summit conference at Yalta 4–11 February 1945, attended by Churchill, Roosevelt, and Stalin, at which plans were made for the disposition of territories freed from German occupation

IN PRAISE OF THE DIASPORA
In Praise of the Diaspora was originally serialized in seven instalments indicated here by the breaks in the text.

brought Death ... all our woe!: Milton, *Paradise Lost*, I, 3

Better were it that that day had perished: Job 3:3

Judengasse, Juiverie, Judacaria: Jewish quarters

Sing us ... : Psalms 137:3–4

Abarbanel: properly Abrabanel, a distinguished Jewish-Spanish family of the thirteenth to seventeenth centuries

Shaika Feifer, Motka Chabad, Hershel of Ostropol: all legendary Jewish jesters

aliyot: pilgrimages to Jerusalem, made by Jews in ancient Israel on Passover, Shevuoth, and Succoth

Speak now ... : Exodus 11:2

sheol: 'the netherworld'

Amoraic: pertaining to the *amoraim* (sing. *amora*), the sages of the Talmud, scholars of the post-Mishnaic period, about 200–500 AD

Nakdanim: 'punctators,' scholars of the ninth to fourteenth centuries who provided biblical manuscripts with masoretic apparatus, vowels, and accents

kometz ... patach: similar sounding Hebrew vowel signs
'the will! ... ': Shakespeare, *Julius Caesar* iii.ii
fellahin: Arab peasants

la'azim: glosses with French words (written in Hebrew characters) to
    define certain biblical expressions, used by Rashi in his commentaries

It is not necessary ... : from Klein's poem, '*In Re*: Solomon Warshawer'
The dwarf dictators ... : *ibid.*

Glossary

The following is a short list of frequently recurring Hebrew and Yiddish terms, arranged alphabetically.

al kiddush (kdushas) hashem: 'for the sanctification of God's name,' an
    expression often used in connection with acts of martyrdom
aliyah (pl. aliyoth): 'ascension,' usually refers to immigration to Israel
aretz: 'the land,' usually refers to Israel
Baal Shem Tov: 'Master of the Good Name' (Israel Ben Eliezer, c1700–60),
    founder of Chassidism in the eighteenth century
bar mitzvah: the attainment of religious and legal maturity by Jewish males
    at the age of thirteen
bracha: 'benediction'
chai: 'living' or 'alive.' The numerical equivalent of the letters forming this
    word is eighteen, hence regarded as a number denoting good fortune.
chalutz (pl. chalutzim): 'pioneer,' more specifically the immigrants who culti-
    vated the land of Israel before the establishment of the Jewish State
Chanukah: eight-day celebration commemorating the victory of Judah Mac-
    cabee over the Syrian king Antiochus Epiphanes and the subsequent
    rededication of the Temple in 164 BC
chassidim (sing. chassid): literally 'righteous men'; pietists; a sect of Jewish
    mystics founded in eastern Europe about 1750; a movement whose fol-
    lowers emphasize ecstasy in prayer, charismatic leadership, and learning
cheshbon hanefesh: spiritual examination and self-appraisal
Eretz Israel (Erez Israel): Land of Israel
galut(h): 'exile,' diaspora
gematria: the interpretation of Hebrew words according to the numerical
    value of their letters, used as a method of finding 'hidden' meanings
    of biblical or other texts
geulah: 'redemption,' deliverance
goy (pl. goyim): 'non-Jew'

Haggadah: the 'telling,' a narrative of the exodus from Egypt, presented
through a set form of benedictions, prayers, homilies and psalms, recited
by the family at the Passover meal

hora: circular group dance popular in Israel

kashruth: Jewish dietary laws

Knesseth: Israeli parliament

Leviathan: fabulous sea animal reserved as food for the righteous in the
hereafter

luftmensch: a person 'up in the air' without a definite occupation

Machzor: festival prayer book

matzo (pl. matzoth): unleavened bread eaten during the weak of Passover

megillah: 'scroll,' for example, the Scroll or Book of Esther recited on
Purim

mitzva (pl. mitzvoth): religious commandment or duty, good deed, usually
but not necessarily in connection with biblical or rabbinic teaching

Mogen Dovid: 'shield of David,' a symbol of Jewish identification

Passover: seven-day festival starting on the 15th of Nissan (March-April)
commemorating the Israelites' exodus from Egypt

pilpul: a method of Talmudic study involving dialectical argumentation

Purim: festival on the 14th of Adar (February-March) commemorating the
deliverance of the Jews from Haman's plot to kill them, as narrated in
the Book of Esther

Rosh Hashanah: Jewish New Year, first and second days of Tishri (September-
October)

sabra: native Israeli, named after the prickly pear plant

Sambation (Sambatyon): legendary river across which part of the ten lost tribes
of Israel were exiled by the Assyrians. According to legend it rages
constantly except on the Sabbath and hence cannot be crossed.

Seder: 'order,' often refers to the order of ceremonies observed in Jewish
homes on the night of Passover when the Haggadah is recited.

sefer yetzirah: 'Book of Creation,' an early cabbalistic work stressing cosmology and the symbolism of letters and numbers

Shechina: the Divine Presence or Radiance

shechita: 'slaughtering,' usually refers to kosher slaughtering

Shehechianu: 'Who hath kept us alive,' a benediction to mark a joyous or
novel occasion

Shevuoth: the Feast of Weeks, Pentecost, occurring on the fiftieth day after
Passover, commemorating Divine Revelation on Mount Sinai

Shma: Jewish proclamation of monotheism, beginning with the words
'Shma Yisroel ... ' (Hear, O Israel: the Lord Our God is One Lord)
Deuteronomy 6:4, recited frequently in prayers and also on one's
deathbed

shochet: ritual slaughterer

shofar (pl. shofroth): ram's horn sounded on the High Holydays (New Year and Day of Atonement) and at proclamation of great national events, and to be sounded at the coming of the Messiah

Shulchan Aruch: Jewish code of religious law compiled and systematized by Joseph Karo in the sixteenth century

siddur (pl. siddurim): daily prayerbook

Succoth: 'tabernacles,' a seven-day festival beginning on the 15th of Tishri (September-October)

tallis (pl. tallesim): 'prayer shawl'

Talmud: a compendium of discussions by generations of scholars in many academies from the third through to the end of the fifth century. Together with the Bible it constitutes the basis of traditional Jewish law and culture.

Talmud Torah: Jewish religious school

tanna (pl. tannaim): rabbinic teacher of the Mishnaic period, from about the first to the early third century

t'fillin: 'phylacteries'

Torah: the 'Teaching,' the Pentateuch or Five Books of Moses, the most sacred part of the Jewish Bible; by extension all traditional Jewish learning

yahrzeit: anniversary of a person's death

yeshiva (pl. yeshivoth): Jewish Talmudic academy

Yishuv: settlement, more specifically the Jewish community settled in Palestine during the pre-State period

Yom Kippur: 'Day of Atonement,' the most sacred day in the Jewish calendar, occurs on the tenth day following Rosh Hashanah

zaddik (pl. zaddikim): saintly person, or leader venerated as a holy person

Zohar: 'Brightness' or 'Splendour,' the main text of the Jewish mystical tradition, written as a commentary on the Bible

Index

This book
was designed by
WILLIAM RUETER
and was printed by
University of
Toronto
Press